P9-DCJ-632

Please remember that this is a library book,
and that it belongs only temporarily to each
person who uses it. Be considerate. Do
not write in this, or any, library book.

CORRECTIONS IN AMERICA: AN INTRODUCTION

Second Edition

GLENCOE CRIMINAL JUSTICE SERIES

General Editor:

G. DOUGLAS GOURLEY

Former Professor and Chairman
Department of Criminal Justice
California State University at Los Angeles
Los Angeles, California

CORRECTIONS IN AMERICA: AN INTRODUCTION
SECOND EDITION

HARRY E. ALLEN
Director, Program for the Study
of Crime and Delinquency
The Ohio State University
Columbus, Ohio

CLIFFORD E. SIMONSEN
Chairman, Law and Justice Program
City College
Seattle, Washington

GLENCOE PUBLISHING CO., INC.
Encino, California

Collier Macmillan Publishers
London

To My Family

Glencoe Publishing Co, Inc.
17337 Ventura Boulevard
Encino, California 91316
Collier Macmillan Canada, Ltd.

Library of Congress Catalog Card Number: 77-73240

First Printing 1978

ISBN 0-02-470830-5

Contents

Foreword

An ancient Egyptian patriarch once noting the irresponsibility of the times concluded, "And everybody is writing a book." So it might be said of the present age regarding crime and criminals. Not only books, but movies, television shows, and newspaper columns are rife with crime and violence. This is perhaps natural in a culture where crime is one of the great problems in society. It is refreshing, therefore, to find a book such as *Corrections in America* which is not sensational, which does not rant about the failure of corrections, and which presents a wealth of interesting and informative data, especially for students of whatever age or station who want to discover the facts and who may be attempting to find their way through a complex and confusing subject.

In reading *Corrections in America,* one should bear in mind a number of assumptions which are pitfalls in so many current books in criminology. The writer has noted over 20 such misconceptions which appear plausible, but which will skew objective and rational thinking. Some of these assumptions are examined in Chapter 5, "Correctional Ideologies."

Perhaps the most popular of these assumptions is that the penitentiary system is a failure because recidivism rates remain high. To regard recidivism as a test of the effectiveness of a prison or parole system is of course as invalid as to fault a hospital because a patient who was treated for measles and who has since taken up residence in a malaria swamp returns to the hospital with malaria. Correctional treatment, which at best is a short era in a life exposed, both before and after, to a myriad of societal hazards, can play only a small part in the pattern of that life. The reader should remember this when reading about recidivism as a test of correctional treatment.

Another popular notion is that prisons exist to "rehabilitate" offenders. This notion is the outgrowth of the exaggerated hopes of each generation since 1790 and especially of the era 1935 to 1970 when "programs of rehabilitation" attempted to forestall the idleness which resulted from legal restrictions on prison industries. This notion is equally false because no prisoner was ever "rehabilitated" in an institution. "Trimming the prison down to size'' will show that prisons can observe, diagnose, train, possibly even *change criminals a little,* and perhaps, with luck, get them to follow a different path than formerly.

A third popular assumption is that only the "hard-core" prisoners require institutional confinement. Advocates of this assumption frequently ignore the question of how one determines which prisoners constitute the "hard core.'' As any professional operator knows, only the most skillful observation of offenders, often over an extended period of time, can separate the sheep from the goats, and such observation usually requires institutionalization of many convicts who are not "hard core.'' Others who think a record of known criminal acts is sufficient for such classification are relying on symptoms rather than basic problems underlying criminality. Since crime is only one symptom of maladjustment, such simplistic thinking is the most superficial sort of symptomology. It follows the practice of blood-letting as a cure for fever symptoms.

A fourth assumption, which ignores the evidence of 150 years of practice, is the proposal to abandon the indeterminate sentence and parole in favor of mandatory sentences established by lawmakers and made uniform for the same offense and for offenders who are of the same class. As has been demonstrated many times when attempts have been made to set up comparative groups in so-called controlled experiments, there is no similarity among offenders. Neither have lawmakers shown any wisdom in setting sentences. However, someone must decide which prisoners may be released to the community and when. To propose to settle this at the time of sentencing is the most unprofessional sort of *a priori* reasoning. If existing parole boards have proved unsatisfactory, it may be well to establish better criteria for selecting the personnel of such semijudicial bodies. Certainly one should hesitate to throw the baby out with the dirty water.

There are numerous other assumptions which any reader must be wary of; for example, that the penitentiary system has failed to reduce crime, that judicial discretion should be divided or eliminated, that prisons exist to punish and not to treat, that no prison official knows how to treat criminality, that counseling and treatment in prison are coercive, that treatment has nothing to do with readiness for release, that readiness for release can *only* be determined by trial-and-error results of temporary release on furloughs, work or education release, or similar methods of community corrections, and that the penitentiary system lacks a scientific philosophy of corrections.

In presenting a wealth of facts, opinions, and proposals, this text has included the essentials of modern thinking in corrections leaving it to the reader to separate the wheat from the chaff and hopefully to develop a personal philosophy of corrections. The final part, "Summary and Overview,'' gives the reader a correctional program providing a springboard from which to launch one's own ideology.

On the whole, *Corrections in America* is an interesting, readable, and comprehensive text which offers a stimulating introduction to the whole correctional process.

Howard B. Gill
Institute of Clinical Criminology

Preface

This second edition of *Corrections in America: An Introduction* builds upon the principles used by the authors in the original text. As our deliberate break from the traditional college textbook has received gratifying support from both instructors and students, we have retained the same essential concepts, utilizing the comments of those who taught from the first edition to eliminate overlap, to rearrange topics to create a more cohesive flow of ideas, and to add current material to update subjects.

We have continued to place footnotes at the end of each chapter, keeping the body of the text readable and complete in itself, without interruption by extensive notes. To facilitate the reference process, however, we have moved some of the more important biographical descriptions and historical data from the footnotes into the body of the text.

We want to emphasize that we have attempted to write a readable and useful *introductory* text, one that deals with most of the systems, processes, and people across the broad spectrum of the corrections system. As writers of an introductory text, we have not attempted to explore one area of corrections in depth at the expense of others. To the students, we offer this effort in the hope that it will provide both an enjoyable and a productive learning experience. To our colleagues in academia, we offer the hope that the organization and coverage of this text will make that learning experience as effective as possible.

What Is Corrections?

Since this text has been written to provide the new student in the broad discipline of criminal justice with an overview of the development and current status of *corrections* in America, it seems appropriate to address the meaning of this often misused term. Is it a system? Is it a process? Is it a philosophy? Or, is it simply a euphemism used to cover a multitude of sins? The answers to these questions vary with the orientation of the questioner.

Is it a *system?* Somewhat. A popular belief holds that corrections is a coherent subsystem of the overall criminal justice system. It is often assumed that federal, state, and local jails, prisons, halfway houses, parole and probation are all carefully integrated in some master scheme of corrections. A closer look at the corrections *non*system and its relationship to the criminal justice *non*system, however, tends to dispel this belief.

Is it a *process?* Sometimes. A basic assumption of the process model is that a predictable outcome can be obtained by variation in the process, once the process is known. This model is useful in the physical sciences. It is relatively easy to determine the diameter of a ball-bearing and adjust the manufacturing process to keep the diameters within prescribed tolerances. In corrections, however, the student soon perceives a lack of agreement as to what the *outcome* should be, which *processes* are related to which *outcomes,* and, lastly, what *tolerances* in outcomes are considered acceptable. While the basic process is composed of arrest-trial-incarceration-punishment-treatment-parole, it is soon obvious that there are almost as many different variations in processes as there are systems.

Is it a *philosophy?* To some extent. System and process in a given society are greatly affected by that society's philosophical orientation toward the offenders: whether it feels something should be done *to* them or *for* them. Oppressive and inhumane philosophies often lead to oppressive and inhumane systems and processes. While the underlying philosophical intent of corrections seems to be the restoration of the offender to a useful role in society, the student soon finds that the relationship between that intent and economics is also critical. The loftiest ideals are seldom realized without the support, philosophical and financial, of society as a whole.

Is it simply a *euphemism* used to cover a multitude of sins? For some people, "Imprisonment," "confinement," "punishment," "retribution," "rehabilitation," "penitence," "reformation" are but a few of the buzzwords people have used at one time or another to describe the handling of offenders. One must look behind such catchall phrases to see if they have any real significance, or are just new words with old meanings. Correction that does not correct is neither more nor less effective than punishment that does not punish or rehabilitation that does not rehabilitate. Unfortunately, these and other terms have been used by politicians, the media, and even professionals as though they were absolutes. Corrections must not be used as "the Emperor's new clothes," an invisible garment draping the same old body.

As can be seen, the corrections concept covers a wide range of activity. This text will attempt to review where corrections in America originated, where it is today, where it seems to be going from here, and what issues need to be resolved to get there. The reader will soon appreciate that there are no easy answers to the question, "What is corrections?" Corrections programs will emerge as a poorly articulated series of almost independent operations, sometimes with conflicting goals, all trying to effect some kind of change in the offender. This knowledge should stimulate readers to seek appropriate reforms in their chosen sectors of criminal justice.

Whether one is the present or future *police officer* who makes the arrest, the *lawyer* who tries the case, the *judge* who passes sentence, the *prison administrator* who executes the sentence, the *parole officer* who attempts to reintegrate the offender into society, or the *concerned citizen* who is tired of being the victim of past efforts at "corrections," that process must be seen as but one function of the entire socio-legal-economic structure. Whether the social benefits of correctional efforts justify their cost is a question often asked about other social welfare delivery systems as well. Answers to these questions lie in the informed efforts of all persons involved with that particular delivery system known as corrections.

H.E.A.
C.E.S.

Acknowledgments

The authors would be remiss if we did not again acknowledge our debt both to those who contributed to the task of the original preparation of this text and to those who were kind enough to use it and advise us how to make the second edition better. A second edition, in some ways, is more difficult to prepare than the first. We have been made proud and embarrassed, gratified and humbled by the experience of having our colleagues comment on the original effort. We are especially grateful for their continuing use of the text, and for their trust that we will correct the flaws in this second edition. Their comments, both complimentary and critical, have been taken seriously, and we have incorporated them, wherever possible, in this new edition.

We especially appreciate the comments and suggestions of Donal E. J. MacNamara, who read the first edition and was kind enough to write a highly flattering foreword. Howard B. Gill was especially insightful in his comments and advice, and was also kind enough to write a foreword for this edition.

Hal Vetter, Sy Dinitz, and Walter Reckless are again thanked for their continuing and continuous support and assistance. We would also like to thank Reed Adams, Bob Culbertson, Jeff Alpert, June Morrison, and Al Reynolds for their encouragement and helpful comments.

The Federal Bureau of Prisons, the American Correctional Association, the Ohio Department of Rehabilitation and Correction, the Pennsylvania Department of Correction, and the National Clearinghouse for Correctional Programming and Architecture, all receive our deep-felt thanks as well. These agencies were especially helpful in providing historical and current material, as well as most of the photographs used in this text.

Walker and Company, publishers of *The New Red Barn* and *The Human Cage,* must also receive our thanks and acknowledgments for allowing us to use many passages, based on current research, from these two books.

The publication of the National Advisory Commission on Criminal Justice Standard and Goals' many volumes of exceptional material made it possible for us not only to *describe* the correctional milieu, but also to *prescribe* in many areas possible cures for its problems.

It is virtually impossible to acknowledge all of the other colleagues and professionals who assisted and encouraged us in this endeavor. To delineate a list of those who did would result in certain omission of some. You all know who you are, so we hereby acknowledge each of you with heartfelt "thanks."

Bill Bryden, Senior Editor at Glencoe, deserves special mention for his patience, advice, help, and hard work in getting this text far enough along to *require* a second edition. Monique de Varennes also gets a special thanks for her editing of the second edition under strained time constraints while reluctant authors dragged their feet. She helped weld this effort into a cohesive and unified whole.

PART I

History and Evolution of Corrections

1 Early History (2000 B.C.–1700 A.D.)

The descent to hell is easy. The gates stand open day
and night. But to reclimb the slope and escape to the
upper air: this is labor. . . .

VIRGIL
Aeneid, *Book 6*

Introduction

This text is not intended to be a history of corrections or a dissertation on the
legal aspects of the field. It is appropriate, however, to provide at least a
minimum of the historical background, legal and social, needed for a better
understanding of the concepts to be discussed later. In describing this
background, we have tried to avoid technical jargon in order to keep
misunderstanding to a minimum. We begin by tracing the roots of corrections back to the early beginnings of civilization.

Behavior as a Continuum

Behavior in social groups, whether they be primitive tribes or complex
modern nations, can be viewed as points on a simple continuum, as shown
in Figure I-1.

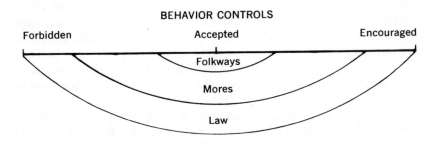

FIGURE I–1. Continuum of Behavior

In all societies, certain acts or groups of acts have been universally forbidden or *proscribed*, such as murder, rape, kidnapping, and treason (or some form of rebellion against the group authority). On the other hand, most societies have encouraged or *prescribed* behavior such as having children, marrying, hunting, growing food, and other actions that seemed in the interest of the common welfare.

Behavior toward the center of the continuum (Figure I-1) is usually controlled by a set of social rules called "folkways." Enforcement of these rules is accomplished by mild *disapproval* (the raising of an eyebrow, staring, or a look of shock) or by mild *encouragement* (applause or a smile). Actions further out on the continuum, which either threaten the existence of the group or serve to perpetuate it, are controlled by a stronger set of rules called "mores." In the very distant past, all mores were enforced solely by the individual's use of strong social *disapproval* (verbal abuse, beatings, temporary ostracism, even death) or strong *encouragement* (dowries, secure social or financial status, fertility rites); and these informal controls still protect certain mores today. But as societies became more complex, they developed more structured sanctions to prevent violation of those mores that were essential to the group survival. These sanctions have been codified in the form of written rules ("laws"), and the reward for obeying them is simply the ability to function as a respected and productive member of society.

Redress of Wrongs

The earliest remedy for wrongs done to one's person or property was simply to take personal retaliation on the wrongdoer. In early primitive societies this personal retaliation was accepted and even encouraged by members of the tribal group. This ancient concept of personal revenge could hardly be considered "law." Yet it has colored the development of most legal systems, especially English criminal law, from which most of American criminal law derives.

The practice of personal retaliation was later augmented by the "blood feud," in which the victim's family or tribe avenged themselves on the family or tribe of the offender. Because this form of retaliation can easily escalate and result in an endless vendetta between the injured factions, some method of control had to be devised to make these blood feuds less costly and damaging.

The practice of retaliation usually begins to develop into a system of criminal law when it becomes customary for the victim of the wrongdoing to accept pecuniary satisfaction in place of blood vengeance. This custom, when established, is usually dictated by tribal tradition and the relative strengths of the injured party and the wrongdoer. Custom has always exerted great force among primitive societies. The acceptance of vengeance in the form of a payment (e.g., cattle, food, personal services) was usually not compulsory and the victim was still free to take whatever vengeance he wished. Legal historians Albert Kocourek and John Wigmore have described this retaliatory pressure from kinsmen and tribesmen:

> It must not be forgotten that the right of personal revenge was also in many cases a duty. A man was bound by all the force of religion to avenge the death of his kinsman. This duty was by universal practice imposed upon the nearest male relative—the avenger of blood, as he is called in the Scripture accounts.[1]

The custom of atonement for wrongs by payment to appease the family or tribe of a victim became known as "lex salica"[2] (or "Wergeld,"[3] in Europe). It is still in effect in many Middle and Far East countries, with the amount of payment based on the rank and position of the injured person.

Fines and Punishments

How did these simple, voluntary systems become part of an official system of fines and punishments? As tribal leaders, elders, and (later) kings came into power they began to exert their authority on negotiation proceedings. Wrongdoers could choose to stay away from the procedures; this was their right. If they refused to abide by the sentence imposed, however, they were declared outside the law of the tribe (nation, family), or an "outlaw." There is little doubt that outlawry, or exile, was the first punishment imposed by society,[4] and it heralds the beginning of criminal law as we know it.

Criminal law, even primitive criminal law, requires an element of *public* action against the wrongdoer—as in a pronouncement of outlawry. Prior to this development, the backgrounds of law and public sanctions seem to be parallel in all legal systems. The subsequent creation of legal codes and sanctions for different crimes either stresses or refines the vengeance factor, according to the attitudes of the particular society.

Early Codes

Even primitive ethics demanded that a society express its vengeance within a system of regulations and rules. Moses is advised to follow the "eye for eye, and tooth for tooth" doctrine in Exodus 21:24, but this concept ("lex talionis") is far older than the Bible; it appears in the Sumerian codes and in the code of King Hammurabi of Babylon, compiled over 500 years before the Book of the Covenant.[5]

As early societies developed language and writing skills, they began to record the laws of their nations. The Hammurabic Code is viewed by most historians as the first comprehensive attempt at codifying social interaction.

The Sumerian codes[6] preceded it by about a century, and the principle of lex talionis was evident in both. The punishments under these codes were savage and based on vengeance (or *talion*), in many cases inflicted by the injured party. In the Babylonian code, over two dozen offenses call for the penalty of death. Both these codes also prescribed mutilation, whipping, or forced labor as punishments for numerous crimes. The following excerpt illustrates the vengeance principle:

> If either a slave or slave-girl has received anything from the hand of a married woman, the nose and the ears of the slave or slave-girl shall be cut off, the stolen property shall be requited; the man shall cut off his wife's ears. Or if the man has let his wife go free [and] has not cut off her ears, [the nose and ears] of the slave or slave-girl shall not be cut off and [the theft of] the stolen property shall not be requited.[7]

The kinds of punishment applied to slaves and bondsmen have been cited by many scholars[8] as the origin of the punishments which in later law applied to all offenders. As historian Gustav Radbruch states:

> Applied earlier almost exclusively to slaves, [the mutilating penalties] became used more and more on freemen during the Carolingian period [640-1012 A.D.] and specially for offenses which betokened a base and servile mentality. Up to the end of the Carolingian era, punishments "to hide and hair" were overwhelmingly reserved for slaves. Even death penalties occurred as slave punishments and account for the growing popularity of such penalties in Carolingian times. The aggravated death penalties, combining corporal and capital punishments, have their roots in the penal law governing slaves.[9]

The early punishments were considered synonymous with slavery; those punished even had their heads shaved, the mark of the slave.[10] In Roman days the extensive use of penal servitude was spurred by the need for workers to perform hard labor in the great public works. The sentence to penal servitude was reserved for the lower classes and usually meant life in chains working in the mines or galleys building the public works planned by the government. These sentences carried the complete loss of citizenship and liberty and were classed, along with exile and death, as capital punishment. Penal servitude, or "civil death," meant that the offender's property was confiscated in the name of the state and that his wife was declared a widow, eligible to remarry. To society, he was, in effect, "dead."

Crime and Sin

Punishing the individual in the name of the state also involved the concept of superstitious revenge. Here crime was entangled with sin, and punishment in the form of Wergeld (payment to the victim) or Friedensgeld[11] (payment to the state) was not sufficient. If society believed the crime might have offended a divinity, the accused had to undergo a long period of progressively harsher punishment to appease the gods. The zone between church law and state law became more and more blurred. The concept of personal responsibility for one's act was combined with the need to "get right with God."[12] The early codes, even the Ten Commandments, were designed to make the offender's punishment satisfactory both to society and to God.

Roman and Greek Codes

In the sixth century A.D., Emperor Justinian of Rome wrote his code of laws, one of the most ambitious early efforts to match a desirable amount of punishment to all possible crimes. Roman art of the period depicts the "scales of justice," which imply that punishment balances the crime. Justinian's effort, as might be expected, bogged down in the morass of administrative details needed to enforce it.[13] The Code of Justinian did not survive the fall of the Roman Empire, but it left the foundation upon which most of the Western world's legal codes were built.

In Greece the harsh Code of Draco[14] provided the same penalties for freemen and slaves. These included many of the concepts used in primitive societies (e.g., vengeance, outlawry, and blood feuds). The Greeks were the first to allow *any* citizen to prosecute the offender in the name of the injured party. This clearly illustrates that during this period, the public interest and protection of the social order were becoming more important than individual injury and individual vengeance.

The Middle Ages

The Middle Ages were a period of general disorder. Vast changes in the social structure and the growing influence of the Church on everyday life resulted in a divided system of justice. Reformation was viewed as a process of religious, not secular, redemption. As in early civilizations, the sinner had to pay two debts, one to society and another to God. The "ordeal" was the Church's substitute for a trial, until it was abolished in 1215 A.D. In trials by ordeal, guilt or innocence was determined by subjecting the accused to dangerous or painful tests, in the belief that the innocent would emerge unscathed while the guilty would suffer agonies and die. The brutality of most trials by ordeal ensured a very high percentage of convictions.

The Church expanded the concept of crime to include some new areas, reflected in modern codes. Sexual activity was seen as especially sinful during the Middle Ages. The sex offenses generally involved either public or "unnatural" acts. They provoked horrible punishments, as did heresy and witchcraft; the Church justified cruel reprisals as a means of saving the unfortunate sinner from the ways of the Devil. The zealous movement to stamp out heresy brought on the Inquisition[15] and its use of the most vicious tortures imaginable to gain "confessions" and "repentance" from alleged heretics. Untold thousands of persons died at the hands of inquisitioners in Spain and Holland, where these methods were most extensively used. Punishment was not viewed as an end in itself, but as the offender's only hope of pacifying a wrathful God.

The main contribution of the medieval Church to the study of corrections is the concept of "free will." This idea assumes that individuals *choose* their actions, good or bad, and thus can be held fully responsible for them. The religious doctrines of eternal punishment, atonement, and spiritual conversion rest on the assumption that individuals who commit a sin can act differently if they choose to do so.

These early codes and their administration were usually based on the belief that punishment was necessary to provide vengeance for the victim. In early small tribal groups and less complex societies, direct compensation to the victim was used in place of revenge to prevent disintegration of the social structure through extended blood feuds. When these groups concentrated their power in a king or similar ruler, the concept of crime as an offense against the *victim* gave way to the idea that crime—however lowly the victim—is an offense against the state. In the process, Wergeld was replaced by Friedensgeld and the administration of punishment became the responsibility of the king.

Punishment

The most common forms of state punishment over the centuries have been death, torture, mutilation, branding, public humiliation, fines, forfeits of property, banishment, transportation, and imprisonment.[16] These themes, and numerous variations on them, have always symbolized retribution for crimes. Imprisonment and transportation are relatively modern penal practices and will be dealt with in later chapters; other common practices are discussed below.

The death penalty was the most universal form of punishment among early societies. With little knowledge of behavior modification and other modern techniques used to control violent persons, these feared offenders were very often condemned to death by hanging, crucifixion, burning at the stake, drowning, and every other cruel and unusual method the human mind could conceive. As technology advanced, methods for killing offenders became more sophisticated. In a belief that punishment, especially capital punishment, would act as a deterrent to others, executions and lesser punishments were generally carried out in public.

Torture, mutilation, and branding fall in the general category of corporal punishment. Many tortures were used to extract a "confession" from the accused, often resulting in the death penalty for an innocent person.

FIGURE I–2. Early Use of Pillory (Courtesy Federal Bureau of Prisons)

Mutilation was often an attempt to match the crime and the punishment (e.g., a liar's tongue was ripped out, a rapist's genitals were removed, a thief's hands were cut off). Corporal punishment was among those considered a deterrent to other potential offenders. Branding was still practiced as late as the nineteenth century in many countries, including the United States.

Public humiliation of offenders was a popular practice in early America, utilizing such devices as the stocks, the pillory, ducking stools, and branding. The most significant aspect of these punishments was their public nature. Offenders placed in the stocks (hands and feet fastened into a locked frame, sitting down) or in the pillory (standing, with head and hands fastened into a locked frame) were flogged, spit upon, heaped with garbage, and reviled by all who passed by.

The ducking stool and the brank were common public punishments for gossips. The ducking stool was a chair or platform at the end of a long lever which allowed the operator to dunk the victim from the bank of a stream. The brank was a bird-cage-like instrument placed over the offender's head, containing a plate of iron with sharp spikes in it extending into the subject's mouth. Any movement of the mouth or tongue would result in painful injury.

Flogging has been a common punishment in almost all Western civilizations, particularly to preserve discipline in domestic, military, and academic settings. It is usually administered by a short lash at the end of a solid handle about three feet long, or by a whip made of nine knotted lines or cords fastened to a handle (the famed "cat-o'-nine-tails"). Flogging was a popular method of inducing "confessions" at heresy trials. Few men could stand up long against the tongue of the lash.

Deterrence

The extensive use of capital and corporal punishment during the Middle Ages reflected, in part, a belief that public punishment would deter potential wrongdoers—a belief the passing years have refuted: "It is plain that, however futile it may be, social revenge is the only honest, straightforward, and logical justification for punishing criminals. The claim for deterrence is belied by both history and logic."[17] No matter how society tried to "beat the Devil" out of offenders, the only criminal deterred was the one who was tortured to death. Later, enlightened thinkers began to seek more rational deterrents for crime by means of extensive investigation of its cause.

Emergence of Secular Law

The problem of developing a set of laws that applied to the actions of men in earthly communities was compounded by Christian philosophers who insisted that law was made in heaven. In the fourth century A.D., St. Augustine recognized the need for justice, but only as decreed by God. The issue was somewhat clarified by Thomas Aquinas in the thirteenth century when he distinguished among three laws: eternal law (*lex eterna*), natural law (*lex naturalis*), and human law (*lex humana*), which is intended for the common good.[18] The last was considered valid only if it did not conflict with the other two.

As time passed, the secular leaders (kings and other monarchs) became more powerful, and they wanted to detach themselves from the divine legal order and the restrictions it placed on their power. In the early fourteenth century, many scholars advocated the independence of the monarchy from the Pope. Dante, the Italian poet and philosopher, proposed the establishment of a world state.

England's lord chancellor, Sir Thomas More, tried to oppose the forces advocating the unification of church and state, and died on the executioner's block as a result. He refused to bend ecclesiastical law to suit the marital whims of his King, the fickle Henry VIII. More was out of line with his day in another sense as well: as an advocate of the seemingly radical theory that *punishment* could not prevent crime, he was one of the first to see that prevention might require a close look at the *conditions that gave rise to crime*. In the sixteenth century, this line of thought was unfortunately far ahead of its time, but More's ideas eventually provided much of the background for modern theories in criminology and penology.

This early background of law and punishment points up the significance of social revenge as a justification for individual or societal punishment against an offender. This rationale allowed the development of penal slavery and civil death as retaliation for wrongs against the Crown. The idea of *correcting* an offender was entirely incidental to *punishment*. Imprisonment served purely for detention. Offenders condemned to the galleys or the sulphur mines suffered a form of social vengeance far more painful than loss of freedom alone, often including the lash and other physical abuse. The offender was placed in dungeons, galleys, or mines to *receive* punishment, not *as* punishment.

This idea of punishment to repay society and to expiate one's transgressions against God explains in part why most punishments were cruel and barbarous. Presumably, the hardships of physical torture, social degradation, exile, or financial loss (the four fundamental types of punishment[19]) would be rewarded by eternal joy in heaven. Ironically, these punishments did little to halt the spread of crime: "Even in the era when extremely severe punishment was imposed for crimes of minor importance, no evidence can be found to support the view that punitive measures materially curtailed the volume of crime."[20]

Early Imprisonment

What kinds of prisons existed during this early era? It is important to examine some aspects of these early prisons which relate to later correctional practices. Some form of detention for offenders, whether temporary or

FIGURE I-3. Early Congregate Confinement (Courtesy Federal
Bureau of Prisons)

permanent, has been a social institution from the earliest times. Offenders
were, of course, detained against their will, but the concept of imprisonment
as a punishment in itself is a fairly recent one. Formerly, imprisonment was
primarily a means of holding the accused until the authorities had decided on
his or her real punishment, chosen from the variety described above.

Those condemned to penal servitude in the Roman public works must
have been kept in some special place at night. Unfortunately, little is known
about this form of imprisonment. Most early places of confinement were
basically cages. Later, stone quarries and similar places designed for other
purposes were used to house prisoners. The only early Roman place of
confinement we know much about is the Mamertine Prison, a vast system of
dungeons built under the main sewer of Rome in 64 B.C.[21]

In the Middle Ages, after the fall of Rome, fortresses, castles, bridge
abutments, and town gates were built very strongly and securely to provide
defense against roving bands of raiders. With the advent of gunpowder the
fortress cities lost much of their value and these massive structures were
used as places of confinement. Many became famous as places to house

political prisoners.[22] Not until the twelfth century were prison chambers specifically included in castle plans.

The Christian church had followed the custom of sanctuary or asylum[23] since the time of Constantine, placing the wrongdoer in seclusion to provide an atmosphere conducive to penitence. This form of imprisonment developed into more formalized places of punishment within the walls of monasteries and abbeys. Long periods in solitary confinement for alleged transgressions against canon law were common. The prisons built for use during the Inquisition were similar in concept, if not in operation, to later cellular prisons in America. The idea of reformation by isolation and prayer had some influence on our first penitentiaries. In general, however, the impact of these early prisons is hard to evaluate.

Workhouses

Bridewell, a workhouse built for the employment and housing of London's riffraff in 1557, was based on the work ethic[24] that was developing with the breakup of feudalism and the increased movement of the population to urban areas. The workhouse was so successful that by 1576 Parliament required the construction of a "bridewell" in every county in England. The same unsettled social conditions prevailed in Holland, and the Dutch began building workhouses in 1596. These were soon copied all over Europe.

Unfortunately, workhouses did not typify the places of confinement used for minor offenders and other prisoners in the seventeenth and eighteenth centuries. Most cities had to make prisons out of buildings erected for some other purpose. No attempt was made to keep the young from the old, the able from the sick, or even the males from the females. No food was provided for those without money, and sanitary conditions were usually deplorable. Exploitation of inmates by other inmates and jailers resulted in the most bestial acts of violence. Jail fever (typhus) spread easily to surrounding cities and seemed to be the main method of keeping the country's population down. By the beginning of the eighteenth century, workhouses, prisons, and houses of correction in Europe and England had deteriorated into shocking condition. Housing in such miserable prisons was perhaps the most ruthless—if abstract—social revenge of all the punishments thus far described. "Out of sight, out of mind," was the watchword of that period.

We have seen the principle of punishment pass from an individual's response to a wrong, to a blood feud that involved the family, to an abstract action taken by some bureaucracy in the name of the state. This abstract approach to justice and punishment allowed the places of confinement to develop into human cesspools. It took the brilliant and dedicated reformers of the eighteenth century to establish the basis for modern penal philosophy. The works of these great men are examined in the next chapter.

REVIEW QUESTIONS

I. Find the answers to the following in the text:

   1. What is the difference between folkways, mores, and laws?

   2. At what point in the development of a society does retaliation begin to develop into criminal law?

   3. What effect did the increasing power of kings have on punishment?

   4. What was the first punishment imposed by *society?*

   5. What is meant by civil death?

   6. What is meant by the concept of ''free will''?

   7. What form of punishment has been most widely used?

   8. What is meant by ''deterrence as a result of punishment''?

   9. What were some of the earliest forms of imprisonment?

   10. From what does most American law derive?

II. Words to identify and remember:

   1. vendetta

   2. Wergeld

   3. outlawry

   4. lex talionis

   5. Friedensgeld

   6. sanctuary

   7. Inquisition

   8. Bridewell

   9. heresy

   10. corporal punishment

NOTES

1. Albert Kocourek and John Wigmore, *Evolution of Law, Vol. II: Punitive and Ancient Legal Institutions* (Boston: Little Brown and Company, 1915), p. 124.

2. *Lex salica* was the fine paid for homicide, and it usually varied according to the rank, sex, and age of the murdered person. In Sweden this was known as *kinbote,* or compensation for homicide. In general, lex salica refers to a payment for death or injury.

3. *Wergeld*, which means *man-money*, originally applied to the death of an individual and the individual's supposed value to his or her family. It later applied to personal injury as well.

4. Kocourek and Wigmore, *Evolution of Law, Vol. II*, p. 126.

5. *The Code of Hammurabi* is estimated to have been written about 1750 B.C.

6. The *Sumerian Codes* were those of Kings Lipit-Ishtar and Eshnunna and are estimated to date from about 1860 B.C.

7. G. R. Driver and John C. Mills, *The Assyrian Laws* (Oxford: Clarendon Press, 1935), p. 383.

8. Thorsten Sellin, "A Look at Prison History," *Federal Probation* (September 1967):18.

9. Gustav Radbruch, *Elegantiae Juris Criminalis*, 2d ed. (Basel: Verlag fur Recht and Gesellshaft A. G., 1950), p.5.

10 Slaves were also marked by branding on the forehead or by metal collars that could not easily be removed.

11. *Friedensgeld* was the practice of paying restitution to the crown, in addition to individuals, for crimes. It later replaced payment to individuals altogether and became the system of fines paid to the state.

12. This religious requirement brought the two issues of sin and crime into the same arena and broadened the scope of the Church courts. The offender was obligated to make retribution to both God and the state.

13. *Emperor Justinian I* (483-565) was a great preserver of Roman law who collected all imperial statutes, issued a digest of all writings of Roman jurists, and wrote a revised code and a textbook for students. His *Corpus Juris Civilis* became the foundation of law in most of continental Europe.

14. *Draco*, ruler of Greece in 621 B.C., drew up a very harsh and cruel code that used corporal punishment so extensively that it was said to be written not in ink but in blood.

15. *The Inquisition* was a tribunal established by the Catholic Church in the Middle Ages with very wide powers for the suppression of heresy. The tribunal searched out heretics and other offenders rather than waiting for charges to be brought forward (somewhat in the manner of Senator Joseph McCarthy, rooting out "Communists" in the early 1950s). Emperor Frederick II made it a formal institution in 1224. The Inquisitor was supreme in matters of heresy and reported only to the Pope. The Inquisitor was provided with an itinerant court of vicars, lieutenants, advisors, spies, and sergeants at arms. The testimony of two witnesses was all that was needed to convict an accused. The convicted heretics were eventually turned over to secular authority for punishment, usually burning at the stake. Although the Spanish Inquisition is the most famous of the various European tribunals, it was not the worst, just the longest. The Inquisition came to an end in 1834.

16. Walter C. Reckless, *The Crime Problem*, 4th ed. (New York: Appleton-Century-Crofts, 1969), p. 497.

17. Harry Elmer Barnes and Negley K. Teeters, *New Horizons in Criminology*, 3d ed. (Englewood Cliffs, N.J.: Prentice-Hall, 1959), p. 286.

18. Stephen Schafer, *Theories in Criminology* (New York: Random House, 1969), p. 25.

19. Edwin H. Sutherland, *Criminology* (Philadelphia: Lippincott, 1924), p. 317.

20. Reckless, *The Crime Problem,* p. 504.

21. Norman Johnston, *The Human Cage: A Brief History of Prison Architecture* (Washington, D.C.: The American Foundation, 1973), p. 5.

22. Johnston, *The Human Cage,* p. 6.

23. The practice of granting a criminal sanctuary from punishment was generally reserved to holy places. It was abandoned in England in the seventeenth century.

24. *Work ethic* refers to the generally held belief in the Judeo-Christian world that hard work is good for the soul and the society.

2 A Century of Change (1700–1800)

The vilest deeds like poison weeds
Bloom well in prison air;
It is only what is good in man
That wastes and withers there.
Pale anguish keeps the heavy gate
And the warder is Despair.

OSCAR WILDE
"The Ballad of Reading Gaol"

A New Era Begins

As chapter 1 suggests, the underlying principle of public revenge for private wrongs invariably tipped the scales of justice in favor of the state. Corporal and capital punishment were the rule; executioners in sixteenth- and seventeenth-century Europe had at least thirty different methods to choose from. These ranged from hanging and burning at the stake to breaking on the rack. Public punishment and degradation were commonly prescribed for even minor offenses. Imprisonment served only as a preface to some gory punishment, carried out in the name of justice. With over 200 crimes in England alone punishable by death, that nation witnessed some 800 executions a year. As the seventeenth century drew to a close, the concept of retributive punishment by the state (with its implication that pity and justice are forever locked in opposition) was firmly entrenched in the laws of England and the European countries.

The events of the eighteenth century are especially important to the student of corrections. It was this period—later known as the Age of Enlightenment—that saw the recognition of humanity's essential dignity and imperfection by some of the most brilliant philosophers in our history. The movement for reform was led by such giants as Montesquieu, Voltaire, Beccaria, Bentham, Howard, and Penn. The impact of their work, while not confined to any one area, was particularly devastating with regard to the treatment of criminals. The basic contribution made by each is discussed briefly below.

Montesquieu and Voltaire, the French Humanists

The French thinkers Charles Montesquieu and François Voltaire, along with Denis Diderot, epitomized the Enlightenment concern for the rights of humanity. In his *Persian Letters*,[1] Montesquieu used his mighty pen to bring the abuses of criminal law to the foreground. Voltaire became involved in a number of trials that challenged the old ideas of legalized torture, criminal responsibility, and justice. Their humanitarian efforts paralleled the work of the most influential criminal law reformer of the era, Cesare Beccaria.

Charles Louis Secondat, Baron de la Brede et de Montesquieu (1689–1755) was a French historian and philosopher who analyzed law as an expression of justice. He believed that harsh punishment would undermine morality and felt that appealing to moral sentiment was a better means of preventing crime. He wrote *Persian Letters* and *The Spirit of Laws*.

Voltaire (François Marie Arouet) (1694–1778) was the most versatile of the eighteenth-century philosophers. He believed that the fear of shame was a deterrent to crime. He fought the legally sanctioned practice of torture, winning reversals—even after the convicted felons had been executed—on convictions so obtained under the old code. He was imprisoned in the Bastille in 1726 and was released on condition of leaving France. Voltaire was also a great writer and a master of satire.

Denis Diderot (1713–1784) was a French encyclopedist and philosopher. He was thrown into prison in 1749 for his work *Lettre sur les Aveugles* (*Letter on the Blind,* a strong attack on orthodox religion). He worked for twenty years on his twenty-eight-volume Encyclopedia, along with Voltaire, Montesquieu, and other greats of the time. His Encyclopedia became a real force for change in the eighteenth century.

Beccaria, the Father of the "Classical" School

The best-known work of Cesare Beccaria is his essay, *Crimes and Punishment*—a primary force in the transition from punishment to corrections. It established these principles:

1. The basis of all social action must be the utilitarian conception of the greatest happiness for the greatest number.

2. Crime must be considered an injury to society, and the only rational measure of crime is the extent of that injury.

3. Prevention of crime is more important than punishment for crimes; indeed punishment is justifiable only on the supposition that it helps to prevent criminal conduct. In preventing crime it is necessary to improve and publish the laws, so that the nation can understand and support them; to reward virtue; and to improve the public's education both in regard to legislation and to life.

4. In criminal procedure secret accusations and torture should be abolished. There should be speedy trials. The accused should be treated humanely before trial and must have every right and facility to bring forward evidence in his behalf. Turning state's evidence should be done away with, as it amounts to no more than the public authorization of treachery.

5. The purpose of punishment is to deter persons from the commission of crime and not to provide social revenge. Not severity, but certainty and swiftness in punishment best secure this result. Punishment must be sure and swift and penalties determined strictly in accordance with the social damage wrought by the crime. Crimes against property should be punished solely by fines, or by imprisonment when the person is unable to pay the fine. Banishment is an excellent punishment for crimes against the state. There should be no capital punishment. Life imprisonment is a better deterrent. Capital punishment is irreparable and hence makes no provision for possible mistakes and the desirability of later rectification.

6. Imprisonment should be more widely employed but its mode of application should be greatly improved through providing better physical quarters and by separating and classifying the prisoners as to age, sex, and degree of criminality.[2]

When the essay was first published it was judged far superior to its author, who had attempted to remain anonymous so as to "defend the truth without becoming her martyr.''[3] After two hard years of writing he felt he had made enough of a contribution, and he did his best to avoid persecution for his sharp criticism of the conditions of the time. It was soon evident that he was not to be persecuted, but hailed as a genius, and when his identity was disclosed he was promptly invited to Paris by Domenico Morellet.[4] He did not want to leave his home and young wife, however, and when he finally made the trip had a miserable time. The great philosophers who came to Paris found the brilliant and fiery writer to be a shy, withdrawn, and slightly disturbed young man of twenty-six. He refused to debate with anyone and soon returned to Milan, never to journey away again. In later years he even refused an invitation from Catherine II of Russia to be her legislative advisor at court.

While Beccaria himself did not seek or receive great personal fame, his small volume was praised as one of the most significant books produced by the Age of Enlightenment. Four of his more unprecedented ideas were incorporated into the French Code of Criminal Procedure in 1808, and into the Penal Code of 1810. They are:

1. An individual should be regarded as innocent until he is proven guilty.

2. An individual should not be forced to testify against himself.

3. An individual should have the right to employ counsel and to cross-examine the state's witnesses.

4. An individual should have the right to a prompt and public trial and, in most cases, a trial by jury.

Obviously, the philosophers who took careful note of Beccaria's ideas included the authors of the United States Constitution. It seems we owe a great deal to this shy Italian writer of the eighteenth century.

Cesare Bonesana, Marchese de Beccaria (1738–1794) wrote the *Essay on Crimes and Punishment* published anonymously in 1764—the most exciting essay on law of the eighteenth century. It proposed a reorientation of criminal law toward humanistic goals. Beccaria proposed that judges should not interpret law, but rather that law should be made more specific. He believed that the real measure of crime was its harm to society. He is regarded as the founder of the classical school of criminology.

Bentham and the "Hedonistic Calculus"

Jeremy Bentham was the leading reformer of the British criminal law system during the late eighteenth and early nineteenth centuries. He strongly advocated a system of graduated penalties to more closely relate the punishment to the crime. As political equality became a dominant philosophy, new penal policies were required to accommodate this new emphasis. Thorsten Sellin states:

> Older penal law had reflected the views dominant in societies where slavery or serfdom flourished, political inequality was the rule, and sovereignty was assumed to be resting in absolute monarchs. Now the most objectionable features of that law, which had favored the upper classes and had provided often arbitrary, brutal and revolting corporal and capital punishments for the lower classes, were to be removed and equality before the law established. Judicial torture for the purpose of extracting evidence was to be abolished, other than penal measures used to control some conduct previously punished as crime, and punishments made only severe enough to outweigh the gains expected by the criminal from his crime. This meant a more humane law, no doubt, applied without discrimination to all citizens alike in harmony with the new democratic ideas.[5]

Bentham believed that an individual's conduct could be influenced in a more scientific manner. Asserting that the main objective of an intelligent person is to achieve the most pleasure while receiving the least amount of pain, he developed his "hedonistic calculus,"[6] which he applied to all his efforts to reform the criminal law. He, like Beccaria, believed that punishment could act as a deterrent, but only if made appropriate to the crime. This line of thought, adopted by active reformers Samuel Romilly and Robert Peel in the early nineteenth century, has been instrumental in the development of the modern prison.

Jeremy Bentham (1748–1832) was the greatest leader in the reform of English criminal law. He believed that if punishments were designed to negate whatever pleasure or gain the criminal derived from crime, the crime rate would go down. He wrote prodigiously on all aspects of criminal justice. Something of a crackpot in his later years, he devised his ultimate prison: the Panoptican. This monstrosity was never constructed, but debate over it slowed down progress in English penology.

Sir Samuel Romilly (1757–1818), a follower of Bentham, was an able lawyer and the greatest leader in direct and persistent agitation for reform of the English criminal code. He pressed for construction of the first modern English prison, Millbank, in 1816. This prison idea was taken up by Romilly's followers, Sir James Mackintosh (1765–1832) and Sir Thomas Fowell Buxton (1786–1845).

Sir Robert Peel (1788–1850) was the leader in the English legislature for reform of the criminal code, pushing through programs that were devised by Bentham, Romilly, and others. He established the Irish constabulary, called the "Peelers" after the founder. In 1829, he started the London metropolitan police known as "Bobbies," also after Sir Robert. He was active in all phases of criminal justice.

John Howard

John Howard gave little thought to prisons or prison reform until he was appointed sheriff of Bedfordshire in 1773. This appointment opened his eyes to horrors he never dreamed could have existed. He was appalled by the conditions he found in hulks[7] and gaols[8] and pressed for legislation to abate some of the abuses and to improve sanitary conditions. He also traveled extensively on the European continent to examine prisons in other countries. He saw similarly deplorable conditions in most areas, but was most impressed by some of the institutions in France and Italy. In 1777, he described these conditions and suggested reforms in his *State of Prisons*. In 1779 Parliament passed the Penitentiary Act, providing four principles for reform: secure and sanitary structures, systematic inspection, abolition of fees, and a reformatory regime.[9] This Act resulted in the first penitentiary, located at Wyndomham in Norfolk, England, and operated by Sir Thomas Beever, the sheriff of Wyndomham. As will be seen, the principles contained in the Act, while lofty in concept, were hard to implement in the atmosphere of indifference which prevailed. It is ironic that this great advocate for better conditions in prisons should himself contract jail fever (typhus) and die of it in the Russian Ukraine in 1790. John Howard's name has become a synonym for prison reform, and the John Howard Society carries his ideas forward to this day.[10]

William Penn and the "Great Law"

The American colonies were governed by the British under codes established by the Duke of York in 1676, and part of the older Hampshire code established in 1664. These codes were similar to those followed in England, and the use of capital and corporal punishment was the rule of the day. Branding, flogging, the stocks, the pillory, and the brank were also in vogue.

The concept of more humanitarian treatment of offenders was brought to America by William Penn, the founder of Pennsylvania and leader of the Quakers. The Quaker movement was the touchstone of penal reform, not only in America but also through its influence on such advocates as Beccaria in Italy and Howard in England. In comparison to the harsh colonial codes in force at the time, the "Great Law" of the Quakers was quite humane. This body of laws envisioned hard labor as a more effective punishment than death for serious crimes, and capital punishment was eliminated from the original codes. Later, in supplementary acts, murder and manslaughter were included as social crimes. Only premeditated murder was punishable by death; other acts were treated according to the circumstances.

FIGURE I–4. John Howard, Early Jail Reformer (Courtesy Federal Bureau of Prisons)

It is interesting to note that the Quakers' "Great Law" did away with most religious offenses and stuck to strictly criminal jurisprudence. This was a vast departure from the codes of other colonies and the earlier European codes. Under the Great Law, a "house of corrections" was established where most punishment was meted out in the form of hard labor. This was the first time that correctional confinement at hard labor was used as punishment for serious crimes, and not merely as a *preface* to punishment scheduled for a later date. This Quaker code of 1682 was in force until 1718, when it was repealed, ironically, just one day after the death of William Penn. The Great Law was replaced by the English Anglican Code, and the mild Quaker philosophy gave way to harsh punishments. This new code was even worse than the previous codes of the Duke of York. Capital punishment was prescribed for thirteen offenses[11] and mutilation, branding, and other corporal punishments were restored for many others.

The influence of Montesquieu, Voltaire, Beccaria, Bentham, Howard, and Penn was felt throughout colonial America. Much of the idealism embodied in the United States Constitution reflects the writings of these progressive eighteenth-century leaders. With their philosophies in mind, we can consider some of the major developments in correctional practice in that era of reform.

Houses of Correction, Workhouses, and Gaols

The proliferation of Bridewell-style houses of correction in England was originally intended as a humanitarian move. In 1576, as previously mentioned, Parliament ordered that each county in England should construct such an institution. These were not merely extensions of almshouses or poorhouses, but were actually penal institutions for all sorts of misdemeanants. While the bloody penalties for major offenses were growing in number, not even the most callous would advocate harsh physical punishment for all offenders. All sorts of rogues, from idlers to whores, were put into these bridewells where they were compelled to work under strict discipline at the direction of hard taskmasters. The house of correction and the workhouse are generally regarded as synonymous today. Actually the workhouse was intended to be used not as a penal institution, but as a place for the training and care of the poor. In practice, however, the two soon became indistinguishable, first in England and later in America. Conditions and practices in these institutions were no better than in the gaols (jails) by the turn of the eighteenth century.

The use of gaols for the detention of prisoners has a grim and unsavory history. As the eighteenth century began, gaol administration was pretty much left up to the whim of the gaoler, usually under the control of the sheriff. Gaols were often used to extort huge fines from those who had the means by holding them indefinitely in pretrial confinement until they gave in and paid. The lot of the common "gaolbird"[12] was surely not a happy one. Many of the prisoners perished long before their trial date. The squalid and unhealthy conditions gave rise to epidemics of gaol fever that spread to all levels of English life. John Howard claimed that more people died from this malady between 1773 and 1774 than were executed by the Crown.[13] Ironically, prisoners and not prison conditions were blamed for the spread of this deadly disease, and even more sanguinary penalties for offenses were devised. Robert Caldwell describes the typical English gaol:

> Devoid of privacy and restrictions, its contaminated air heavy with the stench of unwashed bodies, human excrement, and the discharge of loathsome sores, the gaol bred the basest thoughts and the foulest deeds. The inmates made their own rules, and the weak and the innocent were exposed to the tyranny of the strong and the vicious. Prostitutes plied their trade with ease, often with the connivance and support of the gaolers, who thus sought to supplement their fees. Even virtuous women sold themselves to obtain food and clothing, and frequently the worst elements of the town used the gaol as they would a brothel. Thus, idleness, vice, perversion, profligacy, shameless exploitation, and ruthless cruelty were compounded in hotbeds of infection and cesspools of corruption. These were the common gaols of England.[14]

It is depressing to think that John Howard, shocked into humanitarian reform efforts when he found himself responsible for one of these human cesspools, was the only sheriff to consider such action.

Transportation Systems

One of the earliest forms of social vengeance was banishment. In primitive societies the offender was cast out into the wilderness, usually to be eaten by wild beasts or to succumb to the elements. As we have seen, places of imprisonment and capital punishment were later developed as substitutes for banishment. Banishment to penal servitude was, in effect, *civil* death. Banishment to the gaols, however, more often than not ended in *physical* death.

The wandering and jobless lower classes, in the period following the breakup of feudalism, were concentrated mostly in high crime slums in the major cities. As economic conditions worsened, the number of imprisonable crimes was increased to the point where the available prisons were filled. In England, from 1596 to 1776, the pressure was partially relieved by deporting or "transporting" malefactors to the colonies in America. Estimates of how many American settlers arrived in chains vary greatly. Margaret Wilson estimates between 300 to 400 annually;[15] other authorities put the figure as high as 2,000 a year. The use of convict labor was widespread prior to the adoption of slavery in the colonies. Even though the entering flow of dangerous felons was somewhat slowed by the introduction of slavery, the poor and the misdemeanant continued to come in great numbers.

Transportation to America was brought to an abrupt halt in 1776 by the Revolution. But England still needed to send the vast numbers of criminals overloading their crowded institutions *somewhere*. Captain James Cook had discovered Australia in 1770, and as soon as possible the system of transportation was transferred to that continent. It was planned that the criminals would help tame that new and wild land. Over 135,000 felons, roughly, were sent to Australia between 1787 and 1875, when the British finally abandoned the system.

The ship's felons were transported in what have been described as "floating hells"[16]—an understatement. The conditions below decks were worse than those of the gaols. Many died on the long voyages, but enough survived to make it a profitable venture for shipowners, who fitted out ships specifically for this purpose. Other nations turned to transportation in the nineteenth century, as we will discuss later.

Hulks: A Sordid Episode

From 1776 until 1875, when transportation to Australia was terminated, the increased prisoner loads wreaked havoc in England's few available facilities. The immediate solution to that problem created one of the most odious episodes in the history of penology and corrections: the use of old "hulks," abandoned or unusable transport ships anchored in rivers and harbors throughout the British Isles, to confine criminal offenders. The brutal and degrading conditions found in the gaols, houses of correction, and work-houses paled in comparison with these fetid and rotting human garbage dumps.

Those responsible for the hulks made no attempt to segregate young from old, hardened criminals from poor misdemeanants, or even men from women. Brutal flogging and degrading labor soon bred moral degeneration in both inmates and keepers. The hulks were originally intended only as a temporary solution to a real problem, but they were not completely abandoned until eighty years later, in 1858. (Hulks were used in California in the nineteenth century, and one state, Washington, made extensive plans to use decommissioned U.S. Navy warships as prisons in 1976.) This episode in penal history becomes relevant later when the problems of overcrowding in our maximum security prisons are examined.

Early Cellular Prisons

In his travels on the continent, John Howard was most impressed by Jean Jacques Vilain's Maison de Force (stronghouse) at Ghent, Belgium, and by

FIGURE I–5. Convict Hulk, Nineteenth-Century England (Courtesy Federal Bureau of Prisons)

the Hospice (hospital) of San Michele in Rome. Although these institutions had developed along entirely different lines, both made a lasting impression on Howard. Both served as workhouses, but otherwise they had little in common; their differences are more important than their similarities.

Predecessors of the Belgian workhouses were those in neighboring Amsterdam, constructed around 1596. Most were intended to make a profit, not to exemplify humanitarian ideals, and were seen as a way to put rogues and able-bodied beggars to work. The workhouses were modeled after the Bridewell institution in England and followed a similar pattern of hard work and cruel punishment. By the eighteenth century, Belgium too was faced with increasing numbers of beggars and vagrants, and the government called on administrator and disciplinarian Jean Jacques Vilain for help. His solution—the "Maison de Force" built in Ghent in 1773—followed the basic workhouse pattern established in Holland and England, but in many respects it was far more just and humane.

Vilain's efforts at improving the administration of the workhouse have earned him an honored place in penal history. He was one of the first to develop a system of classification to separate women and children from hardened criminals, and felons from minor offenders. Although he was a stern disciplinarian, he was opposed to life imprisonment or cruel punishment.

Rather, discipline was defined by the biblical rule: "If any man will not work, neither let him eat." Vilain's use of individual cells and a system of silence while working resembled procedures observed at the Hospice of San Michele in Rome. His far-reaching concepts of fair and just treatment, when viewed against the harsh backdrop of that era, mark Vilain as a real visionary in the correctional field.

The Hospice of San Michele was built in 1704 by Pope Clement XI. The Pope himself placed an inscription over the door which remains to this day: *"It is insufficient to restrain the wicked by punishment unless you render them virtuous by corrective discipline."* This concept of expiation and penance, applied to corrections, was new and exciting to John Howard. His Puritan ethic could see the value of repentance and hard work as demonstrated by the program there. The use of separate cells for sleeping and a large central hall for working became the model for penal institutions in the nineteenth century.

The Hospice of San Michele was designed for incorrigible boys and youths under twenty. As such it is recognized as one of the first institutions that undertook to handle juvenile offenders exclusively. The rule of strict silence was enforced by ready flogging of violators. They were administered massive doses of scripture and hard work in hopes that this regime would reform them. Under somewhat different policies, the Hospice of San Michele is still used as a reformatory for delinquent boys today.

The main concepts that carried over from these early cellular institutions were the monastic regime of silence and expiation, the central community work area, and solitary individual cells for sleeping. The philosophy of penitence and monastic contemplation of past wrongs espoused by these institutions was reflected in the Quakers' early prison efforts in America.

The Walnut Street Jail

As we have seen, the world of the eighteenth century had prisons as such, but they were generally used only as places of detention for minor offenders and for pretrial confinement.

One of the earliest recorded American attempts to operate a state prison for felons was located in an abandoned copper mine in Simsbury, Connecticut. This underground prison began operation in 1773 and quickly became the site of America's first prison riots, in 1774. Although some have called it the first state prison, it was really not much more than a throwback to the sulphur pits of ancient Rome, and it did nothing to advance the state of American corrections. The prisoners were housed in long mine shafts and the administration buildings were placed near the entrances. Underground "mine shaft" prisons constituted one of several American attempts to make a special place in which to house and work the convicted felon. These efforts reached a focal point in Pennsylvania in 1790.

FIGURE I–6. The Walnut Street Jail, Philadelphia, 1790 (Courtesy
Federal Bureau of Prisons)

It is hard to imagine a time when there were no long-term penitentiaries
for felons, but prior to 1785, in England, that was the case. Ironically, in
1790 the first penitentiary in America and the "father" of the modern prison
system was born in the same city which spawned the fledgling United States
as a nation. Philadelphia, Pennsylvania, the home of the Declaration of
Independence, is also—thanks to the Quakers—the home of the Walnut
Street Jail,[17] the first true correctional institution in America.

Despite earlier efforts at prison reform, the Quakers had been thwarted in
their humanistic goals by the repeal of Penn's Great Law in 1718. In 1776,
the first American Penitentiary Act was passed, but its implementation was
delayed because of the War of Independence. In 1790, with the Revolution
behind them, the Quakers reasserted their concern with the treatment of
convicted criminals.[18] After much prodding, they convinced the Pennsylvania legislature to declare a wing of the Walnut Street Jail as a penitentiary
house for all convicted felons except those sentenced to death.[19] Thus,
although prisons, gaols, dungeons, and workhouses had existed before, this
wing was the first to be used *exclusively* for the *correction* of convicted
felons.

Some of the concepts embodied in the Walnut Street Jail had their
antecedents in the charter of William Penn in 1682. Those provisions,
repressed by the harsh Anglican Code, were:

1. all prisoners were to be bailable;

2. those wrongfully imprisoned could recover double damages;

3. prisons were to be free as to fees, food, and lodging;

4. the lands and goods of felons were to be liable for double restitution to injured parties;

5. all counties were to provide houses to replace the pillory, stocks, and the like.[20]

While not all of these idealistic reforms were adopted, the direction of change had been established. The system of prison discipline developed at the Walnut Street Jail became known as the "Pennsylvania system." The Pennsylvania system was developed through the ideas and efforts of such reformers as Benjamin Franklin and Benjamin Rush, building on the humanitarian ideals of Howard, Bentham, Beccaria, and Montesquieu. Patriot and war hero William Bradford, who drafted the codes that implemented the system, praised the European reformers in the state legislature.

As originally conceived, the basic element of the Pennsylvania system called for solitary confinement without work. It was assumed that this method would result in quicker reformations. Offenders could reflect on their crimes all day and would soon repent so that they might rejoin humanity. The terrible effects of such isolation—physical and psychological—soon became apparent. Some kind of work had to be provided, as well as moral and religious instruction, to maintain the prisoners' mental and bodily health. The work schedule was from eight to ten hours a day in isolation, usually in the form of piecework or handicrafts.

More and more convicts were sent to the new state prison, and overcrowding shattered early hopes for its success. Even the original system of separate areas for women and children broke down with the flood of inmates. Despite the ultimate failure of the Walnut Street program, it represented a major breakthrough. New prisons were soon in demand throughout America. The Walnut Street Jail was copied extensively, in at least ten states and many foreign countries.[21]

Benjamin Franklin (1706–1790) founded the American Philosophical Society in Philadelphia in 1743. He served as Pennsylvania's appointed agent to England and as a member of the Second Continental Congress (1775) committee to draft the Declaration of Independence, which he signed. He was plenipotentiary to France and negotiated to obtain that country's help in the Revolution. He was a statesman, scientist, and philosopher.

Benjamin Rush (1745–1813), physician and political leader, was a member of both Continental Congresses (1776, 1777) and a signer of the Declaration of Independence. He established the first free dispensary in the U.S. (1786), and was an advocate of prison reform and humane treatment.

William Bradford (1721–1791), the "Patriot Printer of 1776," was one of the early advocates of a Continental Congress. He was a member of the Sons of Liberty, a rival of Benjamin Franklin, and an active reformer of the hard British codes. As a major in the army, he became a hero of the Revolution.

Bentham's Panoptican

Jeremy Bentham was more than a philosopher and an idealist; he was also a practical man and an architect. The tragic situation of the hulks on the rivers and in the harbors of England created a stir in the British Parliament; members saw the need for some alternative to these horrors for the housing of convicted felons and other offenders. A national penitentiary system was considered a viable solution. Bentham had been working on the design of a national penitentiary, in line with John Howard's four principles: secure and sanitary conditions, systematic inspection, abolition of fees, and a reformatory regime. Parliament passed a bill to erect one or more national institutions in 1779, but never provided the funds. In 1799 that defunct bill was superseded by a contract with Bentham to furnish the design of a building which he called a Panoptican (inspection-house). While this monstrosity was never actually constructed, some of the principles Bentham followed in designing it are worth discussing.

Essentially, the Panoptican plan called for a huge structure covered by a glass roof. A central cupola allowed the guards to see into all the cells, which were arranged around it in a circular arrangement like spokes on a wheel. It was Bentham's notion that the visibility of the cells would make it easier for custodians to manage the inmates. There was a great amount of controversy over this radically new concept, and, in the end, Bentham spent almost all of his time and most of his family fortune in vain attempts to get it built.

While the British government was not convinced of the Panoptican's worth, many U.S. prisons were based on that principle. Perhaps the Western penitentiary in Pennsylvania came closest to Bentham's plans. The radiating spoke design, constructed on a large scale, characterized many of the massive institutions built in the nineteenth century.

The End of an Era

As the eighteenth century drew to a close, the move for prison reform was sparked by a new feeling of vigor and energy. The decade after the Walnut Street Jail opened was full of bright hope for the concepts embodied there, however imperfectly. It would be an oversimplification to say that the Walnut Street Jail was the world's first real attempt at a prison for convicted felons. The eighteenth century produced many such attempts, both in Europe and in America. Some of the principles behind the Walnut Street Jail, however, had a *permanent* influence on the development of correctional institutions throughout the world. Connecticut's abortive attempt to establish a state prison at Simsbury failed because the mine shafts could not be made habitable and because there was little public enthusiasm for the project. The compassionate efforts of the Quakers, while much more humane, were doomed to failure by the lack of public and political support, incompetent personnel, and enforced idleness. With the industrial age came overcrowded prisons, which forced the new administrators to consider much larger and more productive kinds of institutions. As America entered the nineteenth century, it also entered an age of bigness and expansion. The prison movement adopted this growth-oriented philosophy, and, as we shall see in the next chapter, the nineteenth and early twentieth centuries became the age of prisons.

REVIEW QUESTIONS

I. Find the answers to the following in the text:

1. What was Beccaria's main contribution to corrections?

2. What were John Howard's four principles for a penitentiary system?

3. Many reformers tried to improve prison conditions in the eighteenth century. Name at least three and describe their major contributions.

II. Words to identify:

1. hulks

2. transportation

3. gaols

4. workhouse

5. jail fever

6. Maison de Force

7. Panoptican

8. penitentiary

9. Walnut Street Jail

10. Anglican Code

NOTES

1. The *Persian Letters* was a satirical essay by Montesquieu on the abuses of current criminal law. The essay had a great influence upon Beccaria. This, along with Voltaire's activities, led Beccaria to write his "Crimes and Punishments."

2. Harry Elmer Barnes and Negley K. Teeters, *New Horizons in Criminology,* 3d ed. (Englewood Cliffs, N.J.: Prentice-Hall, 1959), p. 322.

3. Cesare Beccaria, *An Essay on Crimes and Punishment* (Philadelphia: P. H. Nicklin, 1819).

4. *Domenico Morellet* (1727-1819) was a French philosopher who worked with Diderot on the Encyclopedia.

5. Thorsten Sellin, "A Look at Prison History," *Federal Probation* (September 1967): 20.

6. *Hedonistic calculus* was a term derived by Jeremy Bentham to describe the idea that "to achieve the most pleasure and the least pain is the main objective of an intelligent man."

7. Convict *hulks* were the earliest application of imprisonment as a method of dealing with criminals. The hulks, sometimes called "hell holds," were broken-down war vessels. They were stripped and anchored on bays and rivers around England. They were unsanitary, full of vermin, and unventilated. Disease ran rampant and often wiped out the whole prisoner population, and sometimes the crew and neighboring citizens as well. The last European hulk was still maintained at Gibraltar as late as 1875.

8. *Gaols* (jails) were used primarily as places of detention. Some prisoners waited to be tried, others could not pay their fines, and others awaited execution. No attempt was made to segregate prisoners by age, sex, or degree of crime. Food was often sold by the sheriff at inflated prices, and those who could not pay or have food brought in starved. Early efforts of reformers like John Howard helped to clean them up, but even today jails are usually the worst disgrace of the criminal justice system.

9. Barnes and Teeters, *New Horizons in Criminology,* p. 335.

10. *The John Howard Society* is a nonprofit organization supported by contributions. It provides casework service to inmates and their families. It also works to promote community understanding of prison problems and provides technical assistance to correctional agencies. (608 South Dearborn Street, Chicago, Illinois 60605.)

11. Only larceny was exempt from capital punishment. All other major crimes were punishable by death.

12. *Gaolbird* (jailbird) was coined because of the large cagelike cells used to confine the prisoners in unsegregated bunches, like "birds in a cage."

13. John Howard, *The State of Prisons* (New York: E. P. Dutton and Co., 1929).

14. Robert G. Caldwell, *Criminology* (New York: The Ronald Press, 1965), p. 494.

15. Margaret Wilson, *The Crime of Punishment* (New York: Harcourt, Brace, and World, 1931), p. 224.

16. Transportation ships are described in Barne's *The Story of Punishment* (p. 74):

> Hired transports were employed to convey the convicts from England to New South Wales. Contractors received between £20 and £30 per head. The more convicts carried the greater the profit would be, thus as many were usually crammed on board as the ships would hold. As a result of such a state of confinement the most loathsome disease was common and the death rate was extremely high. Out of 502 who were placed on the "Neptune" in 1790 for conveyance to Australia, 158, and in 1799, 95 out of the 300 on board the "Hillsborough" died on the voyage. Those who did arrive were so near dead that they could not stand, and it was necessary to sling them like goods and hoist them out of the ships, and when first landed they died at the rate of ten or twelve a day. The government attempted in 1802 to correct these evils by sending convicts twice a year in ships specially fitted out for the purpose, and placed under the direction of a transport board and commanded by naval officers. Although the transports continued to be crowded, health conditions apparently had greatly improved as it was reported in 1819 by Sir T. B. Martin, the head of the transport board, that within the past three years only 53 out of 6,409, or at the rate of 1 in 112, had died. Out of the 10 transports which had recently sailed only one or two had died.

17. *The Walnut Street Jail,* until the innovation of solitary confinement for felons, was typical of colonial jails. These are described in David J. Rothman's *Discovery of the Asylum* (Boston: Little-Brown, 1971), p. 55:

> [J]ails in fact closely resembled the household in structure and routine. They lacked a distinct architecture and special procedures. When the Virginia burgess required that county prisons be "good, strong, and substantial," and explicitly recommended that they follow "after the form of Virginia housing," results were in keeping with these directions. The doors were perhaps somewhat sturdier, the locks slightly more impressive, but the general design of the jail was the same as for an ordinary residence. True to the household model, the keeper and his family resided in the jail, occupying one of its rooms; the prisoners lived several together in the others, with little to differentiate the keeper's quarters from their own. They wore no special clothing or uniforms and usually neither cuffs nor chains restrained their movements. They walked—not marched—about the jail. The workhouse model was so irrelevant that nowhere were they required to perform the slightest labor.

18. Barnes and Teeters, *New Horizons in Criminology,* p. 336.

19. Negley K. Teeters, *The Cradle of the Penitentiary* (Philadelphia: Pennsylvania Prison Society, 1955).

20. Donald R. Taft, *Criminology,* 3d ed. (New York: Macmillan, 1956), p. 478.

21. Harry Elmer Barnes, *The Story of Punishment,* 2d ed. (Montclair, N.J.:Patterson Smith, 1972), p. 128.

3 The Age of Prisons (1800–1960)

To the builders of this nitemare
Though you may never get to read these words I pity you;
For the cruelty of your minds have designed this Hell;
If men's buildings are a reflection of what they are,
This one portraits the ugliness of all humanity.
IF ONLY YOU HAD SOME COMPASSION
on a prison wall

The Pennsylvania System

With the advent of the nineteenth century, and the social upheaval produced by the Industrial Revolution, the citizens of Pennsylvania began to exert leadership in the development of a penitentiary system. The Walnut Street Jail had been fairly effective for a decade, and that Pennsylvania system was copied extensively in both architectural design and administration. But when the Philadelphia Society for the Alleviation of the Miseries of Public Prisons[1] observed the many emerging problems at the Walnut Street Jail, a radically new prison was proposed for the state. It was proposed that solitary confinement without labor be used as the sole reformatory process. As mentioned in the previous chapter, the rationale here was that complete isolation would work as a quick reformer.

Pennsylvania	Walnut St. Jail, Philadelphia	1790
Pennsylvania	Walnut St. Jail, Philadelphia	1790
New York	Newgate Prison, New York City	1797
New Jersey	State Penitentiary, Lamberton	1798
Kentucky	State Penitentiary, Frankfort	1800
Virginia	State Penitentiary, Richmond	1800
Massachusetts	State Prison, Charlestown	1805
Vermont	State Prison, Windsor	1809
Maryland	State Penitentiary, Baltimore	1812
New Hampshire	State Prison, Concord	1812
Ohio	State Penitentiary, Columbus	1816
Georgia	State Penitentiary, Milledgeville	1817

Early American Prisons—Prior to 1825

FIGURE I–7. Eastern State Penitentiary, Philadelphia (Courtesy Federal Bureau of Prisons)

The Western Pennsylvania Prison at Pittsburgh, built in 1826, was based on the cellular isolation wing of the Walnut Street Jail. Essentially, the Western prison amounted to a poor imitation of Bentham's Panoptican. This octagonal monstrosity, as proposed, originally provided for solitary confinement and no labor. The legislature amended the program in 1829, maintaining solitary confinement but adding the provision that inmates perform some labor in their cells. In 1833 the small, dark cells were torn down and larger outside cells were built. These efforts influenced the development of the Eastern Penitentiary, in Philadelphia.

The Eastern Penitentiary became the model and primary exponent of the Pennsylvania or "separate" system. This prison was built somewhat like a square wheel, with the cell blocks arranged like spokes around the hub, or central rotunda. The routine at Eastern—solitary confinement, silence, and labor in "outside"[2] cells—clearly stressed the *separation* of each inmate from the others.

While the Pennsylvania system aroused great interest among foreign nations, it was adopted by only two other states. The New Jersey State Penitentiary in Trenton began operations in 1837 along the lines of the separate system—soon abandoned, however, in favor of that used at Auburn, New York. Rhode Island followed the same pattern as New Jersey. Their first prison, built in 1838 along the lines of the Eastern Penitentiary, had abandoned the separate system by 1852. By contrast, many European countries wholeheartedly adopted the Pennsylvania model.[3]

FIGURE I–8. Cleaning the "Slop Jars," Early Auburn-Style Prison
(Courtesy American Correctional Association)

The Auburn System

The major evils of the jails and other confinement facilities prior to 1800 were indiscriminate congregate confinement and enforced idleness. The rapid debasement of the prisoners, when kept in filthy conditions with men, women, and children thrown together under a regime of neglect and brutality, appalled the early reformers. The long-term prisons established in the last decade of the eighteenth century were not just a substitute for capital and corporal punishment; they were total administrative and custodial systems intended to provide relief from the evils of the old methods. In the first quarter of the nineteenth century, administrators were experimenting with many new systems. The leading contenders for the world's attention were the Eastern Penitentiary, described above, and the New York State Prison at Auburn, opened in 1819.

The Auburn prison administrators developed a system that was almost the opposite of that used at the Eastern Penitentiary. The building itself was based on a new "inside" cell design,[4] and the cells were small when compared to those at Eastern. These small cells were designed just for sleeping, not for work. In addition, a new style of discipline was developed at Auburn, which became known as the Auburn or "congregate" system.

In the early years of the Auburn prison, administrators tried an experiment to test the efficacy of the Pennsylvania system. They selected eighty of the

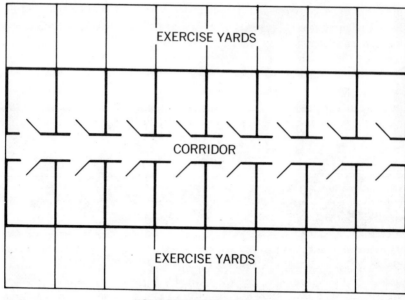

EXERCISE YARDS

CORRIDOR

EXERCISE YARDS

"OUTSIDE" CELL DESIGN

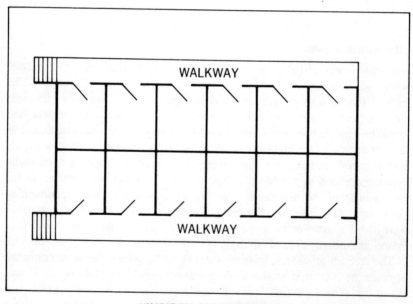

WALKWAY

WALKWAY

"INSIDE" CELL DESIGN

FIGURE I–9. Cell Designs

most hardened convicts and placed them in solitary confinement and enforced idleness from Christmas 1821 through Christmas 1823. So many of
these men succumbed to sickness and insanity that the experiment was
scrapped. The Auburn administration claimed failure for solitary confinement, where idleness was a condition. Given the small inside cells at
Auburn, their claim is no doubt a valid one. However, the Auburn experiment cannot be considered a fair test of the Pennsylvania system, since it
used large outside cells and provided for handicraft and other labor in the
cell.

An unfortunate by-product of the badly planned Auburn experiment was
the use of solitary confinement as a means of punishment within the prison.
Other elements of the discipline regimen that developed at Auburn included
congregate work in the shops in the daytime, separation of prisoners into
small individual cells at night, silence at all times, lock-step marching
formations, and a congregate mess at which the prisoners sat face-to-back.[5]
There was great emphasis on *silence*. In the belief that verbal exchange
between prisoners was contaminating, conversation was prevented by liberal
use of the whip. An excellent description of the Auburn system, in its early
stages, is contained in the classic *Story of Punishment* by the great
criminologist and historian Harry Elmer Barnes, in the form of a letter from
Louis Dwight:

> At Auburn we have a more beautiful example still of what may be
> done by proper discipline, in a prison well constructed. It is not
> possible to describe the pleasure which we feel in contemplating this
> noble institution, after wading through the fraud, and the material and
> moral filth of many prisons. We regard it as a model worthy of the
> world's imitation. We do not mean that there is nothing in this
> institution which admits of improvement; for there have been a few
> cases of unjustifiable severity in punishments; but, upon the whole, the
> institution is immensely elevated above the old penitentiaries.
>
>   The whole establishment, from the gate to the sewer, is a specimen
> of neatness. The unremitted industry, the entire subordination and
> subdued feelings of the convicts, has probably no parallel among an
> equal number of criminals. In their solitary cells they spend the night,
> with no other book but the Bible, and at sunrise they proceed, in
> military order, under the eye of the turnkeys, in solid columns, with
> the lock march, to their workshops; thence, in the same order at the
> hour of breakfast, to the common hall, where they partake of their
> wholesome and frugal meal in silence. Not even a whisper is heard;
> though the silence is such that a whisper might be heard through the
> whole apartment. The convicts are seated, in single file, at narrow
> tables, with their backs towards the center, so that there can be no
> interchange of signs. If one has more food than he wants, he raises his

left hand; and if another has less, he raises his right hand, and the waiter changes it. When they have done eating, at the ringing of a little bell, of the softest sound, they rise from the table, form the solid columns, and return, under the eye of the turnkeys, to the workshops. From one end of the shops to the other, it is the testimony of many witnesses, that they have passed more than three hundred convicts, without seeing one leave his work, or turn his head to gaze at them. There is the most perfect attention to business from morning till night, interrupted only by the time necessary to dine, and never by the fact that the whole body of prisoners have done their tasks, and the time is now their own, and they can do as they please. At the close of the day, a little before sunset, the work is all laid aside at once, and the convicts return, in military order, to the solitary cells, where they partake of the frugal meal, which they were permitted to take from the kitchen, where it was furnished for them as they returned from the shops. After supper, they can, if they choose, read Scripture undisturbed and then reflect in silence on the errors of their lives. They must not disturb their fellow prisoners by even a whisper.[6]

Harry Elmer Barnes (1889–1968) was a great American educator and sociologist. He co-authored many books on penology, punishment, and criminology.

Louis Dwight (1793–1854) organized the Prison Discipline Society of Boston. He was originally trained for the ministry, but injured his lungs and could not preach. In 1824 he rode through the countryside distributing Bibles to prisoners. He was the most vocal advocate of the Auburn system, and his writings as director of the Prison Discipline Society of Boston from 1825 to 1854 are the best source of information on this era of American prisons.

The Auburn system became the pattern for over thirty state prisons in the next half century. Sing Sing Prison in New York followed the Auburn pattern in 1825. Wethersford Prison in Connecticut copied the Auburn system, but used a more moderate form of the brutal punishment employed at Auburn and Sing Sing. Later prisons modeled their discipline systems after Wethersford, in preference to the earlier New York systems.

New York (Sing Sing) 1825	Michigan (Jackson) 1838
Connecticut (Wethersford) . . .1827	Iowa (Ft. Madison) 1840
Massachusetts (a wing) 1829	Alabama (Wetumpka) 1841
Maryland (a wing) 1829	Georgia 1841
Vermont 1831	Kentucky 1842
Tennessee (Nashville) 1831	Indiana (Jeffersonville) 1842
New Hampshire 1832	Mississippi (Jackson) 1842
Illinois (Alton) 1833	Maine (Thomaston) 1845
Ohio (Columbus) 1834	New York (Clinton) 1845
Louisiana (Baton Rouge) 1835	Texas (Huntsville) 1848
Missouri (Jefferson City) 1836	Minnesota (Stillwater) 1851
California (San Quentin) 1852	Kansas (Lansing) 1864
Wisconsin (Waupun) 1852	Nevada (Carson City) 1864
Illinois (Joliet) 1858	South Carolina (Columbia) . .1865
Indiana (Michigan City) 1860	W. Virginia (Moundsville) . .1866
Idaho (Boise) 1863	Nebraska (Lincoln) 1869

Early American Prisons—after 1825

Auburn's structural design—inside cells and wings composed of cell tiers (cell blocks)—became the model for most prisons built in the following 150 years. Variations on the Auburn concept are shown in Figure I-10. The most popular of these types, first constructed in 1898 at Frenes, France, became known as the "telephone pole" design. Regardless of the cell block arrangement, the inside-cell design became the most common model in America.

One of the more important, but less noted, aspects of the early prison architecture was the grand scale and sheer size of these institutions. "Bigger is better" (and cheaper) was the watchword of early prison builders. These huge, gothic-style structures achieved an effect similar to the cathedrals of Europe in the Middle Ages, that of making the people inside seem small and insignificant. This feeling was further enhanced by the systems of stern and severe discipline employed in these huge castles of despair. Size will be discussed again in later chapters, but it should be noted at this point that the size of these early prisons gave rise to a subtle pressure to keep them filled with the castoffs of society.

Prison Discipline

The main theme in both the Pennsylvania and Auburn systems was the belief that a regimen of *silence* and *penitence* would prevent cross-infection and encourage behavior improvement in the prisoner. Supporters of the

1

Original Auburn
1816–1826

2

Eastern Penitentiary
1819–1829

3

Standard Auburn
1835–1935

4

Telephone (Fresnes)
1898

5

Hollow Square
1704–1940

6

Panoptican (Stateville)
1917–1918

7

"Last Word" (Terre Haute)
1940

8

"Sky-light" Super-Security
Fed. Bur. Pr. 1949

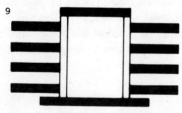

9

Dormitory (Lorton)
1916–1926

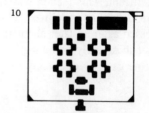

10

Community (Norfolk)
1927–34

FIGURE I–10. Types of Prison Structure (© Howard B. Gill, 1960. Reproduction permitted by Institute of Correctional Administration, Boston, Mass.)

Pennsylvania system claimed it was superior because the system made it easier to *control* the prisoners, gave more consideration to their *individual needs, prevented contamination* by complete separation of prisoners from each other, and provided more opportunity for *meditation* and repentance. Another advantage they cited was that prisoners could leave that system with their background known only to a few administrators.

On the other hand, supporters of the Auburn, or congregate, system argued that it was *cheaper to construct* and get started, *provided better vocational training,* and *produced more money* for the state.[7] The persuasive power of economics finally decided the battle, and the congregate system was adopted in almost all other American prisons, even in Pennsylvania. The Western Penitentiary was converted in 1869, and finally in 1913 the Eastern Penitentiary. The capitulation of the Pennsylvania system followed many long years of fierce controversy between the two systems. "The only gratifying feature of the controversy was that both systems were so greatly superior to the unspeakable. . . system which they displaced that their competition inevitably worked for the betterment of penal conditions."[8]

As mentioned in chapter 1, the prisons can be viewed as yet another method of social vengeance for wrongs against society. Europeans examining the Auburn and Pennsylvania systems made a keen observation on the American society and its prisons:

> It must be acknowledged that the penitentiary system in America is severe. While society in the United States gives the example of the most extended liberty, the prisons of the same country offer the spectacle of the most complete despotism.[9]

In this context, the individual citizen's sense of guilt when he inflicts brutal or cruel punishment on another is diffused by the need for revenge on criminal offenders as a class and for the protection of society. The "out of sight, out of mind" principle was especially evident in the early nineteenth-century prisons. Most of them were located far out in the countryside, free from either interference or inspection by the communities which supplied the prisoners. It is not too hard to understand why rules and procedures emphasized the smooth and undisturbed operation of the prison rather than efforts to modify the individual prisoner's behavior. Administrators were judged by the prison's production record and the number of escapes, not by the number of successful rehabilitations. Because of this, rules were designed to keep prisoners under total control. It is these early and well-established prison practices that have been the most difficult to overcome.

These practices, sometimes called the "old prison discipline," have been outlined by Howard B. Gill:

Hard labor.—Through productive work from "making little ones out of big ones" to constructive prison industries, or through nonproductive punitive labor such as the tread-mill and the carrying of cannon shot from one end of the prison yard to the other.

Deprivation.—Of everything except the bare essentials of existence.

Monotony.—Of diet and drab daily routine.

Uniformity.—The warden's proudest boast: "We treat every prisoner alike."

Mass movement.—Mass living in cell blocks, mass eating, mass recreation, even mass bathing. In this monolithic type of program the loss of individual personality was characteristic. One watched the dull gray line with its prison shuffle where the faces of men were as if shellacked with a single mask.

Degradation.—To complete the loss of identity prisoners became numbers. Housed in monkey cages, dressed in shoddy nondescript clothing, denied civil contacts even with guards like the one who snarled: "Who the hell are you to wish me a Merry Christmas?" Degradation became complete.

Subservience.—To rules, rules, rules—the petty whims of petty men.

Corporal punishment.—Brutality and force prevailed. In Tennessee the paddle, in Colorado the whip, in Florida the sweat box, etc.

Noncommunication.—Silence or solitary confinement; limited news, letters, visits, or contacts of any normal kind.

Recreation.—At first none; later a desultory or perfunctory daily hour in the yard.

No responsibility.—"No prisoner is going to tell me how to run my prison." Actually prisoners were relieved of every social, civic, domestic, economic, or even personal responsibility for the simplest daily routines.

Isolation.—Often 16 hours a day. Psychologically the admonition to "do your own time" with no thought for the other fellow only increased the egocentricity of the lone wolves.

No "fraternization" with the guards.—The rule found in many prisons that guards must not talk with prisoners about their personal problems or their crimes prevented any attempt at solving the criminal problem.

Reform by exhortation.

Now that psychology has come of age, we know that such a discipline denied every normal, basic need of the human personality and its corresponding opposite essential to a healthy and normal life. These included love and a proper comprehension of its opposite, hate; independence and the right kind of dependence; constructive use of imagination and truth; achievement and learning how to meet failure;

identity and a decent humility which recognized the dignity of the individual; intimacy and its opposite—discrimination; creativity and constructive criticism; integration and concentration.

These 16 human needs are recognized today as basic in the making of a healthy personality. Yet the prison discipline which was current for 100 years prior to 1925 denied every one of these basic needs. More than this, such a discipline fostered every pathology which results from a malfunctioning of these needs, namely, rejection, doubt, guilt, inferiority, inadequacy, diffusion, self-absorption, apathy, despair. Is it any wonder that men left prison worse than when they entered?[10]

Elam Lynds, warden of Auburn and later Sing Sing (which he built), was one of the most influential persons in the development of early American prison discipline. He is described as a strict disciplinarian who believed that all convicts were cowards who could not be reformed until their spirit was broken. To this end he devised a system of brutal punishments and degrading procedures, many of which remained as accepted practice until very recent times.

As mentioned, the imposition of *silence* was seen as the most important part of the discipline program. The rule of absolute silence and non-communication was maintained and enforced by the immediate use of the lash for the slightest infraction. Flogging was advocated by Lynds as the most effective way to maintain order. He sometimes used a "cat" made of wire strands, but more often a rawhide whip. One remembers the stereotyped ex-con from the movies of the 1930s and '40s who was always shown talking out of the side of his mouth; this technique actually developed earlier, in the "silent" prisons, to get around the silence rules.

Another bizarre form of discipline developed at Auburn was the lock-step formation. Prisoners were required to line up in close formation with their hands on the shoulders or under the arms of the prisoner in front. The line then moved rapidly toward its destination as the prisoners shuffled their feet in unison, without lifting them from the ground. Because this nonstop shuffle was "encouraged" by the use of the lash, any prisoner who fell out of lock-step risked a broken ankle or other serious injury from the steadily moving formation. Breaking the rule of silence during formation was considered especially objectionable and was punished viciously.

The use of degrading prison garb was also initiated at Auburn and Sing Sing. Early prisoners were allowed to wear the same clothing as the free society. At Auburn and Sing Sing different colors were used for the first-time offenders and for repeaters. These bizarre outfits served to reveal the prisoners' classification at a glance, to further institutionalize them, and to facilitate identification of escapees. The famous "prison stripes" came

FIGURE I–11. Lock-Step and Prison Stripes (Courtesy American Correctional Association)

into being in 1815 in New York. Only very recently were the stripes abandoned in most prisons.[11]

The methods used to prevent conversation or communication during meals were also bizarre. As mentioned earlier, prisoners were required to sit face-to-back. They were given their meager, and usually bland and unsavory, meal to eat in silence. If they wanted more food they would raise one hand, if they had too much they raised the other. Any infraction of the rule of silence resulted in a flogging and the loss of a meal. This kind of entrenched procedure, very resistant to modern reforms, has been the source of many prison riots.

One of the earliest and most well-known forms of prison discipline was the "prison-within-a-prison," or solitary confinement, used as punishment for violation of institutional rules. While the early experiment with total solitary confinement at Auburn showed that it could not serve as the basis of a *permanent* prison system, the administrators saw its possibilities as an ultimate *punishment* for infractions of prison rules. Most of the prisons designed along the Auburn model, therefore, had a block of cells somewhere inside the walls often referred to as the "hole."[12] Usually a sentence to solitary confinement was accompanied by reduced rations as well, often only bread and water. Solitary confinement is frequently used to discipline prisoners even today, although under somewhat more humane conditions.

Although many new prisons appeared in the century after the Eastern Penitentiary and the Auburn prison were built, they made few, if any, contributions to the development of penology or corrections. The two major innovations, which still persist today, were prison industries and the massive structures using the interior cell block. Enforced silence was finally seen as a failure and has generally been abandoned. Cruel and barbaric punishments, while publicly decried, are still in use—largely because most prisons are isolated from society and its controls. The development of corrections between 1800 and 1870, branching into procedures and philosophies that were unjust, still produced better methods than the universally accepted capital and corporal punishment which preceded it. And in the following era the swing toward a more realistic and humanistic correctional approach began.

Beginnings of Prison Industry

The handicrafts introduced into the solitary Eastern Penitentiary cells represented the origin of prison industries in America. In Europe and England, the infamous efforts to provide labor in the workhouses and bridewells had resulted in such fruitless activities ,as the treadmill.[13] The modern pressure to provide vocational training or earnings for inmates did not concern early American prison administrators; rather, they wanted to make the prisons self-sustaining. Toward this goal, the prison workshops were merely extensions of the early factory workshops. When the factory production system was introduced into prisons, and when the prisons began to show actual profits from their output, legislators were quickly convinced that prison industries were a sound operation. The Auburn system held out over the less efficient Pennsylvania system because it paid better returns on the taxpayer's investment. By the 1860s the system of absolute silence had begun to fall apart due to the necessity for communication in the industrial shops. Production became the paramount goal of prisons. As a report of that period stated: "There is not a state prison in America in which the reformation of the convict is the supreme object of the discipline."[14] Early prison industries, in effect, exploited the available free labor for the sole purpose of perpetuating the institution itself. Some leaders in the field, however, saw that a change in emphasis could make the industries an important factor in prisoner rehabilitation.

Maconochie and Crofton: A New Approach

The reformatory system in America owes a great deal to the work of an Englishman, Captain Alexander Maconochie, and an Irishman, Sir Walter Crofton. Taken together, they laid the foundation for the development of reformative rather than purely punitive programs for the treatment of criminals. In 1840, Captain Maconochie was put in charge of the British penal colony on Norfolk Island, about a thousand miles off the coast of Australia. To this island were sent the criminals who were "twice condemned": they had been shipped to Australia from England, and then from Australia to Norfolk. Conditions were so bad at Norfolk that men reprieved

FIGURE I–12. The "Hole" (Courtesy American Correctional Association)

from the death penalty wept, and those who were to die thanked God.[15] This was the kind of hell that Maconochie inherited.

The first thing Maconochie did was to eliminate the flat sentence, which allowed no hope of release until the full time had been served.[16] Then he developed a "mark system" whereby a convict could earn his freedom by hard work and good behavior. This put the burden of his own release on the convict. As Maconochie said, "When a man keeps the key of his own prison, he is soon persuaded to fit it into the lock." The system had five basic principles:

1. Release should not be based on the completing of a sentence for a set period of time, but on the completion of a determined and specified quantity of labor. In brief, time sentences should be abolished, and task sentences substituted.

2. The quantity of labor a prisoner must perform should be expressed in a number of "marks" which he must earn, by improvement of conduct, frugality of living, and habits of industry, before he can be released.

3. While in prison he should earn everything he receives. All sustenance and indulgences should be added to his debt of marks.

4. When qualified by discipline to do so, he should work in association with a small number of other prisoners, forming a group of six or seven, and the whole group should be answerable for the conduct and labor of each member.

5. In the final stage, a prisoner, while still obliged to earn his daily tally of marks, should be given a proprietary interest in his own labor and be subject to a less rigorous discipline, to prepare him for release into society.[17]

It is a sorry fact that Maconochie's visionary efforts toward rehabilitation were not appreciated or supported by the benighted bureaucrats above him. His results were disclaimed and the colony fell back into its former brutalized routine almost as soon as he left it.

Fortunately, Maconochie's ideas did reach beyond the shores of Norfolk Island. His successful use of the indeterminate sentence[18] showed that imprisonment could be used to prepare a convict for eventual return to the community. If this were true, then the length of sentence should not be an arbitrary period of time, but should be related to the rehabilitation of the offender. Sir Walter Crofton of Ireland used this concept in developing what he called the "indeterminate system," which came to be known as the

"Irish system." He reasoned that if penitentiaries are places where offenders think about their crimes and can decide to stop their criminal misbehavior ("repent"), then there must be a mechanism to determine that this decision has in fact been made, as well as a mechanism for getting the inmate out when penitence has been done. The indeterminate sentence was believed to be the best mechanism.

The system Crofton devised—like Maconochie's—consisted of a series of stages, each bringing the convict closer to the free society. The first stage was composed of solitary confinement and dull, monotonous work. The second stage involved assignment to public works and a progression through various grades, each grade shortening the length of stay. The last stage was assignment to an intermediate prison where the prisoner worked without supervision and moved in and out of the free community. If his conduct continued to be good and if he were able to find employment, he was returned to the community on a conditional pardon or "ticket-of-leave." This ticket could be revoked at any time within the span of his original fixed sentence, if his conduct was not up to standards established by those who supervised his conditional pardon. Crofton's plan was the first effort to establish a system of conditional liberty in the community, the system we know today as parole.

The Reformatory Era (1870–1910)

Leaders in United States penology and prison administration met at the American Prison Congress of 1870[19] to discuss the direction corrections practices should take next. They were especially concerned about over-crowding, and they discussed what new kinds of prisons should be built to

FIGURE I-13. Elmira Reformatory Prisoner Regiment (Courtesy Federal Bureau of Prisons)

alleviate this problem. Many urged that Maconochie's and Crofton's plans be adopted in America. This idea was endorsed by the members, and the Reformatory Era in American corrections was born.

The first reformatory in America, built in Elmira, New York, in 1876, became the model for all that followed it. Zebulon Brockway, the first superintendent, had introduced some new educational methods at the Detroit House of Corrections, and he expanded on this concept at Elmira. Elmira was originally built for adult felons, but it was used instead for youths from sixteen to thirty years of age who were serving their first term in prison. One observer cites the following characteristics as the basis for Elmira, and many of these reappeared in its imitators:

1. The material structural establishment itself. The general plan and arrangements should be those of the Auburn system, modified and modernized; and 10 percent of the cells might well be constructed like those of the Pennsylvania system. The whole should be supplied with suitable modern sanitary appliances and with abundance of natural and artificial light.

2. Clothing—not degradingly distinctive, but uniform, . . . fitly representing the respective grades or standing of the prisoners. . . . Scrupulous cleanliness should be maintained and the prisoners appropriately groomed.

3. A liberal prison dietary designed to promote vigor. Deprivation of food, by a general regulation, is deprecated. . . .

4. All the modern appliances for scientific physical culture; a gymnasium completely equipped with baths and apparatus; and facilities for field athletics.

5. Facilities for manual training sufficient for about one-third of the population. . . . This special manual training covers, in addition to other exercises in other departments, mechanical and freehand drawing; sloyd [manual training] in wood and metals; cardboard constructive form work; clay modeling; cabinet making; clipping and filing; and iron molding.

6. Trade instruction based on the needs and capacities of individual prisoners. (Where a thousand prisoners are involved, thirty-six trades may be usefully taught.)

7. A regimental military organization with a band of music, swords for officers, and dummy guns for the rank and file of prisoners.

8. School of letters with a curriculum that reaches from an adaptation of the kindergarten ... up to the usual high school course; and, in addition, special classes in college subjects. ...

9. A well-selected library for circulation, consultation, and for occasional semi-social use.

10. The weekly institutional newspaper, in lieu of all outside newspapers, edited and printed by the prisoners under due censorship.

11. Recreating and diverting entertainments for the mass of the population, provided in the great auditorium; not any vaudeville or minstrel shows, but entertainments of such a class as the middle cultured people of a community would enjoy. ...

12. Religious opportunities ... adapted to the hereditary [and] habitual ... denominational predilection of the individual prisoners.

13. Definitely planned, carefully directed, emotional occasions; not summoned, primarily, for either instruction, diversion, nor, specifically, for a common religious impression, but, figuratively, for a kind of irrigation.[20]

The only real differences between the programs at Elmira and the adult prisons were the emphasis on reforming youth, increased academic education, and more extensive trade training. Two major outstanding features were adopted for the reformatories, though: the indeterminate sentence and a grading system based on marks which could lead to parole.

Zebulon Reed Brockway (1827–1920), along with Enoch C. Wines and Franklin Benjamin Sanborn, was the third member of the "big three" of penology in 1870. He served on many commissions to improve prisons, and even developed the U.S. Army Disciplinary Barracks at Fort Leavenworth. Later, he was the first superintendent at Elmira Reformatory, where he used military organization and discipline to govern the prisoners. His book *Fifty Years of Prison Service* (Montclair, N.J.: Patterson-Smith, 1969) is a classic.

Elmira was copied, in one form or another, by eighteen states between 1876 and 1913. Brockway's leadership produced the first attempt to provide some programs of education and reformation to *all* inmates, adult or youth. Trade training, academic education, and the military type of discipline utilized at Elmira undoubtedly also influenced the programs of many of the older prisons. Some aspects of the indeterminate sentence and parole concepts were finally extended to the state prisons. In an era when public education was considered the answer to so many problems in the free world, it is not surprising that it was viewed as an answer to crime as well. Since the same physical plants and the same underpaid and poorly qualified personnel assigned to prisons were also assigned to reformatories, however, they were soon reduced to junior prisons with the usual institutional routine. The old "prison discipline" was still the most dominant factor in any penal program.

While the two main contributions of the Reformatory Era were the indeterminate sentence and parole, the seeds of education, vocational training, and individual rehabilitation had been sown. While these radical ideas could not flourish in the barren and hostile environment of that period, they took root and grew to fruition in later years.

New York (Elmira) 1876	Ind. (Jeffersonville) 1897
Michigan (Ionia) 1877	Wis. (Green Bay) 1898
Mass. (Concord) 1884	New Jersey (Rahway) 1901
Pa. (Huntingdon) 1889	Washington (Monroe) 1908–09
Minnesota (St. Cloud) 1889	Oklahoma (Granite) 1910–11
Colorado (Buena Vista) 1890	Maine (S. Windham) 1912–19
Illinois (Pontiac) 1891	Wyoming (Worland) 1912
Kansas (Hutchinson) 1895	Nebraska (Lincoln) 1912–13
Ohio (Mansfield) 1896	Conn. (Cheshire) 1913

Early Reformatories

Post-Civil War Prisons

The sixteen states that built prisons between 1870 and 1900 were almost all in the northern or western part of the country. Their only claims to improvement were the general introduction of plumbing and running water. All were of the Auburn type and the only modifications in the older prison routine were the abandonment of the silent system and the use of the indeterminate sentence and parole.

In the South, devastated by the Civil War, the penitentiary system had been virtually wiped out. Some states attempted to solve their prison

Oregon (Salem)	1871	Kentucky (Eddyville)	1883
Iowa (Anamosa)	1873	New Mexico (Santa Fe)	1884
Arizona (Yuma)	1875	Washington (Walla Walla)	1886
N. Carolina (Raleigh)	1875	Montana (Deer Lodge)	1889
Colorado (Canon City)	1876	Michigan (Marquette)	1889
Illinois (Menard)	1878	S. Dakota (Sioux Falls)	1891
California (Folsom)	1880	Tennessee (Brushy Mt.)	1895
N. Dakota (Bismarck)	1883	Utah (Salt Lake City)	1896

Post–Civil War Prisons

problems by leasing out their entire convict populations to contractors.[21] Others took in contract work, or devised combinations of leasing out prisoners and taking in contracts. The freed blacks were thus replaced by yet another group of slaves: the convicted felons. The South was unique in that it ignored the Auburn and Reformatory systems. The South's agrarian economy made exploitation of cheap labor both easy and desirable. A large portion of the prison population in the South was composed of plantation blacks with no influence or resources, and they were treated with no mercy. Leasing was eventually replaced by prison farms in most Southern states, but the practice was not completely erased until the mid-1920s. This sordid period in penal history, brought to light again in the 1960s in Arkansas,[22] simply confirms the depths to which even "civilized" people can sink in the treatment of their castoffs. This Southern correctional experience made only a negative contribution, in both procedure and discipline.

The Twentieth Century and the Industrial Prison

From the beginning of the twentieth century until 1935, the number of inmates in United States prisons increased by 140 percent.[23] Ten new Auburn-style prisons and one based on Bentham's Panoptican were built during this period—often referred to as the industrial era for prisons in America—which reached its zenith in 1935. These new prisons were considered "as cold and hard and abnormal as the prisoners whom they were intended to persuade toward better things."[24]

The industrial prison really had its origins in the profits turned by the first state prisons. Early in the nineteenth century, however, mechanics and cabinetmakers began to complain about the unfair competition they faced from the virtually free labor force available to prisons. The use of lease and contract systems further accelerated this aggravation and led to a series of investigations that reached national prominence in 1886. The emergence of the labor union movement, coupled with abuses of the contract and lease systems of prison labor, eliminated these systems in the northern prisons by

FIGURE I–14. A Typical Industrial Prison (Courtesy Pennsylvania
Bureau of Corrections)

the end of the nineteenth century. They were replaced by "piece-price"[25]
and "state account"[26] systems. Opposition to prison industries resulted in
enforced idleness among the increasing inmate population. This forced the
adult prisons to adopt reformatory methods in some measure, but made
self-sustaining institutions a thing of the past.

The story of the prison industry's battle with organized labor is a history
in itself and will not be covered here. The beginning of the end for
large-scale prison industries, those which could keep all inmates employed
in some kind of work, was the enactment of two federal laws which
controlled the character of prison products. The Hawes-Cooper Act, passed
in 1929, defined prison products as subject to the laws of any state they were
shipped to. The Ashurst-Sumners Act, passed in 1935, essentially stopped
the interstate transport of prison products by requiring that all prison
products shipped out of the state be labeled with the prison name, and
prohibiting interstate shipment where state laws forbade it. Excerpts from
these two important acts are reproduced below.

Hawes-Cooper Act, chap. 79:

*Be it enacted by the Senate and House of Representatives of the
United States of America in Congress assembled,* That all goods,
wares, and merchandise manufactured, produced, or mined, wholly
or in part, by convicts or prisoners, except convicts or prisoners
on parole or probation, or in any penal and/or reformatory
institutions, except commodities manufactured in Federal penal and
correctional institutions for use by the Federal Government,

transported into any State or Territory of the United States and remaining therein for use, consumption, sale, or storage, shall upon arrival and delivery in such State or Territory be subject to the operation and effect of the laws of such State or Territory to the same extent and in the same manner as though such goods, wares, and merchandise had been manufactured, produced, or mined in such State or Territory, and shall not be exempt therefrom by reason of being introduced in the original package or otherwise.

SEC. 2. This Act shall take effect five years after the date of its approval.

Approved, January 19, 1929.

Ashurst-Sumners Act, chap. 412:

Be it enacted by the Senate and House of Representatives of the United States of America in Congress assembled, That it shall be unlawful for any person knowingly to transport or cause to be transported, in any manner or by any means whatsoever, or aid or assist in obtaining transportation for or in transporting any goods, wares, and merchandise manufactured, produced, or mined wholly or in part by convicts or prisoners (except convicts or prisoners on parole or probation), or in any penal or reformatory institution, from one State, Territory, Puerto Rico, Virgin Islands, or District of the United States, or place noncontiguous but subject to the jurisdiction thereof, or from any foreign country, into any State, Territory, Puerto Rico, Virgin Islands, or District of the United States, or place noncontiguous but subject to the jurisdiction thereof, where said goods, wares, and merchandise are intended by any person interested therein to be received, possessed, sold, or in any manner used, either in the original package or otherwise in violation of any law of such State, Territory, Puerto Rico, Virgin Islands, or District of the United States, or place noncontiguous but subject to the jurisdiction thereof. Nothing herein shall apply to commodities manufactured in Federal penal and correctional institutions for use by the Federal Government.

SEC. 2. All packages containing any goods, wares, and merchandise manufactured, produced, or mined wholly or in part by convicts or prisoners, except convicts or prisoners on parole or probation, or in any penal or reformatory institution, when shipped or transported in interstate or foreign commerce shall be plainly and clearly marked, so that the name and address of the shipper, the name and address of the consignee, the nature of the contents, and the name and location of the penal or reformatory institution where produced wholly or in part may be readily ascertained on an inspection of the outside of such package.

SEC. 3. Any person violating any provision of this Act shall for each offense, upon conviction thereof, be punished by a fine of not more than $1,000, and such goods, wares, and merchandise shall be forfeited to the United States, and may be seized and condemned by like proceedings as those provided by law for the seizure and forfeiture of property imported into the United States contrary to law.

SEC. 4. Any violation of this Act shall be prosecuted in any court having jurisdiction of crime within the district in which said violation was committed, or from, or into which any such goods, wares, or merchandise may have been carried or transported, or in any Territory, Puerto Rico, Virgin Islands, or the District of Columbia, contrary to the provisions of this Act.

Approved, July 24, 1935.

In 1940, the Ashurst-Sumners Act was amended to prohibit fully the interstate shipment of prison products.

The economic strains of the Great Depression[27] led thirty-three states to quickly pass laws which prohibited the sale of prison products on the open market. These statutes tolled the death knell for the industrial prison. With the exception of a few license plate and state furniture shops, most state prisons took a giant step backward to their original purposes: punishment and custody. Fortunately, another model was emerging at the same time: the "new penology" of the 1930s and the rising star of the Federal Bureau of Prisons under the leadership of Sanford Bates.

Sanford Bates (1884–1972), a legendary figure in American corrections, was president of the American Correctional Association in 1926. He became the first superintendent of federal prisons in 1929 and the first director of the United States Bureau of Prisons in 1930. In 1937 he became the executive director of the Boys' Clubs of America. Later he served as commissioner of the New York State Board of Parole and commissioner of the New Jersey Department of Institutions and Agencies. He was also an active consultant and author.

The Period of Transition (1935–1960)

The quarter century between 1935 and 1960 was one of great turmoil within the prisons. Administrators, stuck with the huge fortresses of the previous century, were now deprived of the ability to provide meaningful work for inmates. The depression and the criminal excesses of the '20s and '30s hardened the public's attitude toward convict rehabilitation, at a time

FIGURE I-15. Alcatraz, the Super-Maximum Prison (Courtesy Federal
Bureau of Prisons)

when behavioral scientists were just beginning to propose hopeful reforms in
prisoner treatment. J. Edgar Hoover led the battle against "hoity-toity
professors" and the "cream-puff school of criminology." His war on crime
helped to give the world the super-maximum prison, Alcatraz.[28] Located on
an island in San Francisco Bay, Alcatraz was constructed to house the
hardest criminals in America. When it was built in 1934, it was seen as the
answer to the outrages of such desperate criminals as John Dillinger,[29]
Bonnie and Clyde,[30] and Ma Barker.[31] Eventually the Federal Bureau of
Prisons abandoned this idea as another failure and Alcatraz was closed in
1963.

Early efforts toward diagnostic classification and casework were pio-
neered by such notables as Bernard Glueck at Sing Sing in the period
between 1915 and 1920, Edgar Doll and W. G. Ellis in New Jersey in 1925,
and A. W. Stearns in Massachusetts in 1930. Sanford Bates introduced these
procedures into the Federal Bureau of Prisons in 1934. While sometimes
"borrowing" principles from states across the nation, the Federal Bureau of
Prisons gradually emerged as the national leader in corrections, introducing
many new concepts that have been copied by state systems. Two major
contributions were diagnosis and classification, and the use of professional
personnel such as psychiatrists and psychologists to help rehabilitate inmates. The federal system also led the way to more humane treatment and
better living conditions. But, no matter how they were cleaned up, prisons
remained monuments to idleness, monotony, frustration, and repression.
Despite attempts to tear down the massive walls around some prisons, the

forces of "lock psychosis"[32] continued to hold out. Prison inmates were feared as the "convict bogey,"[33] which could be dealt with only by locking and relocking, counting and recounting.

It is not too surprising that the long hours of idleness, forbidding architecture, growing populations, and unnecessarily repressive controls created unbearable tensions among inmates. The first riots in this country, as noted earlier, were at the mine-shaft prison in Simsbury, Connecticut. Riots at the Walnut Street Jail were reported in the early 1800s as well. The mid-nineteenth century, when prison industries provided extensive work for convicts, was a time of few riots. Presumably inmates were either too tired to riot or control was too strict. As the prison industries died out, riots began to take place more regularly, adding evidence to support the theory that enforced idleness causes restlessness and discontent among caged men. There was a wave of riots in the prisons between 1929 and 1932. During the Second World War there were few problems, but in 1946 there was even a riot in Alcatraz, the super-prison.

Whether the Alcatraz publicity provided an incentive, or whether the rising prosperity of the 1950s simply presented too sharp a contrast to the bleak life on the inside, there was an explosion of prison discontent during that decade. Over one hundred riots or other major disturbances troubled American prisons between 1950 and 1966 alone. The American Correctional Association investigated the riots and reported what appeared to be the main causes:

- inadequate financial support, and official and public indifference;

- substandard personnel;

- enforced idleness;

- lack of professional leadership and professional programs;

- excessive size and overcrowding of institutions;

- political domination and motivation of management;

- unwise sentencing and parole practices.[34]

The period of transition saw many resort to drastic measures, inside and outside the walls of America's prisons, to get across the point that mass-treatment prisons had failed. The giant fortresses to futility, built to house prisoners in silence and hard labor, were still being used for inmates no longer silent and forbidden to compete with outside labor. They were becoming the "hulks" of the twentieth century.

With a few exceptions, the principles established at the first prison congress in 1870—untried and untested to this day—were crushed by the administrators' need to maintain custody and control at any cost. As America entered the 1960s, the emphasis turned slowly toward the individual prisoner's needs, and some of the technology and ability that led us into the Atomic Age was finally focused on the problems of corrections.

REVIEW QUESTIONS

I. Find the answers to the following in the text:

　　1. Which of the two early nineteenth-century prison systems won out in America? Why?

　　2. What effect did the industrial revolution have on prisons and prison discipline?

　　3. What were the major differences between prisons and reformatories?

II. Words to identify:

　　1. inside cells

　　2. outside cells

　　3. lock-step

　　4. congregate system

　　5. the hole

　　6. mark system

　　7. ticket-of-leave

　　8. conditional release

　　9. lease system

　　10. state account system

　　11. Alcatraz

　　12. Depression

　　13. Auburn system

　　14. stripes

　　15. penitence

NOTES

1. *The Philadelphia Society for the Alleviation of the Miseries of Public Prisons* was originally formed by a group of concerned citizens meeting at the home of Benjamin Franklin in 1787. Dr. Benjamin Rush outlined the state of public punishment in Pennsylvania. Due to their continued efforts, the law of 1790 was passed and the Walnut Street Jail was remodeled to accommodate felons in solitary confinement.

2. *Outside cells* were each about six feet wide, eight feet deep, and nine feet high with a central corridor extending the length of the building in between. Some of them had individual yards added on the outside with high walls between.

3. That system, in modified form, is used in Belgium, France, and West Germany to this day.

4. *Inside cells* are built back-to-back in tiers within a hollow building. Doors open onto galleries or runs which are eight to ten feet from the outside wall. Cells are small and intended only for sleeping. The interior cell block has become characteristic of American prisons.

5. Walter C. Reckless, *The Crime Problem,* 4th ed. (New York: Appleton-Century-Crofts, 1969), p. 548.

6. Harry Elmer Barnes, *The Story of Punishment,* 2d ed. (Montclair, N.J.: Patterson Smith, 1972), p. 136.

7. Robert G. Caldwell, *Criminology,* 2d ed. (New York: Ronald Press, 1965), p. 506.

8. Barnes, *The Story of Punishment,* p. 140.

9. G. de Beaumont and A. de Tocqueville, *On the Penitentiary System in the United States and its Application in France* (Philadelphia: Francis Lieber, 1833).

10. Howard B. Gill, "A New Prison Discipline: Implementing the Declaration of Principles of 1870," *Federal Probation* (June 1970): 29-30.

11. *Prison stripes* were a development of the various forms of attire used to degrade and identify prisoners. Wide alternating black-and-white horizontal bands were placed on the loose-fitting heavy cotton garments. Stripes were still in use in the South as late as the 1940s and 1950s. They have been generally replaced by blue denims or whites in most security prisons.

12. The *hole,* or solitary confinement, was generally located in the lower levels of the prison. Most were small four-by-eight cells with no light and solid walls and doors, usually painted black. Time in the hole was usually accompanied by reduced rations and loss of all privileges. Today solitary confinement is used for administrative or disciplinary segregation, usually in cells similar to all others except for their single occupancy.

13. The *treadmill* was devised to provide an exercise outlet for prisoners in the workhouses in England. They were actually man-powered squirrel cages, and although sometimes used to power some mills and factory tools, their primary function was to keep prisoners busy. The lack of activity in the Walnut Street Jail caused the treadmill to be introduced in the early 1800s. The term "on the treadmill" refers to motion without going anywhere, like the prisoners on the great wheels of the treadmills.

14. George C. Killinger and Paul F. Cromwell, Jr., *Penology* (St. Paul, Minn.: West Publishing, 1973), p. 40.

15. John V. Barry, "Captain Alexander Maconochie," *The Victorian Historical Magazine* 27 (June 1957): 5.

16. *Flat sentence* refers to a specific period of time (e.g., 5 years, 10 years) in confinement for an offense, with no time off for any reason.

17. Harry Elmer Barnes and Negley K. Teeters, *New Horizons in Criminology,* 3d ed. (Englewood Cliffs, N.J.: Prentice-Hall, 1959), p. 419.

18. An *indeterminate sentence* generally has broad beginning and end figures (3-5 years, 1-10 years, etc.) instead of a certain fixed period. Prisoners are allowed to earn their freedom by means of good conduct.

19. Progressive penologists of the era met in Cincinnati, Ohio, on October 12, 1870, to plan the ideal prison system. Two earlier attempts to gather had failed, but this meeting of the American Prison Congress developed into the National Prison Association, later the American Correctional Association. (4321 Hartwick Road, College Park, Md. 20740).

20. Barnes and Teeters, *New Horizons in Criminology,* p. 426.

21. Georgia, Florida, Mississippi, Louisiana, and Arkansas, in particular, followed this procedure.

22. Tom Murton and Joe Hyams, *Accomplices to the Crime: The Arkansas Prison Scandal* (New York: Grove Press, 1967).

23. Killinger and Cromwell, *Penology,* p. 48.

24. Wayne Morse, *The Attorney General's Survey of Release Procedures* (Washington, D.C.: U.S. Government Printing Office), 1940.

25. Under the "piece-price" system, a variation of the contract system, the contractor provided the raw material and paid a price for each finished product delivered.

26. In the "state account" or "public account" system, all employment and activity is under the direction of the state and products are sold on the open market. The prisoner receives a very small wage and the profit goes to the state. Usually binder twine, rope, and hempsacks were produced this way; it provided a lot of work for prisoners, but little training.

27. The *Great Depression* spanned the period from 1929 to 1940. It began with the great Wall Street crash in 1929.

28. *Alcatraz* is a twelve-acre island in San Francisco Bay. Starting in 1859, it was the site of an Army Disciplinary Barracks, which was replaced in 1909 by a military prison. In 1934 the military prison was converted to a federal prison which was considered virtually escape-proof. It was closed in 1963.

29. *John Herbert Dillinger* (1902-1934) was an infamous American gangster and bank robber. He deserted the Navy in 1923. In 1924 he was imprisoned for nine years following assault to rob a grocery. He committed his first bank robbery in 1933. Another famous gangster, "Baby Face" Nelson, was part of his gang. Dillinger robbed and killed across the Midwest until he was killed by the F.B.I. outside the Biograph Cinema in Chicago. Anna Sage, a madame and friend of Dillinger's, betrayed him for the reward.

30. *Bonnie Parker* (?-1934) and *Clyde Barrow* (1910-1934) were the leaders of the Barrow gang which terrorized the Midwest in 1933 and 1934. They were gunned down in a Ford V-8 during a famous ambush in 1934. Clyde's dead hands clutched a shotgun with seven notches on the stock, Bonnie's a pistol with three. Bonnie had sent a song, "The Story of Bonnie and Clyde," to a music publisher to be released after her death. It caught the imagination of the country and was a hit, making pseudoheros of these cheap killers (who were restored to fame again in the 1967 movie glorifying their exploits).

31. *Kate Clark ("Ma") Barker* (1872-1935) was the co-leader of another infamous gang in the 1933-1934 era of crime waves in the Midwest. Her husband and four sons made up the nucleus of the gang. Alvin Karpis was also a member. They robbed banks and plundered around the St. Paul, Minnesota, area. In early 1935 "Ma" Barker and her husband, Fred, were surrounded and killed in a cabin on Lake Weir, Florida. She was found with a submachine gun in her hands.

32. *Lock psychosis* has come to mean the unreasonable fear of prison administrators that leads them to lock prisoners behind several layers of barred doors and other barricades. The huge ring of keys carried by most prison personnel is an outward manifestation of this psychosis. Counts are usually conducted several times a day to ensure that all prisoners are locked up.

33. The *convict bogey* refers to society's exaggerated fear of the convict and ex-convict, which is usually far out of proportion to the real danger they present. The tough escaped convicts shown in the movies and on television are a contributing factor to this unreasonable fear of convicts as a group.

34. Barnes and Teeters, *New Horizons in Criminology*, p. 385.

4 The Modern Era

The failures within our correctional institutions are part
of our larger failures throughout society.

A simultaneous war against poverty and racism must
accompany the war against crime.

HON. A. LEON HIGGINBOTHAM, JR.
United States District Judge

Introduction

The modern era of corrections began about 1960, and it followed the pattern
of change that was to highlight the next decade. The 1960s in the United
States were noted for turbulent and violent confrontations at almost every
level of activity affecting human rights. The forces for change at work in the
overall society were reflected in great pressures for change in corrections as
well. The drastic reinterpretations of criminal law, the civil rights movement, violent and nonviolent demonstrations in the streets, the assassinations
of a popular president and two other important national figures, the longest
and most unpopular war in American history—all these outside pressures
were also felt inside the walls of the nation's prisons. Reaction took the form
of periodic violent prison riots and disorders. The Supreme Court of the
United States emerged as the primary external agent for the enforced
recognition of the basic rights of those swept up in the criminal justice
system. This external pressure was generated by a long series of significant
judicial interpretations. Finally, leadership and funding by the federal
government were provided to corrections administrators and planners at the
state and local levels, enabling them to create, implement, and evaluate new
policies and practices. The impetus for change continues to the present day.

Internally Sought Reform

Early prisons were less secure than modern ones, and escape was far more
common. It was also relatively easy to "disappear" into early American
society, with a new name and a new start. Improved measures for inmate

security and control, developed in recent years, have made escape from prisons difficult and escape into society almost a hopeless dream.

When the prisons became so secure that escape was cut off, inmate frustrations and disturbances turned inward. Prisoners in this "total institution"[1] used disturbances and riots to express their desire for reforms and changes in rules and conditions. Disturbances also served to resolve power struggles between inmate groups. The early disturbances were characterized by disorganization and rapid dispersion; inmates used them to settle old grudges, refusing to fall in line behind any kind of leadership. In the 1950s and '60s, disturbances were commonplace in most large state systems, reflecting the usual grievances: crowded living conditions, harsh rules, poor food, excessive punishment, and guard brutality. The growing awareness of individual rights on the outside in the 1960s, however, led inmates to seek the same rights in prison.

Beginning about 1966, the nature of the demands changed from basic conditions to basic rights. In that year the Maryland Penitentiary in Baltimore was the scene of a riot involving over 1,000 inmates. The warden claimed it was caused by heat waves and overcrowding, but "The riot had to have social overtones," said Joseph Bullock, a member of the State House of Delegates. "If they don't stop telling these people (blacks) about their *rights,*" Bullock went on, "things will get worse" [emphasis added].[2] Rioting and violence spilled over from the streets into the prisons of America. The "political prisoner" label, particularly for blacks and Chicanos, offered a more acceptable way for minority groups to state their feelings of deprivation. They struck out at a system that gave them an unequal start in life, then jailed them for failing to live up to the rules of that system.[3] Clearly, outside social behavior and conditions do carry over into prison. Little that is new in society *starts* in prison.

Of the dozen or so major prison riots after 1966, many had racial overtones. A riot at the California State Penitentiary in San Quentin, in 1967, stemmed from conflict between Black Muslim and white inmates.[4] On July 4, 1970, while Bob Hope, Billy Graham, and 350,000 people were celebrating "Honor America Day"[5] in Washington, D.C., a major riot took place at Holmesburg Prison in Philadelphia. Ninety percent of the 1,300 inmates at Homesburg were black. Superintendent Hendricks placed the blame for this riot, which left 80 prisoners and 25 guards injured, on "hard-core Black militants."[6] Statements on civil rights and political liberation for blacks, made at Soledad and San Quentin prisons in 1971, contributed to the tense atmosphere that produced shootings and riots in several prisons.[7]

In September 1971, the tense situation at the New York State Penitentiary at Attica erupted and made nationwide newspaper headlines. At the final count, thirty-two prisoners and eleven guards had been killed in this terrible prison riot. The governor of New York appointed a commission to study the reasons for the Attica tragedy and to search for ways to prevent a recurrence. The results of this study showed that riot leaders were using Attica as an arena to highlight the despair of and inhumane treatment toward the so-called "political prisoners."[8] Winston E. Moore, Executive Director of the Cook County Department of Corrections, an outspoken prison reformer and black himself, says that while the civil rights movement helped cut down racial discrimination and similar abuses outside prison walls, practically nothing has changed inside. Thus, he finds that: "The recent killings in Attica and other prisons have served notice that racist practices will no longer be tolerated by the inmates."[9]

Change, though often temporary, does come about as a result of prison riots. More often today, new voices can help shape prison policies—through an inmate council, or inmates serving on regular prison committees, following a collaborative model. Some systems also use an "ombudsman" as a link between the prisoner and the establishment.[10] These methods are thought to be effective, and their continued use appears to be the trend for the future. Inmate self-government, tried in the 1800s at Elmira Reformatory in New York and more recently at the Washington State Penitentiary in Walla Walla, does not appear to offer the same promise as selected individual representation.[11]

The advent of community-based corrections will not eliminate the prison riot from the scene, however. Paradoxically, prison riots will probably pose a *greater* threat in the fewer and smaller maximum security prisons envisioned for the future. As more and more offenders are treated in the community, the "hard core" that must be kept in institutions will require very careful supervision to avoid major problems in control and treatment. The prison riot has not been the most effective tool for expression of inmate grievances, but it has helped focus public attention on prison problems.

Changing the internal administration of prisons is another, although less sensational, method of reform. In the Arkansas system, then prison administrator Tom Murton, appointed to act in the role of "reformer" by Governor Winthrop Rockefeller, managed to unearth various scandals in the state prison system, thereby achieving temporary reform.[12] The threat of institutionalization is real to the staff as well as the inmate, however. The routine of the standard prison setting is one that leads to staff burnout in a relatively short time.[13] Internally initiated reform by the staff is, therefore, often short-lived; either conditions return to the old routine, or the reforms settle into a new but equally sterile routine. Unless *real* reform occurs at *all levels* of the correctional system, there is little incentive for the continuation of new programs. The most lasting reforms appear to be those that are accomplished either as a result of outside pressure or with the knowledge and support of outside community and public leaders. How are these external pressures brought to bear?

Externally Induced Reform

Corrections, as a social system, is above all a political unit established by an authorizing mandate, supported by tax revenues, and subject to political influences. It reflects both the system of justice and the overall sociocultural environment. The latter is the source of externally induced reform. *In externally induced reform, changes are effected by individuals or groups outside the correctional system.*[14]

At the state and local levels, correctional reform is usually accomplished through legislative or executive action. Examples of reform by legislation range from the complete revision of a state's criminal code to passage of simple amendments to bills, allowing such benefits as educational and home furloughs. The executive branch of government can also exert a direct effect on correctional reform through executive orders. These orders can accomplish small but important changes, such as the abolition of mail censorship,[15] the appointment of a task force composed of involved citizens to seek correctional reform,[16] and the withholding of support for clearly unsound correctional programs.[17]

At the federal level, the most active agent for external reform has been the courts—particularly the United States Supreme Court, which has traditionally upheld the principle of individual rights in the face of government power. Major court cases that produced prison reforms include *Gideon* v. *Wainwright* (right to counsel), *Johnson* v. *Avery* (jailhouse lawyers), and *Furman* v. *Georgia* (death penalty); some details on these and other cases are supplied below.

Reform by the Courts

During the 1960–72 era, American criminal law passed from a state of evolution to a state of revolution.[18] The extension of the various federal constitutional guarantees of individual rights to the states, step by step, has clearly been the goal of the courts' quiet but effective revolution. The decisions of the much-maligned—or revered—Warren Court are more readily understood when viewed from this perspective. During the 1960s nearly all the guarantees of the Fourth, Fifth, Sixth, and Eighth Amendments of the Constitution[19] were made binding on the states. The Fourteenth Amendment[20] (due process clause) provided the primary leverage in these landmark decisions, described below. The extension of constitutional guarantees to all persons accused in state proceedings has produced dramatic and significant changes in criminal law and criminal procedures and important effects on corrections.

A. *Mapp* v. *Ohio* (exclusionary rule): 367 U.S. 643. This 1960 case opened a Pandora's box of Fourteenth Amendment rulings. A crack in the armor of state proceedings, it paved the way for the flood of cases heard by the Court during the next decade, in reference not only to illegally obtained evidence but to all areas of individual rights. The basic finding in *Mapp* v. *Ohio* asserts that evidence obtained during an illegal search or seizure is "fruit of the poisoned tree," and therefore inadmissible in both federal and state courts. *Mapp* v. *Ohio* dealt primarily with illegally obtained evidence and as such had little effect on corrections. Its primary interest here lies in the Court's use of the Fourteenth Amendment to support its decision.

B. *Robinson* v. *California* (cruel and unusual punishment): 370 U.S. 660. The Eighth Amendment's clause forbidding cruel and unusual punishment was made binding on state proceedings in this 1961 California case. The case involved the arrest of the subject on the charge of *being* a drug addict, even though he had neither used drugs in the state nor was in any way guilty of irregular behavior. The majority opinion stated that a law which imprisons a person for being sick inflicts a cruel and unusual punishment in violation of the Eighth Amendment and due process under the Fourteenth Amendment.[21] Although few of the many issues raised by the cruel and unusual punishment clause have been considered since that time, the Eighth Amendment has again come under scrutiny in the recent decisions on the death penalty.

In *Furman* v. *Georgia,* 408 U.S. 238 (1972), the issue of cruel and unusual punishment as applied to the death penalty was raised in a petition by several states for clarification of this long-standing dilemma. In June of 1972 the United States Supreme Court held that any statute which permits a jury to demand the death penalty is unconstitutional. The majority stated that the death penalty, left to the discretion of a jury, violates the Eighth Amendment—not because it is inherently intolerable, but because it is applied "so wantonly and freakishly" that it serves no deterrent purpose and, therefore, constitutes cruel and unusual punishment.[22]

In a series of decisions initiated on July 2, 1977, however, the U.S. Supreme Court held that the death penalty was not an unconstitutional punishment *if* judges and juries were given both discretion and guidance in determining guilt and in considering the circumstances of the capital crime and character of the individual defendant (*Proffitt* v. *Florida,* No. 75-5706).

C. *Gideon* v. *Wainwright* (right to counsel): 372 U.S. 335. In this crucial 1963 decision, the Court held that defendants in noncapital cases are entitled to assistance of counsel at trial as a matter of *right*. This right was extended to state proceedings, again under the provisions of the Fourteenth Amendment. This decision opened the door to a number of subsequent decisions involving not only the right to counsel under the Sixth Amendment, but also the protection against self-incrimination under the Fifth Amendment. *Morrissey* v. *Brewer* (408 U.S. 471) provided the right to counsel at parole board revocation hearings.

A significant 1969 decision provided prisoners in state penal institutions with legal assistance in preparing habeas corpus proceedings. In *Johnson* v.

Avery (393 U.S. 483), the Court held that states not providing adequate legal assistance would have to put up with "jailhouse lawyers"[23]—prisoners determined to research and conduct their own and others' appeals. Some states, although not in a position to provide the vast number of lawyers required, have accommodated the prisoners through the use of law students and trained lay persons. Law libraries are being set up in many state correctional institutions, with the help of the Law Enforcement Assistance Administration.[24] Right to counsel has been firmly established, and responsibility for maintaining this right lies squarely on the shoulders of correctional administrators. On April 27, 1977, the U.S. Supreme Court reinforced this right with the decision that law libraries must be made available to prisoners who seek legal assistance.[25]

D. *Miranda* v. *Arizona* (self-incrimination): 384 U.S. 436. The application of the Fifth Amendment protections against self-incrimination, as noted earlier, was influenced by the *Gideon* decision. An interim decision was rendered in 1964 by the Supreme Court in *Escobedo* v. *Illinois* (378 U.S. 478), which required certain procedural safeguards against self-incrimination by the police in an interrogation at the station house. Confusion as to the nature of procedures and the time at which they should be applied resulted in the court's most controversial decision of the criminal justice revolution. For the first time, in the 1966 decision of *Miranda* v. *Arizona,* a set of specific and detailed police warnings to the arrested person were required, through the due process clause, at specific and distinct points in the criminal process.[26] The key phrase in the *Miranda* decision stated that the privilege against self-incrimination "is available outside of criminal court proceedings and serves to protect persons in all settings in which their freedom of action is curtailed *in any significant way* on being compelled to incriminate themselves" [emphasis added]. While some law enforcement officers have claimed to be "handcuffed" by the *Miranda* warnings, the safeguards appear to be effective and have not materially hindered the securing of confessions.[27] Although court decisions made in 1976 have tempered the conditions necessitating the *Miranda* warnings, they are still the law of the land and have established an important procedural precedent.

In summary, the student can see how external pressure from the United States Supreme Court has modified and clarified the criminal law and provided basic constitutional guarantees for all persons, including those incarcerated in state and federal prisons. Such pressures, especially in the area of corrections, can be expected to continue marching under the banner of the Fourteenth Amendment until all other federal constitutional protection provisions are also imposed on the states.

This effort to return the control over prison conditions to the courts, following the abandonment of the "hands-off doctrine," has resulted in over 1,500 court decisions in the past 15 years. The return of the power of the courts over correctional administration is a hopeful sign for the modern era. The erosion of this power, which had its gradual beginning in 1970, and the subsequent assumption of power by the executive branch have been at the core of many of the problems noted at the beginning of this chapter.[28]

External pressure is also brought to bear by private organizations and some groups composed of former prisoners. The John Howard Association,[29] the American Correctional Association,[30] and the National Council on Crime and Delinquency[31] seek reform through prison visits and suggestions to correctional administrators. These efforts help keep the major problem areas in corrections before the public view. Organizations of ex-offenders who work with prisoners, such as the Seventh Step Foundation,[32] Man-to-Man,[33] and the Fortune Society[34] also seek correctional reform.

Reform by Legislation

Passage of meaningful reform legislation, especially in the corrections area, has been painfully slow. Even more difficult has been the provision of adequate funding to accomplish reform. The turbulence of the early 1960s prompted federal enactment of the Law Enforcement Assistance Act of 1965. That act, designed to test the value of granting federal funds to assist local law enforcement, was a symbol of things to come. After release of the findings of President Lyndon Johnson's criminal justice commission, entitled *The Challenge of Crime in a Free Society* (1967), legislation was introduced to vastly expand the Law Enforcement Assistance Act, with direct grants to state and local governments focusing on causation research, prevention, and control of crime. But the U.S. Senate moves slowly; the bill was deadlocked in committee when the congressmen were shocked from their apathy by the assassination of presidential aspirant Senator Robert Kennedy. This dramatic demonstration of the nation's need for more effective crime control prompted quick passage.

The final version of the bill, known as the "Omnibus Crime Control and Safe Streets Act of 1968," replaced direct grants to local governments with block grants to the states, but was otherwise passed substantially as submitted. This far-reaching act, implemented by the Law Enforcement Assistance Administration (LEAA), provided billions of dollars to states for action programs, research, education, evaluation, training, and administration of the criminal justice system.[35] Amendments in 1970 created a category of funds especially earmarked for corrections.[36]

The policy change embodied in this act was a reaction to overemphasis on police needs in previous years, and it reflected a new awareness of the realities of local political structures. The criminal justice system, however loosely structured it may be, is still subject to the rules of any social system. When too much effort was expended on improving the police ability to *catch* criminals, judicial and correctional sectors were overwhelmed by the impact of their success. Most experts now recognize that corrections *also* must improve, or we will simply continue to recycle the same or similar people through the system indefinitely. As Chief Justice Burger stated in 1967: "The total process is a deadly serious business that begins with an arrest, proceeds through a trial, and is followed by a judgment and a sentence to a term of confinement in a prison or other institution. The administration of criminal justice in any civilized country must embrace the idea of *rehabilitation* of the guilty person as well as the protection of society"[37] [emphasis added].

Reform by Executive Order

Not since 1929, when President Hoover established the National Commission on Law Observance and Enforcement (commonly known as the Wickersham Commission), had the executive office undertaken an in-depth examination of crime in America. The Great Depression, World War II, the Korean War, subsequent adjustments to peace—all led a series of presidents to assign a low priority to criminal justice reforms.

The outbreak of violence on the streets of America in the early 1960s changed all that. From the embattled ghettos of Los Angeles and Detroit to the assassination of the president in Dallas, events highlighted the problems of crime and violence across the nation. On July 23, 1965, President Lyndon B. Johnson established a Commission on Law Enforcement and Administration of Justice with a mandate to examine every area of the American criminal justice system. The Commission's report on *The Challenge of Crime in a Free Society* and its more detailed papers have become the basic reference points for progress on all fronts of the criminal justice system.

The President's Commission confirmed in many respects the earlier Wickersham Report. Many recommendations were found to be as pertinent in 1967 as they had been in 1929. At that time, the 3,000 federal and state prisons, reformatories, workhouses, and county/city jails were cited for basic deficiencies in prisoner classification, employment, education, parole, and probation. They were characterized by outdated physical facilities, untrained and inadequate staffs, and inmates beset by idleness. Identical problems, with few exceptions, were found in the massive study of corrections in America completed in 1967. The president's involvement, through his Commission, pushed such issues as crime on the streets, corrections, and judicial processes to the top of the list for legislative proposals and action. Finally spurred to action, Congress provided federal funds to states, through LEAA, to work on the problems.

Disturbed by the problems in their own states, a number of governors also became involved in examining, evaluating, and improving the conditions of their criminal justice system, especially the corrections sector. Using the citizens' task force concept as a model, they searched for ways to reform prison operations. Federal funding enabled them to implement many key suggestions from their state task forces. This was particularly important where a needed reform required more than state funds or a simple executive order. Notable among the citizen task forces were those in Ohio and Wisconsin.

Corrections in the 1970s

The need for correctional reforms, and for structured plans to achieve them, has been documented by the Wickersham Commission, President Johnson's Task Force on Corrections, and the various state task forces. The early 1960s emerge as a period of seeking alternative methods, programs, treatment procedures, and designs for facilities—all in line with the new emphasis on *correction* of offenders. This search took place in hundreds of feasibility studies and test programs throughout the nation.

As a result of these evaluations and programs, many of the treasured beliefs of the public, correctional administrators, and practitioners were shown to be folklore at best, if not totally false. The most astonishing and significant findings included the following:

1. Long sentences are self-defeating, in terms of rehabilitation.

2. Most offenders—perhaps as many as 85 percent—do not need to be incarcerated and could function better back in the community under supervision.

3. Most inmates derive maximum benefit from incarceration during their first two years; after that period, it becomes less and less likely that they could function as productive citizens if returned to society.

4. Community-based corrections are more realistic, less expensive, and at least as effective as incarceration.

5. Corrections, as a system, must encompass all aspects of rehabilitative service, including mental health, employment services, education, social services, and so on.

6. Some offenders—due to their dangerousness—will require extensive incarceration and treatment programs especially designed and implemented in secure institutions. The staff in these institutions must be extensive and of high quality.

7. Most inmates are not mentally ill, but suffer from a variety of educational, medical, psychological, maturational, economic, and interpersonal handicaps which are seldom reduced or resolved in contemporary correctional systems.

8. Inmates must be given the opportunity and capability to earn a living wage. Thus, they might be able to compensate the victims of their crimes and support their own families, keeping them off public assistance rolls.

9. Pay for inmates presently incarcerated is too low to be regarded as wages. Rates of pay must be increased to at least the minimum wage on the ouside for similar labor.

10. Laws which prohibit the meaningful development of prison industries must be replaced. The private economic sector must be sought out and used to provide both training and work programs that will produce employable workers at the end of the corrections cycle.

From these assumptions, findings, and funding trends, it is clear that the shape of corrections for the next decades tends toward a community-based emphasis. The potential for community-based corrections can only be exploited if it is recognized that the problems of the offender in the community are complex and demanding. Many alternative approaches and various stages of entry into and exit from the community must be developed and employed.

Community-based Corrections: Direction of the Future

In the sense used here, community treatment applies to probation and parole, after-care halfway houses (halfway-in and halfway-out), community-based institutions, and nonresidential work and group therapy programs.

If the present trends continue, it is reasonable to expect that the typical state correctional system will include a variety of custodial and treatment modes, from which the judiciary and correctional administrators can select the most appropriate approach for any offender.

The sentencing judge will have at his or her disposal the options of probation, probation without supervision, halfway-in programs, community (out-patient) therapy centers, and shock probation (an early release procedure which provides probation following a short term of imprisonment), and will be able to commit the offender to the state correctional authority for disposition in any of the available treatment modes.

The state department of corrections will process incoming felons through a classification procedure, and assign individual inmates to the appropriate treatment and custody programs.

As can be seen, corrections is slowly becoming an integrated and functional portion of the criminal justice system. Only when the various elements of this system are truly coordinated, rather than ill-matched and

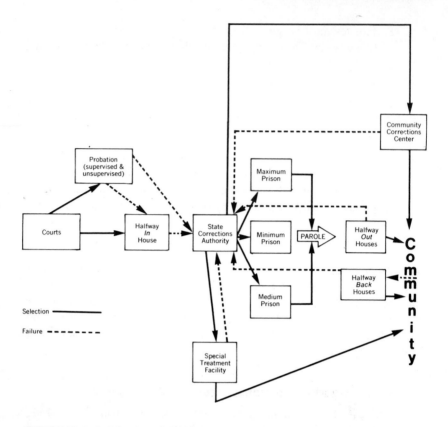

FIGURE I–16. Custody and Treatment Modes

incompatible, will the model be a workable one. The chapters that follow will discuss the ideologies, practices, clients, and programs of the corrections system in the modern era.

REVIEW QUESTIONS

I. Find the answers to the following in the text:

1. Which has the most lasting effect, prison riots or internal administrative changes?

2. What has been the most effective outside force for prison reform? Why?

3. What amendment to the Constitution has had the most effect on reform in criminal justice? Explain the reason for this effect.

II. Words to identify:

    1. racism

    2. Chicano

    3. Attica

    4. Soledad

    5. jailhouse lawyers

    6. task force model

    7. due process clause

    8. *Miranda* warning

    9. LEAA

    10. ombudsman

NOTES

1. Irving Goffman, "On the Characteristics of Total Institutions: Staff-Inmate Relations," in D. R. Cressey, ed., *The Prison* (New York: Holt, Rinehart & Winston, 1966), pp. 16-22. This concept refers to the sum of conditions created by a large number of people living around the clock within a close space . . . with tightly scheduled sequences of activity coordinated by a central authority.

2. *New York Times,* July 9, 1966, p. 9., col. 2.

3. James W. L. Park, "What Is a Political Prisoner? The Politics of Predators," *American Journal of Corrections* 34 (November/December 1972): 22-23.

4. *New York Times,* January 19, 1968, p. 69, col. 8.

5. *Honor America Day* was conducted to try to bolster a sagging spirit in the nation following the riots of 1968 and 1969 on the streets and the continued escalation of the Vietnam War. Top entertainers donated their time for a nationally-televised live show on the mall in Washington, D.C. Bob Hope was the chairman.

6. Law Enforcement Assistance Administration, *Outside Looking In: A Series of Monographs Assessing the Effectiveness of Corrections* (Washington, D.C.: U.S. Department of Justice, 1970).

7. Statements attributed to George Jackson, San Quentin Prison, June 11, 1971.

8. *McKay Commission Report* (New York: September 1972). A "must" reading for serious students of penology.

9. Winston E. Moore, "My Cure for Prison Riots: End Prison Racism," *Ebony* (December 1971): 85-95.

10. *Ombudsman* comes from the Swedish and New Zealand practices of appointing a representative to receive and investigate complaints made by individuals against abuses or capricious acts of public officials.

11. Prison self-government systems in a total institution are subject to the pressures of the inmate subculture, making it very difficult to achieve the goals of true inmate representation.

12. Tom Murton and Joe Hyams, *Accomplices to the Crime: The Arkansas Prison Scandal* (New York: Grove Press, 1967).

13. *Staff burnout* refers to the development of a pattern that takes place after a staff member has worked for a certain period of time in a total institution. Innovative ideas and concern for the inmate give way to routine and concern for the institution.

14. H. E. Allen, *The Task Force Model as a Vehicle for Correctional Change: Liability or Asset?*, paper presented at the Interamerican Congress of the American Society of Criminology and the Interamerican Association of Criminology, Caracas, Venezuela, November 20, 1972.

15. J. J. Gilligan, Governor, Ohio, Administrative Orders 814, 814A, 814B, August 5, 1971.

16. For example, Ohio Citizens' Task Force on Corrections, February 1971; Wisconsin Citizens' Study Committee on Offender Rehabilitation, May 1971.

17. An example of such withdrawal is the abolition of prison farm programs throughout the nation. Farming has ceased to be a relevant vocational training vehicle for primarily urban offenders, and it is too expensive to operate in most states.

18. Editors of "Criminal Law Reporter," *The Criminal Law Revolution and Its Aftermath,* 1960-71 (Washington, D.C.: BNA Book, 1972).

19. *Fourth Amendment:* The right of the people to be secure in their persons, houses, papers, and effects, against unreasonable searches and seizures, shall not be violated, and no Warrants shall issue, but upon probable cause, supported by Oath or affirmation, and particularly describing the place to be searched, and the persons or things to be seized.

    Fifth Amendment: No person shall be held to answer for a capital, or otherwise infamous crime, unless on a presentment or indictment of a Grand Jury, except in cases arising in the land or naval forces, or in the Militia, when in actual service in time of War or public danger; nor shall any person be subject for the same offense to be twice put in jeopardy of life or limb; nor shall be compelled in any criminal case to be a witness against himself, nor be deprived of life, liberty, or property, without due process of law; nor shall private property be taken for public use, without just compensation.

    Sixth Amendment: In all criminal prosecutions, the accused shall enjoy the right to a speedy and public trial, by an impartial jury of the State and district wherein the crime shall have been committed, which district shall have been previously ascertained by law, and to be informed of the nature and cause of the accusation; to be confronted with the witnesses against him; to have compulsory process for obtaining witnesses in his favor, and to have the Assistance of Counsel for his defense.

    Eighth Amendment: Excessive bail shall not be required, nor excessive fines imposed, nor cruel and unusual punishment inflicted.

20. *Fourteenth Amendment:* Section 1. All persons born or naturalized in the United States, and subject to the jurisdiction thereof, are citizens of the United States and of the State wherein they reside. No State shall make or enforce any law

which shall abridge the privileges or immunities of citizens of the United States; nor shall any State deprive any person of life, liberty, or property, without due process of law; nor deny to any person within its jurisdiction the equal protection of the laws.

21. The Court declared that sickness may not be made a crime, nor may sick people be punished for being sick. Since narcotics addiction is a sickness, a state cannot make it a punishable offense any more than it could put a man in jail "for the 'crime' of having a common cold."

22. All nine members of the Court delivered separate opinions; Justices Douglas, Brennan, Stewart, White, and Marshall writing concurring remarks, with Chief Justice Burger and Justices Blackman, Powell, and Rehnquist writing dissenting opinions.

23. Mr. Justice Fortas, who wrote the majority opinion, acknowledged that the state has an interest in preservation of prison discipline. However, he emphasized that interest "must yield to a prisoner's habeas corpus rights."

24. Illinois, for example, has established law libraries at each of its adult institutions.

25. "Court Rules on Prison Law Libraries," *Corrections Digest* 8 (May 11, 1977): 3-4.

26. *Miranda* warnings: (1) You have the right to remain silent. (2) Any statement you make may be used as evidence against you in a criminal trial. (3) You have the right to consult with counsel and to have counsel present with you during questioning. You may retain counsel at your own expense or counsel will be appointed for you at no expense to you. (4) Even if you decide to answer questions now without having counsel present, you may stop answering questions at any time. Also, you may request counsel at any time during questioning.

27. Actually, the Miranda warnings *have* caused the police to upgrade the quality of their investigative activity. This originally created some problems, but the long-term effect has been better cases and a better police image

28. Howard K. Gill, based on comments before the Philadelphia Bar Association and in *William and Mary Law Review* 5, no. 1 (1964): 30-45.

29. *The John Howard Association,* named after the famous prison reformer, seeks reform by visits and inspections to prison systems. (537 South Dearborn Street, Chicago, Illinois 60605.)

30. *The American Correctional Association,* the major professional organization of practicing penologists, was founded in 1870. It publishes the *American Journal of Corrections.* (4321 Hartwick Road, College Park, Md. 20740.)

31. *National Council on Crime and Delinquency* is a voluntary citizens' organization that operates a clearing house for criminal justice information and attempts to develop innovations in corrections and to influence legislation. (NCCD Center, 291 Route 17, Paramus, New Jersey 07652.)

32. *Seventh Step Foundation* is an ex-offender organization formed by Bill Sands (*My Shadow Ran Fast*). This organization works inside and outside prisons in a manner similar to Alcoholics Anonymous. (136 East Maple, Independence, Missouri 64058.)

33. *Man-to-Man Associates, Inc.,* is a volunteer organization that contacts programmed release prisoners six months prior to their actual release and starts their adjustment. Members meet prisoners on their release day and help wherever needed. (935 East Broad Street, Columbus, Ohio 43205.)

34. *Fortune Society* is an ex-offender organization with the goal of helping former inmates back into society by providing limited shelter and help in finding a job. (1545 Broadway, New York, New York 10036.)

35. Actual appropriations were $63 million in 1969, $268 million in 1970, $529 million in 1971, $699 million in 1972, $856 million in 1973, $871 million in 1974, $895 million in 1975, $1.01 billion in 1976, and an anticipated $754 million in 1977.

36. "The new funds, beginning in FY 1972, will amount to at least 20 percent of the total funds allocated for regular action programs." Third Annual Report of the LEAA, FY 1971, p. 14.

37. "Paradoxes in the Administration of Criminal Justice," *Journal of Criminal Law, Corrections and Police Science* (1967): 428. Based on a commencement address delivered at Ripon College, May 21, 1967.

5 Correctional Ideologies: The Pendulum Swings

> The mood and temper of the public with regard to the treatment of crime and criminals is one of the most unfailing tests of the civilization of any country.
>
> *SIR WINSTON CHURCHILL*

Conflicting Correctional Ideologies

Underlying the field of corrections—and the materials which follow—are three basic ideologies regarding the offender and the societal response to illegal behaviors. In order to understand the current state of corrections, its problems and issues, and its possible futures, we turn first to a discussion of ideologies.

An *ideology,* according to Webster's, is a "systematic body of concepts, especially about human life or culture." A *correctional ideology,* then, refers to a body of ideas and practices that relate to the treatment of offenders. Obviously, the actions of various correctional authorities and organizational units are shaped in large part by the particular ideologies to which they subscribe. In the history of treatment and punishment of offenders, the ideologies of different societies have provided both the basis and the rationalization for the broad range of efforts—vengeful to semi-humane—aimed at getting criminals off the streets. When a given effort is clearly a failure, the ideology eventually shifts to justify a different approach.

In modern times, a strong belief in the efficacy of one correctional ideology or another has sometimes led administrators to commit vast sums to an unproven approach, thus shackling themselves to a possibly worthless plan for an indefinite period. By the same token, if the administrator's ideology happens to conflict with the approach favored by the society he or she serves, the administrator may try to resolve the conflict in one of two ways: by working out a compromise or by trying to sabotage the system. If cottage leaders, for example, feel that the superintendent of a juvenile institution is trying to bring about change so rapidly that it threatens their personal security, they may encourage or even trigger frequent escapes and walk-aways from their institution. In corrections, where the backgrounds and ideologies of the keepers and the kept often diverge sharply, it is difficult to convince *both* groups that they can work toward a mutual goal.

Most of the ideologies applied to correctional actions over the years fall in one of three major categories: *punishment, treatment,* or *prevention.* These often overlap, of course—punishment and treatment are usually justified as means to prevention, rather than ends in themselves—but the division is useful for the purpose of this analysis.

The Punishment Ideology

Since the first system of laws was developed, punishment has been officially sanctioned as a means of regulating criminal behavior. The punishment ideology holds that the criminal is an enemy of society who deserves severe punishment, including banishment or death, for willfully breaking its rules. This philosophy has its roots in a societal need for retribution. As noted in chapter 1, early punishment came in the form of immediate and personal retribution, administered by either the victim or the victim's family. Society's authorization of punishment can be traced to this individual need for retaliation and vengeance. There are many theories as to the reason for the transfer of the vengeance motive from the individual to the state:[1]

> Philosophers have debated the reasons for this transfer to government of the victim's desire to strike back at the offender. Heinrich Oppenheimer lists several theories. Three of them are as follows: (1) In the *theological* view, retaliation fulfills a religious mission to punish the criminal. (2) In the *aesthetic* view, punishment resolves the social discord created by the offense and re-establishes a sense of harmony through requital. (3) In the *expiatory* view, guilt must be washed away through suffering
>
> Ledger Wood advances a fourth explanation, a *utilitarian theory*. Punishment is considered to be a means of achieving beneficial and social consequences through application of a specific form and degree of punishment deemed most appropriate to the particular offender after careful individualized study of the offender [emphasis added].[1]

Yet another reason for punishment of criminals is the belief that such actions have a deterrent effect, specifically on the offender, or generally on others who might consider a similar act.[2] In order for punishment to serve as a deterrent, it must be swift, closely linked to the forbidden action so that it negates future recurrences of that crime, certain, and categorical (all persons committing a certain crime will receive the *same* punishment). Furthermore, the state and its representatives must uphold superior values and conforming behavior, to serve as irreproachable examples of good citizenship. Finally, after punishment, offenders must be allowed to resume their prior positions in society, without stigma or disability.

The failure of early penologists to recognize that uniform punishment was not as effective as selective and specialized punishment contributed to the failure of prisons based on the punishment ideology. *Over*punishment has little deterrent effect as well, because when the compliance point has been passed and punishment continues, the offender ceases to care. For example, even after an offender has successfully completed a punishment-oriented correctional process, the stigma of conviction and imprisonment must be carried for the rest of the ex-offender's life. Finding it almost impossible to get a job because of a criminal past, the ex-offender decides, "If I'm going to have the name, I might as well play the game." At that point, neither the punishment nor the stigma is an effective deterrent and the offender is likely to return to crime.

A third reason to punish the offender derives from the concept of incapacitation. This theory asserts that there is no hope for the individual as far as rehabilitation is concerned, and that the only solution is to temporarily isolate, remove, or cripple such persons in some way. This approach is sometimes referred to as the "theory of disablement," a euphemism for death, banishment, or mutilation. Ideally, the disablement should relate to the crime (e.g., in some countries castration has been used to punish sex criminals). Current research, however, has seriously undermined the logic behind the punishment ideology.

It is recognized that some punishment can be effective when applied in the right amounts and at the right time. But when this ideology is applied in a correctional institution, the result is usually negative for both the punished and the punisher: correctional personnel tend to watch for minor rule infringements or nonconformism so that punishment can be applied, and they overlook any positive actions by offenders. Often the rules that are prepared for a punishment-oriented environment surround the offender with a wall of "do nots," leaving almost no leeway to *do* anything. Punishment by the law, as evidenced by the rising crime rate, does not seem to create much respect for the law, even in relatively backward jurisdictions where punishment may indeed be swift, harsh, and certain. Overuse of punishment in a society that claims to be open and free creates a situation where the punished can characterize their punishers as persecutors of the poor and helpless, turning attention away from their crimes and giving rise to the concept of the "political prisoner." Thus, minority group members are likely to blame their incarceration on "repression by the rich," "political persecution," or "attempted genocide." Punishments are then made more and more severe, in a hopeless effort to compensate for their ineffectiveness. Often such punishment motivates offenders to study to be more sophisticated criminals (rather than noncriminals) in a belief (no doubt valid) that the more skilled one is at a trade, the less likely one is to be caught. The offenders become hardened to punishment while the administrators learn to dole it out automatically, as their only means of control. Both parties are degraded in the process.

The argument that the use of punishment can halt crime is refuted by history and science.

> Punitiveness is a complex of attitudes about social revenge having as component parts strong sanctions and retributions through a severe system of penalties and punishment. Institutionalization is a critical variable in punitiveness. It should also be noted that older age and maturation, in conjunction with incarceration, produces less punitive attitudes. These two findings, in particular, suggest that it may be the type and degree of legal treatment relative to the *mala acta* that calls forth the maximum efficacy in the alteration of attitudes.
>
> Durkheim stated, when he wrote of the function of crime in society, that the group must victimize offenders in order that non-offenders may be reinforced in law-abiding behavior. This victimization with attendant punitiveness is intended to insure conformity to norms.
>
> If the behavior of those whom society punishes is frequently unaltered by such treatment, perhaps it is time to seek more satisfactory and effective techniques of rehabilitation; this can and must be done within the framework of a system which punishes violations since the general public seems unwilling to forego its almost blind faith in punitiveness as the principal vehicle of social control.[3]

Many factors contribute to make punishment the least effective means of reducing crime:

1. The use of punishment for deterrence must avoid the over-severity of application which arouses public sympathy for the offender.

2. Those persons most likely to be imprisoned are already accustomed to experience deprivations and frustration of personal goals routinely in daily life.

3. It is impossible to fashion a practical legal "slide rule" which will determine exact degrees of retribution appropriate for a list of crimes ranging from handkerchief theft to murder.

4. The simple application of naked coercion does not guarantee that the subjects of its force will alter their behavior to conform to new legal norms or to

improve their conformity with norms previously violated.

5. The possibility of deterrence varies with the chances of keeping the particular type of crime secret and consequently of avoiding social reprobation.[4]

It must be understood that the significance of punishment as an ideology in correctional practice lies in the viewpoint of the punished offenders. If they see the punishment as an unjust imposition of the will and power of the "establishment," and if they are reinforced in this belief by peers (other offenders), punishment will only encourage them to maintain negative behavior patterns. On the other hand, if offenders feel that their punishment is both deserved and just, and their social group agrees, the punishment may have a startlingly different and more positive result. If a prosocial criminal (one who is not totally committed to a life of crime) is justly treated, this offender may abandon crime; but excessive punishment may push the offender over the edge and destroy every chance of reform. The punished and stigmatized offenders turn to those who are most like them for support and values. If they are embittered by the punishment they have received, they are likely to reject the very values the punishment was intended to reinforce.

The punishment ideology is very attractive to those with a strong hostile urge just below the surface—although they may appear to be upright and productive citizens. Thus, justifications for the punishment ideology have been found in theories on theology, aesthetics, and utility, the idea being that the suffering and "expiation" of the offender serves to cleanse and re-establish accord throughout the society as a whole. While all kinds of logical arguments for punishment can be devised, it has been an obvious failure when set up as a uniform and inflexible response to negative behavior. The routine use of punishment in institutions designed to correct offenders can be viewed as more degrading to society than the offenses themselves in many cases. The punishment *ideology* soon becomes a punishment *procedure* that is applied without regard to the individual nature of those being punished. Because of this, prisons become places where inmates look to one another for support and values, and the agents of the law become the enemy. This is one of the major reasons that many authorities on corrections refer to prisons as "schools of crime." The punishment ideology is still a major factor in correctional programs.[5] For a while it gave way to the therapeutic ideology, but around 1975 punitiveness became fashionable once again. Selective punishment is an important and effective tool for correctional administrators, but only if it is designed to suit an individual offender and an individual situation. General and uniform punishment is still the rule rather than the exception, and the movement toward a treatment or preventive model is slow.

The Treatment Ideology

A major trend in corrections today favors approaching the offender much as one would the mentally ill, the neglected, or the underprivileged. This more humane ideology, the *treatment model,* sees criminal behavior as just another manifestation of pathology that can be handled by some form of therapeutic activity. While the criminal may be referred to as "sick," the treatment ideology is not analogous to a medical approach. The most essential comparison with physical illness lies in the need for offenders to recognize the danger and undesirability of their criminal behavior, and then to make significant efforts to rid themselves of that behavior. The treatment model does not "remove" criminal behavior, as one might remove an infected limb; rather, the "patient" (inmate) is made to see the rewards of positive behavior and encouraged and equipped to adopt it as a model.

The treatment ideology does *not* mean that inmates are coddled and allowed to do as they please within the institution. It is a fairly common belief among many elements of the criminal justice system that any program that is not punitive or restrictive is being "soft" or "running a country club." In fact, some form of treatment ideology can be applied in even the most restrictive and security-oriented institution. The major difference between the treatment and punishment ideologies is that in the former, offenders are assigned to the institution for a correctional program intended to prepare them for readjustment to the community, not just for punishment and confinement. There is room for punishment and for security in the treatment approach, but little room for treatment in the punitive approach. The more humane treatment methods are intended to be used in conjunction with the employment of authority in a constructive and positive manner, but inmates must be allowed to try and to fail. Authoritarian procedures, used alone, only provide the offender with more ammunition to support a self-image as an "oppressed and impotent pawn of the power structure."

Treatment procedures are almost as varied as the imaginations of the treatment staff that designs them. When one thinks of the therapeutic approach to treatment, the most common conception is the psychiatrist and his or her efforts to assist the offender to adjust. Actually, the use of classic psychiatric treatment techniques in the correctional institution is relatively rare. A more common approach is the use of group therapy programs, which include staff members as well as offenders. These are more in tune with the belief that most criminal behavior is learned from and encouraged by the offender's associates. Group therapy programs are intended to transfer the offender's allegiance from the values and activities of the criminal group to those of the noncriminal group. If that group can be labeled as desirable in terms of future associations, the offender will develop a new behavior model which will represent status and security. Groups conducted in a routine manner, as just another duty inmates and personnel must perform, have little chance for success. Rather, the leader must be a skilled and dedicated therapist, with the ability to stimulate intense exchanges and help participants—offenders *and* staff—understand what they are learning about themselves.

The main purpose of the treatment approach in corrections is to provide a means by which the individual who has some kind of a defect or problem can hope to overcome it. The offender is placed into confinement to identify and treat this problem, not to be punished for criminal actions without regard for the underlying causes. Treatment in the correctional field is still fraught with problems. The needs of the institution often take precedence over the needs of the individual, such that treatment programs may be temporarily suspended due to institutional activity or disciplinary actions. For example, inmates who violate institutional rules may be placed in a disciplinary cell (or isolation) for a period of time without books or materials. If they are enrolled in an academic program, they may fall so far behind the rest of their class that they will have to drop out until the next class starts, and it may be six months before they can resume their education. Similarly, encounter groups can be broken up, thus losing their effect, when the needs of the institution are paramount.

Despite this handicap, however, group therapy is becoming increasingly popular as a form of institutional treatment. Group programs which involve correctional personnel can benefit not only the offenders, but the staff members themselves as well. Regular interaction between staff and inmates tends to break down barriers between them and provides insights on the problems of both sides.

The administrator who wants to instill a treatment atmosphere in a formerly punishment-oriented institution faces many difficulties. The security staff, generally indoctrinated to believe in the punitive model, will resist change as a threat to institutional order. Because treatment programs are usually much more expensive than control models, legislators are slow to assign the necessary funds. The public, like the staff, exhibits unreasonable fear of crime and presses for *more* punishment when treatment alternatives are proposed; and politicians often bow to the wishes of the voters, even in the face of evidence suggesting that a treatment model is more effective. Criminal activities come to the public's attention via the media more vividly today than ever before. It is difficult to convince average citizens that prisoners deserve expensive treatment when they have seen the Attica riots on TV, live and in color. Like their colleagues in law enforcement, correctional administrators seem to make the headlines only during times of crisis or adversity. The real hope for the acceptance of the treatment ideology in corrections is to ensure sufficient security and control so that the successes are not drowned out by failure headlines. Punishment can be part of a treatment program as long as it is a disciplinary procedure, not the focus of the program.

Both punishment and therapy are geared to deal with offenders *after* they have been convicted of an offense. The more recent trend is to anticipate offenders *before* they enter the criminal justice system, in hopes of preventing future offenses entirely.

The Prevention Ideology

As mentioned earlier, the problem of crime cannot be surgically divided from the individual offender. In a sense, the problem can be removed from the community by sending the offender off to prison. Almost all offenders are eventually released, however, and the problem returns unless it has been effectively treated while the offender is in the prison. Because of the minimal success of present correctional programs (recidivism rates of from 40 to 70 percent),[6] many communities and governmental agencies are turning to crime prevention as a possible solution. Prevention methods have a dual focus: the individual and the environment in which he or she lives.

Much crime prevention activity is designed to steer potential delinquents away from a life of trouble. Such programs generally begin at the school level, where truancy and dropping out are often the precursors of criminal activity. These early programs, for the most part, attempt to identify the first signs of criminal behavior. Prediction is a complex process, even when carefully controlled. The famous studies by Sheldon and Eleanor Glueck illustrate the problems inherent in most prediction efforts.[7] Prevention programs in schools today aim to treat the problem child by providing specialized classes, vocational education, and counseling; they do not aim to force the juvenile out of the picture by expulsion from school. The prevention ideology recognizes that problem children must have supportive help, or they are very likely to use crime as an outlet for unhappiness and insecurity.

Those who advocate the preventive ideology are well aware that total prevention of crime is probably an impossibility. Emile Durkheim believed that crime in some form was an inevitable accompaniment to human society, and that if serious crime was prevented, authorities would focus their attention on minor offenses.[8] Essentially, the prevention ideology holds that crime may at least be reduced by attacking the social and emotional problems that encourage a child's criminal inclinations.

The individual's environment is recognized as a crucial focus in the prevention of crime; the prevention ideology emphasizes the need to structure the environment so that criminal *opportunity* is minimized. As an example, it has been said that the greatest crime prevention device ever invented was the street light. The movement toward crime prevention through environmental design is one that has great promise for the future. The object of such an approach is not only the provision of *barriers* to crime (i.e., bars on windows, fences, locks, airport security checks, etc.) but also the *enhancement* of existing features which tend to discourage crime (i.e., more lighting around homes and apartment buildings, more windows in dark hallways, community projects aimed at getting to know your neighbors). The conditions that produce a high or low crime rate in a given area are not all physical, however; the environment includes the people, activities, pressures, and ideas to which an individual is exposed every day. The preventive ideology would advocate the maximum use of resources in areas with special problems such as poverty and overcrowding—funds allocated for crime prevention rather than prison construction.[9]

The preventive ideology is combined with treatment in the emergence of community corrections.[10] The emphasis is on identification and treatment of the problems that have caused past criminal behavior, to prevent its recurrence. Eventually, the emphasis may lead to a closer, more interdependent relationship between the agencies now involved in crime prevention and community services. As they presently operate, criminal justice agencies actually tend to create more problems for minor offenders, instead of treating the problems that got them into trouble. If schools, churches, service agencies, and similar organizations could become more integrated with the criminal justice system, as alternatives to formal processing, many criminal careers could be prevented before they start. Diversion and non-judicial approaches to offenders are seen as potentially valuable alternatives to a more formal punishment-oriented reaction to the problem of crime. A combination of preventive and therapeutic ideologies would constitute the most promising and humane organization of corrections beliefs and practices.

The Pendulum Swings

In 1975, due in part to increasing crime rates, reactionary rhetoric, a sudden lurch to the political right, and forceful dissent from *The Challenge of Crime in a Free Society*, a number of significant arguments and changes emerged in corrections. Heralded by a controversial article by Robert Martinson,[11] several thoughtful treatises were published. Most attacked some aspect of the "treatment" or "medical" model, and many called for the acceptance of punishment as the basic rationalization for responding to crime, mandatory prison sentences, incarceration for deterrence reasons, "flat sentences," and the abandonment of probation and elimination of such early release procedures as parole.[12]

It should be noted that, at present, both the correctional "liberals" (treatment advocates) and "conservatives" (punishment ideologists) are forming an uneasy coalition to advocate the continued use of imprisonment. The conceptual glue which has brought these disparate groups together has been the ever-increasing crime rates; in 1976, these took a significant downturn. The effects that this decrease in the serious crime rates will have on the coalition and on the efforts of punishment advocates remain to be seen.

Only when American society decides which ideology or combination of ideologies most deserves its support will the problems facing the correctional administrator be properly addressed. It may be that some combination will be the only possible answer, given the wide variety of problems offenders present. Offenders may respond only to a punitive ideology, at least until we are able to develop treatment techniques that offer greater potential for success and are constitutionally acceptable. The offender who can respond to treatment, however, must be given a chance to receive it—without being totally free of control, as the protection of society remains a paramount concern. The prevention ideology offers great promise, but it seems too idealistic to suffice in and of itself. As prison populations become increasingly unmanageable, it may become necessary to introduce ex-offenders into the prison environment, as leavening and change agents working with the correctional administration. These ideas will undoubtedly lead to the development of further alternatives to incarceration, and some possibilities are discussed in later sections. To comprehend the current issues in corrections, one must examine the decision process and options available to the prosecution, judiciary, and releasing authorities. This process and these options are described in the next section.

REVIEW QUESTIONS

I. Find the answers to the following in text:

   1. What basic ideologies have determined the handling of offenders over the years? Which is the oldest?

   2. What criteria must be met if punishment is to act as a deterrent?

   3. How does the treatment ideology differ from punishment? Are they necessarily exclusive of each other?

   4. What are some of the significant changes presently taking place in the clientele of the correctional system?

II. Words to identify:

   1. ideology

   2. theological

   3. aesthetic

   4. expiation

   5. utilitarian

   6. disablement

7. therapeutic approach

8. genocide

9. selective punishment

10. criminal opportunity

NOTES

1. Elmer H. Johnson, *Crime, Correction, and Society* (Homewood, Ill.: Dorsey, 1964), p. 355.

2. Norman Carlson, "A More Balanced Correctional Philosophy," *FBI Law Enforcement Bulletin* 46 (January 1977): 22-25.

3. Christine G. Schultz and Harry E. Allen, "Inmate and Non-Inmate Attitudes Toward Punitiveness," *Criminologica* 5 (August 1967): 40-45.

4. Johnson, *Crime, Correction, and Society*, pp. 358-361.

5. There is a current rebirth of the punishment ideology, described in detail by Donal E. J. MacNamara, "The Medical Model in Corrections: *Requiescat in Pace*," *Criminology* 14 (February 1977): 439-448.

6. The effectiveness of correctional programs is under scrutiny and criticism. See Robert Martinson, "What Works?—Questions and Answers about Prison Reform," *Public Interest* 35 (Spring 1974): 22-55. This study is to be updated by 1978. In an unusual shift, after arguing that little in the area of correctional treatment has any demonstrable effect on recidivism, Martinson has recently argued that recidivism rates are considerably lower than previously estimated—in the less than one-third rate area. See: "New Martinson/Wilks Analysis Shows That Recidivism Is Much Lower Than Previously Believed—and Dropping," *Criminal Justice Newsletter* 7 (October 25, 1976): 1-2.

7. Eleanor and Sheldon Glueck conducted a number of large research projects in the 1930s, 1940s, and 1950s to develop predictive instruments. The reliability and efficacy of these instruments are still in question.

8. Emile Durkheim, *Division of Labor in Society*, trans. George Simpson (Glencoe, Ill: The Free Press, 1947).

9. William Minor, "Skyjacking Crime Control Models," *The Journal of Criminal Law and Criminology* 66 (March 1975): 94-105.

10. C. Ray Jeffery, *Crime Prevention Through Environmental Design* (Beverly Hills, Ca.: Sage, 1977).

11. Martinson, "What Works? Questions and Answers about Prison Reform."

12. See MacNamara, "The Medical Model in Corrections" for a list of the most important of these writers.

RECOMMENDED READING LIST

Allen, Harry E., and Beran, Nancy. *Reform in Corrections*. New York: Praeger, 1977.

Bagdikian, Ben H. *The Shame of Prisons*. New York: Pocket Books, 1972.

Barnes, Harry Elmer. *The Story of Punishment*. 2d ed. Montclair, N.J.: Patterson Smith, 1972.

Barnes, Harry Elmer, and Teeters, Negley K. *New Horizons in Criminology*. 3d ed. Englewood Cliffs, N.J.: Prentice-Hall, 1959.

Boesen, Povl G., and Grupp, Stanley. *Community-Based Corrections*. Santa Cruz, Calif.: Davis, 1976.

Carter, Robert M.; Glaser, Daniel; and Wilkins, Leslie T. *Correctional Institutions*. New York: J. B. Lippincott, 1972.

Criminology: An Interdisciplinary Journal 14:4 (February 1977). Special issue devoted to incarceration.

Johnston, Norman. *The Human Cage: A Brief History of Prison Architecture*. New York: Walker & Company, 1973.

Joint Commission on Correctional Manpower and Training. *Perspectives on Correctional Manpower and Training*. Lebanon, Pa.: Sowers Printing, 1970.

Killinger, George C., and Cromwell, Paul F., Jr. *Penology: The Evolution of Corrections in America*. St. Paul, Minn.: West, 1973.

Nagel, William. *The New Red Barn*. New York: Walker, 1973.

National Advisory Commission on Criminal Justice Standards and Goals. *Corrections*. Washington, D.C.: U.S. Department of Justice, 1973.

National Conference on Corrections. *We Hold These Truths . . .* Richmond, Va.: Division of Justice and Crime Prevention, 1971.

The President's Commission on Law Enforcement and Administration of Justice. *Task Force Report: Corrections*. Washington, D.C.: U.S. Government Printing Office, 1967.

Radzinowicz, Leon, and Wolfgang, Marvin E. *The Criminal in Confinement*. New York: Basic Books, 1971.

Reckless, Walter C. *The Crime Problem*. 4th ed. New York: Appleton-Century-Crofts, 1969.

Rothman, David J. *The Discovery of the Asylum*. Boston: Little, Brown, 1971.

Schafer, Stephen. *Theories in Criminology*. New York: Random House, 1969.

PART II

Law and the Correctional Process

6 Misdemeanants and Felons: A Dual System

Crime is normal because a society exempt from it is utterly impossible.

EMILE DURKHEIM

Common Law Origins of Crime

Most crimes fall into one of two categories, felonies or misdemeanors. Felonies are a group of offenses that are considered serious enough to deserve severe punishment or even death in most societies. Although they vary somewhat in their specific names, the major felony crimes are remarkably similar for all jurisdictions. In the United States, we have come to define most "common law" crimes as felonies, because we inherited many of them from the English common law statutes. Under the common law, which developed by history and precedent, there were three categories of crimes: treason, felony, and misdemeanor.[1] Originally, the distinction between felonies and misdemeanors was based on the fact that all felonies were capital offenses, also involving forfeiture of all lands and property of the perpetrator, whereas misdemeanors received lesser penalties. While the United States adopted many aspects of English common law, the severity of felony punishment was modified to reflect the American way of life.

The distinction between a felony and a misdemeanor in America is generally based on either the type of institution in which the offender will be incarcerated or the length of the sentence imposed. Most felony convictions would require a sentence of at least *one year* in the state prison. This guideline is not infallible, but it may serve as a good rule of thumb in determining which crimes are generally considered to be felonies. Most legal agencies tend to lump the various kinds of felonies into categories which relate to the social harm involved: offenses against the person, offenses against the habitation, offenses against property, offenses against morality and decency, etc. A brief look at these categories and the correctional clients they produce is in order.

Crimes against the Person

It is significant to note that four of the seven major or "index" offenses cited in the Federal Bureau of Investigation's *Uniform Crime Reports* are usually labeled *crimes against the person*.[2] These four crime categories (murder and non-negligent manslaughter, aggravated assault, forcible rape, and robbery) are "headline crimes," which create public fear and promote support for stronger law enforcement. Despite their shock effect, these four offenses accounted for only 9.1 percent of the index crimes reported in 1975 (1,026,280 out of 11,256,600).[3] The emphasis placed on these crimes is demonstrated by the higher percentage which are cleared by arrest; it is only logical that the principal resources of our law enforcement agencies should be marshaled to solve the crimes that the public fears most. An average of 55 percent of the crimes in these four categories are cleared by arrest, compared to only 17 percent in crimes against property. Murder and non-negligent manslaughter lead with a clearance rate of 78 percent, aggravated assault follows with 64 percent, forcible rape has a 51 percent rate, and robbery has only a 27 percent rate.[4]

A nationwide survey of 191,400 prisoners in the custody of state correctional authorities in 1974 revealed the following offenses for which they were currently incarcerated (instant offense):

Robbery	23%	Assault	5%
Homicide	18	Sexual Assault	5
Burglary	18	Major Drug Offense	4
Larceny	6	Forgery, Fraud, Embezzlement	4
Minor Drug Offense (possession)	6	All other offenses	11
			100%

An estimated 71 percent of the offenders in custody had been incarcerated at least once before.[5]

Crimes against the person are also those which have the most severe penalties for the convicted offender. All of these offenses either are, or have been, capital offenses in the United States. A contemporary example of the seriousness of these offenses is found in the sentences and penalties attached to them in the Ohio Criminal Code:[6]

1. Murder: death penalty or life imprisonment.

2. Forcible Rape: 4-25 years (life imprisonment if victim was under 13 years of age).

3. Aggravated Assault: 4-25 years.

4. Robbery: 4-25 years.

TABLE 1. MURDER CIRCUMSTANCES, 1966–1975 (Percent distribution)

YEAR	TOTAL NUMBER	SPOUSE KILLING SPOUSE	PARENT KILLING CHILD	OTHER FAMILY KILLINGS	ROMANTIC TRIANGLE AND LOVERS' QUARRELS	OTHER ARGU- MENTS	KNOWN FELONY TYPE	SUS- PECTED FELONY TYPE
1966	10,950	16.3%	4.2%	8.3%	8.5%	40.9%	14.8%	7.0%
1969	14,640	13.1	3.7	8.4	7.0	41.3	19.3	7.2
1972	18,520	12.5	2.9	8.9	7.1	41.2	22.1	5.3
1975	20,510	11.5	3.0	7.9	7.3	37.9	23.0	9.4

At one time or another, murder has been a capital offense on the statutes of nearly all countries in the Western world. An attempt to understand the correctional client who commits crimes against the person might well begin with the murderer, as described in the *Uniform Crime Reports* for 1975. Since murder is generally considered the most completely reported, cleared, and resolved crime, it is a good vehicle for examining the offender who commits crimes against the person. First, one cannot fail to observe that a disproportionate number of blacks are the *victims* of murder (47 percent) and the *offenders* arrested for murder (54 percent). It is also notable that over 45 percent of the persons arrested for murder in 1975 were under twenty-five years old. Those aged between twenty and twenty-four, in fact, accounted for one in four of the arrests for murder. The report shows that 55 percent of the adults arrested for murder in 1975 were prosecuted during that year, and that 54 percent of these were found guilty as charged. Of the remaining 46 percent, 14 percent were convicted of some lesser charge and the remainder were either acquitted or dismissed. It is clear from the analysis of the processing of murder cases that they are considered important and get more thorough attention than less publicized crimes.

The American murderer, then, is often a young black male who kills his victim in the course of an argument or over a family problem. The profile of the circumstances under which murder occurs is shown in Table 1.

While there is serious public alarm and concern about murderers,[7] in prison they are generally the least problematic of all offenders, frequently are given "honor" status, and often work in the warden's quarters as domestics.

The rates of prosecution and conviction for aggravated assault and forcible rape are very similar to those for murder.[8] While a major study by the Law Enforcement Assistance Administration suggests that the actual crime rate may be as much as three to five times the reported crime rate,[9] this does not change the fact that many of the persons convicted and sentenced to state prisons are young and aggressive, and have committed prior violent offenses.

Crimes against Property

Of the estimated one and one-half million individuals who are under correctional supervision in America each day, the vast majority are placed there for *offenses against property*. Even with the low clearance by arrest percentages, the sheer volume of the property crimes tends to keep our prisons full. Reported incidents of burglary, for example, totaled 3,252,100 in 1975; the clearance by arrest rate for burglary was 18 percent, and of this group 71 percent were brought to prosecution and 60 percent were found guilty.[10] When the mathematics involved here are computed, one ends up with about 249,300 clients for some aspect of the corrections subsystem. Similar figures apply to both larceny and auto theft, with convictions for all three of these offenses totaling approximately one-half million clients for the correctional system.

The offender against property is generally young. The number of auto theft cases alone that must be referred to juvenile authorities is 55 percent of the total for those offenses. The same is true for 40 percent of the larceny and 57 percent of the burglary cases reported. Persons under twenty-one accounted for almost two-thirds of the larcenies and 73 percent of the auto thefts; persons under twenty-five accounted for 83 percent of the burglaries.[11] Crimes against the person may account for the longer sentences, but crimes against property contribute most to the *volume* in the correctional pipelines.

Burglary is generally considered a *crime against the habitation,* and is the most common crime reported in the crime index. There were over three and one-quarter million burglaries reported in 1975, an increase from 1971. Since 64 percent of these burglaries are committed in dwellings, it is a crime that alarms the citizens. There is a great amount of fear, sometimes resulting in overreaction by the victim, that forcible entry into one's home necessarily implies violence against one's person. The homeowner's zeal for self-preservation results in a number of tragic accidents each year, even though burglary offenders are seldom aggressive. It has been estimated that billions of dollars in property each year is taken to obtain money for drugs, but this claim has been seriously challenged.[12] Drug abuse may be one of the reasons that *daytime* burglaries are on the increase, however, especially with the increased chance of absence of both adults in a family, as more women take jobs. Since the crime of burglary involves stealth and cunning, offenders are seldom caught at the scene. More often, they can be arrested when they attempt to sell the stolen goods. Although the clearance by arrest rate was only 18 percent in 1975, this is a deceptive figure.[13] Some burglaries are perpetrated by more than one offender, but in other cases one person may be responsible for numerous offenses. Unless arrested offenders choose to *confess* to more than the offense for which they were caught, many thousands of burglaries go unsolved.

Crimes against Morality and Decency

Crimes that may get even more publicity than murder are those that have a sexual connotation. The child molester, for example, excites widespread public alarm and high interest in the media. This individual also assumes the lowest position in the inmate social system in most prisons; other bizarre sex crimes, with the possible exception of rape, are also considered repulsive by the inmate subculture. Rape is at least vaguely linked to the manhood role and is sometimes, in a perverse way, viewed as an accomplishment of some note. Although homosexuals are looked upon as "weirdos" in prisons, they can be welcome to other inmates, although they create dissension and trouble for correctional administrators. Many of the so-called "acts between consenting adults" are being removed from the criminal codes,[14] leaving only the forcible assaultive homosexuals to be sent to prison. This may aggravate an already growing problem in the control of the offender population in the prisons of America.

Rape is possibly the most under-reported crime in America. It has been argued that the stigma and prosecution problems for the *victim* in this type of case are often more damaging than the penalty for the *offender*. There were 56,090 forcible rapes reported in 1975, but some experts place the actual occurrence at as much as five times that number. Although the victim has good reason to remember her assailant, only 51 percent of forcible rapes were cleared by arrest. This demonstrates the victim's reluctance to follow through with a complaint. Only 42 percent of the persons prosecuted for rape were found guilty of that offense, a result that again can be traced to the reluctance and fear of the victim to testify in court. In the case of rape, usually the only witness is the victim. In the absence of physical or other testimonial evidence, the rapist often goes free. The greatest number of rapists were found in the sixteen- to twenty-four-year-old group, and the white/black percentages were 52 to 45, respectively. The rapist, then, is also young, probably from an urban area, and another aggressive problem for the correctional administrator.[15] Many states have made the crime of rape, and many other crimes against morality and decency, a nonprobational offense.[16] This means that most of these offenders will spend some time—and frequently a long time—in prison before they can hope to be on the streets. Sex crimes that involve extremely peculiar acts or psychopathic personality are discussed in chapter 20.

Misdemeanants

While the number of annual admissions is about 200,000 for adult felony institutions, there are almost three *million* arrests for misdemeanors or crimes classified as misdemeanors.[17] The projections to 1975 by President Johnson's Commission showed average daily prison populations of 771,000 for adult felons and 482,000 for misdemeanants. If other factors remain constant, the number of misdemeanor arrests for 1977 should approximate eight million.[18] It is obvious that the misdemeanant offender problem touches all the related subsystems of the criminal justice system, affecting plans, workloads, and personnel.

The misdemeanant category contains most of the offenders who are confined, but their sentences are relatively short. Of the 9.3 million arrests reported in 1975, an estimated three million were for misdemeanor offenses.[19] A misdemeanor conviction generally involves a sentence of less than one year, usually served at a jail or workhouse rather than a state prison. A misdemeanor can also be punished by the assessment of a fine. This broad definition varies from jurisdiction to jurisdiction, but the standard of less than one year's imprisonment is fairly common.

Alcoholics and the Revolving Door

In some parts of the country one can stagger down the sidewalk in drunken splendor and seldom run afoul of the law.[20] In most areas, however, the "common drunk" is the major source of clients for the misdemeanor facilities. Over 50 percent of misdemeanor arrests are for drunkenness or offenses directly related to drinking. One study found that 43 percent of the states' imprisoned male felons were drinking at the time they perpetrated their crimes. It is estimated that over two million arrests are made each year for public drunkenness alone.[21] Of course, this creates several problems for the police, not the least of which is assignment of great numbers of personnel to handle these drunks. The second area to feel the crunch of this huge volume is the lower court system. The packed dockets are not able to cope with the numbers and tend to dish out "assembly line justice" in order to function at all. It is estimated that approximately 50 percent of the convicted jail population could be treated in facilities other than jails, if such facilities were available.

Alcoholism is a problem of major proportions in America. In terms of number, it is our leading drug abuse problem. It is estimated that there are at least nine million alcoholics in the United States, most of whom do not recognize their problem. The "skid rows"[22] of America are populated with the derelicts and dregs of a society that treats the drinking problem as *criminal* when revealed to the public. Most of the offenders arrested for public drunkenness are chronic, having been arrested many times before. The conditions in most jails allow for little more than a drying-out period, followed by the inevitable return to the streets and the bottle. The situation has been evaluated by Austin MacCormick,[23] former President of the American Correctional Association, as follows:

The appallingly poor quality of most of the county jails in the United States is so well known that it is probably not necessary to discuss this point at any great length. The fact that the majority of all convicted alcoholics go to these institutions, however, makes it imperative that the public, and particularly those thoughtful citizens who are interested in the treatment of alcoholics, never be allowed to forget that our county jails are a disgrace to the country . . . and that they have a destructive rather than a beneficial effect not only on alcoholics who are committed to them but also on those others who are convicted of the most petty offenses.[24]

The alcoholic is neither deterred nor cured by frequent trips to jail. All that is accomplished is the provision of a brief period of sobriety and removal from public view. The system of misdemeanant corrections is unable to deal with the alcoholic, either medically or from a social standpoint, and jail is usually the only available local response.

In several court cases petitioners have attempted to draw an analogy between public drunkenness for an alcoholic and the logic of *Robinson* v. *California*. In this case, it will be recalled, the United States Supreme Court found that an individual could not be punished simply for being a drug addict. The argument for applying this logic to the alcoholic was finally reviewed in 1968 by the Supreme Court in the case of *Powell* v. *Texas*. The Court found that being drunk in public was not a compulsion symptomatic of the disease; therefore, arrest and confinement for it did not constitute cruel and unusual punishment. As stated by Justice Marshall:

[A]ppellant was convicted, not for being a chronic alcoholic, but for being in public while drunk on a particular occasion. Texas thus has not sought to punish a mere status, as California did in *Robinson;* nor has it attempted to regulate appellant's behavior in the privacy of his own home. Rather, it has imposed upon appellant a criminal sanction for public behavior which may create substantial health and safety hazards, both for appellant and . . . the general public, and which offends the moral and esthetic sensibilities of a large segment of the community. This seems a far cry from convicting one for being an addict, being a chronic alcoholic, being "mentally ill or a leper."

Robinson so viewed brings this Court but a very small way into the substantive criminal law. And unless *Robinson* is so viewed it is difficult to see any limiting principle that would serve to prevent this Court from becoming, under the aegis of the Cruel and Unusual Punishment Clause, the ultimate arbiter of the standards of criminal responsibility, in diverse areas of the criminal law, throughout the country. . . . The entire thrust of *Robinson's* interpretation of the

Cruel and Unusual Punishment Clause is that criminal penalties may be inflicted only if the accused has committed some act, has engaged in some behavior, which society has an interest in preventing, or perhaps in historical common law terms, has committed some actus reus. It thus does not deal with the question of whether certain conduct cannot constitutionally be punished because it is, in some sense, "involuntary" or "occasioned by a compulsion."[25]

This was a setback for those attempting to decriminalize the drunkenness laws, but the Court has not completely barred the door to alternative constitutional approaches to the problem.

The sheer volume of drunkenness cases makes it imperative to discover alternatives to the automatic jailing of the chronic drunk. In one study of only *six* chronic offenders in Washington, D.C., it was found that the group had amassed a total of 1,409 arrests for drunkenness and had spent, altogether, over 125 years behind bars.[26] The increasing use of alternatives to incarceration for alcoholics and drunkenness offenders suggests that they are proving somewhat effective in rehabilitating these chronic offenders, especially as opposed to more conventional techniques. The most popular form of diverting alcoholics from the criminal justice system is the *detoxification center,* now being used in numerous jurisdictions.

The detoxification center is a *civil,* treatment-oriented alternative to the police station as the processing point for offenders whose only crime is drunkenness. Offenders are retained there until they have been restored to a stable and sober condition. The option of treatment beyond the initial "drying out" period[27] is usually left up to the individual, and in most detoxification centers, the majority elect to stay for more treatment. Detoxification centers are generally staffed with medical and other professional staff to determine the exact needs of each individual. In the case of serious complications, the patient can be transferred to a public hospital for more extensive care. An example of the concept in practice is the Dayton, Ohio, "Pilot Cities" program, sponsored by the U.S. Department of Health, Education, and Welfare. The structure and goals of the project are outlined in the HEW evaluation report:

> A screening and detoxification center, located in the City Mission, is designated to diagnose medical problems and provide medical treatment to persons suffering from the physical symptoms associated with drinking. Persons coming to the center may be referred from a variety of sources: Police, courts, probation department, hospitals, social agencies, the correctional farm, and volunteer admissions. Disposition of persons from the screening centers can occur in a variety of ways: (1) persons with acute medical problems will be sent to local hospitals; (2) persons progressing in the reduction of medical

problems will be sent to a halfway house; (3) persons not having a serious or chronic drinking problem will be returned to society; (4) persons may elect another rehabilitation program such as the one at the City Mission.

The planned procedure to bring persons to the screening center by the police merits special comment. Instead of arresting persons for public drunkenness, police are to bring such persons to the screening center unless the offender refuses or exhibits violent behavior, in which case he is arrested. However, there is no legal compulsion imposed on an individual to participate in the program. He may terminate his individual involvement at any time without suffering legal consequences.[28]

The removal of over two million such "customers" from the workload of the country's law enforcement agencies, permitting the agencies to concentrate on more serious threats, would be no small step toward the reduction of major crime in America. One model for a comprehensive system for the diversion of the public drunk is shown in Figure II–1.

Misdemeanor or Felony: Offender or Offense?

Does the misdemeanor offender graduate to more serious crime, or is he or she usually a felon to begin with, who has plea-bargained[29] down a charge? The answer to this two-part question seems to be *yes,* in both cases. It is a common practice to plea-bargain a felony charge down to a misdemeanor, especially in the case of a first offense. Some studies show that misdemeanants (excluding the drunkenness offenders) tend to repeat and eventually are convicted for a felony. How do we go about drawing a line between a misdemeanor and a felony?

The definition of a misdemeanor, as mentioned earlier, varies from state to state. The legal definition is usually rooted in the statutes, according to how severe the penalty is for the act, the level of government at which the offender is tried, or some specific list of offenses. In many cases, the term is a catchall, with any crime not specifically listed as a felony automatically considered to be a misdemeanor. The gray area between a misdemeanor and a felony is even further confounded in some jurisdictions, which attempt to differentiate between "high" or "gross" misdemeanors and the regular garden variety. In general, however, the term misdemeanor applies to such offenses as drunkenness, vagrancy, disorderly conduct, breach of the peace, minor assaults, larcenies of small amounts, small-scale gambling and other forms of "vice," shoplifting, and other minor offenses.

Most felonies also contain the elements of some misdemeanor. If they have a weak felony case, prosecutors will often try to persuade the defendant to plead guilty to a lesser, included offense. This usually costs the state

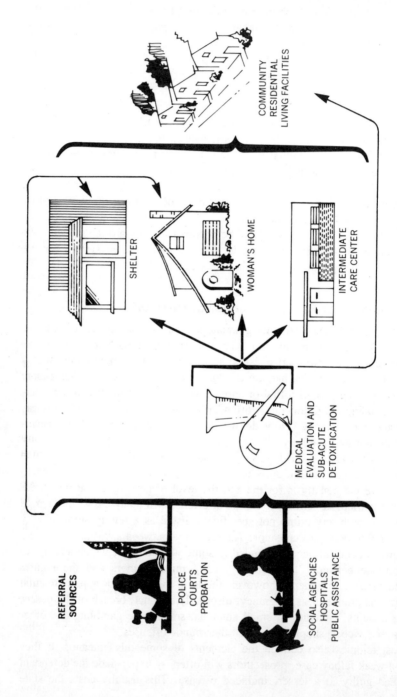

FIGURE II–1. Comprehensive Public Inebriate Diversionary Program (National Institute of Law Enforcement and Criminal Justice. *Diversion of the Public Inebriate from the Criminal Justice System* (Washington, D.C.: U.S. Department of Justice, 1973). p. 7.)

much less in the way of time and money, if the accused will accept the deal. It also gives the offender one more opportunity to remain free of a felony record. Almost nothing is empirically known about the disposition of misdemeanor offenders in America, so any attempt to state the frequency with which prosecutors use this form of plea bargaining would be mere conjecture. Plea bargaining is discussed in detail in chapter 7.

Many felonies and misdemeanors are very similar in nature. The major difference, as noted above, lies in the kind of treatment offenders can expect, depending upon whether they are handled as felons or as misdemeanants. The convicted felon can expect to receive, in the majority of cases, a better chance for probation services, institutional programs, and parole services when released. On the other hand, as the system now works, those advantages are more than offset by the loss of civil rights and later employment problems that make a felony conviction a serious and permanent handicap. While there are efforts under way to adopt licensing standards and restore civil rights for ex-offenders, movement in this area is extremely slow. For this reason, many offenders avoid the stigma of a felony conviction by the expedient of a misdemeanor guilty plea. The correctional system must be adapted to provide similar services to *all* convicted offenders, whether they are felons or not. A false distinction between the *offenses* does not change the basic problems that lead the offender to commit the act in the first place. When correctional treatment can be placed on a sensible continuum, so that procedures are related to the needs of the individual *offender,* the stigma of being called a "felon" will be reduced and real corrections may take place.

REVIEW QUESTIONS

I. Find the answers to the following in the text:

1. What are the four major crimes against the person?

2. Explain why the clearance by arrest rate is higher for crimes against the person than for other crimes.

3. Explain why the alcoholic represents a serious problem in the correctional system.

4. Explain the difference between a felony and a misdemeanor.

II. Words to identify:

1. common drunk

2. alcoholism

3. fines

4. detoxification

5. treason

6. infractions

7. index crime

8. burglary

9. skid row

10. drying-out

NOTES

1. Rollin M. Perkins, *Criminal Law and Procedure,* 4th ed. (Mineola, N.Y.: Foundation Press, 1972), p. 4.

2. Crimes against the person as defined in the *Uniform Crime Reports* are:

> 1. *Criminal homicide.* (a) Murder and non-negligent manslaughter: all willful felonious homicides as distinguished from deaths caused by negligence. Excludes attempts to kill, assaults to kill, suicides, accidental deaths, or justifiable homicides. Justifiable homicides are limited to: (1) the killing of a person by a peace officer in line of duty; (2) the killing of a person in the act of committing a felony by a private citizen. (b) Manslaughter by negligence: any death which the police investigation establishes was primarily attributable to gross negligence of some individual other than the victim.

> 2. *Forcible rape.* Rape by force, assault to rape and attempted rape. Excludes statutory offenses (no force used—victim under age of consent).

> 3. *Robbery.* Stealing or taking anything of value from the care, custody, or control of a person by force or violence or by putting in fear, such as strong-arm robbery, stickups, armed robbery, assaults to rob, and attempts to rob.

> 4. *Aggravated assault.* Assault with intent to kill or for the purpose of inflicting severe bodily injury by shooting, cutting, stabbing, maiming, poisoning, scalding, or by the use of acids, explosives, or other means. Includes attempts. Excludes simple assault, assault and battery, fighting, etc. (1971, p. 57).

3. Clarence M. Kelley, *Uniform Crime Reports* (Washington, D.C.: U.S. Department of Justice, 1975), p. 11.

4. Kelley, *Uniform Crime Reports,* p. 40.

5. "Nationwide Survey Describes State Inmates," *Criminal Justice Newsletter* 7 (May 24, 1976): 5.

6. Ohio House Bill 511, which went into effect on January 1, 1974.

7. Kelley, *Uniform Crime Reports,* p. 19.

8. Kelley, *Uniform Crime Reports,* pp. 20-24.

9. Law Enforcement Assistance Administration, *National Crime Panel: Preliminary Report* (Washington, D.C.: U.S. Department of Justice, 1973).

10. Kelley, *Uniform Crime Reports,* pp. 26-31.

11. Kelley, *Uniform Crime Reports,* p. 42.

12. The Drug Abuse Foundation, *Heroin Addiction: The Issues* (Washington, D.C.: DAF, 1973).

13. Kelley, *Uniform Crime Reports,* p. 40.

14. Acts between consenting adults are generally defined as sexual activity that does not involve coercion or force and takes place in private.

15. Kelley, *Uniform Crime Reports,* pp. 22-24.

16. In Ohio this can apply generally to any repeat or dangerous offenders. The court must consider: risk that offender will commit another offense; nature and circumstance of offense; history, character and condition of offender. Those who fall into the non-probationable category generally serve much longer prison terms.

17. Kelley, *Uniform Crime Reports,* p. 37.

18. The President's Commission on Law Enforcement and Administration of Justice, *Task Force Report: Corrections* (Washington, D.C.: U.S. Government Printing Office, 1967), p. 7.

19. Kelley, *Uniform Crime Reports,* p. 37.

20. The President's Commission on Law Enforcement and Administration of Justice, *The Challenge of Crime in a Free Society* (Washington, D.C.:U.S. Government Printing Office, 1967), p. 234.

21. *The Challenge of Crime in a Free Society,* p. 233.

22. *Skid rows* were used in the Pacific Northwest as a route through the underbrush and timber for dragging logs to the rivers. The most famous of these skid rows ended up at Puget Sound in Seattle, Washington, near what is now called Pioneer Square. The poorer sections of the city were situated along the course of the skid row and it became associated with being down on your luck, or "on the skids."

23. *Austin MacCormick* (1893-   ) was born in Georgetown, Ontario, Canada. He graduated (1915) from Bowdoin College where he became interested in prison reform. His studies of penal institutions in the U.S.A. led to his writing the *Handbook of American Prisons* (1926), *Handbook of American Prisons and Reformatories* (1929), and *Education of Adult Prisoners* (1931). MacCormick was Assistant Director of the U.S. Bureau of Prisons (1929-33) and Commissioner of Corrections in New York (1934-40). In 1946 he became Executive Director of the Osborne Association, a leading penological research and welfare organization. He was appointed Professor of Criminology at the University of California (Berkeley) in 1951.

24. *The Challenge of Crime in a Free Society,* p. 234.

25. *Powell* v. *Texas,* 392 U.S. 514, 88 S. Ct., 2145, 20 L. Ed. 2d 1254 (1968).

26. *The Challenge of Crime in a Free Society,* p. 233.

27. *Drying out* refers to the period required for the alcoholic's body to readjust to a lowered level of alcohol. This is often a very severe shock to the system, resulting in withdrawal symptoms like those of the drug user who goes ''cold turkey.''

28. Community Research, Inc., *Evaluation of the Alcoholic Rehabilitation Program, Dayton-Montgomery County Pilot Cities Program* (Dayton, Ohio: CRI, 1972).

29. *Plea bargaining* is a process by which an offender negotiates with the prosecutor to plead guilty to a lesser charge in order to reduce the penalty. (See also chap. 7, note 8.)

7 The Correctional Funnel

In the halls of justice the only justice is in the halls.

LENNY BRUCE

Introduction

The first requirement for any correctional process is a *client* (or inmate, prisoner, resident, felon, etc.). Whether one examines the largest maximum security prison in the world[1] or a rural jail, the common denominator is always some individual who has been placed there for detention, punishment, or rehabilitation. Why was one person incarcerated while another was freed or placed under some other kind of supervision in his or her home community? American corrections is a diversified mix of facilities, theories, techniques, programs, and practices. This amalgam is also part of a poorly articulated combination of police, courts, juvenile authorities, probation, prisons, and parole that is somewhat simplistically referred to as our "criminal justice system."

A better understanding of the nonsystematic nature of criminal justice in America can be gained by examining the prevailing sentiments and goals at the two extremes of the process: *police* and *corrections*. The police, in their law-and-order role, are working hard to get offenders off the streets and *out* of the community. If offenders are locked up, no matter how temporarily, they are no longer a "police problem." In this role, police are often viewed as agents of banishment by the public. In the course of their work, the police see offenders at their worst, often while they are committing the offense. It is, therefore, understandable that the police reaction to offenders sometimes leans toward the ideologies of retribution and punishment rather than reintegration and rehabilitation.

Correctional personnel, on the other hand, are attempting to get the offender *out* of prison and back into society. Accomplishing this involves taking calculated risks and releasing some offenders who might return to crime. Usually, only the *worst* risks fail to abide by the law; unfortunately, these failures are the only examples of "corrected" felons who come in contact with the police. Thus, the police—already overworked and saddled with an often thankless job—view attempts to reintegrate former felons into their communities as a threat and an extra work burden.

The offender, if caught, passes through most of the different stages of the criminal justice (non-)system on his way to prison. Many do not pass through every procedural step but fall out of the system at different stations along the way. Therefore, it is essential to examine this screening process, called the "correctional funnel," to determine at what point and for what reasons certain offenders are dropped from the system.

The Elements of the Criminal Justice System

The popular myth that our criminal justice system provides fair and uniform treatment of offenders was recently exploded by our own Department of Justice:

> A substantial obstacle to development of effective corrections lies in its relationship to police and courts, the other subsystems of the criminal justice system. Corrections inherits any inefficiency, inequity, and improper discrimination that may have occurred in any earlier step of the criminal justice process. Its clients come to it from the other subsystems; it is the consistent heir to their defects.
>
> The contemporary view is to consider society's institutionalized response to crime as the criminal justice system and its activities as the criminal justice process. This model envisions interdependent and interrelated agencies and programs that will provide a coordinated and consistent response to crime. The model, however, remains a model—it does not exist in fact. Although cooperation between the various components has improved noticeably in some localities, it cannot be said that a criminal justice "system" really exists.[2]

The American criminal justice system is, in fact, many *separate* systems of institutions and procedures. The thousands of American villages, towns, cities, counties, states—and even the federal government—all have criminal justice "systems" of sorts. While they may appear similar in that all function to apprehend, prosecute, convict, and sentence lawbreakers, no two are exactly alike.

A diagrammatic representation of the flow of offenders through police, prosecution courts, and corrections is shown in Figure II–2. This diagram emphasizes the points at which the "typical" criminal justice system

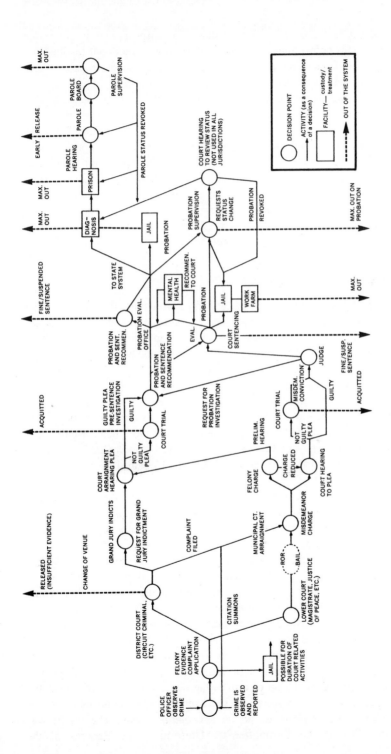

FIGURE II–2. Criminal Justice System (National Clearinghouse for Correctional Programming and Architecture. *Correctional Environments.* (Washington, D.C.: U.S. Department of Justice, 1973). p. 46.)

provides alternate courses of action, so that many suspects may be processed out of the system before they even come close to a correctional institution.

The criminal justice system is composed of three separate subsystems: police, courts, and corrections, each with its specific tasks. These subsystems are by no means mutually exclusive of one another, however, and what is done in one has a direct effect upon another. Courts receive their raw material from the police; the corrections sector receives clients from the courts; and the cycle goes on when the released offenders are again arrested by the police. Any increased success by the police impacts on courts and corrections by overloading already heavy work schedules. Also, if corrections cannot succeed in its rehabilitation efforts, the police are overloaded with repeat offenders (recidivists). This circular process is the focal point for much controversy among the three parts. Each subsystem, with its effect on the correctional funnel, is examined below.

Discretion and the Police

In the criminal justice subsystem, particularly corrections, there has been an increasing focus on those situations and circumstances where guidelines, operating policies, and procedures are missing, contradictory, or unwritten. The potential abuse of discretionary power has become an area for considerable concern and angry debate. This concern, evident in all subsystems, may be illustrated by the police sector.

Decision making in most administrative agencies is usually the responsibility of an organization's top executive. This individual is probably the highest-paid, best-educated, most experienced, and most mature individual in the organization. The executive is provided a staff to marshal information needed to make decisions and usually is given sufficient time to deliberate on them.

The police system, it can be argued, appears to be just the opposite. The decision to arrest or not to arrest, to shoot or not to shoot is usually made in a split second and often by young, inexperienced officers at the *bottom* of the organizational ladder. In most cases they are also in the lowest pay bracket, with little education, experience, or maturity. They have no staff to provide them with data, but must make decisions based on whatever training they have and how they perceive the situation at the moment. It is small wonder that use of this broad discretionary power at the lowest levels tends to arouse general distrust of police statistics that show an ever-increasing crime rate and to create hostility between the subsystems.

The basic document for any attempt to determine the rates of crime in America is the Federal Bureau of Investigation's *Uniform Crime Reports*.[3] This report is an accumulation of crimes known to the police from over ten thousand police agencies in America. The agencies which contribute data for the *Uniform Crime Reports* do so on a *voluntary* basis. The report was started in 1930 by the Committee on Uniform Crime Records of the

International Association of the Chiefs of Police. Since that time, its statistical coverage has extended to 93 percent of the population in America. The term "crimes known to the police" is explained in the *Uniform Crime Reports* for 1972:

> Law enforcement does not purport to know the total volume of crime because of the many criminal actions which are not reported to official sources. Estimates as to the level of unreported crime can be developed through costly victim surveys but this does not eliminate the reluctance of the victim to report all criminal actions to law enforcement agencies. In light of this situation, the best source for obtaining usable crime counts is the next logical universe, which is the offenses known to the police. The crimes used in the Crime Index are those considered to be most constantly reported and provide the capability to compute meaningful crime trends and crime rates.[4]

Over 11,250,000 crime index offenses were reported by law enforcement agencies in 1975.[5] Of this number, 8,198,613 were eventually classified as "known" offenses. During this same period approximately 150,000 individuals were admitted to prisons in America. Where did the other 11,000,000 disappear? This is the correctional funnel in action.

First of all, most of the crimes known to the police are never solved. The rate of *clearance by arrest* for various crimes varies greatly, from 86.2 percent for murder to 7.4 percent for auto theft (in the New England states).[6] The aggregate number of serious (index) crimes cleared by arrest[7] in 1975 was only 21 percent, with 44 percent clearance for violent crimes and 18.5 percent for property crimes. Of course, this means that 79 percent (almost 4 out of 5 index crimes) did *not* result in an offender entering the criminal justice system. Even if one assumes that any one criminal may be responsible for many offenses, there is a *major* narrowing of the funnel at the entry point, leaving us with only about one and three-quarter million offenses cleared by arrest in 1975.

The Prosecutor's Decision

The next step in the flow of criminals is the prosecutor's office. It is here that prosecutors implement their broad discretionary power to dismiss the charges or reduce them to charges for which the defendant will plead guilty. Recent studies indicate that as many as 50 to 80 percent of the felony cases initiated by the police are dismissed by prosecutors. A high percentage of charges not dismissed are reduced through "plea bargaining"[8] to a less serious charge, to which the defendant agrees to plead guilty. The usual explanation for this further narrowing of the correctional funnel is that high caseloads and limited resources force prosecutors to dispense with much of their caseload as quickly as possible in order to avoid overwhelming the courts. The time factor does not explain, however, why some cases are prosecuted and others dismissed. Here, the wide discretionary power given to prosecutors becomes a crucial issue.

The effectiveness of prosecutors is usually measured by the number of convictions they get while they are in office. Since their political survival depends on their success in securing convictions, it is not too surprising that they will dismiss or bargain away those cases which show little promise of conviction. They may even bargain for probation without prosecution ("deferred prosecution") in cases they could not possibly win. The general public is seldom concerned with prosecutors' methods of obtaining convictions, as long as they get them:

> When a case finally reaches the trial court, the prosecutor earnestly prepares for a real battle, not for justice, but for a conviction. His professional reputation is at stake. He must resort to all the oratory and psychological trickery he can mobilize. He is ethically no better and no worse than the defense lawyer in this judicial bout. The average trial, unfortunately, becomes more a show or contest than a struggle for justice. The judge acts as referee—to see that there is something like fair play. The jury sits in amazement, at times flattered at the compliments paid them by the lawyers, and at times incensed at the threats and insults exchanged by the lawyers in reckless fashion.
> During the court recess the two lawyers may often be seen slapping each other on the back in perfect amity. Here is a basic American institution in action, with tragic implications that most Americans do not grasp.[9]

The prosecutor's discretion to dismiss or bargain further helps to explain the gap between the number of reported crimes and the number of actual imprisonments.

Since this part of the decision process is so critical for offenders, it will be helpful to review it in detail. The decision to charge an offender occurs after the police have made their arrest and presented their information to the prosecuting attorney. Except in those few police departments with legal advisors on call twenty-four hours a day, prosecutors are the first *legally trained* individuals to examine the facts. It is their job to decide whether to charge the suspect or to dismiss ("no paper"[10]) the case.

The legal decision to proceed will be made only if the alleged crime displays certain essential elements.[11] There must be a narrowly defined unlawful act and the presence of criminal intent. The offender must have *intended* to commit the specific unlawful act, or the case is on shaky legal ground. Many crimes may include a number of lesser crimes within their definition. Alternatives to the charge of first degree murder, which is very difficult to prove, might be unpremeditated murder (manslaughter), aggravated assault, assault with intent to kill, etc. With a bit of imagination, good prosecutors can make the intent and the unlawful acts match up well enough to assure a fairly strong case for conviction. If they think they can get a defendant to plead guilty to a lesser charge (and accept a lesser penalty), they may well bargain for it. Often, if the defendant will not accept the lesser charge, the case is dropped because of its low potential for conviction if pursued (thereby maintaining the good track record the prosecutor needs for reelection or advancement). At least 90 percent of the defendants convicted will have pled guilty (or "no contest") to a charge.

Aside from the "legal sufficiency" issue, a complaint will also be considered by the prosecutor from the extralegal standpoint. Often the most important of the extralegal considerations are determined by the matter of equity or by department policy. Age, sex, race, prior convictions, and similar factors have no bearing on guilt, but they are obviously taken into account in the charging decision. If established department policy diverts all first offenders or all those under eighteen years of age to nonjudicial programs, the prosecutor will act accordingly. By the same token, a tough department position on certain offenses means that almost everyone who commits such an offense will be charged and processed through the courts.

The initial screening by the prosecuting attorney is the most important point for most suspects in the criminal justice system. Although more statistics are being gathered on this critical process, it is still a cloudy area. As early as 1933, criminologist N. Baker wrote:

> How much more significant would it be to have figures on the situations arising behind closed doors in the prosecutor's office! Court statistics are enlightening to such an extent that it is now almost commonplace to designate the prosecutor as the most powerful official in local government. If we had some means of checking the decisions of the prosecutor when the question "to prosecute or not to prosecute?" arises, such figures would go much farther to substantiate such a statement.[12]

Almost fifty years later we still know only that the funnel narrows sharply at this point and we have little real insight into the factors that determine which suspects are charged, and which are not.

The Court's Dilemma

The criminal court is at the core of the American criminal justice system. The courts are highly structured, deeply venerated, and circumscribed by law and tradition. The rest of the system is dependent upon and responsible to the courts. The police and their procedures are molded and restricted by decisions of the courts; prosecutors must weigh the legal and extralegal issues surrounding the cases before them in light of the court which will try them; and the correctional system is dependent upon the court for its workload. The formal processes that take place in the courtroom are not merely symbolic, but are often crucial for the protection of the individual suspect and of society.

Judges are elected or appointed to office. In either case, they can be put in a position where they owe a political debt to their backers. Because of the corrupt practices of a very few judges, it is often felt that judges in general are responsive only to pressure groups and will dismiss cases if told to do so by those in power. Actually, the discretion of a judge in a criminal court is quite limited.

Dean Wigmore[13] is credited with originating the "sporting theory" of justice as a description of a court trial.[14] The trial can boil down to a legal contest between two highly skilled lawyers, with the judge playing the role of a referee. Our adversary system of justice pits two lawyers against each other in an attempt to prove the *technical* guilt or innocence of the suspect. The judge, who may be considerably less skilled at law than either the prosecutor or defense attorney, simply determines the outcome of various procedural disputes. If he or she makes one wrong decision, the offender may question it on appeal, and that alone can suffice to overturn the conviction. It is a basic concept of the American system of justice that many offenders should be permitted to go free, rather than risk the conviction of one innocent person because the procedures that protect his or her rights were not observed to the letter.

The courts, like the prosecutor, may work to narrow the correctional funnel in several ways. Cases may be lost because the court finds there was a mistake in either the charges or the facts, and dismisses them at the early stages of the trial. The court itself may allow damaging or false evidence to be admitted, which would cause the case to be reversed later by an appellate court. Also, the court may divert the convicted offender into treatment systems which are alternatives to the state's correctional institutions. Thus, many potential correctional clients who enter the court process do not actually end up in a prison.

Although prosecuting attorneys may have good cause to believe that a certain suspect committed a particular offense, cause to charge that suspect, and cause to bring the suspect to trial, they sometimes make errors. These errors are usually brought to the court's attention by the defense attorney, in the suspect's preliminary appearance before the judge. A judge who is convinced at this point that the charges are in error can dismiss the case. He or she will usually accompany this dismissal with a few unkind words to the prosecutor for presenting such a poor case. It is this kind of problem that the ambitious prosecutor seeks to avoid at all costs.

Sometimes, though seldom as often as television might lead one to think, the case against a suspect falls apart during the trial. The lawyers make critical motions in attempts to suppress evidence or restrict certain testimony. Judges must rule on these crucial issues, knowing that their ruling might be reversed on appeal. If they make a decision that later is appealed and overruled, their reputation may suffer. On the other hand, they might agree with the motions and dismiss the case at that point, saving the state the expense and bother of a long string of appeals. In either case, yet another client may fall out of the correctional funnel.

In earlier days, the choices for a judge were relatively simple. The suspect would be found guilty and sentenced to prison, or innocent and then released. A few were found "not guilty by reason of insanity," but most of those convicted were sentenced to the prisons of early nineteenth- and twentieth-century America. Today, a guilty finding means the judge must choose among a broad range of alternative paths. A few of these are mentioned below, and many will be covered in detail later.

Probation[15] has become by far the most popular alternative to incarceration in state prisons. Judges have seen this approach as an opportunity to allow guilty individuals who present little or no danger to society to continue a productive life, on condition of good behavior. Probation is used in as many as 60 percent of the cases in some states. A variation on probation, called "shock probation,"[16] has been initiated in Ohio, Kentucky, and Indiana. In this system the offender is given the maximum sentence for a crime, then released after a short taste of prison life (up to ninety days) and returned to the community on regular probation. The initial results of this system in Ohio are quite promising, and judges find it a desirable way to punish offenders whose crimes are slightly more serious than those for which regular probation is clearly an effective and appropriate remedy.[17]

Another method of diverting clients from the corrections system is to place them in the mental health system instead. Many states have "psychopathic offender" or "habitual offender" statutes[18] that allow the court to have offenders examined and committed after conviction, but before sentencing. Still others have systems that provide this path before conviction. The pleas of "incompetency to stand trial"[19] and "not guilty by reason of insanity"[20] are also available to the defendant in most jurisdictions.

All of these procedures provide temporary or permanent escape from the corrections system and further accelerate the funneling process. One result of this process, it appears, is that the group of offenders who are eventually incarcerated is significantly different in composition from the group that includes all those arrested.

Even those offenders who are found guilty and sentenced to the corrections system are often destined for units other than prisons. A broad range of community correctional programs[21] has sprung up across the nation. Some (such as halfway houses) are designed to provide a place for housing and treatment while the offender attempts to maintain family and job ties in the community. The sharply increased emphasis on and use of these programs herald the beginning of the end to treatment methods predicated on the fortress prisons of the past. Judges are more inclined to choose a treatment option that provides a measure of humanity and hope. The community-based correctional programs are believed to offer great promise in this regard.

While the above offer the most widespread options for judges in their sentencing decisions, others are available as well. With minor crimes, a fine or restitution to the victim may be required in place of a prison sentence in several jurisdictions. Public service has also been used as a substitute for prison. Weekend imprisonment, evening imprisonment, and attendance centers have also been used in attempts to replace full-time incarceration. All of these attempts recognize the importance of offenders' remaining in the community and holding their jobs, while paying for their crimes in some reasonable way. (A more detailed discussion of these attempts is found in chapter 28.)

Although the criminal process at times may seem unwieldy and inefficient, this very lack of efficiency reflects our American concern for justice, as suggested by President Johnson's Crime Commission:

> [T]he basic procedures of the criminal court must conform to concepts of "due process" that have grown from English common law seeds. A defendant must be formally notified of the charge against him and must have an opportunity to confront witnesses, to present evidence in his own defense, and to have this proof weighed by an impartial jury under the supervision of an impartial judge. In addition, due process has come to incorporate the right of a defendant to be represented by an attorney. Unquestionably adherence to due process complicates, and in many instances handicaps, the work of the courts. They could be more efficient—in the sense that the likelihood and speed of conviction would be greater—if the constitutional requirements of due process were not so demanding. But the law rightly values due process over efficient process. And by permitting the accused to challenge its fairness and legality at every stage of his prosecution, the system provides the occasion for the law to develop in accordance with changes in society and society's ideals.[22]

This system allows many clients to slip through the correctional funnel, but it also provides a safeguard for defendants in cases of doubtful merit.

Another Look at Crime Statistics

It can now be seen that the extent of the crime picture in America depends upon where you are in the system with respect to the correctional funnel (see Figure II–3). Statistics are very helpful, keeping us informed about how many people have been arrested, prosecuted, convicted, acquitted, committed, and placed on probation or parole. They can also be very deceptive,

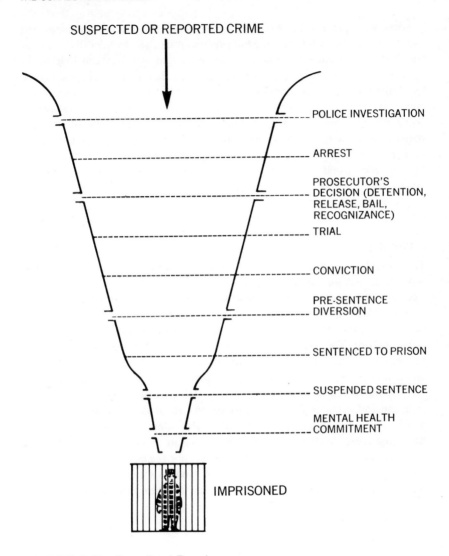

FIGURE II–3. The Correctional Funnel

because so many cases fall out of the process along the way. It is far too easy for the beginning student of corrections or criminal justice to assume that the number of prisoners in our correctional institutions reflects an accurate picture of the crime problem. The preceding description of the screening process, with its limiting effect on the number of cases actually incarcerated, suggests the error of this assumption. There is a great discrepancy between the vast number of actual crimes (reported and unreported) and the number of incarcerated felons.

When you consider that most of the early studies on crime were conducted using incarcerated offenders in adult prisons, it is small wonder that some of our theories are unsound. There is no doubt that statistics can help us in deciding new procedures or processes, but statistics used in criminal justice have some strange characteristics, and these must be taken into consideration. Law professor Thorsten Sellin, discussing the problems of analyzing crime records, stated as his "second principle": "The value of criminal statistics as a basis for the measurement of criminality in geographic areas decreases as the procedure takes us farther away from the offense itself."[23] Since prisons usually represent the farthest possible point from the offense, clearly one must be very skeptical in drawing conclusions from statistics which originate in prison.

Summary

The correctional funnel provides us with a problem and an advantage. The problem is that we know the number of incarcerated felons is quite different from the number of crimes known to the police or arrest figures shown in the *Uniform Crime Reports*. This means that those programs aimed at the small sample of criminals who actually end up in prison are attacking only the tip of the iceberg. The advantage this knowledge gives criminal justice administrators is the recognition that their efforts must be redirected toward the *real* crime problems. Without a thorough knowledge of the funneling process, much effort could be wasted on a very small part of the problem.

In the following chapters and discussions about law and the correctional process, we will examine the practices and alternatives available. While following these discussions, you should keep in mind the drastic effect the correctional funnel exerts on those who cannot manage to avoid imprisonment. One recalls the famous line from George Orwell's political satire, *Animal Farm:* "All pigs are equal, but some are more equal than others."[24]

REVIEW QUESTIONS

I. Find the answers to the following in the text:

1. What are the major elements of the criminal justice system?

2. What are the *Uniform Crime Reports?*

3. What effect does the correctional funnel have on crime statistics?

II. Words to identify:

1. discretion

2. no-paper

3. plea bargaining

4. elements of crime

5. index crime

6. cleared by arrest

7. incompetency

8. insanity

9. shock probation

10. UCR

11. deferred prosecution

NOTES

1. The largest prison in the Western world is the State Prison of Southern Michigan at Jackson. It was built in 1926 and can hold over 3,000 prisoners.

2. National Advisory Commission on Criminal Justice Standards and Goals, *Corrections* (Washington, D.C.: U.S. Department of Justice, 1973), pp. 5-6.

3. The *Uniform Crime Reports Program* is the product of a voluntary cooperative law enforcement effort to produce national crime statistics. Approximately 10,000 law enforcement agencies, covering 93 percent of the United States population, submit monthly and annual reports to the F.B.I. so that information can be assembled to depict the current crime problem. This program is entirely voluntary on the part of the law enforcement agencies.

4. Clarence M. Kelley, *Crime in the United States: 1972 (Uniform Crime Reports)* (Washington, D.C.: U.S. Government Printing Office, 1973), p. 1.

5. Kelley, *Uniform Crime Reports* (1975), p. 10.

6. Kelley, *Uniform Crime Reports* (1975), pp. 168-169.

7. In the Uniform Crime Reports Program, police clear a crime when they have identified the offender, have sufficient evidence to charge the offender, and actually take the offender into custody.

8. *Plea bargaining* refers to the practice by prosecutors of permitting the defendant to plead to a lesser charge than the one he or she was arrested for, usually because the prosecutor does not feel the case is strong enough on the more serious charge, or because the prosecutor hopes to persuade the defendant to provide information about other crimes or offenders.

9. Harry Elmer Barnes and Negley K. Teeters, *New Horizons in Criminology*, 3d ed. (Englewood Cliffs, N.J.: Prentice-Hall, 1959), p. 242.

10. A *no-paper action* means that the prosecutor has decided there is not enough likelihood of conviction to warrant filing an information.

11. The term *elements of a crime* refers to specific and precise statutory conditions of fact that *must* exist in order for that crime to have taken place. (E.g., it must be *dark* for "burglary in the night season" to take place.)

12. N. Baker, "The Prosecutor—Initiation of Prosecution," *Journal of Criminal Law, Criminology and Police Science* 23 (1933): 771.

13. *John Henry Wigmore* (1863-1943) was probably the world's foremost authority on the law of evidence. His *Treatise on the Anglo-American System of Evidence Trials at Common Law,* written in 1904-05, is generally regarded as one of the world's greatest law books. He had great influence on the reform of evidentiary law.

14. Roscoe Pound, *Criminal Justice in America* (New York: Holt, Rinehart, and Winston, 1929), p. 163.

15. *Probation* is a sentence not involving confinement which imposes conditions to restrain the offender's actions in the community and retains authority of the sentencing court to modify the conditions of sentence or to resentence the offender if he or she violates the conditions (see chapter 10).

16. *Shock probation* is the imposition of a short prison term as a condition of probation. This is designed to give the offender a taste of incarceration in the belief that it will deter future criminal activity.

17. On the other hand, shock probation may work to expose the offender to the least desirable elements of both probation and incarceration, an argument used by many critics of the plan. For a discussion of this and other arguments for and against shock probation, see David Petersen and Paul Friday, "Shock of Imprisonment: Short-Term Incarceration as a Treatment Technique," *International Journal of Criminology and Penology* 1 (November 1973): 319-326.

18. Psychopathic offender and habitual offender statutes received a great impetus in the late 1930s and the early 1940s. Their main function is to permit an examination to determine if the offender is psychopathic or an habitual criminal, as a basis for possible commitment (see chapter 20).

19. *Incompetency to stand trial* means that the defendant's mental or physical condition is such that he or she cannot assist counsel in his or her own defense. Specific statutes vary greatly between jurisdictions.

20. *Not guilty by reason of insanity* generally refers to the M'Naghten test, established in England in 1843 (see chapter 20). To establish a defense on the grounds of insanity, it must be clearly proved that when the crime was committed, the offender's mind was so unsound that the offender did not know what he or she was doing—or did not realize the act was wrong.

21. *Community corrections* generally refers to programs that take place in the community or draw heavily on community resources in their operation (see chapter 28).

22. The President's Commission on Law Enforcement and Administration of Justice, *The Challenge of Crime in a Free Society* (Washington, D.C.: U.S. Government Printing Office, 1967), p. 125.

23. Thorsten Sellin, "The Significance of Records of Crime," *The Law Quarterly Review* 67 (October 1951): 498.

24. George Orwell, *Animal Farm* (New York: Harcourt, Brace, and World, 1954).

8 Sentencing

My object all sublime
I shall achieve in time—
To let the punishment fit the crime,
The punishment fit the crime.

WILLIAM S. GILBERT
The Mikado

The Sentencing Decision

Defendants who reach the sentencing stage of the criminal proceeding are those who have not escaped the correctional funnel. At this point they have either pled guilty to or been found guilty of a crime. The court must now decide how to dispose of them, often the most complicated and difficult task for the sentencing judge. If the sentence had no purpose except to punish the offender, as was the case until fairly recently, the judge's job would be easily prescribed by statute. In modern times, however, sentencing is also intended to be the cornerstone for rehabilitation. These broadly divergent objectives create a paradox which may force judges to choose between equally unwise alternatives based on the *offense* rather than the *offender*. This choice is often further complicated by subtle pressures from police, prosecutors, and the public to incarcerate certain offenders for long periods of time.

One of the main problems with the sentencing decision is that it requires that judges *predict* human behavior. As judges ask themselves if specific offenders will respond to prison in a positive way or perhaps benefit more from psychiatric help, they have little factual information to guide them. In the final analysis, most judges must rely on a presentence investigation and their own intuition, experience, and imagination to produce the best decision.

The Presentence Investigation

Only about one-fourth of the states make a presentence report *mandatory* for offenses for which imprisonment can be more than one year. It is estimated

FIGURE II–4. A Modern Courtroom (Courtesy National Clearinghouse
for Criminal Justice Planning and Architecture)

that over 85 percent of the states do prepare some kind of presentence report
on felony cases, although the variation in usefulness and quality from one
report to the next may be extreme. The presentence report, if properly
researched and prepared, can be a most valuable document for trial judges in
their sentence decisions.

The presentence investigation is usually prepared by the court's probation
officer, or by any available staff of social workers. The defense attorney
usually reviews, and may challenge, points in the presentence report in order
to help the judge make a sentencing decision which is based on information
from all sources. Walter C. Reckless points up the essential elements of a
workable presentence investigation report:

> A presentence investigation report, when written up and presented to
> the judge, should include in summary form such information as:
> present offense (including the person's attitudes toward it and his role
> in it); previous criminal record; family situation (including tensions
> and discord and the factors affecting his happiness); neighborhood
> environment; school and educational history; employment history
> (especially the skills and the efficiency and stability as a worker);
> associates and participation; habits (including alcohol, gambling,
> promiscuity, and so forth); physical and mental health (as reported by
> various sources and by special examinations); summary and

recommendations. Although most presentence investigations will emphasize such objective facts in a case as age, grade reached in school, number of children, and so on, it is important that the investigating officer capture as much subjective content as possible, especially how the defendant looks at things and the meaning of various plights and difficulties to him. The defendant's perspective on life and the way he approaches it, as well as his attitudes toward the objects and the relationships of his milieu, are the most crucial items in a presentence investigation, just as they are in more elaborate case studies. Subjective data, in short, give the more revealing clues as to what has shaped the destiny of the defendant so far and what the possibilities of his future are.[1]

Judicial vs. Administrative Sentencing

Traditionally, the sentencing process has involved a *judicial* determination of the appropriate punishment for a specific crime. Extensive changes in judicial power have taken place in the last century, however. In the early days, when a judge sentenced an offender to ten years in prison, it was almost a certainty that the offender would serve ten years *to the day*. As administrative forms of sentence-shortening (such as good-time, pardon, parole, and clemency) became more common, the correlation between the judge's sentence and the time the offender served largely disappeared. In practice, courts can establish minimum and maximum sentences within the sentencing statutes, but the actual length of the sentence is often left up to the administrators of the correctional system—to the executive rather than the judicial branch of government.

Some states, such as California, have formalized this *administrative* sentencing method by forming centralized Adult Authorities. Even though a centralized, statewide administrative system is different from the judicial system in its political and bureaucratic context, it is strikingly similar in operation and results. Administrative sentence-fixing is envisioned as providing standards and policies that will tend to equalize sentence lengths for similar offenses. In the case of California, the facts do not seem to bear out this hope (because the standard application of penalties to the *offense* does not acknowledge vast differences among *offenders*).

A comparison of the judicial and administrative styles of decision-making in sentencing reveals some similar criteria:

> 1. [A] determination of how much time is right for the kind of crime at issue, with the decision-maker's own sense of values and expectations usually (but not always) heavily influenced by the pressures of his environment and what he perceives to be the norms of his colleagues;

2. classification within that crime category of the offender's particular act as mitigated, average or aggravated;

3. his past criminal record (slight, average or aggravated);

4. the extent of his repentance, his attitude toward available "treatment," and the official prognosis of his reformability; or

5. the anticipated public (usually meaning law enforcement) reaction to a proposed disposition. Not all of these criteria are used or even relevant in every case and many other variables may be raised because of the existence of particular facts (such as strong middle-class background and allegiance) or the peculiarities or hangups of an individual decision-maker. Something approximating the basic list given, however, appears to comprise the critical factors in most sentence-fixing. Presumably very similar criteria are involved in prosecutorial sentence-bargaining at the pre-arraignment stage.[2]

Practical Problems in Sentencing

As we have seen previously, a flow chart of the criminal justice process reveals at every step along the way an imbalance of input to output (number of arrests vs. number of incarcerations). Many cases are winnowed out in the early stages, and it is a highly select group of prisoners who end up in the Atticas and San Quentins of America. In a statistical sense, the negative selection process which admits the offender to prison may be considered more discriminating than the positive one which admits students to most Ivy League colleges. But for the practical need to spread limited resources over an overwhelming number of cases, scores of fellow offenders would join each of the relatively few offenders who do end up in prison.

The state and federal correctional systems are finite in size. The sentencing decision must take into account decisions at the other end of the funnel process, which determine release rates. The system can become blocked if sentences do not approximately balance releases, and dangerous overcrowding results. Sentencing, therefore, must reflect both the number of prisoners in the institutions and the limited resources for handling them.

Diminution of Power in Sentencing

The most pronounced loss of sentencing power by the courts has been in the area of determining the actual duration of imprisonment. As the penitentiary system rose to prominence in the mid-nineteenth century, it was used more and more as the primary method of punishment for adult felons. It had been generally accepted that the power to determine the place and duration of imprisonment was vested in the courts. Sometimes there were certain restrictions, such as a mandatory life sentence or mandatory death penalty for certain offenses,[3] but usually there was room for judicial discretion within the prescribed legislative limits. The only outside influence on duration in these earlier days was the governor's power to pardon.[4] While pardons were sometimes granted in massive doses, the occasion was usually overcrowded prisons or certain holidays.[5] The finality of the judge's decisions was not seriously eroded by these early executive practices.

The steady assumption of discretionary power by prison management and correctional personnel has shifted the decision on sentence duration from the judge's shoulders. Essentially, five different sentencing structures are used by American jurisdictions today. The classifications are generally determined according to the balance of power in a state between courts and the parole authorities. A concise description of each classification is drawn from *The Correctional Process,* a text that should be a part of every correctional professional's library:

> [T]he statutes are discussed in a general order of increasing indeterminacy, an index of which is increasing power in the parole board and consequent decreasing powers in the courts.

> 1. *Maximum and minimum term fixed by the court.* The statutes in eight states provide that the court must set a minimum and maximum term of imprisonment within the applicable statutory limits for the offense charged. In three states, the court may, in its discretion, impose a sentence of this kind. In two states such sentences are authorized only for some offenses and for these they are mandatory. In two other states, such sentences may be imposed for some offenses.
>
> The significance of the minimum term imposed by the court normally inheres in its effect on parole eligibility. In six of the aforementioned states, a prisoner is eligible for parole at the expiration of such term less good behavior credits; and in four after a certain fraction of the minimum has expired. In the remaining four states parole eligibility is not affected by the minimum fixed by the court.
>
> Although these statutes are normally denominated indeterminate sentencing schemes, the indeterminacy of sentence may be severely limited in those six states in which the minimum sentence imposed, or such minimum less good behavior

credits, determines eligibility for parole, since the sentence is indeterminate only for the period of time separating the maximum and minimum terms, and the court may cause that period to be extremely short. It should also be noted that where parole eligibility is governed by the minimum sentence imposed, the incidence of unreasonable disparities in parole eligibility of different prisoners is greater than where parole eligibility is statutorily fixed at a fraction of the maximum sentence imposed.

2. *Maximum term fixed by statute, minimum term fixed by the court.* Hawaii and Michigan have sentencing schemes under which the maximum sentence imposed is the statutory maximum for the offense charged, while a minimum term is fixed by the courts. Under the Hawaiian system, the sentencing court is required to sentence the defendant for the statutory maximum term immediately upon conviction unless the statutory maximum is life imprisonment. Within three months the parole board is required to conduct an intensive presentence investigation and in-confinement study of the prisoner's character and background and to fix the minimum term of imprisonment to be served before he shall become eligible for parole. Such minimum must then be submitted to the sentencing court, which may approve, reduce, or increase the minimum so fixed subject to the condition that there must be a "reasonable period" between the maximum and minimum sentence imposed. The Hawaii formula thus vests final discretion in the courts while assuring that such exercise of discretion will be based on more information regarding the background, character, and potential reformation of the prisoner than is normally available to the courts in other jurisdictions. The parole board retains full discretion to parole the prisoner during the "reasonable period" that must separate the maximum and minimum term. The policies and practice of both the courts and the parole board are integrated by the dual sentence fixing arrangement.

In Michigan, power to determine length of incarceration gravitates somewhat more toward the courts since there is no apparent requirement that the minimum period of confinement fixed by the court be separated in any substantial degree from the statutory maximum. Flexibility of release and integration of policies is furthered by allowing paroles before the minimum sentence expires with the written permission of the court. Because of the greater interaction between the parole authorities and the courts in these two states, the restrictions on indeterminacy that may arise in states in which the minimum and maximum sentences are fixed by the court alone seem less likely to occur.

3. *Maximum and minimum term fixed by the court, but minimum not to exceed a certain fraction of maximum.* In four states, the District of Columbia, and under a recent act making indeterminate sentences optional in the federal courts, the power to fix minimum and maximum terms is given to the court but is subject to the following limitations: for federal offenses, and in the District of Columbia, the minimum imposed, if any, may not exceed one-third of the maximum imposed; in Alaska the same limitation exists but the court may, in its discretion, impose the statutory minimum; in Pennsylvania, it may not exceed one-half of the maximum imposed; and in New York and Maine it may not exceed one-half the statutory maximum. The purpose of the limitation in each case is to allow a reasonable period of parole eligibility by eliminating sentences in which the minimum and maximum sentences imposed are not substantially separated, but the New York and Maine statutes only prevent the imposition of sentences that are *both* long and unduly restrictive of the discretion of the parole board, since indeterminacy is guaranteed only to the extent that the maximum imposed exceeds one-half the statutory maximum for the offense.

4. *Maximum term fixed by the court, minimum fixed by law.* In eighteen "fixed" sentence jurisdictions, the maximum term of imprisonment is fixed by the court, while the minimum period of confinement, if any, is determined by the parole law. In seven other jurisdictions this procedure may be employed at the court's option; in five its application is authorized for some cases only, but is then mandatory; in two use of this procedure is mandatory for some offenses, and is discretionary for all others.

In eight of the fixed sentence jurisdictions, a prisoner may be paroled at the expiration of a certain fraction of the sentence imposed. In nine others a prisoner alternatively becomes eligible for parole after a certain number of years have been served, regardless of the sentence imposed, thereby vitiating the potential power of the courts to unduly postpone parole eligibility for some multiple offenders by imposition of extremely long sentences. In nine jurisdictions, parole is apparently authorized at any time, although there are numerous exceptions in two of these states, and the court is empowered to recommend a minimum period of incarceration in another. In three states the prisoner may be released after the statutory minimum for the offense has expired, although in one of these, the court may provide that there shall be no minimum term of incarceration. In one state parole eligibility varies with the age and recidivism of the offender. In two states, no statute authorizing parole for prisoners sentenced to "fixed" terms was found.

Although often denominated as "fixed" sentence plans, the statutes in most of these states determine parole eligibility in a way that assures at least some parole flexibility and thus allow the date of parole release to be determined in accordance with reformative progress, a result that may not always obtain in those jurisdictions in which the courts are given unlimited freedom in fixing the parole eligibility date. It has been argued that prison terms in this country are generally too long and that "fixed" sentences have the added advantage of tending towards shorter incarceration. Although statistical data might appear to support this conclusion, it is open to serious question. Professor Tappan has pointed out that the reasons for the relative brevity of incarceration in "fixed" sentence states may well be unrelated to the nature of the sentencing scheme. It is his belief that the limited use of probation in many of the states that employ "fixed" sentences leads to the imposition of short prison terms for offenders who might have been placed on probation elsewhere. Furthermore, in those states in which the deterrent aspect of sentencing is considered highly important due to high crime rates prison terms naturally tend to be longer, and most of these states employ indeterminate sentence plans. As further support for his position Professor Tappan noted that where both "indeterminate" and definite sentences are authorized, there is no considerable difference in the length of incarceration according to the nature of the sentence. It might be added to these arguments that in all but one jurisdiction where jury sentencing is authorized, "fixed" sentences are employed. In eleven of these twelve jurisdictions, the sentencing structure provides a check on the imposition of long sentences not available elsewhere since the court may reduce, suspend in part or suspend entirely sentences thought to be excessively long, although it may not increase a legal sanction imposed by the jury. It would thus appear that there is no demonstrable merit in the view that "fixed" sentences result in shorter prison terms.

5. *Statutory maximum and minimum term to be imposed by the court.* In six states, the trial judge is required to impose the maximum and minimum term, if any, fixed by statute for the offense. In another two states this procedure may be employed at the court's option, and in four more, the statutorily fixed minimum and maximum must be imposed for some cases. Insofar as the use of such provisions is discretionary, these statutes go no further towards indeterminacy than those that authorize the court to fix a minimum and maximum sentence since a judge favoring indeterminacy could, under the latter scheme, similarly impose sentence for the statutory minimum and maximum term. When imposition of the statutory minimum and maximum is mandatory, however, control over length of incarceration, within the statutory limits for the offense, rests entirely with the parole board, and the courts have no sentencing discretion except insofar as a plea to a lesser crime may be accepted or the defendant may be placed on suspended sentence or probation. Moreover, even the availability of these release procedures is restricted to less serious felonies in seven of these states.

In Washington and California the correctional authorities who also administer the parole law are required to make a thorough background investigation and in-confinement study of the prisoner after the court has imposed a sentence to the statutory minimum and maximum, and to fix within these statutory limits a definite period of incarceration that is subject to reconsideration at a later date. This procedure gives the prisoner a fairly definite idea of the date of his release and is thus thought by some to avoid the deleterious effects of sentences of extremely uncertain duration. The term so fixed serves different purposes in each state: in

California, parole eligibility is entirely governed by
statute, and the sentence fixed or refixed by the
correction authority within statutory limitations
merely governs final discharge; in Washington, the
prisoner is not eligible for parole until the expiration
of the period of incarceration fixed or refixed by the
board, less up to one-third off for good behavior. In
seven of the remaining jurisdictions, the prisoner
may be paroled at the expiration of the statutory
minimum for the offense or some fraction thereof,
less good behavior credits in some cases. In the
other two states most prisoners may be paroled at
any time. It should be noted that in at least five
states, the court may recommend a specific period
of incarceration, but such recommendation is not
binding on the board.[6]

It appears that the movement toward the indeterminate sentence will tend
to shift the balance of the power in the direction of parole and correctional
authorities.

Problems with Penal Codes

The penal codes of most jurisdictions are a potpourri of social thinking from
past eras. Most of the earlier penal codes were devised in response to a
specific event or set of events, often a particularly heinous crime or
repugnant act. Such acts bring public pressure on legislators, and, if that
pressure is persistent enough, a new law is created with a formula for
punishment attached. Unfortunately, these laws, with punishments which are
often irrationally severe, remain on the books for decades after the incident
and the legislators are long forgotten.

Many states are in the process of updating and revising their entire
criminal codes. This is a long and arduous task, however, and there is a
great temptation to use the old as a model for the new. It is felt by many that
sentence-fixing should not be part of penal legislation. The obvious failure
of early penal codes, designed to mete out specific punishment for specific
offenses, has reinforced the belief that legislators and judges should be
excluded from the sentence-fixing process. One alternative that has been
advocated is the use of professional psychologists, trained to understand
human behavior, as a replacement for legislators and jurists in fixing the
penalties for crimes.

President Johnson's Crime Commission reported in 1967 that: "A common characteristic of American penal codes is the severity of sentence
available for almost all felony offenses."[7] This background of severity has
inhibited meaningful change in penal codes. In examining sentencing prac-

tices, one must review both the system of criminal justice and the erratic quality of justice dispensed by that system. Failure to observe the difference between justice *in* the law and justice *before* the law can result in unfair criticism of the judge.

The "Model Penal Code"[8] drafted by the American Law Institute addresses the problems of severity and inconsistency of present penal codes with regard to sentencing. Imprisonment is seen as a last resort, to be used only when:

1. there is undue risk that during the period of suspended sentence or probation the defendant will commit another crime; or

2. the defendant is in need of correctional treatment that can be provided most effectively by commitment to an institution; or

3. a lesser sentence will depreciate the seriousness of the defendant's crime.[9]

These criteria are intended as a guide for extreme cases only. The Model Code envisions that every alternative to imprisonment will be explored in a given case before the criteria are applied. The New York Revised Penal Law[10] uses these standards for imprisonment.

The major problems with penal code revision involve the need to make codes conform to modern-day standards and capabilities. The American Bar Association has outlined some general principles for statutory structure:

a. All crimes should be classified for the purpose of sentencing into categories which reflect substantial differences in gravity. The categories should be very few in number. Each should specify the sentencing alternatives available for offenses which fall within it. The penal codes of each jurisdiction should be revised where necessary to accomplish this result.

b. The sentencing court should be provided in all cases with a wide range of alternatives, with gradations of supervisory, supportive and custodial facilities at its disposal so as to permit a sentence appropriate for each individual case.

c. The legislature should not specify a mandatory sentence for any sentencing category or for any particular offense.

d. It should be recognized that in many instances in this country the prison sentences which are now

> authorized, and sometimes required, are
> significantly higher than are needed in the vast
> majority of cases in order adequately to protect the
> interests of the public. Except for a very few
> particularly serious offenses, and except under the
> circumstances set forth (in the section dealing with
> special terms for certain types of offenders), the
> maximum authorized prison term ought to be five
> years and only rarely ten.[11]

Another major issue in penal code revision is disparity of sentencing for the same or similar offenses. The emphasis today is on rehabilitation, but prisoners who feel that they have been unfairly treated in sentencing may well reject all efforts to rehabilitate them. This kind of disparity also destroys public confidence in the criminal justice system. The elimination or revision of antiquated statutes and the adoption of principles that are widely accepted by both the judiciary and correctional administrators will go a long way toward encouraging consistent and appropriate sentencing.

Sentence Length

Once the practical problems are overcome, and within the legislative framework provided, the court must decide how long the offender's sentence is to be. We have seen disparity between sentence length and actual time spent in prison. To compound this disparity, the factor of sentence ranges may arise. Take, for example, an offense which has a range of twenty years. Even if most of the offenders in this category are usually sentenced to about five years, it would still be possible for a sentence to range from five to *twenty* years, or much longer than necessary. The point is not that long sentences are always inappropriate, but that the law often does not reflect the current practice.

One of the reasons some crimes may be punished by such long sentences lies in the "worst offender" nature of these statutes at the time they were passed. As noted above, this simply means that most of the extremely long sentence laws date from an incident which so shocked the public that the legislature quickly established a long sentence for that offense, to protect society in case of a recurrence. These incidents involve a minute sample of the criminal population, but laws may be applied to anyone who commits a similar, though far less aggravated, offense. The sad fact is that longer maximum penalties tend to drive up the actual sentences in cases where it might be unwarranted. One judge might choose five to eight years as an appropriate sentence under a twenty-year maximum statute. Others might impose as much as fifteen years for the same offender. Thus, the drafters of penal statutes face a quandary. They must provide a sentence stiff enough to handle the occasional "worst offender," but short enough to be applied to the offenders who are not unusual risks.

How should the jurist arrive at the proper length of sentence for an offender? The present system, sometimes referred to as the "hunch" system,[12] results in discriminatory sentences by the same judge, and between different judges, on the same offenses. Over a quarter of a century ago, reformers felt that "It should be no great task to set up a diagnostic clinic for administration of persons sentenced. In this clinic, impartial, disinterested scientists would function under conditions which never exist in the courts."[13] Diagnostic clinics have been very slow in coming, but at least the "presentence" clinic is in wider use than before.

Ten points were made in regard to more appropriate sentencing at the 1971 National Conference on Corrections in Williamsburg, Virginia:

1. It should be mandatory that trial judges have presentence reports in all felony cases. These reports should be prepared by qualified probation or corrections officers. Subsidiary to this, Professor Sweat proposed that a copy of the report be made available to defense counsel at sentencing, and that a copy should go to the confining facility if the man is sentenced to confinement. The report should also be made a part of the record for any sentence appeal which may be permitted.

2. Diagnostic facilities should be made available to all judges.

3. Indeterminate sentencing should be available to judges in all felony cases.

4. Jury sentencing should be abolished.

5. Sentencing judges should be required to record the reasons for each sentence. These reasons are to be made known to the defendant, with copies to the corrections personnel involved and to the appellate courts in those instances in which the sentences are appealed.

6. The corrections system should provide for appellate review.

7. Sentencing judges should educate their communities on the philosophy of sentencing.

8. Defense counsel and the prosecutor should be consulted by the judge before imposing sentence.

9. Probation officers and judges should receive instructions in sentencing, perhaps attend sentencing institutes.

10. Trial judges should be elected or appointed in as non-political a way as possible.[14]

The Model Penal Code of the American Law Institute would reduce all crimes to five grades, three for felonies and two for misdemeanors. A maximum penalty would be assigned to each grade, shorter in most cases than those now used by the states. Minimums would be set at one year for most felonies and at three years for only the very serious felonies. If the offense was especially dangerous, the judge would be able to extend the maximum. Judges would be granted the flexibility they need to fit the sentence to the particular case. While the Model Penal Code has great appeal to the practitioners in the field of corrections, it has had slow acceptance in legislatures which must choose between a humane and workable code and the outcry of an enraged citizenry when the harsh "law and order" codes are struck down.

Another approach to sentencing reform has been devised by David Fogel, the executive director of the Illinois Law Enforcement Commission. In his "justice model," which groups crimes into five categories, each category would have a flat sentence of from two to twenty-five years, depending on the offense. Sentencing judges would be allowed a 20 percent leeway in either direction under this legislative plan, but each circumstance that might affect the severity of the sentence would be spelled out in detail.[15]

Summary

While the problem of sentencing the convicted felon remains the burden of the judiciary, much of the judge's power to implement sentencing decisions has been eroded by administrative procedures in corrections. The jurist is torn between trying to retain this sentencing power and letting it pass to some form of expert sentencing tribunal. In addition to the understandable desire to protect their domain, the judges distrust the behavioral scientists, with their "easy solutions to real problems," and see them as a threat to the power and structure of the law. Many committees and commissions have discussed the dilemma of the sentencing process, but the basic burden still remains with the court.

Some states have moved toward a more realistic set of penal codes, but most continue to use the spur-of-the-moment statutes born in the limelight of some horrible crime. The availability of excessively long maximum sentences almost ensures their abuse. The Model Penal Code is but one approach that offers promise for the future. Presentence investigations, revision of the penal codes, and a general overhaul of the procedures are recommended almost universally.

REVIEW QUESTIONS

I. Find the answers to the following in the text:

1. What has been the major source of diminution in the judge's sentencing power?

2. Evaluate the five basic sentencing structures described in the chapter.

3. What are some of the aids available to the judge in the sentence-fixing decision?

II. Words to identify:

1. judicial sentencing

2. maximum sentence

3. indeterminacy

4. mandatory sentencing

5. administrative sentencing

6. presentence investigation

7. Model Penal Code

8. fixed sentence

9. worst offender

10. diagnostic sentencing

NOTES

1. Walter C. Reckless, *The Crime Problem,* 4th ed. (New York: Appleton-Century-Crofts, 1967), pp. 673-674.

2. Caleb Foote, "The Sentencing Function" in *A Program for Prison Reform,* Roscoe Pound, ed. (Cambridge, Mass.: American Trial Lawyers Foundation, 1973), p. 30.

3. The *mandatory life sentence* was reserved for certain serious crimes and for repeat offenders. In some states a fourth conviction required mandatory life. *Mandatory death* was usually reserved for murder in conjunction with some other heinous felony (e.g., kidnap-murder, rape-murder, child molesting-murder).

4. *Pardon* involves excusing an offense without exacting the penalty. It usually means that all rights have been restored and responsibility for guilt has been removed. It is an executive function.

5. This is especially true around Christmas, and the policy has come to be called "Christmas clemency" in many jurisdictions.

6. Frank W. Miller et al., *The Correctional Process* (New York: Foundation Press, 1971), pp. 973-976.

7. The President's Commission on Law Enforcement and Administration of Justice, *The Challenge of Crime in a Free Society* (Washington, D.C.: U.S. Government Printing Office, 1967), p. 142.

8. American Law Institute, *Model Penal Code, Proposed Official Draft* (Philadelphia: ALI, 1962).

9. American Law Institute, *Model Penal Code.*

10. New York State Commission on Revision of the Penal Law and Criminal Code, *Proposed New York Penal Law* (Albany, N.Y.: State of New York, 1964).

11. American Bar Association, *Standards Relating to Sentencing Alternatives and Procedures* (New York: Office of the Criminal Justice Project, 1968).

12. Harry Elmer Barnes and Negley Teeters, *New Horizons in Criminology,* 3d ed. (Englewood Cliffs, N.J.: Prentice-Hall, 1959), p. 264.

13. Barnes and Teeters, *New Horizons in Criminology,* p. 264.

14. *National Conference on Corrections, Williamsburg, Virginia* (Washington, D.C.: U.S. Government Printing Office, 1971).

15. Michael S. Serrill, "Critics of Corrections Speak Out," *Corrections Magazine* (March 1976): 23.

9 Appellate Review

We are under a Constitution, but the Constitution is
what the judges say it is.

CHARLES EVANS HUGHES

The Issue of Due Process

A basic tenet of the criminal justice process in America is that every
defendant is presumed innocent until proven guilty. Not only does our
system demand proof of guilt, it also requires that this proof be obtained
fairly and legally, and the process of appellate review helps ensure that it
will be. In effect, appellate review acts as a shield for the defendant caught
up in the processes of criminal trial, incarceration, or supervision in the
community. The state has considerable resources to prosecute those it
considers offenders, and the Constitution protects us from the kind of
government "railroading"[1] that could deprive us of life, liberty, or property
without the benefit of due process of law. Due process has been a
constitutional right for all Americans under federal law since the passage of
the Fourteenth Amendment in 1868.[2] It was not until the "criminal law
revolution"[3] of the 1960s, however, that the due process clause of the
Fourteenth Amendment was also made binding on all the states, through a
series of Supreme Court decisions. In the field of corrections, like every
other segment of criminal justice, these decisions have created a climate of
great challenge and rapid change. This chapter includes a brief examination
of the appeal process and procedure, a glance at several significant cases,
and an analysis of trends that appear to be emerging in pending appeals.

One of the problems with due process of law is not that it is due—that is,
something we are entitled to—but rather *how much* of it is due. Only a few
decades ago, very few criminal cases were appealed. Since the case of
Gideon v. *Wainwright* (see chapter 4), however, the picture has radically

changed. The securing of the right to counsel for all defendants, stemming from that landmark decision, has opened the floodgates in the review courts across America. In some jurisdictions the rate of appeals is as high as *90 percent* of all convictions. Collateral attack,[4] or the filing of an appeal in the federal system while the state case is still undecided—almost unknown prior to the 1960s—is now routine in most state courts. The result of this overload in the review system has been a monumental increase in the workload for state and federal judges. It has also created extended periods of litigation, often stretched out over several years, eroding any lingering belief that a conviction for a criminal offense must be considered final. The review procedure involves as many as eleven steps in some state systems, and it is not unusual for a defendant to explore at least four or five. The major steps are:

1. New trial motion filed in court where convicion was imposed;

2. Appeal to state intermediate appellate court (in states where there is no intermediate appellate court this step would not be available);

3. Appeal to state supreme court;

4. Petition to U.S. Supreme Court to review state court decision on appeal;

5. Postconviction proceeding in state trial court;

6. Appeal of postconviction proceeding to state intermediate appellate court;

7. Appeal to state supreme court;

8. Petition to U.S. Supreme Court to review state court decision on appeal from postconviction proceeding;

9. Habeas corpus petition in federal district court;

10. Appeal to U.S. Court of Appeals; and

11. Petition to U.S. Supreme Court to review court of appeals decision on habeas corpus petition.[5]

It is easy to see why the review process can take so long, especially when some steps may be utilized several times in a single appeal, with reviews of the same case taking place simultaneously in different court systems. Thus due process may be a long and complicated procedure; and when appeal is part of the scheme, it can become a seemingly endless cycle.

The Path of a Criminal Case

There are so many points in the criminal proceeding to which appellate actions can be directed that it is worthwhile to re-examine the steps in which the courts become participants. The first point at which most defendants come into contact with the criminal justice system is their *arrest,* usually by a police officer. Even at this early step, the potential for a later appeal is great. It is all too true that the "guilty often go free because the constable blundered." A suspect's Fourth and Fifth Amendment rights have been clearly established by decisions such as *Mapp* v. *Ohio* and *Miranda* v. *Arizona* (see chapter 4). The failure of law enforcement officers to comply with the procedural safeguards established as a result of these landmark cases could mean an overturned conviction in a review court later on.

The next stage of the criminal justice process is generally the *initial appearance* before a judge. Often the court where this appearance takes place may not have the jurisdiction to actually try the defendant, but the defendant has the right to state his or her case before a court as soon as possible after arrest.[6] This initial appearance is usually accompanied by the presentation of a complaint by the prosecution. The judge at the initial appearance has several tasks to perform, and failure to perform them correctly can result—as with the arresting officer—in a successful appeal at a later time. The defendant must be made aware of the charges against him or her and warned against making any self-incriminating statements. If the accused is to be assigned an attorney at state expense, this procedure is initiated. When the initial court does not have the jurisdiction to try a particular case, a decision must be made as to the continued detention of the accused (in the case of dangerous persons) or some arrangement must be made for the accused's release prior to trial before the court of primary jurisdiction. The defendant can be released on his or her own recognizance[7] or may be required to post bail.[8] In the first instance, the judge believes that the defendant will appear in court as required because he or she has nothing to gain—and a reputation to lose—by running away. In the second, the defendant "posts" a certain sum of money that is forfeited if he or she fails to appear. In both cases, the object is to encourage the defendant's appearance at further proceedings on the case.

If the case does not fall under the jurisdiction of the initial court, the defendant has the right to request a *preliminary hearing,* to examine the merits of binding the case over to a higher court. The preliminary hearing gives both defense and prosecution the opportunity to gather evidence and witnesses and present them informally. It constitutes a sort of "preview" of the case for both sides, and for the judge. To the defendant, the preliminary hearing offers an informal evaluation of his or her chances in the later trial. *It is at this point that many defendants decide to plead guilty to their charge, or to negotiate a plea to a lesser count.*[9]

The next important step is the filing of the *formal criminal charge* in the court that will try the case. If a federal crime punishable by death, imprisonment, hard labor, or loss of civil or political privileges has been committed, the filing of charges may be preceded by another review of the facts by a grand jury.[10] If the grand jury agrees there is probable cause that the offense has occurred and the defendant might have done it, a document is issued which constitutes the formal charging of the accused. This document is called an *indictment.* A defendant has a right to participate in the preliminary hearing but is not usually allowed to appear before the grand jury, unless special permission is obtained.

The federal government permits the waiver of a grand jury in noncapital cases, and it has been used less and less often in recent years (Watergate would be one instance of a case where a grand jury was considered necessary). If the grand jury inquiry is not required, the prosecutor simply files a document called an *information,* which contains the formal criminal charge. Many challenges are made in regard to this portion of the process. Some of the challenges *must* be made at the time or they cannot be used as grounds for later appeal. As a matter of fact, the resolution of issues raised at this point—in regard to search and seizure, police interrogation techniques, and other questions as to the admissibility of evidence—may consume more court time than the actual trial.

The next critical point is the *arraignment,* the offender's first formal appearance before the trial court. At this point the defendant is asked how he or she will plead. If the defendant chooses to stand mute, a plea of "not guilty" is entered automatically. It is when the defendant pleads guilty at this point (in about 90 percent of the cases) that the judge must exercise care about procedural errors that might result in an appeal. The defendant who pleads guilty must understand the nature of the charges against him or her and the consequences of a guilty plea. The judge should have some basis for accepting the plea, usually evidence from the prosecutor that tends to indicate or establish guilt. Although there is little error on this last point, probably because those who plead guilty seldom appeal, it is another legal basis for appeals.

The *trial,* so memorably dramatized on television and in the movies, appears to be the main target for the appellate procedure. It is the trial that best illustrates the impact of our adversary system[11] on the process of criminal justice. Grounds for appeal abound in the trial, from the selection of the jury to the finding of guilt or innocence. The burden of proof of guilt is on the prosecution throughout. Many defense motions[12] are made only to establish grounds for later efforts at appeal. After a determination of guilt or innocence, the trial is completed. The effect of most appeals is to require that a new trial be held—not to ensure an overturned conviction for the accused.

The last step in the court process is *sentencing* by the court. The judge generally prescribes the sentence, but it can be done by a jury in some jurisdictions. In the case of a guilty plea, the sentencing usually follows the completion of a pretrial or presentencing investigation of the defendant, who has become the convicted offender. The sentencing process has not generated extensive appeal actions, probably because sentences are usually determined by specific statutes rather than the discretion of the judge. Excessive or cruel sentencing practices do come under appeal, however, and the indeterminate sentence has been attacked many times.

The Mechanics of an Appeal

Now that we have seen the points at which appealable errors are most likely to occur, the effects of some of the major cases, and the potential of future appeals, it is important to know how one goes about making an appeal following a criminal conviction. The process is highly fragmented and cumbersome, but there is a basic scheme that applies to most jurisdictions. Although there are many alternatives to this basic model, it covers most of the avenues for appeals.

The entire process stems, of course, from a conviction of *guilt* by some court system, at the municipal, county, state, or federal level. In each case, the procedure for appeal is determined by the court of record for that case. These appeals, known as "postconviction remedies," were not generally available until after the seventeenth century. They are usually made by the defendant. The state is unlikely to appeal a decision, regardless of the outcome: if the accused is convicted, that is the result the state was after, and if the accused is declared innocent, the state cannot appeal—the Constitution guarantees that someone who is found innocent cannot be placed in "double jeopardy" (subjected to a second trial). The effect of an appropriately introduced appeal is a stay in the execution of the original sentence until the appeal is decided. As soon as possible, if not immediately after the sentence is pronounced, the defendant's counsel must either move for a new trial or make an appeal on some reasonable grounds, since appellate courts usually make short work of "frivolous" appeals. But as long ago as 1933, the significance of the appeal process was firmly established:

> Appellate courts . . . do not reverse decisions simply because they disagree with them. Reversal must proceed from error of law and such error must be substantial. But if this account is to be veracious I must call attention to a fact familiar to every experienced lawyer, yet not apparent in the classical literature of the law, and probably not consciously admitted even to themselves by most appellate judges.

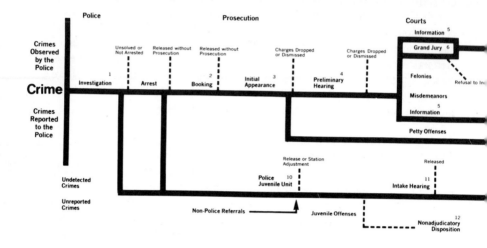

1 May continue until trial.

2 Administrative record of arrest. First step at which temporary release on bail may be available.

3 Before magistrate, commissioner, or justice of peace. Formal notice of charge, advice of rights. Bail set. Summary trials for petty offenses usually conducted here without further processing.

4 Preliminary testing of evidence against defendant. Charge may be reduced. No separate preliminary hearing for misdemeanors in some systems.

5 Charge filed by prosecutor on basis of information submitted by police or citizens. Alternative to grand jury indictment; often used in felonies, almost always in misdemeanors.

6 Reviews whether government evidence sufficient to justify trial. Some states have no grand jury system; others seldom use it.

FIGURE II–5. General Flow of the Criminal Justice System

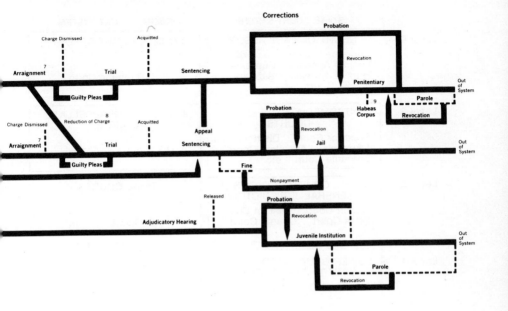

7 Appearance for plea; defendant elects trial by judge or jury (if available); counsel for indigent usually appointed here in felonies. Often not at all in other cases.

8 Charge may be reduced at any time prior to trial in return for plea of guilty or for other reasons.

9 Challenge on constitutional grounds to legality of detention. May be sought at any point in process.

10 Police often hold informal hearings, dismiss or adjust many cases without further processing.

11 Probation officer decides desirability of further court action.

12 Welfare agency, social services, counselling, medical care, etc., for cases where adjudicatory handling not needed.

	STATE COURT SYSTEM	FEDERAL COURT SYSTEM
Level 4	COURT OF LAST RESORT "Supreme Court" "Court of Criminal Appeals" "Supreme Court of Appeals" "Supreme Judicial Court," etc.	COURT OF LAST RESORT U.S. Supreme Court
Level 3	INTERMEDIATE APPELLATE COURTS "Superior Court" "District Court of Appeals" "Appellate Court" "Supreme Court," etc.	INTERMEDIATE APPELLATE COURTS U.S. Courts of Appeals
Level 2	TRIAL COURTS (COURTS OF GENERAL JURISDICTION) "Circuit Court" "District Court" "State Court" "County Court," etc.	TRIAL COURTS U.S. District Courts
Level 1	LOWER COURTS (COURTS OF LIMITED JURISDICTION) "Municipal Court" "Justice of the Peace" "Small Claims Court" "Traffic Court" "Magistrate's Court," etc.	LOWER COURTS U.S. Magistrates and Specialized Courts

FIGURE II–6. Parallels between State Court Systems and the Federal Court System

TABLE 2. COURTS OF APPEAL BY LEVEL OF JURISDICTION AND ORGANIZATION, BY STATE

STATE	COURTS OF LAST RESORT	COURTS OF INTERMEDIATE APPEALS
Alabama	Supreme Court	Court of Civil Appeals Court of Criminal Appeals
Alaska	Supreme Court	None
Arizona	Supreme Court	Court of Appeals (2 Departments)
Arkansas	Supreme Court	None
California	Supreme Court	Court of Appeals (5 Districts)
Colorado	Supreme Court	Court of Appeals
Connecticut	Supreme Court	None
Delaware	Supreme Court	None
District of Columbia	Court of Appeals	None
Florida	Supreme Court	Court of Appeals (4 Districts)
Georgia	Supreme Court	Court of Appeals
Hawaii	Supreme Court	None
Idaho	Supreme Court	None
Illinois	Supreme Court	Appellate Court (5 Districts)

TABLE 2. COURTS OF APPEAL BY LEVEL OF JURISDICTION AND ORGANIZATION, BY STATE (CONT.)

STATE	COURTS OF LAST RESORT	COURTS OF INTERMEDIATE APPEALS
Indiana	Supreme Court	Court of Appeals
Iowa	Supreme Court	None
Kansas	Supreme Court	None
Kentucky	Court of Appeals	None
Louisiana	Supreme Court	Court of Appeals (4 Circuits)
Maine	Supreme Judicial Court	None
Maryland	Court of Appeals	Court of Special Appeals
Massachusetts	Supreme Judicial Court	None
Michigan	Supreme Court	Court of Appeals
Minnesota	Supreme Court	None
Mississippi	Supreme Court	None
Missouri	Supreme Court	Court of Appeals (3 Districts)
Montana	Supreme Court	None
Nebraska	Supreme Court	None
Nevada	Supreme Court	None
New Hampshire	Supreme Court	None
New Jersey	Supreme Court	Appellate Division of Superior Court
New Mexico	Supreme Court	Court of Appeals
New York	Court of Appeals	Appellate Division of Supreme Court (4 Departments)
North Carolina	Supreme Court	Court of Appeals
North Dakota	Supreme Court	None
Ohio	Supreme Court	Court of Appeals (11 Districts)
Oklahoma	Supreme Court Court of Criminal Appeals (3 Districts)	Court of Appeals
Oregon	Supreme Court	Court of Appeals
Pennsylvania	Supreme Court	Superior Court Commonwealth Court
Rhode Island	Supreme Court	None
South Carolina	Supreme Court	None
South Dakota	Supreme Court	None
Tennessee	Supreme Court	Court of Appeals Court of Criminal Appeals
Texas	Supreme Court Court of Criminal Appeals	Court of Civil Appeals (14 Districts)
Utah	Supreme Court	None
Vermont	Supreme Court	None
Virginia	Supreme Court of Appeals	None
Washington	Supreme Court	Court of Appeals (3 Divisions)
West Virginia	Supreme Court of Appeals	None
Wisconsin	Supreme Court	None
Wyoming	Supreme Court	None

National Survey of Court Organization (Washington, D.C.: U.S. Department of Justice, 1971), p. 4.

> Practically every decision of a lower court *can* be reversed. By that I
> mean practically every record contains some erroneous rulings [and]
> they can nearly always find some error if they want grounds for
> reversal.[13]

Each state has an appellate tribunal which serves as the "court of last
resort." Titles are variable (as shown by Figure II–6), but no matter what
the title, a pathway for appeal is open to all in the American judicial system.

Table 2 illustrates the Courts of Appeal of each state, by level of
jurisdiction. The level immediately above the trial court is usually called the
court of appeals. In some states, and in the federal system, there is more
than one level of appeal. In these cases, the highest level of appellate court
is generally called the *supreme court*. The Supreme Court of the United
States is the court of last resort; cases decided there are considered final. The
Supreme Court of the United States will hear cases from the state systems
only after the defendant has exhausted all state remedies and the case has
been finally adjudicated.

In most state systems, the court of appeals reviews the decisions of the
trial court for judicial error. The facts in a case are not in question, and the
trial court's decisions on that aspect of the case are binding on the appellate
court. Because of this aspect of appellate review, evidence on the facts of
the case is not presented to the court of appeals; rather, review is based on
the trial record. An appellate court cannot reverse the factual findings of the
trial court unless they are totally erroneous. In states where there is a second
level of review, the trial record and the intermediary court's decision are
examined. Usually, the refusal to hear an appeal over a lower appellate
court's ruling is the same as upholding the decision and the case stops there,
unless an appeal is filed separately in a federal court of appeals on some
constitutional issue.

The federal court system currently includes ninety-one trial courts (federal
district courts) and eleven intermediary review courts (courts of appeal)
between the state trial courts and the United States Supreme Court. The
federal courts of appeal are spread across the country in eleven "circuits" to
facilitate servicing the ninety-one trial courts. Federal courts are restricted in
their powers to:

> . . . cases arising under the Constitution, federal laws or treaties,
> all cases affecting ambassadors, public ministers, and consuls,
> admiralty and maritime cases, controversies where the United States is
> a party, controversies between states, between a state and a citizen
> of another state, between citizens of the same state claiming lands
> under grants from different states, and in cases between a state or
> citizens of a state and foreign states, citizens or subjects.[14]

The federal courts of appeal are very similar to the state courts of appeal in that they review for error the cases tried by the federal district courts:

> The Supreme Court is the ultimate interpreter of the Constitution and federal statutes. It reviews the decisions of the courts of appeals, and some direct appeals from district courts. The Supreme Court also reviews the decisions of state courts involving matters of federal constitutional rights where the case has been finally adjudicated in the state court system. Besides its appellate function, the court has original jurisdiction in suits where a state is a party and in controversies involving ambassadors, ministers and consuls.[15]

Appeals from Behind the Walls

In the early twentieth century, most appeals were based on the issues in the trial. In the 1960s, appeals began to move toward issues related to individual rights under the United States Constitution. Using the Fourteenth Amendment as a lever, the Supreme Court affirmed these rights to individuals in the separate states on a piecemeal basis. Under the "hands off" doctrine established by Chief Justice Felix Frankfurter, the Court had restricted its early decisions to the actions of judges. Later, abandoning the Frankfurter policy, the Court began to impose procedural guidelines on law enforcement, corrections, and every other element of the criminal justice system. Constitutional rights of prisoners (to be discussed in Part IV) were more sharply defined by decisions of the appellate courts. Many of these appeals came from desperate people behind prison walls.

No prison is without its share of "jailhouse lawyers," prisoners who have become familiar with the substance of the law and courtroom procedures from first-hand experience. In the days when the indigent (poor) suspect's right to an attorney—in court or in prison—had not been established, these jailhouse lawyers helped their fellow inmates assemble cases for appellate review. With time on their hands, and great personal interest in their causes, these inmates paved the way for appeals by the prisoners of today. Probably the most famous early appeal was that of Clarence Earl Gideon, an indigent prisoner in Florida's Raiford Prison:

> Gideon was a fifty-one-year-old white man who had been in and out of prisons much of his life. He had served time for four previous felonies, and he bore the physical marks of a destitute life: a wrinkled, prematurely aged face, a voice and hands that trembled, a frail body, white hair. He had never been a professional criminal or a man of violence; he just could not seem to settle down to work, and so he had made his way by gambling and occasional thefts. Those who had

known him, even the men who had arrested him and those who were
now his jailers, considered Gideon a perfectly harmless human being,
rather likeable, but one tossed aside by life. Anyone meeting him for
the first time would be likely to regard him as the most wretched
of men.

And yet a flame still burned in Clarence Earl Gideon. He had not
given up caring about life or freedom; he had not lost his sense of
injustice. Right now he had a passionate—some thought almost
irrational—feeling of having been wronged by the state of Florida, and
he had the determination to try to do something about it.[16]

His petition, submitted to the United States Supreme Court, was done as a
pauper (*in forma pauperis*) under a special federal statute. This statute
makes great allowances for those unable to afford the expense of counsel
and administrative technicalities. As an example, the court usually requires
forty typewritten copies of a petition; Gideon submitted *one*, handwritten in
pencil on lined yellow sheets.[17] Although Gideon did not have counsel for
his trial in 1961 when he was accused of breaking into a pool hall, when his
petition was heard before the Supreme Court in the 1962-63 term he was
magnificently represented—for free. Abe Fortas,[18] one of Washington's
most successful lawyers, who later was to become a Supreme Court Justice,
was appointed by the Court as Gideon's attorney for this case. The Court's
decision was unanimous (as opposed to an awkward 5-4 split, which might
have decreased its impact):

In deciding as it did—that "appointment of counsel is not a
fundamental right, essential to a fair trial"—the Court in *Betts* . . .
made an abrupt break with its own well-considered precedents. In
returning to these old precedents, sounder we believe than the new, we
but restore constitutional principles established to achieve a fair system
of justice. Not only these precedents but also reason and reflection
require us to recognize that in our adversary system of criminal justice,
any person summoned into court, who is too poor to hire a lawyer,
cannot be assured a fair trial unless counsel is provided for him.[19]

As if to emphasize the Court's finding, when Gideon was finally retried
with counsel, he was acquitted. Subsequently, in decision after decision the
Supreme Court has ruled in favor of the right to counsel at a "critical stage"
in the defendant's case. This "critical stage" has been extended from initial
police contact to the preparation of a brief for appeal and even to assistance
in having transcripts of the trial prepared. It is easy to see how this case
signaled an avalanche of appellate cases which has not yet abated.

A flood of appeals made with the help of court-appointed lawyers filled
the dockets of the appeal courts in the 1960s. As rights were established in

the obvious areas *outside* prison walls (arrest, search and seizure, privacy and intrusion, cruel and unusual punishment), they were eventually tested with regard to events inside the walls as well. The autonomous and discretionary control over inmates was finally lifted, as the right to counsel moved into the prison as well as the courtroom. A milestone case was decided in the 1967-68 Supreme Court term, when *Mempa* v. *Rhay*[20] extended the right to counsel to state probation revocation hearings, previously considered an essentially administrative action. The Court held that the application of a deferred sentence was a "critical point" in the proceeding.

The right to counsel for defendants both inside and outside the walls of America's prisons has created strain on the entire criminal justice system. As more and more aspects of the criminal justice system are challenged, often by court-appointed lawyers, the real problem becomes the need for a routine way to reduce the flow of frivolous cases into the system.

Breaking the Appellate Logjam

The criminal courts have been forced to become almost administrative in nature because of the vast overload of cases. Since as many as 90 percent of convictions are appealed, the review courts are equally inundated. The National Advisory Commission on Criminal Justice Standards and Goals expended a great deal of effort in trying to find ways to reduce the court caseload. The first recommendations that were made included a number of alternatives.

One of the methods suggested was to place more stress on *screening;* the basic guidelines for screening offenders vary greatly from jurisdiction to jurisdiction. To help in developing fundamental criteria for screening suspected offenders out of the process, the following suggestions were made by the Commission:

> An accused should be screened out of the criminal justice system if there is not a reasonable likelihood that the evidence admissible against him would be sufficient to obtain a conviction and sustain it on appeal. In screening on this basis, the prosecutor should consider the value of a conviction in reducing future offenses, as well as the probability of conviction and affirmance of that conviction on appeal.
>
> An accused should be screened out of the criminal justice system when the benefits to be derived from prosecution or diversion would be outweighed by the costs of such action. Among the factors to be considered in making this determination are the following:
>
> 1. Any doubt as to the accused's guilt;
>
> 2. The impact of further proceedings upon the accused and those close to him, especially the

likelihood and seriousness of financial hardship or
family life disruption;

3. The value of further proceedings in preventing
future offenses by other persons, considering the
extent to which subjecting the accused to further
proceedings could be expected to have an impact
upon others who might commit such offenses, as
well as the seriousness of those offenses;

4. The value of further proceedings in preventing
future offenses by the offender, in light of the
offender's commitment to criminal activity as a way
of life; the seriousness of his past criminal activity,
which he might reasonably be expected to
continue; the possibility that further proceedings
might have a tendency to create or reinforce
commitment on the part of the accused to criminal
activity as a way of life; and the likelihood that
programs available as diversion or sentencing
alternatives may reduce the likelihood of future
criminal activity;

5. The value of further proceedings in fostering the
community's sense of security and confidence in
the criminal justice system;

6. The direct cost of prosecution, in terms of
prosecutorial time, court time, and similar factors;

7. Any improper motives of the complainant;

8. Prolonged nonenforcement of the statute on which
the charge is based;

9. The likelihood of prosecution and conviction of the
offender by another jurisdiction; and

10. Any assistance rendered by the accused in
apprehension or conviction of other offenders, in
the prevention of offenses by others, in the
reduction of the impact of offenses committed by
himself or others upon the victims, and any other
socially beneficial activity engaged in by the
accused that might be encouraged in others by not
prosecuting the offender.[21]

Narrowing the correctional funnel at this point would result in a great
workload reduction throughout the rest of the criminal justice system.

A second major effort in the drive to reduce the number of cases brought
to trial involves the *diversion* of offenders before conviction. Diversion is

quite different from screening; it assumes that the individual will participate in some treatment program in return for removal from the criminal justice process before trial. In screening, the individual is dropped out of the process before it really begins, with no threat of continued prosecution or promise of special programs for his or her cooperation. Diversion programs may be run by agencies within the criminal justice system, or by private and public agencies entirely outside it. The primary benefit from both screening and diversion programs is their ability to offer services to offenders without placing the stigma of further criminalization on them. Overcriminalization, usually a result of too many antiquated laws remaining on the books, is one of the reasons why so many cases sit on dockets. The Commission also suggested guidelines for when diversion should take place:

> In appropriate cases offenders should be diverted into noncriminal programs before formal trial or conviction.
>
> ·Such diversion is appropriate where there is a substantial likelihood that conviction could be obtained and the benefits to society from channeling an offender into an available noncriminal diversion program outweigh any harm done to society by abandoning criminal prosecution. Among the factors that should be considered favorable to diversion are: (1) the relative youth of the offender; (2) the willingness of the victim to have no conviction sought; (3) any likelihood that the offender suffers from a mental illness or psychological abnormality which was related to his crime and for which treatment is available; and (4) any likelihood that the crime was significantly related to any other condition or situation such as unemployment or family problems that would be subject to change by participation in a diversion program.
>
> Among the factors that should be considered unfavorable to diversion are: (1) any history of the use of physical violence toward others; (2) involvement with syndicated crime; (3) a history of antisocial conduct indicating that such conduct has become an ingrained part of the defendant's lifestyle and would be particularly resistant to change; and (4) any special need to pursue criminal prosecution as a means of discouraging others from committing similar offenses.
>
> Another factor to be considered in evaluating the cost to society is that the limited contact a diverted offender has with the criminal justice system may have the desired deterrent effect.[22]

Diversion programs are another recognition of the situational nature of many crimes. By expanding the base of available services and keeping the offender out of the damaging stages of the criminal justice process, society gives the offender a much better chance to adjust *in the community.*

Where Are the Next Areas of Appeal?

As has been shown, the appellate system has brought rights and reform to the criminal justice system as a whole, and to the sector known as corrections in particular. If the stone walls that surround our American fortress prisons cannot be torn down, then at least the basic rights available to those outside must be brought in. This process has only begun, but thanks to the efforts of inmates like Clarence Gideon, attorneys like Abe Fortas, and many other prisoners and lawyers, the courts are whittling down the dictatorial powers formerly held by prison administrators.

The basic rights granted citizens under most of the constitutional amendments have been extended to the inmates in our prisons. In the next years the peripheral issues will be examined. Two of the most controversial will be the *right to treatment* and its corollary—the right to *refuse* treatment. These issues stem from the widespread use of the treatment model in most of our adult correctional systems. Lack of prison industries and enforced idleness have encouraged the development of treatment programs to fill time. The long-term value of such programs is questionable at best, and they are coming under attack.

Following an interim decision in *Wyatt* v. *Stickney*,[23] in which the United States District Court held that the states had to provide adequate treatment for patients involuntarily confined in mental institutions, the United States Supreme Court also ruled on this issue in *O'Connor* v. *Donaldson*.[24] The decision in this case leaves little question that civilly committed mentally ill persons have a right to treatment. The Court stated that every person has a constitutional right to liberty. It also concluded:

> A state cannot constitutionally confine . . . a nondangerous individual who is capable of surviving safely in freedom by himself or with the help of willing and responsible family members or friends. Since the jury found, upon ample evidence, that O'Connor, as an agent of the State, knowingly did so confine Donaldson, it properly concluded that O'Connor violated Donaldson's constitutional right to freedom.[25]

Since the justification for the indefinite commitment of mentally disturbed offenders (i.e., the incompetent to stand trial, the not guilty by reason of insanity, and, by some court interpretations, those adjudicated psychopathic offenders) is a need for treatment, this right might easily be extended to this class of residents of mental health institutions.

As in the right to treatment for the mentally ill, cases supporting the right to rehabilitation have been argued on both statutory and constitutional grounds. For instance, if state statutes clearly define the purpose of confinement as rehabilitation, the major responsibility of the administering organization could easily be conceived of as the provision of rehabilitation opportunities. A number of states include in their criminal codes some reference to the rehabilitation goals of incarceration. Ohio, for example, even changed the name of the state department responsible for incarceration of offenders to the Department of *Rehabilitation* and Correction. Although these statutes state rehabilitative purposes, the enforcement of rights based on these statutes has been delayed because societal values emphasize other goals and because corrections appears to lack knowledge of proven rehabilitative methods.

Arguments for a constitutional right to treatment derived from the Eighth Amendment prohibition of cruel and unusual punishment were made applicable to state actions in 1962.[26] Since that time, federal courts have increasingly intervened in prison administration, making decisions on the right-to-treatment issue. Some decisions uphold the view that governmental entities have no constitutional duty to rehabilitate prisoners.[27] Others withhold constitutional affirmation of the right to rehabilitation but conclude that the absence of rehabilitation programs, in conjunction with other prison conditions, may result in the definition of a specific prison's setting as cruel and unusual punishment.

The courts have yet to specifically define a right to rehabilitation, but many feel that the constitutional identification is inevitable, if not imminent. The right to treatment for the mentally ill has progressed slowly through the courts; the impediment of defensive and punitive public opinion has delayed implementation of the humanitarian philosophy of a right to treatment for prisoners, but this right should not be ignored. The indications are numerous and strong that the time for such recognition is near and that collateral consequences will be substantial. In addition to the signs from the judiciary, a Harris poll conducted in 1967 reported that 72 percent of Americans felt the main emphasis in prisons should be on rehabilitation.[28] Practitioners in the field of corrections would do well to anticipate and prepare for the likely effects of this new emphasis.

Obviously, the resolution of this problem could decide whether the future of corrections lies in real *correction* efforts or a return to old-fashioned imprisonment. Unless some highly effective *treatments* for criminal behavior are found, backed by solid evaluation, the treatment programs are in serious trouble.

A final area of future appeals will relate to treatment programs that are directed at the *motivation* of an offender, rather than the *specific actions* which brought him to prison. One such program is *behavior modification*. In a 1973 case, *Mackey* v. *Procunier,* the Ninth Circuit Court raised the issue of "impermissible tinkering with the mental processes." Later the same year, in the case of *Kaimowitz* v. *Michigan Department of Mental Health* (which involved lobotomy operations), such tinkering was labeled a violation of the First Amendment by the Michigan Circuit Court.

Appeals will continue until inmates behind prison walls are granted the same constitutionally guaranteed protections accorded their counterparts in the free world. When appeals do fail, however, convicted and sentenced offenders must pay a debt to society in the correctional process—the subject of the next part of this text.

REVIEW QUESTIONS

I. Find the answers to the following in the text:

    1. Explain the difference between a court of appeals and a supreme court.

    2. Who was Clarence Gideon? Explain the actions he took to make his appeal.

    3. Why is there such a logjam in the appellate system? What are some suggestions for easing the pressure?

II. Words to identify:

    1. collateral attack

    2. habeas corpus

    3. initial appearance

    4. preliminary hearing

    5. indictment

    6. information

    7. arraignment

    8. jailhouse lawyer

    9. *in forma pauperis*

    10. screening

    11. railroaded

NOTES

1. The term *railroaded* has become a part of American slang. It has its origin in the practice by early state prisons of having a train pick up prisoners at various points along the route and drop them at the prison. Sometimes undesirables were put on the prison train and ended up in prison under less than due process conditions.

2. The relevant clause is: "nor shall any State deprive any person of life, liberty, or property, without due process of law. . . ."

3. See chapter 4.

4. National Advisory Commission on Criminal Justice Standards and Goals, *Courts* (Washington, D.C.: U.S. Government Printing Office, 1973), p. 113:

> [T]raditional or direct appellate review is circumscribed by rules that limit the court's consideration to matters in the trial record and thereby prevent a total review of the case. Matters outside the record cannot be considered even

though they may undercut the legality. As a result of those restrictions, the defendant not only has an opportunity to obtain collateral review, but he can seek, and sometimes obtain, multiple reviews.

A state defendant can pursue collateral litigation through both state and federal courts. On federal habeas corpus the courts have been skeptical about relying on prior adjudications and have been reluctant to insist on adherence to procedural rules governing the assertion of issues in the regular course of trial and appeal.

5. National Advisory Commission, *Courts,* p. 113.

6. This is what is generally called the right to *habeas corpus.*

7. *Recognizance* means that the court feels that the defendant will be available for trial without the need to exact a financial penalty for nonappearance. In a sense, it means "on the defendant's word of honor."

8. *Bail* is the creation of a financial incentive for an appearance at trial. A large enough amount is put into trust (usually by a bondsman, for a 10 percent fee) and it is forfeited if the defendant "skips" bail.

9. This is a classic example of *plea bargaining* (see chapter 7).

10. A *grand jury* is usually composed of twenty-three or more members and does not determine guilt. The *petit jury* is composed of six to twelve members and hears the facts to determine guilt.

11. The adversary system refers to the battle that takes place between the prosecution and defense attorneys during a trial when each cross-examines and attacks witnesses and facts presented by the other.

12. Such motions usually concern the admissibility of evidence and are aimed to suppress the presentation of evidence which might hurt the defense attorney's case.

13. Joseph N. Ulman, *The Judge Takes the Stand* (New York: Alfred A. Knopf, 1933), pp. 265-266.

14. U.S. Constitution, Article III, Section 2.

15. John Palmer, *Constitutional Rights for Prisoners* (Cincinnati, Ohio: Anderson, 1973), p. 10.

16. Anthony Lewis, *Gideon's Trumpet* (New York: Vintage Books, 1966), pp. 5-6.

17. Lewis, *Gideon's Trumpet,* p. 4.

18. Abe Fortas (1910–   ) was Lyndon Johnson's first appointee to the Supreme Court, on July 29, 1965. A close advisor to President Johnson, he represented "Bobby" Baker in the scandal over his business activities. Fortas left the Supreme Court in 1969.

19. Editors of The Criminal Law Reporter, *The Criminal Law Revolution and Its Aftermath* (Washington, D.C.: BNA Books, 1972), p. 25.

20. *Mempa* v. *Rhay,* 389, U.S. 128, 2d Cir. 3023 (1968). A petitioner filed a habeas corpus claiming a denial of the right to counsel at the probation revocation and sentencing proceedings. The Supreme Court of the State of Washington denied the petition. The U.S. Supreme Court reversed the previous decision, asserting the necessity that counsel be present at such a hearing.

21. National Advisory Commission, *Courts,* pp. 20-21.

22. National Advisory Commission, *Courts*, p. 32.

23. *Wyatt* v. *Stickney*, 325 F. Supp. 781 (M.D. Ala. 1971). 344 F. Supp. 373, and 374 F. Supp. 387 (1972).

24. *O'Connor* v. *Donaldson*, 43 L.W. 4929 (1975).

25. *O'Connor* v. *Donaldson* at 4933.

26. *Robinson* v. *California*, 370 U.S. 660 (1962).

27. See *McLaramore* v. *State*, 257 S.C. 413 (1972).

28. Joint Commission on Manpower and Training, *The Public Look at Crime and Corrections* (Washington, D.C.: U.S. Government Printing Office, 1968), p. 7.

RECOMMENDED READING LIST

Carter, Robert M.; Glaser, Daniel; and Wilkins, Leslie T. *Correctional Institutions.* New York: J. B. Lippincott, 1972.

Clinard, Marshal B., and Quinney, Richard. *Criminal Behavior Systems: A Typology,* New York: Holt, Rinehart & Winston, 1967.

Dawson, Robert O. *Sentencing: The Decision as to Type, Length and Conditions of Sentence.* New York: Little, Brown, 1969.

Dinitz, Simon, and Reckless, Walter C. *Critical Issues in the Study of Crime.* New York: Little, Brown, 1968.

Doleschal, Eugene. *Graduated Release.* Paramus, N.J.: National Council on Crime and Delinquency, 1969.

Dressler, David. *Practice and Theory of Probation and Parole.* New York: Columbia University Press, 1969.

Editors, The Criminal Law Reporter. *The Criminal Law Revolution and Its Aftermath: 1960-1971.* Washington, D.C.: Bureau of National Affairs, 1972.

Ennis, Phillip. *Criminal Victimization in the United States: A Report on a National Survey,* Washington, D.C.: U.S. Government Printing Office, 1967.

Leinwand, Gerald. *Prisons.* New York: Pocket Books, 1972.

Morris, Norval, and Hawkins, Gordon. *The Honest Politician's Guide to Crime Control.* Chicago: University of Chicago Press, 1970.

National Advisory Commission on Criminal Justice Standards and Goals. *Courts.* Washington, D.C.: U.S. Department of Justice, 1973.

Packer, Herbert L. *The Limits of the Criminal Sanction.* Stanford, Calif.: Stanford University Press, 1968.

Toomey, Beverly; Allen, Harry E; and Simonsen, Clifford E. "The Right to Treatment: Professional Liabilities in the Criminal Justice and Mental Health Systems." *The Prison Journal* 54:43-56.

PART III

The Correctional Process

10 Probation

Humane treatment may raise up one in whom the divine
image has long been obscured. It is with the
unfortunate, above all, that humane conduct is
necessary.

DOSTOEVSKI

Sanctuary and Suspended Sentence

Following a determination of guilt, the courts have a number of options for
dealing with the offender. In recent times the option most often selected is
probation; approximately 57 percent of convicted felons are placed on
probation in a given year.

Probation is a derivative of the suspended sentence, handed down to us
somewhat indirectly by way of past judicial procedures. Both suspended
sentences and probation involve mitigation of punishment for an offender
through a judicial procedure, and their earliest antecedent is found in the
right of sanctuary,[1] frequently cited in the Bible. In many cultures, holy
places and certain cities were traditionally set aside as places for sanctuary.

The right of sanctuary was written into Mosaic law.[2] To escape the blood
vengeance of a victim's family, a killer could go to certain specified cities
and find refuge. During the Middle Ages, many churches were able to offer
sanctuary for those hiding from harsh secular law. The practice of sanctuary
disappeared in England in the seventeenth century and was replaced with
"benefit of clergy." This practice, originally reserved for clerics, was
eventually extended to those who could pass the "Psalm 51" test—a test of
the offender's ability to read the verse which begins "Have mercy upon
me." The result was a form of suspended sentence, and the offender was
able to move about in society.

The suspended sentence differs from probation, though the terms are
sometimes used interchangeably. The suspended sentence does not require
supervision and usually does not prescribe a specified set of goals for the

offender to work toward. It is merely a form of quasi-freedom which can be revoked, and a prison sentence imposed at the instruction of the court. Sentence can usually be suspended in two different ways:

1. The sentence is imposed, but execution of it is suspended.

2. The imposition and execution of the sentence are both suspended.

Of these two, the second is considered the more desirable because of reduced stigma. The practice of suspending sentences, like sanctuary, outlived its usefulness and has generally been replaced with supervised probation in America. Sentences may be vacated by the sentencing judge, and the offender may be placed at liberty in the community. This is a relatively infrequent occurrence.

Under the European model of suspended sentence, or *sursis* (surcease), the offender has satisfactorily fulfilled the conditions if no further offense is committed during the period established. Once the sentence has been suspended, little control or supervision is provided, with the result that most offenders with suspended sentences are denied the specialized or therapeutic services needed to prevent further criminal involvement.

Following a directive from the Ministers' Deputies of the Council of Europe,[3] European countries have generally employed the suspended sentence. Conditions similar to probation are used to regulate behavior. These specified conditions, which do not constitute punishment in the traditional sense, govern the following areas:

1. place of residence and living conditions;

2. leisure activities and associations;

3. employment;

4. payment of damages to the victim or other means of compensation for the offense;

5. use of alcohol;

6. use of special services, such as psychiatric clinics, health clinics, etc.; and

7. fulfillment of family obligations, such as child support.

The Birth of Probation

John Augustus,[4] a Boston shoemaker, is credited with being the "father" of probation. He liked to spend his spare moments observing what transpired in the courts, and was disturbed by the fact that common drunks were often forced to remain in jail because they had no money to pay their fines. He convinced the authorities to allow him to pay their fines and provided them friendly supervision. Between 1841 and 1848 he bailed out almost two thousand men, women, and girls. He was sharply critized for his "strange" ideas, which have been described by criminologist Sheldon Glueck:[5]

> His method was to bail the offender after conviction, to utilize this favor as an entering wedge to the convict's confidence and friendship, and through such evidence of friendliness as helping the offender to obtain a job and aiding his family in various ways, to drive the wedge home. When the defendant was later brought into court for sentence, Augustus would report on his progress toward reformation, and the judge would usually fine the convict one cent and costs, instead of committing him to an institution.[6]

Augustus' efforts encouraged his home state of Massachusetts to pass the first probation statute in 1878. Four more states had followed suit by 1900.[7] Probation was established as a legitimate alternative to incarceration, and a strong impetus to employ it came with the creation of the first Juvenile Court in 1899:[8] the need to supervise young offenders and keep them out of adult prisons.

The Spread of Probation

Juvenile probation service developed with the growing movement for juvenile courts. By 1910 thirty-seven states and the District of Columbia had passed a children's court act and forty had provided some kind of probation service for juveniles. Every state had provided juvenile probation service in some measure by 1925, as the practice became firmly entrenched.

Not until 1956, however, was probation available for adult offenders in every state. Variations in the organization and operations of probation services make it difficult to compare them across states, but the growth in the number of persons registered as probation officers attests to the rapid acceptance of this area of corrections. In 1907, the first directory of probation officers identified 795 volunteers, welfare workers, court personnel, and part-time personnel serving as officers. Most of these were in the juvenile system. By 1937 the figure had grown to over 3800, of which 80 percent were in full-time service. By 1970, probation and parole officers were listed together and numbered over 25,000. Probation is seen as one of the brightest hopes in the field of corrections, and probation officers continue to grow in number.

What Is Probation Today?

Probation, often confused with the suspended sentence, is actually a form of sentence in itself. The American Bar Association defines probation as:

> A sentence not involving confinement which imposes conditions and retains authority in the sentencing court to modify the conditions of sentence or to resentence the offender if he violates the conditions. Such a sentence should not involve or require suspension of the imposition or execution of any other sentence. . . .
>
> A sentence to probation should be treated as a final judgment for purposes of appeal and similar procedural purposes.[9]

Across the nation, probation is administered by hundreds of separate agencies, with a wide variety of rules and structures within the states. Often one agency may be required to serve juvenile, misdemeanant, and felony offenders. But while some agencies handle all three types, others handle these offenders separately. The term "probation" has multiple meanings within the multiple areas of corrections.

As a disposition, probation was first seen as a new type of suspended sentence. If convicted offenders could meet certain conditions established by the court, they were allowed to remain in their communities under limited freedom. These conditions vary greatly from jurisdiction to jurisdiction and judge to judge, but they usually include prohibitions regarding drinking, travel, and association with undesirable persons. Currently, probation is used as a sentence in its own right.

As a *status,* probation has many advantages for offenders. While their freedom is somewhat limited, their status is considered better than that of confined offenders. They are neither completely free nor totally restricted; they can work, keep their families off welfare, avoid the stigma of incarceration, and make restitution to their victims.

As a *subsystem* of the criminal justice system, probation has many different structures and organizational variations. In this context, it refers to the administrative agency that provides the probation service to juvenile or adult offenders.

The set of functions, activities, and services which probation performs for its administrative agency and the offender is the probation *process.* The process model for probation service is usually seen as a series of interlinking activities between the courts, the offender, and the offender's community and its resources. The process includes the offenders' *reporting* regularly to their probation officers; the *servicing* of their needs through treatment, counseling, and so on; and the officer's *supervision* of probationers to ensure that the rules of the probation order are observed.

So, probation today is a *process* which provides the judge with an alternative *disposition* that resuls in an improved *status* for the offender within a *subsystem* of the criminal justice system. Knowledge of the multiple meanings of probation will generate a thorough understanding of probation today.

Organization and Administration

The problems associated with a lack of organizational coherence in the criminal justice system are exemplified in probation services. Under the original concept, it was envisioned that judges would administer the probation services themselves. For small jurisdictions this may still be the case in some instances, and these judges may be the best-informed decision makers in the criminal justice system. Most states, however, administer probation through a wide range of organizational and operational systems which are often unresponsive to each other's goals or efforts. The most frequent plan is to provide local probation service at the county level. Even in those states which have attempted to form a state-administered probation[10] system, county participation has sometimes been maintained, at the discretion of local officials. This concept of local autonomy is an American tradition, but it hampers efforts to develop integrated probation services on a statewide basis.

While considerable controversy surrounds the issue of state vs. local probation administration, a number of advantages have been cited for a state system:

> A state-administered system can more easily organize around the needs of a particular locality or region without having to consider local political impediments. It also can recommend new programs and implement them without requiring additional approval by local political bodies.
>
> A state-administered system provides greater assurance that goals and objectives can be met and that uniform policies and procedures can be developed. Also, more efficiency in the disposition of resources is assured because all staff members are state employees and a larger agency can make more flexible use of manpower, funds, and other resources.
>
> When it is simply not possible for a state to administer a probation system, the state, through a designated agency in the executive branch, should be responsible for developing standards for local probation systems that provide for a minimum acceptable level of functioning. State standards have a greater chance of being implemented if the state indicates a willingness to share the costs with local governments when standards are met and maintained.
>
> In addition to setting standards for local jurisdictions, the state agency should be responsible for establishing policies, defining statewide goals, providing staff training, assisting in fiscal planning and implementation, collecting statistics and data to monitor the operations of local probation agencies, and enforcing change when necessary. Through these means, a state-supervised program can bring

about some degree of uniformity in operations throughout the state,
but not to the same degree as a state-administered program.[11]

Some state administrators have tried to encourage local probation systems
to comply with state standards by assistance with either personnel or
subsidies. In Michigan, for example, parole officers on the state payroll are
assigned to work alongside local officers. In New York, where local
communities are reimbursed up to 50 percent of probation service costs if
they meet state standards, the number of probation officers has increased by
over 28 percent from 1965 to 1972.[12] Washington and California have
adopted a novel and promising approach:

> These states attempt to resolve a problem that is inherent when
> probation is a local function; namely, that financing probation is a
> local responsibility. However, when juveniles or adults are sent to
> correctional institutions, these are usually administered and financed
> by the state. A consequence often is the shifting of financial
> responsibility from the local government to the state government by
> sentences of incarceration rather than probation.
>
> California and Washington have developed probation subsidy
> programs in which counties are reimbursed in proportion to the
> number of individuals that remain in the community rather than being
> sent to state institutions. The subsidy program in California was
> developed as a result of a study that indicated that some individuals
> eligible for commitment to state correctional institutions could safely
> be retained on probation and that with good probation supervision,
> they could make a satisfactory adjustment. It was estimated that at
> least 25 percent of the new admissions to state correctional institutions
> could remain in the community with good probation supervision.
>
> California estimates that, even with expanded probation services,
> the cost of probation runs little more than one-tenth of the cost of
> incarceration, approximately $600 per person annually for probation,
> compared to $5,000 annually for institutionalization. In all, the
> program has resulted in substantial savings to taxpayers. In the six
> years between 1966 and 1972, California canceled planned
> construction, closed existing institutions, and abandoned new
> institutions that had been constructed. Almost $186 million was saved
> in these ways, while probation subsidy expenditures came to about $60
> million. Furthermore, although there has been a general decrease in
> commitments to state institutions throughout the United States, the
> decrease is sharper in those counties in California that participate in
> the subsidy program. The decrease in those counties almost doubles
> that of California counties not participating in the subsidy program.

The state of Washington has had a similar experience with the probation subsidy program begun in January 1970. Its purpose was to reduce the number of commitments to institutions from county juvenile courts. In the two years the program has been in operation there has been a marked reduction in the number of children and youth sent to state institutions. To illustrate, in 1971, the state received 55 percent fewer commitments than expected.[13]

The means of administering probation programs are as varied as the types of organizations. Many are administered by judges, some by social workers, and a few by persons trained in public administration. The need for public administration training for probation personnel has been expressed in at least two major studies.[14] Since the methods of most probation officers reflect the background and training of their administrators, there is little uniformity in their approaches. Different perspectives at different levels within the same agency can result in poorly defined goals and policies within the organization. The deeply rooted tradition of placing and keeping probation under court supervision, combined with rapid expansion of services, has undermined the effectiveness of those agencies. This problem is especially critical in those states which have not made an effort to train their administrators, especially at the executive and middle-management levels. Training of probation officers in the field is a highly commendable goal, but change must begin at the management level to ensure maximum benefit from the officers' increased skills.

Probation Services

The average probation officer suffers from the problem of serving two masters. He or she is generally required to meet with probationers to discuss their progress and troubles (casework)[15] and to provide the court with reports and recommendations about them. The idea that the probation officer must often act as a social worker has had a profound effect on the development of probation services. Earlier, overemphasis on casework and the medical model of the probation officer as "therapist" resulted in a narrow focus on the relationship between probationer and officer. As a result, many officers overlooked the social factors that might have contributed to the offender's criminal behavior, such as poverty, unemployment, poor housing, racism, poor health, and lack of education. The undesirability of the casework emphasis was expressed in a report by the National Advisory Commission on Criminal Justice Standards and Goals:

> The social task in corrections seems to call for social workers rather than for caseworkers or group workers. All social workers in

corrections work with individuals, groups and communities, with less emphasis on the use of one method than is characteristic of many social work jobs.[16]

One inherent drawback in the casework model is the likelihood that the officer will try to exceed the limited function assigned to probation. Placement of probationers in foster homes, operation of shelters for them, and attempts to deal with such extreme problems as alcoholism, drug addiction, and mental illness should properly be the concern of the appropriate community agency, not the probation officer. Probation officers cannot possess the background required to handle all the problems of their probationers. But probation officers are expected to account for their probationers if they get into trouble again. One of the first questions asked by the court in this circumstance is usually "When did you last see your client?" In a system that demands accountability of this kind, probation officers often overextend themselves in an effort to prevent or justify their clients' failure.

Large caseloads have been the probation officer's most common excuse for failure and a traditional reason for expanding probation staffs. A standard load of fifty cases per officer was considered desirable as early as 1917, but no research was conducted to validate this figure. The San Francisco Project,[17] a 1969 study of the relationship between recidivism and probation caseloads, shattered many of these long-held beliefs:

Four levels of workloads were established: (1) ideal [50 cases]; (2) intensive [25, i.e., half the ideal]; (3) normal [100, twice the ideal]; and (4) minimum supervision [with a ceiling of 250 cases]. Persons in minimum supervision caseloads were required only to submit a monthly written report; no contacts occurred except when requested by the probationer. It was found that offenders in minimum caseloads performed as well as those under normal supervision. The minimum and ideal caseloads had almost identical violation rates. In the intensive caseloads, the violation rate did not decline, but technical violations increased.

The study indicated that the number of contacts between probationer and staff appeared to have little relationship to success or failure on probation. The conclusion was that the concept of a caseload is meaningless without some type of classification and matching of offender type, service to be offered, and staff.[18]

The concept of an optimum or ideal caseload (such as thirty-five cases) is handy when calculating rough estimates of resources. The danger is that these figures seem to translate into a "standard" caseload which each officer should carry, regardless of the fact that different probationers require different kinds and degrees of service. A frequent response to the pressures resulting from these highly mixed caseloads is to establish a standardized procedure for all cases, regardless of their complexity. A broad system of differential treatments, involving assignment of specific kinds of cases to specific types of probation officers, is a crucial need. Methods of applying the probation service are undergoing a rapid evolution. Continued evolution requires further steps, as suggested by the National Advisory Commission:

1. Develop a goal-oriented service delivery system.
   The probation services system should be goal-oriented, directed toward removing or reducing individual and social barriers that result in recidivism among probationers. To achieve this goal, the probation system should provide a range of services directly and obtain others from existing social institutions or resources. The goal should be to help persons move from supervised care in their own communities to independent living.

2. Identify service needs of probationers systematically and periodically, and specify measurable objectives based on priorities and needs assessment.
   An inventory of needs should be developed by involving probationers rather than relying solely on probation staff to identify what it believes probationers' problems to be. More specifically, needs assessment requires:

   • Knowledge of the target group in terms of such factors as age, race, education, employment, family status, availability of transportation.

   • Identification of what services the offender most wants and needs to remove individual and social barriers.

   • Identification of services available and conditions under which they can be obtained.

   • Determination of which needed and wanted services do not exist or are inadequate.

3. Differentiate between those services that the probation system should provide and those that should be provided by other resources.
   Generally the kinds of services to be provided to probationers directly through the probation system should:

   • Relate to the reasons the offender was brought into the probation system.

- Help him adjust to his status as a probationer.

- Provide information and facilitate referrals to needed community resources.

- Help create conditions permitting readjustment and reintegration into the community as an independent individual through full utilization of all available resources.

4. Organize the system to deliver services, including purchase of services for probationers, and organize the staff around workloads.

The system should be organized to accomplish the following work activities:

- Needs assessment—ongoing assessment of probationers' needs and existing community resources.

- Community planning and development—establishing close working relationships with public and private social and economic groups as well as community groups to interpret needs; identifying needs for which community resources do not exist; and, in concert with appropriate groups, developing new resources.

- Purchase of services—entering into agreements and monitoring and evaluating services purchased.

- Direct services—receiving and assessing probationers; obtaining and providing information, referral, and follow-up; counseling; and supervising.

5. Move probation staff from courthouses to residential areas and develop service centers for probationers.

Probation services should be readily accessible to probationers. Therefore they should be based in that part of the community where offenders reside and near other community services.

Services to offenders should be provided in the evening hours and on weekends without the usual rigid adherence to the recognized work week. The problems of offenders cannot be met by conventional office hours. Arrangements should be made to have a night telephone answering service available to probationers.

6. Redefine the role of probation officer from caseworker to community resource manager.

> While some probation officers still will have to
> carry out counseling duties, most probation officers
> can meet the goals of the probation services system
> more effectively in the role of community resource
> manager. This means that the probation officer will
> have primary responsibility for meshing a
> probationer's identified needs with a range of
> available services and for supervising the delivery of
> those services.[19]

The future growth of probation may well depend on the successful adoption of these ideas.

Restrictions and Conditions

Restrictions on and conditions of probation are usually a result of statutory requirements, coupled with the opinion of the sentencing court about the offender. Most states have a number of statutory restrictions for felony cases, usually related to the type of offense. Often probation will be denied for an offender with a prior record, or for those convicted of murder or sex crimes. Murder and rape are the most universally recognized offenses which do not permit probation. Otherwise, restrictive offenses and standards vary greatly between states. The most important aid in the decision to deny or grant probation is the provision of detailed and accurate presentencing information to the judge. A second important factor is to ensure that the decision-making process focuses on the *offender*, not the *offense*, insofar as the statutes will allow. This is difficult when statutory limitations are extensive, but many states are moving toward the elimination of these mandatory exclusions.

Rules or conditions for probation cannot be formulated as a set of standard operating procedures. The conditions for continuance of probation should be tailored to the needs of the individual offender. Unfortunately, the court's frequent delegation of rule-making power to probation officers puts them in the almost impossible position of being lawmakers, enforcers, and confidants. The most effective way to ensure that rules are not established arbitrarily is to have them carefully reviewed by the court. In a situation where probation officers are devising too many rules, violations will soon overload the court.

It is generally conceded that probation rules should not extend to every kind of conduct. A number of courts require the probation officer who makes the presentence investigation to recommend the conditions for the offender's probation, which are usually based on the officer's expectations about where the offender will be living, how he or she will make a living, and so on. The terms are discussed by the judge with the probation candidate, his or her counsel, and the probation officer. Decisions made in this manner will usually result in a few important restrictions, giving the probationer a clear idea of what constitutes acceptable behavior.

Victim Compensation

A common condition for probation is the requirement that victims be compensated for their losses or injury. The emphasis on the study of victimization[20] in the last few years has resulted in some state compensation of crime victims, by payment of medical costs and other financial reimbursement. In the case of probationers, however, the victim is often repaid by the offender. It is important that probation authorities link the amount of payment to the offender's ability to pay. Installment payment is generally the most realistic approach. In some cases a partial restitution may be all that is reasonably possible (e.g., in the case of an arsonist who burns down a multi-million-dollar building).

In addition to the establishment of reasonable installment payments, compensation provisions must ensure that failure to make a payment does not mean automatic revocation of probation. It is possible that certain hardships and other conditions beyond their control would prevent probationers from making an occasional payment. The most effective approach to victim compensation by probationers is to include a careful financial report on the defendant and a recommended plan for reimbursement in the presentence investigation. This plan would be discussed with the prospective probationer, his or her attorney, the probation officer, and the judge. If adopted, the financial reimbursement plan would become a condition of probation.

Shock Probation

The recent practice by some courts of imposing a short jail term as a condition of probation has gained much attention. This practice, commonly called the *mixed sentence* is designed to give the offender a taste of incarceration, as a deterrent to future criminal activity.

Correctional personnel in the United States have been opposed to this approach on the grounds that the deterrent effect is negated by the job loss and broken community ties that usually follow incarceration, however brief. They argue that the purpose of probation is to avoid incarceration, not supplement it. It is further argued that even a short incarceration might "contaminate" the individual and reduce his or her chances for rehabilitation. Such short-term stays, presumably, can harden negative attitudes, expose the probationer to more criminals, and lead to a general resentment of society.[21] The most telling argument holds that prison and probation are at opposite ends of the punishment scale—are mutually exclusive—and therefore should not be mixed. Shock probation opponent Eugene N. Barkin has stated: "Once having determined that a person can be trusted to remain in the community and can benefit most under community supervision, no appreciable benefits can be derived from committing to a short period of incarceration.[22]

Only a few studies have been conducted on the impact of mixed (or "split") sentences. Limited statistical or empirical results are available from Sweden,[23] Denmark,[24] and Poland.[25] The results show no conclusive evidence to either support or reject the practice of mixed sentencing. The main question is when, and under what conditions, such sentencing should be used. Shortly after the practice was legally established, Judge Richard Hartshorne observed two conditions that seemed to call for shock probation:

1. When probation is not sufficient on the merits of the case (e.g., the nature of the crime and societal reaction to it).

2. When the individual has already demonstrated that he has violated a probation order.[26]

Ohio passed a law in 1965 providing for early release from prison of convicted felons by placing them on probation.[27] This law provides many of the features described as essential to an effective split-sentence program:

1. A way for the courts to impress offenders with the seriousness of their actions without a long prison sentence,

2. A way for the courts to release offenders found by the institutions to be more amenable to community-based treatment than was realied by the courts at the time of sentence,

3. A way for the courts to arrive at a just compromise between punishment and leniency in appropriate cases,

4. A way for the courts to provide community-based treatment for rehabilitable offenders while still observing their responsibilities for imposing deterrent sentences where public policy demands it, and

5. . . . it affords the briefly incarcerated offender a protection against absorption into the "hard rock" inmate culture.[28]

The Ohio statute is unique in that shock probation is not part of the original sentence. The offender must file a petition to the court no sooner than thirty and no later than sixty days from the original sentence date.[29] The petitioner does not know whether he or she will be granted probation until the court acts (within ninety days). By this procedure the Ohio act has added uncertainty to the shock effect of short-term incarceration. Of 1,674 inmates released on shock probation between 1966 and 1970, only 165 (9.8 percent)[30] have been reinstitutionalized. The Ohio experiment provides possible answers to many questions in regard to the use of mixed sentences. Several other states are observing the Ohio experience prior to making a decision; Kentucky adopted a similar statute in 1972, Indiana's statute became effective in 1974, and both Georgia and Michigan are considering the adoption of similar statutes.

Split sentencing may be an appropriate response to research findings that have shown no relationship between time served in prison and probability of recidivism (return to crime after release). Actually, it appears that rehabilitation chances are *decreased* by extended institutionalization. The negative effects of imprisonment and the positive effects of probation are both brought to bear in shock probation. It is likely that this form of judicial punishment will be used more extensively once its value has been clearly established.

Probation without Adjudication

Once the court has decided that probation will be used, the sentencing judge has another major question: whether to declare offenders guilty and label them as "convicted felons" or to place them on probation without the stigma of that label. This dilemma has been outlined by Paul Murchek:

> Although adjudication of guilt may provide certain safeguards to society such as: requiring criminal registration, serving notice to prospective employers that the applicant has been convicted of a criminal offense, preventing the offender from voting, holding public office, serving on a jury and perhaps making it more difficult to obtain firearms, it appears to provide very little appreciable effect in providing protection to society. It does, in fact, seriously hamper the offender's chances of rehabilitation.
>
> The withholding of adjudication of guilt, on the other hand, is consistent with the philosophical concepts of probation which combine community-based treatment with the full utilization of available community resources as a viable alternative to imprisonment and the accompanying degradation and stigma associated with same.[31]

Actually, probation without adjudication was the original practice at the time of John Augustus. Augustus convinced the judge to withhold sentencing on those released to him for a period of three weeks, after which the offender would return for sentencing. This procedure gave offenders a chance to prove themselves and usually resulted in a simple fine rather than imprisonment in the House of Corrections. This system of delayed or postponed sentence had the advantage of keeping offenders in the community, under supervision, without a criminal record and its inherent handicaps. The ability to function in the community without the stigma of a criminal conviction provides a great psychological uplift to offenders and improves their desire to reform.

Olin Lee Turner summed up the argument for probation without adjudication at the Southern Conference on Corrections in February 1973:

> I cannot see where the court would be relinquishing any of its hold or authority on the offender by using the delayed sentence or postponed sentence, as compared to our present system of pronouncing sentence and then placing the offender on probation. It would be just simply a matter of giving the offender an opportunity to prove on a trial basis his ability to adjust and reform without the threat of going to prison for a number of years, already established by the sentence, if he fails to do so. The threat of going to prison would not be removed in the delayed sentence act, since the offender on this type of probation would realize he can still be brought before the court for sentencing, but again, the stigma of already having been convicted and sentenced would be removed and the offender would realize that should his adjustment be satisfactory he could avoid the possibility of ever having a record of conviction, that in many ways could affect his entire life. I feel this could and would serve as a big incentive to many offenders to adjust while on probation.[32]

Perspectives on Probation

Probation is viewed as the bright hope for the future of corrections. It is generally conceded, however, that the full potential of this alternative to imprisonment cannot be reached without some effort to fulfill two major needs: (1) development of an effective system to determine which offenders should receive probation, and (2) provision of support and services to the probationers in the community to allow them to live independently in a socially accepted way. To achieve these goals, probation services must be better organized, staffed, and funded. The shifting of money and resources to the efforts of community-based projects is necessary to make probation a viable alternative. The National Commission on Criminal Justice Standards and Goals has recommended the national use of probation as the preferred disposition, preferably without adjudication of guilt. It has also recommended that probation, which started as a volunteer service, seek out volunteers to serve in all capacities.

The persuasive arguments favoring probation over imprisonment focus on reduced stigma, community help, and other advantages to the offender. Perhaps one of the most telling arguments, from the public's point of view, is that probation is so much *cheaper* than imprisonment. The taxpayer can easily appreciate the fact that while it costs about $3,500 a year (excluding capital costs) to keep the average adult offender in prison, probation runs about one-tenth that figure. If one includes the average capital cost of over $25,000 a bed for the average correctional institution, plus the cost of welfare for unsupported families and loss of tax revenue from prisoners who would otherwise be employed, the difference in dollars and cents becomes more obvious. Some states have shown even more spectacular financial savings. Ohio, for example, has a combined probation and parole service (probation services provided on a county option basis) and reported an institution cost rate of $4,574 and a parole/community services cost rate of $641 per offender for twelve months ending July 1, 1976.[33]

Probation has established itself as the new wave in corrections. It appears that such actions as the moratorium on prison construction and the emphasis on probation as the preferred disposition will keep it in the forefront of correctional reform. If a comparison of costs between prison and probation is considered, the taxpayer must rule in favor of probation. As the population grows, the number of offenders will surely increase as well. Students of probation concur that the practice is approximately 75 percent effective on a national basis; some states (particularly Ohio) report a 90 percent success rate. An alternative to imprisonment which is about one-tenth to one-twelfth as costly (and at least as effective) has great appeal, and clearly answers the need for a sound and economical approach to corrections.

REVIEW QUESTIONS

I. Find the answers to the following in the text:

1. Define the purpose of probation and describe the methods by which it is generally administered.

2. What organizational system is best suited for probation? Why?

3. What are some of the restrictions often applied to probation? What kinds of offenders are usually denied probation?

4. Discuss the effectiveness of probation, as compared to imprisonment.

II. Words to identify:

1. sanctuary

2. *sursis*

3. bail

4. shock probation

5. probation subsidy

6. casework

7. medical model

8. probation conditions

9. probation restrictions

10. victim compensation

11. split sentence

12. adjudication

13. suspended sentence

14. asylum

15. probationer

NOTES

1. Norman Johnston, *The Human Cage: A Brief History of Prison Architecture* (New York: Walker and Company, 1973), p. 8: "The concept of imprisonment as a substitute for death or mutilation of the body was derived in part from a custom of the early church of granting asylum or sanctuary to fugitives and criminals."

2. See Numbers 35:6 and Joshua 20:2-6.

3. European Committee on Crime Problems, *Probation and Aftercare in Certain European Countries* (Strasburg, Austria: Council of Europe, 1964).

4. *John Augustus* (1785-1859), a philanthropist par excellence, literally worked himself to death by his efforts to help the poor unfortunates caught up in the court systems. He is said to have bailed out at least 1,946 persons between 1842 and 1858. He operated completely independent of any sect or society. The work of this humble but successful shoemaker has formed the basis for modern probation services.

5. *Sheldon Glueck* (1896–   ) is an American criminologist noted for his extensive long-range research in criminal careers. These studies followed the history of many groups of young people, in an effort to develop a prediction device for determining who might become delinquent. He has written many books with his wife, Eleanor, who was equally famous as a criminologist.

6. Harry Elmer Barnes and Negley K. Teeters, *New Horizons in Criminology,* 3d ed. (Englewood Cliffs, N.J.: Prentice-Hall, 1959), p. 554.

7. Missouri (1897), Rhode Island (1899), New Jersey (1900), Vermont (1900).

8. The first juvenile court in the United States was established in Chicago in 1899.

9. American Bar Association Project on Standards for Criminal Justice, *Standards Relating to Probation* (New York: Institute of Judicial Administration, 1970), p. 9.

10. New Jersey, California, Michigan, and Washington.

11. National Advisory Commission on Criminal Justice Standards and Goals, *Corrections* (Washington, D.C.: U.S. Department of Justice, 1973), p. 315.

12. National Advisory Commission, *Corrections,* p. 315.

13. National Advisory Commission, *Corrections,* p. 315.

14. The two studies are: Joint Commission on Correctional Manpower and Training, *Corrections 1968: A Climate for Change* (Washington, D.C.: JCCMT, 1968), p. 30; and Herman Piven and Abraham Alcabes, *The Crisis of Qualified Manpower for Criminal Justice: An Analytic Assessment with Guidelines for New Policy,* vol. 1 (Washington, D.C.: U.S. Government Printing Office, 1969). A new national study for the U.S. Department of Justice is almost completed.

15. *Casework* generally refers to the social worker model of providing services to the client based on an analysis of the case which is obtained by contacting significant members of the client's family and community.

16. National Advisory Commission, *Corrections,* p. 318.

17. James Robinson et al., *The San Francisco Project,* Research Report No. 14 (Berkeley, Calif.: University of California School of Criminology, 1969).

18. National Advisory Commission, *Corrections,* p. 319. See also R. Adams and H. J. Vetter, "Probation Caseload Size and Recidivism Rate," *British Journal of Criminology and Deviant Behavior* 11 (1974).

19. National Advisory Commission, *Corrections,* pp. 320-323.

20. *Victimization* is the study of the role of the victim in encouraging crime. This is a relatively new field and the focus on the victim has revealed many surprising factors in certain kinds of crime.

21. Kenyon J. Scudder, "In Opposition to Probation with a Jail Sentence," *Federal Probation* 23 (June 1959): 12-17. The bulk of the material in this section on shock probation was drawn from a paper ("Shock of Imprisonment: Comparative Analysis of Short-Term Incarceration as a Treatment Technique," by Paul Friday and David Petersen) presented at the InterAmerican Congress of the American Society of Criminology and the InterAmerican Association of Criminology at Caracas, Venezuela, November 19-25, 1972. See also "Shock of Imprisonment: Comparative Analysis of Short-Term Incarceration as a Treatment Technique," *Canadian Journal of Criminology and Corrections* 281 (1973). Footnotes 3-6 are referenced in the Caracas paper.

22. Eugene N. Barkin, "Sentencing the Adult Offender," *Federal Probation* 26 (June 1962): 11-16.

23. Hakan Wunderman, "Klientelet vid Skyddstillsynsanstalten Asptuna" (Stockholm: Kriminalvetenskapliga Institut, 1968).

24. Karen Bernsten and Karl O. Christiansen, "A Resocialization Experiment with Short-term Offenders," in *Scandinavian Studies in Criminology,* vol. 1 (Oslo: University Forlaget, 1965), pp. 35-54.

25. Mieczysaw Rudnik, "Spoeczna Efektywnosc Kary Pozbawwienia Wolnosci," in *Socjotechnika,* vol. 2 (Warsaw: Ksiazka i Wiedza, 1970), pp. 364-399.

26. Richard Hartshorne, "The 1958 Federal Split-sentence Law," *Federal Probation* 23 (June 1959): 9-12.

27. Ohio Revised Code, 2947.06.1, July 1965.

28. Paul C. Friday and David M. Petersen, *Shock of Imprisonment: Comparative Analysis of Short-term Incarceration as a Treatment Technique* (paper presented at the 1972 InterAmerican Congress), p. 11.

29. The early release procedures under the Ohio statute can be initiated by the judge as well.

30. Friday and Petersen, *Shock of Imprisonment,* p. 8.

31. Paul Murchek, "Probation without Adjudication," in *Proceedings, 18th Annual Southern Conference on Corrections* (Tallahassee, Fla.: School of Criminology, 1973), p. 27.

32. Olin Lee Turner, "An Opinion on Probation without Adjudication," in *Proceedings, 18th Annual Southern Conference on Corrections,* p. 131.

33. Ohio Department of Rehabilitation and Correction, *Annual Report: Fiscal Year 1976* (Columbus, Ohio: Ohio Department of Rehabilitation and Correction, 1977), p. 27.

11 Imprisonment

As he went through Cold-Bath Fields he saw
A solitary cell;
And the Devil was pleased, for it gave him a hint
For improving his prisons in Hell.

SAMUEL TAYLOR COLERIDGE

The Philosophy of Imprisonment

Organized society has dealt with criminal offenders in a variety of ways. As we saw in Part I, when victims were responsible for dealing with offenders their approach reflected the motive of revenge or compensation for loss. As the state began to intervene and act in the name of the victim, retribution became the basic motive. The death penalty was the most common form of retribution for criminal acts. Death or mutilation by the state, in the name of justice, were common practices by the end of the sixteenth century. In most societies, the purpose of confinement was only to detain offenders until some more severe form of punishment could be imposed.

The Church was evidently the first social institution to use confinement as a form of punishment. In *The Human Cage,* Norman Johnston describes how the philosophy of imprisonment as a punishment evolved:

> The concept of imprisonment as a substitute for death or mutilation of the body was derived in part from a custom of the early church of granting asylum or sanctuary to fugitives and criminals. Begun largely during the reign of Constantine, this ancient right existed earlier among Assyrians, Hebrews, and others. The church at that time had under its aegis a large number of clergy, clerks, functionaries, monks and serfs, and, except the latter, most of these fell under the jurisdiction of the church courts. Traditionally forbidden to shed blood and drawing on the Christian theme of purification through suffering, these canon courts came to subject the wrongdoer to reclusion and even solitary cellular confinement, not as punishment alone, but as a

FIGURE III–1. Men in Cages (Courtesy American Correctional Association)

way of providing conditions under which penitence would most likely occur.

. . . Some of the monastic quarters provided totally separate facilities for each monk so that it was a simple matter to lock up an errant brother for brief periods.

As "mother houses" of monastic orders had satellite houses often located in less desirable places, it was also the practice to transfer monks for periods of time to such locations. There is some evidence that some of these satellites came to be regarded as punitive facilities.[1]

The church built several kinds of prisons. In monastic prisons, offenders lived in solitary confinement, supervised by monks, for long periods of time. The Inquisition used underground cells for lifetime imprisonment of heretics, witches, sorcerers, and others spared from the death penalty. The Church also played a major role in the development of workhouses. The workhouses were organized by the church to keep deviants and the unemployed off the streets while teaching them the work ethic.

The penitentiary, as noted in Part I, was basically an American idea. From the creation of a few solitary cells in the Walnut Street Jail to the new federal institution at San Diego, built in 1975,[2] prisons are characteristically American in philosophy and construction. Conceived at a time when the new nation was breaking away from all the old connections with European ideas, the American prison has come to represent both a monument and an obstruction to the development of corrections. Prisons in America quickly outgrew the function originally conceived by the early reformers—another example of a good idea poorly implemented and oversold. Today, with most judges well aware that prisons tend to be badly run at best, prison sentences are often a last resort.

This chapter examines the background and current state of imprisonment practices in America, focusing on the institutions for the adult male felons and their effect on inmates. Institutions for juveniles and women are discussed in Part V.

A basic philosophical tenet underlying the use of imprisonment in America appears to be a belief in the perfectability of people. The Revolution had inspired a great zeal for reform. Hated codes from the past were struck down and incarceration became the American substitute for England's indiscriminate use of the death penalty. A rational system of corrections, with punishment certain but humane, was expected to deter offenders from a life of crime. Early American efforts to reform the penal codes were strongly influenced by Cesare Beccaria's comments on laws as they relate to punishment:

> If we glance at the pages of history, we will find that laws, which surely are, or ought to be, compacts of free men, have been, for the most part, a mere tool of the passions of some. . . . The severity of punishment of itself emboldens men to commit the very wrongs it is supposed to prevent. . . . They are driven to commit additional crimes to avoid the punishment for a single one. The countries and times most notorious for severity of penalties have always been those in which the bloodiest and most inhumane of deeds were committed. . . . The certainty of a punishment, even if it be moderate, will always make a stronger impression than the fear of another which is more terrible but combined with the hope of impunity. . . . Do you want to prevent crimes? See to it that the laws are clear and simple and that the entire force of a nation is united in their defense.[3]

The passage of "clear" laws was seen as the most important aspect in the deterrence of deviant behavior. If the old British codes had encouraged crime, the new American codes would, it was believed, soon end the problem. Actually, it was the general reaction against the cruel practices of the British penal codes rather than faith in the penitentiary system that encouraged this belief. Unfortunately, this emphasis on *law* rather than the law*breaker* drew attention away from the prisons and prison conditions. The *fact* of imprisonment, not the internal routine within the prison, became the chief concern. David J. Rothman points out that, as the emphasis moved away from the legal system, systematic change occurred within prisons:

> The focus shifted to the deviant and the penitentiary, away from the legal system. Men intently scrutinized the life history of the criminal and methodically arranged the institution to house him. Part of the cause for this change was the obvious failure of the first campaign. The faith of the 1790s now seemed misplaced; more rational codes had not decreased crime. The roots of deviancy went deeper than the certainty of a punishment. Nor were the institutions fulfilling the elementary task of protecting society, since escapes and riots were commonplace occurrences. More important, the second generation of Americans confronted new challenges and shared fresh ideas. Communities had undergone many critical changes between 1790 and 1830, and so had men's thinking. Citizens found cause for deep despair and yet incredible optimism. The safety and security of their social order seemed to them in far greater danger than that of their fathers, yet they hoped to eradicate crime from the new world.[4]

America embraced prisons with its typical zeal for "humanitarian" advances, and built the fortresses of the late nineteenth and early twentieth centuries on the theory of reformation by confinement. "Lock 'em up" may have become the American replacement for "Off with their heads." Even after over a century and a half of failure, imprisonment is still practiced as the primary response to criminal behavior.

Maximum Security Prisons

The basic purposes of confinement have been *punishment, deterrence, quarantine, rehabilitation,* and, more recently, *integration into the community.*[5] The specific goals and the settings for their achievement are dictated by the particular society's dominant orientation, whether toward individual rights or toward collective security. Because both orientations command a strong following in America, neither one has entirely superseded the other. The scales have tipped in favor of security more often than equity, however, and the battle continues. We are currently witnessing a swing toward incarceration for purposes of punishment and deterrence.

Prisons were originally built as places that would stress maximum security above all other concerns. Typically, they are surrrounded by a high wall, usually thirty to fifty feet high and several feet thick, equipped with towers, manned by armed guards trained and prepared to prevent possible escapes or riots, lit by floodlights after dark, and sometimes bounded by electrified wire fences to further discourage escape attempts. These stone fortresses are placed far out in the rural countryside, away from the mainstream of contemporary American life.

The walled prison was so popular that it was not until 1926 that the first unwalled prison appeared in the United States.[6] It is clear upon approaching a typical maximum security prison that they are designed for punishment. The fearsome and forbidding atmosphere of the Auburn style of prison exemplifies the penal philosophy that prisoners must not only do time for their misdeeds, but most do so under a discipline which emphasizes rejection, doubt, guilt, inferiority, diffusion, self-absorption, apathy, and despair.[7] It is small wonder that these prisons generally release men who are emotionally less stable than when they entered.

A vivid description of the nineteenth-century maximum security prison is found in *The Human Cage:*

> In 1825 prisoners arrived in leg shackles from Auburn at a site on the Hudson River, later to be known as Sing Sing, to construct a new prison. The plan was similar: tiny cells back to back on five tiers, with stairways on either end in the center of the very long range. Cell doors were iron with grillework in the upper portion, and they fastened with gang locks. Cells received small amounts of light coming through a tiny window located nine feet away in the outer wall opposite the cell door. These cells were extremely damp, dark and poorly ventilated and, like those at Auburn, contained no toilet facilities except buckets. The East House, which alone contained 1,000 cells and continued in use until 1943, was to become the prototype for most American prison cellhouse construction, rather than the earlier Auburn prison from which the system took its name.
>
> For the remainder of the nineteenth century in this country, the characteristic layout for nearly all prisons was to consist of a central building housing offices, mess hall and chapel, usually flanked and joined on each side by a multitiered cell block. In the prison enclosure formed by the wall would be shops, hospital and power plant. In 1834 Ohio opened a prison on this plan in Columbus. Five tiers of tiny cells (7 x 3½ x 7 feet) back to back were built with convict labor. Wisconsin opened a similar type of prison at Waupun in 1851. The Illinois Penitentiary at Joliet (1856-1858), the Rhode Island Penitentiary at Cranston (1873-1878), the Tennessee Penitentiary at Nashville (1895) and a number of others were on this plan. The largest prison of this sort was the Western Penitentiary at Pittsburgh (1882) with 1,100 cells on five tiers. A few such institutions were erected following the turn of the century—Cheshire, Connecticut, was opened

FIGURE III-2. Ohio State Penitentiary, Maximum Security, Now a Reception and Medical Center (Courtesy Ohio Department of Rehabilitation and Correction)

in 1913 and Monroe, Washington, in 1908—but by that time nearly all the states had built maximum security prisons and little prison building would occur again until the 1930s.[8]

These great Gothic-style[9] monoliths had been built in the belief that this kind of architecture, as part of the total system, would aid in the restoration of prisoners. This idea was discredited by the beginning of the twentieth century, however, and both American and European penologists began to concentrate on treatment strategies. But because America was stuck with almost 60 of these monstrosities,[10] built before 1900 with only economy, security, and isolation in mind, the new programs had to be designed to fit the structure. Of course, it should have been the other way around; the physical plants should have been built to fit the programs. Though corrections philosophy has changed drastically in the past fifty years, America is still tied to the approaches of a century and a half ago by the outmoded architecture of most maximum security prisons.

Classification: A Move toward Corrections

Enforced idleness and the demoralizing influence of the maximum security prisons have resulted in two major movements in corrections over the last half-century. One course of action has been to continually upgrade living conditions and humanitarian treatment within the security prisons. The second action involves the introduction of "classification," a term borrowed from psychology, into the imprisonment process. Classification in prison generally refers to two actions:

1. a differentiation of the prisoner population into custodial or security groups, thus permitting a degree of planned custodial flexibility not possible previously;

2. opening of the prisons to the teacher, psychologist, social worker, psychiatrist, and others.[11]

The advent of classification in the post-World War II era marks a substantial shift from imprisonment to correction as a goal for the prisons of America. The timing was fortuitous, as unionism and federal legislation of the 1930s severely restricted prison industries. The idleness which followed the restrictive federal laws would have been even more troublesome were it not for the Prison Industries Reorganization Administration. Operating between 1935 and 1940, this agency developed programs of constructive activities for prisons which contributed to the rehabilitation programs more characteristic of prisons between 1940 and 1973.

The movement toward increased use of classification was accompanied by a great amount of rhetoric on the concept of "correctional treatment." Some of the more positive aspects of this strategy have been outlined by the American Correctional Association:

The offender was perceived as a person with social, intellectual, or emotional deficiencies which should be diagnosed carefully and his deficiencies "clinically" defined. Programs should be designed to correct these deficiencies to the point that would permit him to assume a productive, law-abiding place in the community. To achieve the goals of correctional treatment, it would be necessary only to maintain the pressure on the inmate for his participation in the treatment programs, to continue to humanize institutional living, to upgrade the educational level of the line officer, and to espand the complement of professional treatment and training personnel. The coordination of the variety of treatment and training programs would be assured by the establishment of a division of "classification, treatment and training" or some similar designation, either in the central office, in the institution, or both. This model of the "progressive prison" continues to be advocated as the standard pattern of the contemporary prison.[12]

"Correctional treatment," however, defies definition, especially when attempted in a maximum security institution where the overriding emphasis is on custody. According to current convention, almost everything done to, for, with, or by the inmate is immediately covered by the umbrella categorization of correctional treatment.

Correctional treatment is generally assumed to begin with the classification process. Classification procedures are conducted in a reception unit located within the existing prisons or in special reception and classification centers. They are sometimes carried out by classification committees, reception-diagnostic centers, or community classification teams. The purpose of classification varies among institutions, but generally it serves to provide assistance in management or treatment planning.

Management classification dates back to the earliest efforts to segregate prisoners by categories. The European "Standard Minimum Rules for the Treatment of Offenders" is a good example of a representative classification scheme, using segregation as a management tool:

> The different categories of prisoners shall be kept in separate
> institutions or parts of the institution, taking account of their sex, age,
> criminal record, the legal reasons for their detention, and the
> necessities of their treatment. Thus, (a) men and women shall so far as
> possible be detained in separate institutions. In an institution which
> receives both men and women, the whole of the premises allocated to
> women shall be entirely separate; (b) untried prisoners shall be kept
> separate from convicted prisoners; (c) persons imprisoned for debt and
> other civil prisoners shall be kept separate from persons imprisoned by
> reason of criminal offense; (d) young prisoners shall be kept separate
> from adults.[13]

While management categories are valuable for the correctional administrator, continuing status evaluation and reclassification are critical. If treatment in the correctional setting is to be effective, the inmate must be reclassified and different treatments designed and applied. Unfortunately, many a well-conceived treatment plan has failed due to inaccurate or nonexistent reclassification.

Management and treatment classification plans must be based on procedures that can be readily implemented within the prison environment. The 1967 report by President Johnson's Task Force on Corrections stressed this point:

> [I]t would be of great help to have some relatively simple screening
> process, capable of administration in general day-to-day correctional
> intake procedures, that would group offenders according to their

management and treatment needs. To the extent that such screening procedures could be regularized, the errors attendant upon having a wide variety of persons make decisions on the basis of different kinds of information and presumptions would be reduced.[14]

That this "simple screening process" has not appeared on the correctional horizon is readily apparent. Until such a process has been designed, most classification systems will retain their crude orientation toward security and custody.

The general model for classification is a variation on the caseworker plan, adopted from the social work profession, which assumes that offenders are "sick" and therefore require "help"[15] from the treatment team, whether they want it or not. In most cases the goals for this kind of "help" are established by caseworkers and the treatment staff. This model, which has been shown to be ineffective, violates two basic principles of social casework. It does not recognize that *offenders* may not perceive themselves as "sick," and therefore may lack the motivation to seek help. It also ignores the offenders' potential ability to establish their own goals. It is a "catch-22"[16] situation for the prisoners:

> In order to use them as a foundation for practice, it is necessary to assume that all offenders are sick. That is, "We know you're sick. If you deny that you're sick, you're really sick. But if you acknowledge that you're sick, then you really *must* be sick or you wouldn't admit it [emphasis added]."[17]

The usual purpose for classification, from the staff viewpoint, is to create a plan that will "correct" prisoners and send them back to society as changed people. The prisoners, on the other hand, see the classification process only as a way to get *out*. They try to determine what they are supposed to do to prove they are ready for release, and then *do* it. Because the emphasis on what they must do tends to shift in accordance with the convenience of the administration, the composition of the treatment staff, or "suggestions for improvement" from the paroling authority, this is not an easy task. An inmate may be classified as deficient in education, for example, so he begins day classes. But because he is a skilled baker, he is needed in the kitchen and must shift to that role to earn a "good attitude" rating. In the complex organization of the prison, institutional needs must be met, even at the expense of correcting the offenders.

Classification was hailed as a new revolution in corrections, moving the focus from the mass-production tactics of the past to individualized treatment. The failure of classification and advanced social work techniques lies partly in the fact that the establishment is very resistant to change, and partly in the poor environments for change provided in the prisons themselves.

Several states have abandoned classification reception-diagnostic centers as counterproductive, since the centers raised inmate and staff aspirations above the level of possible achievement. The treatment model has a place in corrections, but not in maximum security prisons.

The National Advisory Commission on Criminal Justice Standards and Goals still holds hope for classification, but only if reorganized along the lines of their recommended standard:

Each correctional agency, whether community-based or institutional, should immediately reexamine its classification system and reorganize it along the following principles:

1. Recognizing that corrections is now characterized by a lack of knowledge and deficient resources, and that classification systems therefore are more useful for assessing risk and facilitating the efficient management of offenders than for diagnosis of causation and prescriptions for remedial treatment, classification should be designed to operate on a practicable level and for realistic purposes, guided by the principle that:

   a. No offender should receive more surveillance or "help" than he requires; and

   b. No offender should be kept in a more secure condition or status than his potential risk dictates.

2. The classification system should be developed under the management concepts discussed [earlier] . . . . and issued in written form so that it can be made public and shared. It should specify:

   a. The objectives of the system based on a hypothesis for the social reintegration of offenders, detailed methods for achieving the objectives, and a monitoring and evaluation mechanism to determine whether the objectives are being met.

   b. The critical variables of the typology to be used.

   c. Detailed indicators of the components of the classification categories.

   d. The structure (committee, unit, team, etc.) and the procedures for balancing the decisions that must be made in relation to programming, custody, personal security, and resource allocation.

3. The system should provide full coverage of the offender population, clearly delineated categories, internally consistent groupings, simplicity, and a common language.

4. The system should be consistent with individual dignity and basic concepts of fairness (based on objective judgments rather than personal prejudices).

5. The system should provide for maximum involvement of the individual in determining the nature and direction of his own goals, and mechanism for appealing administrative decisions affecting him.

6. The system should be adequately staffed, and the agency staff should be trained in its use.

7. The system should be sufficiently objective and quantifiable to facilitate research, demonstration, model building, intrasystem comparisons, and administrative decision-making.

8. The correctional agency should participate in or be receptive to cross-classification research toward the development of a classification system that can be used commonly by all correctional agencies.[18]

Inside the Walls

After classification, the offender may be transported to one of the more than 100 maximum security prisons still in operation. If he is fortunate he will be placed in one of the smaller institutions; if not, he will enter one of the giant walled cities. He will pass through a double fence or stone wall surrounded by manned guard towers. As the large steel main gate slams shut behind him, the process of prisonization begins. Donald Clemmer, the originator of this concept, describes it best:

Every man who enters the penitentiary undergoes prisonization to some extent. The first and most obvious integrative step concerns his status. He becomes at once an anonymous figure in a subordinate group. A number replaces a name. He wears the clothes of the other members of the subordinate group. He is questioned and admonished. He soon learns that the warden is all-powerful. He soon learns the ranks, titles, and authority of various officials. And whether he uses the prison slang and argot or not, he comes to know their meanings. Even though a new man may hold himself aloof from other inmates

FIGURE III–3. Inside a Maximum Security Penitentiary of the 1930s
(Courtesy American Correctional Association)

and remain a solitary figure, he finds himself within a few months
referring to or thinking of keepers as "screws," the physician as the
"croaker" and using the local nicknames to designate persons. He
follows the examples already set in wearing his cap. He learns to eat in
haste and in obtaining food he imitates the tricks of those near him.

After the new arrival recovers from the effects of the swallowing-up
process, he assigns a new meaning to conditions he had previously
taken for granted. The fact that food, shelter, clothing, and a work
activity had been given him originally made no especial impression. It
is only after some weeks or months that there comes to him a new
interpretation of these necessities of life. This new conception results
from mingling with other men and it places emphasis on the fact that
the environment *should* administer to him. This point is intangible and
difficult to describe in so far as it is only a subtle and minute change in
attitude from the taken-for-granted perception. Exhaustive questioning
of hundreds of men reveals that this slight change in attitude is a
fundamental step in the process we are calling prisonization.[19]

The effort to depersonalize and routinize is seemingly without respite. The maximum security prison is geared to supervision, control, and surveillance of the inmate's every move. Every other human consideration is weighed against its possible effect upon security.

The pragmatic penal leaders in the last half of the nineteenth century began to accept imprisonment as a valid end in itself, rather than a means to reform. This opened prisons up as a dumping ground for America's poor and "different" masses. Foreign immigrants, blacks, and anyone who did not fit the "all-American" mold were likely candidates for these remote asylums. The reformers' rhetoric spoke of rehabilitation, but the actions of corrections administrators belied this emphasis. Prisons were built to keep the prisoners in, but also to keep the public out. To justify the imprisonment of such a heterogeneous group of offenders under such rigid control required a theory of uniform treatment and uniform punishment, without regard to individual differences.

The new inmate is reminded of this principle as he is processed into the prison. The buildings, policies, rules, regulations, and control procedures are all designed to minimize his control over his environment. No privacy is allowed in his windowless and open cell. Even the toilet is open to view, and showers are taken under close supervision. Every consideration is given by the designers and operators to prevent intrusion or contact from the outside. Visits are carefully supervised and many visitor contacts with inmates are possible only by special communication devices[20] that allow conversation but no physical contact. A body search of the inmate, including all body cavities, is invariably conducted if contact has been made. Everything is locked, and all movements involve short trips between locked doors.

This description offers only a rough idea of a "typical" maximum security prison on the inside. Nothing can substitute for an actual visit to or confinement in one of these monuments to man's triumph of external control over internal reform. Some of these human cages are over 150 years old, some are relatively new; but the differences involve only minor construction refinements, not basic philosophical changes. These prisons form the backbone of corrections because they house well over 100,000 inmates[21] and because they are both expensive and durable. The national average cost per square foot of covered floor space in the United States is $45 (1973 dollars).[22]

In general, prisons vary so greatly from state to state that generalizations are dangerous. But the comments of Alexis de Tocqueville in this regard, though made over a century ago, are still valid today.[23] He wrote in 1833 that, aside from common interests, the several states "preserve their individual independence, and each of them is sovereign master to rule itself according to its own pleasure. . . . By the side of one state, the penitentiaries of which might serve as a model, we find another whose prisons present the example of everything which ought to be avoided."[24]

FIGURE III–4. A Typical Maximum Security Prison of the Early 1900s
(Courtesy Ohio Department of Rehabilitation and Correction)

Medium and Minimum Security Institutions

In the twentieth century, a broad range of experimental alternatives to the maximum security approach was launched. Much of the construction in corrections over the past half-century has been for *medium* security institutions. About one-third of all state prisoners are now housed in these medium security facilities. Early medium security prisons were hard to distinguish from maximum security institutions; control was still the dominant concern. But even though security may be almost as tight in a medium security prison, the prisoners are not made so *aware* that they are being watched. Also, medium security prisons are usually smaller, without the overwhelming impersonality of the maximum security monoliths, and the offender's routine is somewhat less regimented.

Some of the most recent medium security prisons are patterned after the so-called "campus" design, including attractive residence areas with single rooms (not cells) and dormitories for inmates. External fences and subtle features installed within buildings to maintain security and protect the inmates from each other are the only obvious signs that prisoners are under observation. Sophisticated electronic and other surveillance equipment is used, but unobtrusively. Assistance for the effective design of these new correctional facilities is provided by organizations such as the National

FIGURE III–5. Robert F. Kennedy Youth Center, an Open Institution
(Courtesy Federal Bureau of Prisons)

Clearinghouse for Correctional Programming and Architecture.[25] If we
continue to use imprisonment as a response to criminal behavior, these new
medium security systems may well represent the first wave of the future for
corrections in America.

Two other grades classify correctional institutions today: the *minimum* and
open institutions, designed to serve the needs of rural farm areas and public
works rather than those of the offender. Prisoners with good security
classifications are assigned to these programs, which range from plantation-
style prison farms to small forestry and road camps.

In many ways the minimum and open facilities are beneficial. They rescue
relatively stable inmates from the oppressive rigors of confinement and from
personal danger in the large stifling prisons. As long as we continue to
imprison offenders who are little threat to themselves or the public for long
periods, the open facilities are preferable to traditional prisons. On the other
hand, if we develop more programs of education, vocational training, and
treatment within the maximum and medium security institutions, those in the
minimum security, work-oriented camps will miss those opportunities. Also,
as community-based corrections programs begin to drain off the least
dangerous and more treatable offenders, the open facilities will lose their
value—they are not suited to the hard-core offenders who remain. Professionals in the corrections field will have to resist efforts to place men into
minimum security or open facilities for *economic* reasons, rather than
placing them into community-based programs for *correctional treatment*
reasons. Some aspects of this dilemma are outlined by the National Advisory
Commission in describing an innovative minimum security facility:

One remarkable minimum security correctional center was opened in 1972 at Vienna, Ill., as a branch of the Illinois State Penitentiary. Although a large facility, it approaches the quality of the nonpenal institution. Buildings resembling garden apartments are built around a "town square" complete with churches, schools, shops, and library. Paths lead off to "neighborhoods" where "homes" provide private rooms in small clusters. Extensive provision has been made for both indoor and outdoor recreation. Academic, commercial, and vocational education facilities equal or surpass those of many technical high schools.

This correctional center has been designed for 800 adult felons. Unfortunately, most of them will come from the state's major population centers many miles away. Today this open institution is enjoying the euphoria that often accompanies distinctive newness. One may speculate about the future, however, when community correctional programs siphon from the state's prison system many of its more stable and less dangerous offenders. Fortunately, this facility will not be rendered obsolete by such a development. The nonprisonlike design permits it to be adapted for a variety of education, mental health, or other human service functions.[26]

The minimum security institution is a logical step between the medium security prison and community-based corrections for the future. The abandonment of the fortress-style prisons of a bygone era is a necessary step in this movement. A few very small maximum security facilities could be built or renovated to house the estimated 15 to 20 percent of the incarcerated felons who need this kind of protection.

Prison Populations Increase

During the period from 1962 to 1969, the prison population in America decreased from 220,000 inmates to a low of 187,000. In 1970, however, the population figure began a dramatic turnaround, and, in the twelve months between January 1976 and January 1977, it soared to an all-time high of 275,578. In addition to that astounding figure, another 7,690 inmates sentenced to state prisons were being held in county jails and detention facilities. The resultant overcrowding of the system means that offenders are doubled up in cells meant for one, packed into makeshift dormitories, and bunked in the basements, corridors, converted hospital facilities, tents, trailers, warehouses, and program activity areas of the nation's prisons. There are currently 131 Americans in prison for every 100,000 citizens—the highest rate for any democratic nation. If present trends continue, there will be over 380,000 Americans in prisons by 1985.[27]

TABLE 3. TOTAL POPULATION OF U.S. STATE AND FEDERAL PRISONS—1962–1977
(Figures are in thousands—as of January 1.)

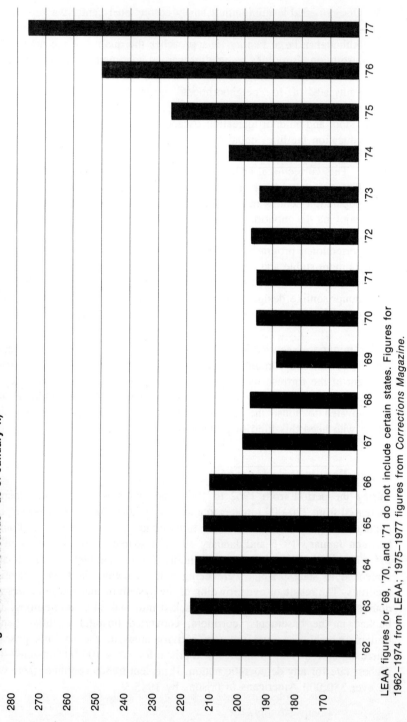

LEAA figures for '69, '70, and '71 do not include certain states. Figures for 1962–1974 from LEAA; 1975–1977 figures from *Corrections Magazine*.

While such rapid overcrowding is not easily explained, it appears that possible explanations include a hardening of public attitudes toward crime, which produces more and more "get tough" policies in the criminal justice system. The courts are under pressure to use their sentencing discretion to deter others by giving longer sentences. They are using probation less often and are themselves pressing for better legislation in the area of probation. The legislators respond by passing more mandatory sentencing laws, limiting the judges' latitude to grant probation or reduce the minimum time for parole consideration.

Another factor contributing to the increase of the prison population as a whole is the increase in the population in the 20- to 30-year-old age group. This is seen as the "population at risk," since crime is generally a young person's activity. This group is a direct result of the baby boom following World War II, which clogged the school systems of America in the fifties and sixties·and has now impacted on yet another area—urban crime. This group is also the one with the highest unemployment rate and, in a time of general underemployment, will continue to commit crime out of proportion to its size.

Currently, billions of dollars are programmed for prison construction, with many projects already underway. Until they are available, or community corrections programs are expanded, prison administrators must be careful to redouble efforts at early diagnosis, classification, and separation of different categories of offenders. The dangerous must be separated from the young and the weak, the permanently sick from those who are able to respond to treatment. While increased staffs will help, prison administrators will need to devote increasing amounts of time and resources to the development and maintenance of rational programming and segregation of the more explosive members of the offender population.

Sex and Corrections

The subject of homosexuality and other sexual problems in prisons has always been highly controversial. Homosexuality is no longer a matter of great concern in the free community, where many states have passed legislation decriminalizing this practice between "consenting adults." Yet great pains are taken to prevent such activity in an institution that is filled with sexually experienced individuals who are forced to exist in a one-sex society. The sexual drive is not one that can be turned off when the offender is placed in an institution. The standard beliefs about sex in prison are based on a number of unfounded assumptions and misleading implications:

- that the incidence of homosexual rape is high;
- that homosexual rape is the characteristic form of prison homosexuality;

- that there exist two distinct role types—an aggressor and an unwilling victim;

- that solutions would require establishing alternative outlets for the sexual drives.

Actually, recent evidence and theory suggest that none of these assumptions or implications is true. It is important, therefore, that any discussion of prison homosexuality begin by stripping away the myths and rationalizations which surround the subject. One such approach is to focus initially on the prison context in which such behavior takes on meaning to the participants.[28]

It is estimated that there is a relationship between prior homosexual experience and the intensity of such activity in institutional custody:

> The relationship between prison homosexuality and preinstitutional homosexual experience is also an issue requiring further elucidation. Working on the assumption that 40 to 50 percent of a penal population will have homosexual experience in prison, Gagnon has estimated that 5 to 10 percent will have had no prior homosexual experience, 25 to 30 percent will have had casual or intermittent prior experience, and 5 to 10 percent will have had extensive or nearly exclusive homosexual commitment in the free community. Gagnon bases his estimates in part on interview data from the Institute for Sex Research which found that in a group of 888 white prisoners, about 7 percent had homosexual experience for the first time while in prison. Based on continuing study of long term maximum security institutions, Thomas finds 30 percent with a prior commitment to homosexual adjustment strong enough to suggest clinical fixation, while 60 percent have negligible prior experience, but undertake homosexual behavior in prison due to regression occasioned by the emotionally impoverished environment.
>
> Even with these relatively high *incidence* figures, it seems quite clear that the *frequency* of homosexual contact is usually quite low, even among cellmates; and in no sense does it approach the rates of heterosexual or homosexual behavior of these same prisoners on the outside, except possibly for those prisoners who come into the institution with well-developed homosexual commitments and who become the "passive" partner in homosexual liaisons. In some prisons, usually those with a very low order of custody inside the walls, high rates of homosexual behavior may be achieved; however, these are not the prevalent conditions in most prison systems.[29]

Most of this research is based on fragmentary evidence, and it is probable that homosexuality is much less common in prison than popular mythology would lead us to believe. At least one researcher, however, believes that homosexual rape in prison is increasing and that it reflects an attempt by minority group members to "get even" with a repressive society.[30] Probably the most universal sexual outlet in prison is masturbation, a practice not unknown in the free world.

The problem of how to deal with sex in prison is a difficult one for the correctional administrator, since intervention in this area is one of the major sources of violence in the institutional setting. Some of the administrator's problems are made clear in the following excerpt from *Homosexuality in Prisons:*

> What is clear is that it is not the sexual drive itself that makes a prison full of unrest and that as a matter of fact most males survive the deprivation of the sexual outlet and usually even survive transitory homosexual commitments to return to relatively conventional heterosexual lives on the outside.
>
> What the sexual problem in the male prison does represent is a series of land mines, some for the administration, more for the inmates. In the case of the inmates, men get into relationships which have some potential for shaping their future commitments to sexuality; relationships which leave them open to exploitation and especially for those who take the passive role, the possibility of distortion of their self-conceptions. Further, there is some jealousy. When a relationship deteriorates or when a transfer of affection takes place, there is a distinct possibility of violence. The violence that does occur often is extreme, and at this point becomes a serious matter for prison management.
>
> The dilemma for the prison manager is that often he is not aware of the relationships until they erupt into violence. Attempts at intervention in this process through getting inmates to aid in the identification of those involved may result in serious scapegoating of these persons out of the sexual anxieties of the other prisoners. The segregation of these prisoners has also been attempted. However, one major difficulty with this measure seems to be that when the most obvious homosexuals are removed from the situation there is a tendency to co-opt other persons to take their place. This tendency is also noted when the aggressive male is removed, though the policy has usually been to remove only those men who are conventionally obvious, that is, who appear excessively effeminate.[31]

The conjugal visit has been a frequent proposal for the solution to the problem of an institution with no heterosexual outlets. The adoption of this practice is inhibited by the American society's reluctance to accept any sexual relationship outside of marriage, limiting the benefits of conjugal visits to inmates with an intact family. The practice of home furlough, without supervision, is a more reasonable and natural response to the inmate's need for relationships outside the prison, whether sexual or other-wise. The treatment of more and more offenders in a community environment is another reasonable and viable response.

The main cause of the sexual problems that arise in prisons is probably the prison environment itself. As the prison becomes the last resort for a small percentage of the inmate population, appropriate means for providing the residual prisoners with sexual outlets will need to be found. A society that uses sex appeal in almost every aspect of its mass media and sales promotional material should not raise an eyebrow at the news that sexually experienced and relatively normal persons cannot be deprived of this outlet for months and years without problems. One of the major issues to be resolved by future correctional administrators will be the possibility of accepting homosexual activity between consenting prisoners, when it is legally accepted in the free world.

The Future of Imprisonment

It has been frequently shown that the large adult prisons operated by the state are the least effective way to rehabilitate and reintegrate offenders. Despite findings to this effect, in the 1920s,[32] the '30s,[33] the '60s,[34] and again in the '70s[35] the building and filling of maximum security prisons has continued. The advent, and relative success, of community-based treatment of criminal offenders has begun to dent the armor of the diehards who advocate punitive prison as the ultimate correctional solution. It is the threat that these new programs pose to the old-line institutional staff that must be overcome before the present system, which exists primarily to perpetuate itself, can undergo any real change.

The reasons for the static nature of the present have been well-documented. Long sentences are one problem: it is difficult to provide programs and promise to a man who will not be released for ten years or more. Laws which restrict the employment of ex-offenders make the vocational training programs in many prisons a mockery. Also, to expect a man who has been earning $500 a day as a drug pusher to return to the same environment and work cheerfully as a janitor for $2 an hour is totally unreasonable. The street conditions which make such high illegal earnings possible cannot be controlled by the correctional staff, but they impact heavily on the results of their efforts.

We must again turn to the efforts of the National Advisory Committee and their recommendations as to what can and should be done to at least improve the environment of present institutions:

> Each correctional agency operating juvenile or adult institutions, and each institution, should undertake immediately to reexamine and revise its policies, procedures, and practices to bring about an institutional social setting that will stimulate offenders to change their behavior and

to participate on their own initiative in programs intended to assist them in reintegrating into the community.

1. The institution's organizational structure should permit open communication and provide for maximum input in the decision-making process.

   a. Inmate advisory committees should be developed.

   b. A policy of participative management should be adopted.

   c. An ombudsman independent of institutional administration should receive and process inmate and staff complaints.

   d. Inmate newspapers and magazines should be supported.

2. The correctional agency and the institution should make explicit their correctional goals and program thrust.

   a. Staff recruitment and training should emphasize attitudes that support these goals.

   b. Performance standards should be developed for programs and staff to measure program effectiveness.

   c. An intensive public relations campaign should make extensive use of media to inform the public of the agency's goals.

   d. The institution administration should be continuously concerned with relevance and change.

3. The institution should adopt policies and practices that will preserve the individual identity of the inmate and normalize institutional settings.

   a. Each offender should be involved in program decisions affecting him.

   b. Offenders should be identified by name and social security number rather than prison number.

   c. Rules governing hair length and the wearing of mustaches and beards should be liberalized to reflect respect for individuality and cultural and subcultural trends.

d. Where possible, uniforms should be eliminated and replaced with civilian dress, with reasonable opportunity for individual choice of colors, styles, etc.

e. Institutional visitation should be held in an environment conducive to healthy relationships between offenders and their families and friends.

f. Home furloughs should be allowed to custodially qualified offenders to maintain emotional involvement with families.

g. Telephone privileges, including reasonable provisions for long-distance calls, should be extended to all inmates.

h. No limitation should be imposed upon the amount of mail offenders may send or receive.

4. Each institution should make provision for the unique problems faced by minority offenders and take these problems into consideration in practices and procedures.

a. Subcultural groups should be formally recognized and encouraged.

b. Ethnic studies courses should be provided.

c. Staff members representative of minority groups in the institution should be hired and trained.

d. Minority residents of the community should be involved actively in institution programs.

5. The institution should actively develop the maximum possible interaction between community and institution, including involvement of community members in planning and in intramural and extramural activities.

a. Institutionally based work-release and study-release programs with an emphasis on community involvement should be adopted or expanded.

b. Ex-offenders and indigenous paraprofessionals should be used in institutional programs and activities.

c. Joint programming between the institution and the community should be developed, including such activities as drug counseling sessions,

Alcoholics Anonymous meetings, recreation programs, theatre groups, and so on.

d. Offenders should be able to participate in educational programs in the community, and community members should be able to participate in educational programs in the institution.

e. Police officers should become involved, acquainting offenders with pertinent sections of the law and in general playing a supportive role.

f. Offenders should have opportunities to travel to and to participate in worship services of local churches, and representatives of the churches should participate in institutional services.

g. The institution should cultivate active participation of civic groups, and encourage the groups to invite offenders to become members.

h. The institution should arrange for representatives of government agencies to render services to offenders by traveling to the institution or by enabling offenders to appear at agency offices.

i. The institution should obtain the participation of business and labor in intramural and extramural programs and activities.

j. The institution should seek the participation of volunteers in institutional programs and activities.

6. The institution should apply only the minimum amount of security measures, both physical and procedural, that are necessary for the protection of the public, the staff, and inmates, and its disciplinary measures should emphasize rewards for good behavior rather than the threat of punishment for misbehavior.

a. Committed offenders initially should be assigned the least restrictive custodial level possible, as determined by the classification process.

b. Only those mechanical devices absolutely necessary for security purposes should be utilized.

c. Institutional regulations affecting inmate movements and activities should not be so restrictive and burdensome as to discourage

FIGURE III–6. Southern Ohio Correctional Facility, Lucasville (1973)
(Courtesy Ohio Department of Rehabilitation and Correction)

participation in program activities and to give offenders a sense of oppression.

d. Standards concerning disciplinary procedures should be adopted, including the promulgation of reasonable rules of conduct and disciplinary hearings and decisions respecting the rights of offenders.

e. An incentive system should be developed to reward positive behavior and to reinforce desired behavioral objectives.

f. Security and disciplinary policies and methods should be geared to support the objective of social reintegration of the offender rather than simply to maintain order and serve administrative convenience.[36]

This litany of cures for correctional ills may seem to be a replay of previous efforts. The significant difference today lies in the interest and assistance of the federal government in the form of funds, technical advice, and planning assistance through the efforts of the Law Enforcement Assistance Administration (see chapter 4).

The kind of patchwork effort recommended by the National Advisory Commission is a good beginning. Prison problems are relentless, however, and even the most humane reformers are subtly changed by the enormous problems that face them. They become cold, callous, and finally prisonized themselves. William Nagel, in *The New Red Barn,* quotes early twentieth-century scholar and penologist Frank Tannenbaum:

> We must destroy the prison, root and branch. That will not solve our problem, but it will be a good beginning. . . . Let us substitute something. Almost anything will be an improvement. It cannot be worse. It cannot be more brutal and useless.[37]

Although this is a laudable goal, the realities of prison population increases will make it difficult to attain in the foreseeable future.

REVIEW QUESTIONS

I. Find the answers to the following in the text:

1. What are the main purposes of confinement?

2. Differentiate between classification for management and for treatment.

3. Describe a typical maximum security prison. Explain the main differences between maximum, medium, and minimum security institutions.

II. Words to identify:

1. punishment

2. classification

3. deterrence

4. Gothic

5. rehabilitation

6. correctional treatment

7. quarantine

8. custody grade

9. integration

10. catch-22

11. prisonization

12. open institution

13. depersonalization

14. perfectability

15. management classification

NOTES

1. Norman Johnston, *The Human Cage: A Brief History of Prison Architecture* (New York: Walker and Company, 1973), p. 8.

2. The U.S. Bureau of Prisons completed a new 500-bed facility in San Diego in 1975 at a cost of $14,859,000, or $29,718 per cell.

3. Cesare Beccaria, *On Crimes and Punishments,* trans. Henry Paolucci (Indianapolis, 1963), pp. 8, 43-44, 58, 94.

4. David J. Rothman, *The Discovery of the Asylum* (Boston: Little Brown, 1971), p. 62.

5. William G. Nagel, *The New Red Barn: A Critical Look at the Modern American Prison* (New York: Walker and Company, 1973), pp. 11-13.

6. The District of Columbia Reformatory, built at Lorton, Virginia, in 1926.

7. Howard B. Gill, "Correctional Philosophy and Architecture," *Journal of Criminal Law, Criminology, and Police Science* 53 (1962): 312-322.

8. Johnston, *The Human Cage,* p. 40.

9. Gothic architecture was designed to overwhelm the person who entered such structures. The famous Gothic churches of Europe were known to make people feel small and insignificant.

10. Maximum security prisons in America:

Prior to 1830	6
1831 to 1870	17
1871 to 1900	33
1901 to 1930	21
1931 to 1960	15
1961 to 1975	21
Total	113

11. Benjamin Frank, "Basic Issues in Corrections," *Perspectives on Correctional Manpower and Training* (Washington, D.C.: The American Correctional Association, 1970).

12. American Correctional Association, *Manual of Correctional Standards,* 3d ed. (Washington, D.C.: The American Correctional Association, 1966).

13. United Nations Department of Economic and Social Affairs, *Standard Minimum Rules for the Treatment of Prisoners and Related Recommendations* (New York: United Nations, 1958).

14. The President's Commission on Law Enforcement and Administration of Justice, *Task Force Report: Corrections* (Washington, D.C.: U.S. Government Printing Office, 1967), p. 20.

15. "Help" in this context would include the full array of services available—medical, psychological, psychiatric, educational, vocational, and others.

16. "Catch-22" means that you can escape from an unpleasant situation only by meeting certain conditions, but if you meet those conditions, you can't escape. The expression was popularized by Joseph Heller's novel of that name, about an

army pilot constantly required to fly suicidal missions. He knew it was crazy to fly the missions, but according to the army, *because* he knew it was crazy, he was perfectly sane. And if he was sane, he could continue to fly the missions.

17. National Advisory Commission on Criminal Justice Standards and Goals, *Corrections* (Washington, D.C.: U.S. Department of Justice, 1973), p. 199.

18. National Advisory Commission, *Corrections*, p. 210.

19. Donald Clemmer, "The Process of Prisonization," in *The Criminal in Confinement*, ed. Leon Radzinowicz and Marvin Wolfgang (New York: Basic Books, 1971), pp. 92-93.

20. Special devices for communicating include such things as telephones on either side of bulletproof glass, booths with wire screen between, etc.

21. National Advisory Commission, *Corrections*, p. 344.

22. Ohio Department of Rehabilitation and Correction (Columbus, Ohio), *The Communicator* 1, no. 12:12.

23. Alexis de Tocqueville was one of the French commissioners who visited America in 1833 and wrote a treatise on what he observed in the American penitentiary system. (See note 24.)

24. Gustave de Beaumont and Alexis de Tocqueville, *On the Penitentiary System in the United States and Its Application in France* (Carbondale, Ill., Southern Illinois University Press, 1964), p. 48.

25. The National Clearinghouse for Correctional Programming and Architecture is located at the University of Illinois, Department of Architecture, Urbana, Illinois.

26. National Advisory Commission, *Corrections*, p. 345.

27. Rob Wilson, "U.S. Prison Population Again Hits New High," *Corrections Magazine* 3 (March 1977): 3-22.

28. Peter C. Buffum, *Homosexuality in Prisons* (Washington, D.C.: U.S. Department of Justice, 1972), pp. 2-3.

29. Buffum, p. 13.

30. Anthony Scacco, Jr., *Rape in Prison* (Springfield, Ill.: Charles C. Thomas, 1975).

31. Buffum, pp. 28-29.

32. National Commission on Law Observance and Enforcement (The Wickersham Commission), 1929.

33. *Attorney General's Survey of Release Procedures*, 1939.

34. The President's Commission on Law Enforcement and Administration of Justice, 1967.

35. The National Advisory Commission on Criminal Justice Standards and Goals, 1973.

36. National Advisory Commission, *Corrections*, pp. 362-363.

37. Nagel, *The New Red Barn*, p. 148.

12 Parole

The problems of crime bring us together. Even as we join in common action, we know that there can be no instant victory. Ancient evils do not yield to easy conquest. We cannot limit our efforts to enemies we can see. We must, with equal resolve, seek out new knowledge, new techniques, and new understanding.

LYNDON B. JOHNSON

Indefinite Sentences and Conditional Release

Earlier in American history, offenders were sentenced to prison for a fixed period, and they were not released until they had "jammed their time." In the Middle Ages, the fixed period of time was often for *life,* leaving the prisoners with little hope for release or incentive to change their ways. Beccaria's general theorem of punishment bears review:

> In order for punishment not to be, in every instance, an act of violence of one or of many against a private citizen, it must be essentially public, prompt, necessary, the least possible in the given circumstances, proportionate to the crimes, dictated by the laws.[1]

This theorem, of course, was not observed by those who devised the long, excessively severe, and far from public punishments meted out in the early prisons. One of the great breakthroughs in the development of corrections was the indeterminate (sometimes called indefinite) sentence, preceded by a form of sentence reduction called "good time" laws. This term did not refer to fun within the walls, but to taking days off the offender's sentence as a result of conduct and behavior in accordance with the institutional rules. New York, in 1817, was the first state to pass a good time law. The rules were firm and fairly straightforward, varying from state to state. New York's enabled the correctional administrator to "reduce by one fourth the sentence of any prisoner sentenced to imprisonment for not less than five years, upon certificate of the principal keeper and other satisfactory evidence, that such prisoner had behaved well, and had acquired in the whole, the net sum of 15 dollars or more per annum.''[2] Every state in the union and the District of Columbia had passed some kind of good time law by 1916.

While the good time laws were a step forward, they were really not much better than the methods used to gain pardon[3] for prisoners. Pardons were often sought to relieve offenders of oppressively heavy sentences. In some cases the juries *themselves* petitioned the governor to grant pardon, because the only sentence the law allowed them to recommend was extremely long. The power of pardon was often used to empty out the prisons so that courts would have some place to send newly sentenced offenders. In addition, that power made weak governors succumb to pressure from rich or influential offenders. The good time laws were a help, but they were usually bound by a fixed formula, so that many prisoners were kept long after officials had agreed that they were ready for release. By 1832 a new concept was being developed and discussed: indeterminate sentencing.

The idea of the indeterminate sentence is generally attributed to the efforts of England's Alexander Maconochie and Ireland's Sir Walter Crofton (see chapter 3). The effectiveness of Crofton's "Irish System" was discussed at the meeting of the National Prison Association in 1870. Crofton himself presented a paper on the indeterminate sentence at the meeting. Zebulon Brockway, who had influenced the Michigan legislature to pass an indeterminate sentence act in 1867 and used it in his position as Superintendent of the Detroit House of Corrections,[4] also advocated its widespread usage. The indeterminate sentencing and parole ideas espoused by Brockway and Crofton in 1870 were finally put into practice at Elmira Reformatory in 1876. A form of parole was worked out at Elmira which kept the prisoner under the supervision and control of the prison authorities for an additional six months after release.

The use of a true indeterminate sentence has won acceptance more slowly than the use of parole. A genuine indeterminate sentence has no minimum and no maximum, with release based entirely on the offender's willingness to conform to whatever model is used to determine his or her ability to return to free society. Many judges are reluctant to give up such a large part of their sentencing power. Others fear that it is dangerous to leave such a broad power over the inmate in the hands of correctional administrators, since it could result in a life sentence for a minor offense if an administrator bore a grudge against an inmate. Most indeterminate sentence laws have, therefore, been designed with some kind of a minimum and maximum time that still allows broad discretion to the administrator. In most jurisdictions, the minimum sentence is no more than half of the maximum (e.g., 10-20, 15-30, 5-10), although the minimum can be as *low* as deemed necessary (e.g., 6 months–3 years, 1-20, 3-30). The general consensus is that the practice of parole, while not totally dependent on the indeterminate sentence, could not have developed without it. The indeterminate sentence, sometimes attacked as too lenient, is in fact a sound alternative. It gives deserving offenders a chance to get out from under the oppressive sentencing practices of earlier judges, while providing a means of retaining the incorrigibles in custody. It can also be used by the paroling authority to reduce or eliminate disparities in sentencing.

Origins of Parole

Most offenders who enter the prisons of America eventually end up back on the streets of the neighborhoods they came from. Unless prisoners die in prison (from natural causes or otherwise), they *will* come out someday. The cruelly long sentences of the nineteenth century usually meant that the few offenders who did leave the prisons were bitter, broken, or both. Today the odds are heavy that offenders will leave prison on parole, usually long before the expiration of their maximum sentences. In recent years, the number and percentage of prisoners released on parole has climbed steadily. In 1966, the prisoners released on parole numbered 61 percent of the total, but this figure jumped to 72 percent by 1970.[5] In some states prisoners on parole account for 100 percent of the releases.[6] The significance of parole is clear when one recognizes that the only alternative means of relief are clemency, completion of sentence, or death.

In the days of extensive capital punishment and life sentences, death in prison was a strong possibility. The prisoner might die as a result of natural causes, an accident, or homicide inside the walls. Another way out—sometimes not much more satisfactory, from the offender's viewpoint—is to be forced to serve the entire maximum sentence before release (to "max out").

Infinitely better, but rare, is executive clemency, in the form of a pardon or similar action by the governor. A full pardon usually involves complete exoneration of blame for the offense and relieves the prisoner of the stigma of guilt. One version of the pardon is amnesty, which may be granted to a group or class of offenders. The United States has a long tradition of granting amnesty to soldiers who deserted in major wars. And in countries where it is customary to imprison any and all political dissidents, the government may use mass amnesty to gain public favor. Another executive power is the use of a reprieve, usually in the case of the death penalty. (One remembers the old "B" grade movies in which the star is granted a last-minute reprieve while being strapped into the electric chair.) A reprieve does not usually result in a release, but merely a reduction in the severity of the punishment. Another version of this power to lessen punishment is the use of commutation (shortening the sentence by executive order). Usually the commutation is based on time already spent in jail and prison, and results in almost immediate release of the petitioner. Another form of release, discussed in chapter 9, results from some sort of appellate review action. These procedures, along with parole (and, of course, escape) cover the possible ways that a prisoner can expect to be released from prison.

The classic definition of parole is "release of an offender from a penal or correctional institution, after he has served a portion of his sentence, under the continued custody of the state and under conditions that permit his reincarceration in the event of misbehavior."[7] The term "parole" is generally attributed to Dr. S. G. Howe of Boston,[8] who used it in a letter to the Prison Association of New York in 1846. It is the amount of supervision exercised over the parolee that distinguishes American parole procedures from those of other countries. As the state parole systems developed in America, the reliance on rules and supervision became a crucial element. As the nation entered the twentieth century, parole had gained a strong foothold as a way for prisoners to return to the free world. Today, every state has some system of parole supervision for released offenders, even though some states are in the process of reducing or eliminating its use.

The Parole Board

If prisoners want to be released on parole, they must be recommended and reviewed by some procedure that will select them for this option. When parole selection procedures were first developed, many states had a single Commissioner of Parole, appointed by the governor. This kind of political patronage soon led to corruption and a great deal of controversy, and was generally abandoned after World War II. Two general models for parole recommendation have replaced it: (1) parole boards that are linked to, or actually part of, the correctional system staff; and (2) parole boards that are independent of correctional institutions and the administrators of the system. A third model, a consolidation of all correctional and parole services, will be discussed later.

The correctional system model tends to perceive the parole decision as merely another in a series of decisions which relate to the offender. The institutional staff feels that it is best suited, because of its intimate contact with the offender, to make the parole decision. This argument, however, is based on the false assumption that strict obedience to the conditions and rules that dominate prison life somehow relates to a healthy adjustment on the outside. In other words, the kind of behavior that might lead the staff to conclude an inmate was ready for parole could in fact cripple his or her efforts to cope on the outside. Complete subordination to rules and regulations and suppression of individuality—the desired behavior in institutions, to ensure a smooth operation—are hardly the requisite skills for survival in the free world. Another potential problem if parole decisions are made by the institutional staff could be a twisted use of that procedure: as an easy way to get rid of prison troublemakers. Institutional decision making can be buried too readily in the invisible activity behind the walls. Removed from public scrutiny or control, the parole decision soon becomes just another mechanical process that treats offenders, vitally concerned with the decision, as only incidental to the outcome.

In time, the independently authorized parole authority became the most widely used model in adult corrections. As a matter of fact, today *no* adult parole releasing authority is controlled directly by the staff of a penal institution.[9] The obvious purpose of this independent authority was to remove the decision-making procedure from the atmosphere outlined in the previous paragraph. It was felt that the institutional parole authorities were too easily swayed by the subjective input of the staff.

While an independent board may well be more objective than the correctional bureaucracy in making parole recommendations, it is not a perfect system. Board members' lack of knowledge about the programs, policies, and conditions within the prisons create an organizational gap, critics have argued, that causes unnecessary conflict between prison authorities and the Boards:

> First, the claim is made that such boards tend to be insensitive to institutional programs and fail to give them the support they require. Second, independent boards are accused of basing their decisions on inappropriate considerations, such as the feelings of a local police chief. Third, their remoteness from the institutional program gives independent boards little appreciation of the dynamics in a given case; their work tends to be cursory, with the result that too often persons who should be paroled are not, and those who should not be paroled are released. Fourth, the argument is made that independent systems tend to place on parole boards persons who have little training or experience in corrections.[10]

An attempt to solve the problems that have plagued the institutional and independent systems has resulted in the newest and most popular model, the *consolidated board*. The consolidated model places the authority for parole decisions in the department of corrections, but includes independent powers in the decision-making process. This arrangement reflects the general move toward the consolidation of *all* correctional services, such as institutional programs, community-based programs, and parole and aftercare programs, under state departments of correction. The consolidation model views the treatment of offenders as they pass through the correctional system as a continuum, rather than a series of separate, unrelated experiences. It is claimed that removal of the decision-making authority to a level above the institutions, but still within the system, tends to foster objectivity while maintaining a sensitivity toward the programs and problems of the prison administrators. This approach is gaining wide acceptance, and over 60 percent of the state parole boards responsible for release of adult offenders now function as part of an administrative structure that includes other agencies for offenders.[11] While this system is preferable to the alternatives outlined above, it still must struggle to maintain its autonomy through careful selection of board members and avoidance of automatic tenure, with explicit delineation of parole board tasks and responsibilities. The National Advisory Commission has made six recommendations with regard to the organization of parole authorities:

Each state that has not already done so should, by 1975, establish parole decisionmaking bodies for adult and juvenile offenders that are independent of correctional institutions. These boards may be administratively part of an overall statewide correctional services agency, but they should be autonomous in their decisionmaking authority and separate from field services. The board responsible for the parole of adult offenders should have jurisdiction over both felons and misdemeanants.

1. The boards should be specifically responsible for articulating and fixing policy, for acting on appeals by correctional authorities or inmates on decisions made by hearing examiners, and for issuing and signing warrants to arrest and hold alleged parole violators.

2. The boards of larger states should have a staff of full-time hearing examiners appointed under civil service regulations.

3. The boards of smaller states may assume responsibility for all functions; but should establish clearly defined procedures for policy development, hearings, and appeals.

4. Hearing examiners should be empowered to hear and make initial decisions in parole grant and revocation cases under the specific policies of the parole board. The report of the hearing examiner containing a transcript of the hearing and the evidence should constitute the exclusive record. The decision of the hearing examiner should be final unless appealed to the parole board within five days by the correctional authority or the offender. In the case of an appeal, the parole board should review the case on the basis of whether there is substantial evidence in the report to support the finding or whether the finding was erroneous as a matter of law.

5. Both board members and hearing examiners should have close understanding of correctional institutions and be fully aware of the nature of their programs and the activities of offenders.

6. The parole board should develop a citizen committee, broadly representative of the community and including ex-offenders, to advise the board on the development of policies.[12]

The Parole Selection Process

How is an offender selected for parole? This question has been asked by many researchers, and they have found little concrete evidence that any reasonably objective criteria are used. The most extensive studies show that the main factor considered in the selection process is the "seriousness of the crime" for which the offender was convicted.[13] Perhaps a good way to analyze this process is to walk through a typical parole review and selection effort.

Most parole boards operate by assigning cases to individual board members, who review the cases in detail and then make recommendations to the board as a whole. In most cases the recommendation of the individual member is accepted, but sometimes the assembled board will request more details. At this point, the prisoner will often be asked to appear. Some states send individual board members to the institutions to interview the inmate and the prison staff; others convene the entire board at the various institutions on a regular schedule. If inmates do not meet whatever mystical standards the board has established for parole, their sentences are continued and they are "flopped."[14] In the case of acceptance, they are prepared for turnover to the adult parole authority, for a period of supervision determined by the parole board.

A major problem in the administration of parole decisions lies in the tendency of most boards to disregard the right of offenders to know what standards they are expected to meet (and, if they fail, the reasons for it):

> It is an essential element of justice that the role and processes for measuring parole readiness be made known to the inmate. This knowledge can greatly facilitate the earnest inmate toward his own rehabilitation. It is just as important for an inmate to know the rules and basis of the judgment upon which he will be granted or denied parole as it was important for him to know the basis of the charge against him and the evidence upon which he was convicted. One can imagine nothing more cruel, inhuman, and frustrating than serving a prison term without knowledge of what will be measured and the rules determining whether one is ready for release. . . . Justice can never be a product of unreasoned judgment.[15]

This criteria problem also affects the correctional staff, who should know the "rules of the game" so they can guide inmates in the direction desired by the parole board.

Another problem facing potential parolees is the lack of an appeal process. Because criteria for granting parole and reasons for denying it are not specified, inmates—and concerned citizens—have often questioned the validity of board decisions. Future parole selection processes *must* include self-regulating internal appeal procedures, or the courts will be deluged with relevant cases until the Supreme Court, no doubt, will have to establish a basis for rules and procedures under the rubric of the Fourteenth Amendment. Some states, recognizing the handwriting on the wall, have begun to establish criteria and develop appeal procedures before they are forced to do so by court decisions based on class action suits.

Conditions for Parole

The rules for conditional release developed under Crofton's Irish System form the basis for most parole stipulations, even today. The conditions for parole should be related to the general objectives of a parole system, as follows:

1. Release of each person from confinement at the most favorable time, with appropriate consideration to requirements of justice, expectations of subsequent behavior, and cost.

2. The largest possible number of successful parole completions.

3. The smallest possible number of new crimes committed by released offenders.

4. The smallest possible number of violent acts committed by released offenders.

5. An increase of general community confidence in parole administration.

The methods by which these objectives can be carried out would include the following:

1. A process for selecting persons who should be given parole and for determining the time of release.

2. A system for prerelease planning both inside the institution with the offender and outside the institution with others in the community at large.

3. A system for supervision and assistance in the community.

4. A set of policies, procedures, and guidelines for situations in which the question of reimprisonment must be decided.[16]

Designed in the belief that these conditions should be followed to the letter, and in the awareness that the public saw the paroled offender as a "convict bogey," many early programs were based on unreasonable restrictions. Many of these rules were no more than convenient techniques for ensuring the quick return of parolees to prison if they created even a slight stir for the parole supervisors. An example of such rules, in force as recently as 1962, is displayed in Figure III–7. More recently, that rigid formula was replaced with the simple and commonsense statement presented in Figure III–8.

1. Upon leaving the institution I will go directly to the place to which I have been paroled and will report as directed to my parole officer.

2. I will remain in the county and state to which I have been paroled unless I obtain written permission to leave through my parole officer. I will consult with my parole officer and obtain the officer's approval before changing my address or residence within the county to which I have been paroled.

3. I will submit true written reports of my activities to my parole officer as directed. A false report will constitute a violation of my parole.

4. I will reply promptly to any communication from the Adult Parole Authority or any of their officers.

5. I will report in person to such person or persons at such time and in such place and manner as may be directed by the Adult Parole Authority.

6. I will make every effort to obtain and keep satisfactory employment as is approved by my parole officer. If my employment should stop for any reason I will immediately report this fact to my parole officer. I will not voluntarily change my place or type of employment without first obtaining permission from my parole officer.

7. I will support to the best of my ability those persons for whom I am responsible.

8. I will enter into marriage only after I have received the written permission of my parole officer. Under no circumstances will I cohabit with anyone not my legal spouse.

9. I will associate and communicate only with persons of good reputation. I will avoid contact with persons who have criminal records or persons who are on probation or parole. I will not visit persons or frequent places or areas forbidden by my parole officer.

10. I will get written permission from my parole officer before purchasing, owning or operating any motor vehicle, aircraft, or powerboat, in addition to satisfying any conditions which might apply to my particular case. I understand this permission will be given only after I have a valid operator's license and such liability insurance as is approved by my parole officer.

11. I will not purchase, own, possess, use or have under my control any deadly weapon or firearm. I understand there will be no exceptions to this rule while I am on parole.

12. I will not have in my possession, use, sell, distribute or have under my control any narcotic drugs, barbiturates, marijuana, paregoric, or extracts containing them in any form or instruments for administering them except on prescription of a licensed physician.

13. I will not use intoxicants to such an excess that in the opinion of my parole officer my health or the safety or welfare of others is placed in jeopardy, or that it interferes with meeting financial obligations, employment, my family relations, or acceptable behavior.

14. I will obey all municipal ordinances, state and federal laws, and will at all times conduct myself as a respectable law-abiding citizen.

FIGURE III–7. Rules of Parole (1962)

Special Conditions

In addition to agreeing to abide by the above conditions of parole, I understand and accept that while on parole I do not have the right to vote, serve on juries, or hold public office.

I further understand that if I am granted permission to be in another state or if I should be there without permission and my return to [my home state] is authorized, I hereby waive extradition to the [said] state . . . and agree not to contest efforts to effect such return.

By affixing my signature below I signify my acceptance of these conditions of parole and any other special conditions which the Adult Parole Authority might impose. I agree to abide by and follow any instructions given by the Adult Parole Authority or any of its supervisors or officers and I accept them as part of the conditions of my parole.

These conditions of parole have been explained to me and I understand them.

Witness _____   Signed _____

Date _____ [17]

FIGURE III–7. (CONT.)

The Members of the Parole Board have agreed that you have earned the opportunity of parole and eventually a final release from your present conviction. The Parole Board is therefore ordering a Parole Release in your case.

Parole Status has a two-fold meaning: One is a trust status in which the Parole Board accepts your word you will do your best to abide by the Conditions of Parole that are set down in your case; the other, by state law, means the Adult Parole Authority has the legal duty to enforce the Conditions of Parole even to the extent of arrest and return to the institution should that become necessary.

1. Upon release from the institution, report as instructed to your Parole Officer (or any other person designated) and thereafter report as often as directed.
2. Secure written permission of the Adult Parole Authority before leaving the [said] state.
3. Obey all municipal ordinances, state and federal laws, and at all times conduct yourself as a responsible law-abiding citizen.
4. Never purchase, own, possess, use or have under your control, a deadly weapon or firearm.
5. Follow all instructions given you by your Parole Officer or other officials of the Adult Parole Authority and abide by any special conditions imposed by the Adult Parole Authority.
6. If you feel any of the Conditions or instructions are causing problems, you may request a meeting with your Parole Officer's supervisor. The request stating your reasons for the conference should be in writing when possible.
7. Special Conditions: (as determined). I have read, or have had read to me, the foregoing Conditions of my Parole. I fully understand them and I agree to observe and abide by my Parole Conditions.

Witness _____   Parole Candidate _____

Date _____ [18]

FIGURE III–8. Statement of Parole Agreement (1973)

One can imagine that conforming to the early rule requiring the parolee to "only associate with persons of good reputation" would be difficult for a man whose wife was a prostitute, or whose father was an ex-convict. The emphasis on such rules gave parole officers great discretionary power over parolees. The parolees knew that they could be returned to prison for a technical violation[19] of their parole conditions at almost any time the parole officer desired, a situation hardly conducive to reform and respect for the law. Parolees who had committed some minor violation might decide, "If I'm going to get busted for a technical violation, I might as well do something *really* wrong." The revised, nonrestrictive rules in the 1973 statement are aimed at eliminating the need for this kind of rationale.

Even with the new and simpler rules, of course, technical violations[19] are possible; and Ohio has taken special steps to handle them. If parolees have violated one of the simple conditions, but have not committed another convictable offense, they may be sent to a Community Reintegration Center.[20] There they are given guidance to help them deal with complete freedom in the community without the need to return them to a penal institution. Ohio's Reintegration Centers, located in three communities, give parolees a chance to continue their employment and other community contacts while proving to the parole authorities that they can adjust to their problems without further incarceration. The centers are still too new to determine the extent of their effectiveness, but they seem to represent a hopeful model for the problem of handling technical violations by parolees. A combination of rules that are easy to grasp and follow, plus an alternative to reincarceration for those who slip up occasionally, is a more humane, less expensive, and less damaging solution than return to prison.

Personnel and Caseload Problems in Parole

As the fastest-growing segment of the corrections field, the parole area offers great opportunities and challenges for career-oriented professionals in criminal justice. It was estimated that over 140,000 offenders would be under parole supervision in America by 1975;[21] the number of parole officers will have to increase dramatically to match further increases. It is essential that well-qualified individuals seek careers in parole supervision. In the past, a lack of such qualified personnel forced recruitment of parole officers whose basic orientation stemmed from other disciplines (e.g., law enforcement officers, teachers, investigators, custodial personnel from prisons, etc.). These officers often favored the "watchdog" model of parole supervision, whereby the officer's constant expectation that the parolee would fail did indeed produce such failure (a variation on the "self-fulfilling prophecy").[22] The vast expansion of parole services in the last two decades has attracted more professionals from the social sciences, especially social workers. This trend, if it continues, will assist in the overall goal of professionalizing corrections as a whole.

Since social workers are becoming more prominent in the field of parole supervision, the old caseload issue has arisen as a persistent and continuing problem. As early as 1931, the government's *Report on Penal Institutions, Probation and Parole* (the Wickersham Report) recommended that the caseload for parole officers should average no more than fifty[23]—at a time when only a little over 50 percent of all offenders were released on parole supervision. In 1967, the average caseload for parole officers ran from a low of 40 to a high of 93, depending on the state. (If the officers' probation cases and other workloads are added in, the low becomes 73 and the high 245!) Even the increased number of officers today could not begin to handle the 1967 caseload on a 50-per-officer basis—and the current load is at least 14 percent greater than it was in 1967.

Actually, research has shown that it is not the number of cases each parole officer handles that makes the biggest difference in outcome.[24] Rather, the *type* of case as it relates to the background and experience of the parole officer is the key to his or her effectiveness. Some officers can handle as many as 100 fairly simple cases in which parolees require little assistance to lead a crime-free existence in the community, while the same officers could barely handle a caseload of ten complicated cases. The message is clear. Administrators must emphasize a differential assignment of cases, keeping in mind such factors as the complexity of the cases, the type of offenders, and the background and ability of the parole officer. A proper assignment would match parolees who need minimal attention and reporting with officers whose background stresses enforcement and custody, and parolees whose problems are more extensive with officers who have had social work experience. The National Advisory Commission on Standards and Goals addresses this issue in drawing up its standards:

Measures of Control

Each state should take immediate action to reduce parole rules to an absolute minimum, retaining only those critical in the individual case, and to provide for effective means of enforcing the conditions established.

1. After considering suggestions from correctional staff and preferences of the individual, parole boards should establish in each case the specific parole conditions appropriate for the individual offender.

2. Parole staff should be able to request the board to amend rules to fit the needs of each case and should be empowered to require the parolee to obey any such rule when put in writing, pending the final action of the parole board.

3. Special caseloads for intensive supervision should be established and staffed by personnel of suitable skill and temperament. Careful review procedures should be established to determine which offenders should be assigned or removed from such caseloads.

4. Parole officers should develop close liaison with police agencies, so that any formal arrests necessary can be made by police. Parole officers, therefore, would not need to be armed.

Manpower for Parole

By 1975, each state should develop a comprehensive manpower and training program which would make it possible to recruit persons with a wide variety of skills, including significant numbers of minority group members and volunteers, and use them effectively in parole programs.

Among the elements of state manpower and training programs for corrections that are prescribed [elsewhere], the following apply with special force to parole.

1. A functional workload system linking specific tasks to different categories of parolees should be instituted by each state and should form the basis of allocating manpower resources.

2. The bachelor's degree should constitute the requisite educational level for the beginning parole officer.

3. Provisions should be made for the employment of parole personnel having less than a college degree to work with parole officers on a team basis, carrying out the tasks appropriate to their individual skills.

4. Career ladders that offer opportunities for advancement of persons with less than college degrees should be provided.

5. Recruitment efforts should be designed to provide a staff roughly proportional in ethnic background to the offender population being served.

6. Ex-offenders should receive high priority consideration for employment in parole agencies.[25]

Clearly, the rising number of parolees creates a fertile field for the criminal justice professional.

Emerging Issues in Parole

While parole has taken its place as one of the most important areas of the correctional spectrum, it still presents some problems for administrators, and it has its share of enemies. One of the most crucial problems is the selection of parole authority personnel. It is very difficult to decide between candidates from *within* the department, who might be hesitant to challenge a system that gave them their chance, and candidates from *outside* the system, who might be uninformed and politically motivated individuals willing to use the position for personal gain. Standards have been suggested for the selection of parole authority personnel,[26] but they do not guarantee that boards will display the expertise and skills required. The only really effective way to ensure qualified boards is to make the standards part of the statutes—thus removing the selection process from the political arena. Among other considerations, these statutory measures should permit qualified ex-offenders to serve, especially as hearing examiners.[27] No one could be as sensitive as an ex-offender to an inmate's tension and uncertainty when trying to present his or her case to the parole board. In addition to careful selection of board members based on statutory criteria, administrators must require that parole personnel undergo extensive training in recent legal decisions, advances in technology, and current correctional practices in the institutions they will serve. The government's Standards and Goals Commission has recommended that such training be provided on a national scale.[28]

Another major problem is the board's need for adequate information from which to make a parole decision. Daniel Glaser has suggested a revised reporting system, in which staff members having the most contact with the inmate (invariably the custodial personnel) would provide a different kind of data for the board's decision.[29] Currently, the principal source for data is staff reports describing the inmate's adjustment to *institutional* life; a focus on the inmate's potential for reintegration into the *free* community would be much more helpful to the board.

By the time inmates have fully adjusted to the institutional life (become *institutionalized*), it may be difficult if not impossible to reintegrate them into the free world. Techniques for determining their "readiness" for parole must be as efficient as possible, since studies have shown that once they go beyond that *ready* point, their chances for successful readjustment are significantly diminished. Modern informational technology could provide such data, if correctional administrators and parole authorities were willing to develop and use the required procedures.

One critical issue that has begun to shape parole procedures in recent years concerns court intervention. In the past, courts viewed hearings to grant and revoke parole as administrative matters, outside court jurisdiction—the "hands off" doctrine. Starting in 1963 with *Hyser* v. *Reed*,[30] however, the courts began to chip away at the informal and discretionary structure of the revocation hearings. The due process question was perhaps expressed best in a 1970 federal circuit court case, *Murray* v. *Page:*

> Therefore, while a prisoner does not have a constitutional right to parole, once paroled he cannot be deprived of his freedom by means inconsistent with due process. The minimal right of the parolee to be informed of the charges and the nature of the evidence against him and to appear to be heard at the revocation hearing is inviolate. Statutory deprivation of this right is manifestly inconsistent with due process and is unconstitutional; nor can such right be lost by the subjective determination of the executive that the case for revocation is "clear."[31]

This issue was finally decided in 1972 by the United States Supreme Court in *Morrissey* v. *Brewer*. The Supreme Court held that:

> [T]he liberty of a parolee, although indeterminate, includes many of the core values of unqualified liberty and its termination inflicts a "grievous loss" on the parolee and often on others. It is hardly useful any longer to try to deal with this problem in terms of whether the parolee's liberty is a "right" or a "privilege." By whatever name the liberty is valuable and must be seen as within the protection of the Fourteenth Amendment. Its termination calls for some orderly process, however informal.[32]

Now that the courts have seen fit to apply the due process issue to parole *revocation* hearings, it seems probable that hearings to *grant* parole will be held up to the same standards.

The last major issue concerns the provision of community services to the parolee. While many parolees could probably do quite well with little or no supervision, others require extensive help in the community. The need to provide services in such areas as mental health, family counseling, employment, personal relations, and the whole spectrum of human problems will change and expand the role of parole officers. They must become services brokers, thoroughly acquainted with the forms of assistance available to their clients. This new role requires a broad knowledge of the organizational structure and power base of the community in which they must operate. The present prejudices against the ex-offender population will be magnified as more and more are supervised in the community on parole. The parole officers of the future will need considerable negotiation and administrative skills to make the system operate successfully.

Summary

We have seen that nearly every offender who enters prison is eventually released in some fashion. The question to ask is not "When?" but more precisely "How?"; and most often, today, the answer is *parole*. Two basic functions are involved in parole: the *surveillance* function, ensuring adequate supervision and control (in the form of a parole officer) to prevent future criminal activity, and the *helping* function, marshalling community resources to support the parolee in establishing noncriminal behavior patterns.

The parole process is a series of steps which include an appearance before a parole authority, establishment of a set of conditions to be met by the parolee, the assignment to a parole officer followed by regular meetings with the officer, appearance at a revocation hearing if parole is violated, and the eventual release from conditional supervision. This process has been changed or modified by the heat of public opinion and court decisions.

While the parole process is a valuable aid to the corrections system, it is far from perfect.[33] The quality of personnel, at both the parole authority and parole officer levels, must be greatly improved. Salary levels, tenure regulations, and professional standards have been described and recommended. If these standards are met, the parole officer will become a true professional in a short period of time.

All offenders should be placed on parole as soon as they are first eligible unless one of the following conditions exists:

1. There is a substantial indication that they will not conform to conditions of parole.

2. Their release at that time would depreciate the seriousness of the crime or promote disrespect for the law.

3. Their release would have substantially adverse effects on institutional discipline.

4. Their continued correctional treatment, medical care, or vocational or other training in the institution will substantially enhance their capacity to lead a law-abiding life when released at a later date.[34]

The greatest need in parole is a method to determine the moment when inmates are most likely to benefit from parole, so that quick action can be taken to release them from the institutional setting at that time.

REVIEW QUESTIONS

I. Find the answers to the following in the text:

    1. Differentiate between determinate and indefinite sentences.

    2. What are the three basic models of parole boards?

    3. What are the basic differences between parole and probation?

    4. Why should parole boards be independent of institutions?

II. Words to identify:

    1. flopped

    2. good time

    3. pardon

    4. conditional release

    5. commutation

    6. amnesty

    7. self-fulfilling prophecy

    8. institutionalized

    9. revocation

    10. surveillance

NOTES

1. Cesare Beccaria. *An Essay on Crimes and Punishments*, trans. Henry Paolucci (Indianapolis, In.: Bobbs-Merrill, 1963), p. 99.

2. Harry Elmer Barnes and Negley K. Teeters, *New Horizons in Criminology*, 3d ed. (Englewood Cliffs, N.J.: Prentice-Hall, 1959), p. 568.

3. See chapter 8, note 4.

4. Brockway pressed for the use of parole and the indeterminate sentence mainly because of the prostitutes who were being shuttled in and out of the Detroit House of Corrections.

5. National Advisory Commision on Criminal Justice Standards and Goals, *Corrections* (Washington, D.C.: U.S. Department of Justice, 1973), p. 389.

6. New Hampshire and Washington.

7. Wayne Morse, *The Attorney General's Survey of Release Procedures* (Washington, D.C.: U.S. Government Printing Office, 1939).

8. Dr. Samuel G. Howe, husband of famed suffragist and reformer Julia Ward Howe, is credited with the first use of the word "parole" in its present sense. It originally meant "word" (of honor) not to commit further crimes.

9. National Advisory Commission, *Corrections*, p. 396.

10. National Advisory Commission, *Corrections*, p. 396.

11. National Advisory Commission, *Corrections*, p. 397.

12. National Advisory Commission, *Corrections*, p. 412.

13. Joseph E. Scott, "An Examination of the Factors Utilized by Parole Boards in Determining the Severity of Punishment" (Ph.D. dissertation, Indiana University, 1972), pp. 57-59.

14. *Flopped* is inmate slang for failure to meet the parole board standards for acceptance. A flop usually means that the inmate will not be eligible to come up before the board until after another six months or more of observation in the institution.

15. Everette M. Porter, "Criteria for Parole Selection," in *Proceedings of the American Correctional Association* (New York: ACA, 1958), p. 227.

16. The President's Commission on Law Enforcement and Administration of Justice, *Task Force Report: Corrections* (Washington, D.C.: U.S. Government Printing Office, 1967), p. 185.

17. Walter C. Reckless, *The Crime Problem*, 4th ed. (New York: Appleton-Century-Crofts, 1967), p. 761.

18. State of Ohio, Department of Rehabilitation and Correction, Adult Parole Authority, *Statement of Parole Agreement (APA-271)* (Columbus, Ohio: State of Ohio, 1973).

19. A *technical violation* generally refers to a violation that is not criminal, but is prohibited by the conditions of the parole agreement. It is the technical violation that has generated concern about the possibility of capricious and arbitary parole revocation by the officer.

20. "Reintegration Centers" are located in Columbus, Cleveland, and Cincinnati. They are designed to house technical parole violators for 60-90 days and treat their immediate problems through programmed learning techniques and concerned supervision.

21. *Task Force Report: Corrections*, p. 8.

22. Robert K. Merton is credited with elucidating the concept of the self-fulfilling prophecy: If those around a prison *expect* an inmate to behave in a certain way—to be stupid or brilliant, successful or a failure—their expectations will tend to shape his or her behavior.

23. National Commission on Law Observance and Enforcement, *Report on Penal Institutions, Probation and Parole* (Washington, D.C.: U.S. Government Printing Office, 1931), p. 325.

24. James Robinson et al., *The San Francisco Project*, Research Report No. 14 (Berkeley, Calif.: University of California School of Criminology, 1969).

25. National Advisory Commission, *Corrections*, p. 435.

26. National Advisory Commission, *Corrections*, p. 420.

27. See P. McAnany and E. Tromanhauser, "Organizing the Convicted: Self-Help for Prisoners and Ex-cons." *Crime and Delinquency* 23 (January 1977): 68-74.

28. National Advisory Commission, *Corrections,* p. 414.

29. Daniel Glaser, *The Effectiveness of a Prison and Parole System* (New York: Bobbs-Merrill, 1964), chap. 9.

30. *Hyser* v. *Reed,* 318 2d 225, 235 (D.C. Cir. 1963). The United States Court of Appeals, District of Columbia, held that constitutional due process does not require the Board of Parole to conduct adversary proceedings like a nonjury trial in order to revoke parole and does not require the appointment of counsel for indigent parolees, cross-examination of sources of information, disclosure of the Board's files, or compulsory process granting court authority to the parolee to subpoena witnesses.

31. *Murray* v. *Page,* 429 F. 2d 1359 (10th Cir. 1970). The court established that although prisoners do not have a constitutional right to parole, they cannot be deprived of their freedom, once paroled, by means inconsistent with due process. More specifically, as parolees they retain the right to be informed of the charges and nature of evidence against them and the right to be heard at the revocation hearing.

32. *Morrissey* v. *Brewer,* 408 U.S. 471 (1972). The court held that at a revocation of parole hearing, the following elements of due process are required: (1) written notice of the charges, (2) disclosure to parolees of the evidence against them, (3) the opportunity for parolees to be heard, (4) the right of parolees to confront and cross-examine witnesses, and (5) a neutral hearing body.

33. For a critique, see John R. Manson, "Determinate Sentencing," *Crime and Delinquency* 23 (April 1977): 204-207. See also the "Comments" which follow, pp. 207-214.

34. Glaser, *The Effectiveness of a Prison and Parole,* chap. 9.

RECOMMENDED READING LIST

American Bar Association, *Criminal Appeals.* Washington, D.C.: ABA, 1969,

American Bar Association. *Post-Conviction Remedies.* Washington, D.C.: ABA, 1968.

Carter, Robert M.; Glaser, Daniel; and Wilkins, Leslie T. *Correctional Insititutions.* New York: J.B. Lippincott, 1972.

Clinard, Marshal B., and Quinney, Richard. *Criminal Behavior Systems: A Typology.* New York: Holt, Rinehart & Winston, 1967.

Dawson, Robert O. *Sentencing: The Decision as to Type, Length and Conditions of Sentence.* New York: Little, Brown, 1969.

Dinitz, Simon, and Reckless, Walter C. *Critical Issues in the Study of Crime.* New York: Little, Brown, 1968.

Doleschal, Eugene. *Graduated Release.* Paramus, N.J.: National Council on Crime and Delinquency, 1969.

Dressler, David. *Practice and Theory of Probation and Parole.* New York: Columbia University Press, 1969.

Editors, The Criminal Law Reporter. *The Criminal Law Revolution and Its Aftermath: 1960-1971*. Washington, D.C.: Bureau of National Affairs, 1972.

Ennis, Phillip. *Criminal Victimization in the United States: A Report on a National Survey*. Washington, D.C.: U.S. Government Printing Office, 1967.

Gough, A. R. "The Expungement of Adjudication Records of Juvenile and Adult Offenders." *Washington University Law Quarterly* (1966): 147-190.

Leinwand, Gerald. *Prisons*. New York: Pocket Books, 1972.

Morris, Norval, and Hawkins, Gordon. *The Honest Politician's Guide to Crime Control*. Chicago: University of Chicago Press, 1970.

National Advisory Commission on Criminal Justice Standards and Goals. *Courts*. Washington, D.C.: U.S. Department of Justice, 1973.

Packer, Herbert L. *The Limits of the Criminal Sanction*. Stanford, Calif.: Stanford University Press, 1968.

Robinson, Sophia M. "A Critical View of the Uniform Crime Reports." *Michigan Law Review* 64: 1031-1054.

PART IV

The Rights of the Convicted Criminal

13 Prisoner Rights in Confinement

The price we pay for continued reliance on a system
which fails to rehabilitate, and worse, which distorts
and prevents human capabilities, is the specter of an
increasing number of embittered and alienated
individuals who will continue to explode in the faces of
our children and their children.

SAMUEL DASH

What Is the Convicted Offender's Status?

When defendants have been through the whole criminal justice process,
including all appeals, and their sentences have been upheld, they officially
acquire the status of *convicted offender*. They may already have spent a long
time in prison, as their appeals made their tedious way through the courts.
But with the final guilty verdict in, the offenders' relationship to the
correctional system undergoes a significant change. In this section, we will
examine the offenders' new status and their rights during and after incarceration. Over the years, a body of folklore has grown up about the rights of
prisoners and ex-prisoners. This chapter will explode some of these myths
and clarify recent developments in this critical area.

In early imprisonment sentences, the conviction often involved "civil
death," a cruel form of punishment expressly acknowledging a prisoner's
permanent removal from the free society. In a perverse sense, the civil death
sentence was viewed as a benefit to the prisoner's family; the "widows" of
male prisoners were able to remarry and rebuild a shattered life. Today,
except in rare cases, convicted offenders eventually return to the community
from which they came. Their families may try to hold together until they are
released, when the ex-prisoners must begin to cope again with the free
world.

Imprisonment by its very nature deprives the offender of some constitutional rights. It is not clear, however, which of those rights must be
completely sacrificed and which may be retained, perhaps in modified form.
Prison officials have always been able to wield enormous power over the
lives of incarcerated offenders. In the days when the entire purpose of

imprisonment was *punishment*, the rights of offenders seemed unimportant. Because they seldom returned to the community, neither they nor their families were likely to complain that the offenders' rights had been infringed. As the philosophy of penology moved toward rehabilitation, however, the complete deprivation of rights became intolerable.

With over one and one-half million[1] people subject to the control of some kind of correctional authority in America each day, the status of those convicted offenders poses a significant question. Correctional officials have been slow to develop internal policies and procedures to guide their administrators in protecting the rights of offenders. Under the "hands-off" policy mentioned earlier, the courts were reluctant to criticize decisions and procedures developed by correctional administrators. That policy was abandoned in the mid-'60s, opening the door to case after case in regard to prisoners' rights with no end in sight. Prison practices with regard to convicted offenders' rights have ranged from total loss upon conviction to many shades of loss in between, but the new movement is toward the standards recommended by the National Advisory Commission:

> Each state should immediately enact legislation that defines and implements the substantive rights of offenders. Such legislation should be governed by the following principles:
>
> 1. Offenders should be entitled to the same rights as free citizens, except where the nature of confinement necessarily requires modification.
>
> 2. Where modification of the rights of offenders is required by the nature of custody, such modification should be as limited as possible.
>
> 3. The duty of showing that custody requires modification of such rights should be upon the correctional agency.
>
> 4. Such legislation should implement substantive rights.
>
> 5. Such legislation should provide adequate means for enforcement of the rights so defined. It should authorize the remedies for violations of the rights of offenders, where they do not already exist.[2]

Community Ties: A Basic Need

The vestiges of civil death are probably most visible in those correctional practices which relate to the privilege of having visitors. There is continuous debate as to whether the visitor privilege is in fact a right. The practice is not new; occasional visitors were allowed even as early as the Walnut Street Jail. If a prisoner were diligent and good, he was allowed a visit from a close family member . . . but only once every three months, for fifteen minutes, through two grills, and under the scrutiny of a keeper.[3] This procedure may seem absurdly strict, but it closely resembles current practices in many correctional institutions. The security psychosis at most prisons dictates that visits be limited and subject to highly regimented conditions, likely to discourage close physical or emotional contact. The dehumanizing rules and procedures for visiting do not accord with modern goals of rehabilitation and correction. While security is important in maximum security prisons, it would seem that security could be tempered with humanity in such a personal thing as a visit from a friend or family member.

Limitations on visiting hours, restricted visitor lists, overcrowded visiting rooms, and the constant presence of guards all contribute to the inmate's difficulty in maintaining ties with the outside world. Most institutions are located far from large urban centers (where most inmates' families live), requiring long hours of travel and expense for visitors.[4] Not only family ties, but friendships as well must wither under these conditions. This alienation creates serious problems for both the inmate and the institution. Typically, an inmate receives a visitor once a month, usually a member of his or her immediate family. This is hardly representative of social life in contemporary America.

For the married inmate, family ties are inevitably weakened by long separation. The social consequences of near-inevitable divorce to the family, community, and institution are incalculable; imprisonment itself is grounds for divorce in some jurisdictions.[5] Institution officials often face severe problems caused by deterioration of an inmate's family situation. When, for example, a wife does not write, or the inmate hears through the grapevine that she has a lover, violence can and often does result—expressed in attacks against prison personnel or another prisoner, or even in escape.

Deprived of even a semblance of normal relations with the outside, the inmate turns to the other inmates and the inmate subculture for solace. It seems ironic that inmates are cut off from both friends and relatives and drawn entirely into the company of criminals, while some parole rules forbid association of the parolee with known ex-offenders. Such paradoxical situations seem to counter the basic premises of American corrections. There is no better way to combat the inmate social system and prepare an inmate for freedom than by strengthening his or her ties with the outside world. The Ohio Citizens' Task Force on Corrections recommended that:

1. Every effort be made to bring the community into the prison and the prisoner into the community.

2. With due regard for the well-being of the individual and the welfare of the institutional community,

relatives, appropriate friends, civic groups, church groups and volunteers be encouraged to visit individual prisoners and to participate in group programs in our institutions.

3. Visiting rules be standardized and made as liberal as possible.

4. Visiting hours be so arranged as to give the greatest possible latitude to families arriving from a distance.

5. Visiting hours be extended to weekends and evenings at all institutions, *even* if this necessitates hiring additional staff.[6]

Another form of visitation, employed in many foreign countries and at least one state,[7] is the so-called conjugal visit. In Sweden this is generally referred to as an unsupervised visit. The strong feelings generated over this issue relate to the common belief that part of the inmate's punishment should be the loss of his or her sexual outlet. In the Swedish system the sexual aspect of the visit is not questioned. As Torsten Eriksson, former Director of Prisons in Sweden, has stated:

> The question whether an inmate shall be permitted to have sexual intercourse with his wife or a female inmate with her husband within the institution is the subject of considerable discussion in many countries. In the Latin American countries this is regarded as obvious and even necessary to the inmate's mental health; the Anglo-Saxons, on the other hand, usually regard it as an impossibility. In Sweden we generally allow unsupervised visits in the open institutions. An inmate may take a visitor to his private room, whether it is his father, mother, brother, sister, wife, fiancée, or someone else close to him. Since the inmate has a key to his room, nobody pays any attention if he locks himself in with his visitor. Moreover, unsupervised visits in special rooms may be permitted in closed institutions also. I do not know whether sexual intercourse occurs during such visits, although I can always hazard a guess. In our opinion, sexuality is strictly a personal matter. We do not ask questions, we make no special provisions. We merely ask whether the individual inmate can be trusted to receive a visitor without supervision.[8]

Research on the relative effectiveness of conjugal visiting or unsupervised visits in the United States has not been extensive, but conjugal visiting is believed to strengthen family ties, reduce homosexuality among inmates, lessen tensions between officers and inmates, make inmates easier to manage, and lessen isolation from the outside community. Opponents argue that it puts too much emphasis on the physical aspects of marriage, is unfair to the unmarried resident, raises welfare costs through increased family size, and decreases the intensity of punishment to offenders.

It seems probable that our Anglo-Saxon heritage will negate conjugal visitation reforms in this country on a par with those in Sweden. The logical solution here, used increasingly, is the home furlough. This permits the deserving prisoner to visit his or her family under unsupervised circumstances in a natural situation. So far, where it has been used, the home furlough has not resulted in mass escapes or crime waves. This is but another step in the march toward community corrections. Ties with family and friends are critical to the rehabilitation of offenders, and correctional administrators must provide them with maximum opportunities to maintain these ties. The National Advisory Commission also addressed the problem of the prisoner's access to the public:

Each correctional agency should develop and implement immediately policies and procedures to fulfill the right of offenders to communicate with the public. Correctional regulations limiting such communication should be consistent. Questions of right of access to the public arise primarily in the context of regulations affecting mail, personal visitation, and the communications media.

MAIL. Offenders should have the right to communicate or correspond with persons or organizations and to send and receive letters, packages, books, periodicals, and any other material that can be lawfully mailed. The following additional guidelines should apply:

1. Correctional authorities should not limit the volume of mail to or from a person under supervision.

2. Correctional authorities should have the right to inspect incoming and outgoing mail, but neither incoming nor outgoing mail should be read or censored. Cash, checks, or money orders should be removed from incoming mail and credited to offenders' accounts. If contraband is discovered in either incoming or outgoing mail, it may be removed. Only illegal items and items which threaten the security of the institution should be considered contraband.

3. Offenders should receive a reasonable postage allowance to maintain community ties.

VISITATION. Offenders should have the right to communicate in person with individuals of their own choosing. The following additional guidelines should apply:

1. Correctional authorities should not limit the number of visitors an offender may receive or the length of such visits except in accordance with regular institutional schedules and requirements.

2. Correctional authorities should facilitate and promote visitation of offenders by the following acts:

   a. Providing transportation for visitors from terminal points of public transportation. In some instances, the correctional agency may wish to pay the entire transportation costs of family members where the offender and the family are indigent.

   b. Providing appropriate rooms for visitation that allow ease and informality of communication in a natural environment as free from institutional or custodial attributes as possible.

   c. Making provisions for family visits in private surroundings conducive to maintaining and strengthening family ties.

3. The correctional agency may supervise the visiting area in an unobtrusive manner, but should not eavesdrop on conversations or otherwise interfere with the participants' privacy.

MEDIA. Except in emergencies such as institutional disorders, offenders should be allowed to present their views through the communications media. Correctional authorities should encourage and facilitate the flow of information between the media and offenders by authorizing offenders, among other things, to:

1. Grant confidential and uncensored interviews to representatives of the media. Such interviews should be scheduled not to disrupt regular institutional schedules unduly unless during a newsworthy event.

2. Send uncensored letters and other communications to the media.

3. Publish articles or books on any subject.

4. Display and sell original creative works.

As used in this standard, the term "media" encompasses any printed or electronic means of conveying information to the public including but not limited to newspapers, magazines, books, or other publications regardless of the size or nature of their circulation and licensed radio and television broadcasting. Representatives of the media should be allowed access to all correctional facilities for reporting items of public interest consistent with the preservation of offenders' privacy.

Offenders should be entitled to receive any lawful publication, or radio and television broadcast.[9]

Use of the Mails

The mail system is closely tied to visitation, as another essential contact with the outside world. As in the case of visits, stated reasons for the limitation and censorship of mail are tied either to security or to the orderly administration of the prison. Although the use of the mail system is a right, case law has established that correctional administrators can place *reasonable* restrictions on prisoners in the exercise of this right.[10] As with most situations behind the walls, over the years mail rules were systematically stiffened to facilitate the smooth operation of the institutions. If it became too much of an administrative burden to read all the incoming and outgoing mail, the number of letters or the list of correspondents was reduced. Eventually, a small maximum of allowed letters and very restrictive lists of correspondents became the standard. As long as the prisoners could not turn to the courts, this practice did not create a stir. When the attorneys appointed to help prisoners began to see the unjustness of restrictions concerning mail and other "privileges," they began to question the rules and reestablish these "privileges" as rights.

How much mail should a prisoner receive? Administrators have usually restricted it to an amount which could readily be censored. During personnel shortages (e.g., wars) the amount of mail was often limited to one letter a month. Outgoing mail was similarly restricted. The general rule for communications with an attorney is that they may be opened and read, but not censored unless they refer to plans for illegal activity or contain contraband.[11] More recently court decisions have tended to imply that most censorship of communications between inmates and their lawyers is unconstitutional; this direction also appears in decisions regarding communications with the news media.

In the situation where an inmate wishes to communicate with a second inmate, either a friend or "jailhouse lawyer," at another institution, the courts have stuck to a hands-off policy, leaving this problem to the discretion of the administrators. The general policy has been to prohibit the passage of any correspondence between inmates. This policy is under attack, however, and has been rejected by some states.[12] In most court cases, the test for permissibility of mail and literature has been the "clear and present danger" standard:

We accept the premise that certain literature may pose such a clear and present danger to the security of a prison, or to the rehabilitation of prisoners, that it should be censored. To take an extreme example, if there were mailed to a prisoner a brochure demonstrating in detail how to saw prison bars with utensils used in the mess hall, or how to provoke a prison riot, it would properly be screened. A magazine detailing for incarcerated drug addicts how they might obtain an euphoric "high," comparable to that experienced from heroin, by sniffing aerosol or glue available for other purposes within the prison walls, would likewise be censorable as restraining effective rehabilitation. Furthermore, it is undoubtedly true that in the volatile atmosphere of a prison, where a large number of men, many with criminal tendencies, live in close proximity to each other, violence can be fomented by the printed word much more easily than in the outside world. Some censorship or prior restraint on inflammatory literature sent into prisons is, therefore, necessary to prevent such literature from being used to cause disruption or violence within the prison. It may well be that in some prisons where the prisoners' flash-point is low, articles regarding bombing, prison riots, or the like, which would be harmless when sold on the corner newsstand, would be too dangerous for release to the prison population.[13]

Ohio took the lead in the reform of mail censorship, eliminating all of it in Ohio's prisons on August 3, 1973.[14] Under the Ohio system, both incoming and outgoing mail is merely inspected for contraband and delivered unread. Each inmate may write and receive an unlimited number of items of mail. Since the adoption of these standards, they apparently have caused few if any problems.

Religion in Prison

The basic idea underlying the penitentiary was drawn from religious precepts. It seems ironic that there would be any conflict in providing freedom of religion in prisons, but this has been the case. The early efforts to restore the criminal through penitence and prayer were conducted in small homogeneous communities. As immigration to America expanded, it became the most heterogeneous nation in the world. Since the United States was founded on a belief that freedom of worship could not be infringed by the government, the First Amendment addressed these issues: "Congress shall make no law respecting an *establishment* of religion, or prohibiting the *free exercise* thereof . . . [emphasis added]."[15] It is the basic conflict between what constitutes an *established* religion and the individual's right to exercise it that has caused grief in the nation's prisons.

A clear example of this problem would be the Black Muslim decision, which has dominated case law for over a decade. After a long string of cases,[16] the courts finally held that the Black Muslim faith *did* constitute an established religion, and that the Muslims were therefore entitled to follow the practices that religion prescribed. The resolution of the Black Muslim issue means that the standards applied there can be applied to any duly recognized religion. This puts a strain on the prison administrator, who must allow equal protection for all inmates. The question of whether the state really grants each inmate "free exercise" simply by ensuring access to a minister of his or her particular faith is still being settled. It is clear that totally free exercise of all religions would result in chaos in a closed environment such as a prison. However, administrators have been alerted that religious freedoms are of special interest to the courts and will receive strong review, with the burden resting on the correctional administration to prove why restrictions were imposed.

Access to Court and Counsel

Access to the federal courts was not established as a constitutional right for inmates until 1940, in a case called *Ex Parte Hull*.[17] In this decision, the United States Supreme Court established that "the state and its officers may not abridge or impair a petitioner's right to apply to a federal court for a writ of habeas corpus." Despite this clear ruling, the courts still maintained a strict hands-off policy in this regard until the 1969 case of *Johnson* v. *Avery*.[18] This case established the right of prisoners who could not afford adequate legal assistance to use "jailhouse lawyers" in the preparation of habeas corpus proceedings. The need for the smooth operation of the prison was subordinated to the right to habeas corpus.

Once the prisoners' right to use jailhouse lawyers was established, inmates needed to be assured of an adequate supply of legal research materials. And in 1971, the case of *Younger* v. *Gilmore*[19] guaranteed the inmate writ writers such assistance. But the *extent* of materials provided has varied considerably, from complete law libraries in the state prisons to the bare essentials elsewhere. It seems that the courts must continue to require that administrations provide adequate legal counsel to inmates, or they will have to live with the continued use of jailhouse lawyers and the problems that result.

The right to consult with counsel has been clearly established. The problem, before *Gideon* and the cases it generated, was that most inmates could not afford a lawyer to defend them or prepare later appeals. And early prison rules restricted the use of jailhouse lawyers, so few prisoners were able to file writs in the federal courts. After the courts established the right to counsel, those administrative agencies that could not or would not comply were covered by *Johnson* v. *Avery*. While not all jurisdictions have been able to provide counsel for all inmates, the remedies incorporated in the court decisions have helped to fill the void—incidentally creating a flood of writs.

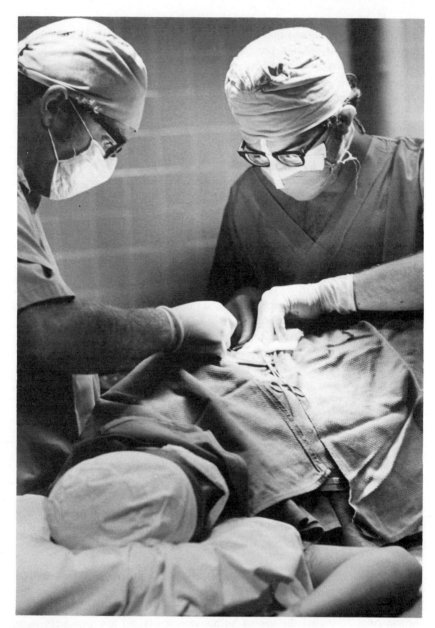

FIGURE IV–1. Surgical Treatment in a Federal Prison (Courtesy
Federal Bureau of Prisons)

The Right to Medical Treatment and Services

The issue of adequate medical care in our prisons has finally prompted a
decision from the United States Supreme Court. Only when a constitution-

ally guaranteed right has been violated has the Court become involved in the provision of medical care. Because both medical programs and the backgrounds of prison medical personnel are extremely diversified, the quality of medical aid varies among institutions.

The U.S. Supreme Court has chosen to take the position that inmates in state prisons should seek remedy in the state courts. In the 1976 case of *Estelle* v. *Gamble*[20] this position was made even more clear. While suits in the past have shown that prisoners' rights to proper diagnosis and medical treatment of illness have been violated on a grand scale, the courts have moved slowly in this area. In *Estelle* v. *Gamble,* however, the Court stated: "We therefore conclude that deliberate indifference to serious medical needs of prisoners constitutes the unnecessary and wanton infliction of pain . . . proscribed by the Eighth Amendment. This is true whether the indifference is manifested by prison doctors in their response to the prisoner's needs or by prison guards in intentionally denying or delaying access to medical care or intentionally interfering with the treatment once prescribed."[21] This is a giant step forward in provision of medical treatment, but it still falls short of the individual remedies provided by decisions in other areas.

Gamble provides a position of sympathy for complaints about the systemwide failure to provide adequate and humane medical care. The test of *deliberate indifference,* however, a requirement for evoking the Eighth Amendment, seems to be a major hurdle for most who chose to use *Gamble* as a basis for action. Mere negligence or malpractice leaves the prisoner with remedy only in a state civil case. Total deprivation of medical service seems to be the current standard for application of Constitutional prohibitions.

Many times the federal courts have been forced to overlook the issue of constitutional rights to correct situations involving a flagrant disregard of the need for adequate medical service. This disregard has often produced prison riots in the past, and it will continue to be a factor in right-to-treatment cases over the next decade. Right to treatment is covered in detail in chapter 24.

Remedies for Violations of Rights

The first steps to remedy the almost standard practice of depriving convicted offenders of *all* rights have been taken, starting with the recognition that the Constitution does entitle these individuals to retain a substantial portion of their rights, even while incarcerated. The push for this recognition has come from the offenders themselves, often with the assistance of jailhouse lawyers, and has resulted in active and sympathetic judicial intervention. The writ of habeas corpus, designed as a tool for prisoners to test the legality of their confinement, has been the main weapon in the battle for prisoner rights. This battle continues today, especially with regard to increased maintenance of community ties and the abolition of the death penalty.

Strengthening the offender's rights has been a major area of study for the National Advisory Commission. This issue is highly charged, and correctional authorities are understandably concerned that the press for rights may disrupt the programs at their institutions. The standards suggested by the Commission attempt to address the central problems:

> Each correctional agency immediately should adopt policies and procedures, and where applicable should seek legislation, to insure proper redress where an offender's rights are abridged.

1. Administrative remedies, not requiring the intervention of a court, should include at least the following:

   a. Procedures allowing an offender to seek redress where he believes his rights have been or are about to be violated.

   b. Policies of inspection and supervision to assure periodic evaluation of institutional conditions and staff practices that may affect offenders' rights.

   c. Policies which:

      (1) Assure wide distribution and understanding of the rights of offenders among both offenders and correctional staff.

      (2) Provide that the intentional or persistent violation of an offender's rights is justification for removal from office or employment of any correctional worker.

      (3) Authorize the payment of claims to offenders as compensation for injury caused by a violation of any right.

2. Judicial remedies for violation of rights should include at least the following:

   a. Authority for an injunction either prohibiting a practice violative of an offender's rights or requiring affirmative action on the part of governmental officials to assure compliance with offenders' rights.

   b. Authority for an award of damages against either the correctional agency or, in appropriate circumstances, the staff member involved to compensate the offender for injury caused by a violation of his rights.

c. Authority for the court to exercise continuous supervision of a correctional facility or program including the power to appoint a special master responsible to the court to oversee implementation of offenders' rights.

d. Authority for the court to prohibit further commitments to an institution or program.

e. Authority for the court to shut down an institution or program and require either the transfer or release of confined or supervised offenders.

f. Criminal penalties for intentional violations of an offender's rights.[22]

The remaining chapters in this section address some of the issues these standards focus on, as they affect the operation of America's correctional institutions.

A New Shift in Direction

A string of Supreme Court decisions has slowed the trend toward judicial recognition of prisoner rights:

- In two cases, the high court reversed lower courts and upheld blanket prohibitions against reporters' interviews with prisoners (*Pell* v. *Procunier* and *Saxbe* v. *Washington Post Co.*). The cases arose from litigation against the U.S. Bureau of Prisons and the California penal system.

  Justice Potter Stewart, writing for the court, noted that the regulations barring most face-to-face communications with newsmen were promulgated because such interviews had deleterious effects on prison security and discipline. Justice William O. Douglas, joined by Justices William J. Brennan, Jr., and Thurgood Marshall, objected to giving such unfettered powers to administrators without safeguards.

- The court in *Woff* v. *McDonnell* refused to grant prisoners in disciplinary hearings, where they were threatened with loss of good time or solitary confinement, the full panoply of procedural rights permitted in parole and probation revocation hearings in the famous *Morrissey* v. *Brewer* and *Gagnon* v. *Scarpelli* cases. The court ruled that inmates must be given written notice of the alleged infraction at least twenty-four hours prior to the hearing and said that reasons for its decision should be given in writing by the disciplinary panel. However, the court refused to hold that inmates are entitled to counsel or to cross-examine the witnesses against them.

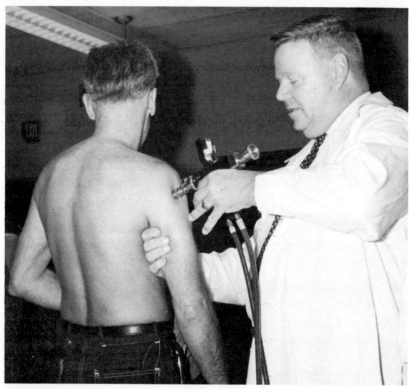

FIGURE IV–2. Immunization, a Part of Most In-Processing (Courtesy Ohio Department of Rehabilitation and Correction)

- The tribunal ruled that the Fourteenth Amendment, which permits disenfranchisement for "participation in rebellion, or other crime," permits California to deny voting rights to ex-convicts (*Richardson* v. *Ramirez*). The three-judge dissent argued that the California Supreme Court's judgment invalidating the law rests on an adequate and independent state ground and therefore should not be taken up by the U.S. high court. (In 1974, California voters altered the state constitution so that ex-convicts would be allowed to vote.)

- The Supreme Court ruled that a judge does not have to give reasons for sentencing a youth as an adult rather than under the applicable provisions of the Youth Corrections Act of 1960 (*Dorszynski* v. *U.S.*)[23]

If the Burger Court continues to de-emphasize prisoner rights (as seems likely), reformers will have to focus their efforts on correctional administrators. The movement toward change will lose some impetus, at least for the next few years, but it will not come to a standstill.

REVIEW QUESTIONS

I. Find the answers to the following in the text:

    1. Why is it important for offenders to retain their ties with the community?

    2. What is the difference between conjugal visits and unsupervised visits?

    3. What is the name of the writ which tests the legality of confinement?

II. Words to identify:

    1. jailhouse lawyer

    2. habeas corpus

    3. conjugal visit

    4. censorship

    5. contraband

    6. hands-off policy

    7. Black Muslims

    8. establishment of religion

    9. free exercise of religion

    10. legal remedy

NOTES

1. National Advisory Commission on Criminal Justice Standards and Goals, *Corrections* (Washington, D.C.: U.S. Government Printing Office, 1973), p. 558.

2. National Advisory Commission, *Corrections,* p. 439.

3. Harry Elmer Barnes and Negley K. Teeters, *New Horizons in Criminology,* 3d ed. (Englewood Cliffs, N.J.: Prentice-Hall, 1959), p. 505.

4. Ohio Citizens' Task Force on Corrections, *Final Report* (Columbus, Ohio: Ohio Department of Urban Affairs, 1972), p. C-66.

5. Imprisonment is grounds for divorce in Ohio and a number of other states.

6. Ohio Citizens' Task Force, p. C-67.

7. The only state where the conjugal visit is a matter of statutory right is Mississippi.

8. Torsten Eriksson, from a speech to a group in Sydney, Australia, unpublished. He was the Director of Prisons in Sweden.

9. National Advisory Commission, *Corrections,* p. 66.

10. *Brown* v. *Wainwright,* 419 F.2d 1308 (5th Cir. 1969); *Ortega* v. *Ragen,* 216 F.2d 561 (7th Cir. 1954); *Medlock* v. *Burke,* 285 F. Supp. 67 (E.D. Wisc. 1968). These three decisions found insufficient justification for federal court interference on behalf of inmates against prison authorities. The *Brown* decision

refused a prisoner's request that a three-judge court be convened to enjoin prison censors from removing postage stamps from his outgoing mail. In *Ortega* v. *Ragen,* civil rights action was denied to a prisoner alleging the warden's failure to deliver letters of appeal. The *Medlock* decision refused the prisoner's appeal for court intervention to prevent alleged deprivation of medical care.

11. *Contraband* is any material that might be used for an escape or to take advantage of the other prisoners inside the prison. Such items as matches, money, pornographic pictures, lubricants, drugs, weapons, and tools are generally considered as contraband. Any items can be placed on the prohibited list if they become a threat to the orderly operation of the prison.

12. Mail between prisoners is allowed in Ohio with no restrictions, except for contraband.

13. *Sostre* v. *Otis,* 330 F. Supp. 941, 944-945 (S.D.N.Y. 1971). The District Court upheld the prisoner's petition against prison officials for interfering with his receipt of literature.

14. Executive Order Number 814 for incoming mail, 814A for outgoing mail, Office of the Governor, State of Ohio, August 3, 1973.

15. First Amendment to the Constitution of the United States (1791).

16. *Knuckles* v. *Prasse,* 435 F. 2d 1255 (3rd Cir. 1970); *Sewell* v. *Pegelow,* 304 F. 2d 670) (4th Cir. 1962); *Banks* v. *Havener,* 234 F. Supp. 27 (E.D.Va. 1964). These three cases dealt with the right of Black Muslim inmates to freedom of religion. In *Knuckles* v. *Prasse,* the Court of Appeals held that prison officials were not required to make available to prisoners Black Muslim publications not properly interpreted by a trained Muslim minister which urged defiance of prison authorities and thus threatened prison security. In the *Sewell* decision, a clear instance of discrimination against a Black Muslim prisoner was brought before the Court of Appeals, which dismissed the case on the grounds that it properly came under the jurisdiction of the District Court. In *Banks* v. *Havener,* responding to a petition under the Civil Rights Act by Black Muslim prisoners, the District Court held that the antipathy of inmates and staff occasioned by the Black Muslims' belief in Black supremacy, standing alone, was not sufficient to justify suppression of the practice of the Black Muslim religion.

17. *Ex Parte Hull,* 312 U.S. 546 (1940). This case upheld the right to petition for a writ of habeas corpus for a parolee whose parole was revoked for committing a second offense.

18. *Johnson* v. *Avery,* 393 U.S. 483, 484 (1969). Through a writ of certiorari, a Court of Appeals decision was reversed in favor of an inmate who had been disciplined for violating a prison regulation which prohibited inmates from assisting other prisoners in preparing writs. The Court of Appeals had reversed a District Court decision which voided the regulation because it had the effect of barring illiterate prisoners from access to general habeas corpus.

19. *Younger* v. *Gilmore,* 92 S.Ct. 250 (1971).

20. *Estelle* v. *Gamble,* 97 S.Ct. 285 (1976).

21. *Estelle* v. *Gamble.*

22. National Advisory Commission, *Corrections,* p. 70.

23. "Supreme Court Decisions May Signal Halt to Expansion of Prisoner's Rights," *Criminal Justice Newsletter* 5 (August 12, 1974): 1.

14 The Use of Force

We decree that no one shall be killed or hung for any misdeeds, but rather that his eyes be plucked out and his feet, hands and testicles cut off, so that whatever part of his body remains will be a living sign to all of his crime and inequity.

WILLIAM THE CONQUEROR

Custody and Control: The Driving Force

The prisons of America are not populated by the cream of polite society. Placed behind walls and deprived of many of their rights and most of the pleasures of society, prisoners sometimes explode in acts of violence. These incidents, over the years, have shaped a custodial philosophy which boils down to "you can't *treat* 'em if you ain't *got* 'em!" In turn, this philosophy has encouraged the development of extensive and detailed prison rules and procedures dealing with every aspect of prisoner control and custody. Searches and shakedowns, tool and key control, property control, visiting, and correspondence are all covered by "rules and regulations." Vernon Fox has compiled the twenty-one most commonly found rules from a sample of over a dozen prison rulebooks across the country:

1. Address employees respectfully.
2. No insolence.
3. No fighting, suffering, or violence [suffering refers to masochistic behavior].
4. No attacking employees.
5. No forcing way through gate.
6. Remove cap when entering chapel, administration building, and other specified places.
7. No gambling.
8. No writing of notes or contacting other inmates.

9. Smoking only in designated places.

10. No profane use of language.

11. No contraband.

12. No trafficking, bartering, or trading.

13. All confiscated articles will be considered contraband and not returnable.

14. When wearing a coat, at least two buttons shall be buttoned.

15. No staring, gesticulating, or speaking to outside visitors.

16. No running—walk!

17. No catcalls, whistling, hissing, or derisive shouting.

18. No sexual perversion.

19. No money.

20. Work on your own case only, making no legal writs for anybody else.

21. Subject to search at any time.[1]

These explicit rules were created to maintain order in the prison, and clearly a prisoner who followed them religiously would have a hard time readjusting to the free world. But the officials who wrote the rules were concerned with controlling the prisoners inside the walls, not with their future after they left.

Most prisons in America are categorized according to the degree of custody employed. They are generally classified as *extreme* security, *maximum* security, *medium* security, and *minimum* security. All except the minimum security prisons also employ secondary grades of custody (according to security requirements) within the primary category. In the supersecure prisons, the maximum security grade prisoners will work, move about, and even receive visitors "under the gun."[2] Lower custody grades move about freely within the walls, or under supervision on outside work details. Grading is based on some evaluation or prediction of the safety risk a given inmate represents to other prisoners, to the staff, or to the offender himself. This determination, often made as the offender is processed into the prison, is usually based in great part on his or her offense. In the interests of security, most prisoners are initially placed in maximum grades until they have proven themselves to be at least reasonable safety risks. Revocation of an offender's favorable custody grade, with the privileges that accompany it, is one of the most common forms of discipline inside the walls. More severe violations of the rules and regulations can sometimes result in loss of "good time" as well.

Another important aspect of control and custody is the *count*. Prisoners in some maximum security prisons are counted as often as every two hours. Any discrepancy in the count results in the triggering of escape alarms, a general upheaval, and paralysis of operations throughout the prison. The usual procedure is to have all prisoners return to their cells and conduct a full head-count in place. The prisoners are usually required to remain in their cells until administrators have verified that no one is missing. Obsession with counting is one of the more visible manifestations of oversupervision in prisons. While so many counts seem unnecessary to the uninformed outsider, they are a reality of institutional life, and this "numbers game" can become a serious headache for the liberal administrator. Fear of the "convict bogey" pressures administrators to continually reconfirm that all prisoners are present and accounted for.

Prisons are geared to provide maximum supervision, surveillance, and control of inmates. Institutional programs, architectural design, and inmate activities are all designed to optimize security. Since the introduction of the Auburn system, prison procedures have been based on the assumption that inmates are untrustworthy. Thus, their personal and social needs take a back seat to security. Technological developments have facilitated this approach, providing the advocates of tight custody with much more effective tools with which to enforce it.

Custodial staff in maximum security prisons are generally undertrained for their jobs, prisonized, and strongly dependent on one another for aid, especially in time of stress. Since they know many of their charges are violence-prone, organized, and aggressive, with a high level of frustration and resultant hostility, they feel a legitimate anxiety for their own safety—coupled with a desire for strict regulations. Thus, the emphasis on external controls in our prisons has triumphed over attempts at internal reform (see chapter 4). The "best" prisoner, in the view of the custodial staff, is one who obeys all the rules and does not make any trouble. It is not too surprising that force is sometimes used in order to make prisoners toe the mark.[3]

How Much Force?

The history and evolution of corrections (Part I) suggests that almost unrestrained force was the rule in keeping America's early prisoners under control. The infamous Elam Lynds set the example at Auburn with his almost fanatical belief in the power of the whip to create order. Force, usually in the form of corporal punishment, was the standard discipline measure in most nineteenth-century prisons. In recent times, force has customarily been used to quell prison riots, though negotiations are sometimes tried first. How much force should be considered justifiable, and under what conditions? It is obvious that those who become the keepers of large groups of prisoners, many of whom are incarcerated for crimes of violence, will sometimes face situations in which response by force is the only immediate answer. John Palmer addresses this question in discussing the prisoner's constitutional rights:

> Every person, including an incarcerated felon, has the rights to be free from the *fear* of offensive bodily contact and to be free from *actual* offensive bodily contact. Any person who violates either of these rights can be held liable, both civilly and criminally, unless such conduct is privileged.
>
> It has generally been recognized that prison officials have a privilege to use force against inmates in five fact situations. These areas are: (1) self-defense; (2) defense of third persons; (3) enforcement of prison rules and regulations; (4) prevention of escape; and (5) prevention of crime.[4]

Palmer is listing the *conditions* that may justify a use of force. The amount, or *degree,* of force to be used is a more complicated issue. A fairly safe rule of thumb for officials might be to gauge the amount of force they should employ by the amount the *inmate* is using; another general rule would be to use *only* that amount of force required to overcome the inmate. Excessive force can often result in tragedy. Although Governor Nelson Rockefeller of New York consistently indicated that only minimum force should be used to control the Attica uprising, many deaths occurred. The Attica Commission's *Report* offered some explanations:

> The hostages were indistinguishable in their dress from inmates.
>
> The state police were equipped with shotguns, loaded with ''00'' buckshot pellets which would spread at distances exceeding 30 yards and hit unintended targets, creating a high risk of injury and death to unresisting inmates and hostages when discharged in or into the prison yard. No specific safeguards were developed to avoid hitting hostages and unresisting inmates with the spread and overfire from shotgun blasts.
>
> The tactical plan left the decision on whether to discharge a weapon to the discretion of each individual trooper. Gas masks inhibited verbal communication and no alternative means, such as hand signals, were developed for transmitting fire and cease-fire orders or other instructions once the assault was under way.
>
> Many correction officers fired their weapons from the blocks during the assault as the Governor's orders that they should not participate was never communicated to them.
>
> There was much unnecessary shooting. Troopers shot into tents, trenches, and barricades without looking first.

Finally, the Commission concluded that the deficiencies in the assault plan were not the result of callous indifference on the part of police officials, nor were they the result of a casual attitude toward the enormous situation confronting them. They were the result, rather, of assigning a new kind of mission to a force of men that was neither trained nor equipped for the occasion. The deficiencies in the plan were not perceived—and are still not acknowledged in all instances—by the police commanders or state officials. No one reviewed or questioned the assault plan except superficially. It is doubtful that state leaders even realized that the only prospect for retaking the prison without indiscriminate shooting rested on the individual judgment and self-restraint of 211 tense, frightened, frustrated, angry men and their separate "reasonable beliefs."[5]

"Deadly force"[6] is perhaps the correctional official's ultimate weapon in keeping control inside prisons. It need not involve the use of deadly weapons. Factors in determining the degree of force include: areas of the body struck, the skill of the one applying the force (e.g., an expert in Kung Fu[7] would be considered more deadly than the average person), and the victim's physical condition at the time. Our society generally frowns upon forcible control methods, but understands that they are sometimes necessary, within reason. The high value that Americans place on human life has made the use of deadly force an absolute *last resort* for prison administrators.

When to Use Force

One instance where force is considered justifiable is that of *self-defense*. All Americans, including prison guards, have the right to defend themselves against personal attack. If guards are assaulted by inmates, various court cases[8] have determined that the guards have the right to respond. This right has not been equally extended to the inmates, however. Early control practices involved excessive punishments (beating and whipping). The inmates, assumed to have no rights, could not defend themselves. Under the thin veneer of modern penological techniques, this old philosophy remains in effect, as the Attica aftermath illustrates:

> Injured prisoners, some on stretchers, were struck, prodded or beaten with sticks, belts, bats or other weapons. Others were forced to strip and run naked through gauntlets of guards armed with clubs which they used to strike the bodies of the inmates as they passed. Some were dragged on the ground, some marked with an "X" on their backs, some spat upon or burned with matches, and others poked in the genitals or arms with sticks. According to the testimony of the

inmates, bloody or wounded inmates were apparently not spared in this orgy of brutality.[9]

Though state officials expected immediate physical reprisals against inmates in the aftermath of the rebellion, they did nothing to prevent them. National Guardsmen and other outside observers, as well as a few troopers and correction officers, confirmed the almost universal inmate descriptions of widespread beatings, proddings, kickings, and verbal abuse of the vilest nature. Reprisals were especially severe in segregation, where the suspected leaders of the uprising were taken. Forty-five percent of the inmates who had been in D yard suffered bruises, lacerations, abrasions, and broken bones.[10]

One of society's most brutal tendencies is the one that permits an attack on those who are in no position to respond, physically or otherwise.

A second situation which justifies force is the need to defend a *third person*. The rule of reasonableness applies here also—the force should be the minimum required to regain control of the situation. Obviously, this principle is all too easy to abuse. Guards coming to the aid of an inmate or another guard might easily become overzealous in their attempt to reestablish control. This possibility was discussed in the court decision on a California case involving a prisoner's attack on a guard:

> The amount of force used cannot be measured by a micrometer, nor can it be considered separate and apart from the circumstances existing at the time. The three men were in or about to enter the locker room. Without warning or provocation Riddle hit Stanley on the jaw, bruising it and loosening two teeth. The three fell to the floor and Riddle hit or kicked Stanley. The latter, who was unarmed, reached for the baton, tried to subdue Riddle by hitting him on the kneecap, and when that failed hit him on the head. The last blow had the desired effect. It is certainly too bad that Stanley hit him so hard. It is tragic that his skull was fractured. But Stanley, under the circumstances could not, reasonably, be expected to measure carefully the precise amount of force he should use.[11]

The enforcement of prison rules and regulations, prevention of crime, and prevention of escape are other situations in which the use of force has been established as permissible by case law. Regarding enforcement of prison rules, the general guideline is *reasonable* force. *Deadly* force could almost never be appropriate in this context, unless the situation had escalated to the point where self-defense standards might apply. Prevention of crime within correctional settings is a valid function of prison officials, but deadly force is considered valid only in the case of felonies, and then only after all other means have failed. In order to justify the use of deadly force in the event of attempted escape, practically every state has passed a law making the *act* of escape a felony. Most prisons have guard towers positioned around the high walls, with armed marksmen inside, to prevent escapes with deadly force if necessary.

In summary, the use of force is justified in many circumstances, although the use of deadly force is highly circumscribed. The more brutal methods of control used in the past may erupt again in tense situations. Progressive correctional administrators are aware of the dangerous effects the institutional process may have on guards and inmates, and have prescribed specific guidelines governing *when* and *how* force can be used.

Is Corporal Punishment Necessary?

The use of corporal punishment for discipline is deeply ingrained in our society. From preschool days, children are told that if they are bad they will get a "spanking" from a parent. To early prison authorities, corporal punishment was just another vested power; the whipping of convicts has been a recognized method of prison discipline for centuries. As recently as 1963, a federal circuit court held that use of the whip did not violate either state or federal constitutions.[12] Many other forms of corporal punishment, by contrast, were dropped soon after early correctional reforms began. Since the concept of corporal punishment is a part of our culture, it is seldom questioned unless it is grossly abused. How effective *is* corporal punishment as a means of discipline?

The advocates of corporal punishment make great claims, often in the face of contrary facts, for its utility in deterring future rule infringements. The American Correctional Association, however, adamantly opposes corporal punishment, stating flatly that it "should never be used under any circumstances." The Association's *Manual of Correctional Standards* continues:

> Punishments out of all proportion to the offense, employing inhumane and archaic methods and dictated by brutality coupled with ignorance, incompetence, fear and weakness, are demoralizing both to inmates and staff. Staff punishments substantially increase the chances that the inmates will continue to be disciplinary problems in the institution and will return to crime after release.[13]

Only in 1968, in the case of *Jackson* v. *Bishop*,[14] did a court find that whipping violated the Eighth and Fourteenth Amendments to the Constitution. This opinion, from the United States Court of Appeals for the Eighth Circuit, was written by Judge Harry Blackmun, now a Justice on the United States Supreme Court. Whipping was held to be "cruel and unusual punishment" for these reasons:

1. We are not convinced that any rule or regulation as to the use of the strap, however seriously or sincerely conceived and drawn, will successfully prevent abuse. . . .

2. Rules in this area often seem to go unobserved. . . .

3. Regulations are easily circumvented. . . .

4. Corporal punishment is easily subject to abuse in the hands of the sadistic and the unscrupulous.

5. Where power to punish is granted to persons in lower levels of administrative authority, there is an inherent and natural difficulty in enforcing the limitations of that power.

6. There can be no argument that excessive whipping or an inappropriate manner of whipping or too great frequency of whipping or the use of studded or overlong straps all constitute cruel and unusual punishment. But if whipping were to be authorized, how does one, or any court, ascertain the point which would distinguish the permissible from that which is cruel and unusual?

7. Corporal punishment generates hate toward the keepers who punish and toward the system which permits it. It is degrading to the punisher and to the punished alike. It frustrates correctional and rehabilitative goals. . . .

8. Whipping creates other penological problems and makes adjustment to society more difficult.

9. Public opinion is obviously adverse. Counsel concede that only two states still permit the use of the strap.[15]

It seems unlikely that any subsequent cases will change the Appellate Court's ruling. The elimination of whipping as a legitimate method of punishment in prisons spelled the end to all overt efforts to use it or other forms of corporal abuse to enforce institutional rules.

Liability of Prison Officials

When the use of force is determined to be excessive, who is responsible? In most of the cases focusing on this problem, the citation reads *"Prisoner* v. *Warden."* Does this mean that the warden is personally responsible? How do prisoners conduct attempts to sue their keepers? The doctrine of "sovereign immunity," which says that the state may not be sued without its consent, is a major hurdle facing the prisoner. Even in states where this policy has been dropped or waived, it is not easy to stand up against the massed power of the state government. When the state retains its immunity from suit, the prisoner is still allowed to sue the correctional official on a personal level (in a *tort* case, a civil action involving personal injury to one person by another).

If a constitutional right is involved, the prisoner can usually obtain an *injunction:* a court writ forbidding the prison officials to repeat the punishment until the case is decided. Only recently has this procedure been possible; previously, the "hands-off" doctrine led courts to reject all cases where the inmates sued their correctional officials. The courts are still reluctant to interfere in matters essentially the concern of the correctional administration, but they *will* move when there is evidence that an inmate's civil rights have been infringed.

Unresolved is the question of possible civil liability for officials acting in their governmental roles. Unfortunately, the picture is quite confused. It is a basic precept of governmental service that one must be freed from fear of civil damage liability while acting in an official capacity. To prison officials, the many civil suits brought by inmates are a nuisance that decreases their administrative effectiveness. Many of these harassed officials are trying to fight several suits at once. It is part of the correctional argot today that you aren't "established" until you have been sued for a million dollars. Damages are seldom awarded in these suits, unless a prisoner can prove that the wrongs were inflicted in a wrongful and malicious manner. A leading authority explains the problem:

What the law of tort liability of public officers and employees most needs is an expansion of tort liability of governmental units. If the particular governmental unit is liable for the tort, so that the loss will thus be properly spread, then the courts will be relieved from the need for choosing between leaving a deserving plaintiff without remedy and imposing liability upon the individual officer or employee, who is usually either ill-equipped to bear the loss or is performing the type of function that can be properly performed only if the officer is free from the need of considering his own pocket book. The public interest in fearless administration usually should come first, so that officers must be immune from liability even when the plaintiff asserts that the officers have acted maliciously; when this is so, the only proper way to compensate deserving plaintiffs is to impose liability on the governmental unit. When the public gets the benefit of a program, the public should pay for the torts that may be expected in carrying out the program. The only satisfactory solution of many problems about liability of officers and employees is to compensate the plaintiff but to hold the officer or employee immune.[16]

A wide variety of remedies is available to inmates today in their quest to rectify past wrongs and prevent future violations of their constitutional rights. The erosion of the hands-off doctrine has created a climate in which the courts are receptive to suits originating from behind the walls. Since most adult felons are confined in *state* prisons, it is appropriate to examine some of the remedies available in the states.

The states are generally protected by the rule of sovereign immunity, but this rule depends on whether the actions of the correctional official are "ministerial"[17] or "discretionary"[18] in nature. In the first case, it is clearly the *duty* of correctional officials to provide a particular service or privilege to the inmate. In this capacity they have no right to act, or fail to act, in a way that would result in denial of that service or right to the inmate. Discretionary duties, by contrast, are those the officers themselves decide to administer—and they include, of course, punishment. Some states have interpreted this area very broadly, to the extent that administrators can feel practically immune to lawsuit. If the discretion is grossly abused, however, the officials become liable. Prisoners now appear to have the right to protest any offensive bodily contact that is intentionally inflicted upon them.[19] The civil suit in this kind of case can be brought in the same manner as any other tort.

The declaratory judgment[20] is another form of state remedy, similar to the federal remedy, that has been completely ignored for state actions. The Federal Declaratory Judgment Act reads in part:

> In a case of actual controversy within its jurisdiction . . . any court of the United States, upon the filing of an appropriate pleading, may declare the rights and other legal relations of any interested party seeking such declaration. . . .[21]

This act allows the court to establish that a certain procedure or rule in use by the correctional administration is unconstitutional, but still gives the prison officers a chance to revise the procedures or submit plans to remedy the problem to the court. Many states have passed similar acts. State remedy in the form of criminal prosecution of the offending officials has been successful in only a few cases. It is difficult to prove a criminal act by correctional personnel unless there is a specific statute that applies to the particular situation. (Although it is hard to get a conviction under the general criminal codes, it has been done.)[22] Governors were found to be immune from suit in a 1971 case.[23]

Yet another remedy is the use of contempt of court proceedings against the correctional officials in their capacity as officers of the sentencing court. Arizona[24] and Rhode Island[25] have endorsed the use of contempt proceedings to punish officials for mistreatment of inmates.

The most common remedy in use in the federal court system is Section 1983 of the Civil Rights Act. This provision of the Act states:

> Every person who, under color of any statute, ordinance, regulation, custom, or usage, of any State or Territory, subjects, or causes to be subjected, any citizen of the United States or other person within the jurisdiction thereof to the deprivation of any rights, privileges, or immunities secured by the Constitution and laws, shall be liable to the party injured in an action at law, suit in equity, or other proper proceeding for redress.[26]

The ability to bring these "1983" suits against state prison officials was extended to inmates in the case of *Cooper* v. *Pate*,[27] in 1963. Generally the United States Supreme Court requires that petitioners exhaust all remedies available to them in the state courts before bringing a case to the highest level. Cases brought under the Civil Rights Act, however, do not require that all other remedies be exhausted—the idea being that violation of civil rights is a constitutional issue and can move into federal courts more rapidly. Even so, exhaustion of state remedies is recommended and makes a stronger case for the appellant. The prisoner's best guide is to determine whether the unconstitutional acts will be discontinued by an administrative action at some future date. If this is the case, exhaustion of state remedies *is* required. If the acts seem likely to continue indefinitely, the exhaustion of state remedies is not necessary and the inmate can bring the case directly into the federal court system.

Monetary damages have been awarded in civil rights suits, on occasion.[28] In one case, the warden and state commissioner of corrections were ordered to pay damage costs of $9,300 to the inmate. Punitive damages were not required, however, as the court found that no malice was intended on the officials' part. Another federal relief is found in the use of an injunction[29] under the Civil Rights Act. This action prevents continued deprivation of the inmate's right while he or she awaits a decision from the courts. The case of *Jones* v. *Wittenberg*,[30] which attacked the totally deplorable conditions in an Ohio county jail, illustrated the power of the injunction in seeking relief from unconstitutional conditions. Other federal remedies—criminal prosecution, contempt proceedings, and habeas corpus—parallel those available in state courts.

Review and Forecast

The use of force as a control tool by prison administrators is as old as the concept of confinement itself. Prisoners naturally attempt to resist the control of their keepers; since the performance of those keepers is rated in part on how calm their institutions are, they are willing to squelch this resistance by almost every kind of force imaginable, the most popular method being the whip. When most prisoners served life sentences, permanently removed from their communities, little notice was paid to the control methods used. As the states began to use parole more frequently, the stories of brutal treatment behind the walls came out. Corporal punishment decreased due to the movement to restore rights and humane treatment to the nation's prisoners. The 1971 uprising at Attica, New York, however, showed us that brutal incidents are still possible.

Excessive force and cruel punishment have also been attacked in federal courts under the Civil Rights Act. Force has been deemed necessary in some conditions, primarily for self-defense, defense of a third party, prevention of a felony, enforcement of prison rules, or to prevent an escape. Prison rules continue to be reformed through court action, in a movement toward providing an atmosphere inside the walls that begins to resemble conditions on the outside.

The legal liability of public officials, whatever their capacity, has been severely limited by the sovereign immunity doctrine. This doctrine has been eroded by case law to the point where prison officials and correctional administrators have been found liable for monetary damages. The threat of financial loss if an official deprives prisoners of their constitutional rights heralds major changes in institutional operations and procedures. Strong state and federal remedies have been supplied for prisoners who seek redress for alleged constitutional wrongs. The provision of legal assistance has encouraged inmates to avail themselves of these remedies.

The future of correctional control is somewhat paradoxical. At a time when inmate rights—especially as they apply to the use of force—are being protected against the state, the prisons are experiencing rapidly increasing populations. This creates a problem and a challenge for modern correctional administrators. How do they control the uncontrollable without resorting to excessive force? The answer to this question includes a rapid upgrading of personnel skills at all levels and the development of small, maximum security prisons, reserved for the dangerous criminal, that will eventually replace our present structures. These prisons will need to be secure, but they should not be inhumane. Highly skilled professionals must be brought in to concentrate on changing the behavior of these troublesome prisoners as much as possible. It will be a strong challenge to the correctional professional to work with the real losers who will compose the population of the prisons of the future.

REVIEW QUESTIONS

I. Find the answers to the following in the text:

 1. What are the security classifications of the prisons in America?

 2. When are prison officials authorized to use force?

 3. Explain the difference between ministerial and discretionary actions of prison officials.

4. What remedies are currently available to inmates today to rectify past wrongs and prevent future violations of their constitutional rights?

II. Words to identify:

1. count

2. toe the mark

3. deadly force

4. self-defense

5. reasonable force

6. sovereign immunity

7. ministerial actions

8. discretionary actions

9. declaratory judgment

10. 1983 suit

NOTES

1. Vernon Fox, *Introduction to Corrections* (Englewood Cliffs, N.J.: Prentice-Hall, 1973), pp. 160-161.

2. *Under the gun* applies to any kind of work or recreational activity which is supervised by armed guards, including tower guards.

3. *Toe the mark* derives from the former practice of painting lines on the floor in various parts of the prison. If prisoners wanted to communicate with a guard, or pass to another area, they were required to stand with their toes on the mark until ordered to pass it.

4. John Palmer, *Constitutional Rights of Prisoners* (Cincinnati, Ohio: Anderson Press, 1973), p. 15.

5. William L. Wilbanks, "The Report on the Commission on Attica," *Federal Probation* (March 1973): 7.

6. *Deadly force* refers to the amount of force which is normally expected to result in the death of the individual upon which it is used.

7. *Kung Fu* is an Oriental form of hand-to-hand combat in which blows are directed toward vital parts of the anatomy. Experts in Kung Fu or Karate, or professional boxers are considered to possess great advantage over the average person.

8. *In re Riddle,* 57 Cal. 2d 848, 372 P. 2d 304, 22 Cal. Rptr. 472 (1962); *In re Jones,* 57 Cal. 2d 860, 372 P. 2d 304, 22 Cal. Rptr. 478 (1962). The State Supreme Court turned down a petition for writ of habeas corpus from a prisoner demanding to be released from San Quentin Prison. The prisoner alleged that a prison guard hit him, thus subjecting him to cruel and unusual punishment.

9. Palmer, p. 17.

10. Wilbanks, p. 7.

11. *In re Riddle.*

12. *Jackson* v. *Bishop,* 404 F. 2d 571 (8th Cir. 1968). The Court held that any use of a strap as a disciplinary measure against a prisoner violates the constitutional injunction against cruel and unusual punishment.

13. American Correctional Association, *A Manual of Correctional Standards,* 3d ed. (Washington, D.C.: American Correctional Association, 1966), p. 417.

14. *Jackson* v. *Bishop,* 268 F. Supp. 804, 813 (E.D. Ark. 1967). Aff'd., 404 F. 2d 571 (8th Cir. 1968).

15. *Jackson* v. *Bishop.*

16. K. Davis, *Administrative Law Treatise* (St. Paul, Minn.: West Publishing Co., 1959), p. 26.07.

17. *Ministerial duties* are generally those which are stipulated by statute and which permit little room for deviation.

18. *Discretionary duties* are those which involve a broad range of alternative approaches from which the administrator may choose.

19. Palmer, p. 146.

20. *A declaratory judgment* is a judgment which establishes or interprets a legal right.

21. 28 U.S.C., §2201 (1970).

22. *State* v. *Mincher,* 172 N.C. 895, 90 S.E. 429 (1916). The State Supreme Court of North Carolina upheld the conviction of a prison guard for assault and battery and excessive use of corporal punishment, the plaintiff having claimed he had been whipped by the guard in prison.

23. *Parker* v. *McKeithen,* 330 F. Supp. 435 (E.D. La. 1971). The court rejected the plaintiff's claim that he was deprived of equal protection and freedom from cruel and unusual punishment when he was stabbed by another inmate because prison officials knew of the existence of such weapons in the prison but failed to adequately protect the other prisoners against them.

24. *Howard* v. *State,* 28 Ariz. 433, 237 P. 203 (1925). The court held that the plaintiff, who had been placed in a dark cell for thirty days without reason or official charges, had been subjected to unreasonable and harsh treatment.

25. *State* v. *Brant,* 99 R.I. 583, 209 A. 2d 455 (1965). The warden was held in contempt for holding a prisoner in solitary confinement beyond the thirty days allowed for security reasons.

26. 42 U.S.C., §1983 (1970).

27. *Cooper* v. *Pate,* 324 F. 2d 165 (7th Cir. 1963).

28. *Wiltsie* v. *California Department of Corrections,* 406 F. 2d 515 (9th Cir. 1968). The Court of Appeals upheld the plaintiff's claim that he was deprived of his civil rights by prison officials who beat him.

29. An *injunction* is a writ granted by a court which requires one to do or refrain from doing a specified act.

30. *Jones* v. *Wittenberg,* 323 F. Supp 93 (N.D. Ohio 1971), aff'd. sub. nom. *Jones* v. *Metzger,* 456 F. 2d 854 (6th Cir. 1972). This case determined that prisoners have the right to engage in civil rights actions.

15 The Death Penalty

The useless profusion of punishments, which have never made men better, induces me to inquire, whether the punishment of *death* be really useful in a well governed state? What *right,* I ask, have men to cut the throats of their fellow-creatures?

CESARE BECCARIA

The Death Penalty as a Public Spectacle

As discussed in Part I, the death penalty was perhaps the earliest form of punishment—and, until recent years, the most common. At one time there were over two hundred crimes for which the death penalty applied in England. The basic argument supporting the death penalty, its theoretical deterrent power, led to frequent public executions. This practice was finally stopped in England, legend has it, partly to curb the flourishing pickpocket business at the executions (picking pockets, ironically, was a capital offense). Early public executions in America were well-attended, to say the least:

> The day of the execution was dark and cloudy. A slight, drizzling rain fell during the greater part of the morning, and the streets presented an unbroken surface of slop and mud. A large crowd had gathered from the country at an early hour—"arriving by the first trains from the east, west, north and south. Many came into town on horseback and in carriages and wagons," and the streets were thronged with a moving mass of human beings, eager to gratify curiosity.
> A rope had been stretched across the enclosure in which the gallows stood, at a distance of forty or fifty feet from it, and guards, armed with muskets, were stationed inside of the rope to keep the crowd from pressing upon the place of execution. Outside of the stretched rope the streets were filled. . . . The only incident that diverted the intense interest of this vast multitude was the appearance of a traveling auctioneer, who had selected that time to cry his goods and dispose of his wares.[1]

The last public execution in the United States took place in Owensboro, Kentucky, on August 14, 1936.[2] It is estimated that over twenty thousand people crowded into the small Kentucky town to witness the spectacle. Various reform groups, disturbed that such a solemn event should take place in a holiday atmosphere, moved to transfer it behind the high stone walls of our prisons. As the executions began to take place in private, methods were improved in order to make them more efficient. Without the alleged deterrent power of an audience, the task of execution became a sort of ritualistic slaughter. Many prisoners have died in the gas chamber or the electric chair since Ramsey Bethea was hanged in Kentucky in 1936. As this book goes to press, a convicted murderer in Texas is attempting to have his execution broadcast on live television. There has been speculation as to whether such a spectacle will "turn off" the public to the execution of criminals (as it is postulated that the televising of the Vietnam war did in regard to wars in general), or whether the execution will turn the public on to a new thrill in an era of increasing television violence.

America's most innovative solution to the prison execution was probably the electric chair. While this invention was extolled as a more humanitarian way to kill the offender, many considered it merely a promotional scheme of the New York electrical company that developed it. The first electrocution was conducted at Auburn Penitentiary, New York, in 1890.

Opponents of the chair, claiming that it must be excessively painful (a claim vehemently denied by prison administrators who use it) advocated lethal gas as the most humane execution method. It is interesting to note that Texas and Oklahoma have both passed legislation to use an injection of a lethal chemical as the form of execution. It seems that we are still seeking a way to make the *process,* if not the practice, of execution more humane.

The physical pain of the execution is probably the smallest concern of victims during their prolonged wait in the death house, often lasting eight to ten years.[3] The mental anguish they must endure, which that wait can only intensify, has been a primary focus of the widespread controversy recently surrounding the death penalty, as the more industrialized societies moved to abolish it. The use of the death penalty in the United States peaked in the crime-laden 1930s, when a total of 1,513 prisoners were executed,[4] at an average rate of about twelve per month. The number of appeals increased in the 1960s, and in 1972 the United States Supreme Court placed a moratorium on capital punishment.

Origins of the Death Penalty

In earlier chapters, brief references have been made to some of the issues involved with capital punishment, or the death penalty. The frequency with which this topic occurs demonstrates how deeply intertwined it is with all the other aspects of criminal justice. The term "capital punishment" generally applies to the execution, in the name of the state, of a person who has been convicted of some serious crime. The crimes for which this punishment has been applied have varied over the centuries, but murder and rape have been the most common. The means by which the punishment has been carried out have varied even more. In preindustrial society, the death penalty was relatively simple to carry out. Offenders were usually forced out into the wilderness (banished), where their demise was relatively certain. When human skills and culture developed, the chances for wilderness survival increased, and the effectiveness of banishment diminished. When society began to execute (rather than banish) individuals for serious trans- gressions (usually murder, based on *talion*), the procedure remained simple. Society has always been able to devise countless imaginative and cruel methods for the destruction of a condemned offender.

The condemned have been hanged, burned, flayed alive, boiled in oil, thrown to wild beasts, crucified, drowned, crushed, impaled, stoned, shot, strangled, torn apart, beheaded, disemboweled, electrocuted, buried alive, smothered, gassed, and now, injected with lethal drugs. This list only partially exhausts the methods that executioners have employed through history. In search of vengeance against the condemned, society has also resorted to all sorts of ritual punishment, with mutilation and degradation preceding the final coup de grace.

Early executions were almost always administered as a public spectacle, in the hope that they would serve as a warning and a deterrent to others. It could be argued that the human desire to obtain retribution for crimes was transferred from individual to state in a way that finally became repugnant to most enlightened societies. Still, long after the elimination of the more bloody aspects of capital vengeance, controversy still centers on the possible deterrent value of the death penalty. Executions are less cruel and less public, but the philosophy behind them remains equally questionable.

Deterrence: Individual or General?

The term *deterrence* refers to the theory that some action against a convicted offender will help prevent similar crimes—either by the same offender (*individual* deterrence) or other potential criminals (*general* deterrence). It should be obvious that, in the case of capital punishment, individual deterrence is totally effective. The individual deterrent effect can also be seen as a method of *correction,* however, with the value of the ultimate sanction lying in its *non*-use and the offender's reaction to it. Howard Gill sees the death penalty as a possible *correctional force in treating persons convicted of a capital offense.* In what was later referred to as the "only intelligent testimony *in favor* of the death penalty" given before the Committee of the Judiciary of the U.S. House of Representatives, he noted:

> To abolish the death penalty is to remove this most potent force in
> changing persons convicted of a capital offense. By retaining the death

penalty, but providing for its modification through constructive use of it as a motivating factor, turns it from an "irrational and archaic institution," as claimed by the abolitionists, into a constructive force for reform.

What I propose is briefly—

1. That all persons convicted of a capital offense be sentenced conditionally to capital punishment;

2. With a finding by the jury of either aggravating or mitigating circumstances;

3. That such convicted persons be remanded to a diagnostic center for thorough observation and diagnosis;

4. That on findings as to the probable problem or problems underlying the offense, the convict be given the opportunity for treatment toward change;

5. That as long as constructive change is demonstrated, the execution of the sentence shall be held in abeyance;

6. If in the opinion of those in charge of such treatment, such change is sufficient to warrant release under supervision (either work-release or parole), recommendations to this effect shall be made to the committing court, and if approved, the convicted person shall be released under such conditions as are appropriate; and finally,

7. If no adequate change is noted, their recommendations for execution of the sentence shall be made to the court, and appropriate action follow.[5]

With the rush of so many states to write new capital punishment legislation, it might be well to consider the efficacy of the plans suggested by Gill.

It is the value of capital punishment as it applies to *general* deterrence, however, which has sparked debate over the centuries. This argument centers on the *threat* of capital punishment and its alleged deterrent effect on the potential offender.

Thorsten Sellin states four basic outcomes that would prove the death penalty's effectiveness as a deterrent:

a. Murders should be less frequent in states that have the death penalty than in those that have abolished it, other factors being equal. Comparisons of this

nature must be made among states that are as alike
as possible in all other respects—character of
population, social and economic conditions, etc.—in
order not to introduce factors known to influence
murder rates in a serious manner but present in only
one of these states.

b. Murders should increase when the death penalty is
abolished and should decline when it is restored.

c. The deterrent effect should be greatest and should
therefore affect murder rates most powerfully in
those communities where the crime occurred and its
consequences are most strongly brought home to
the population.

d. Law enforcement officers would be safer from
murderous attacks in states that have the death
penalty than in those without it.[6]

Many studies have attempted to prove or disprove these apparently simple
propositions. Almost all those conducted in the United States have demonstrated that the death penalty has little if anything to do with the relative
occurrence of the crimes to which it applies. A short excerpt from *Meet the
Murderer,* by Lewis E. Lawes, illustrates the conclusion these studies seem
to require—the death penalty is not going to stop a potential murderer:

Before Morris Wasser's execution, when I told him that the governor
had refused him a last-minute respite, he said bitterly: "All right,
Warden. It doesn't make much difference what I say now about this
here system of burning a guy, but I want to set you straight
on something."

"What's that?" I asked.

"Well, this electrocution business is the bunk. It don't do no good,
I tell you, and I know, because I never thought of the chair when I
plugged that old guy. And I'd probably do it again if he had me on
the wrong end of a rod."

"You mean," I said, "that you don't feel you've done wrong
in taking another man's life?"

"No, Warden, it ain't that," he said impatiently. "I mean that you
just don't think of the hot seat when you plug a guy. Somethin'
inside you just makes you kill, 'cause you know if you don't shut him
up it's curtains for you."

"I see. Then you never even thought of what would happen to you
at the time."

"Hell, no! And lots of other guys in here, Harry and Brick and
Luke, all says the same thing. I tell you the hot seat will never stop a

guy from pullin' a trigger.'' That was Wasser's theory, and I've heard it echoed many times since.[7]

The deterrence argument is further eroded by the theory that the state's practice of killing convicted offenders actually *increases* the chance for violence. Many cornered offenders are believed willing to try to escape arrest by shooting their way out—at the risk of killing someone—rather than surrender to a more certain death by capital punishment. Its apparent failure as a deterrent and its infrequent use in recent years have led to the ''cruel and unusual punishment'' attack on the death penalty, under the Eighth Amendment to the Constitution.

Cruel and Infrequent Punishment

To better understand the magnitude of the death penalty issue, one must examine the somewhat incomplete records on the subject. The total executions in this country between 1930 and 1977 are shown in Table 4. As mentioned earlier, the death penalty has most often been prescribed for murder and rape. One would reasonably expect a fairly high correlation between the number of such offenses and the number of executions. In the 1930s, the earliest period for which relatively reliable statistics are available, the average number of executions was about 165 per year. The number of murders and rapes reported per year during the 1930s averaged about 3,500 and 3,800, respectively.[8]

It is worth noting that 80 percent of those executed for rape between 1930 and 1977 were black. All 405 of these executions took place in the Deep South with the exception of seven in Missouri, a border state (see Table 5). This tends to indicate that, in the case of rape, the death penalty was most readily applied to blacks in the South, where the idea of interracial sex relations stirred deep emotions.

Also significant is the number of executions in different states and regions. As Figure IV–3 indicates, the vast majority of executions have taken place in the South (over 50 percent of the total in the ten states of Texas, Arkansas, Louisiana, Mississippi, Tennessee, Alabama, Georgia, Florida, South Carolina, and North Carolina). The six industrial states that extend from Illinois to New York account for another 22 percent of the executions. When California is added into the equation, these seventeen states account for over 80 percent of the executions in America between 1930 and 1977. This leaves an average of only twenty-two executions per state for the remaining thirty-three, between 1930 and 1977. Seven states had no executions during that period (North Dakota, Minnesota, Wisconsin, Michigan, Maine, Alaska, and Hawaii).

The broad gap between the number of capital crimes and the number of executions is even more evident when examining data for the 1960s. From 1960 to 1967, the year the moratorium on the death penalty took effect,

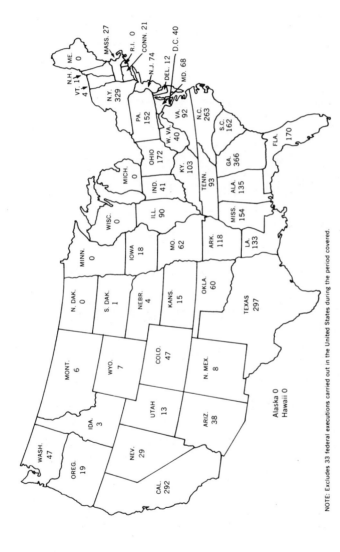

NOTE: Excludes 33 federal executions carried out in the United States during the period covered.

FIGURE IV–3. Executions 1930–1977. Prisoners Executed under Civil Authority in the United States, by State (Ramsay Clark, *National Prisoner Statistics: Executions 1930–1967* (Washington, D.C.: U.S. Department of Justice, June 1968). p. 4.)

TABLE 4. PRISONERS EXECUTED UNDER CIVIL AUTHORITY IN THE UNITED STATES BY RACE, OFFENSE, AND YEAR: 1930–1977
(Years 1930–1959 exclude Alaska and Hawaii except for three federal executions in Alaska: 1939, 1948, 1950)

YEAR	ALL OFFENSES Total	White	Negro	Other	MURDER Total	White	Negro	Other	RAPE Total	White	Negro	Other	OTHER OFFENSES[b] Total	White	Negro
All years[a]	3,860	1,752	2,066	42	3,335	1,665	1,630	40	455	48	405	2	70	39	31
Percent	100.0	45.4	53.5	1.1	100.0	49.9	48.9	1.2	100.0	10.6	89.0	0.4	100.0	55.7	44.3
1977	1	1	—	—	1	1	—	—	—	—	—	—	—	—	—
1968–1976	—	—	—	—	—	—	—	—	—	—	—	—	—	—	—
1967	2	1	1	—	2	1	1	—	—	—	—	—	—	—	—
1966	1	1	—	—	1	1	—	—	—	—	—	—	—	—	—
1965	7	6	1	—	7	6	1	—	—	—	—	—	—	—	—
1964	15	8	7	—	9	5	4	—	6	3	3	—	—	—	—
1963	21	13	8	—	18	12	6	—	2	—	2	—	1	1	—
1962	47	28	19	—	41	26	15	—	4	2	2	—	2	—	2
1961	42	20	22	—	33	18	15	—	8	1	7	—	1	1	—
1960	56	21	35	—	44	18	26	—	8	—	8	—	4	3	1
1959	49	16	33	—	41	15	26	—	8	1	7	—	—	—	—
1958	49	20	28	1	41	20	20	1	7	—	7	—	1	—	1
1957	65	34	31	—	54	32	22	—	10	2	8	—	1	—	1
1956	65	21	43	1	52	20	31	1	12	—	12	—	1	1	—
1955	76	44	32	—	65	41	24	—	7	1	6	—	4	2	2
1954	81	38	42	1	71	37	33	1	9	1	8	—	1	—	1
1953	62	30	31	1	51	25	25	1	6	—	6	—	5	5	—
1952	83	36	47	—	71	35	36	—	12	1	11	—	—	—	—
1951	105	57	47	1	87	55	31	1	17	2	15	—	1	—	1
1950	82	40	42	—	68	36	32	—	13	4	9	—	1	—	1
1949	119	50	67	2	107	49	56	2	10	1	9	—	2	—	2
1948	119	35	82	2	95	32	61	2	22	1	21	—	2	2	—

TABLE 4. PRISONERS EXECUTED UNDER CIVIL AUTHORITY IN THE UNITED STATES BY RACE, OFFENSE, AND YEAR: 1930–1977 (CONT.)
(Years 1930–1959 exclude Alaska and Hawaii except for three federal executions in Alaska: 1939, 1948, 1950)

YEAR	ALL OFFENSES				MURDER				RAPE				OTHER OFFENSES[b]		
	Total	White	Negro	Other	Total	White	Negro	Other	Total	White	Negro	Other	Total	White	Negro
All years[a]	3,860	1,752	2,066	42	3,335	1,665	1,630	40	455	48	405	2	70	39	31
Percent	100.0	45.4	53.5	1.1	100.0	49.9	48.9	1.2	100.0	10.6	89.0	0.4	100.0	55.7	44.3
1947	153	42	111	—	129	40	89	—	23	2	21	—	1	—	1
1946	131	46	84	1	107	45	61	1	22	—	22	—	2	1	1
1945	117	41	75	1	90	37	52	1	26	4	22	—	1	—	1
1944	120	47	70	3	96	45	48	3	24	2	22	—	—	—	—
1943	131	54	74	3	118	54	63	1	13	—	11	2	—	—	—
1942	147	67	80	—	115	57	58	—	25	4	21	—	7	6	1
1941	123	59	63	1	102	55	46	1	20	4	16	—	1	—	1
1940	124	49	75	—	105	44	61	—	15	2	13	—	4	3	1
1939	160	80	77	3	145	79	63	3	12	—	12	—	3	1	2
1938[b]	190	96	92	2	154	89	63	2	25	1	24	—	11	6	5
1937	147	69	74	4	133	67	62	4	13	2	11	—	1	—	1
1936	195	92	101	2	181	86	93	2	10	2	8	—	4	4	—
1935	199	119	77	3	184	115	66	3	13	2	11	—	2	2	—
1934	168	65	102	1	154	64	89	1	14	1	13	—	—	—	—
1933	160	77	81	2	151	75	74	2	7	1	6	—	2	1	1
1932	140	62	75	3	128	62	63	3	10	—	10	—	2	—	2
1931	153	77	72	4	137	76	57	4	15	1	14	—	1	—	1
1930	155	90	65	—	147	90	57	—	6	—	6	—	2	—	2

[a]Figures revised to reflect one white federal bank robber who was erroneously carried in previous bulletins as a murderer.

[b]Includes 23 armed robbery, 20 kidnapping, 11 burglary, 6 sabotage, 6 aggravated assault, and 2 espionage.

Ramsey Clark, *National Prisoner Statistics: Executions 1930–1967* (Washington, D.C.: U.S. Department of Justice, June 1968). p. 7.

TABLE 5. EXECUTIONS FOR MURDER AND RAPE BY OFFENSE, RACE, AND STATE: 1930–1977

REGION AND STATE	ALL OFFENSES				MURDER				RAPE			
	Total	White	Negro	Other	Total	White	Negro	Other	Total	White	Negro	Other
SOUTH	2,306	637	1,659	10	1,824	585	1,231	8	443	43	398	2
Delaware	12	5	7	—	8	4	4	—	4	1	3	—
Maryland	68	13	55	—	44	7	37	—	24	6	18	—
Dist. of Columbia	40	3	37	—	37	3	34	—	3	—	3	—
Virginia	92	17	75	—	71	17	54	—	21	—	21	—
West Virginia	40	31	9	—	36	28	8	—	1	—	1	—
North Carolina	263	59	199	5	207	55	149	3	47	4	41	2
South Carolina	162	35	127	—	120	30	90	—	42	5	37	—
Georgia	366	68	298	—	299	65	234	—	61	3	58	—
Florida	170	57	113	—	133	55	78	—	36	1	35	—
Kentucky	103	51	52	—	88	47	41	—	10	1	9	—
Tennessee	93	27	66	—	66	22	44	—	27	5	22	—
Alabama	135	28	107	—	106	26	80	—	22	2	20	—
Mississippi	154	30	124	—	130	30	100	—	21	—	21	—
Arkansas	118	27	90	1	99	25	73	1	19	2	17	—
Louisiana	133	30	103	—	116	30	86	—	17	—	17	—
Oklahoma	60	42	15	3	54	40	11	3	4	—	4	—
Texas	297	114	182	1	210	101	108	1	84	13	71	—
WEST	510	406	83	21	497	394	82	21	—	—	—	—
Montana	6	4	2	—	6	4	2	—	—	—	—	—
Idaho	3	3	—	—	3	3	—	—	—	—	—	—
Wyoming	7	6	1	—	7	6	1	—	—	—	—	—
Colorado	47	41	5	1	47	41	5	1	—	—	—	—
New Mexico	8	6	2	—	8	6	2	—	—	—	—	—
Arizona	38	28	10	—	38	28	10	—	—	—	—	—
Utah	14	14	—	—	14	14	—	—	—	—	—	—
Nevada	29	27	2	—	29	27	2	—	—	—	—	—
Washington	47	40	5	2	46	39	5	2	—	—	—	—
Oregon	19	16	3	—	19	16	3	—	—	—	—	—
California	292	221	53	18	280	210	52	18	—	—	—	—
Alaska	XX[a]	XX	XX	XX	XX	XX	XX	XX	XX	XX	XX	XX
Hawaii	XX	XX	XX	XX	XX	XX	XX	XX	XX	XX	XX	XX

TABLE 5. EXECUTIONS FOR MURDER AND RAPE BY OFFENSE, RACE, AND STATE: 1930–1977 (CONT.)

REGION AND STATE	ALL OFFENSES				MURDER				RAPE			
	Total	White	Negro	Other	Total	White	Negro	Other	Total	White	Negro	Other
NORTHEAST												
Maine	XX	XX	XX	XX	XX	XX	XX	XX	—	XX	XX	XX
New Hampshire	1	1	—	—	1	1	—	—	—	—	—	—
Vermont	4	4	—	—	4	4	—	—	—	—	—	—
Massachusetts	27	25	2	—	27	25	2	—	—	—	—	—
Rhode Island	—	—	—	—	—	—	—	—	—	—	—	—
Connecticut	21	18	3	—	21	18	3	—	—	—	—	—
New York	329	234	90	5	327	232	90	5	—	—	—	—
New Jersey	74	47	25	2	74	47	25	2	—	—	—	—
Pennsylvania	152	95	57	—	152	95	57	—	—	—	—	—
	608	424	177	7	606	422	177	7	—	—	—	—
NORTH CENTRAL	403	257	144	2	393	254	137	2	10	3	7	—
Ohio	172	104	67	1	172	104	67	1	—	—	—	—
Indiana	41	31	10	—	41	31	10	—	—	—	—	—
Illinois	90	59	31	—	90	59	31	—	—	—	—	—
Michigan	XX	XX	XX	XX	XX	XX	XX	XX	XX	XX	XX	XX
Wisconsin	XX	XX	XX	XX	XX	XX	XX	XX	XX	XX	XX	XX
Minnesota	XX	XX	XX	XX	XX	XX	XX	XX	XX	XX	XX	XX
Iowa	18	18	—	—	18	18	—	—	—	—	—	—
Missouri	62	29	33	—	52	26	26	—	10	3	7	—
North Dakota	1	1	—	—	1	1	—	—	—	—	—	—
South Dakota	—	—	—	—	—	—	—	—	—	—	—	—
Nebraska	4	3	—	1	4	3	—	1	—	—	—	—
Kansas	15	12	3	—	15	12	3	—	—	—	—	—
TOTAL STATE	3,827	1,784	2,063	40	3,320	1,655	1,627	38	453	46	405	2

aXX signifies that state has no death penalty.
Ramsey Clark, *National Prisoner Statistics: Executions 1930–1967* (Washington, D.C.: U.S. Department of Justice, June 1968), pp. 10–11.

there were only 135 executions in America, an average of only a little over seventeen a year. Actually, as the sixties progressed the number per year dropped to only seven in 1965, one in 1966, and two in 1967. When one considers that the number of murders and rapes reported during that period averaged about 10,000 and 25,000 per year, respectively,[9] one tends to agree with Justice Brennan:

> When a country of over 200 million people inflicts an unusually severe punishment no more than 50 times a year, the inference is strong that the punishment is not being regularly and fairly applied. To dispel it would indeed require a clear showing of non-arbitrary infliction.[10]

Even if one agrees that the number of murders and rapes committed does not necessarily reflect the number for which the death penalty might have been a possible sentence, the difference is still staggering. As Justice Stewart characterizes it, the death penalty is "freakishly" or "spectacularly" rare in its occurrence. In a telling argument in *Furman* v. *Georgia,* Justice Brennan sums up the arbitrary nature of the death penalty:

> *When the punishment of death is inflicted in a trivial number of cases in which it is legally available, the conclusion is virtually inescapable that it is being inflicted arbitrarily.* Indeed, it smacks of little more than a lottery system. The states claim, however, that this rarity is evidence not of arbitrariness, but of informed selectivity: Death is inflicted, they say, only in "extreme" cases.
>
> Informed selectivity, of course, is a value not to be denigrated. Yet presumably the states could make precisely the same claim if there were ten executions per year, or five, or even if there were but one. That there may be as many as fifty per year does not strengthen the claim. When the rate of infliction is at this low level, it is highly implausible that only the worst criminals or the criminals who commit the worst crimes are selected for this punishment. No one has yet suggested a rational basis that could differentiate in those terms the few who die from the many who go to prison. Crimes and criminals simply do not admit of a distinction that can be drawn so finely as to explain, on that ground, the execution of such a tiny sample of those eligible. Certainly the laws that provide for this punishment do not attempt to draw that distinction; all cases to which the laws apply are necessarily "extreme." Nor is the distinction credible in fact. If, for example, petitioner Furman or his crime illustrate the "extreme," then nearly all murderers and their murders are also "extreme."
> Furthermore, our procedures in death cases, rather than punishment, actually sanction an arbitrary selection. For this Court has held that

juries may, as they do, make the decision whether to impose a death sentence wholly unguided by standards governing that decision. *McGautha* v. *California,* 402 U.S. 183, 196-208 (1971). In other words, our procedures are not constructed to guard against the totally capricious selection of criminals for the punishment of death.[11]

This argument is further reinforced by the fact that the two crimes of murder and rape have accounted for nearly 99 percent of the executions in the United States since 1930, with 87 percent of the total for murder alone.

It appears that the original practice of mandating the death penalty for murder has become repugnant to American society as a whole. This is demonstrated by the reluctance of juries to convict in these cases, despite the efforts of state legislators to pass laws that call for mandatory executions for certain types of murder. The concept of "malice aforethought,"[12] generally an essential element of proof in the capital murder statutes, provided a rationale for juries to opt for a lesser penalty. The legislature finally recognized that the juries were using this concept to avoid the death penalty, and passed statutes which attempted to differentiate between the *degrees* of various capital crimes (e.g. first and second degree murder, first and second degree rape), retaining mandatory execution for only the first offenses. In response, juries simply refused to convict in cases where they felt—arbitrarily—that the death penalty was inappropriate. The further refinement of the distinction between capital and noncapital cases was abandoned by legislation in many jurisdictions, and juries were given legal discretion to continue the practice they had already established in fact. The sentence of death is now discretionary in virtually every jurisdiction in which it is still used. Many states have done away with the death penalty entirely, and others prescribe it only in very rare cases.[13]

As of December 31, 1975, the death penalty was illegal in 10 States that had no statutory provisions for capital punishment. In 11 other jurisdictions (10 States and the District of Columbia), the death penalty statutes predated the *Furman* decision and were either of questionable validity or, as in the cases of Massachusetts, Missouri, New Jersey, and Washington, had specifically been declared unconstitutional by the courts. Legislatures in the remaining 30 States had enacted new or revised death penalty statutes since *Furman.* These statutes provide the courts authority to invoke the death penalty for a restricted number of crimes, usually specific types of murder or rape. In Illinois, however, the revised statutes were declared unconstitutional during 1975. The Federal Criminal Code contains death penalty statutes predating *Furman;* these have not been revised except for that section of the Code relating to the death penalty for aircraft piracy, which was revised in 1974.

Revised capital punishment statutes have been designed to comply with the U.S. Supreme Court ruling as they formerly tended to be imposed in an arbitrary and capricious manner, inconsistent with the Eighth Amendment prohibition against "cruel and unusual punishment." The revised statutes reflect the goal of eliminating the discretionary application of the death penalty by requiring that it be mandatory for persons found guilty of committing certain crimes. Specifically defined types of murder, such as the killing of a law enforcement officer, murder by a prisoner serving a life sentence, murder for pecuniary gain, and murder during the perpetration of a felony are included among the relevant offenses. Some States continue to authorize the death penalty for premeditated murder, for rape, and, more rarely, for treason. In addition to stipulating in detail the types of offenses requiring the death penalty, many of the revised statutes also make imposition of capital punishment contingent upon the existence of at least one aggravating circumstance and no mitigating circumstances to the crime. These circumstances, varying according to jurisdiction, are spelled out separately in the statutes and are generally weighed by the jury or judge at separate sentence hearings.[14]

As the power of imposition of death moved from the impersonal and mandatory statutory approach to the hands of the jurors, the use of this final punishment declined to the point of insignificance. Of course, this decline was not so insignificant to the few who were still being executed by the state. Thus, in the 1960s another series of cases attacking the death penalty on the grounds of cruel and unusual punishment appeared.

The Eighth Amendment vs. the Death Penalty

American jurisprudence has borrowed much from the English law. The ban against cruel and unusual punishment embodied in the Eighth Amendment clause was lifted from the English Bill of Rights of 1689. As Justice Marshall indicates in *Furman* v. *Georgia:*

Perhaps the most important principle in analyzing "cruel and unusual" punishment questions is one that is reiterated again and again in the prior opinions of the Court: i.e., the cruel and unusual language *"must draw its meaning from the evolving standards of decency that mark the progress of a maturing society."* Thus, a penalty which was permissible at one time in our nation's history is not necessarily permissible today.

The fact, therefore, that the Court, or individual Justices, may have in the past expressed an opinion that the death penalty is constitutional is not now binding on us.[15]

This reference to *unusual* punishment helps to clarify the relationship between this particular Amendment and the customs and practices of any given period. The death penalty, while perhaps deemed cruel by today's standards, was surely not unusual in the early nineteenth century.

Cruelty was examined by the Supreme Court in 1878 in *Wilkerson* v. *Utah*.[16] It was Utah's practice to punish premeditated murderers by shooting them at a public execution. In this case, the concept of the developing frontier and the execution practices in vogue in other areas around the world were examined. The court did not stick to the doctrine of traditional practice, but examined contemporary thought on the matter of *cruel* punishment. It found that the case against Utah was not cruel in the context of the times, but left open the door for future Court examinations of the cruelty issue:

> Difficulty would attend the effort to define with exactness the extent of the constitutional provision which provides that cruel and unusual punishments shall not be inflicted: but it is safe to affirm that punishments of torture . . . and all others in the same line of unnecessary cruelty, are forbidden by that amendment to the Constitution.[17]

Only with the introduction of the electric chair in New York was the issue of cruel and unusual punishment raised again. The 1890 case of *In re Kemmler* challenged the use of this new form of execution as cruel and unusual punishment. The Court was unanimous in its decision that electrocution was not unconstitutional just because it was unusual. It also came very close to employing the due process clause of the Fourteenth Amendment in this case, giving early warning that it might do so at a later, more substantial hearing. In the 1892 case of *O'Neil* v. *Vermont,* the Court again affirmed that the Eighth Amendment did not apply to the states, but this time there were three strong dissenting opinions. One of the dissenting Justices wrote:

> That designation [cruel and unusual], it is true, is usually applied to punishments which inflict torture, such as the rack, the thumbscrew, the iron boot, the stretching of limbs and the like, which are attended with acute pain and suffering. . . . The inhibition is directed not only against punishments of the character mentioned, but against all punishments which by their excessive length or severity are greatly disproportioned to the offenses charged. The whole inhibition is against that which is excessive. . . .[18]

This logic, while in the minority at the time, prevailed to dominate the 1910 "landmark" case of *Weems* v. *United States*[19]—the first time the Court invalidated a penalty because they found it *excessive.* Clearly, excessive punishment had become as objectionable to the Court as that which was inherently cruel.

Not until 1947 did the Court decide another significant case on the issue of whether the Eighth Amendment applied to the states. In the case of *Louisiana ex rel. Francis* v. *Resweber*,[20] the Court was virtually unanimous in its agreement that the infliction of unnecessary pain is forbidden by traditional Anglo-American legal practice. This unusual case involved a convicted murderer (Francis) who was sentenced to die in the electric chair. The electrical system malfunctioned at the execution and Francis was not killed the first time the current passed through his body. Pleading that a second attempt at electrocution would be cruel and unusual punishment, Francis took his case to the Supreme Court. While this case brought out many of the crucial Eighth Amendment issues, it stopped short of enforcing that Amendment on the states, and Francis lost his appeal on a 5-4 split. He was finally executed, but his case paved the way for several that came in the 1960s.

The 1967 case of *Robinson* v. *California*[21] suggested that the Court was now prepared to consider cases that dealt with excessive punishment in any form, even if the punishment were only a ninety-day sentence. The *Robinson* case involved the California statute which made it a crime to "be addicted to the use of narcotics." In this case, the defense argued that the cruel and unusual punishment clause is not *static,* but a living interpretation of the contemporary standards of society. Thus, some penalties can be seen as excessive and cruel, even if they are widely applied. This matter was clarified in *Powell* v. *Texas,*[22] where the same logic was applied to a case of public drunkenness. The punishment in the *Powell* decision was not found to be excessive or cruel, but the precedent of the Court's willingness to examine these issues in a rapidly changing society was firmly established.

The 1968 *Powell* case was the last to be heard on the issue of cruel and unusual punishment until the landmark 1972 case on capital punishment, *Furman* v. *Georgia*. The decision of the Court was 5-4 in favor of a ban on the use of capital punishment as it is presently being practiced. The Justices were so widely divided on the issue that each wrote a separate opinion.[23] Only two of the Justices (Brennan and Marshall) held that the death penalty was cruel and unusual punishment under all circumstances. The due process clause of the Fourteenth Amendment was evoked, leaving the states the problem of providing legislation that meets the Court's requirements, as described in the opinion of Chief Justice Burger:

> The legislatures are free to eliminate capital punishment for specific crimes or to carve-out limited exceptions to a general abolition of the penalty, without adherence to the conceptual strictures of the Eighth Amendment. The legislatures can and should make an assessment of

FIGURE IV–4. The Electric Chair, Modern Science's Answer to the Gallows (United Press International Photo)

the deterrent influence of capital punishment, both generally and as affecting the commission of specific types of crimes. If legislatures come to doubt the efficacy of capital punishment, they can abolish it either completely or on a selective basis. If new evidence persuades them that they have acted unwisely, they can reverse their field and reinstate the penalty to the extent it is thought warranted. An Eighth Amendment ruling by judges cannot be made with such flexibility or discriminating precision.[24]

While the minority opinion seemed to feel that the Court had overstepped its jurisdiction, the tenor of the dissenting remarks made it clear that they were willing to hear a new appeal when the findings in *Furman* were challenged. The high level of legislative activity in the states, seeking to reinstate the death penalty under the Court's new guidelines, suggested that there would be a challenge in the near future. While *Furman* gave a new lease on life to the over six hundred men who had been sitting on death row,[25] a number of new death sentences have been handed down since, awaiting final resolution of the issue.

On January 17, 1977, the firing squad of the Utah State Prison ended the moratorium on the death penalty that the *Furman* decision had imposed for a decade. Amid a great amount of controversy and in a circus-like atmosphere, Gary Mark Gilmore made his way into the history books as the first American to be executed in the nation's third century. The Supreme Court, in a series of cases, had clarified the conditions in which the death penalty could and could not be imposed.

The 1976 Decisions

Five cases were decided on the same date, July 2, 1976, in regard to the death penalty—specifically as to whether certain state provisions were acceptable under the *Furman* decision. The statutes of three states (Texas, Florida, and Georgia) were affirmed, and the statutes of two (North Carolina and Louisiana) were struck down. The case of *Gregg* v. *Georgia* is the model for those that were upheld. As noted in that decision:

> We think that the Georgia court wisely has chosen not to impose
> unnecessary restrictions on the evidence that can be offered at such a
> hearing and to approve open and far-ranging argument. So long as the
> evidence introduced and the arguments made at the presentence
> hearing do not prejudice a defendant, it is preferable not to impose
> restrictions. We think it desirable for the jury to have as much
> information before it as possible when it makes the sentencing
> decision.
>   Finally, the Georgia statute has an additional provision designed to
> assure that the death penalty will not be imposed on a capriciously

selected group of convicted defendants. The new sentencing procedures require that the state supreme court review every death sentence to determine whether it was imposed under the influence of passion, prejudice, or any other arbitrary factor, whether the evidence supports the findings of a statutory aggravating circumstance, and "[w]hether the sentence of death is excessive or disproportionate to the penalty imposed in similar cases, considering both the crime and the defendant." In performing its sentence review function, the Georgia court has held that "if the death penalty is only rarely imposed for an act or it is substantially out of line with sentences imposed for other acts it will be set aside as excessive." The court on another occasion stated that "we view it to be our duty under the similarity standard to assure that no death sentence is affirmed unless in similar cases throughout the state the death penalty has been imposed generally . . ."

It is apparent that the Supreme Court of Georgia has taken its review responsibilities seriously. In *Coley*, it held that "[t]he prior cases indicate that the past practice among juries faced with similar factual situations and like aggravating circumstances has been to impose only the sentence of life imprisonment for the offense of rape, rather than death." It thereupon reduced Coley's sentence from death to life imprisonment. Similarly, although armed robbery is a capital offense under Georgia law, the Georgia court concluded that the death sentences imposed in this case for that crime were "unusual in that they are rarely imposed for [armed robbery]. Thus, under the test provided by statute, . . . they must be considered to be excessive or disproportionate to the penalties imposed in similar cases." The court therefore vacated Gregg's death sentence for armed robbery and has followed a similar course in every other armed robbery death penalty case to come before it.

The provision for appellate review in the Georgia capital-sentencing system serves as a check against the random or arbitrary imposition of the death penalty. In particular, the proportionality review substantially eliminates the possibility that a person will be sentenced to die by the action of an aberrant jury. If a time comes when juries generally do not impose the death sentence in a certain kind of murder case, the appellate review procedures assure that no defendant convicted under such circumstances will suffer a sentence of death.

The basic concern of *Furman* centered on those defendants who were being condemned to death capriciously and arbitrarily. Under the procedures before the Court in that case, sentencing authorities were not directed to give attention to the nature or circumstances of the crime committed or to the character or record of the defendant. Left unguided, juries imposed the death sentence in a way that could only

THE RIGHTS OF THE CONVICTED CRIMINAL

be called freakish. The new Georgia sentencing procedures, by contrast, focus the jury's attention on the particularized nature of the crime and the particularized characteristics of the individual defendant. While the jury is permitted to consider any aggravating or mitigating circumstances, it must find and identify at least one statutory aggravating factor before it may impose a penalty of death. In this way the jury's discretion is channeled. No longer can a jury wantonly and freakishly impose the death sentence; it is always circumscribed by the legislative guidelines. In addition, the review function of the Supreme Court of Georgia affords additional assurance that the concerns that prompted our decision in *Furman* are not present to any significant degree in the Georgia procedure applied here.

For the reasons expressed in this opinion, we hold that the statutory system under which Gregg was sentenced to death does not violate the Constitution. Accordingly, the judgment of the Georgia Supreme Court is affirmed.[26]

The decision in *Gregg* has already set off a chain of legislative actions in state houses across the nation, aimed at providing death penalty statutes that meet the Supreme Court's challenge. The case of *Woodson* v. *North Carolina* displayed the flawed logic that eventually resulted in reversal by the high court:

It is now well established that the Eighth Amendment draws much of its meaning from "the evolving standards of decency that mark the progress of a maturing society." *Trop* v. *Dulles,* 356 U.S., at 101 (plurality opinion). . . . [O]ne of the most significant developments in our society's treatment of capital punishment has been the rejection of the common-law practice of inexorably imposing a death sentence upon every person convicted of a specified offense. North Carolina's mandatory death penalty statute for first-degree murder departs markedly from contemporary standards respecting the imposition of the punishment of death and thus cannot be applied consistently with the Eighth and Fourteenth Amendments' requirement that the State's power to punish "be exercised within the limits of civilized standards."

A separate deficiency of North Carolina's mandatory death sentence statute is its failure to provide a constitutionally tolerable response to *Furman's* rejection of unbridled jury discretion in the imposition of capital sentences. Central to the limited holding in *Furman* was the conviction that the vesting of standardless sentencing power in the jury violated the Eighth and Fourteenth Amendments. It is argued that North Carolina has remedied the inadequacies of the death penalty statutes held unconsitutional in *Furman* by withdrawing all sentencing discretion from juries in capital cases. But when one considers the long and consistent American experience with the death penalty in first-degree murder cases, it becomes evident that mandatory statutes enacted in response to *Furman* have simply papered over the problem of unguided and unchecked jury discretion.

. . . [T]here is general agreement that American juries have persistently refused to convict a significant portion of persons charged with first-degree murder of that offense under mandatory death penalty statutes. The North Carolina study commission reported that juries in that state ''[q]uite frequently'' were deterred from rendering guilty verdicts of first-degree murder because of the enormity of the sentence automatically imposed. Moreover, as a matter of historic fact, juries operating under discretionary sentencing statutes have consistently returned death sentences in only a minority of first-degree murder cases. In view of the historic record, it is only reasonable to assume that many juries under mandatory statutes will continue to consider the grave consequences of a conviction in reaching a verdict. North Carolina's mandatory death penalty statute provides no standards to guide the jury in its inevitable exercise of the power to determine which first-degree murderers shall live and which shall die. And there is no way under the North Carolina law for the judiciary to check arbitrary and capricious exercise of that power through a review of death sentences. Instead of rationalizing the sentencing process, a mandatory scheme may well exacerbate the problem identified in *Furman* by resting the penalty determination on the particular jury's willingness to act lawlessly. While a mandatory death penalty statute may reasonably be expected to increase the number of persons sentenced to death, it does not fulfill *Furman's* basic requirement by replacing arbitrary and wanton jury discretion with objective standards to guide, regularize, and make rationally reviewable the process for imposing a sentence of death.

A third constitutional shortcoming of the North Carolina statute is its failure to allow the particularized consideration of relevant aspects of the character and record of each convicted defendant before the imposition upon him of a sentence of death. In *Furman*, members of the Court acknowledged what cannot fairly be denied—that death is a punishment different from all other sanctions in kind rather than degree. A process that accords no significance to relevant facets of the character and record of the individual offender or the circumstances of the particular offense excludes from consideration in fixing the ultimate punishment of death the possibility of compassionate or mitigating factors stemming from the diverse frailties of humankind. It treats all persons convicted of a designated offense not as uniquely individual human beings, but as members of a faceless, undifferentiated mass to be subjected to the blind infliction of the penalty of death.

This Court has previously recognized that ''[f]or the determination of sentences, justice generally requires consideration of more than the particular acts by which the crime was committed and that there be taken into account the circumstances of the offense together with the character and propensities of the offender.'' Consideration of both the offender and the offense in order to arrive at a just and appropriate sentence has been viewed as a progressive and humanizing development. While the prevailing practice of individualizing sentencing determinations generally reflects simply enlightened policy rather than a constitutional imperative, we believe that in capital cases the fundamental respect for humanity underlying the Eighth Amendment requires consideration of the character and record of the individual offender and the circumstances of the particular offense as a constitutionally indispensable part of the process of inflicting the penalty of death.

This conclusion rests squarely on the predicate that the penalty of death is qualitatively different from a sentence of imprisonment, however long. Death, in its finality, differs more from life imprisonment than a 100-year prison term differs from one of only a year or two. Because of that qualitative difference, there is a corresponding difference in the need for reliability in the determination that death is the appropriate punishment in a specific case.

For the reasons stated, we conclude that the death sentences imposed upon the petitioners under North Carolina's mandatory death sentence statute violated the Eighth and Fourteenth Amendments and therefore must be set aside. The judgment of the Supreme Court of North Carolina is reversed insofar as it upheld the death sentences imposed upon the petitioners, and the case is remanded for further proceedings not inconsistent with this opinion.[27]

After a long and tortuous process, the Court has finally made clear what it feels are the boundaries for imposition of the death penalty. Despite this effort, many states still feel that the death penalty is too harsh a punishment to impose. The arguments in the Supreme Court may be, at least for the time being, settled, but the arguments in the society as a whole continue.

A Matter of Life or Death

Another major argument of the abolitionists is that the death penalty is not as effective a deterrent as the life sentence. There is perhaps no problem in criminal justice more complicated than the attempt to determine the deterrent effect of the death penalty. As we mentioned earlier, the effect on individual deterrence is absolute; it is the general deterrence that is questioned. Every time a capital offense occurs, we can argue that deterrence has failed, whatever the punishment. We can easily count the failures, but counting the individuals who actually may have been deterred from capital crimes for fear of the punishment is more difficult, if not impossible. The argument in favor of capital punishment as a deterrent was perhaps best summarized by noted English jurist Sir James Stephen in 1864:

> No other punishment *deters men so effectually* from committing crimes as the punishment of death. This is one of those propositions which it is difficult to prove, simply because they are in themselves more obvious than any proof can make them. It is possible to display ingenuity in arguing against it, but that is all. The whole experience of mankind is in the other direction. The threat of instant death is the one to which resort has always been made when there was an absolute necessity for producing some result. . . . No one goes to certain inevitable death except by compulsion. Put the matter the other way. Was there ever yet a criminal who, when sentenced to death and brought out to die, would refuse the offer of a commutation of his sentence for the severest secondary punishment? Surely not. Why is this? It can only be because "All that a man has will he give for his life." In any secondary punishment, however terrible, there is hope; but death is death; its terrors cannot be described more forcibly.[28]

The abolitionists, using the logic of Professor Sellin (outlined in the first part of this chapter), try to amass vast statistical bases to show the lack of correlation between capital crime *rates* and the presence or absence of capital punishment *statutes* in various jurisdictions. While such evidence is not without flaws, the abolitionists have a clear and convincing case that the death penalty is not useful as a deterrent to crime in America.

What is the alternative to a death penalty in punishment of offenders who have committed crimes such as murder and rape? Life imprisonment is considered the most logical substitute, though prison administrators claim that offenders who know they are in prison for life will feel they have nothing to lose if they commit further crimes behind the walls. In fact, there is an overwhelming body of evidence that the presence or absence of the death penalty has no effect on the homicide rate inside prisons. Murderers (who account for almost 90 percent of capital cases) are usually model prisoners. It has even been postulated that the death penalty itself creates an atmosphere that fosters violence in prison. The day of an execution is charged with extreme tension. The prisoners are often placed under more security than usual, and acts of violence in defiance of the authorities seem to be more prevalent.

Many who oppose the life sentence as a replacement for the death penalty observe that the parole laws in many states make it possible for a "lifer" to get out in a relatively brief time. Usually, those who receive life sentences become eligible for parole in thirteen years. The proposed answer to this argument is to remove the hope of parole from a life sentence (*life certain*), but this action would constitute an admission that certain prisoners could not be rehabilitated, and would destroy the offenders' possible incentive to change their behavior patterns. The chance that an innocent person might be convicted also detracts from the acceptability of the irreversible life sentence.

Three Other Arguments

While the deterrence argument is the most popular, other death penalty controversies also continue to rage. The most important of these involve *retribution, economy,* and *protection.* The advocates of capital punishment do not equate retribution with revenge, claiming that the former is a method of uniting society in the fight against especially serious crimes. The law dispenses retribution in relation to the seriousness of crime; by this theory, the punishment the death penalty represents is more important than the fact that it requires the loss of a single life. The abolitionists, on the other hand, point out that the number of crimes for which the death penalty may be imposed has steadily declined. Since a great proportion of the offenders who commit these serious crimes *do not* receive the sentence of death, the retribution factor has been reduced to a meaningless gesture. In *Weems* v. *United States,* the conflict between the two arguments was clarified:

> [T]his contrast shows more than different exercises of legislative judgment. It is greater than that. It condemns the sentence in this case as cruel and unusual. It exhibits a difference between unrestrained power and that which is exercised under the spirit of constitutional limitations formed to establish justice. The state thereby suffers nothing and loses no power. *The purpose of punishment is fulfilled, crime is repressed by penalties of just, not tormenting, severity, its repetition is prevented, and hope is given for the reformation of the criminal.*[29]

The Court made it clear that the demands of retribution may be satisfied without exceptionally severe punishments.

The argument that the death penalty is more *financially economical* than life imprisonment does not stand up under close examination. Prisoners who are awaiting death sentences will use every remedy available to them. This increases the cost to the state in terms of prolonged special security for the condemned, court expenses, provision of counsel, and other outlays that attend a lengthy series of appeals. Many cases drag on for eight years or more. The cost to an offender's family must be considered as well. Many studies have shown that the life sentence is less expensive than the long legal battle resulting in the final act of ritual homicide in the name of the state.

The *protection* theory holds that dangerous persons who commit serious crimes should be eliminated from society to ensure that they will not later repeat those crimes. This argument is reminiscent of the primitive banishment justification. If all those who committed the offenses in question were to be executed, most states would need a regular assembly line of extermination. Actually, so few (less than 1 percent) of these convicted capital cases have been actually sentenced to death that the protection theory seems a shallow one at best. Not even police or correctional personnel, apparently, benefitted from the death penalty; studies have shown no difference in the number of attacks on these officials in jurisdictions with and without the option of capital punishment.

This is a text on corrections rather than criminology, but the principles are certainly applicable to either field. The ritual killing of offenders—in the name of retribution, deterrence, economy, or protection—seems hard to justify, based on the available facts. *The answer seems to lie in the improvement of the entire criminal justice system, to provide equity to all the offenders who come under its control.*

Summary

The Supreme Court has shown that it is willing to take on the knotty issue of capital punishment—head-on. In the *Gregg* decision the Court showed what state provisions it was willing to accept in the post-*Furman* state of the criminal justice system; in *Woodson,* the Court demonstrated the conditions it was *not* about to accept when the life of an offender was involved. With many states rushing to put new capital punishment penalties in their criminal codes, the battle over the administration of the death penalty is sure to be renewed in the near future. Although it may only be upheld in very *restricted* circumstances, the death penalty is considered by some law enforcers an opportunity to gain publicity and to deter the most serious offenders. It is clear, however, that these limited instances will have to be administered on a scrupulously equitable basis, or even this limited sanction will be held unconstitutional. It is hoped that we will choose to work toward improved and innovative correctional treatment, leaving the death penalty ritual for future historians to ponder in amazement, as a symbol of our callous disregard for the value of human life.

REVIEW QUESTIONS

I. Find the answers to the following in the text:

    1. Explain the difference between individual and general deterrence.

2. Explain the basic guidelines that came out of *Furman* v. *Georgia*.

3. Explain the arguments of retribution, economy, and protection as attempts to justify the death penalty.

4. Prepare an argument *for* the retention of the death penalty; then prepare an argument *against* it.

II. Words to identify:

1. deterrence

2. unusual punishment

3. general deterrence

4. retribution

5. life certain

6. coup de grace

7. individual deterrence

8. moratorium

9. malice aforethought

NOTES

1. "Public Executions," *Journal of Prison Discipline and Philanthropy* (July 1859): 117-123.

2. Harry Elmer Barnes and Negley K. Teeter, *New Horizons in Criminology*, 3d ed. (Englewood Cliffs, N.J.: Prentice-Hall, 1959), p. 308.

3. Barnes and Teeters, *New Horizons in Criminology,* p. 309.

4. Federal Bureau of Prisons, *National Prisoner Statistics* 18 (February 1958).

5. Statement of Howard B. Gill, Director of the Institute of Correctional Administration, Boston, Massachusetts, before the Committee on the Judiciary of the United States House of Representatives, March 17, 1972.

6. Thorsten Sellin, "The Death Penalty, Deterrence, and Police Safety" in *The Sociology of Punishment and Correction,* ed. Johnson, Savitz, and Wolfgang (New York: John Wiley & Sons, 1970), p. 371.

7. Lewis E. Lawes, *Meet the Murderer!* (New York: Harper & Row, 1940), pp. 178-179.

8. J. Edgar Hoover, *Uniform Crime Reports* (Washington, D.C.: U.S. Government Printing Office, 1931-1939). A rough average of these crimes known to the police is presented here.

9. Hoover, *Uniform Crime Reports, 1960-1967.* Again, an average of these crimes known to the police is presented. A note of caution: The reported crimes in the early era of the *Uniform Crime Reports* are not to be compared with the later reports. They are presented only to call attention to the difference between crimes which *can* result in the death penalty and those which *did* result in an execution.

10. Justice William J. Brennan, *Furman* v. *Georgia,* 408 U.S. 238.

11. Brennan, *Furman* v. *Georgia.*

12. *Malice aforethought* means malice in fact or implied malice in the intent of one who has had time to premeditate an act which is unlawful or harmful.

13. The states without the death penalty (prior to *Furman* v. *Georgia*) were:

State	Date Abolished	Special Conditions
Rhode Island	1852	
Wisconsin	1853	
Maine	1887	
Minnesota	1911	
North Dakota	1915	Treason, or first-degree murder while serving a term for murder.
Hawaii	1957	
Alaska	1957	
Michigan	1963	
Oregon	1964	
Iowa	1965	
West Virginia	1965	
Vermont	1965	For first-degree murderers who commit a second murder or kill a law enforcement officer.
New York	1965	Killing a peace officer on duty, or a guard or inmate while confined or escaping.

14. U.S. Department of Justice, *Capital Punishment 1975* (Washington, D.C.: U.S. Government Printing Office, 1976), p. 5.

15. Justice Thurgood Marshall, *Furman* v. *Georgia.*

16. *Wilkerson* v. *Utah,* 99 U.S. 130 (1878). The State Supreme Court of Utah upheld a lower court decision sentencing a prisoner convicted of murder in the first degree to be publicly shot.

17. Justice Nathan Clifford, *Wilkerson* v. *Utah,* 99 U.S. 130 (1878).

18. Justice Stephen Field, *O'Neil* v. *Vermont,* 144 U.S. 323 (1892).

19. *Weems* v. *United States,* 217 U.S. 349 (1910). This decision represented a broad interpretation of the Eighth Amendment, asserting that cruel and unusual punishment could apply to prision sentences of a length disporportionate to the offense.

20. *Louisiana ex rel. Francis* v. *Resweber,* 329 U.S. 459 (1947). The State Supreme Court of Louisiana denied a writ of habeas corpus against a second attempt to execute a prisoner convicted of murder, the first attempt at electrocution having failed because of mechanical difficulty.

21. *Robinson* v. *California,* 370 U.S. 660, 82 S.Ct. 1417, 8 L.Ed. 2d 758 (1962). The U.S. Supreme Court reversed a lower court decision upholding a California law making the petitioner's narcotics addiction a criminal offense. The Court maintained that the statute violated the Eighth Amendment of the Constitution.

22. *Powell* v. *Texas,* 392 U.S. 514, 88 S.Ct. 2145, 20 L.Ed. 2d 1254 (1968). The U.S. Supreme Court upheld a county court decision in favor of the defendant's claim that a statute making it unlawful to be drunk in a public place violated the Eighth Amendment of the Constitution. However, two of the justices dissented.

23. For brief analysis of the varied opions, see F. C. Rieber "Supreme Court Bars Death Penalty as It is Now Imposed by the States," *American Journal of Corrections* 35 (1973): 10-14.

24. Chief Justice Warren Burger, *Furman* v. *Georgia.*

25. These included such notable figures as Sirhan Sirhan, the convicted killer of Senator Robert Kennedy; and Charles Manson, leader of the group of mass killers in California known as "the Family."

26. *Gregg* v. *Georgia,* U.S. No. 74-6257, July 2, 1976.

27. *Woodson et al.* v. *North Carolina,* U.S. No. 75-5491, July 2, 1976.

28. Sir James Stephen (as quoted in *Furman* v. *Georgia* by Justice Marshall).

29. *Weems* v. *United States* (emphasis added).

16 Rights of Ex-Offenders

In part the terrible price we are paying in crime is because we have tended—once the drama of the trial is over—to regard all criminals as human rubbish.

CHIEF JUSTICE WARREN E. BURGER

The Legend of the Ex-Con

The highly stylized version of the "ex-con" often presented in the movies and on television usually depicts a tough, scar-faced thug, able to survive on his wits and muscle, with a good-looking blonde always somewhere in the background. He is depicted as a man to be feared and never trusted. With a granite jaw and shifty eyes, he talks out of the corner of his mouth, and he prefers a life of crime. The real-life ex-offender, of course, is something quite different from our gangster legends.

The ex-offenders found in most cities are young, with little experience outside prison walls; poor, with only the funds they have managed to acquire while in prison; uneducated, with less than a high school degree; and frightened, having spent several years away from a rapidly changing world. After release from prison, these individuals must start a new life and make it in the free world while being watched by the correctional authorities, local police, employers, friends, and family. They often return to the same social and environmental conditions in which their trouble arose in the first place. The wonder is not that so many ex-offenders recidivate, but that *more* do not. If one adds to this already heavy burden the legal and administrative restrictions placed on ex-offenders, it is evident that the happy-go-lucky "ex-con" is indeed a legend invented for the reading and viewing public. This chapter examines the restrictions on ex-offenders, and the current status of efforts to provide more rights for them.

Collateral Consequences of Conviction

The conviction for an offense carries with it the punishment imposed by that guilt determination. In addition, the convicted offender must carry several other disabilities and disqualifications that result from the conviction per se. Even after offenders have served their sentences, these secondary problems

continue to plague them, in the form of social stigma, civil rights deprivation, and administrative and legislative restrictions. Each of these areas
interacts with the others, and the sum total of their effect is to negate the
successful reintegration of ex-offenders with the free community. The
problems first surface when ex-offenders attempt to find employment, as this
comment by one such job seeker illustrates:

> Now if you're out there on the bricks and looking for work, Joe, don't
> bother applying for any of those jobs I told you about and you'll save
> yourself a bundle of heartaches. Whenever you apply for any job, my
> advice is not to mention your record. That's right, lie to 'em. If they
> have a place on the employment application where it asks you if
> you've ever been convicted of a crime, put down N-O, no! If you
> don't, you're screening yourself out of 75 percent of all jobs, and
> damned near 100 percent of the better jobs. You have to look ahead
> too, Joe. Big Willie, the trustyland barber, has a brother working for
> one of the big steel companies. A friend got him the job, white collar
> too. That was seven, eight years ago. He's still on the same job, but
> guys who have only been with the company two or three years are
> moving right up the line to higher job classifications and better pay.
> Why? His boss told him why. He's got a record, and the company
> knows it's on his original employment application. His boss told him
> he was terribly sorry, that it wasn't his fault, but the higher-ups passed
> him up because fifteen years ago he served two years in prison. See,
> Joe, crime don't pay, because they ain't never going to let you up once
> they got you down. That's just the way it is.
>
> Go ahead and tell 'em if you want to, Joe. You're taking a chance
> no matter what you do. If you tell 'em you don't get the job most
> of the time. If you don't tell 'em, and they find out, they fire you.
> You know Louie, the cell-house clerk? He got a job and didn't
> tell 'em about his record. Louie's parole officer came around checking
> on him and blowed the job for Louie. How do you like them apples?
> And Gabby, the four block runner, went out and got a job that'll
> knock you out. He was hired as a credit investigator! Yeah, handling
> confidential financial reports all day long. While he was still on parole
> too. His parole officer was an OK guy and said more power to 'em.
> Well, it took about two months because the employment application
> investigation isn't handled by regional offices but is done by the main
> office in New York. One day his boss calls him in, red-faced and all,
> and says to him, why didn't you tell us? Louie says, if I'd told you,
> would you have hired me? His boss says, of course not! Louie was
> canned.[1]

The great dilemma faced by the ex-offender in search of a job is obvious.

The stigma of a prison record seems to ex-offenders a millstone, to be worn around their necks until death. While we pride ourselves that we have advanced beyond the eye-for-an-eye mentality of the past, we do not show it in the treatment of our offenders who have allegedly paid their "debt" to society. Aaron Nussbaum points out some of the problems of stigma for the discharged prisoner:

> It is a grim fact that total punishment for crime never ends with the courts or jails. None can deny that a criminal record is a life-long handicap, and its subject a "marked man" in our society. No matter how genuine the reformation, nor how sincere and complete the inner resolution to revert to lawful behavior, the criminal offender is and remains a prisoner of his past record long after the crime is expiated by the punishment fixed under the criminal codes.
>
> This traditional prejudice and distrust stalks him at every turn no matter what crime he may have committed, or the nature of the punishment meted out to him. It strikes at the first offender as ruthlessly, and with as deadly effect, as upon the inveterate repeater or the professional criminal. It pursues those alike who have served time in imprisonment, of long or short duration, and those who have been merely cloaked with a criminal record in the form of a suspended sentence, a discharge on probation, or even a fine.[2]

The loss of self-esteem, a trait the average American must have to survive in the competitive atmosphere of the free world, makes it difficult to bridge the gap between institutional life and the community. It is this search for self-esteem and status that leads many ex-offenders back to the circle of acquaintances who first led them afoul of the law. The personal disintegration encouraged by the fortress prisons of America makes the discharged offender both a social and economic cripple. Hopefully, the new techniques in corrections, designed to strengthen self-esteem and produce reasonable readjustment in the community, will help to offset this effect.

Most people recognize that released prisoners do not automatically regain all their civil rights, but there is widespread confusion as to which rights are permanently lost and which suspended, and what machinery is available to regain them. Sol Rubin, lawyer and writer on penology, discusses the loss of such rights as voting and certain kinds of employment after release:

> [W]hen a convicted defendant is *not* sentenced to commitment, but is placed on probation, and receives a suspended sentence, he should lose no civil rights. This is a recommendation of the Standard Probation and Parole Act published as long ago as 1955.

It is a contradiction of the purposes of probation and parole that this view does not prevail. A California case cites the following instruction to a new parolee: "Your civil rights have been suspended. Therefore, you may not enter into any contract, marry, engage in business or execute a contract without the restoration of such civil rights by the Adult Authority." A look at the rights restored by the Adult Authority at the time of release on parole is just as sad, hardly more than that on release he may be at large. He may rent a habitation, he is told, buy food, clothing, and transportation, and tools for a job; and he is advised that he has the benefit of rights under Workman's Compensation, Unemployment Insurance, etc.

When the sentence is commitment, the principle of *Coffin* v. *Reichard* ought to apply, that a prisoner retains (or should retain) all rights of an ordinary citizen except those expressly or by necessary implication taken away by law.[3]

The laws in most states *permanently* deprive felons of the right to vote. It seems reasonable that felons, while incarcerated, might be denied this right on grounds that they are not entitled to help determine the outcome of elections during that period. Being able to vote in the free society, however, is important to the ex-offenders' self-esteem. Further, it seems that the goals of rehabilitation would be enhanced by encouraging ex-offenders to partici- pate in the political process and thus to identify with the free society.

Some of the other more common rights that are denied to convicted felons (permanently in many states) are the rights to hold public office, to serve on juries, to testify, and to make contracts or sue in court. Variations in the application of these sanctions among the different states make it impossible to generalize about them. Recognition of the inequities in these denials is expressed in the provisions of Section 306.1(1) of the American Law Institute's Model Penal Code:

> No person shall suffer any legal disqualification or disability because of his conviction of a crime or his sentence on such conviction, unless the disqualification or disability involves the deprivation of a right or privilege which is:
>
> a. necessarily incident to execution of the sentence of the court; or
>
> b. provided by the Constitution or the Code; or
>
> c. provided by a statute other than the Code, when the conviction is of a crime defined by such statute; or
>
> d. provided by the judgment, order or regulation of a court, agency or official exercising a jurisdiction conferred by law, or by the statute defining such

> jurisdiction, when the commission of the crime or the
> conviction or the sentence is reasonably related to
> the competency of the individual to exercise the
> right or privilege of which he is deprived.[4]

While all the problems mentioned so far are certainly significant barriers to the reintegration of ex-offenders into the community, the most significant hurdles in our industrial society stage seem to stem from employment restrictions. The unemployment rate for released prisoners is as much as five times the average for non-offenders. For offenders under twenty years of age, who are involved in one-half the arrests for serious crimes, the rate is as high as 36 percent.[5] The two basic reasons for this high rate of unemployment are the ex-offender's lack of skills or training and the laws, regulations, and practices which prohibit certain jobs to those with a criminal record. The significance of these problems has been acknowledged by the Attorney General of the state of Washington:

> [T]he public is not generally aware of the fact that at the very time
> when it is approving efforts to develop job skills and employment for
> offenders and ex-offenders, there exists a major body of legal barriers
> to meaningful and gainful employment of persons released from
> correctional systems. . . .
> We are thus involved in a system which defeats itself, in a system
> where through the work ethic and the values of our society, we
> applaud hard work and productive activity, while at the same time
> denying exactly that opportunity to do hard work and productive
> activity to persons we expect, in fact demand, to act responsibly. We
> try to rehabilitate, and then we place barriers to rehabilitation and in
> fact initiate an active impetus back to a life of crime.[6]

An American Bar Association study found 1,948 different state statutory provisions that affect the licensing of an ex-offender. Of this number, 134 referred to the commission of a criminal offense as grounds for denial of a license, and 707 required that the applicant have not committed a criminal offense and possess "good moral character."[7] These provisions clearly prohibit the ex-offender from seeking a career in those fields which require licenses. The study also touched on the problem of crimes which involve "moral turpitude."[8] Four hundred ten licensing statutes disqualified the applicant on these grounds, which can be stretched to cover almost any criminal offense. The study referred to these two handicaps:

> In the final analysis, the problem with such so-called licensing
> standards as "good moral character" and "crime involving moral
> turpitude" is that, without definitive guidelines, the terms are too
> imprecise to be adequate tests in determining the applicant's fitness or

capacity to properly perform the duties of the occupation for which he seeks a license. In the absence of guidelines, there is often a failure by licensing agencies to take into account whether the crime committed by the applicant relates to the occupation sought, the age of the individual and surrounding circumstances at the time of the offense, the length of time that has elapsed since the unlawful activity, and the subsequent rehabilitative efforts of the individual. The result is that, without such guidelines, broad discretion is left to persons on the licensing board or agency to exercise their authority in such a manner as to arbitrarily reject any applicant, particularly the former offender, whom they consider unfit.[9]

Such restrictions certainly hamper adjustment by the over 100,000 persons released from prison each year, and complicate the efforts of correctional professionals who supervise the over one million paroled offenders.[10] It is ironic and sobering to recognize that many prisons include vocational training in certain trades which ex-offenders cannot be licensed to practice when they are released.[11]

An Analysis of the Restricted Trades

There are four occupations which the U.S. Department of Labor refers to as "old standbys," i.e., jobs where workers are almost always needed. These four were examined in depth by the American Bar Association study:

> A. *Barber.* Barbering is one of the most restricted occupations. Forty-six states and the District of Columbia have statutory provisions containing restrictions on the licensing of former offenders. Forty-five of these jurisdictions have a requirement of good moral character. Twenty-four jurisdictions deny a license to an applicant convicted of a felony or a crime involving moral turpitude. And in twenty-two jurisdictions, the applicant has to satisfy both conditions for a license; that is, have no conviction for a criminal offense and possess good moral character. Ironically, many correctional institutions offer supervised training programs in barbering for inmates.
>
> Only four states—Alabama, Massachusetts, New Hampshire, and South Carolina—have no statutory provisions on the licensing of ex-offenders as barbers. In 1970, an estimated 180,000 barbers were employed in the United States, most of them men.

B. *Cosmetologist/Beautician.* The occupation of cosmetologist/beautician is even more restrictive to ex-offenders than barbering. Forty-seven states and the District of Columbia limit the licensing for cosmetologist/beautician. Forty-six of these jurisdictions have a requirement of good moral character. Twenty-six jurisdictions deny a license to an applicant convicted of a felony or a crime involving moral turpitude. And in twenty-four jurisdictions, the applicant has to satisfy both conditions before receiving a license. Only three states—Massachusetts, North Carolina, and South Carolina—have no restrictions on the licensing of an ex-offender as a cosmetologist/beautician. In 1970, approximately 485,000 people were employed as hairdressers and cosmetologists, about 10 percent being men.

C. *Practical Nurse.* Practical nursing runs very close to the occupation of cosmetology/beautician in the number of licensing restrictions placed on ex-offenders. Forty-six states and the District of Columbia place restrictions on the hiring of practical nurses with criminal records and forty-six jurisdictions require that they possess good moral character. Twenty-four jurisdictions deny a license to an applicant convicted of a felony or other crime involving moral turpitude. And in twenty-three jurisdictions, an applicant has to satisfy both conditions before receiving a license. Only four states—Indiana, Iowa, Montana, and Pennsylvania—have no restrictions on the licensing of ex-offenders as practical nurses. In 1970, approximately 370,000 licensed practical nurses were employed. It should also be noted that after a year of training, hospital attendants, of which there are approximately 830,000, become eligible to be licensed as practical nurses. The majority of persons in these categories are women, who constitute about 14 percent of all offenders.

D. *Plumber.* There are restrictions on ex-offenders being licensed as plumbers in Connecticut, District of Columbia, Kentucky, Maryland, Michigan, Texas, and Utah. All of these jurisdictions are restricted only by the requirement of good moral character. In 1970, approximately 350,000 plumbers and pipefitters were employed, and this number is expected to increase rapidly during the '70s.[12]

The Problem with a Record

As we have seen, the person with a record of conviction is at a major disadvantage when it comes to reintegration into the community. The deprivation of rights and bars to employment are related to that record, so it is vital to know what having a record means in the "Age of Information." It seems that a record, even a record of mere *contact* with the criminal justice system, is extremely difficult to shed once it has been acquired. This record becomes the basis for special attention by the police and harassment from credit agencies. Once the record has been placed in the computers, it is retrieved whenever requested by an authorized agency and, inevitably, by some unauthorized agencies.

One way to overcome the problem of a record is to develop a system that will annul the conviction after certain specifications are met. The National Council on Crime and Delinquency[13] makes this provision in its Model Act for Annulment of Conviction of Crime:

The court in which a conviction of crime has been had may, at the time of discharge of a convicted person from its control, or upon his discharge from imprisonment or parole, or at any time thereafter, enter an order annulling, canceling, and rescinding the record of conviction and disposition, when in the opinion of the court the order would assist in rehabilitation and be consistent with the public welfare. Upon the entry of such order the person against whom the conviction had been entered shall be restored to all civil rights lost or suspended by virtue of the arrest, conviction, or sentence, unless otherwise provided in the order, and shall be treated in all respects as not having been convicted, except that upon conviction of any subsequent crime the prior conviction may be considered by the court in determining the sentence to be imposed.

In any application for employment, license, or other civil right or privilege, or any appearance as a witness, a person may be questioned about previous criminal record only in language such as the following: "Have you ever been arrested for or convicted of a crime which has not been annulled by a court?"

Upon entry of the order of annulment of conviction, the court shall issue to the person in whose favor the order has been entered a certificate stating that his behavior after conviction has warranted the issuance of the order, and that its effect is to annul, cancel, and rescind the record of conviction and disposition.

Nothing in this act shall affect any right of the offender to appeal from his conviction or to rely on it in bar of any subsequent proceedings for the same offense.[14]

This kind of proposal has aroused some interest, but little action, in state legislatures. Because annulment is in fact the only reasonable way to protect the ex-offender from questions about prior convictions, some courts are getting around the legislative inaction by failing to enter the record of conviction and keeping an informal "vest-pocket" record.[15]

The problem of a record, in this country, is especially critical when an arrest does *not* result in a conviction. In most foreign countries, an arrest with no conviction cannot be used against the person in later actions. In the United States, in most jurisdictions, employment applications can include questions about an arrest, regardless of whether or not a conviction took place. Even a pardon, exonerating the suspect from guilt, does not remove the incident from the record. Not surprisingly, the current attack on this perpetual record is based on the cruel and unusual punishment clause of the Eighth Amendment.[16] Another legal approach is reflected in recent suits claiming that prisoners and ex-offenders are being discriminated against as a *class,* instead of being treated on the basis of individual merit:

> It is a truism that we find hard to accept that the protections of the Bill of Rights against police and other official abuse are for all of us, the criminals and the non-criminals. But when we consider the tens of millions who have a record of arrest, perhaps as many as 50 million, it is clear that the civil rights of those who are in conflict with the law are, indeed, in the most pragmatic way, the interest of all. We are in an era of struggle for civil rights, for Blacks, for women, for the mentally ill, for the young, even the delinquent young. Perhaps we are in a period of civil rights for homosexuals and others whose sexual practices are unreasonably subject to legal condemnation.
>
> It is timely, indeed, that we awake to the excesses in punishing those in conflict with the law. It is a field of great discrimination, and must be remedied, just as much as other discriminations must be remedied. Not all people with a criminal record are vicious or degraded to begin with, or if their crime was vicious, are they doomed to remain as they were; unless, of course, we strive by discrimination and rejection, to make them so.[17]

Registration of Criminals

Registration of criminals has been a practice ever since society started imprisoning individuals. In ancient times, registration was used to identify prisoners in penal servitude; prisoners were branded or marked to decrease their already minimal chances of escape. Since penal slaves had no hope of ever being free, the markings were a sign of their permanent status. The "yellow card" was later used in European countries to identify former prisoners who were lucky enough to live through their sentences.[18] The registration of felons has also been a widespread practice in America, especially at the local level. A problem with local registration provisions is that they tend to single out offenders for special attention from authorities which they would not otherwise be subject to. Most of these requirements are obsolete today. As information on offenders and arrested persons is placed into computer data-banks, a public official can easily query the computer to check the status of almost anyone.

The most common form of local registration concerns sex-related offenses. The "pervert file" is used to check out former offenders in the event of similar crimes. This kind of file is an undoubted asset to law enforcement, but it becomes a real problem for the ex-offender who is seriously trying to conform. These inquiries are legitimate for law enforcement personnel; however, the discretion with which they are conducted can make a great difference to the ex-offender.

The practice of registering felons is on the decline, mainly because of the mobility of the present American society, but it remains in force in many jurisdictions. Registration may be much more subtle than the practice of branding with a scarlet letter,[19] but it also has the potential to become a permanent stigma. There is considerable room to improve on these tactics in an age of modern informational techniques.

Expungement as a Response

It is clear that the vastly debilitating effect of a criminal conviction is often heightened, rather than reduced, when the ex-offender returns to the free society. Some states have recognized this fact and attempted to develop *expungement* statutes, which erase the history of criminal conviction and completely restore the ex-offender's rights by providing for removal of the stigma of a criminal record. This idea was first developed in 1956, at the National Conference on Parole:

> The expunging of a criminal record should be authorized on a discretionary basis. The court of disposition should be empowered to expunge the record of conviction and disposition through an order by which the individual shall be deemed not to have been convicted. Such action may be taken at the point of discharge from suspended sentence, probation, or the institution upon expiration of a term of commitment. When such action is taken the civil and political rights of the offender are restored.[20]

The American Law Institute also saw the need for some way to vacate a conviction record in selected cases. A section of the Institute's *Model Penal Code* was compiled in 1961, recommending that the court make use of its authority to erase a record when an offender ''has been discharged from probation or parole before the expiration of the maximum thereof'' or ''when the defendant has fully satisfied the sentence and has since led a law-abiding life for at least five years.''[21]

These early recommendations of expungement did not specify procedures for the expungement order and did not go into great detail in identifying the real issues. The Model Act for Annulment proposed by the National Council on Crime and Delinquency, containing the comprehensive provisions for expungement quoted above, would give the ex-offender better protection than the *Model Penal Code* provides. But it remains too limited in its application and fails to recommend adequate procedures. Its effect on someone who is convicted is clear, as it only takes effect *after* conviction. But it does not help the individual who is arrested and not convicted. A viable annulment statute must also permit erasure of an arrest record.

As recently as 1970, the American Bar Association Project on Standards for Criminal Justice made the following points in regard for the need to remove the record stigma:

> *Every jurisdiction should have a method by which the collateral effects of a criminal record can be avoided or mitigated following the successful completion of a term on probation and during its service.*
>
> The Advisory Committee is not as concerned with the form which such statutes take as it is with the principle that flexibility should be built into the system and that *effective ways should be devised to mitigate the scarlet letter effect of a conviction once the offender has satisfactorily adjusted.*[22]

Clearly, there is growing support for the principle that ex-offenders (especially those who have demonstrated that they are in fact reformed) should be provided a means of eliminating the brand of the felon.

Efforts at Expungement

Most state expungement schemes suffer from the problems described above. They are usually fairly clear as to *what* is to be expunged, but very vague and general as to *how* this is to be accomplished. In many cases the laws are extremely limited, even when they are well written. California, for example, states explicitly what records will be sealed: ''the record of conviction and other official records of the case.'' In addition, ''conviction, arrest, or other proceedings shall be deemed not to have occurred, and the petitioner may answer accordingly any question relating to their occurrence.''[23] This statute is clearly and precisely written. The problem is that it applies only to misdemeanor offenders under the age of twenty-one, who must petition the court to gain the benefits of the statute. Even then it excludes narcotic offenses, traffic violations, and sex offenses. What started out as a real model statute has become in practice relatively unimportant because of its narrowed scope. Another California statute, however, allows those who complete probation to withdraw a guilty plea (or the verdict may be set aside if they pled not guilty, but were found guilty), and the defendant is then "released from all penalties and disabilities resulting from the offense of crime."[24] While this statute is supposedly mandatory in its application, it has little applicability due to judicial and legislative efforts to restrict it. Nevada has a similar statute.[25]

Another example of the narrowness issue appears in the Texas codes. Again the provision is very definitive as to intended effect:

> a. When the period and terms of a probation have been satisfactorily completed, the court shall, upon its own motion, discharge him from probation and enter an order in the minutes of the court setting aside the finding of guilty and dismissing the accusation or complaint and the information or indictment against the probationer.
>
> b. After the case against the probationer is dismissed by the court, his finding of guilty may not be considered for any purpose except to determine his entitlement to a future probation under this Act, or any other probation Act.[26]

Again, however, the petitioner must apply for the benefits, and can do so only in the case of a misdemeanor. Further, the defendant must never have been convicted of a misdemeanor or a felony for which a term of imprisonment could have been imposed, and must never have been placed on probation in the preceding five years. The age limitations in the first example are not present, but the other provisions make it extremely difficult to obtain this expungement in most cases.

In nearly all states which have some form of expungement remedy on the statutes, the pattern is the same. The laws are beautifully written in the most benevolent phrases, but no practical way is provided to implement the provisions, or the statutes are so restrictive in their application as to be almost useless. Minnesota has perhaps the most promising effort at a workable expungement statute. In that state, any first-time offender may, after completion of his or her sentence, ask for a "pardon extraordinary." This petition goes to the State Board of Pardons, which then examines the character and reputation of the petitioner. When granted, the "pardon extraordinary . . . shall have the effect of restoring such person to all civil rights and shall have the effect of setting aside the conviction and nullifying the same and of purging such person thereof and such person shall never thereafter be required to disclose the conviction at any time or place other than in a judicial proceeding thereafter instituted.''[27] This statute does not expressly exclude any crimes, and it is especially effective in that it restores *all* civil rights. Like most expungement statutes, it does not consider the arrest record problem, but it could readily be expanded and implemented, and bears watching as one of the few that may encourage solid practical results in time.

Four major recommendations, drawn from findings in a major study of the effect of a criminal record, are found in the Georgetown University Law School report on *The Closed Door:*

> A. *Finding*—Many expungement statutes provide no mechanism by which a conviction may be expunged; thus they often have been found to be not effective. Procedures may be difficult, judicial authority may be discretionary and rarely exercised, and few ex-offenders may know of a statute providing that they must petition for expungement. Most statutes apply only in limited cases and some exclude a variety of listed offenses while others apply only to those completing probation or receiving suspended sentences.
>
> *Recommendation*—It is clear that as to criminal conviction, there is still a vast need for some means by which the debilitating effect of a criminal record may be lessened. An effective state expungement practice is by no means the only method by which ex-offenders may be aided, but changes in this area are sorely needed.
>
> Some have suggested that because existing expunging statutes do not work, and because public attitudes are so important, that statutory reform is not a viable method of removing obstacles to employment. The Institute recognizes the importance of public attitudes and rehabilitative efforts, and is not suggesting that the sole answer is statutory and administrative reform. But a proper legal and administrative structure is a requirement before other necessary steps can be effective. It does little good to train an individual for an occupation if a license to practice cannot be obtained or employers are unwilling to hire ex-offenders. In the latter case legislation restricting the use of criminal records when a job is at stake will at least prevent the legal structure from obstructing bona fide efforts at obtaining employment.

B. *Finding*—Most expungement statutes are unclear as to the meaning and effect of expungement.

Recommendation—Most existing expungement laws do not provide for the destruction and obliteration of court and police records because there are many uses for such records. If expungement statutes limit the use of criminal records, destruction or obliteration becomes unnecessary. The statute could provide that when the conviction is annulled or expunged all civil rights are restored to the petitioner. It could further provide that license and job application forms may ask only about *convictions which have not been expunged.* Restricting such questioning may be a far more effective remedy than placing upon the job seeker the burden of concealing a part of his past.

C. *Finding*—Most expungement statutes do not explicitly describe how courts and police departments are to handle expunged records.

Recommendation—Provisions should require courts and police departments to seal expunged records and prohibit their divulgence to any public or private employer. Responses to any inquiries should not be different from those made about persons who have no criminal records. Under such a provision only a court hearing a criminal case involving that particular ex-offender's involvement in a subsequent crime or a police department investigating a crime could gain access.

D. *Finding*—Probation and parole officers are rarely involved in the expungement process.

Recommendation—Should the probationer not utilize the expungement procedure, petitions could be authorized from probation and parole officers as a back-up measure. These officers could, with a minimum of difficulty, set regular schedules as to when they would consider filing such petitions. For example, they might consider filing such petitions one year after the completion of probation or parole and two years after mandatory release from imprisonment for a felony. The Institute has opted for authorizing proceedings immediately after discharge from probation or parole and release from imprisonment on the grounds that legal obstacles to work should not slow up the rehabilitative process.

Vesting this authority in probation and parole officers could well make expungement an integral part, in fact the "graduation ceremony" of the rehabilitative process, and ex-offenders would be more likely to be made aware of expungement. Also, these officers ideally would have the resources for the social investigation demanded by courts.[28]

While expungement is not the only answer to the problem of the burden and consequences of a criminal record, adoption of a sensible approach to the method is sorely needed.

Right to Work vs. Need to Work

Ex-offenders are often faced with a cruel paradox which dictates that they *must* have employment in order to remain free, while the system denies them any hope for employment *because* they have a record. Many studies have shown that employment is one of the critical factors (if not the most critical) in the successful reintegration of the ex-offender into the community. There were times when ex-offenders might have moved on to a new territorial area and established a new identity, thus escaping the stigmatization that goes with a prison record. The advancing frontiers of early America did not ask many questions, but judged individuals on their present actions instead of their past records. In today's world of computerized records on every aspect of life, privacy has become less a right than a very rare privilege. To most people, the informational expansion is a boon; to ex-offenders it is often a catastrophe. Even citizens who find themselves involved in an arrest that does not result in a conviction may suffer the worst consequences of a record, including the failure to obtain a job, or its loss.

Summary

If convicted felons have paid their debt to society, many organizations feel they should have a chance to start fresh, with a clean record. This belief has been translated into statutes which provide for annulment and expungement of criminal records in a number of states, but many of them lack adequate mechanisms to implement the provisions. Only when the general public has fully accepted the idea of a new and fresh start for the ex-offender will our legislators pass the revisions necessary to make the statutes fully effective.

REVIEW QUESTIONS

I. Find the answers to the following in the text:

1. What are the collateral consequences of a conviction? Discuss.

2. How could expungement improve the reintegration process for ex-offenders?

3. Why does registration of criminals have such a drastic effect on the ex-offender? What are the alternatives?

II. Words to identify:

1. expungement

2. stigma

3. civil rights

4. moral turpitude

5. good moral character

6. old standbys

7. criminal registration

8. yellow card

9. scarlet letter

10. annulment

NOTES

1. Georgetown University Law Center, *The Closed Door: The Effect of a Criminal Record on Employment with State and Local Public Agencies* (Springield, Va.: National Technical Information Service, 1972), p. v.

2. Harry Elmer Barnes and Negley K. Teeters, *New Horizons in Criminology,* 3d ed. (Englewood Cliffs, N.J.: Prentice-Hall, 1959), p. 544.

3. Sol Rubin, "The Man with a Record: A Civil Rights Problem," *Federal Probation* (September 1971): 4.

4. American Law Institute, *Model Penal Code; Proposed Official Draft* (Philadelphia: American Law Institute, 1962).

5. American Bar Association, *Laws, Licenses and the Offender's Right to Work* (Washington, D.C.: National Clearinghouse on Offender Employment Restrictions, 1973), p. 2.

6. *Laws, Licenses and the Offender's Right to Work,* p. 3.

7. *Good moral character* is meaningless term in this context; the statutes imply that a record automatically negates "good character."

8. *Moral turpitude* involves an act of inherent baseness in private, social, or public duties which one owes to his fellowmen or to society, or to his country, her institutions, and her government. [*Kurtz* v. *Farrington,* 104 Conn. 257, 132 Atl. 540, 541 (1962)].

9. *Laws, Licenses and the Offender's Right to Work,* p. 7.

10. National Advisory Commission on Criminal Justice Standards and Goals, *Corrections* (Washington, D.C.: U.S. Government Printing Office, 1973), p. 389.

11. For many years barbers were being trained in the prisons in Florida, but could not be licensed as barbers in Florida.

12. *Laws, Licenses and the Offender's Right to Work,* p. 7.

13. The National Council on Crime and Delinquency was founded in 1907. It has 60,000 members and sponsors a number of action programs in the criminal justice sector. (NCCD Center, 291 Route 17, Paramus, New Jersey 07652.)

14. National Council on Crime and Delinquency, *Annulment of a Conviction of Crime, A Model Act* (Paramus, New Jersey: NCCD, 1962).

15. *A vest-pocket record* is an informal record which the court keeps unofficially and holds over the defendant for a set period of time.

16. "Excessive bail shall not be required, nor excessive fines imposed, *nor cruel and unusual·punishment inflicted*" (emphasis added).

17. Rubin, *Federal Probation,* pp. 6-7.

18. Most European countries have generally required residents to carry identification cards, for population control purposes. A "yellow card" (identification card of yellow color) was a sign of an ex-offender in many countries.

19. The *scarlet letter* was a scarlet "A" the Puritans required known women adulterers to wear around the neck as a punitive mark. The practice is fully described in Nathaniel Hawthorne's novel of the same name.

20. *The Closed Door,* p. 58.

21. American Law Institute, *Model Penal Code.*

22. *The Closed Door,* p. 61 (emphasis added).

23. California Penal Code #1203.45.

24. California Penal Code #1203.4.

25. Nevada Revised Statutes #176.225.

26. *The Closed Door.* p. 65.

27. Minnesota Statutes, Annotated #683.02(2) (1969 Supplement).

28. *The Closed Door,* pp. 68-71.

RECOMMENDED READING LIST

Klotter, John, and Kanovitz, Jacqueline. *Constitutional Law for Police.* Cincinnati, Ohio: W. M. Anderson, 1968.

Lockhart, William, et al. *Constitutional Rights and Liberties.* St. Paul, Minn.: West, 1970.

National Advisory Commission on Criminal Justice Standards and Goals. *Corrections.* Washington, D.C.: U.S. Department of Justice, 1973.

Palmer, Hohn. *Constitutional Rights of Prisoners*. Cincinnati, Ohio: W. M. Anderson, 1973.

The President's Commission on Law Enforcement and Administration of Justice. *Task Force Report: Challenge of Crime in a Free Society*. Washington, D.C.: U.S. Government Printing Office, 1967.

The President's Commission on Law Enforcement and Administration of Justice. *Task Force Report: Corrections*. Washington, D.C.: U.S. Government Printing Office, 1967.

The President's Commission on Law Enforcement and Administration of Justice. *Task Force Report: Courts* Washington, D.C.: U.S. Government Printing Office, 1967.

Scacco, Anthony. *Rape in Prison*. Springfield, Ill.: Charles C. Thomas, 1975.

Schrag, Clarence. *Crime and Justice: American Style*. Washington, D.C.: U.S. Government Printing Office, 1971.

Walker, Daniel. *Rights in Conflict*. New York: E. P. Dutton, 1968.

PART V

The Correctional Client

17 Male Offenders

The simple rule for corrections is that the correctional treatments of maximum reformative effect are those that enhance a prisoner's opportunities in legitimate economic pursuits, and those that improve his conception of himself when he identifies with anticriminal persons.

DANIEL GLASER

As we saw in Part I, until very recently incarceration practices were not intended to "correct" the behavior of inmates; consequently, the young and the old, the sick and the well, the women and the men, and the dangerous and the naive were all placed indiscriminately in one facility. As the concepts of penitence and corrections were developed, men and women were segregated in separate institutions. Later, institutions were further specialized, and different kinds of institutions were developed for the younger inmates, who were separated from the more hardened felons (though these are still sometimes hard to tell apart).

If corrections and prisons can be considered as businesses, it becomes necessary to consider inmate groups as *clients* with different needs, problems, and demands. This part of the text addresses the major subdivisions into which the modern day "correctional client" may be categorized: *men, women, juveniles,* and *special category offenders.* We turn now to the plight of the male offender in the jail setting.

Men and Boys in Jail

Of all the institutions through which offenders pass in the correctional funnel, none have a more diverse population or a more sordid past than the jails, facilities operated by a unit of local government for the detention or correction of adults suspected or convicted of a crime.[1] The jail is the first facility within the criminal justice system with which adult males (and many juvenile males) have contact.

Both the felon and the misdemeanant, the first-time and the repeat offender, the adult and the juvenile, the convicted and the accused (not to mention the guilty and the innocent) are housed in America's jails. Others being held in jail include the accused who are awaiting arraignment, transfer to other authorities (mental hospitals, federal courts, the military), trial, or final sentencing. *Only about 45 percent of the nation's jailed are actually serving sentences.*[2] Almost 95 percent of the jail population is male. Based on the latest jail census, there are at least 134,500 men in 3,921 jails on any given day. Men held in jails are in many ways the "losers" of America—in terms of economic status, social status, occupation, marital status, education, and almost any other factor that can be named.

In addition to the diverse legal statuses held by jailed men, there are sharp differences in their socioeconomic characteristics. Blacks comprise a disproportionately large component of the men in jails (42 percent) when compared to whites (56 percent). Roughly one-half of all inmates are young, between the ages of 19 and 29. As one would expect from so young a population, almost half of the inmates have never been married, and the other half are about evenly divided among those who are married and those who are divorced, widowed, or separated.

Poverty and unemployment are common characteristics of men in jail. Two out of every five inmates in pretrial detention are not employed, and only 48 percent are employed full-time at the time of their admission. There is no significant difference in this employment pattern for those serving sentences in jail. It should be of no surprise that, at the time of the survey, nearly half (45 percent) of the men in jail failed to earn an annual income of even $1,999, then the official U.S. poverty-level income for persons with no dependents, before their arrest and incarceration. Only 16 percent of all men in jails met or exceeded the U.S. median income at that time.

The most common offenses which jail inmates have been accused of and held for are burglary (13 percent), robbery (11 percent), drunkenness/vagrancy (10 percent), possession and use of drugs (7 percent), and murder/kidnapping (7 percent). Table 6 provides more detailed figures on this subject.

About one-fourth of all jailed men are denied bail while awaiting trial. It appears that refusal to set bond is not significantly influenced by the offender's race, income, present employment status, marital status, or the number of his dependents. When the custodial nature of incarceration for vagrancy and public drunkenness (both misdemeanors) is excluded, bail denial is most significantly influenced by the nature of the charge; for example, a murder/kidnapping charge is likely to bring a particularly high bail refusal rate (55 percent). Felony charges also result in substantially higher bail amounts, in contrast to charges for lesser offenses. Poor persons are not often able to raise the funds for a high bail bond and are therefore more likely to be detained prior to trial.

TABLE 6. JAIL INMATES, BY MOST SERIOUS OFFENSE, CONFINEMENT STATUS, AND RACE*

Offense	TOTAL				CONFINEMENT STATUS							
					Serving Sentences				Awaiting Trial			
	Total	White	Black	Other**	Total	White	Black	Other	Total	White	Black	Other
Burglary	18,700	57.3%	42.2%	.5%	5,900	57.6%	42.4%	—%	8,200	53.7%	45.1%	1.2%
Robbery	15,900	28.3	71.1	.6	3,200	25.0	71.9	3.1	4,900	32.7	65.3	2.0
Drunkenness/Vagrancy	14,100	72.3	23.4	4.3	10,300	71.8	23.3	4.9	2,000	75.0	25.0	—
Drugs (possession/use)	10,000	63.0	36.0	1.0	4,100	58.6	39.0	2.4	2,000	65.0	35.0	—
Murder/Kidnapping	9,400	37.2	60.7	2.1	1,700	29.4	70.6	—	5,500	36.4	61.8	1.8
TOTAL: ALL***	141,600	56.4	41.6	2.0	60,200	58.8	38.5	2.7	50,800	51.8	46.8	1.4

*These are the five most numerous offenses. Excludes those in other stages of adjudication.
**Mainly American Indians and Orientals.
***Includes all offenses, including the five most numerous offenses.

Survey of Inmates of Local Jails, (Washington, D.C.: U.S. Department of Justice, 1974), p. 17.

Pretrial delay also reflects the nature of the charge. Men charged with kidnapping, murder, robbery, grand larceny, or aggravated assault generally spend between four and five months in jail awaiting trial. Those accused of sale of drugs or rape log an average of about three months, in contrast to the median time of one month of pretrial delay when all offenses are combined.

To the men in most jails, pretrial delay and denial of bail mean months of enforced idleness, minimal opportunities for recreation and services, and prolonged contact with convicted and repeat offenders. Although 60 percent of the jails provide some types of recreational opportunity or entertainment (including television), such diversions are usually quite restricted except in the largest and most affluent county facilities. A rule of thumb is that the larger the jail, the more likely that it will provide the best and most diverse recreational options (exercise yards, radios and television sets, sports equipment, and facilities for showing motion pictures). Only about one in eight jails have in-house medical facilities.

Due to the issues surrounding the provision of rehabilitation services for nonadjudicated men and the legal view that non-offenders do not need rehabilitation, social and rehabilitation services are usually reserved only for *convicted* offenders serving sentences in jails. For these, a combination of local and federal funds has increased both the number and types of programs, particularly in the larger jails. Programs include religious services (in 60 percent of the jails), alcoholic treatment programs (in about 30 percent of the jails), and drug addiction programs (in about 25 percent of the jails). Inmate counseling, vocational training, remedial education, job placement, and agency referral programs are expanding, but they are still available to only slightly more than 10 percent of the inmate population of the nation's jails. Work release programs are now available in about 40 percent of the jails; such programs allow the sentenced inmates to hold outside jobs and spend nonworking hours in confinement. These programs are welcome aids in filling otherwise empty hours in jail, and they should be expanded in the future. As the National Advisory Commission recommended:

> Every jurisdiction operating locally based correctional facilities and programs for adults should immediately adopt the following programming practices:
>
> 1. A decisionmaking body should be established to follow and direct the inmates' progress through the local correctional system, either as a part of or in conjunction with the community classification team concept. Members should include a parole and probation supervisor, the administrator of the correctional facility or his immediate subordinates,

professionals whose services are purchased by the institution, representatives of community organizations running programs in the institution or with its residents, and inmates. This body should serve as a central information-gathering point. It should discuss with an individual inmate all major decisions pertaining to him.

2. Educational programs should be available to all residents in cooperation with the local school district. Particular emphasis should be given to self-pacing learning programs, packaged instructional materials, and utilization of volunteers and paraprofessionals as instructors.

3. Vocational programs should be provided by the appropriate State agency. It is desirable that overall direction be provided on the State level to allow variety and to permit inmates to transfer among institutions in order to take advantage of training opportunities.

4. A job placement program should be operated at all community correctional centers as part of the vocational training program. Such programs should be operated by State employment agencies and local groups representing employers and local unions.

5. Each local institution should provide counseling services. Individuals showing acute problems will require professional services. Other individuals may require, on a day-to-day basis, situational counseling that can be provided by correctional workers supervised by professionals.

6. Volunteers should be recruited and trained to serve as counselors, instructors, teachers, and recreational therapists.

7. A range of activities to provide physical exercise should be available both in the facility and through the use of local recreational resources. Other leisure activities should be supported by access to library materials, television, writing materials, playing cards, and games.

8. In general, internal programs should be aimed only at that part of the institutional population unable to take advantage of ongoing programs in the community.

9. Meetings with the administrator or appropriate staff
   of the institution should be available to all
   individuals and groups.[3]

The men in our jails are subjected to the most degrading forms of behavior
and to personal danger, and they soon learn the meaning of the term "dead
time." The problems in jails, as a function of the correctional system, are
covered in detail in chapter 25.

Prisons: Warehouses for Men

As pointed out in Part I, the prison was one of America's unique contributions to the Western world. While accused offenders were once housed in
detention facilities only until their trial and punishment (which was usually
severe), the Walnut Street Jail of 1790 and its successors provided a facility
for punishment, penitence, treatment, and reformation.

In the nineteenth and early twentieth centuries, America built dozens of
massive bastion-like prisons, capable of warehousing literally thousands of
inmates in their tiered cellblocks. Providing few treatment services, these
castles for losers were rapidly filled with offenders and remained full until
the late 1960s and early 1970s, when prison populations began to drop. This
drop, in part due to increased use of community-based corrections, particularly probation, has come to a halt, and the prison population has begun to
climb to new heights. It appears that a variation of Parkinson's law is
operating in corrections: as rapidly as prisons are built, court commitments
expand to fill all available cells. As Simon Dinitz would say, "Nothing fails
like success."[4] The proliferation of prisons and the almost instant overcrowding of the new institutions seem to doom the men within to *no* help at
best and *too much* help (punishment) at worst.

Who are the prison inmates? What are their needs, and what programs
should be developed to address these needs? What should we know about
their backgrounds? What happens to the men in the prisons of America?

Male Offenders

The offenders who populate America's prisons are increasing in number at
an alarming rate, despite a brief decline in the early 1970s. Between 1976
and 1977, the prison population increased by 13 percent, from 250,042 to
275,578 (excluding another 7,690 inmates sentenced to state prisons by the
courts but currently being held in county facilities due to prison overcrowding). Of this number, 27,665 (10 percent) were incarcerated in federal
facilities under the Bureau of Prisons (see chapter 27), and 247,913 (90

percent) were in state prisons. In total, there were 131 Americans in prison for every 100,000 citizens.[5]

The most common offenses for which offenders in state correctional facilities were serving sentences in 1974 included robbery (23 percent), homicides (18 percent), burglary (18 percent), minor drug offenses, including possession (6 percent), assault (5 percent), sexual assault (5 percent), major drug offenses, excluding possession (4 percent), and forgery, fraud, and embezzlement (4 percent).[6] Another way of looking at these figures is to say that 48 percent of all state prisoners were serving time for crimes against the person (including armed robbery), and 52 percent were imprisoned for crimes against property.

Men in Prison

Males have historically and overwhelmingly predominated the prison population, although the number of females sentenced to prison is increasing rapidly. Ninety-seven percent of the total number of inmates in prison between 1971 and 1974 were male. In corrections, as in the overall criminal justice system, women receive more favorable disposition at each major decision point in the system (see chapter 18). This accounts, in part, for the overrepresentation of men in prisons. Although crimes committed by women account for one out of every six arrests in America, only one out of every 33 female offenders ends up in prison.

One must remember that those in prison are at the bottom of the correctional funnel. As a group, men in prisons are undereducated and underemployed—a function, primarily, of social class and lack of opportunity. These men are often beset with medical and psychological problems. Many, if not most, are poor and have been unable to cope with the complexities of urban life.[7] Often recent arrivals to urban areas, they have limited job skills and do not know how to use available social services in the urban community. Many come from broken homes with low annual incomes, and a large number suffer from drug and alcohol abuse problems. These characteristics suggest the number of treatment challenges faced by correctional administrators whose mandate it is to provide reasonable and effective treatment services while protecting society from the offenders. The problems in meeting this mission are further exacerbated by a hardening of public attitudes and opinions about the male felon.

Jails, detention facilities, and prisons in the U.S. are becoming overcrowded to the danger point, due to the recent flood of commitments. The sheer numbers of inmates create a dangerous situation. It is becoming obvious that the present male prison system will be unable to meet the increasing demands facing it. Not only must we reexamine all of our institutions for male offenders, but we must also give serious consideration to alternatives to incarceration. While there can be no question that some male offenders are extremely dangerous and *must* be isolated from others, it has been estimated that only some 15-25 percent of the male population in prison falls within this category. This situation is, however, changing fast; overcrowding has tended to force correctional administrators to find ways to release those men considered least dangerous back into the community, and this leaves an increasingly greater percentage of violent offenders smoldering in a potential tinderbox.

As stated earlier, male offenders tend to be heavy users of alcohol and drugs. In the 1974 survey made for the Department of Justice, it was found that almost one-half of the men in prison had been drinking at the time of the instant offense, and that another 25 percent were under the influence of drugs. These statistics indicate that drug and alcohol abuse and misuse are serious problems that contribute in a negative way to offenders' behavior, both in the community and in the institution. Drug and alcohol treatment programs in both locations are no longer a luxury—they are a necessity.

Education is an important factor in American society; it is viewed by many as one of the most essential prerequisites for economic stability and success. Education in a postindustrial society such as the United States is a crucial element of the process of getting a job and earning an adequate income. Despite this need for education, the most recent national survey found that one in five Americans can be considered functionally illiterate.[8] This sad situation is deteriorating further as increasing numbers of youths pass through our public school systems without being properly prepared to function in an urban environment with developed and reality-oriented problem-solving skills. Almost seven out of ten of the men in prison in 1974 were employed at the time of their crime, but more than half of them had never finished high school, and six out of ten had earned less than $6,000 in the year prior to their arrest, a figure considerably lower than the national average. It is not too surprising that crime is often chosen as one alternative for survival under these circumstances. It is not enough that many inmates are now given a chance to earn a high school education in prison; the nation as a whole must insist that the education provided by our public school systems supply the skills needed to keep these men out of prison. It seems clear that this is one step that can be taken in the effort to reduce crime to a minimum.

Finally, almost one in four imprisoned men are eligible to be furloughed into an early release procedure, but less than half of those eligible are given the opportunity to take such a furlough. Most inmates (74 percent) have some kind of institutional work assignment, but six out of ten are earning less than twenty cents per hour for their work. It is hard to motivate an incarcerated man to devote serious effort toward learning a trade while working in prison for such low wages, when the same man has made up to $500 a day illegally in his community—and knows it can be done again.

Prisonization

Every venture intended to elevate humanity to new heights (or at least to encourage improvement) has as many unplanned and unwanted effects as desired effects. Efforts to provide male offenders with a setting in which to do penance and to be "reformed" have resulted in a number of such unwanted side effects, ranging from the mental and physical deterioration caused by extreme solitary confinement at Sing Sing to a more contemporary unwanted phenomenon called prisonization. The originator of the term, Donald Clemmer, described this process as ". . . the taking on in greater or less degree of the folkways, mores, customs and general culture of the penitentiary."[9] Clemmer observed that the course of acculturation into the prison community subjects the inmate to certain influences which either breed or deepen criminal behaviors, causing the prisoner to learn the criminalistic ideology of the prison—to become "prisonized." Prisonization is a process which includes accepting the subordinate role into which one is thrust as an inmate; developing new habits of sleeping, dressing, eating, and working; undergoing status degradation; adopting a new language; and learning that one is dependent on others (including one's fellow inmates) for the scarce pleasures found in incarceration, including food, work assignment, freedom from assault, and privileges. Students of prisonization believe that this process not only leads the inmate to identify with criminal codes, goals, and behaviors, but also serves to undercut rehabilitation programs and to lessen the offender's ability to adjust to society after release.

The phenomenon of prisonization appears to exist in all prisons, not just the large Gothic bastions which testify to archaic prison philosophies. It can be brought into the prison by older inmates, but even in new prisons which receive first-time offenders, the pains of imprisonment faced by the inmates can spontaneously generate the prisonization process.

Since prisonization appears in every institution, although to varying degrees, it is necessary to understand the benefits which accrue to the men who adhere to the inmate codes. It is also vital for a future correctional administrator to understand the nature of the pains of imprisonment that encourage socialization into the inmate subculture. These pains are status deprivation, sexual deprivation, material deprivation, and enforced intimacy with other deviants.

The inmate subculture reduces the pains of imprisonment by encouraging the sharing of the few benefits and pleasures inside prisons, by making naked aggression by inmates against other inmates less likely, and by providing a circle of friends who can and will come to an inmate's assistance if he is attacked. It also provides alternative sexual outlets, defines appropriate roles for getting along with other inmates, and supplies companions with whom an inmate can share confidences and interact comfortably.

Additionally, this process makes available contraband drugs (including glue, "home brew," and prescription drugs stolen from prison dispensaries) with which an inmate can get high. There are also many other less tangible benefits.

Fortunately, recent research suggests that the extent, and thus the negative impacts, of prisonization may be reduced through institutional administration and orientation of the staff:

> We would expect to find more solidarity [of the inmate code] and more traditional inmate types in a correctional system with only one institution for adult felons and where that institution is characterized by more severe material and socio-psychological deprivations.[10]

Others have suggested that the nature and extent of endorsement of prisoner norms ("don't rat on another inmate," "mind your own business," "never exploit another inmate," "never cooperate with correctional officers," "do your own time," "be a man," "don't whine") can be significantly reduced. If an institutional administrator and staff emphasize individual and group treatment rather than custody and discipline, if a pattern of cooperation can be developed between informal inmate leaders and institutional authorities, if a medium or minimum custody level can be achieved, and if violations of rules governing the use of force by the correctional staff are consistently sanctioned, *then* the prison culture and the prisonization process can be markedly reduced. Some researchers have suggested that shorter prison terms tend to undercut the power of the prison culture, since inmates can and do participate in "anticipatory socialization" as they near the end of their prison sentences and begin to anticipate their participation in the activities of the free world. It is reasonable to assume that short, fixed periods of incarceration can help to reduce the negative effects of prisonization.

The Prison Population Boom

In the last three years (1975 through 1977), prison populations have sharply increased, much to the dismay of both prisoners and concerned correctional administrators. There is little agreement on the exact reasons for the population boom, although some correctional personnel are quick to note that the police and court elements of the correctional funnel may have increased in efficiency faster than the correctional subsystem. As one anonymous administrator has noted: "The police tooled up, the prosecutor's office expanded along with the use of plea bargaining, and the courts finally stepped in the twentieth century. We in corrections have received the benefits of efficiency through sharply increased commitments."

Others have identified the hardening of public opinion as a factor, pointing out that judges are perceiving considerable local pressure to commit offenders rather than use probation. It could be that the reaction to crime in

America has exceeded the threshold of fear and reached panic proportions, with widespread public clamor for commitments contributing to prison overpopulation.

It is more likely, however, that the major cause is the increase in the "population at risk,"[11] those males in the age range of 18 to 30. Inasmuch as crime is a young man's game, and the number of persons in the high crime rate ages will double by 1985, one would expect the demographic factor of age to contribute heavily to the overpopulation of America's prisons. The "age at risk" problem has been further exacerbated by a population shift in the last decade, during which families with younger sons have moved from rural environments, which provided more wholesome outlets for young men, to urban areas. Historically, such population shifts—regardless of the population group in motion—have meant that the second generation engages in more frequent criminal behavior. In this case, recent population shifts have coincided with an increase in the population at risk, and we can therefore expect the committed population to increase for several more years.

Two factors which could lead to a blunting of this trend are economic in nature: reduced unemployment and expansion of the economy. The population at risk is traditionally overrepresented in the ranks of the unemployed; with a national unemployment rate of over 7 percent, the unemployment rate for the population at risk (men aged 18-30) is reported to be in the 14-28 percent range. If unemployment is reduced, the population at risk will also be reduced and the crime rate should drop. Since a decrease in the rate of unemployment depends on an expanding economy, expansion at a sufficiently high annual growth rate (above 4 percent) is needed to reduce unemployment and, along with it, the crime rate, with its resultant commitments to prison.

America seems determined to resolve its crime problem with a "lock 'em up and throw away the key" philosophy. Although incapacitation is an effective way to prevent crime, a resolve to help these male losers to expand opportunities and enter the mainstream of American society might be more helpful in lowering crime rates and the collateral national costs of incarceration.

Rape in Prisons

In a detailed study of aggression taking place among men behind prison walls, Anthony Scacco suggests that sex is a vehicle for exploitation rather than an expression of pathological personality or situational frustration.[12] The sexual assaults that occur within prisons and jails cannot be categorized solely as homosexual attacks; rather they often are assaults made by heterosexually oriented males for political reasons—that is, in order to show power and dominance over other human beings. It is a depressing fact that victimization, degradation, racism, and humiliation of victims are the foremost reasons why sexual assaults are perpetrated upon men in this setting.

Scacco also addresses a topic seldom openly discussed by correctional administrators: polarization of inmates in prison, a phenomenon which has perhaps accelerated in recent years. Younger and the more aggressive inmates appear to be polarizing into racial groups, and conflict between these groups—and with the correctional staff—has led to increased tension behind the walls. As prison overpopulation continues, polarization will probably also increase.

To reduce the potential for further disturbances among men in prison, Scacco proposes several constructive steps:

1. The staff of a correctional institution should openly admit that they must meet together as a body and discuss their views on sexuality if they are to render assistance to the inmates in their care.

2. Masturbation for relief of sexual tension should be allowed within an institution, not denied to men within prison walls.

3. Classification at reception and orientation centers should keep sexually different and sexually attractive men from mixing with the rest of the inmate population, to keep the weaker and often younger inmates apart from other inmates with sexual desires which they would fulfill through assault.

4. Conjugal visits, which reduce recidivism and homosexuality, are a more socially acceptable solution than rape.

5. Furlough programs should be implemented to maintain normal sexual relations.

6. Coeducational correctional institutions should be expanded, rather than prisons, and populations reduced to the remaining 30 percent of the inmate population which requires confinement.[13]

Alternatives for the Future

The majority of the male offenders are not dangerous men and can be diverted into such programs as deferred prosecution, probation, weekend confinement, restitution programs, and community reintegration centers, which are at least as effective as prisons and cost much less than the outrageous $28,000 per cell and more than $4,500 per year average per-prisoner cost. Such community programs should be expanded, rather than the prisons. Prisons, however, seem to be almost impossible to get rid of, although they require enormous annual outlays for upkeep and corrupt both the keeper and kept. These monuments to an age gone by do not and cannot achieve their stated mission—unless correctional administrators are trained and dedicated, have sufficient resources, abide by the Constitution, and understand the effects of inaction and indecisiveness.

Expanding alternatives for male offenders has another benefit: to the extent that male offenders are integrated into the community, their future criminal behaviors will be sharply reduced, if not eliminated. Community-based corrections can reduce the crime problem in the United States to a far greater extent than current prison operations through the process of actually making offenders useful citizens.

Although men in prisons will be with us for many years, the more cost-effective and cost-beneficial community programs may eventually reduce the numbers of inmates under lock and key to only those who are too dangerous to release. Corrections must and will divert its resources into those programs which provide humane treatment without sacrificing the protection of society. These new programs must provide strong, substantive change; we cannot afford improvements as illusory as "the Emperor's new clothes." Substituting semantics for substance and rhetoric for real change is not the answer. Calling "the hole" in a male institution by the name of "therapeutic isolation" is simply a case of applying new paint to a rotten wall. The ship will still sink and all aboard will perish unless we look to and correct the basic structure of the system, rather than changing terminology to make the public more comfortable about what we are doing for (or to) our male offenders.

Summary

As men engage in illegal activity and are caught up in the criminal justice system, they are eventually concentrated in America's potpourri of jails, workhouses, and prisons. While a few of these are exceptionally well administered facilities, with adequate programs and dedicated staffs, it seems that most male offenders await trial and serve time in units which are lacking in these factors so necessary to the correctional process. The by-products of the public's cavalier inattention to this tragic situation, exacerbated by uninspired correction leadership, are: ruptured family ties, increased welfare rolls, dead time in jails, socialization into a dysfunctional "prisonized" culture, rape in prison, embitterment and hostility, and decreased ability of former inmates to function in the free world. Men in prison sense—even if they cannot articulate—that the gulf between the treatment and expected reformation and the realities of practice is great.[14] The whole process is viewed as a cruel sham perpetuated in the name of an abstract ideal to which only lip service, if that, is given.

The increase in jail and prison populations in the last few years and the probable continued growth in the numbers of caged men do not bode well for the quality of life behind bars. Aggression in prisons, polarization of inmates, riots and disturbances, and inmate attacks on guards are likely to increase in number. Prison crowding in the absence of meaningful programs and concerned administrators is a time-bomb which will eventually explode—unless steps are taken to defuse the situation. Since the population at risk is not expected to decline in the immediate future, programming and diversion alternatives, including community-based corrections, are the avenues that must now be explored (see chapter 28).

REVIEW QUESTIONS

I. Find the answers to the following in the text:

    1. Why have prison populations increased recently? What short-term effects will result from this increase?

    2. What is meant by "population at risk"? How does this contribute to the population problem in male prisons?

    3. Explain the dynamics of rape in prison.

    4. What factors contribute to prisonization?

II. Words to identify:

    1. prisonization

    2. jails

    3. furloughs

    4. inmate polarization

    5. bail denial

    6. therapeutic isolation

    7. prison overcrowding

NOTES

1. U.S. Department of Justice, *Survey of Inmates of Local Jails* (Washington, D.C.: U.S. Government Printing Office, 1974), p. 13.

2. *Ibid.*, p. 1.

3. National Advisory Commission on Criminal Justice Standards and Goals, *Corrections* (Washington, D.C.: U.S. Government Printing Office, 1973), p. 304.

4. Simon Dinitz, "Nothing Fails Like Success." Paper presented at the annual meeting of the Western Society of Criminology, Las Vegas, February 18, 1977.

5. Rob Wilson, "U.S. Prison Population Sets Another Record," *Corrections Magazine* 3 (March 1977).

6. *Survey of Inmates of Local Jails,* p. 12.

7. George Darwin, "The Prisons," *Criminal Justice Newsletter* 4 (November 1976): 1-2.

8. Charles Bailey, "Prison Populations Surging, And Not Just Because of the Nation's Economic Slowdown," *Corrections Digest* 7 (February 1976): 9.

9. Donald Clemmer, *The Prison Community* (New York: Rinehart & Co., 1940), p. 8.

10. Gene Kaseebaum, David Ward and Daniel Wilner, *Prison Treatment and Parole Survival: An Empirical Assessment* (New York: John Wiley & Sons, 1971), p. 301.

11. Rob Wilson, "U.S. Prison Population Sets Another Record," p. 5.

12. Anthony Scacco, *Rape in Prison* (Springfield, Ill.: Charles C. Thomas, 1975).

13. Scacco, *Rape in Prison* pp. 99-116.

14. See Geoffrey Alpert and Donal Hicks, "Prisoners' Attitudes Toward Components of the Legal and Judicial Systems," *Criminology* 14 (February 1977): 461-482.

18 Female Offenders

As women rightly demand equality in social, cultural, and economic pursuits, the special status which they have traditionally held in the criminal justice system will undoubtedly change.

WILLIAM G. NAGEL

Women and Crime

The 1970s is the decade of liberated women, with their equality and rights being asserted, if not established, on almost every front. Yet, only recently has a movement arisen to push for the rights of women offenders in corrections. In a relative sense, women receive differential, even preferential, treatment at almost every station of the criminal justice system, partly in deference to the traditional belief that the female sex is the weaker of the two. This chapter examines the more common kinds of offenses committed by women, dispositional alternatives for women, and some correctional facilities, issues, and programs for women in a rapidly changing environment.

Although the criminal statistics contained in the Federal Bureau of Investigation's *Uniform Crime Reports* are somewhat limited in scope, especially perhaps for crimes involving women, they are the best available; and they can be accepted at least as an indicator of trends. The 1976 figures show that a total of 20 percent (one in five) of the "index crimes" reported in 1976 were committed by females,[1] an increase of 65 percent over the 10-year period between 1967 and 1976. This increase in female criminality is slightly more dramatic for those under 18, a group with the dubious distinction of having increased their crime rate by 68 percent during that period.

The general increase in female criminality can also be seen in the figures for specific crimes from 1960 to 1975. The rate of larceny committed by women has increased 464 percent since 1960, and the rate of robbery has increased 380 percent, a reflection of the changing patterns of criminal opportunity for women. It is interesting to note that arrests for prostitution, the crime Freda Adler calls "the oldest and newest profession,"[2] increased much less (74 percent) over this 15-year span. The changing sexual mores in America are reflected in an actual *decrease* in total arrests for prostitution between 1972 and 1975, from 42,000 to 32,000. But these figures contrast dramatically with the rate of increase in prostitution among females under 18, which rose a whopping 406 percent between 1960 and 1975.

The arrest figures for prostitution, however, undoubtedly indicate only the tip of the iceberg. Since prostitution is one of the so-called "victimless crimes," and clients seldom complain since they would be implicating themselves, the number of arrests for prostitution usually reflects only cases of flagrant solicitation, rampant disease, or a local "cleanup" campaign. Considerable folklore surrounds prostitution, most of it with no basis in fact. Those who profit from prostitution (almost never the prostitutes themselves) are not about to compile statistics or seek publicity. It is a business that thrives on man's oldest weakness, with the ultimate motive of simple profit.

Careers in prostitution range from the corner hooker to the jet-set courtesan, the main difference being the age, beauty, and *price* of the merchandise. The business of organized vice is not a simple question of boy-meets-girl; many levels of profit-taking and payoff winnow down the average prostitute's nightly earnings of $200-250 to the weekly figure of less than $100 that most are allowed to keep. The pimp, the madam, the landlord, the crooked vice cop, and others all take their cut. The real victim of this "victimless" crime is often the prostitute herself.

It is estimated that there are between 200,000 and 250,000 prostitutes in America. Even if one considers this estimate only 50 percent correct, the business is still staggering in its financial potential. At the lowest market price of $20 for a "trick,"[3] with each prostitute averaging six tricks a day, the volume could range between $3.5 and $5 *billion* a year. This tax-free income for prostitution is several times the annual budget for the United States Department of Justice.[4] Small wonder that arrests for prostitution are so few, with such great monetary resources available.

A Differential Justice System for Women?

The 1970s have seen women fighting to gain equality on every front. The scarcity of research in the area of women's equality in general, and their role in the criminal justice system in particular, makes this area the current "gold mine" for researchers and writers. It is unfortunate that much of the literature is still a warmed-over repetition of the old myths and inaccuracies of the 1940s and 1950s, with little truly current material available. In the rapidly changing times of the 1970s, to quote from research done in the late 1960s is to be guilty of describing *history* and not the current scene. With this caveat in mind, we will attempt to describe the little-known area of the path through the criminal justice system followed by females. References are as current as possible, but we have relied on personal knowledge and experience as well.

The first point at which the female offender comes into contact with the criminal justice system is the point of arrest. While arrest is a traumatic experience for the male offender, it provides special problems for the female. It has been estimated that 80 percent of the female offenders in America have dependent children at home, and that a great percentage of these children have no one else to care for them. Concern for the children and a natural tendency among officers to identify female offenders in some ways with their mothers or sisters tend to cause arresting officers to be more liberal in the use of discretion than they might be with a male in the same situation. A recognition of the need to provide more pretrial services for female offenders has prompted many communities to develop volunteer programs to assist with the women's problems at home. It is important to remember that the *children* of female offenders often become residents of juvenile institutions as a result of the actions of their mothers. To the juveniles who are removed from the community and placed in what *they* perceive as a facility for other juveniles that have committed offenses, it becomes hard to accept the fact that *protection,* not punishment, is the state's motivation (see chapter 19).

Yet another reason for the reluctance of the officer to arrest the female offender is caused by age-old customs, mores, and laws that have created great distinctions between men and women under apprehension. While a policeman seldom hesitates to place a male offender "up against the wall" and to respond to force with equal force, he is loath to do so with a female. Most police departments have strict rules and regulations in regard to the apprehension, search, and detention of women. In most cases, a female officer or matron is assigned to detain women and conduct searches of their persons. The female offender is sometimes treated like someone from a far-off planet rather than as a person who has committed a criminal act.

The female offender also seldom spends much time in detention before trial. Her family problems and the lack of adequate female detention facilities or female personnel in the department almost demand the use of relatively frequent pretrial release for women. Also, until quite recently, female offenders usually committed less serious offenses and could therefore be released on bail or on their own recognizance.

This view of the female offender's treatment in the criminal justice system is not shared by all, however, as noted by Rita Simon:

> Others believe that judges are more punitive toward women. They are more likely to throw the book at the female defendant because they believe there is a greater discrepancy between her behavior and the behavior expected of women than there is between the behavior of the male defendant and the behavior expected of men. In other words,

women defendants pay for the judges' belief that it is more in man's
nature to commit crimes than it is in woman's. Thus, when a judge is
convinced that the woman before him has committed a crime, he is
more likely to overact and punish her, not only for the specific offense
but also for transgressing against his expectations of womanly
behavior.

The existence of such statutes as the indeterminate sentence for
women, or the sanctioning of a procedure whereby only convicted
male defendants have their minimum sentences determined by a judge
at an open hearing and in the presence of counsel, while the woman's
minimum sentence is decided by a parole board in a closed session in
which she is not represented by counsel, are cited as evidence of the
unfair, punitive treatment that is accorded to women in the court.[5]

However, as women are arrested in greater numbers for crimes now
committed mainly by men, they can expect the paternalistic attitudes of
judges to diminish rapidly.

While statistics show that about one out of six persons arrested in the
United States is a woman offender, only one woman out of every thirty
arrested is sent to prison. For example, New York State has a population of
18,111,000 and 911,703 index crimes, but the state incarcerated only 375
women in 1974.[6] Crime patterns are changing, but a precipitous rise in the
number of females placed in state correctional facilities should not be part of
that change. The differential treatment accorded women in many cases does
not automatically mean *better* treatment or consideration. As an alternative
to differential treatment, the model of the male prison is sometimes copied,
even to the point of ignoring the obvious physical differences of the female
inmates. At the other extreme, the best programs of differential treatment,
filled with compassionate understanding for the woman residents, could
serve as models for institutions housing either sex—or both:

Built around multilevel and beautifully landscaped courtyards, the
attractive buildings provide security without fences. Small housing
units with pleasant living rooms provide space for normal interaction
between presumably normal women. The expectation that the women
will behave like human beings pervades the place. Education, recreation, and training areas are uncramped and well glazed.
Opportunity for interaction between staff and inmate is present
everywhere.

About 200 yards away from the other buildings are attractive
apartments, each containing a living room, dining space, kitchen, two
bedrooms, and a bath. Women approaching release live in them while
working or attending school in the city. These apartments normally are
out of bounds to staff except on invitation.[7]

This kind of model seems to reflect the relatively humane feeling toward the offender that continues to motivate the male-dominated criminal justice system to send very few women to prison. It is true that men are also being filtered out of the correctional funnel in greater numbers, but it appears that women can be returned to society with less chance of further criminal activity that might endanger society. A four-year follow-up study, reported in the 1975 *Uniform Crime Reports,* indicates that women did better in every age category than men in regard to recidivism.[8]

For these and other reasons, the female offender often receives discretionary treatment by police and prosecutors, with only those women who are considered particularly hard cases finally coming before a judge. It is also true that no politically-oriented prosecutor can be expected to enjoy bringing a mother with three small children to trial. Thus, such trials seldom occur unless the case is both serious and airtight. The result is that cases against women are more often no-papered, and the correctional funnel for them narrows sharply. Those women brought to court are apt to receive consideration for probation, fines, and suspended sentences more often than men who commit comparable crimes. Finally, the few who are sentenced to prison are likely to receive early consideration for parole or other alternative dispositions. Under these circumstances, it is small wonder that the few women's prisons have so little influence and power in the correctional system.

Women behind Bars

What are these female institutions like? The plight of the female behind bars is often a difficult one. In terms of institutions, the male-offender-oriented criminal justice system may totally ignore the special requirements of the female offender. The nature of punishment for female offenders has come a long way from the time in which they were thrown into the holds of hulks as diversions for the incarcerated male felons, but much more needs to be done before treatment of the female offender can be said to be an integrated part of corrections. As noted earlier, the problems with female prisoners start with the requirement for a search in the police station. Many large urban police departments are able to maintain a matron on duty and provide separate facilities for female detainees. In most jurisdictions, however, there are no matrons and no separate facilities.

Confinement for women, at the local level, ranges from a few well-designed jail facilities for female use to whatever can be improvised, such as a separate cell next to those for male offenders. The screening process at the point of arrest creates great problems for jail personnel. Because only the most serious female offenders are selected for arrest and detention, there is a more immediate need for effective security measures. This problem is made more acute because of the lack of qualified personnel and adequate facilities to provide the extensive security required.

In addition, certain tangential problems relate to the detention of a woman. The first is what to do with her children, if she has any. If there is a husband at home, he is likely to be working during the day. The need to detain the female offender should not imply neglect of the innocent children she leaves behind. Provision of adequate services for them requires close coordination with the local child welfare service agencies. These services are often nonexistent in the smaller jurisdictions, and although it requires an imaginative law enforcement effort to deal with such children, often the job is left to men trained to react only to relatively simple situations, if trained at all. Confinement itself is a problem in most jails, and it is often solved by making temporary use of a portion of the facility designed for male use. In some cases law enforcement officials might make arrangements with the local hospital or mental institution to house the female prisoner for a short period of time. Others make arrangements with the larger urban departments to transfer the female prisoner to their facility until trial.

All of these temporary measures create problems for both the corrections administration and the offender. Security and logistics become a drain on resources not planned for such use. The defendant has problems with visiting, contact with counsel, and concern for the welfare of her family. All these problems may be shared by the male defendant, but he is much less likely to have the woman's acute worry for her children—if he has any children there is probably a wife to take care of them, while the woman often has no husband (or one who works). In addition, some of the women are pregnant or require medical attention for other problems unique to their sex. The average small-town police station is hardly prepared to handle this kind of situation. Because of the almost total lack of standards for female confinement, the situation at the local jail or correctional facility is only a token of the problems that characterize state prisons for women.

There are only fifty-four prison units for female juvenile delinquents and thirty-four state institutions for women offenders listed in the American Correctional Association's directory.[9] The picture in regard to the administration of these women's prisons has changed greatly in recent years. In 1966, only ten of the nation's institutions for women were headed by a female correctional administrator. The 1971 directory shows that twenty-six of the thirty-four correctional administrators of these institutions for women were females. As a matter of fact, the president of the American Correctional Association from 1972 to 1973 was the female superintendent of the women's prison at Marysville, Ohio until 1975. She is now the director of the Detroit House of Corrections.[10] Since the conditions in the women's institutions also vary greatly, it would be fruitless to attempt to describe them individually. They are not all horror stories; it is sufficient to state that the best and the worst aspects of the male institution are also in evidence in the women's prison, the only major difference being the variations based on the traits unique to each sex.

Diversionary procedures seem to be especially applicable to the kinds of offenses for which women are corrected, yet almost no diversion is utilized for females once they have been convicted and sentenced. A large percentage of the women incarcerated have children who must be placed in foster homes or under the supervision of child-care agencies. The woman offender is excluded from the decision making that results in the disposition of her children in most cases. Another major problem with the female institutions is the almost total lack of meaningful programs. Most "vocational training" centers on providing "female-type" services for the rest of the correctional system (e.g., laundry, tailoring, mending, making flags, and other traditionally "female" tasks). This kind of program does little to prepare the female offender for an occupation on the outside. As noted penologist and lecturer Edith Flynn observes:

> Rehabilitative programs aimed at the achievement of personal and vocational self-sufficiency would seem to be a better bet for the development of an effective operational treatment theory than futile attempts to produce a more successful adjustment in terms of the woman's dependency on significant others.[11]

The problems of the female correctional institution were addressed in the following recommendations by the National Advisory Commission:

> Each state correctional agency operating institutions to which women offenders are committed should reexamine immediately its policies, procedures, and programs for women offenders, and make such adjustments as may be indicated to make these policies, procedures, and programs more relevant to the problems and needs of women.

> 1. Facilities for women offenders should be considered an integral part of the overall corrections system, rather than an isolated activity or the responsibility of an unrelated agency.

> 2. Comprehensive evaluation of the woman offender should be developed through research. Each state should determine differences in the needs between male and female offenders, and implement differential programming.

> 3. Appropriate vocational training programs should be implemented. Vocational programs that promote dependency and exist solely for administrative ease should be abolished. A comprehensive research effort should be initiated to determine the aptitudes

and abilities of the female institutional population. This information should be coordinated with labor statistics predicting job availability. From data so obtained, creative vocational training should be developed which will provide a woman with skills necessary to allow independence.

4. Classification systems should be investigated to determine their applicability to the female offender. If necessary, systems should be modified or completely restructured to provide information necessary for an adequate program.

5. Adequate diversionary methods for female offenders should be implemented. Community programs should be available to women. Special attempts should be made to create alternative programs in community centers and halfway houses or other arrangements, allowing the woman to keep her family with her.

6. State correctional agencies with such small numbers of women inmates as to make adequate facilities and programming uneconomical should make every effort to find alternatives to imprisonment for them, including parole and local residential facilities. For those women inmates for whom such alternatives cannot be employed, contractual arrangements should be made with nearby states with more adequate facilities and programs.

7. As a 5-year objective, male and female institutions of adaptable design and comparable populations should be converted to coeducational facilities.

   a. In coeducational facilities, classification and diagnostic procedures also should give consideration to offenders' problems with relation to the opposite sex, and coeducational programs should be provided to meet those needs.

   b. Programs within the facility should be open to both sexes.

   c. Staff of both sexes should be hired who have interest, ability, and training in coping with the problems of both male and female offenders. Assignments of staff and offenders to programs and activities should not be based on the sex of either.[12]

The problem of inadequate statistics and information on the female offender, noted briefly by the Commission, is a major one. The significance of this lack of data is highlighted by Edith Flynn:

> Any attempt to analyze the current status of corrections in the area of special problems of female offenders is seriously hampered by an almost incredible scarcity of data. This situation did not change with the completion of the most comprehensive study to date on the problems of crime and corrections in the United States: The President's Commission on Law Enforcement and Administration of Justice did not include a single paragraph or statistic on the female offender, nor could any such material be found in its nine supportive Task Force Reports. What information does exist is, with a few notable exceptions, rather eclectic and frequently dated, which leads us to the conclusion that the problems of the female offender are characteristically regarded as insignificant, no doubt due to the magnitude and extent of male crime and delinquency.[13]

It is hoped that research now in progress will provide a meaningful and useful data base on female correctional facilities.

The Unisexual Institution

The single-sex experience and long-term deprivation of heterosexual outlets create the same kinds of problems in female institutions that are found in male prisons. The recommendations for coeducational institutions may seem extreme to the uninitiated, but the leavening effect of a system that allows at least social contact in daily activity with members of the opposite sex is considerable. Excessive administrative concern about overt signs of friendship as indicative of possible homosexual activity conflicts with many standard practices for women *outside* the walls. If one observed two *males* holding hands as they walked down the street, they would be suspected of deviant behavior. This same behavior, though not considered at all strange for women (and particularly girls) on the outside, is viewed with great suspicion *inside* the walls, for girls and women alike. This situation is described by an inmate:

> It's tough to be *natural*. The thing that most of us are trying to accomplish here, we're trying to get our minds at a point to where we can handle whatever comes our way, to get our emotions balanced, to maybe straighten up our way of thinking. You know, it just makes it hard when you're trying to be a natural person—to react to things normally—when the staff won't let you be normal—when you do a normal thing that being a woman makes it normal, and then have them

say no, you can't do that because if you do, that's personal contact and that's homosexuality. So there's our mental hassle.

I know that when women are thrown together without men or without the companionship of men it makes it pretty rough on them—women being the emotional people that they are. They have to have a certain amount of affection and close companionship. You know, a woman, if she's with a man she'll put her hand on him or maybe she'll reach up and touch him. This is something that a woman does naturally without thinking, and so if a woman has a good friend here, or an affair, she does the same thing because this is her nature. The thing of it is—like I have a friend at the cottage—neither one of us have ever played. We're never gonna play. And if somebody tried to force us into it, we couldn't, wouldn't, or what have you. But being a woman and after being here for quite a while, we put our arms around each other, we don't think there's anything the matter with it, because there's nothing there—it's a friendship. We're walking down the hall, our records are both spotless, she's a council girl, I'm Minimum A (minimum custody classification). I've never had anything on my record that was bad and my god, the supervisor comes out and says, "Now, now, girls, you know we don't allow that sort of thing here." And we look at her and say "What sort of thing?" "This personal contact." And yet this same supervisor, we saw her up at the corner putting her arm around another supervisor the same way we were doing. So this is where part of our mental hassle comes in.[14]

The redefinition of the natural acts described above into something considered evil and proscribed is another reason why institutionalization is so crippling to the long-term prisoner. As inmates, male or female, learn that simple signs of friendship are *prohibited,* they learn to repress their impulses toward interpersonal warmth when they get out. The kind of behavior that makes them acceptable on the inside makes them appear "hard-case" (unfeeling, unresponsive) on the outside. In the male this kind of coldness can be viewed as "tough" or "macho," but in the woman it is almost always considered unattractive.

Very few studies have been conducted on the homosexuality of women prisoners. A lot of speculative conjecture is found in much of the literature, but true scientific research is rare. Even the monumental effort to compile statistics on women offenders by the Gluecks, *500 Delinquent Women,* [15] did not even mention homosexuality.

The freedom from intensive supervision and the variety of these encounters make prevention of such activity difficult. There are never enough personnel to watch all the inmates, so lovers get together despite the efforts of the staff. In many institutions the staff adopts the attitude of "looking the other way" in regard to sexual activity of female inmates. (The same is true in many male institutions; see chapter 17.)

It is possible that homosexuality is an even more prevalent problem in the women's institutions than in men's, because a high percentage of the inmates have been so misused by men that they had already turned to other females to fulfill their sexual needs on the *outside*. It is also quite possible that the impact of imprisonment is significantly different for women, tending to encourage a homosexual response. Women appear more likely to view arrest, jailing, the court trial, and commitment to prison in highly personal terms. This personalized reaction could harden antisocial attitudes and lead to further illegal behavior. One study has identified three psychological deprivations which might lead to homosexual behavior:

1. Affectional starvation and need for understanding.

2. Isolation from previous symbiotic interpersonal relations.

3. Need for continued intimate relationships with a person.[16]

It would be hard to imagine an incarcerated felon who does not suffer these deprivations to some degree.

The Female Sociopath

Approximately one in four felons incarcerated in a maximum security prison for men is a psychopath or antisocial personality offender:

> [They are] basically antisocial [individuals], whose behavior pattern brings them repeatedly into conflict with society. They are incapable of significant loyalty to individuals, groups, or social values. They are grossly selfish, calloused, irresponsible, and unable to feel guilt or to learn from experience. Frustration tolerance is low. They tend to blame others or offer plausible rationalizations for their behavior.[17]

Research has indicated that the incarcerated male sociopath may be biologically different from the more normal person, in ways that encourage psychopathic behavior. A study conducted in Ohio indicates that this does not appear to be the case for incarcerated female felons. No biological differences of significance were found between the nonsociopathic and sociopathic females at the Ohio Reformatory for Women,[18] although there were remarkable differences in familial, social, historical, criminal, and other dimensions of living.

The absence of such offenders in this prison may well mean that the more manipulative, biologically different female sociopathic offender is funneled into the mental hospital, while her aggressive male counterpart is filtered into the reformatory. If this proves to be true, it will further indicate the extent to which the decision-making process in the criminal justice system helps to shape the correctional funnel.

Women's Liberation and Women's Prisons

One of the rallying cries of the women's liberation movement is "equal pay for equal work." In the case of female prisoners, there is a need for equal treatment—for access to some of the new correctional programs, including alternatives to incarceration, being offered to male offenders. Integrated prisons are another possibility, but not in the forseeable future. A third aspect of equalizing treatment involves the addition of more women as members of the criminal justice team.

While equality is a noble goal for the female offender, it also has a negative side. Female arrest and conviction rates will continue to rise dramatically for a while, and these soaring rates will be accompanied by an accelerated change in attitudes toward and treatment of female offenders. In one area, it is clear that this accelerated change is already occurring. Of the 3,870 persons executed in the United States from 1930 to 1977, only 32 (less than 1 percent of those executed) were women. A recent report of those awaiting execution on death rows in America, however, indicated that 8 out of 479 (or almost 3 percent) were women.[19] This may be an indication that sentencing is getting tougher for females and that females have become involved in more serious crimes. Repetition of these kinds of findings will be commonplace for the next few years as the criminal justice system adjusts to the "liberated" female offender.

The great wall of mystery as to the handling of the female offender must be broken down so that more of those who need treatment will be placed in the right programs. Screening as drastic as that which takes place in the female offender system is perhaps counterproductive to the goals of rehabilitation. At this stage of the development of the correctional subsystem in America, these comments represent pure speculation; it is possible, of course, that the recidivism rate for those women informally screened is very low.

Summary

Bearing in mind that incarceration intensifies a woman offender's antisocial attitudes, thereby increasing the likelihood of her return to criminal behavior, two major alternatives are suggested:

1. Diversionary programs should be made available for handling suspected or convicted female offenders, including increased use of the summons, probation, deferred prosecution, community treatment centers, halfway houses, and so on.

2. Those women who are incarcerated in prison should have maximal contact with the outside world, including more frequent visitation privileges, uncensored mail, home visitations, and home furloughs.

Further examination, too, is needed regarding the approximately twenty-nine out of every thirty convicted female offenders who are *not* imprisoned. Perhaps, as suggested above, the recidivism for this group is very low. Perhaps the discretionary diversion presently employed with non-incarcerated female offenders may well be a model for the rest.

REVIEW QUESTIONS

I. Find the answers to the following in the text:

    1. What are some of the major reasons why women are treated so differently in the correctional system?

    2. What are the major crimes for which women are convicted? Explain why.

    3. How would a more ''equal'' system of criminal justice for women impact on the correctional system?

II. Words to identify:

    1. hard case

    2. antisocial

    3. Women's Liberation

    4. prostitution

    5. trick

    6. masked criminality

    7. unisexual institution

NOTES

1. Clarence M. Kelley, *Uniform Crime Reports* (Washington, D.C.: U.S. Department of Justice, 1976), p. 176.

2. Freda Adler, *Sisters in Crime* (New York: McGraw-Hill, 1975).

3. A *trick* is one act of intercourse, generally considered completed by the orgasm of the male participant.

4. The annual budget for the Department of Justice for 1974 was approximately $1,834,000,000.

5. Rita Simon, *The Contemporary Woman and Crime* (Washington, D.C.: U.S. Department of Health, Education and Welfare, 1976), p. 50.

6. U.S. Department of Justice, *Prisoners in State and Federal Institutions 1974* (Washington, D.C.: U.S. Government Printing Office, 1976), p. 36.

7. National Advisory Commission on Criminal Justice Standards and Goals, *Corrections* (Washington, D.C.: U.S. Government Printing Office, 1973), p. 346. This is a description of the Women's Treatment Center, Purdy, Washington.

8. Kelley, *Uniform Crime Reports,* p. 47.

9. American Correctional Association, *Manual of Correctional Standards* (Washington, D.C.: ACA, 1969).

10. Matha A. Wheeler, Director, Detroit House of Corrections, Detroit, Michigan.

11. Edith E. Flynn, "The Special Problems of the Female Offenders," in *We Hold These Truths* (Richmond, Va.: Virginia Division of Justice and Crime Prevention, 1972).

12. National Advisory Commission, *Corrections,* p. 378.

13. Edith E. Flynn, "The Special Problems of Female Offenders," in *National Conference On Corrections* (Williamsburg, Va.: Virginia Division of Justice and Crime Prevention, 1971), p. 113.

14. David Ward and Gene Kassebaum, "Sexual Tensions in a Women's Prison," in *The Criminal in Confinement* (New York: Basic Books, 1971), pp. 149-150.

15. Sheldon and Eleanor Glueck, *500 Delinquent Women* (New York: A.A. Knopf, 1934).

16. David Ward and Gene Kassebaum, *Women's Prison: Sex and Social Structure* (Chicago: Aldine, 1965), pp. 9-10.

17. American Psychiatric Association, *Diagnostic and Statistical Manual* (Washington, D.C.: APA, 1969).

18. Christine G. Schultz, "Sociopathic and Non-sociopathic Female Offenders" (Ph.D. dissertation, The Ohio State University, 1973), p. 90.

19. U.S. Department of Justice, *Capital Punishment 1975* (Washington, D.C.: U.S. Government Printing Office, 1976), p. 2.

19 Juveniles: Punish or Protect?

> The essential idea of chancery is welfare or balancing
> of interests. It stands for flexibility, guardianship and
> protection rather than rigidity and punishment.
>
> *HERBERT H. LOU*

The Juvenile Crime Problem

Approximately one out of every six boys, and one out of every nine children
in the United States, will be referred to a juvenile court before their
eighteenth birthdays.[1] The rise in juvenile crime is the most serious aspect of
the crime problem in America. In 1976, 25 percent of the crimes cleared by
arrest were committed by persons under eighteen years of age. Juvenile
offenders accounted for 34 percent of the robberies, 52 percent of the
burglaries, and 53 percent of the auto thefts in 1976.[2] At these rates, which
we know reflect only reported crimes—a small part of the true picture—
almost 667,000 crimes against property and 75,000 crimes against persons
cleared by arrest in 1976 involved a juvenile offender. While these percentages are not significantly higher than those reported by President Johnson's
Commission in 1967, they still constitute a significant and alarming portion
of the crime problem.[3]

Juveniles today are handled differently and separately from adults in
almost every phase of the criminal justice system. Extensive use of differential treatment and the exercise of discretion by individual officials at various
stages of the criminal process cloud the juvenile crime picture and problem.
Some major adjustments have taken place in the juvenile justice system in
the past few years, and many more will probably be initiated in the next
decade. Since some 35 percent of incarcerated male felons spent time as
boys in training institutions and schools for delinquents, it is necessary to
examine briefly the development and function of the juvenile courts and the
juvenile system, starting with the philosophy that produced them.

FIGURE V–1. Juvenile Offenders in the 1930s (Courtesy American Correctional Association)

Juvenile Justice: *Parens Patriae*

Like most of American criminal practice, our juvenile justice system derives from the common law of England. The English common law in regard to criminal responsibility was based on three assumptions concerning age. First, children under the age of seven were presumed to be *incapable* of forming criminal intent. Second, from eight to fourteen offenders were not held responsible unless the *state* could prove that they could clearly distinguish between right and wrong. Lastly, if offenders were over the age of fourteen, they were assumed to be responsible for their acts and therefore deserving of punishment. In this last case, the burden was on the *defendants* to prove that they were not responsible.

The king was considered the father of his country *(parens patriae)*, who assumed responsibility for the protection of all orphans and otherwise dependent children. In England this responsibility was fulfilled by the chancery courts,[4] in which the needful child became a ward of the state, under the protection of *parens patriae*. The chancery court was designed to act more flexibly than the more rigid criminal courts. The main concern was for the welfare of the child, and legal procedures that might hamper the court in its beneficial actions were either circumvented or ignored. Thus, there were two concepts under the common law: the presumption that children under certain ages are not responsible for their actions, and that a certain category of children was in need of protection by the state. It was not until the ages indicating possible responsibility were raised to sixteen and eighteen that these two concepts merged into the idea of juvenile delinquency.

Despite concern for the welfare of their children, most communities have a tolerance point for behavior of juveniles. When children go beyond this point, they can be taken into custody and recorded as delinquents. The mixing of juvenile offenders and adult felons was a practice that had been in existence for centuries, but was looked upon as repugnant in America's early history. It was not until 1899, however, that the delinquent juvenile began to receive differential attention in the courts. The first juvenile court was established in that year in Chicago, and the delinquent joined the dependent and neglected child as a ward of the state. When the juvenile delinquent was thus placed under the cloak of *parens patriae,* he or she was removed entirely from the formal *criminal* justice system. The general procedures for handling of juvenile delinquents today have been outlined by author and specialist in juvenile delinquency Ruth Cavan:

1. Police intercept a child in misconduct, respond to a child, or on investigation find evidence that a child has been involved in certain misconduct. The child is taken to the police station. Depending upon the organization of police services and the policy of the police, and of the juvenile court, the child is either reprimanded and released, or turned over to the police juvenile bureau (if there is one), or referred to a social agency or to the juvenile court.

2. If the child is referred to a fully developed juvenile court, his case is reviewed by an intake department. Certain children are released; others are referred to social agencies for treatment, and some are held for a hearing before the juvenile court judge. A minority of children reach court attention through direct referral by parents, school officials or others without reference to the police. The court hearing and subsequent procedures are the same as when the police refer a child.

3. If an interval of time must elapse before the hearing the child may be released to his parents or held in detention in jail or a special juvenile detention center.

4. When the judge hears the case, he has information available not only on the offense but also on the child and his family, assembled by social workers

or probation officers attached to the court. If intervals of time elapse during the course of the hearing, the child may continue to live at home or be held in the place of detention.

5. The child may be dismissed with a warning to him and his parents.

6. The child may be placed on probation, under supervision of the probation officer or of some agency in the community. He usually continues to live at home, attend school, and follow a normal round of activities.

7. If his home is unsuitable for him, he may be placed in a foster home (if a young child) or in a private institution for borderline delinquents (if an older child).

8. If he has committed a serious offense or is a recidivist, he may be committed to a state correctional school for a period of time.

9. When he is released from the school, he is usually placed under the supervision of a parole officer.

10. Eventually he is discharged from probation or parole.

11. In some states, if his offense is a serious adult-type crime, he may be tried in the adult criminal court. Somewhat the same procedure is followed but in a more formal manner; if he is found guilty he may be sentenced to an adult prison, perhaps for a sentence that will keep him imprisoned for many years. In extreme cases, an older adolescent may be given a death sentence, although this rarely happens.[5]

A Whole New Vocabulary

Even after the juvenile delinquent has been officially removed from the criminal justice system, administrators continued to observe many aspects of that system in dealing with juveniles. Various terms used in the criminal courts were changed to apply to juvenile justice, but the meanings remained the same. It is essential in understanding the juvenile justice process to recognize how the new terms relate to the old. For example, *petition* replaces "complaint," *summons* is used in place of "warrant," *finding of involvement* replaces "conviction," and *disposition* is the new term for "sentencing." The glossary below covers most of the significant terms used in the juvenile system. (A detailed glossary of terms used in the criminal justice system as a whole may be found at the end of this text.)

The words "child," "youth," and "youngster" are used synonymously and denote a person of juvenile court age. Juvenile court laws define a "child" as any person under the specified age, no matter how mature or sophisticated he may seem. Juvenile jurisdictions in at least two-thirds of the states include children under 18; the others also include youngsters between the ages of 18 and 21.

Juvenile Term	*Adult Term*
1. Adjudication: decision by the judge that the child has committed delinquent acts.	Conviction of guilt
2. Adjudicatory hearing: a hearing to determine whether the allegations of a petition are supported by the evidence beyond a reasonable doubt or by a preponderance of the evidence.	Trial
3. Adjustment: the term refers to matters which are settled or brought to a satisfactory state so that parties are agreed without official intervention of the court.	Plea bargaining
4. After-care: the supervision given to a child for a limited period of time after he is released from the training school but still under the control of the school or of the juvenile court.	Parole
5. Commitment: a decision by the judge that the child should be sent to a training school.	Sentence to imprisonment
6. Court: the court having jurisdiction over children who are alleged to be or found to be delinquent. Juvenile delinquency procedures should not be used for neglected children or those in need of supervision.	Court of record
7. Delinquent act: an act that if committed by an adult would be called a crime. The term "delinquent acts" does not include such ambiguities and noncrimes as	Crime

"being ungovernable," "truancy,"
"incorrigibility," and
"disobedience."

8. Delinquent child: a child who is
found to have committed an act
that would be considered a crime if
committed by an adult.

Criminal

9. Detention: temporary care of a
child alleged to be delinquent who
requires secure custody in
physically restricting facilities
pending court disposition or
execution of a court order.

Holding in jail

10. Dispositional hearing: a hearing
held subsequent to the
adjudicatory hearing in order to
determine what order of disposition
should be made concerning a child
adjudicated as delinquent.

Sentencing hearing

11. Hearing: the presentation of
evidence to the juvenile court
judge, his consideration of it, and
his decision on disposition of the
case.

Trial

12. Petition: an application for an
order of court or for some other
judicial action. Hence, a
"delinquency petition" is an
application for the court to act in
the matter of a juvenile
apprehended for a delinquent act.

Accusation or
indictment

13. Probation: the supervision of a
delinquent child after the court
hearing but without commitment to
a training school.

Probation (with the
same meaning)

14. Residential child care facility:
a dwelling other than a detention or
shelter care facility, which provides
living accommodations, care,
treatment, and maintenance for
children and youth and is licensed
to provide such care. Such
facilities include foster family
homes, group homes, and halfway
houses.

Halfway house

15. Shelter: temporary care of a child in physically unrestricting facilities pending court disposition or execution of a court order for placement. Shelter care is used for dependent and neglected children and minors in need of supervision. Separate shelter care facilities are also used for children apprehended for delinquency who need temporary shelter but not secure detention.	Jail
16. Take into custody: the act of the police in securing the physical custody of a child engaged in delinquency; avoids the stigma of the word *arrest*.[6]	Arrest

By 1945, juvenile courts had been established in every state, and it became apparent that different terms were being used for the same old things. One of the major problems developed from the practice of combining all the different categories of juveniles under the same rubric of *parens patriae*.

Categories of Juveniles

Essentially three kinds of children come into contact with the juvenile court system—a very significant event in their lives. The children in two of these categories have committed no offense and are generally referred to today as "status offenders," since their only problem is their *status*. They are either *dependent* (without family or support) or *neglected* (have a family situation that is harmful to them). The only category that involves an offense is the *delinquent* juvenile.

Dependent children are those who need the protection of the state to meet their basic life needs. Usually their parents have died, and they have no other adult relatives who can take care of them. In the early days of America, these unfortunates were taken in by other families. Later, when their numbers increased, orphans and other dependent children gravitated to the growing cities, and various types of institutions were developed to handle them. Orphanages, common in the nineteenth century, are seldom seen in America today. Some of the dependent children were kept in almshouses and other institutions, public and private, to provide them with food and shelter. Dependent children now are wards of the state, subject to at least some control by the courts; whenever possible, they are placed in foster homes.

Neglected children have problems similar to those of dependent children. However, they need the protection of the state not because their parents are dead, but because their parents either mistreat or ignore them. Often these children are the victims of a tragic circumstance known as the "battered child syndrome," where the parents' mental problems lead them to hurt their offspring. The child who is physically abused by a parent or guardian usually comes to the attention of the authorities through reports from neighbors, friends, or relatives. Even when badly abused, children are usually very loyal to their parents, and neglect is seldom reported to the authorities by the child. Sexual abuse by parents (incest) is also seldom reported by the young victims.

The care of neglected and dependent children is important, of course, but the juvenile courts were established primarily to handle the *delinquent* juvenile. For judicial purposes, delinquents are divided into several categories. The first is composed of children who have allegedly committed an *offense that would be a crime if it had been committed by an adult.* This group makes up about 75 percent of the population of the state institutions for delinquent juveniles.[7] The second category of delinquents is those who have allegedly violated regulations that generally apply *only to juveniles:* curfew restrictions, required school attendance, and similar rules and ordinances. The third and last group is labeled the "incorrigible" juveniles (those who have been declared unmanageable by their parents and the court). The second and third groups are often referred to as PINS (persons in need of supervision) or MINS (minors in need of supervision). Most concerned juvenile correctional officials would like to remove children in these PINS and MINS classifications (as well as status offenders) from the facilities designed primarily for custody of the first category of delinquent juveniles.[8]

In addition to the three major categories of juveniles, the court may also have to deal with other children's problems such as: adoption, termination of parents' rights, appointment of guardian, custody in divorce, nonsupport, and related situations. *It is this broad overreach of the juvenile court and the resultant conglomeration that takes place in juvenile detention and correctional facilities that generate most attacks on the system.* Juvenile facilities, while generally of much more humane quality than the adult system, have had and still have many major drawbacks.

Juvenile Detention Facilities

Schools built to house the homeless and dependent children who roamed the streets of Europe in the nineteenth century became the model for many later established in the United States. In England, the Reformatory School Acts of 1854, 1857, and 1866 provided methods whereby courts could send offenders under the age of sixteen to reformatories and, later, industrial schools.

The New York City House of Refuge became the first real American response to the juvenile problem in 1825.[9] These early efforts were prison-like structures, and the courts were still allowed to send juvenile offenders to actual adult prisons instead if they so desired. Juvenile institutions attempted to protect the children from the bad influence of the adult institutions, even though the system was crude and decentralized. Most of these schools were established by private organizations that recognized the need for speical attention to both juvenile offenders and neglected or dependent children. The first cottage housing systems for juveniles, now the most popular systems, were founded in Massachusetts (1854) and Ohio (1858).[10] Not until 1899, however, in Chicago, was the juvenile court system coordinated within a political jurisdiction, as an integral part of the county's criminal justice system. Since that time the juvenile court system has extended to cover every jurisdiction in the country, and a fairly standard pattern of juvenile confinement has developed.

The major type of facility for juveniles is the detention "home," where juvenile *victims* of crime are often kept in the same facilities as juvenile *offenders,* with the same treatment afforded both, under *parens patriae.* A survey conducted in 1969 identified 288 detention homes in America, which admitted about 488,800 juveniles a year.[11] These figures, while only an estimate, clearly suggest the enormity of the juvenile detention problem. Even more tragic is the fact that most jurisdictions do not have enough youthful offenders to justify construction of separate juvenile detention facilities, so an estimated 50,000 to 100,000 juveniles are being held in local jails and police lockups each year.[12] Many states have statutory provisions for the detention of juveniles in jails, as long as they are segregated from adult offenders. Some states have statutes or policies prohibiting the deten-tion of juveniles in jails, but practical problems require the frequent violation of such statutes.

Facilities designated exclusively for juvenile detention are usually not the best examples of how an ideal juvenile correctional facility should be designed and operated. Most of these structures were originally built for some other purpose and converted to their present use with as little expenditure as possible. The average capacity of juvenile detention facilities is about sixty-one, but most are overcrowded before they reach that number.[13] In the adult institutions the emphasis is on custody, and the same preoccupation with security shapes the programs and the general environ-ment in the juvenile detention facilities. Most of them are located in urban areas and are virtually sealed off from the community by their physical structure and other security measures. The youths are placed in dormitory-style housing, or single cells in some cases, often with the fixed furniture and dreary interiors that are typical of adult institutions. Most juvenile detention centers lack services and programs that might improve the resi-dents' chances of staying away from crime. They are denied most of the good in adult programs, and are subject to the worst aspects of institutional programs. The National Advisory Commission made specific recommendations with regard to juvenile detention facilities:

1. The detention facility should be located in a residential area in the community and near court and community resources.

2. Population of detention centers should not exceed 30 residents. When population requirements significantly exceed this number, development of separate components under the network system should be pursued.

3. Living area capacities within the center should not exceed 10 or 12 youngsters each. Only individual occupancy should be provided, with single rooms and programming regarded as essential. Individual rooms should be pleasant, adequately furnished, and homelike rather than punitive and hostile in atmosphere.

4. Security should not be viewed as an indispensable quality of the physical environment but should be based on a combination of staffing patterns, technological devices, and physical design.

5. Existing residential facilities within the community should be used in preference to new construction.

6. Facility programming should be based on investigation of community resources, with the contemplation of full use of these resources, prior to determination of the facility's in-house program requirements.

7. New construction and renovation of existing facilities should be based on consideration of the functional interrelationships between program activities and program participants.

8. Detention facilities should be coeducational and should have access to a full range of supportive programs, including education, library, recreation, arts and crafts, music, drama, writing, and entertainment. Outdoor recreational areas are essential.

9. Citizen advisory boards should be established to pursue development of in-house and community-based programs and alternatives to detention.

10. Planning should comply with pertinent state and
    federal regulations and the Environmental Policy
    Act of 1969.[14]

State Training Schools

According to a 1970 survey, there are 135 training schools in the United
States,[15] with an inmate population of 42,371. The average offender cost of
institutional confinement for the fiscal year of 1974 was $11,660, a figure
which should be compared with the costs of $5,500 for community residen-
tial facilities and less than $2,500 for foster home placement.[16] The
population is decreasing, probably due to increased use of alternatives to
institutionalization for juveniles. The state training schools were intended to
act as small reformatories and provide a place where the delinquent under
the age of eighteen could be trained and prepared for a productive future.
The large reformatories, like that in Elmira, New York, were generally used
to house and rehabilitate offenders who fall between the juvenile and adult
categories. Many state training schools are little more than miniature
reformatories, while others have programs that provide educational and
vocational opportunities in good surroundings.

The whole issue of whether it is productive to place juveniles into
institutions is being hotly debated in correctional circles. One state has
closed all of its juvenile institutions[17] and others are phasing them out as
soon as is practical.[18] Various Supreme Court decisions in the 1960s and
'70s, described below, have influenced the programs of the state training
schools, to some extent; but many continue to operate with business-as-
usual.

Institutions are the most expensive and the least successful method of
handling juvenile offenders. But until the services needed to provide supervision and treatment in the community are forthcoming, the judges often
have no other choice but to commit offenders. The junior prisons are not all
bad, but the custody philosophy is the prevailing model, and it creates the
same problems at this level as at the adult level. The dangers that these
institutions present to the civil rights of the juvenile offender were forcefully
brought to public attention in a Supreme Court decision in 1967.

In re Gault: A Turning Point

In 1966, the case of *Miranda* v. *Arizona* signaled a turbulent period for the
criminal justice system. In 1967, the juvenile justice system also received a
major jolt, again from the state of Arizona, in the most far-reaching case of
that term: *In re Gault*.[19] This case focused not on any single right, but on a
number of the rights incorporated into the Fourteenth Amendment's "due
process" clause. Gerald Gault, fifteen years old, was sentenced to confine-

ment for the "remainder of his minority" (six years) for an offense (lewd and indecent phone calls) where the *maximum* penalty for an adult would have been only two months. During the course of his hearings, he was deprived of most of the privileges that various Court decisions had granted his adult counterparts. His appeal was heard by the United States Supreme Court on the issues of: notice of the charge, right to counsel, right to confrontation and cross-examination, privilege against self-incrimination, right to a transcript of the proceedings, and right to appellate review. The decision—that Gault was indeed entitled to those rights—helped to reshape the direction of the juvenile justice system and replaced the concept of *parens patriae* with due process.

As pointed out by Justice Fortas, the common practice of informality and procedural laxity in the juvenile court inevitably gave way to stern discipline in the correctional facility, causing the committed juvenile to feel he or she had been tricked. Justice Fortas held, with regard to the place of commitment and the constitutional questions raised in *Gault,* that:

> [I]t is of no constitutional consequence—and of limited practical meaning—that the institution to which he is committed is called an Industrial School. The fact of the matter is that, however euphemistic the title, a "receiving home" or an "industrial school" for juveniles is an institution of confinement in which the child is incarcerated for a greater or lesser time. His world becomes "a building with white-washed walls, regimented routine and institutional laws. . . ." Instead of mother and father and sisters and brothers and friends and classmates, his world is peopled by guards, custodians, state employees, and "delinquents" confined with him for anything from waywardness to rape and homicide.
>
> In view of this, it would be extraordinary if our Constitution did not require the procedural regularity and the exercise of care implied in the phrase "due process." Under our Constitution, the condition of being a boy does not justify a kangaroo court. The traditional ideas of juvenile court procedure, indeed, contemplated that time would be available and care would be used to establish precisely what the juvenile did and why he did it—was it a prank of adolescence or a brutal act threatening serious consequences to himself or society unless corrected? Under traditional notions, one would assume that in a case like that of Gerald Gault, where the juvenile appears to have a home, a working mother and father, and an older brother, the Juvenile Judge would have made a careful inquiry and judgment as to the possibility that the boy could be disciplined and dealt with at home, despite his previous transgressions. Indeed, so far as appears in the record before us, except for some conversation with Gerald about his school work and his "wanting to go to . . . Grand Canyon with his father," the points to which the judge directed his attention were little different

from those that would be involved in determining any charge of violation of a penal statute. The essential difference between Gerald's case and a normal criminal case is that safeguards available to adults were discarded in Gerald's case. The summary procedure as well as the long commitment were possible because Gerald was 15 years of age instead of over 18.[20]

In regard to the notice of charges, Justice Fortas continues:

It is obvious, as we have discussed above, that no purpose of shielding the child from the public stigma of knowledge of his having been taken into custody and scheduled for hearing is served by the procedure approved by the court below. The "initial hearing" in the present case was a hearing on the merits. Notice at that time is not timely; and even if there were a conceivable purpose served by the deferral proposed by the court below, it would have to yield to the requirements that the child and his parents or guardians be notified in writing of the specific charge or factual allegations to be considered at the hearing, and that such written notice be given at the earliest practicable time, and in any event sufficiently in advance of the hearing to permit preparation. Due process of law requires notice of the sort we have described—that is, notice which would be deemed constitutionally adequate in a civil or criminal proceeding. It does not allow a hearing to be held in which a youth's freedom and his parents' right to his custody are at stake without giving them timely notice, in advance of the hearing, of the specific issues that they must meet. Nor, in the circumstances of this case, can it reasonably be said that the requirement of notice was waived.[21]

The issue of whether a juvenile has the same right to counsel provided to his adult counterpart by *Gideon* v. *Wainwright* was the next to be discussed.

At the habeas corpus proceeding, Mrs. Gault testified that she knew that she could have appeared with counsel at the juvenile hearing. This knowledge is not a waiver of the right to counsel which she and her juvenile son had, as we have defined it. They had a right expressly to be advised that they might retain counsel and to be confronted with the need for specific consideration of whether they did or did not choose to waive the right. If they were unable to afford to employ counsel, they were entitled in view of the seriousness of the charge and the potential commitment, to appointed counsel, unless they chose waiver. Mrs. Gault's knowledge that she could employ counsel is not an "intentional relinquishment or abandonment" of a fully known right.[22]

The issues of confrontation, self-incrimination, and cross-examination were dealt with as interrelated, and the Justice's conclusion was:

> The "confession" of Gerald Gault was first obtained by Officer Flagg, out of the presence of Gerald's parents, without counsel and without advising him of his right to silence, as far as appears. The judgment of the Juvenile Court was stated by the judge to be based on Gerald's admission in court. Neither "admission" was reduced to writing, and, to say the least, the process by which the "admissions" were obtained and received must be characterized as lacking the certainty and order which are required of proceedings of such formidable consequences. Apart from the "admission," there was nothing upon which a judgment or finding might be based. There was no sworn testimony. Mrs. Cook, the complainant, was not present. The Arizona Supreme Court held that "sworn testimony must be required of all witnesses including police officers, probation officers and others who are part of or officially related to the juvenile court structure." We hold that this is not enough. No reason is suggested or appears for a different rule in respect of sworn testimony in juvenile courts than in adult tribunals. Absent a valid confession adequate to support the determination of the Juvenile Court, confrontation and sworn testimony by witnesses available for cross-examination were essential for a finding of "delinquency" and an order committing Gerald to a state institution for a maximum of six years.[23]

On the final issue, appellate review, the opinion of the Court was clear, and it established that the procedures discussed above were to apply in the future:

> This Court has not held that a state is required by the Federal Constitution "to provide appellate courts or a right to appellate review at all." In view of the fact that we must reverse the Supreme Court of Arizona's affirmance of the dismissal of the writ of habeas corpus for other reasons, we need not rule on this question in the present case or upon the failure to provide a transcript or recording of the hearings—or, indeed, the failure of the juvenile court judge to state the grounds for his conclusion. [See] *Kent* v. *United States,* where we said, in the context of a decision of the juvenile court waiving jurisdiction to the adult court, which by local law, was applicable: ". . . it is incumbent upon the Juvenile Court to accompany its waiver order with a statement of the reasons or considerations therefor." As the present case illustrates, the consequences of failure to provide an appeal, to record the proceedings, or to make findings or state the grounds for the juvenile court's conclusion may be to throw a burden

upon the machinery for habeas corpus, to saddle the reviewing process
with the burden of attempting to reconstruct a record, and to impose
upon the juvenile judge the unseemly duty of testifying under
cross-examination as to the events that transpired in the hearings
before him.

For the reasons stated, the judgment of the Supreme Court of
Arizona is reversed and the cause remanded for further proceedings
not inconsistent with this opinion.[24]

These decisions have had a far-reaching effect on the juvenile courts in
America. With the assumption of due process as a right for juveniles in their
proceedings, juvenile courts have been forced to become *courts* first and
social control agencies second. The *parens patriae* doctrine may remain in
effect, but in those cases where the juvenile is threatened with criminal
proceedings, the concept of the due process should take precedent.

The Correctional Funnel for Juveniles

In chapter 7, we saw the effect of the "correctional funnel." A similar
process is at work in the juvenile system. While the effect of the correctional
funnel and the use of discretion at various points of the justice system are
severe in the adult system, a number of other factors, which will be
discussed below, are also at work in the juvenile system. The problem is
sometimes referred to as "hidden delinquency." In an attempt to get to the
bottom of this problem, the Law Enforcement Assistance Administration set
aside $10 million for research projects in the diversion of juveniles from the
system. The problem of "hidden delinquency" was addressed in the
program announcement:

> Most of the early studies of delinquency in the United States were
> based upon police and juvenile court statistics which suggested that
> delinquent behavior was by and large confined to the poor, inner-city
> dwellers, blacks and children from broken homes. Studies based on
> these data resulted in etiological conclusions which located the causes
> of delinquent behavior in deleterious social circumstances. However,
> recent research has shown youthful misbehavior to be widespread in
> the United States, rather than being relatively uncommon and
> restricted to working-class neighborhoods.
>
> The pioneering study of "hidden" delinquency by Porterfield[25]
> involved a comparison of college students and actual juvenile court
> cases. The offenses of the juvenile court cases were incorporated into a
> questionnaire which was administered to several hundred college
> students. Virtually all of the latter reported committing at least one of
> the delinquent acts. The major difference between the two groups

centered about offense seriousness, with college students admitting less serious violations than those committed by the official delinquents.

However, it should be emphasized that nearly all of the inquiries into "hidden delinquency" indicate that the majority of undetected offenders confess to relatively petty acts of misconduct. These studies *do not* show that "hidden" offenders are involved in serious and repetitive acts of delinquency to the extent observed among offenders who have been adjudicated by juvenile courts. Nettler's review of these studies concluded: "While some criminality is normal, persistent and grave violations of the law are the experience of a minority. *This holds whether the measure is confessions or official* statistics" [emphasis in the original].[26]

The "hidden" delinquency studies indicate that some unknown but very large proportion of all American youths engage in delinquent acts of varying degrees of seriousness at some time during their adolescent years. In turn, some unknown segment of this group falls into the hands of the police. The FBI *Uniform Crime Reports* (1975) indicate that 2,078,450 juvenile arrests were reported by 8,050 police agencies. However, these statistics do not cover all police departments in the nation. Moreover, we have no way of determining the precise number of lawbreaking youths who are *not* arrested by the police.

The police perform a major sifting operation with apprehended juveniles, as they send some further into the juvenile justice system while releasing others outright. FBI statistics for 1973 indicate that the reporting agencies counseled and released 45.2 percent of the arrested juveniles while sending 49.5 percent of them to juvenile court intake. However, police referral policies are not uniform from one jurisdiction to another. Bordua[27] has presented data for over 2,000 police agencies in 1965, showing wide variations in the number of youths referred to court. Some agencies released over 95 percent of the youths they encountered, while other departments sent nearly all of the apprehended juveniles to juvenile court. In short, delinquency statistics are often a more revealing measure of police agency activity than they are an index of youthful misbehavior in the community.

What are the determinants of police decisions to refer or not refer a youth to juvenile court? Studies conducted in various communities around the country have provided information on this question. Most of them stress offense seriousness as a paramount consideration in police decision-making, while a number also suggest that racial background and socioeconomic status of the offender also weigh fairly heavily in police dispositions. These inquiries have produced somewhat discordant results, for some investigators contend that racial and economic factors are only incidentally associated with offense seriousness, while others have claimed that the police tend toward harsher dispositions directed at blacks and low income group members, even when offense seriousness is controlled.

Once a youth has been referred to juvenile court there is considerable discretion involved in disposition of the case. Court intake officers can counsel, warn and release a youth; they can place a youngster on probation, refer him to another agency; or send him on for petition and court hearing of the case. The decision-making criteria used by court workers are complex ones, although it appears that much the same types of information are taken into account by intake officers as by police.

The research on dispositional decision-making by police and court officers presents a somewhat confused picture, but it does reveal how the juvenile justice system filters out certain youths while sending others on through the system. Starting with a cohort of norm violators, the number moving through the juvenile justice system is steadily reduced to the point where very few are held in custody following adjudication.[28]

The rising number of juvenile offenders and offense rates are shown graphically in Table 7 (data from the period 1962–1972 are the most recent available as this text goes to press, but show a clear trend upward). As more of the status offenders are removed from the juvenile process, these rates will appear to decline, but the serious offenses can be expected to continue according to the trends now indicated.

The effect of the correctional funnel on the juvenile offender and the number of juveniles who end up in a juvenile institution are shown by the data in Figure V–2. (It is interesting to note that the commitment rates at the bottom of the funnel for the adult and juvenile systems in 1973 were almost identical, .022 and .024 respectively.) This similarity in rates will change dramatically in later statistics, as more and more juveniles are removed from contact with the justice system and more "hidden delinquents" are discovered and processed in the post-*Gault* era.

The Direction of Juvenile Justice

The juvenile crime problem is a great one, with the number of juveniles involved in serious crime increasing each year. The number of juvenile cases reaching the courts is also increasing, partly due to the aftermath of *Gault*. In 1970 and 1971, the number of cases that reached the courts increased by 7 percent, while informally handled cases increased only 3 percent.[35] In 1975, almost 900,000 juvenile offender cases were referred to juvenile court. It is recognized that community alternatives give the offender a better chance than the court processes, and the decline in their use compared with the use of the courts is a serious matter.

TABLE 7. NUMBER AND RATE OF DELINQUENCY CASES DISPOSED OF BY JUVENILE COURTS, UNITED STATES, 1957–1972

YEAR	DELINQUENCY CASES[a]	CHILD POPULATION 10 THROUGH 17 YRS. OF AGE (in thousands)	RATE[b]
1962	555,000	26,989	20.6
1963	601,000	28,056	21.4
1964	686,000	29,244	23.5
1965	697,000	29,536	23.6
1966	745,000	30,124	24.7
1967	811,000	30,837	26.3
1968	900,000	31,566	28.5
1969	988,500	32,157	30.7
1970	1,052,000	32,614	32.3
1971	1,125,000	32,969	34.1
1972	1,112,500	33,120	33.6

[a]Data for 1962–1969 estimated from the national sample of juvenile courts. Data for 1970, 1971, and 1972 estimated from all courts reporting, whose jurisdiction included more than three-fourths of the population of the U.S.
[b]Based on the number of delinquency cases per 1,000 U.S. child population 10 through 17 years of age.
U.S. Department of Health, Education, and Welfare (1973)

Because the nature of a juvenile's initial contact with the law is known to affect the likelihood of recidivism, the movement in the juvenile justice system has been toward nonjudicial alternatives. Intake screening and other methods for diverting all but a few of the juveniles from official sanctioning in the judicial system is an important trend. This kind of service is most commonly described as "informal adjustment" and "informal probation." Illinois has a good example of the kind of statutory authority that can be provided for adjustment proceedings.

1. The court may authorize the probation officer to confer in a preliminary conference with any person seeking to file a petition under Section 4–1, the prospective respondents and other interested persons concerning the advisability of filing the petition, with a view to adjusting suitable cases without the filing of a petition.

2. In any case of a minor who is in temporary custody, the holding of preliminary conferences does not operate to prolong temporary custody beyond the period permitted by Section 3–5.

3. The probation officer may not prevent the filing of a petition by any person who wishes to file a petition under this Act.

FIGURE V-2. The Delinquency Filtering Process

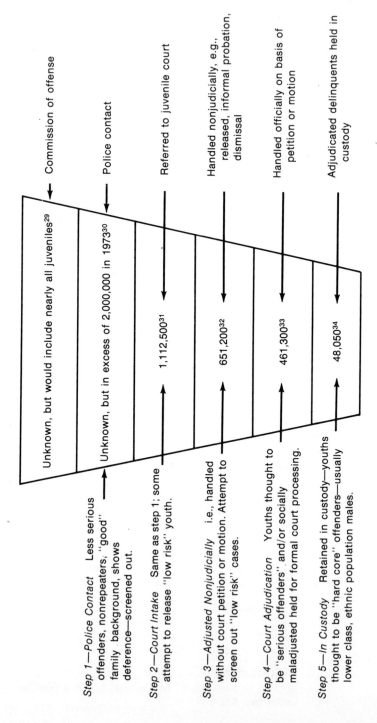

Attributes of those youth filtered into or out of system at each stage of processing

Stages in the juvenile justice process

Commission of offense

Police contact

Referred to juvenile court

Handled nonjudicially, e.g., released, informal probation, dismissal

Handled officially on basis of petition or motion

Adjudicated delinquents held in custody

Unknown, but would include nearly all juveniles[29]

Unknown, but in excess of 2,000,000 in 1973[30]

1,112,500[31]

651,200[32]

461,300[33]

48,050[34]

Step 1—Police Contact Less serious offenders, nonrepeaters, "good" family background, shows deference—screened out.

Step 2—Court Intake Same as step 1; some attempt to release "low risk" youth.

Step 3—Adjusted Nonjudicially i.e., handled without court petition or motion. Attempt to screen out "low risk" cases.

Step 4—Court Adjudication Youths thought to be "serious offenders" and/or socially maladjusted held for formal court processing.

Step 5—In Custody Retained in custody—youths thought to be "hard core" offenders—usually lower class, ethnic population males.

4. This Section does not authorize any probation officer to compel any person to appear at any conference, produce any papers, or visit any place.

5. No statements made during a preliminary conference may be admitted into evidence at an adjudicatory hearing or at any proceeding against the minor under the criminal laws of this state prior to his conviction thereunder.

6. Efforts at adjustment pursuant to rules or orders of court under this Section may not extend for a period of more than 3 months.[36]

Because of the informal nature of these procedures, little is known as to their effectiveness. This is not necessarily a handicap, however, as the basic reason for closing most of these cases after a period of informal handling is that no further problems have arisen with the juvenile.

Informal probation is described in the National Advisory Commission report:

Informal probation, another method of nonjudicial handling of juvenile cases coming to the attention of the court, permits informal supervision of young persons by probation officers who wish to reserve judgment regarding the necessity for filing a petition until after a child has had the opportunity for some informal treatment. There are several recognized advantages to this type of disposition:

- It does not interrupt school or job attendance.

- It avoids the stigma of a delinquent record and a delinquent reputation.

- It does not reinforce antisocial tendencies, as formal adjudication has a tendency to do.

- It is less costly than formal probation.[37]

It is recognized that these informal proceedings could be abused, resulting in coercion of the juvenile and misuse of the procedure. In order to preserve equity and to protect the rights of all juveniles, the following procedural safeguards are suggested:

1. The facts of the case should be undisputed, and all parties including the juvenile should agree to the informal probation disposition.

2. The juvenile and his parents should be advised of their right to formal adjudication procedures, should they so desire.

3. Self-incriminating statements made during the informal process should not be used if formal adjudication procedures ensue after the informal settlement attempt.

4. A reasonable time limit (between three and six months) should be placed on the informal probation period.

5. A petition on the original complaint should not be allowed after an agreement has been worked out with all parties involved.[38]

The move toward more informal disposition of juvenile cases accords with current developments in the adult system. In both systems, incarceration is coming to be viewed as a last resort. In juvenile cases, the National Advisory Commission found, formal proceedings should be used only when:

• Accusations are in dispute, and, if borne out, court-ordered disposition and treatment appear desirable.

• Detention or removal from the home is indicated.

• The nature or gravity of the offense warrants official judicial attention.

• The juvenile or the parents request formal adjudication.[39]

It seems that juvenile justice in America will continue to follow the ideals of *parens patriae,* but with the Supreme Court watching to see that the rights of young citizens are not abused.

It is reasonable to argue that the relatively high proportion of adult felons who were processed through the juvenile treatment delivery systems and training institutions as youths may decrease sharply as alternatives to formal processing, institutionalization, and labeling are developed for juveniles. The poor facilities in juvenile correctional institutions, the inmate social system, and the reduction of services due to a heavy emphasis on custody and a fossilized bureaucratic organization—all contribute to the relative ineffectiveness of the juvenile system. With recognition of this problem, and the development of alternatives, the burden which inadequate treatment of juvenile delinquents places on the adult correctional system can be reduced—a double benefit to the American citizenry.

REVIEW QUESTIONS

I. Find the answers to the following in the text:

1. Explain the concept of *parens patriae*. How does this apply today?

2. Describe and differentiate between the three kinds of children who come into contact with the juvenile courts.

3. What were the major findings in the case of *In re Gault?*

4. What effect does differential treatment have on juvenile justice? Explain.

II. Words to identify:

1. *parens patriae*

2. chancery court

3. adjudication

4. adjudicatory hearing

5. after-care

6. commitment

7. delinquency

8. dependency

9. detention

10. hearing

11. neglected

12. PINS/MINS

13. status offenders

14. state training school

15. summons

NOTES

1. President's Commission on Law Enforcement and Administration of Justice, *Task Force Report: Corrections* (Washington, D.C.: U.S. Government Printing Office, 1967), p. 131.

2. Clarence M. Kelley, *Uniform Crime Reports* (Washington, D.C.: U.S. Department of Justice, 1976), p. 183.

3. *Task Force Report: Corrections,* p. 120.

4. *Chancery courts* date back to the feudal days of England. They traditionally had broad authority over the welfare of children, but exercised this authority almost exclusively on behalf of minors whose property rights were in jeopardy. In America, this was extended to minors in danger of personal as well as property attacks.

5. Ruth S. Cavan, *Juvenile Delinquency,* 2d ed. (New York: Lippincott, 1969), p. 360.

6. This list was developed from a composite of items from: National Advisory Commission on Criminal Justice Standards and Goals, *Corrections* (Washington, D.C.: U.S. Government Printing Office, 1973), p. 248, and Ruth S. Cavan, *Juvenile Delinquency,* p. 367.

7. President's Commission on Law Enforcement and Administration of Justice, *Task Force Report: Juvenile Delinquency* (Washington, D.C.: U.S. Government Printing Office, 1967), p. 4.

8. See "Hearings Open on FY 1978 Juvenile Act Reauthorization," *Criminal Justice Newsletter* 7 (June 7, 1976): 5.

9. *Task Force Report: Juvenile Delinquency,* p. 3.

10. The *cottage* system generally involves a series of small houselike structures within a compound. These usually provide open living and sleeping areas or separate rooms for residents, and a separate living area for the cottage "parents."

11. Nicholas A. Reuterman, *A National Survey of Juvenile Detention Facilities* (Edwardsville, Ill.: Southern Illinois University, 1970), p. 39.

12. National Advisory Commission on Criminal Justice Standards and Goals, *Corrections* (Washington, D.C.: U.S. Government Printing Office, 1973), p. 258.

13. Reuterman, p. 87.

14. National Advisory Commission, *Corrections,* p. 269.

15. Reuterman, p. 87.

16. See "Training School Still Predominates Juvenile Corrections," *Criminal Justice Newsletter* 7 (January 5, 1976): 1-2.

17. Massachusetts juvenile institutions were closed by Director Jerome Miller in 1972.

18. California is moving in that direction.

19. *In re Gault* 387 U.S. 1, 87 S.Ct. 1428, 18 L.Ed. 2d 527 (1967). The U.S. Supreme Court held that juvenile delinquency proceedings which may lead to commitment to state institutions must adhere to the essentials of due process and fair treatment: notification of the child or the parents of the allegations, the right to be represented by counsel, and the right against self-incrimination.

20. *In re Gault,* 1967.

21. *In re Gault,* 1967.

22. *In re Gault,* 1967.

23. *In re Gault,* 1967.

24. *In re Gault,* 1967.

25. A. L. Porterfield, "Delinquency and its Outcome in Court and College," *American Journal of Sociology* 44 (November 1943): 199-208.

26. G. Nettler, *Explaining Crime* (New York: McGraw-Hill, 1974).

27. D. J. Bordua, ''Recent Trends: Deviant Behavior and Social Control,'' *Annual of the American Academy of Political and Social Science* 359 (January 1967): 149-161.

28. U.S. Department of Justice, *Diversion of Youth from the Juvenile Justice System* (Washington, D.C.: U.S. Government Printing Office, 1976), pp. 16-21.

29. D. C. Gibbons, *Delinquent Behavior,* 2d ed. (Englewood Cliffs, N.J.: Prentice-Hall, 1976), pp. 16-33.

30. While actual numbers are unknown, the 1973 *Uniform Crime Reports,* p. 19, show that 49.5 percent of juveniles taken into custody are referred to juvenile court, while 45.2 percent are handled within the department and released.

31. U.S. Department of Health, Education and Welfare, *Juvenile Court Statistics 1973* (Washington, D.C.: U.S. Government Printing Office, 1973), p. 8.

32. U.S. Department of Health, Education and Welfare, *Juvenile Court Statistics 1973,* p. 8.

33. U.S. Department of Health, Education and Welfare, *Juvenile Court Statistics 1973,* p. 8.

34. U.S. Department of Jusrice, *Detention Status of Children in Juvenile Facilities* (Washington, D.C.: U.S. Government Printing Office, 1972), p. 7.

35. National Advisory Commission, *Corrections,* p. 250.

36. Illinois Annotated Statutes, Chapter 37, paragraphs 703-708, Smith-Hurd Supplement (1967).

37. National Advisory Commission, *Corrections,* p. 255.

38. National Advisory Commission, *Corrections,* p. 255.

39. National Advisory Commission, *Corrections,* p. 257.

20 Special Category Offenders

For every zealot who heralds psychiatric concepts and treatment as the only answer to the crime problem, there is a critic who believes that psychiatric contributions to criminology are unscientific and misleading.

SEYMOUR HALLECK

A Special Kind of Deviant

What kind of illness would lead civilized people to reject their own members in the most barbaric fashion, and brand them with a stigma so severe that they are stuck with it even if they seek and achieve a cure? These unfortunates—the mentally ill—used to be scorned and burned, but in more enlightened times we have built backwoods fortresses for them, presumably to protect ourselves from contagion. They have been executed as witches, subjected to exorcisms, chained, or thrown into gatehouses and prisons to furnish horrible diversion for the other prisoners.[1] In some countries they were gathered together and placed on a "Ship of Fools" *(das Shiff der Narren)* and shipped off to uninhabited lands where they were left to wander on their own. The methods recommended by Celsus, a first-century Roman scholar, established the pattern of treatment for the years to come: "When he [the mentally ill person] has said or done anything wrong, he must be chastised by hunger, chains, and fetters."[2] In line with that approach, throughout human history the mentally ill have been subjected to misguided, cruel, sadistic, and fear-based treatment ranging from burning at the stake to banishment from society.

This chapter deals with the evolution of the diagnosis and treatment of the so-called *special-category offenders,* a group of human beings selected for special stigma and treatment. In order to understand the development of the laws, treatments, and institutions which apply to these offenders, one must review the early history of treatment for the mentally ill.

The first insane asylum was constructed in Europe in 1408.[3] From that date until very recently, the asylum has been viewed as a dumping-ground for all the mentally ill we could neither understand nor cure. During the Renaissance, many diseases of the body such as leprosy began to be controlled by medicine and more sanitary conditions, but diseases of the mind were still a mystery. It has been speculated that the vacating of more than 19,000 leprosaria in Europe during this period helped lead to the next logical step for the socially unfit: confinement.[4] Only in modern times has society applied different sanctions to the vagrant, indigent, common criminal, and insane (both benign and raving). Not until 1843, when the M'Naghten Rule[5] was adopted in England, did the insane receive any different treatment under the law than their sane brothers. "As late as 1750 Robert Francois Damiens, a palpably insane man who pricked Louis XV of France with a penknife as the king was leaving the palace, was exposed to an incredibly barbaric execution: his flesh was torn with red hot pincers, the hand that wielded the knife was burned off with lighted sulpher, his tongue was torn out at the root, and finally he was drawn and quartered."[6]

Prior to the Middle Ages, considerable tolerance was shown to the mentally disturbed. They were generally cared for locally, by members of their own family, tribal system, or primitive society. The advent of widespread poverty, disease, and religious fanaticism in the Middle Ages, however, seemed to trigger intolerance for *any* deviation. The mentally disturbed were thought to be possessed by devils and demons and punished harshly because of it. At that time, the insane were driven out of society; during the next ages they were to be *confined* (another form of isolation from society).

The Emergence of the Asylum in America

Until relatively recent times it was assumed that the *intellect* was involved in the process of mental illness. This assumption, however, did not explain the perverted and criminal behavior of people who seemed to have a clear perception of reality—a "normal" intellect—*except* in the area of social morality. We see this concept of the "moral idiot" (or psychopath) first described in modern terms by Philippe Pinel. His classification of *manie sans délire* (mania without delusions) shed light on this previously unexplained phenomenon.[7] The American psychiatrist Benjamin Rush spoke of moral alienation: defective organization of moral faculties and deranged will. Rush, like Pinel, saw that mental illness could involve faculties other than intellectual.

While the scholars and psychiatrists of the early 1800s pondered the paradox of the "moral imbecile," the asylum for the insane found its way into pre-Civil War America. Only Virginia supported a public insane asylum prior to 1810. But in the next few decades, twenty-eight of the thirty-three states built asylums for the insane.[8] The unfounded but enthusiastic claims of psychiatrists as to their ability to "cure" the mentally ill was a strong catalyst for the cult of the asylum as the ultimate solution to the problems of mental illness. It was these claims for curability that inflated the hopes of those sincerely concerned with *helping* the mentally ill. Leaders of the asylum movement, such as Dorothea Dix,[9] were overenthusiastic and overwhelming in their claims for cures, if only legislators would build an asylum that would provide the insane with respite from the open and fluid American society. The states, one after another, responded to this compelling cry and built numerous institutions during the mid-1800s.

The inflated claims could not stand up against the process of institutionalization, however, and long-term commitments, not cures, became the rule of the day. Commitment procedures were entirely too casual in the early period of the insane asylum in America, sometimes requiring only the request of the husband or guardian. Mrs. Elizabeth Parker Ware Packard, an ex-patient, set out in the 1860s to arouse public concern against the practice of "railroading to lunatic asylums."[10] Most of the formal commitment guarantees available today are in great part the result of this courageous woman's efforts.

Two Ways to Escape the Death Penalty

There are two basic justifications defendants can invoke to relieve themselves of criminal responsibility for an act. The first is "not guilty by reason of insanity"; the second is "incompetent to stand trial." In the first instance offenders do not question the commission of the act, but assert that they did not have the capacity to understand the nature of the act, or that it was wrong. The second instance is based on the common law criteria that defendants must be able to understand the charges against them, and to cooperate with their counsel in the preparation of their own defense. The procedures for determining competency vary considerably from jurisdiction to jurisdiction, but most make it a court decision based on psychiatric testimony. In some states a jury to determine competency may be impaneled if requested by the defendant, and in three states the court has the discretion to impanel such a jury.[11] If defendants are found incompetent to stand trial, they are usually committed to a mental institution until declared competent.

Both of these defenses grew out of the overuse of the death penalty in England. The common law development of the insanity plea reflected a major shift in emphasis, away from the excessively cruel criminal justice practices of the early nineteenth century. The defense of insanity—a *legal*, not a medical term—stems from the famous case of Danny M'Naghten, mentioned earlier. In 1843, M'Naghten set out to assassinate the British Prime Minister, but killed the Prime Minister's secretary instead, in the belief that he *was* the Minister. M'Naghten's attorney held that since M'Naghten was not in his right mind when he shot the secretary—i.e., he did not understand what he was doing, or that it was wrong—he should not be subjected to the same penalty that would be accorded a cold-blooded killer. This defense gave the courts an optional method for the disposition of these serious offenders, short of sentencing them to death, and thus produced a new category of offenders: the *criminally insane*.

The Criminally Insane

With the advent of legal insanity and incompetency as defenses against criminal conviction came the development of special asylums for the criminally insane, in most cases just another form of prison, without due process protections. These institutions are reserved for the following categories of offender:

   a. persons adjudicated incompetent to enter a plea or stand trial;

   b. defendants found not guilty by reason of insanity;

   c. persons adjudicated under special statutes, e.g., "sexually dangerous persons," "defective delinquents," "sexual psychopaths," etc.;

   d. convicted and sentenced offenders who have become mentally disturbed while serving a prison sentence and have been transferred to a mental health facility;

   e. other potentially hazardous mentally ill persons requiring special security during the course of their evaluation and treatment.[12]

There are presently seventy-three such institutions in the United States.

The Psychopath

Even as the number of patients and institutions for treatment of the insane increased, doubts arose as to how possible it was to "cure" or even change the category previously identified by Pinel and others as the "moral idiot." About this time, Italy's legal authority Baron Raffaele Garofalo[13] addressed the issue of moral insanity by suggesting the presence of biological factors:

> Should [such moral anomalies as the sociopath] be regarded as a new nosologic [medically classifiable] form—the moral insanity [described by] the English writers? The existence of this form of alienation is questionable, to say the least. In spite of utmost efforts to discover traces of insanity, one is often obliged to admit that the individual under examination possesses an intelligence which leaves nothing to

be desired, that he exhibits no nosologic symptom, unless it be the absence of a moral sense, and that, to quote a French physician, whatever be the subject's unit of mind, "the psychic keyboard has only one false note and only one."[14]

Garofalo substituted the term *constitutional inferiority* for *moral insanity.* His ideas on the treatment of these unfortunates, who seemingly did not deserve *pity,* involved the application of some form of his "relative elimination," usually by marooning in an uninhabited land.

Another member of Italy's "positive" school of criminology, Cesare Lombroso,[15] viewed psychopaths as moral imbeciles, noting that they were guiltless, highly aggressive, impulsive, boastful, and particularly insensitive to social criticism and physical pain.[16] Lombroso felt that the asylum was a good place for such persons:

> At first sight this proposition seems absurd. . . . But proper attention has not been paid to the fact that it is just such . . . cases, intermediate between reason and insanity, in which, therefore, the criminal asylums are most useful and of most service in guaranteeing the public safety.[17]

The term *psychopath* was used first by the ancient Greeks to designate those behaviors that medicine could not explain. The literal translation of the Greek components of the word—*suffering mind*—suggests that our cultural ancestors approached this behavior with some understanding. Historically, psychiatrists have been ambivalent in accepting "psychopath" as a valid designation. As shown previously, Pinel and others chose to refer to this condition as some form of moral insanity. Attempts to give specific content to the term have generally failed because they approached it only in relation to *other* terms. In American psychiatry, "psychopath" is either used as a strict categorization or rejected entirely. Noted psychiatrist H. Cleckley[18] established an effective case for the psychopathic condition as a meaningful one and listed sixteen characteristics common to the class, concluding with his classic definition:

1. Superficial charm and intelligence.

2. Absence of delusions and other signs of irrational thinking.

3. Absence of "nervousness" or neurotic manifestations.

4. Unreliability.

5. Untruthfulness and insincerity.

6. Lack of remorse or shame.

7. Antisocial behavior without apparent compunction.

8. Poor judgment and failure to learn from experience.

9. Pathologic egocentricity and incapacity for love.

10. General poverty in major affective relations.

11. Specific loss of insight.

12. Unresponsiveness in general interpersonal relations.

13. Fantastic and uninviting behavior with drink and sometimes without.

14. Suicide threats rarely carried out.

15. Sex life impersonal, trivial, and poorly integrated.

16. Failure to follow any life plan.

"He mimics the human personality but is unable to *feel*." [19]

While psychiatry continued to try to find a way to identify and *treat* this kind of condition, the law began to see special problems with the offender who, while not troubled by various forms of delusions or other problems of the intellect, was "unable to feel." These offenders, when placed in a mental institution, showed rapid progress and were released, soon getting into trouble again. The response to this perceived threat to society was the first psychopathy law, passed by Massachusetts in 1911. Known as the Briggs Act, it created a distinct class of habitual criminal offenders, known as *defective delinquents*. [20]

Sexual Psychopath Laws

The Massachusetts statute was soon copied by other states, and eventually the first *sexual* psychopath law was passed by Michigan in 1937. This created a flood of such laws in the late 1930s and 1940s, and they are now on the books in twenty-eight states and the District of Columbia. There was little resistance to passage of these laws in most jurisdictions. Most required building new facilities or modifying existing state mental hospitals to house the convicted offenders. Thus, as shown in Figure V–3, a concentric series of asylums developed: first, some form of asylum or institution for the mentally ill; second, a special kind of asylum to contain the criminally insane (so that they do not escape punishment for their crimes); and last, a special kind of asylum for an offender who is not legally insane, but presumably represents a threat to the public safety, especially in the sexual context.

This kind of legislation is based on a series of unproven assumptions. It is generally assumed that sex crimes present the greatest danger to women and children and that most sex crimes are committed by *sexual psychopaths,* who repeat their crimes throughout their lifetime. Further, as mentioned earlier, it is assumed that psychiatrists can diagnose and identify this type of deviant behavior; that sexual psychopaths who are so identified should then be confined as irresponsible and dangerous persons; and that they should not be released until pronounced cured of their "malady" by a judge. The latter judgment is usually made on the basis of a psychiatric examination report.

It is this last proposition that reveals the connection between sexual psychopath legislation and the courtroom significance of insanity. Sexual psychopath laws are sometimes regarded as an extension of the criminal defense of insanity. In fact, the insanity plea is under attack, and abolition of the insanity defense for all federal courts was proposed by then-President Nixon in 1972. Psychiatrist and author S. Brakel argues that the purpose of sexual psychopath statutes seems to be twofold: (1) to relieve from criminal sanctions a group of social deviants who do not properly fall within the boundaries of "normality," and (2) to protect society from the "menace" of the sexual psychopath through his indefinite commitment to a state institution for treatment until recovery.[21] The provision of treatment for these persons while committed to a mental institution marks, at least in theory, the passage from the traditional retributive aims of the criminal justice system to the rehabilitative objectives of society.

It is precisely the *treatment* aspect of these indefinite commitment statutes that has brought them under heavy attack on constitutional grounds. Alabama, for example, has had its sexual psychopath law declared unconstitutional by the U.S. District Court.[22] "Such persons," the court stated, "have been legally detained for therapeutic purposes and have received little or no treatment. . . ."

Michigan, the first state to draft a sexual psychopath law, repealed that law in 1968 in order to stay within the bounds of constitutionality and avoid prolonged indefinite commitments. It is ironic that the state that led the way for the rash of laws in the 1930s and 1940s is now showing the way back.

Institutions throughout the United States vary in their procedures and treatment programs. From the obvious failure in Alabama to the more enlightened operations of the Patuxent Institution in Maryland, we have a full spectrum of institutional types. It took the case of *Tippett* v. *Maryland,*[23] however, to temporarily assure the citizens of that state that the institution at Patuxent was not just another dumping ground for a special category of hard-to-handle offenders. The treatment programs at Patuxent, the case indicated, had responded to the recent emphasis on community-based treatment. This is also true for efforts by the Ohio Division of Forensic Psychiatry, based primarily on increased medical knowledge about the condition referred to as *psychopathy.*

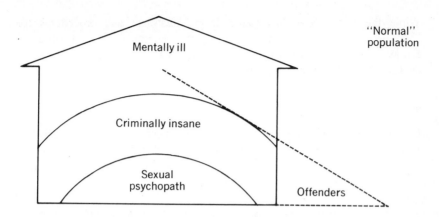

FIGURE V–3. Institutions for the Special Category Offender

Problems with Semantics

The term *sociopath* has become a fairly common one, due to a study of fifty sociopaths by Partridge, which led him to conclude:

> [The sociopathic] personality is a persistent behavior pattern or tendency in which there is usually excessive demand. . . . [When] there is a failure of direct or immediate satisfaction, [there is] a tendency to develop characteristic ways of dominating situations: by emotional displays we call tantrums, by sulks, by running away. . . .[24]

To reflect current knowledge and theory, the term *psychopath* has been replaced by *sociopath,* with subcategories of *antisocial sociopathic personality, dyssocial reaction, sexual deviation,* and *addiction.* The term *antisocial personality* is currently used as a synonym for the sociopath. The three latter conditions are described as follows:

> Dyssocial reaction refers to habitual criminals who utilize their illegitimate gains for particular ends, show strong motivation in behavior, attempt to avoid the consequences of their antisocial behavior, and show loyalty to other group members and their codes. Sexual deviation refers to individuals whose sexual interests are limited primarily toward objects other than people of the opposite sex, or acts, sexual in nature, not usually associated with coitus; this category includes homosexuality, fetishism, transvestism, etc. Finally, addiction refers to alcoholism and drug addiction, suggesting habitual use and interference with normal and personal functions.[25]

While the terminology has changed, the treatment and procedures for handling sexual psychopaths (or sociopaths) continue, by and large, to follow the pattern established in the mid-1800s of consigning them to another form of human warehouse.

The Problem of Prediction

One of the most unfortunate aspects of commitment for mental illness is that long indeterminate sentences often reflect a fear that those committed might be a problem in the *future*. Lewis Carroll presented the problem very effectively in *Through the Looking Glass:*

> "[T]here's the King's Messenger," said the Queen. "He's in prison now, being punished; and the trial doesn't even begin till next Wednesday; and of course the crime comes last of all."
>
> "Suppose he never commits the crime?" said Alice.
>
> "That would be all the better, wouldn't it?" the Queen said, as she turned the plaster round her finger with a bit of ribbon.
>
> Alice felt there was no denying *that.* "Of course it would be all the better," she said, "but it wouldn't be all the better his being punished."
>
> "You're wrong *there,* at any rate," said the Queen. "Were you ever punished?"
>
> "Only for faults," said Alice.
>
> "And you were all the better for it, I know!" the Queen said triumphantly.
>
> "Yes, but then I *had* done the things I was punished for," said Alice. "That makes all the difference."
>
> "But if you hadn't done them," the Queen said, "that would have been better still; better, and better, and better!"[26]

It is the requirement for prediction of criminal *inclination* that makes the programs for treatment of the sexual psychopath so subject to question. Who can predict potential dangerousness with any degree of accuracy? Bernard Rubin says that "the belief in the psychiatrist's ability to predict the likely dangerousness of a patient's future behavior is almost universally held, yet it lacks empirical support." And, he adds, "labeling of deviancy as mental illness or predicting dangerousness is just a convention to get someone to treatment. Once in treatment the concept of dangerousness is forgotten."[27] This becomes critical because most sexual psychopath laws do not differentiate between the various types of the so-called sex offenses. They lump together such deviant behaviors as "making improper exposure of the person in the presence of a child" (exhibitionism) and the crime of violent rape. Some statutes have added the category of "sexually dangerous offender" in order to distinguish (at least in theory) the degrees of seriousness in different sex crimes. In practice, however, these statutes take a more rigid position, often labeling as dangerous what is merely misconduct in sexual matters.

For these reasons, among many, it has been argued that the concept of sexual psychopath is "meaningless and incomprehensible, or in any case, far too broad and unspecific." It does not permit "evaluation of deviation to be used according to objective legal, medical, or common sense standards. This very indefiniteness permits and necessitates judgments that are left to the accidental, or relative morality, to the social and cultural bias, and to the unstated evaluative criteria of the judge, the superintendent, the staff of the state hospital or the examining psychiatrist."[28] More recently, however, Kozol conducted a study of 592 male convicted offenders and seemed able to develop prediction models of dangerousness with a high rate of reliability. Only 6.1 percent of the patients released upon his staff's recommendation were subsequently involved in serious assaultive crimes.[29]

So, we see the paradox of requiring psychiatrists to *predict* behavior and attach a label to offenders, when this might result in an indefinite, or even lifelong, commitment to a mental institution for someone who is not really dangerous. Further, this individual is then labeled for custody and treatment in a special area *within* that institution. When one considers the wealth of folklore surrounding mental institutions, it becomes clear that a dreadful stigma accompanies the label of "sexual psychopath." Recent reform efforts, such as the Patuxent institution and the work of Kozol and others, show that there is a more effective way to handle these unfortunates. In general, though, little is being done to replace the nineteenth-century bastions we have been stuck with. Far from the mainstream of life, filled with society's castaways, the asylums lend themselves to isolation, mystery, and myth.[30] Until the walls between the public and the patient have been *physically* removed, as in some community-based projects, or until hospitalized psychopathic offenders sue their keepers for nontreatment,[31] reform or restoration of the sexual psychopath will continue to be a rare accident.

The Correctional Troublemaker

The significance of the incarcerated psychopathic offender lies not so much in the vagueness of the classification and treatment plan—it cannot be definitive because there is no known effective treatment for such prisoners[32]—but in the effect of the psychopath's behavior on the prison atmosphere. Hostile, aggressive, explosive, and exploitive, the psychopathic inmate necessitates a security emphasis in prisons, negating the rehabilitation potential of other inmates. Further, psychopaths tend to condition public thinking about offenders. Indeed, experts have argued that were it not for these offenders, there would be cosiderably more acceptance of and support for alternatives to incarceration, such as halfway houses, community treatment centers, parole and probation, work and education release, and home visits. Until effective treatments are developed for such psychopathic offenders, the current prison unrest, riots, and security emphasis will continue well into the future. Research is vitally needed in this area, to produce innovative programs and radically new approaches.

Summary

Mental illness has been identified as the nation's largest and most costly health problem, affecting one of every ten citizens, with treatments varying from barbaric to progressive and humane, and costs soaring to the $20 billion-a-year mark.[33] All these factors, added to the current trend in "right to treatment" cases (discussed later, in chapter 24), bode well for the future of treatment of the mentally ill, including special categories such as the sexual psychopath and the criminally insane. The finger of blame is often pointed at attendants, overworked and undertrained staff, legislators, and courts. In the final analysis, however, it will be society's emphasis on the care and treatment of its "losers" that will determine what is done for, and to, these castoffs of our communities in the next decade.

REVIEW QUESTIONS

I. Find the answers to the following in the text:
1. What spurred the growth of asylums in America?
2. What are an offender's two basic justifications for rejecting criminal responsibility?
3. Describe the history of psychopathic offender laws in America.

II. Words to identify:
1. ship of fools
2. moral idiot
3. psychopath
4. sociopath
5. *manie sans délire*
6. incompetent to stand trial
7. not guilty by reason of insanity (NGRI)
8. sexual psychopath
9. mental illness
10. special category offender

NOTES

1. G. Ives, *A History of Penal Methods* (London: S. Paul & Co., 1914).

2. J. Wilpers, "Animal, Vegetable or Human Being?" *Government Executive* (May 1973), p. 32.

3. Wilpers, "Animal, Vegetable or Human Being?" p. 33.

4. N. Kittrie, *The Right to Be Different* (Baltimore, Md.: The Johns Hopkins University Press, 1971), p. 194.

5. *The M'Naghten Rule:* To establish a defense on the ground of insanity, it must be clearly proved that, at the time of the committing of the act, the party accused was laboring under such a defect of reason, from disease of the mind, as not to know the nature and quality of the act he was doing; or, if he did know it, that he did not know he was doing what was wrong.

6. Kittrie, *The Right to Be Different,* p. 58.

7. Harry E. Allen, *Sociological and Biological Correlates of Two Types of Anti-Social Sociopaths* (Ph.D. dissertation, The Ohio State University, 1969), p. 12.

8. D. Rothman, *The Discovery of the Asylum* (New York: Little, Brown and Company, 1971), p. 130.

9. *Dorothea Dix* (1802-1887) was an American social reformer and pioneer in the movement for specialized treatment of the insane. For many years she ran a school in Boston. In 1841 she visited a jail in East Cambridge and was shocked at conditions there, especially at the indiscriminate mixing of criminals and the insane. She began inspecting other places in Massachusetts and in 1842 wrote a famous memorial to the state legislature. Her crusades resulted in the founding of state hospitals for the insane in many states, and her influence was felt in Canada and Europe. She also did notable work in penology. During the Civil War she was superintendent of women war nurses.

10. Kittrie, *The Right to Be Different,* p. 65.

11. S. Brakel and R. Rock, *The Mentally Disabled and the Law* (Chicago: University of Chicago Press, 1971), p. 343.

12. National Institute of Mental Health, *Directory of Institutions for the Mentally Disordered Offenders* (Washington, D.C.: U.S. Government Printing Office, 1972).

13. *Baron Raffaele Garofalo* (1852-1934) was born to an Italian noble family of Spanish origin. Being of this elite class, he was educated in law and became a "Magistrate" (which in Italy is a separate profession). His brillance passed him quickly through the various grades. He was, at one time or another: President of the Civil Tribunal of Pisa, Substitute Procurator-General at the Court of Cassation in Rome, "Sezione" (President of Division) of the Court of Appeal in Naples, and Procurator-General at the Court of Appeal in Venice. He was also a Senator of the Kingdom of Italy, Professor of Criminal Law at the University of Naples, and a member of the Royal Academy of Naples. Of the "Holy Three of Criminology," he is the one who ranks nearest to the legalistic style as it focuses on the *criminal*. He, along with the other two (Lombroso and Ferri), make up the three protagonists of the "Italian Positive School."

14. Raffaele Garofalo, *Criminology* (Boston: Little, Brown and Company, 1914), p. 126.

15. *Cesare Lombroso* (1835-1909) was the originator of the "born criminal" theory which assumed the criminal to be an atavistic throwback whose criminal tendencies could be detected by physical measurements. Lombroso was a member of the postive school of Italian criminology. His book *L'Uomo Delinquente* is a classic in the field of criminal behavior. Although his atavism theory was never proved, it sparked the scientific approach to crime and its causation.

16. Cesare Lombroso, *Crime: Its Causes and Remedies* (Boston: Little, Brown and Company, 1911).

17. Lombroso, *Crime,* p. 423.

18. Dr. Harvey Cleckley is one of the foremost experts on the psychopath. His book *The Mask of Sanity* is a classic in the field. He is also well known for the book *Three Faces of Eve,* which he co-authored and which became an Academy Award winning movie.

19. H. Cleckley, *The Mask of Sanity* (St. Louis, Mo.: Mosby, 1970), pp. 355-356.

20. Kittrie, *The Right to Be Different.*

21. S. Brakel and R. Rock, *The Mentally Disabled and the Law* (Chicago: University of Chicago Press, 1971), p. 343.

22. "Alabama Sexual Psychopath Act Declared Unconstitutional." *American Psychiatric Association Newsletter* (April 18, 1973).

23. *Tippett* v. *State of Maryland* 436 F. 2d 1153 (1971). The Court of Appeals held that the Maryland Defective Delinquent Act was consititutional—it did not offend due process and provided adequate procedural safeguards to protect constitutional rights of persons committed to institutions for defective delinquents.

24. Sydney Maughs, "A Concept of Psychopathy and Psychopathic Personality: Its Evolution and Historical Development," *Journal of Criminal Psychopathology* 2 (April 1941): 465-499.

25. Allen, *Sociological and Biological Correlates . . . ,* p. 1.

26. Lewis Carroll, *Alice's Adventures in Wonderland and Through the Looking Glass and What Alice Found There* (London: Oxford University Press, 1971).

27. B. Rubin, "Prediction of Dangerousness in Mentally Ill Criminals," *Archives of General Psychiatry* 27 (September 1972): 397-407.

28. F. Hacker and M. Frym, "The Sexual Psychopath Act in Practice: A Critical Discussion," *California Law Review* 43 (1955): 766.

29. Kozol et al., "The Diagnosis and Treatment of Dangerousness," *Crime and Delinquency* (October 1972): 371-392.

30. Erving Goffman, *Asylums* (New York: Anchor Books, Doubleday and Company, 1961).

31. B. Toomey, H. Allen, and C. Simonsen, "The Right to Treatment: Professional Liabilities in the Criminal Justice and Mental Health Systems," *The Prison Journal* 54 (1974): 43-56.

32. For a more detailed examination of the problems psychopaths pose, as well as a statement of the current level of the art of treating these offenders, see Allen et al., "Social and Bio-Medical Correlates of Sociopathy," *Criminologica* 5 (August 1967): 68-75. See also Allen et al., "Sociopathy: An Experiment in Internal Environmental Control," *American Behavioral Scientist* 20 (Novermber/December 1976): 215-226.

33. Wilpers, "Animal, Vegetable or Human Being?" p. 34.

RECOMMENDED READING LIST

American Correctional Association. *Manual of Correctional Standards*. 3d ed. Washington, D.C.: ACA, 1966.

American Friends Service Committee. *Struggle for Justice*. New York: Hill & Wang, 1971.

American Psychiatric Association. *Standards for Psychiatric Facilities Serving Children and Adolescents*. Washington, D.C.: APA, 1971.

Boches, Ralph E., and Goldfarb, Joel. *California Juvenile Court Practice*. Berkeley, Calif.: The University of California Press, 1968.

Cavenaugh, W.E. *Juvenile Courts, the Child and the Law*. Bungay, England, 1967.

Comment. "Competency to Stand Trial: A Call for Reform." *Journal of Criminal Law, Criminology, and Police Science* 59 (1968): 569.

Comment. "Constitutional Limitations on the Conditions of Pretrial Detention." *Yale Law Journal* 79 (1970): 941.

Eldefonso, Edward. *Law Enforcement and the Youthful Offender: Juvenile Procedures*. New York: John Wiley & Sons, 1967.

Empey, LaMar T. *Alternatives to Incarceration*. Washington, D.C.: U.S. Government Printing Office, 1966.

Engelbert, Steven L. "Pretrial Criminal Commitment to Mental Institutions: The Procedure in Massachusetts and Suggested Reforms." *Catholic University Law Review* 17 (1967): 163.

Fox, Sanford J. *The Law of Juvenile Courts in a Nutshell*. St. Paul, Minn.: West, 1971.

Giallombardo, Rose. *Soceity of Women: A Study of a Women's Prison*. New York: John Wiley & Sons, 1966.

Kaufman, Harold. "Evaluating Competency: Are Constitutional Deprivations Necessary?" *American Criminal Law Review* 10 (1972): 465.

Kenney, John P., and Pursuit, Dan G. *Police Work with Juveniles and the Administration of Juvenile Justice*. Springfield, Ill.: Charles C. Thomas, 1954.

Moyer, Frederic D., et al. *Guidelines for the Planning and Design of Regional and Community Correctional Centers for Adults*. Urbana, Ill.: University of Illinois, 1971.

Mumford, Gilbert H.F. *A Guide to Juvenile Court Law*. London: Jordan, 1968.

National Council on Crime and Delinquency. *Model Rules for Juvenile Courts*. New York: NCCD, 1969.

National Council on Crime and Delinquency. *Standards and Guides for the Detention of Children and Youth*. New York: NCCD, 1961.

National Sheriffs' Association. *Manual on Jail Administration*. Washington, D.C.: NSA, 1970.

Pollack, Otto. *The Criminality of Women*. Cranbury, N.J.: A.S. Barnes, 1950.

Simon, Rita J. *The Contemporary Woman and Crime*. Washington, D.C.: U.S. Government Printing Office, 1976.

Simonsen, Clifford E., and Gordon, Marshall S. *Juvenile Justice in America*. Encino, Ca.: Glencoe Publishing Co., 1978.

U.S. Bureau of Prisons. *Female Offenders in the Federal Prison System*. Washington, D.C.: U.S. Bureau of Prisons, 1977.

U.S. Bureau of Prisons. *Handbook of Correctional Psychiatry*. Vols. I and II. Washington, D.C.: U.S. Bureau of Prisons, 1968.

PART VI

Correctional Administration

21 Organizational Structures

Too often we are fighting the wrong war, on the wrong
front, at the wrong time; so that our capacity to fight
where we might be protective of the community and
useful to the convicted offender is attenuated.

NORVAL MORRIS

Fragmentation of Corrections

The preceding chapters have examined the various components of the
correctional system and their development, and the clients they serve. It
should now be apparent that the segment of the criminal justice system we
call *corrections* is actually a poorly connected network of many other
subsystems, most of them directed to a specific kind of clientele. Probation
and parole are often not in tune with institutional programs; juvenile courts,
adult institutions, and community programs often vie with each other for
resources and personnel. Women's institutions and special-category offender
programs are pushed into the background, while operation of the larger
correctional units gets top priority. These various programs all compete for
the same limited dollars in state and local correctional budgets, often
resulting in an attempt by administrators to distribute shortages equitably,
rather than making a coordinated and effective use of whatever funds are
available. The fragmentation of the criminal justice system as a whole is one
of the major problems in developing effective rehabilitative programs;
disorganization at the correctional level only aggravates an already critical
situation.

The correctional subsystem is divided basically into seven major administrative areas: (1) jails and detention facilities, (2) probation, (3) adult
institutions, (4) community corrections, (5) juvenile corrections, (6) special
category institutions, and (7) parole. (The military offender belongs in a
separate and distinct category with an organizational structure of its own, not
generally integrated into state and local correctional programs.) This chapter
examines these separate and semi-autonomous organizational subcategories
and their characteristics.

There are over 5,000 correctional facilities of various types in the United States and almost 2,500 probation and parole agencies. It is estimated that only some 16 percent of the adult and juvenile correctional facilities are operated at the state level. The remaining 84 percent, consisting mostly of jails and detention facilities, are operated by the counties and cities of the nation. The major organizational issues are addressed in a 1971 report by the Advisory Commission on Intergovernmental Relations:

> All but four states have highly fragmented correctional systems, vesting various correctional responsibilities in either independent boards or noncorrectional agencies. In forty-one states, an assortment of health, welfare, and youth agencies exercise certain correctional responsibilities, though their primary function is not corrections.
>
> In over forty states, neither state nor local governments have full-scale responsibility for comprehensive correctional services. Some corrections services, particularly parole and adult and juvenile institutions, are administered by state agencies, while others, such as probation, local institutions and jails, and juvenile detention, are county or city responsibilities.
>
> More than half of the states provide no standard-setting or inspection services to local jails and local adult correctional institutions.[1]

The details of these organizational problems, with regard to each of the basic areas in the correctional subsystem, are discussed below.

Jails and Detention Facilities

The local jail or detention facility is essentially used for the holding of accused persons prior to trial and sentencing. Most jurisdictions also use such facilities to hold a mixture of other categories as well, including those awaiting transfer to a prison, those on appeal, those serving short misdemeanor sentences, some who are serving longer sentences, mentally ill persons, juveniles, federal and military offenders awaiting transfer, etc. The jails have remained, in large part, under local control. They are used for a variety of short-term detention purposes, becoming a convenient warehouse for the storage of assorted suspects, offenders, and social outcasts. Two of the major problems with the administration of these facilities are the demand that they accept and handle almost any kind of problem offender presented to them, and the expectation that they *can* deal with such cases. When such offenders are thrust upon officials who often lack facilities and personnel to cope with them, there is little hope for organizational development beyond whatever stop-gap operations can be devised to maintain minimal functions.

County jails are generally operated by a sheriff, an elected official who is usually more concerned with law enforcement than with rehabilitation. Often the actual operation of the jail is delegated to some less-than-qualified deputy who acts merely as a "turnkey," a person charged with little more than seeing that prisoners are fed and do not escape. Most deputies try to avoid the turnkey assignment. It is easy to see that this kind of organizational arrangement results in little more rehabilitation than that which was available at the time of John Howard. In a few jails, the relatively small number of prisoners encourages the use of part-time jailers or turnkeys; it is not unheard-of for the sheriff's wife to fulfill this role.

The organizational structure of the jails and detention facilities across America is as varied as might be imagined. Some common characteristics do exist, however. Since most are operated by a law enforcement officer, either a county sheriff or a municipal police chief, the major emphasis is generally on security rather than rehabilitation. These law enforcement officers impose their own background and personal orientation on the care and treatment of prisoners; more often than not their approach is at odds with advanced corrections philosophy and movements today. The jail and detention facility units constitute by far the most neglected area of the criminal justice system. The National Advisory Commission has addressed the problem of fragmented, localized jail services, and the need to merge them into a state-controlled system:

> All local detention and correctional functions, both pre- and postconviction, should be incorporated within the appropriate state system by 1982.
>
> 1. Community-based resources should be developed initially through subsidy contract programs, subject to state standards, which reimburse the local unit of government for accepting state commitments.
>
> 2. Coordinated planning for community-based correctional services should be implemented immediately on a state and regional basis. This planning should take place under jurisdiction of the state correctional system.
>
> 3. Special training and other programs operated by the state should be available immediately to offenders in the community by utilizing mobile service delivery or specialized regional centers.
>
> 4. Program personnel should be recruited from the immediate community or service area to the maximum extent possible. Employees' ties with the

> local community and identification with the offender
> population should be considered essential to
> community involvement in the correctional program.
> At the same time, professional services should not
> be sacrificed, and state training programs should be
> provided to upgrade employee skills.[2]

Such a plan, as one might expect, will meet considerable resistance at the local level, but the transitions could be encouraged by increased state funding, periodic state inspection, and state-established operational standards to be phased in over a period of time. Personnel training, facility improvement, and program development should be taken over by the states as soon as possible. Only when the detention stage—the stage at which most offenders enter the corrections process—begins to stress *service* over *custody* can the process as a whole work effectively. Improvement in jails and other detention institutions (the largest segment of the process in terms of volume of prisoners and number of facilities) is essential if the goals of the entire criminal justice system are to be realized.[3]

Organization of Probation

Which government agency should be responsible for the probation system— the correctional authority in the executive branch or the courts in the judicial branch—has been the focus of recent controversy. This argument is further aggravated by proponents of a statewide system, who wish to avoid the problems of local control and local politics. At present, most states include probation with the correctional components in the executive branch, while others have optional or mixed arrangements. Ohio's probation system illustrates how complicated the issue can become:

> Variations in the way probation has been organized and placed within
> the government framework have created differences between states as
> well as within states. Ohio provides an example of the complicated
> arrangements that have developed. There, juvenile probation is a local
> function in the judicial branch, but the state aid program is in the
> executive branch. Adult probation can be either a state or local
> function. A state agency in the executive branch can provide probation
> service to local courts, or they may establish their own. Where local
> probation exists, the control may be shared by both branches in an
> arrangement under which the county commissioners and judges of the
> court of common pleas must concur on appointments.[4]

The fragmentation of such an important alternative to incarceration seriously handicaps efforts to develop a consistent correctional pattern within and between states.

The probation and parole systems, similar in function and goals, have been combined in many jurisdictions, usually at the state and federal level. Those who argue for the maintenance of separate probation services at the local level and under the judicial branch are frequently opposed to a similar arrangement for the parole system. There are valid arguments for both sides of this issue of statewide versus local control of probation, but most of the large urban states have opted for local control, usually at the county level. Several advantages are seen in this approach: probation is more closely tied to the community, there is less bureaucratic red tape in processing, and there is better support from local citizens.

If one examines some of the largest local probation agencies, however, it is difficult to see how a coordinated statewide program could be any *less* responsive. In the final analysis, it may well be the individual jurisdiction that must weigh the advantages and disadvantages and decide which way to organize for effective probation services. No matter which type of organization is finally employed, the state must become more involved in the planning, funding, and maintaining of standards for probation services to see that they are uniform and effective across both large and small jurisdictions.

Adult Institutions

It is difficult to describe a "typical" organizational structure for correctional institutions. There are so many different kinds of adult institutions that one can only analyze the major functions most of them are supposed to fulfill. Two of these functions—*custody* and *treatment*—are so complicated that they are covered by separate chapters in this part of the text; we will touch on them only briefly in this discussion of adult institutions. *Adult institutions* include state and federal prisons for both men and women. There are enough similarities among these facilities to consider them as a group in discussing organizational components. Exceptions are special rules or laws that apply only at a particular level of government or to a particular sex; these are discussed later.

Figure VI–1 displays an organizational chart for a "typical" adult correctional institution. At the top of the prison staff is the sperintendent; the title of *warden* is less common today, because that title has negative associations for many people. As the staff member whose job most often involves contact with the *outside* world, the superintendent is responsible for the effective operation of the institution and the quality of the personnel who run it. Thus, the superintendent is considered the "outside" administrator for the correctional institution. The "inside" administrator is one of the superintendent's deputies, usually the deputy in charge of custody rather than treatment. The original purpose of prisons and, therefore, of the prison staff was to keep prisoners confined. The concepts of rehabilitation and correction are relatively new, and the idea of a professional treatment staff is even newer. Modern prisons are the scene of a continuing power struggle between treatment and custody staffs regarding whose function is more important and who deserves the greater share of power and resources inside the walls. The remaining functions, listed in Figure VI–1, are more straightforward; there is no argument as to the necessity and importance of the basic services involved, so personnel have less of a stake in any internal power struggle. As Figure VI–1 suggests, the organization of the correctional institution is primarily designed to ensure a calm and secure operation.

Community Corrections

Corrections has undergone great change in the years since the emphasis shifted from custody to rehabilitation. Public safety demands that the convicted offender emerge from our correctional system a better person, and certainly no *worse*, than when he or she entered it. These high expectations have stimulated the search for more effective ways to handle offenders. One course of the pressure to create what has become known as "community-based corrections" has been the recognition that prisonization can actually *aggravate* an offender's criminality. It is clear that the future of corrections lies in these community-based programs. A major obstacle is the existence of the institutional model, with its physical plants and other programs in operation, while no organized community program has yet gained widespread acceptance. One problem is that, thus far, these programs have generally emerged as demonstration projects or individual experiments, rather than as the product of systematic interaction between police, courts, and conventional correctional services.

Community-based correctional systems vary in scope from state-controlled networks of halfway houses and reintegration centers to volunteer programs operating a single residential unit for as few as six inmates or for a single court. The goals of such programs are seen as humanitarian, restorative, and economic. These goals are discussed in detail in chapter 28, but it is important to understand why they offer greater potential for rehabilitation than past institutional goals. It is not necessary to belabor the humanitarian aspects of community corrections; incarceration, clearly, involves a series of destructive situations. For the offender, the custody model intensifies the likelihood of physical danger, deprivation of human values, and loss of self-esteem. It is a basic humanitarian concept that only offenders who pose a threat to society should be subjected to the trauma of incarceration. This last issue demands, of course, a valid system of diagnosis, classification, and evaluation.

The restorative goal provides the foundation for an effective community-based correctional structure. The nature of that structure will vary, of course, from one community to another. It is the task of local correctional administrators to develop an organization that will provide the necessary

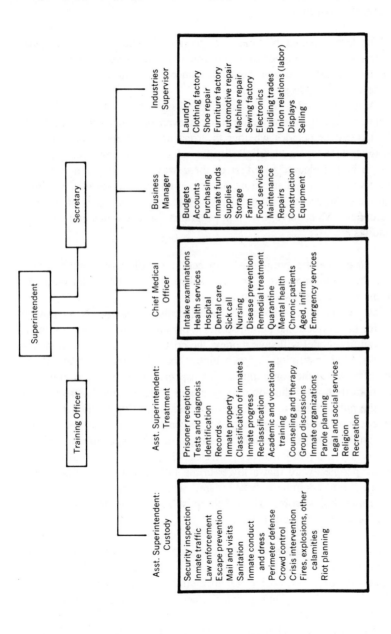

FIGURE VI–1. Organization of Prison Staff and Functions (Clarence Shrag, *Crime and Justice: American Style* (Washington, D.C.: U.S. Government Printing Office, 1971). p. 193.)

services, in coordination with other agencies and programs. The following definition of "community-based corrections" highlights the complexity of the organizational problem:

> [T]he term "community-based corrections" includes all correctional activities that take place in the community. The community base must be an alternative to confinement of an offender at any point in the correctional process.
>
> At the beginning of his experience as a subject of criminal justice decisionmaking, the offender has not even been defined as such. A police officer decides whether to arrest or give him a summons. A magistrate rules on his eligibility for release on his own recognizance or on bail. Released in either of these ways, he may or may not receive correctional attention. Some communities have court employed projects. Some have informal probation for certain types of juvenile offenders. More have diversion programs for alcoholics and narcotics addicts.[5]

It seems clear that the progressive correctional professional must seek to establish these programs as a modern substitute for the custody-oriented institutions of the past two centuries.

The last of the three above-mentioned goals, *economy,* is an obvious concern for the correctional administrator. Any shift from the custody model to a community model will save money; the cost of maintaining an inmate in a state or federal institution is much higher than the cost of programs that keep the offender in the community. This aspect, however, is less important than the contribution of the community model toward *public protection.* At present, the public tends to identify incarceration with protection. In fact, it is believed, most offenders (perhaps 85 percent) of those now incarcerated could probably be released without creating a major danger to the public. It is important for the public to feel protected, but correctional administrators must make people aware that a lower crime rate (and lower welfare costs) may result from community-based care, while imprisonment invariably seems to make things worse. The public must be educated to understand the rationale for community corrections:

> The movement toward community-based corrections is a move away from society's most ancient responses to the transgressor. For thousands of years, society relied mainly on banishment, physical punishment, or the death penalty to accomplish the goals of criminal justice. The world is now too small for any society to eject anyone. Our culture has so changed that we no longer consider imposing capital penalties on the sweeping scale that seemed appropriate to our ancestors.

Out of the realization that the old ways were unacceptable there emerged the prison, a place for artificial banishment or civil death. Nearly two centuries of experience with the penitentiary have brought us to the realization that its benefits are transient at best. At its worst, the prison offers an insidiously false security as those who were banished return to the social scene of their former crimes. The former prisoner seldom comes back the better for the experience of confinement. The effectiveness of the prison as a school for crime is exaggerated, for the criminal can learn the technology of crime far better on the streets. The damage the prison does is more subtle. Attitudes are brutalized, and self-confidence is lost. The prison is a place of coercion where compliance is obtained by force. The typical response to coercion is alienation, which may take the form of active hostility to all social controls or later a passive withdrawal into alcoholism, drug addiction, or dependency.[6]

Juvenile Justice: Courts or Corrections?

The juvenile justice system, like most of the other correctional subsystems, is weakened by fragmentation and lack of agreement on the needs of the juvenile offender, as opposed to the protection requirements of society. The model most used in the past centers on a benevolent judge, acting as a guardian of the youth's rights in the name of the state *(parens patriae)*. The common approach to the juvenile as a *delinquent* rather than a *criminal* has resulted in overly casual juvenile justice procedures. One might expect such informality to benefit the young offender, but a more common result is that his or her rights are ignored and violated instead of protected.

The basic organizational structure of the juvenile court was designed to keep the judge in control at all stages of the procedure, from adjudication to release back to the community. When the concept of corrections and rehabilitation emerged in the adult criminal justice system, the gap between the goals of the two systems narrowed. The provision of due process and many other rights to the adult system highlighted the absence of these basic considerations in most juvenile courts, and this problem was remedied with the U.S. Supreme Court's decision *In re Gault* (see chapter 19). With decreased emphasis on *parens patriae* and the affirmation of due process in the juvenile system, it has become obvious that new organizational structures are necessary.

The President's Commission on Law Enforcement and Administration of Justice proposed a juvenile justice system that includes all the incarceration alternatives and rehabilitation opportunities available to adults. This system (Figure VI–2) is administered by a Youth Services Bureau, which ensures that juvenile offenders have access to these alternatives before the case goes

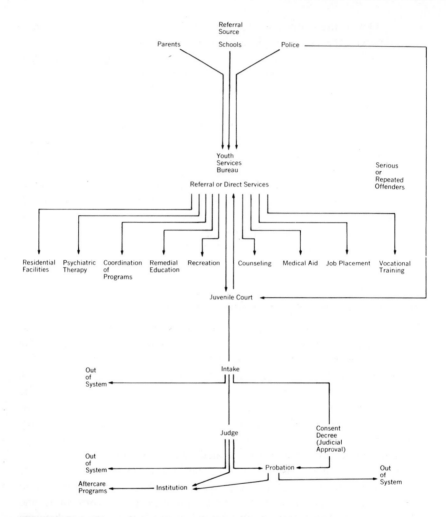

FIGURE VI–2. Proposed Juvenile Justice System (The President's Commission on Law Enforcement and Administration of Justice, *The Challenge of Crime in a Free Society* (Washington, D.C.: U.S. Government Printing Office, 1967). p. 89.)

to court. This correctionally oriented organization tempers the court's authority, furnishing help that applies to the specific needs of youths without necessarily removing them from the community or labeling them as delinquents. The youth services approach is a direction of the future, but the organizational concepts to implement this approach will have to be worked out in each jurisdiction.

Special Category Institutions: In Transition

The special category institutions have traditionally been the domain of mental health administrators. In some states, the administration of these institutions lies in a gray area overlapping corrections and mental health. The issues of right to treatment and indeterminate commitment have created considerable confusion as to appropriate administrative procedures, especially in jurisdictions where inmates in ordinary correctional institutions may be transferred to special category institutions without recourse to due process.

The organizational structure of most special category institutions parallels that of most prisons. Although treatment is usually the stated purpose of these institutions, the main emphasis is on custody and control, often for very long periods of time. Both correctional and mental health authorities want to keep special category offenders out of prison, and their stays in specialized institutions are lengthened accordingly.

The recent emphasis on *forensic* psychiatry (focusing on the specialized legal problems of the mentally disturbed offender) has encouraged the creation of organizational divisions, sometimes under corrections and sometimes under mental health. When these forensic psychiatry divisions are able to provide the same range of services to their special clients that other correctional subsystems offer, and when they are constitutionally required, the threat of continued legal action by these clients to obtain the services will diminish. The community-based correctional system will probably serve as a model for forensic psychiatry programs over the next few decades. A total continuum of services, from outpatient care to maximum security, will be administered by trained professionals who are attuned to the needs of the special category offender. This movement is only just beginning, and it has yet to encounter many of the obstacles that have plagued the development and humanization of all other treatment delivery systems.

Parole: Two Systems in One

Dividing parole into the decision-making and supervision processes helps to demonstrate the major organizational problems involved in this subsystem. The decision-making body, in particular, faces a broad range of problems:

> In addition to issues of equity, parole decisionmakers sometimes respond to actual or anticipated public attitudes. Such concerns for public acceptance of parole generally, and case decisions specifically, govern the kinds of risks that are acceptable and the actions considered feasible by parole decisionmakers. This public reaction issue is particularly acute in cases affecting society's core beliefs. Criteria having little to do with the question of risk may be used by parole

officials in dealing with certain cases, particularly those involving crimes seen as "heinous." The concern is more for meeting general social norms and responding according to public expectations.[7]

As mentioned in chapter 12, the current trend favors a consolidated model. More than 60 percent of state parole boards now integrate their activities with other agencies for offenders through common administrative structures. This positive move helps to relieve the problems of the second area: supervisory services.

In recent years, state correction departments have begun to absorb the supervisory function in adult parole. This trend is described as follows:

> One of the clearest trends in parole organization in the last few years is consolidation of formerly autonomous agencies or functionally related units into expanding departments of corrections. Some of these departments have been made part of still larger units of state government, such as human resources agencies, which embrace a wide range of programs and services. One clear indication of this trend is the number of states that have shifted administrative responsibility for parole officers from independent parole departments to centralized correctional agencies.
>
> Most recently the states of Oregon, New York, and Georgia have made such transfers. A number of smaller states still have parole supervision staffs responsible to an independent parole board. Practically every large state now has adult parole field staff reporting to the same administrative authority as the personnel of the state penal institutions. Today, the majority of parole officers at the state level work for unified departments of correction.[8]

Consolidation of services is a first step toward providing a real spectrum of programs to adult, juvenile, and misdemeanant parolees. These benefits will also accrue to probationers, as they are transferred into state correctional supervised or administered systems.

Organizational Trends

The same theme runs through all the important subsystems of corrections: a movement toward a community-based, service-oriented *system* of programs and policies. The move is also toward consolidated state-level agencies designed to provide a continuum of services in each area. The emphasis at the national level is on funding state correctional programs through a form of revenue sharing and subsidies. This policy has forced the poorer county and municipal political units to reconsider their resistance to consolidation, but there is more resistance in some areas than others. Parole programs are prime examples of how effective statewide consolidated services can be provided without reducing local public protection. The need to extend this consolidation precedent to probation, juvenile, special-category, and community corrections programs represents a great challenge to the correctional administrator. Even the institutional organization will eventually be modified toward a treatment model.

Organizational structures must be responsive to the needs of the offender, who will be treated in great part in the community, but they must also be accountable to the state agency in charge of coordination and funding. There are great advantages to be gained from a broad network of service options which covers the entire spectrum of clients, offering a continuum of services in each of the categories. This ideal concept has met with strong resistance from within and without the corrections subsystem, and reasons for such opposition are discussed in the following chapters.

REVIEW QUESTIONS

I. Find the answers to the following in the text:

1. Describe the seven major administrative areas of corrections.

2. Why is fragmentation of corrections such a problem for the offender?

3. Why is the systems approach the most promising answer to corrections?

4. How would you consolidate correctional services into a single organizational structure?

II. Words to identify:

1. fragmentation

2. inside administrator

3. outside administrator

4. warden

5. superintendent

6. forensic

7. consolidated services

NOTES

1. Advisory Commission on Intergovernmental Relations, *State-Local Relations in the Criminal Justice System* (Washington, D.C.: U.S. Government Printing Office, 1971), p. 15.

2. National Advisory Commission on Criminal Justice Standards and Goals, *Corrections* (Washington, D.C.: U.S. Government Printing Office, 1973), p. 292.

3. "GAO Terms LEAA Jail Projects 'Inadequate,' " *Criminal Justice Newsletter* 7 (May 24, 1976): 5-6.

4. National Advisory Commission, *Corrections,* p. 313.

5. National Advisory Commission, *Corrections,* p. 223.

6. National Advisory Commission, *Corrections,* p. 223.

7. National Advisory Commission, *Corrections,* p. 395.

8. National Advisory Commission, *Corrections,* p. 407.

22 Administrative Problems

> Of all the painful conditions imposed on inmates, none
> is more immediately obvious than the loss of liberty. In
> short, the prisoner's loss of liberty is a double one
> —first, by confinement to the institution and, second, by
> confinement within the institution.
>
> *GRESHAM M. SYKES*

Administrative Problem: Punish, Control, or Treat?

The division of power outlined in the previous chapters suggests some of the reasons why correctional administrators are often confused and hampered in their efforts to correct inmates. While the public is willing to espouse reformatory goals for corrections, it is not willing to provide the support and funding that would make such reform a legislative priority. This inconsistency places dedicated correctional administrators in an awkward position: they can implement only the most meager of programs, and even then they must maintain an overall emphasis on control and punishment. Regardless of the approach taken to this problem, some aspect of operations will suffer. If required to increase the number of security guards, the administrator must obtain the necessary funds by decreasing support to some treatment program. If the administrator tries to amplify the treatment programs, this must be done at the expense of the custody staff.

As if these problems were not enough, a new element has been added in recent years: unionization of the correctional officers in many jurisdictions. Administrators must deal with unions if their institutions are to function effectively, and collective action by the officers has further swung the institutional balance of power in the direction of custody (as opposed to treatment). Preventing a return to outmoded procedures in the face of union strength will be a major task for correctional administrators in the next decade.

Unionization: The Correctional Officers

Unionization, found in almost every sector of business and industry, has spread to the ranks of state and federal employees in recent decades. Most recently, the union movement has extended to the "sworn" officers charged with police, fire, and correctional protection of the public. Police officers and fire fighters have established collective bargaining agencies in most major urban departments, with improved working conditions and wages as a result. Prohibited in many states by law from going on strike to back up their demands, law enforcement and fire protection officers developed the strategy of massive outbreaks of "blue flu" in order to emphasize their plight.[1] In the correctional field, the union movement has taken root more slowly.

As agents of public protection became more successful in their demands, their fellow officers in the correctional institutions took notice. The great move in the late sixties toward more professionalism, reduction of prisoner populations, community corrections, and other programs pointed up some of the needs of the long-neglected correctional officer. Initial efforts to organize met with disapproval from administrators, often because of limited budgets and already-overtaxed security forces in the crowded prisons. Most administrators wanted the few available funds to be used for new personnel, not pay raises for officers they already had. In some cases the correctional officers did go on strike, and their duties were assumed by the administrative and office personnel.[2]

Because correctional institutions tend to be widely scattered, growth of the union movement has been slow and fragmented. In addition, as suggested above, the goals of these collective bargaining agencies sometimes do not correspond to the rehabilitation goals of the administration. Organization and collective action have brought many benefits to correctional officers so far, but they will get little sympathy from the administrators and the public until they show concern for the overall mission of the institution as well as their personal needs.

Inmate Organization: The Social System

Prisons are *total institutions*[3] in which the resident's every activity, moment, movement, and option are carefully regulated by the correctional officer staff. Inmates are given little individual responsibility and autonomy, important characteristics of everyday life in a modern achievement-oriented society. This tight regime compounds their personal inadequacies rather than correcting them. Cut off from ordinary social intercourse, from their families and friends, and isolated in bastion-like prisons, inmates are quickly taught how to exist in this environment by the other residents. The process of learning how to exist in prisons—of learning appropriate attitudes and behaviors, and the norms of prison life—is called "prisonization." This process leads to the adoption of the folkways, mores, customs, and general culture of the prison.[4] Evidently prisonization occurs spontaneously even in newly opened institutions; it is handed down from prisoner to prisoner, remaining a strong force which is transmitted between prisons, working against the rehabilitation goals of even the most enlightened administrator. It impedes rather than facilitates treatment efforts, preventing inmates from acquiring the skills, talents, attitudes, and behavior necessary for successful adjustment in free society. Indeed, the opposite tends to occur; inmates are *infantalized*[5] rather than matured.

This situation has led the President's Commission on Law Enforcement and Administration of Justice to note that "the conditions in which [inmates] live are the poorest possible preparation for their reentry into society, and often merely reinforce in them a pattern of manipulation and destructiveness."[6]

As part of the process of prisonization, inmates learn codes and roles, and they are subjected to a reward and punishment system which encourages them to act appropriately. Prison codes emphasize a number of specific behaviors: loyalty to other inmates ("never rat on a con," "don't be too nosy or talk too much," "never report a grievance against another inmate to the guards"); maintenance of calm ("keep cool," "don't start feuds"); avoidance of trickery or fraud ("always share with your cell-mates," "sell hoarded goods at the going rate"); manliness ("don't complain"); quick-wittedness in prison dealings ("don't be a sucker," "guards are screws, never to be trusted or confided in").

Inmates who conform to these expectations become "real men" who can be trusted and are looked up to by other inmates. They share in the privileges available in prisons, and they can count on support if another inmate attacks them physically. Those who violate the normative structure become outcasts and are referred to by various pejorative terms:

Rats or squealers	Inmates who have betrayed other inmates to the guards.
Gorillas	Inmates who use force or the threat of force to get more than a fair share of the rewards in prison.
Merchants	Inmates who sell goods that others feel should be given or shared.
Wolves	Inmates who assume the homosexual role of the aggressive male; sometimes implies use of force of threats.
Punks	Inmates forced into passive roles in homosexual acts through fear of consequences if they do not comply.
Fags	Inmates who accept the passive homosexual role through choice and for personal reasons.
Toughs	Aggressive fighters who are frequently and easily aroused to violence, fighting both weak and strong inmates.

It should be stressed again that the importance of prisonization lies in its negative impact on attempts to provide rehabilitative programs that encourage inmates to engage in legitimate, noncriminal activities.

Unionization: The Inmates

The prisoner union movement began at California's Folsom Prison in 1970, when the climate was ripe for what then seemed to be revolutionary demands by Folsom inmates. They had just suffered several internal disturbances and been through a nineteen-day strike. The strike had focused on prisoner demands for elimination of indeterminate sentence, and was punctuated by the fatal shooting of three black inmates at Soledad Prison. The "Soledad Brothers" became a rallying point for prisoners who sought to form a union. The three main goals of the California union are:

- The abolishment of the indeterminate sentence system and all its ramifications.

- The establishment of workers' rights for the prisoner, including the right to collectively organize and bargain.

- The restoration of civil and human rights for the prisoners.[7]

The movement spread rapidly, and locals have been established in almost all the California state prisons today. The basic structure of the California model keeps the control function on the outside, in the hands of ex-offenders in the community. These ex-offenders are also active in helping prisoners in other states to set up union operations. New York has a union, established at Greenhaven Prison, which is affiliated with the Distributive Workers of America. Other unions have been established in Massachusetts, North Carolina, Kansas, Georgia, Minnesota, and Washington. The New England Prison Coalition covers Maine, Vermont, Rhode Island, Massachusetts, and New Hampshire.[8]

Internationally, prisoner unions have been most effective in the Scandinavian countries. Criminologist C. Ronald Huff addresses this aspect of prison unionization:

Internationally, the strongest inmate unions are probably to be found in the Scandinavian countries, along with some of the more progressive penal practices. In Sweden, for example, representatives of all five thousand Swedish prisoners negotiated in 1971 with the National Correctional Administration after a hunger strike. Despite the comparatively advanced conditions under which most Swedish prisoners live, they still believe that collective action is necessary to obtain those things which they do not have.[9]

Most correctional administrators in this country strongly oppose inmate unionization, as this comment by a State Director of Corrections suggests: "These men are convicted felons—convicted of breaking the laws of society. Under no circumstances will I recognize their so-called union."[10] Inmate union organizers are often dispersed to other institutions around the state when they begin to become a nuisance. These are only stop-gap resistance measures, however; it appears that the prisoner union is here to stay, and some procedure for collective bargaining seems to be established. Correctional administrators, however, will not cooperate unless inmates can convince them that unions will not threaten security and control within the institution. The concerned administrator's main fear is that the union power will soon gravitate to a few particularly magnetic or authoritative inmates, who will use that power to advance only their own philosophies and interests. Based on the development of such subculture powers in the past, this concern appears to be a valid one.

The right to form a prisoner union is one of the gray areas of correctional law. The general expansion of prisoner rights, which can be interpreted as including the right to form a union, derives from the 1944 decision in *Coffin* vs. *Reichard*.[11] This landmark case held that "a prisoner retains all the rights of an ordinary citizen, except those expressly, or by necessary implication, taken from him by law." The issue was approached more directly in the 1972 decision on *Goodwin* v. *Oswald,* however:

> There is nothing in federal or state constitutional or statutory law of which I am aware that forbids prison inmates from seeking to form, or correctional officials from electing to deal with, an organization or agency or representative group of inmates concerned with prison conditions and inmates' grievances. Indeed, the tragic experience at Attica . . . would make correctional officials, an observer might think, seek more peaceful ways of resolving prison problems than the old, ironclad, solitary-confinement, mail-censoring, dehumanizing methods that have worked so poorly in the past. Promoting or at least permitting the formation of a representative agency might well be, in the light of past experience, the wisest course for correctional officials to follow.[12]

The above may constitute judicial approval of inmate unions, but it offers no solution to the administrative problem of juggling security against inmate rights. Prisoners have always found some way to bargain with their keepers. A formal procedure to accomplish this purpose could have beneficial as well as negative effects in terms of institutional order.

Unionization, for the staff or the inmates, creates many dilemmas for the correctional administrator. How these problems are resolved in the next

decade may either encourage or negate the development of a flexible
corrections approach aimed at rehabilitation and reintegration of offenders.
For example, the need for flexibility would not coincide with the rigid
requirements that tend to develop out of labor union negotiations. It will be
important to meet these challenges so that solutions both flexible and fair to
all sides can be achieved.

The Citizens' Task Force: Help or Hindrance?

Correctional administrators are both hampered and helped in their complex
tasks by well-meaning citizen groups. Some of these groups are organized
into fairly formal organizations and provided with government funding and
broad investigational powers; others are more informal advisory panels.
Whether task forces serve or obstruct the administrator depends on their
composition and purpose. Ohio's example is worthy of examination.

In the early 1970s, Ohio's correctional institutions experienced four major
riots in a relatively brief period of time, and the maximum security Ohio
Penitentiary was plagued by a strike of correctional officers. These events
focused public attention on some of the problems of the Ohio correctional
system, and also on the American approach to corrections in general. In
response to this surge of concern, Ohio Governor John J. Gilligan appointed
a Citizens' Task Force on Corrections in February of 1971 to serve as an
external reform group. The Task Force *Interim Report* appeared in June
1971, and its *Final Report* was completed by December.

Members of the Task Force included a wide range of Ohio public
employees with backgrounds in the criminal justice system, and interested
members of the general public. More specifically, attorneys, state senators,
state representatives, professors of criminal justice, sociologists, judges,
members of labor organizations, institution superintendents, public safety
directors, sheriffs, novelists, clergy, public administrators, correctional officers, a representative from the Governor's office, and a top-management
officer in a medium-sized electronics firm were among the participants. [No
ex-offenders served on the Task Force, although several were employed on
the support staff.]

During the Task Force evaluation and investigation of the state correctional systems, it became apparent that its members could be categorized
according to various types: "Professional," "Facilitator," "Vested Interest," "Bleeding Heart," "Tunnel Vision," "Self-Aggrandizer," and
"Publicity Seeker." In large part, it could be argued the Task Force mission
was accomplished because the professional staff was able to work around the
problems created by these types:

> The "Professional" type was composed primarily of those persons
> capable of understanding corrections as a process, of seeing the
> legitimacy of alternative lines or actions, and of presenting alternatives

to particular problematic situations. These were the workhorses among the Task Force members; each Sub-Committee was chaired by a professional type, whose role was frequently performed at the expense of other duties. Chairmen were in positions of daily contact with some component of the criminal justice system.

The "Facilitator" was also characterized as an in-house politician, lending manipulative skills to potentially politically explosive situations in committee settings and in other closed sessions for testifying and data-gathering from complainants. Frequently anticipating situations, the facilitators would contact appropriate and influential Task Force members to develop possible solutions, and effect compromise when anticipated difficulties arose.

The "Vested Interest" type was concentrated predominately among those persons occupying and playing roles within the correctional system, to whom change would represent threats to their positions, and who would prefer to maintain the status quo. Any shift in power or accommodations to change—unless it represented an increase in their own position or money—was perceived as undesirable, to be at least covertly resisted. Although co-optation did occur, most of these actors began to increase absences from committee work, to decry the presumably deleterious effects of proposed moderate changes, and to resist changes overtly in their official roles in the system, including attempting to scuttle inmate councils and to inform the mass media of both strongly felt and believed reasons why suggested changes would not work and should not be implemented. . . .

The "Bleeding Heart" group was a vocal but not numerically large group occupying positions external to the correctional system. Decrying the dehumanizing effects of the correctional system (especially on naive, prosocial offenders), this type frequently would relate events from personal experiences, to the extent that "story-tellers" could be a synonym. This type would effect change to "save the offender from the system," perceiving the felon as categorically deserving of its efforts. Although cognitively admitting that some offenders could never be released, they paradoxically acted as if they should. If this group had been numerically larger, it is conceivable that the recommendations would have been less acceptable to the general public and to the Executive Branch, resulting in significantly less change. Their most frequently voiced strategem was to suggest changes to make the system more humanitarian and humanistic.

The "Tunnel Vision" type, a less frequent member of this group, characteristically can focus on only one element of the correctional system: either a warden, an institution, or a practice, such as brutality. This type tends to be Quixotic, true-believers, nonemphatic and stereotypic. Due to their visibility and verbosity, they are often able to increase anxiety among correctional administrators and to effect change in the area of their particular but narrow focus.

"Self-Aggrandizers" are characterized as thrusting themselves, rather than the group or mission, into the forefront, by seeking personal gain at the expense of others and of the Task Force, and by both nonattendance at working sessions and unfailing attendance at sessions open to the mass media. There they make publicity-oriented speeches, frequently at sharp variance with formal Task Force positions. This type is the non-reader of material (especially *Interim* and *Final Reports),* and is characterized as the self-styled expert whose frequently uninformed pronouncements can significantly neutralize hard-won gains in judicial, executive, legislative and administrative practices and deliberations. This is the one type for which membership in the Task Force is not a prerequisite; in election years, politicians who have never taken a public stand on any law enforcement issue can be expected to arrive at public sessions.

The "Publicity Seeker" is similar to the "Self-Aggrandizer," but at variance on three dimensions: attendance at all sessions, voluntary and unimpressive contributions (such as position papers, literature reviews, and annual reports), and willingness to perform tasks of any nature. This type frequently drives great distances at early hours, volunteers through telegrams, and can be expected to update vitae as soon as appointed to membership.[13]

A full-time professional staff attached to a citizens' task force on correctional reform (as in the Ohio example) is an expensive adjunct. But if task force members reflect a wide mix of types, if the membership has limited expertise and/or experience in criminal justice, if the system under evaluation is large or complex, and if participation on the force is a part-time affair for the majority of members, professional assistance becomes a necessity.

The more obvious functions of the professional staff include locating experts to offer new ideas and balanced views; maximizing flow of information from one subcommittee to another; responding to inmate communications and maintaining a realistic level of inmate expectations; drawing samples of correctional officers and inmates for interviews; preparing copy of the subcommittee reports; writing position papers; and (to all intents and purposes) writing a final report both for certain subcommittees and for the task force as a whole.

Nine caveats should be considered in developing a task force for correctional reform:

1. Despite the quality, qualifications, and number of persons on the task force, people holding statuses and playing roles within the correction system

("insiders") will perceive of the task force members as outsiders with, therefore, categorically unworkable ideas.

2. People from outside the correctional system will believe insiders will resist *any* change, a condition contrary to fact.

3. The transmission of a report is assumed to be an important change element, but in reality it is used only as a tool by appointing agencies. A small core of informed professionals having access to the executive office *can* make a real contribution to correctional reform.

4. In the appointment of a citizens' task force, it is frequently assumed that all major groups should be represented. This is not necessarily a good idea, and the democratic process may profit more, in the long run, from membership restricted to "professional" types rather than "citizens."

5. It is assumed that much money is necessary to effect adequate correctional reform. However, the most effective reforms are easily made, such as, by executive fiat, abolition of mail censorship and establishment of a grievance ombudsman. These have very little to do with money.

6. There is little political gain to be made by reforming the correctional system, unlike the law enforcement field. The more humanizing the reform, the more costly it is likely to be to the appointing agency or governor.

7. In the final analysis, folk knowledge and belief may still outweigh all rationality; punitiveness, revenge and punishment must constantly be fought in the public sector if corrections will be reformed.

8. Most task force members start with the assumption, which is never formally questioned, that corrections should and can "correct." Thus, there is a "hidden agenda" within almost all members, and the task force process will be an unfolding of this hidden agenda.

9. Each state should not have to establish a task force. Task force reports from a few states (Ohio, Wisconsin, and one or two others) will outline the basic problems and solutions which should apply to most states.[14]

If these caveats are considered and acted on, the task force model can be an effective tool to achieve ongoing correctional reform, until each state has developed a system that meets the dual requirements of social justice and citizen protection.

Managing the "Residual Core"

The nature of inmate populations in major correctional institutions is undergoing great change. As increasing proportions of tractable prisoners are handled through supervisory alternatives to incarceration, the administrator is left with a residue of the most difficult ("hard-core") offenders. The influx of political militants in recent years has added another dimension to this already severe problem. Many of these hard-core prisoners appear to be mentally unstable; as much as 50 percent of the future population of correctional institutions may be classified as psychopathic. The condition is difficult to diagnose, and there seems to be no really effective treatment once it has been diagnosed, though current research has produced some startling discoveries (see chapter 20). Because of the general confusion about this category, the laws are not clear-cut either:

> Most jurisdictions have enacted special legislation designed to deal with the definition and management of the individual who not only manifests the characteristics of this deviant syndrome, but who is also a criminal offender. Like the criminal insanity statutes, this legislation marks the interfaces of the mental health and criminal justice systems.
>
> Not surprisingly, the lack of conceptual certainty among social and behavioral scientists (as reflected in continuing debates over the appropriate label for this deviant syndrome) has been carried over into the legal realm. Thus, statutes are variously called "psychopath laws," "sexual psychopath laws," or laws related to "defective delinquents," "habitual offenders," or "sexually dangerous persons." The first law, known as the "Briggs Act," was passed in Massachusetts in 1911 and was intended to deal with a distinct class of habitual offenders who were called "defective delinquents." Most of the statutes were created, however, in the late 1930s and the 1940s, including the first explicit "sexual psychopath" law (the Goodrich Act) passed by Michigan in 1937.[15]

The split between the correctional and mental health systems with regard to the nature and treatment of psychopaths represents a major problem for administrators in both areas. As more and more people belonging to these marginal categories gravitate to the prisons and hospitals of America, and as overcrowding continues to accelerate, management problems will become more difficult.

Disenchantment with Prisons

The public, correctional officials, and prisoners are becoming tired of a system that has so obviously failed to "rehabilitate" offenders.[16] The huge prisons with their equally huge budgets consume up to seventy cents out of every dollar spent for corrections. Though correctional institutions house less than 25 percent of convicted offenders, they employ more than 75 percent of the people working in corrections. Widespread disenchantment with major expenditures of available resources and personnel on an unsuccessful program means that the new correctional administrator must push for change.

The old bureaucracies, however, are firmly entrenched. Dedicated personnel who have spent many years in correctional institutions are concerned for their jobs and for the safety of themselves and of society. The administrator must shift the emphasis away from the prisons, without creating major upheavals in the process. This delicate and difficult job will undoubtedly tax the ingenuity and resourcefulness of all sectors. It is also important to provide for the relocation and training of all of the individuals displaced by the ultimate shutdown of most of the largest correctional institutions:

Correctional and other agencies . . . should undertake immediate cooperative studies to determine proper redistribution of manpower from institutional to community-based programs. This plan should include the following:

1. Development of a statewide correctional manpower profile including appropriate data on each worker.

2. Proposals for retraining staff relocated by institutional closures.

3. A process of updating information on program effectiveness and needed role changes for correctional staff working in community-based programs.

4. Methods for formal, official corrections to cooperate effectively with informal and private correctional efforts found increasingly in the community. Both should develop collaboratively rather than competitively.[17]

The winds of change are blowing in this direction. In their new roles as "change agents," concerned correctional administrators have begun to develop comprehensive plans for retraining and relocating institutional staff in the community or in small specialized correctional institutions.

The Issue of Treatment: Right or Privilege?

As the correctional administrator has become increasingly dependent upon the treatment staff to provide meaningful activity for inmates, the question of the "right to treatment" has clearly emerged in corrections, as it did earlier in the field of mental health. Attorney Norton Birnbaum was the first to use the term "right to treatment" in an American Bar Association article stressing that society had recognized that criminals had a *moral* right to treatment, but had not established their *legal* right to it.[18] His pioneering article urged the legal profession to move in that direction. The many and diverse treatment programs employed at correctional institutions give rise to two crucial questions. First, does a prisoner have a *right* to treatment or merely just a claim? Second, does the inmate also have the right to *refuse* such treatment?

Philosopher and economist John Stuart Mill has been quoted as saying that a right is a *possession* of the individual, which society must defend against those who would usurp it.[19] In the sense that a right cannot be touched, or seen, or held, it is abstract; but insofar as the state is obliged to respect it, that right becomes a concrete reality.

If criminals and the mentally ill have the right to treatment, do they also have the right to *refuse* such treatment (sometimes called the "right to punishment")? This question arose as the general public learned of behavior modification techniques and their application to offenders. The common belief that these techniques constitute a sophisticated form of brainwashing, encouraged by such fiction as *A Clockwork Orange*[20] and *The Terminal Man*,[21] has hampered the development of specialized correctional programs. The refusal of treatment, from participation in the completion of a high school education to an extensive group therapy program, has served as grounds for institutional disciplinary action in the past. When the definition of *treatment* as opposed to *vocational training* is more clearly established, the right to accept or refuse it will become crucial. Perhaps prisoners should be allowed to decide that they would rather serve their time involved in nothing but confinement and work programs. On the other hand, the social sciences are learning to identify those offenders who might benefit most from behavior modification. Whether these individuals will be required to undergo treatment against their will is one of the most important of the emerging issues in corrections. We will soon have the *capability* to modify the personality of selected types of offenders; whether we have the *right* to do so is another matter.[22] This subject is covered in detail in chapter 24.

Lawsuits or Procedures?

As suggested in chapter 9, American courts are presently flooded with cases from the correctional institutions. What is the effect of this litigation on the administrator? In many correctional institutions the result is administrative paralysis—failure to take almost any kind of disciplinary action for fear of legal reprisals. In other institutions, old disciplinary practices are maintained by administrators who choose to ignore the prisoners' rising awareness of their rights; inevitably, these administrators are deluged with lawsuits. What is the answer to this knotty problem?

Clearly, correctional administrators must recognize the *due process* nature of most of the cases brought to court. They can forestall many such cases simply by developing a clear set of procedures and processes to handle any administrative or disciplinary action against inmates.[23] Due process considerations become relevant *when the action may have a significant effect on the status of the inmate.* With this as a general guide, every possible situation can be covered. One important point is the addition of an "exception" clause in all procedures, so that the unusual case can receive due process consideration as well. If such procedures are established, case dismissals and decisions favoring the administrators will become more common. Correctional administrators cannot afford to be so tied up by fear of court action that they fail to take positive and forceful action when needed. Clear and fair procedures would be an effective shield against the nuisance or arbitrary lawsuit from a disgruntled inmate.

Summary

Correctional administrators face a series of challenging tasks that will not be completed for at least the next decade. Not only has the inmate population for which they must provide custody and treatment changed drastically; it has also been alerted to certain rights and provided with counsel to ensure them. Citizen groups, official and unofficial, have begun to take an interest in corrections. Union activity in the correctional staff and the correctional population has begun to spread. As treatment techniques are developed to correct some categories of offenders, the issue is raised as to the administration's right to use them—and the offender's right to receive them. It sometimes appears that every step forward is counteracted by two steps back.

Despite these problems facing the correctional administrator, hopeful signs of progress can be observed. Public disenchantment with the prison as a solution to the rehabilitation and reintegration of offenders has caused a general movement toward the community-based corrections concept. This in turn has stimulated a general upgrading of corrections personnel, accompanied by a movement toward professionalism and collective action by both custody and treatment staffs. The correctional field is becoming a more attractive career for the new graduate of many criminal justice programs at the community colleges and universities across the country, and the infusion of young professionals will be a significant help to hard-pressed correctional administrators as they face the emerging issues of the next decade.

REVIEW QUESTIONS

I. Find the answers to the following in the text:

1. Name some of the major restrictions on the actions correctional administrators are allowed to take with regard to inmates.

2. What is the attitude of most correctional administrators toward prison unions?

3. Why do prisoners feel they must form unions? Why do correctional officers unionize?

4. Give a reasonable explanation of the difference between a right and a privilege.

II. Words to identify:

1. bleeding heart

2. facilitator

3. self-aggrandizer

4. blue flu

5. correctional professional

6. right to treatment

7. right to punishment

8. exception clause

9. prisonization

10. rats

11. gorillas

12. toughs

13. punks

14. fags

NOTES

1. *Blue flu* refers to the practice by uniformed officers of taking "sick leave" en masse to back up their demands regarding raises, working conditions, and similar items. This method gives them negotiating leverage without forcing them to resort to strikes, illegal for sworn officers.

2. Correctional officers have gone on strike as recently as March 1974 at institutions in the Ohio State system. In these cases, administrative personnel or state police are required to temporarily fill the correctional officers' posts.

3. See D. Shichor and H. Allen, "Correctional Efforts in the Educated Society: The Case of Study Release," *Lambda Alpha Epsilon* 39 (June 1976): 18-24.

4. Donald Clemmer, *The Prison Community* (New York: Rinehart, 1940). See also Anthony Scacco, *Rape in Prison* (Springfield, Ill.: Thomas, 1975).

5. Shichor and Allen, "Correctional Efforts in the Educated Society," p. 21.

6. President's Commission on Law Enforcement and Administration of Justice, *The Challenge of Crime in a Free Society* (Washington, D.C.: U.S. Government Printing Office, 1967), p. 159.

7. John Irwin and Willie Holder, "History of the Prisoners' Union," *The Outlaw: Journal of the Prisoners' Union* 2 (January-February 1973): 1-3.

8. C. Ronald Huff. "Unionization behind Walls," *Criminolgoy* 12 (August 1976).

9. Huff, "Unionization behind Walls," p. 185.

10. Huff, "Unionization behind Walls," p. 186.

11. *Coffin* v. *Reichard,* 143 F. 2nd 443 (1944).

12. *Goodwin* v. *Oswald,* 462 F. 2nd 1237 (1972).

13. Harry E. Allen, "The Task Force Model as a Vehicle for Correctional Change: Liability or Asset?" *Georgia Journal of Corrections* 2 (July 1973): 35-39.

14. Allen, "Task Force Model," pp. 38-39.

15. Clifford E. Simonsen, Harry E. Allen, and Aldo Piperno, "A Social-Legal History of the Sexual Psychopath Law: Beyond Sutherland," *Proceedings of the 18th Southern Conference on Corrections* (Tallahassee: Florida State University, 1973).

16. A raging controversy over prison effectiveness currently is focusing on outcome studies. See Robert Martinson, "What Works?—Questions and Answers About Prison Reform," *Public Interest* (Spring 1974): 22-55; Constance Holden, "Prisons: Faith in 'Rehabilitation' Is Suffering a Collapse," *Science* 188 (May 1975): 815-817. A pro-prison statement can be found in Michael Sherrill, "Is Rehabilitation Dead?," *Corrections Magazine* 1 (May 1975): 3-32.

17. National Advisory Commission on Criminal Justice Standards and Goals, *Corrections* (Washington, D.C.: U.S. Government Printing Office, 1973), p. 487.

18. Norton A. Birnhaum, "The Right to Treatment," *ABA Journal* 46 (1960): 499.

19. Thomas Szasz, "The Right to Health," *Georgetown Law Review* 57 (1969): 747.

20. Anthony Burgess, *A Clockwork Orange* (New York: Ballantine Books, 1965).

21. Michael Crichton, *The Terminal Man* (New York: Knopf, 1972).

22. One issue of *The Prison Journal* focuses on professionals in corrections. See particularly the articles discussing the emphasis on punishment: H. Allen and N. Gatz, "Abandoning the Medical Model in Corrections: Some Implications and Alternatives," *The Prison Journal* 54 (Autumn-Winter 1974): 4-14, and the right to treatment: B. Toomey, H. Allen, and C. Simonsen, "The Right to Treatment: Professional Liabilities in the Criminal Justice and Mental Health Systems," *The Prison Journal* 54 (Autumn-Winter 1974): 43-56.

23. See *O'Connor* v. *Donaldson,* 43 LW 4929 (1975).

23 Custody

Public and official preoccupation with violent and incorrigible prisoners thwarts the development of successful treatment programs for the almost 85 percent of our national prison population that can be helped toward reform.

SANGER B. POWERS

Corrections: Bureaucratic Control

The prevailing management climate for corrections is bureaucratic control, especially in state institutions. In most major correctional institutions, control of the inmate population is most often accomplished by means of coercive rules which prohibit certain kinds of behavior and punishments which apply when the rules are broken. Bureaucratic organization is insulated by rules, and violations are punished in the name of *equity*. In institutions which hold thousands of prisoners, each with personal problems, the bureaucratic style is the only functional way to cope with control: the *process* takes precedence over the *individual,* and prisoners become faceless commodities to be housed, worked, fed, secured, and released. This nineteenth-century model stresses warehousing and processing of offenders—any rehabilitation is incidental, a welcome but low-priority by-product. This bureaucratic style, clearly, conflicts with any emphasis on rehabilitation. Rigid and formalized bureaucratic organizations, with separate functions for each element, provide an impoverished climate for behavioral change.

Custody and control in prisons have traditionally been the warden's dominant concerns. Until very recently, the warden's principal advisor was almost always the chief of the guard force. And the prison guard was the main instrument of control, the stereotyped "screw" with little compassion and a ready fist. Even though correctional officers have now replaced the old-time guards in almost all prisons, they often follow the same oppressive custodial procedures, especially in times of unrest. Until the cause-and-effect relationship between bureaucratic organization and institutional disturbance is openly acknowledged, the advocates of strong custodial control will retain their influential role.

Institutions: Custody Is a Way of Life

The Assistant Superintendent for Custody (also known as Deputy Warden) is one of the most important figures in the correctional institution. The main responsibility of such deputies is to know where all prisoners are at all times. Techniques employed to ensure that all prisoners are accounted for have become more humane and permissive in recent years, but (as mentioned earlier), in most institutions the *count* is still the primary method of determining prisoner whereabouts, and counts are sometimes conducted as often as *every two hours*. Preoccupation with counting and recounting prisoners makes it difficult to conduct meaningful programs or permit individualized operations in maximum security institutions. To some extent, however, outside work details and opportunities for educational and vocational training and furloughs have been provided for by more streamlined counting methods. Today, counts are often called in to a central office in the prison's control room and tabulated against the daily tally of inmates, in some cases using computers. While the count is more sensibly administered, it remains one of the most important tasks for which the custody staff is responsible.

Another major function of the custody staff is to establish and maintain security procedures. Security procedures, at a minimum, include inspection of persons and vehicles passing in and out of the institution, usually at a "sally port" at entry and exit points. The sally port is an area enclosed by a double gate. A vehicle or individual enters through the first gate, which is then closed. Before the second gate is opened, the search for forbidden articles (contraband) is made. After the search is completed, the second gate is opened and the individual or vehicle passes through that gate. At no time may *both* gates be open, and many gate systems are mechanically adjusted so that it is impossible to open them both at the same time. Sometimes a visitor feels that it is as hard to get *into* the institution as it is to get *out*. The fear that inmates and visitors will try to smuggle in contraband or other items to assist in escape pervades the maximum security prison. Unfortunately, similarly unreasonable security practices are also adopted by medium and minimum security prisons. It took over a century before America was prepared to build a prison without massive walls; it may take even longer to convince "old guard" custody personnel that less stringent security measures will serve to ensure control.

Inmate Traffic and Its Control

Rules and regulations for inmates are usually detailed and aimed at strict traffic control. Movements of prisoners are carefully planned and controlled in every detail, the model that has been thought to ensure security. In the past, prisoners were all awakened, moved to work, and fed at the same time, always under the eye of custody personnel. This degree of planning has loosened in many institutions; the trend is toward more reasonable controls over inmate traffic within the walls. President Johnson's Commission described how some of the highly restrictive rules came into existence:

> [U]nder conditions of mass treatment and great concern for custody there is a tendency to accumulate numerous restrictions on inmate behavior. Each disturbance inspires an attempt to prevent its recurrence by establishing a new rule. Once established, rules have great success at survival. Rarely is there any systematic review that looks to the elimination of unnecessary restrictions.
>
> When a disturbance occurs, for example, as men are going from one place to another, it is decreed that if any group of five or more men is moving from one building or area to another, they must walk in a line and be accompanied by an officer. Later an argument between two men in such a line escalates into a fist fight, and henceforth no talking is allowed in line. Someone is attacked with a "shiv" made from a table knife smuggled into a cell and sharpened to a point, and henceforth no forks or knives may be used by inmates in the dining hall.
>
> By such accumulations of permanent rules passed in reaction to episodic disturbances, many prisons have evolved into places of extreme regimentation. They go through periods of tense competition, with staff oriented primarily to enforcing rules and inmates to evading them. What is most striking on investigation is that these efforts do not clearly decrease the amount of disorderly or even dangerous behavior.
>
> When the staff treat inmates as if they were dangerous, they become dangerous, although not so much to staff as to each other. For, if alienated from staff, they fall more than ever under threat of domination by other inmates whose claims to authority they resist by counterhostility.[1]

The Commission's suggestion that inmates treated as if dangerous *will become so* is generally considered a valid point. One way to avoid this problem is for staff and inmates to maintain meaningful communications. If the custody staff loses contact with inmates, the latter can respond only to the inmate subculture. All too often, such limited interaction results in violence among inmates. The most effective controls over inmate traffic and movement may well be those that guide our behavior in the free community.

Prison Discipline

Traffic control is only one aspect of the rules designed to regulate inmate behavior. The same kinds of factors—constructive and irritating—that apply to discipline in any situation are also true of prison discipline:

The constructive factors in prison discipline are: (1) it allows inmates to experience the desirable results of obedience to rules for the common good; (2) it permits various recreational and other pursuits which, through transfer training, may help teach inmates the advantages of cooperation with others; (3) it produces a general atmosphere of order and system that includes regular living and soothes; (4) it helps inmates to acquire recreational habits that can be transferred to the community later; and (5) it neutralizes the negative aspects of prison life as much as possible by controlling and reducing disturbing elements.

The irritating factors of prison discipline are (1) restrictions on individual behavior, (2) regimented movement of groups from place to place, (3) complete lack of privacy, (4) constant supervision by uniformed officers representing authority, and (5) limitations on social contacts with friends and relatives outside by limitations placed on correspondence and visits.[2]

Some of the archaic rules may have been necessitated by the widespread use of untrained rural personnel as correctional officers. Many of these individuals were already instilled with the "convict bogey" before undertaking correctional work, a situation which precluded meaningful interaction with inmates, even those with rehabilitation potential. The gap between the cultural backgrounds of basically urban prisoners and rural guards was often filled by unnecessarily severe discipline.

Correctional administrators must acknowledge the importance of such cultural and philosophical differences in order to utilize the personnel they are currently able to attract. Able to offer only low salaries and a low-prestige occupation to the correctional officer, most administrators have been unable to convince their untrained officers that more progressive discipline methods could be effective. The administrators, therefore, are left with a warehousing role.

It should be noted, however, that the majority of correctional officers are dedicated and humane persons, and marshaling their potential is an important challenge to concerned administrators. The situation with regard to educating these officers is improving. Most states offer preservice training to ensure a minimal level of competence in the officers *before* they are placed on the job at an institution. As this trend continues, salaries, the quality of personnel, and working conditions will improve. The tendency to utilize outdated and counterproductive forms of discipline will decrease accordingly, and the correctional officer, long recognized as the single most important agent for change in institutions, will be able to realize his or her potential contribution to the new rehabilitation approach.

Prevention of Escape

Maximum security adult prisons were built as though they had to contain the most dangerous creature imaginable. "A prison is designed to be as strong as the strongest inmate" is an old correctional chestnut. The high walls, corner towers, and armed guards are external signs of preoccupation with escape. The nature of the prison population, however, does not really justify this model.

> [I]t's a mistake to think U.S. jails and prisons are seething with repressed criminals just waiting their chance to get out and ravage the innocent.
>
> The broad facts are quite different. Over 90 percent of felony arrests in the country are for taking money or other property. The percentage is higher for felonies committed by repeaters. Of the approximately 215,000 prisoners in federal and state prisons two-thirds are there for nonviolent crimes, like forgery, embezzling, larceny, auto-theft, and housebreaking. Less than 10 percent are in prison for homicide, rape, and kidnaping. About another 10 percent are in for aggravated assault.
>
> The typical prisoner is more likely to be the tax accountant from Montana who received a sentence of 31 years and 31 days on tax-fraud charges. He was well past middle age, had raised his family, and nowhere in his previous years was there a suggestion of misconduct. A momentary break in a lifetime of rectitude put him behind bars.[3]

If this is an accurate picture, why is there such concern over the possibility of escape? The answer is complex, but revolves around two essential issues. The first is the philosophy of mass treatment, firmly established since the time when lock-step and silence were required for all prisoner movements. The second reason is political. Seasoned superintendents know that frequent escapes will be extremely damaging to their career ambitions and record, so they take extreme measures to prevent them—directed toward all prisoners, rather than toward the few who might actually try to escape. In a few prisons, however, administrators have begun to accept the fact that the tax evader and ax murderer do not have the same potential for escape attempts.

The Federal Correctional Institution at Seagoville, Texas, is perhaps the best model of a truly "open" prison. There is no wall around Seagoville, and entry to the main facilities is through an open gate. The only barrier around the installation is a low chain-link fence similar to those used in residential back yards. The clean, campus-like appearance of the installation demonstrates that it is possible to confine and rehabilitate men without subjecting them to the dreary, claustrophobic atmosphere of the walled prisons. Few escapes take place under the atmosphere of trust and the administration's belief in encouraging inmate responsibility, self-discipline, and judgment. Seagoville serves as a model in the development of prisons

FIGURE VI–3. The Ubiquitous Tower (Courtesy National Clearinghouse for Criminal Justice Planning and Architecture)

that offer both humanity and hope for the inmate. Work release programs and other progressive transitional steps make the adaptation from institution to community-based correctional programs smooth and effective. Security is a normal part of the daily activity at Seagoville, but not the only activity. The Federal Correctional Institution at Pleasanton, California, presents another model of an open institution that is co-correctional. These and other innovations in the federal system will be covered in detail in chapter 27.

Contraband and Shakedowns

Contraband is officially defined as any item that can be used to break a rule of the institution, or to assist in escape. In practice, it usually refers to anything the custody staff designates as undesirable for possession by inmates. The banning power is unrestricted. It can start with a particular object, such as a knife, and extend to anything that might conceivably be made into a knife—a policy that has placed some relatively innocuous items on contraband lists. The following definition provides the extensive power described above:

> Any item that is not issued or not authorized in the jail is contra-band. Control of contraband is necessary for several reasons:
>
> 1. To control the introduction of articles that can be used for trading and gambling;
> 2. To control the collecting of junk and the accumulation of items that make housekeeping difficult; and
> 3. To identify medications and drugs and items that can be used as weapons and escape implements.
>
> Controlling contraband requires a clear understanding of what contraband is, of regulations that are designed to limit its entry into the jail, and of effective search procedures. The definition of contraband given above is simple and clear. However, this definition can become useless if the jail attempts to supplement it with a long list of approved items. If the jail permits prisoners to have packages, the problem of contraband control will be made difficult since the list of authorized items may grow long.[4]

This relatively simple definition is often complicated by long lists of approved and forbidden items. Overdefinition can only result in a bureau-cratic nightmare for correctional officers who must continuously search for contraband. A broad and clear definition, followed by the use of common sense by trained correctional officers, will usually result in better control and less conflict over what is or is not contraband. Excessive prohibition of items on a contraband list is often seen as a challenge to the inmate, and an indication of suppression by prison administrators. Such items as guns, however, are clearly dangerous contraband, and prison administrators must continually check packages, visitors, and correctional officers to detect such material. This is usually accomplished by means of modern metal detecting equipment.

Shakedowns are another source of potential conflict, the most common type being the "frisk" search. This type of search is used when prisoners enter or leave the institution, and when institutional personnel suspect that a prisoner may be hiding contraband on his or her person. Figure VI–4 shows the proper procedures for a frisk.[5]

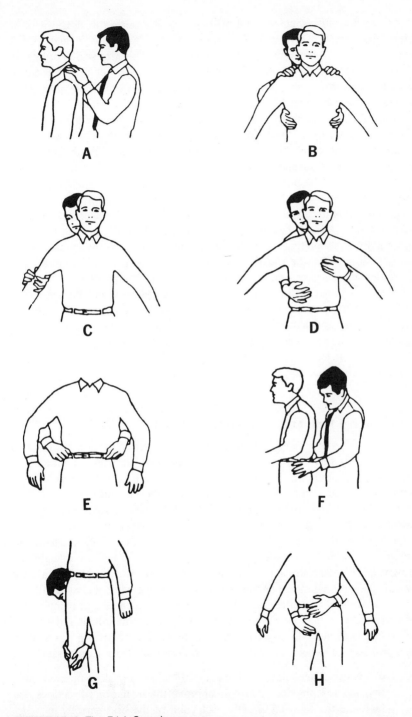

FIGURE VI-4. The Frisk Search

Where it is suspected that the prisoner has had access to drugs or other items that can be secreted on the body or in a body cavity, and a frisk reveals nothing, a strip search may be conducted. The strip search ordinarily should be made in a location where the prisoner will not be subjected to ridicule, and with the assistance of medical personnel, if possible. Suppositories are one way to hide drugs and other small contraband, so body cavities must be examined. The strip search should be a rare event, based on probable cause. In the past, frequent strips were used to debase and abuse prisoners, a practice that greatly increased prison tension. Frisks are a necessary part of institutional security, but if strip searches are made an everyday routine the procedure soon degrades not only the searched but the searcher as well.

As rules prohibiting contraband grow more detailed, inmates seek ways to secrete these items in their living area and throughout the institution. There is virtually no limitation to the ingenuity employed in hiding contraband in prisons. Ironically, the older—and presumably "secure"—institutions and plants lend themselves best to secret hiding places. The process could almost be seen as a game, with correctional officers periodically searching the same old spots. The need for shakedowns is lessened when contraband rules are made realistic and humane; prohibiting such items as family pictures and toothpicks creates a needless irritant. The shakedown also has greater effect if used only to locate items that represent a clear and present danger to the institution, not just for the sake of what inmates call "Mickey Mouse" harassment.

Correctional Officers: The Military Model

The need for an organized and effective control force in prisons has instilled a paramilitary flavor in most security staffs. The adoption of militaristic organizational structures and procedures has made it easier to train a force with limited background to do a specific job. The paramilitary approach is seen in the uniforms, titles, and procedures of custody personnel. Training is directed to the mission of security, and little if any emphasis is placed on interaction with inmates. The model of the aloof but efficient guard has emerged, and hiring of custody personnel is more often based on height and weight criteria than the applicant's ability to work with people. To a great extent, correctional hiring practices bar those people who can best fulfill the newer mission of rehabilitation. The seniority system and the growing power of correctional officer unions may further discourage the infusion of custody personnel with behavioral science backgrounds. The following solutions to this problem have been offered by the National Advisory Commission:

> Correctional agencies should begin immediately to develop personnel policies and practices that will improve the image of corrections and facilitate the fair and effective selection of the best persons for correctional positions.

To improve the image of corrections, agencies should:

1. Discontinue the use of uniforms.

2. Replace all military titles with names appropriate to the correctional task.

3. Discontinue the use of badges, and, except where absolutely necessary, the carrying of weapons.

4. Abolish such military terms as company, mess hall, drill, inspection, and gig list.

5. Abandon regimented behavior in all facilities, both for personnel and for inmates.

In the recruitment of personnel, agencies should:

1. Eliminate all political patronage for staff selection.

2. Eliminate such personnel practices as:

   a. Unreasonable age or sex restrictions.

   b. Unreasonable physical restrictions (e.g., height, weight).

   c. Barriers to hiring physically handicapped.

   d. Questionable personality tests.

   e. Legal or administrative barriers to hiring ex-offenders.

   f. Unnecessarily long requirements for experience in correctional work.

   g. Residency requirements.

3. Actively recruit from minority groups, women, young persons, and prospective indigenous workers, and see that employment announcements reach these groups and the general public.

4. Make a task analysis of each correctional position (to be updated periodically) to determine those tasks, skills, and qualities needed. Testing based solely on these relevant features should be designed to assure that proper qualifications are considered for each position.

5. Use an open system of selection in which any testing device used is related to a specific job and is a practical test of a person's ability to perform that job.[6]

These are a few of the steps that might help span the presently large communication gap between keepers and kept. Correctional officers spend more time with the inmate population than anyone else on the staff. They should relate well to others, since they can be the most positive agents of change in that corrections subsystem. They can also destroy any efforts toward change that are attempted by a treatment staff which tries to bypass them. A move away from the military/police image to the correctional image is critical to effective change in the institutional setting.

Upgrading Correctional Personnel

The most important rehabilitative tool is the impact of one person on another. Thus, a primary goal for the correctional system is the recruitment, training, and retention of employees who are able—physically, emotionally, educationally, and motivationally—to work as a team.

In the correctional system it is hard to hire or keep qualified personnel. This problem was outlined in a recent issue of *Corrections Magazine:*

> With more men and women in prison than ever before, the correctional officer is in a growth industry. Including the prisons and the nation's jails, there are now an estimated 100,000 men and women in custody jobs alone. A *Corrections Magazine* national survey shows that of the total, 42,324 are in state-operated institutions, and their numbers are increasing.
>
> But even during recent difficult economic times, when national unemployment statistics hit new post-Depression peaks, some prison jobs have gone begging. Correctional officer turnover in some places continues at such a rate that some administrators say it is almost impossible to run their institutions with any kind of consistent policy. Officers aren't there long enough to understand the policies. In Louisiana, the annual turnover of correctional officers is 74 percent; in New Mexico it's sixty-five percent. In states with far lower system-wide turnover percentages, the maximum-security institutions report that it's not unusual for them to lose at least half of their new officers in the first year.
>
> But there are exceptions and a few are spectacular. Illinois' Vienna Correctional Center—a tranquil, college-like minimum-security institution—has file cabinets bulging with job requests. Last October it had 1,428 applications on file for the security force alone.
>
> For most shift supervisors and personnel directors, however, the manpower dilemma is not surplus, but shortage. "Supervisors think more in terms of bodies rather than quality—are the job stations going to be filled is the overriding question," says Massachusetts' Frank Gunter, who until recently was superintendent of the maximum-security prison at Walpole.

Because of the almost constant problem of empty slots on various shifts, the burden of filling them falls on officers who stay. At San Quentin in California, some members of the custody force complain about being ordered to work on their days off. They grumble about the inability to schedule vacations. At Walpole, staff shortages this summer resulted in a mandatory sixth work day for every officer.[7]

All salaries are too low, and attempts to raise them have included some unorthodox ideas. In Ohio, for example, hazardous duty and overtime pay for correctional officers was initiated, skewing the salary schedules so that correctional officers could make more than a deputy warden or professional-technical staff with special skills and higher education.

Perhaps more important than salary is the sense of public rejection employees feel, reinforced in some institutions by the belief that administrators do not consult them, treat them fairly, or care what they think. New channels of communication must be opened between administrators and employees, as well as employees and inmates. Administrators should meet with staff to discuss employee problems; custodial and treatment staff should also meet together. These meetings should be regularly scheduled and formally integrated into the institutional procedures.

In most jurisdictions, little or no specialized training is given to new staff members. This lack of training is particularly serious in the case of correctional officers. After two or three weeks of basic orientation, they learn the ways of the institution by working with one or more officers in a modified apprenticeship program, which institutionalizes bad habits of the past.

Correctional officers spend twenty-four hours a day with inmates. The officers' actions, words, training, and skills make the difference between a hostile and destructive environment for prisoners, and one that is constructive and humane. Correctional personnel are too often punitive, contemptuous, and degrading, reflecting a suspicion of inmates which may lead to a self-defeating game of "cops and robbers." It is in this adversary relationship that rehabilitation breaks down.

The following recommendations, to apply to each state, would counteract some of these problems and reduce the conflict between custody and treatment staffs:

1. A position of Program Director should be created, to integrate all services in the institutions. All present Deputy Wardens would report to this individual.

2. The model of the collaborative institution should be adopted. In this model, lines of communication are continuously open between prisoners and staff, and between treatment and security personnel. Inmates, custodial officers, and professional staff meet

regularly to discuss mutual problems and their possible solutions. Under the Program Director, this collaborative effort should engender better treatment as well as better custody.

3. The academy approach to employee training should be adopted. It should be noted that federal funds now support academy programs and in-service training. To achieve the goal of up-grading training, it is absolutely necessary for states to commit themselves to on-going appropriations for the extension and improvement of these training programs.

4. A Corrections Academy should be established in a centrally located area, close to a major university.

5. All persons hired for the management of prisoners should be thoroughly screened through the use of written tests and psychological interviews. This screening process should be followed by at least six months, and perhaps a year, of probationary status on the job.

6. Courses should be designed for all supervisory personnel by the Academy, with special emphasis on the behavioral sciences and rehabilitative penology.

7. New officers should be trained in basic penology before assuming their posts.

8. Continued in-service training should be made mandatory at the Academy and at the institutions.

9. Promotions and salary increases should be contingent on the successful participation in and completion of these in-service training programs, as well as monitoring on the job. This recommendation is contingent upon alterations to existing civil service regulations.[8]

Summary

According to the 1966 Revision of the *Manual of Correctional Standards:*

A fundamental responsibility of prison management is the secure custody and control of prisoners. This is universally prescribed by law, custom and public opinion. Although at times such a concept may seem at variance with attempts to introduce rehabilitative services, it is doubtful that any correctional program which ignores this reality will long endure. Actually services and facilities for rehabilitative treatment can operate effectively only in a climate where control is constant. Conversely, good control cannot be consistently maintained without energizing it with positive correctional and training resources . . . a well-rounded correctional program, including medical, food, educational, industrial, and other rehabilitative services must be correlated with and into a system of sound custody, security and control of inmates.[9]

Historically, correctional institutions probably do a more effective job in security than in any other aspect of the institutional program. Pitfalls in exercising this responsibility include opportunities for excessive use of force by some personnel, the debilitating effects of excessive routinization on inmates, and the frustration of treatment programs when security needs are seen as paramount. These negative possibilities become probabilities because the custodial portion of the institutional program is carried out by the persons least trained in treatment techniques. While the official policy of the institution may be humane, the people who are in direct contact with the inmate may have an entirely different view of their role, leading to degrading and sometimes brutal treatment of the inmate.

Recruitment and hiring standards, practices, and procedures have not established sufficiently high educational or personality standards for the position of corrections officer. Salaries authorized by most legislatures for custodial personnel have not sufficed to attract and retain treatment-minded persons with high levels of educational achievement. It speaks well for today's correctional personnel, generally, that a relative few have been identified as brutal persons. The nature of the situation, however, lends itself to individual expressions of punitiveness.

One of the most vexing problems of prison management is the relationship between security and treatment. Too often, this relationship pits custody and treatment personnel against each other. Both under the law and in fact, the primary emphasis in corrections is on *security*. Thus, the Deputy Warden or Associate Superintendent for Custody becomes the key operating officer of the institution.

Personnel figures from one state reflect this emphasis: in fiscal 1969, for example, correctional institutions employed 1,527 custodial officers. In the same year, for the entire system, there were only 40 social workers and 24 psychologists to deal with family, social, and behavioral problems of the 9,500 inmates. Even when teaching, chaplaincy, and medical staffs are added to this count, the ratio is still approximately ten to one. This ratio, while changing, unfortunately is still the ''norm'' in most states, and is even worse in some of the less progressive states.

Disciplinary infractions and other security considerations can prevent, hamper, or terminate inmate involvement in academic, vocational, educational, and other recommended activities (recreation, Alcoholics Anonymous, visiting, drug therapy, etc.). Furthermore, many important services are generally not available at night, thereby excluding inmates who work during the day. Adequate staffing could permit the expansion of treatment services to the evening hours and weekends.

Treatment-oriented personnel at all levels express concern about the conflict between security and program needs. While institutional rules and regulations play a vital role in the correctional process, unnecessary rules, regimenting minor aspects of daily life, impede the development of individual responsibility. For example, lockdowns, shakedowns, and skin searches are inherently humiliating and engender bitterness and resentment. In a cell shakedown, the inmates' possessions are often knocked to the floor and trampled. It is true that occasional thorough searches of person and premises are necessary for the protection of the institutional community. Nevertheless, the basic principles of human dignity need to be observed. In regard to security, it has been recommended that:

1. Policies be developed to define the relationships between essential security functions and rehabilitative program needs for the institutions. The obvious dichotomy of custody and treatment must be erased and greater recognition given to the fact that each is supportive of the other. Clarification must be made of the essential roles of all aspects of the institutional program so that none can be unduly hampered by the needs of others.

2. Promulgate policies and guidelines for institutional rules and regulations and review all present rules and procedures to insure that the demands of security do not negate the objectives of treatment. In policy formation and in specific rules, the principle of clear and present danger should apply; if the regulation is required for the safety of the institutional community, it should be kept. If not, it should be abolished. These policies should provide for periodic review of institutional compliance. At each institution a permanent standing committee, representing all major services, should be made responsible for implementing these guidelines and policies.

3. In cases where force has been used upon an inmate, in addition to an investigation by institution and/or

Division, a report routinely be submitted to the Commission by the prison physician and by the inmate himself.

4. The Division of Correction respond to requests from families that they be permitted to visit and see an inmate if they believe excessive force has been used against him. If they desire an outside physician to examine the prisoner, this· be granted without delay, in accordance with rules promulgated by the Division of Correction. Copies of all "Use of Force" reports be filed with the Division of Correction and be made available for inspection by the inmate's family, attorney, and, with the inmate's written permission, any other appropriate people.[10]

It is recognized by all involved in corrections that custody and security are vital roles. They are not the *only* goals, however, and the next chapter will deal with *treatment* as another essential goal for corrections.

REVIEW QUESTIONS

I. Find the answers to the following in the text:

1. What is the primary focus of the bureaucratic style of prison management?

2. Where have prison guards been obtained in the past? How does this create problems?

3. Why has the military model been so popular in the prisons?

4. Why do disciplinary and secuirty considerations impact so heavily on treatment programs? How can this be resolved?

II. Words to identify:

1. equity

2. bureaucratic control

3. screw

4. count

5. sally port

6. contraband

7. open prison

8. shakedown

9. frisk

10. collaborative institution

NOTES

1. The President's Commission on Law Enforcement and Administration of Justice, *Task Force Report: Corrections* (Washington, D.C.: U.S. Government Printing Office, 1967), p. 67.

2. Vernon Fox, *Introduction to Corrections* (Englewood Cliffs, N.J.: Prentice-Hall, 1973), p. 163.

3. Robert Ostermann, *Crime in America* (Silver Springs, Ohio: Newsbook, 1966), pp. 149-150.

4. Nick Pappas, *The Jail: Its Operation and Management* (Lompoc, Calif.: Federal Prison Industries, 1971), p. 23.

5. Pappas, *The Jail*, p. 24.

6. National Advisory Commission on Criminal Justice Standards and Goals. *Corrections* (Washington, D.C.: U.S. Government Printing Office, 1973), p. 471.

7. "Prison Guards in America: The Way It Was . . . the Myth . . . and the Reality," *Corrections Magazine* 6 (December 1976): 4.

8. Ohio Citizens' Task Force on Corrections, *Final Report* (Columbus, Ohio: State of Ohio, 1971), pp. C-25–C-26.

9. American Correctional Association, *Manual of Correctional Standards,* 3d ed. (Washington, D.C.: ACA, 1966).

10. Ohio Citizens' Task Force, *Final Report,* pp. C-39–C-40.

24 Treatment

> There is no behavior or person that a modern psy-
> chiatrist cannot plausibly diagnose as abnormal or ill.
>
> *THOMAS S. SZASZ*

The Treatment Model

Treatment services, which generally include vocational training, education, counseling, teaching, casework, and clinical activity, are believed to form a significant part of efforts toward offender rehabilitation. In major institutions, however, the allocation of resources and personnel for treatment bears little if any relation to this assumed significance. As a national average, the resources allocated for treatment services amounts to only about 10 percent of the institutional staffs. This disproportionate distribution of resources was addressed by the 1966 *Manual of Correctional Standards:* "Over the past thirty years, there has been increasing recognition that a major function of a correctional agency is to influence change in the attitude and behavior of the offender. The disciplines of psychiatry, psychology, and social casework have provided corrections with tools which are useful in stimulating change."[1] In the entire corrections system, a very small percentage of institutional personnel are employed in social work or psychological services, and the number of psychiatrists in corrections is infinitesimal. It is important to note that diagnostic workups and testing processes tend to consume the workday of those involved in these services. Treatment personnel must often spend long hours sitting on disciplinary courts, classification and reclassification committees, and honor placement committees. Thus a minute staff has almost no time to spend in ongoing treatment contacts with inmates. In addition, correctional administrators and the treatment staff have to contend with the deeply ingrained antagonism of the staff members who are oriented toward custody, security, and maintenance of calm.

The treatment model for corrections arose from the three basic services first provided to prisoners: religious, medical, and educational. The development of these services will be traced in this chapter, along with the more recent treatment innovations. Much of the public still views treatment as a form of "coddling," and administrators have responded to this view by rejecting new and promising rehabilitation techniques developed by the behavioral sciences. In fact, of course, protection of society, not pampering of offenders, is the basic reason for treatment. If the sources of an individual's criminality can be treated before he or she is referred to the community, they should be. As noted in chapter 23, inmates are most strongly influenced by those persons who spend the most time with them. At present, correctional officers and work supervisors, rather than treatment specialists, are most likely to be influential. Either the sharp split between the treatment and custody staffs must be bridged, or the treatment staff must be increased and given more time with offenders. In any event, the custody staff should become involved not only with *control*, but with *rehabilitation*, a process which actually begins with the initial classification. The treatment model is under attack, however (see chapter 29).

Classification: Security or Treatment?

In chapter 13, we noted that classification is a relatively recent move in corrections. The classification process can frequently intensify the conflict between treatment and custody staffs, if it is not carefully handled. In most correctional classification processes (either at the individual institution or at a central classification facility), there is more concern with the danger new inmates might present to the institution than the possibility that they might respond to treatment. As a result, new inmates are often assigned to higher custody grades than their backgrounds warrant until they can "prove" themselves. This security-oriented classification often excludes inmates from participation in the programs that could lead to their rehabilitation. Their early treatment, in fact, may be restricted to health care—an essential, as most offenders are in poor physical condition when they enter the institution.

Health and Medical Services

Even in the earliest days of American prisons, certain times were set aside for sick call. The treatment provided was and is, of course, less than one would expect to receive at a clinic in the community. In many cases, prisoners use sick call merely to obtain a brief respite from prison labor or from the dull routine. Time wasted on "gold brickers" is time the medical staff cannot give those who really need care. Because the correctional funnel selects out all but the most serious offenders, the cream of society does not often end up in prisons. Thus, the prison doctor must deal with a unique brand of patient:

The prison physician faces one of the most difficult problems in medical service. To him are sent the very essence of society's misfits, for his patients are not only the abnormal, the subnormal, and the maladjusted—the handicapped, the sick, the surgically unfit, the degenerate, the dissipated, the diseased, the psychotic, the psychopathic, the neurotic and the feebleminded, but they are also the socially undesirable—men and women whom society has cast out, who cannot or will not cooperate according to the rules of the game. To this beginning must be added all the complicating forces which are peculiar to a prison and which so materially affect the prison physician's patients. They begin with the mental worry and disgrace of imprisonment and they by no means end with the drab, dull existence which characterizes prison life. Not only does lack of stimulating work weaken the mental keenness of active minds, but lack of any work in most prisons today saps the moral fibre out of the most stalwart spirits. Crowded together in the narrow confines of a walled institution, housed in cages like animals where insufficiency of light and air and no privacy wilt the hardiest, fed on a monotonous diet, allowed only a restricted amount of exercise—the problem of keeping people well under such conditions is itself a problem.[2]

As noted in chapter 13, medical services are often a source of inmate complaints, and frequently become a real headache for administrators. In many areas throughout the country, qualified medical personnel are generally in short supply, and this shortage is felt even more acutely in correctional institutions. To provide the total medical care for which an institution is responsible, it is often necessary to combine the services of full-time medical employees, contractual consultants, and available community resources. Even with all these efforts, inmates and the public often tend to look down on any medically trained person who is willing to become involved with a correctional institution. Any doctor who accepts the prison physician's relatively low income and standard of living, it is thought, must have been a failure in the community.

Proper medical care is very important in the overall rehabilitation effort. In many cases, the offender's health condition is one of the key reasons authorities decided to opt for placement in a correctional institution instead of a road camp unit. Poor diet, drug abuse, a history of inadequate medical attention, and other debilitating conditions are not uncommon among inmates. Once they have been restored to reasonable health, it is often easier to work on the causes behind their problems. In the *most* progressive prisons, cosmetic medicine—plastic surgery—is available on request of the treatment staff, to reshape the offender's self-image and thus increase his or her self-confidence. As a matter of fact, in a survey of over 100 types of treatment it was noted that plastic surgery appeared to be one of the most effective rehabilitation programs. Another major service to the offender is the dental clinic, as most prisoners have very bad teeth. Even in the institution fortunate enough to have good dental care facilities, this service can consume many months for a prisoner who needs a lot of work. The effects of this kind of treatment are similar to those of plastic surgery: improved appearance enhances the offender's feelings of confidence and well-being and he or she may be relieved of chronic pain and irritation as well. The institution fortunate enough to have first-class medical and dental facilities has a great advantage over most other prisons and can include them in treatment and rehabilitation programs.

Chaplaincy Services

One service that has always been available to the incarcerated felon is religious assistance and guidance. Solitary meditation in the Walnut Street Jail was intended to bring offenders to a realization of their sinful ways and render them penitent. Penitence was often encouraged by visits from the local ministers and priests. Later, the large institutions of the early 1800s created the need for a full-time chaplain on the premises. The correctional chaplaincy has been and is currently the least sought-after position among ministers, who evidently prefer to serve more conventional congregations. Part of the problem, too, is the remote location of most prisons, and a widespread public belief (shared by many administrators) that religion in prisons should be confined to the chaplain's traditional duties. A movement has sprung up to establish a core of clinically oriented clerics, but the correctional field is less attractive to them than other kinds of institutions. There is a definite need to upgrade the role of the correctional chaplain, in order to attract the best into the institutions. In this regard, it has been recommended that:

1. A chief of chaplains be appointed who is a clinical pastoral education supervisor accredited by the Association for Clinical Pastoral Education.

2. This person develop programs to advance the professional competency of chaplains within the system.

3. The chief of chaplains develop programs to recruit and train chaplaincy candidates, as well as to help other clergymen understand corrections.

4. Seminary students, when available, should augment chaplaincy services.

5. The chief of chaplains maintain headquarters at the Correction Academy and have some advisory responsibilities to the Superintendents regarding chaplaincy service.

6. Educational leave with pay be allowed for chaplains to take correctional training in other institutions in other states. This would have a cross-fertilization effect helpful to the service.

7. There be an upgrading of salaries for chaplains, and chaplains-in-training. Present pay scales are not competitive.[3]

The new and growing special interest groups inside prisons, those whose religious orientation is toward a particular ethnic, cultural, or subculture group, do not accord with the traditional religious outlets. As discussed in chapter 13, their right to pursue their faiths while confined has been firmly established. The traditional institution has provided Protestant, Roman Catholic, and (sometimes) Jewish chaplains, as representatives of the three major religious groups in this country, because it was not feasible to provide a cleric for each and every religion observed by different inmates. These chaplains offered ecumenical services and tried to provide worship for all prisoners. However, the more vocal members of the smaller sects have protested this arrangement, and the current response leans toward the recommendations of the National Advisory Commission:

Each institution should immediately adopt policies and practices to insure the development of a full range of religious programs.

1. Program planning procedures should include religious history and practices of the individual, to maximize his opportunities to pursue the religious faith of his choice while confined.

2. The chaplain should play an integral part in institutional programs.

3. To prevent the chaplain from becoming institutionalized and losing touch with the significance of religion in free society, sabbaticals should be required. The chaplain should return to the community and participate in religious activities during the sabbatical. Sabbatical leave also should include further studies, including study of religions and sects alien to the chaplain but existing in his institution. Funds should be provided for this purpose.

4. The chaplain should locate religious resources in the civilian community for those offenders who desire assistance on release.

5. The correctional administrator should develop an adaptive attitude toward the growing numbers of religious sects and beliefs and provide all reasonable assistance to their practice.

6. Community representatives of all faiths should be encouraged to participate in religious services and other activities within the institution.[4]

It is possible, if the chaplain's salary and image are sufficiently upgraded, that ministers trained in the behavioral sciences will become part of the contemporary prison scene—a far cry from the Walnut Street missionaries whose sole function was Bible-reading and prayer. These new chaplains might well become an integrated part of the treatment team in future rehabilitation programs.

Education for Inmates

In most state correctional systems, education of incarcerated inmates is a legislative mandate. The largest group of treatment personnel is the teacher category, usually far outnumbering those in counseling services. Although most institutions have some kind of educational program, there are marked differences in kind and extent. Early efforts were aimed simply at teaching prisoners to read. Today, most people have at least a high school education, and the more progressive institutions are even offering courses at the college level. It is acknowledged that lack of education is a serious handicap in the free world; former offenders who cannot get jobs because of insufficient education are likely to return to crime. For this reason, education has long been regarded as a primary rehabilitative tool in the correctional field. The gap between the need for educational services and the provision of adequate educational and vocational training is wide, however, and diminishes the results from programs that are attempted.

One of the first barriers to effective educational programs is, once again, the problem of administrative considerations: operational requirements, security needs, shortage of teachers, shortage of educational materials, and a lack of inmate motivation. Inmates and staff are handicapped by unsuitable or out-of-date textbooks, often below the level of sophistication of the average adult prisoner. Inmates who are prevented from attending classes for disciplinary reasons may have to drop from the rest of the term. Using education as a disciplinary club devaluates its effectiveness as a treatment component.

The classes held in most institutions are conventional and relatively old-fashioned, in contrast to the learning innovations available to students at all levels on the outside. Most prisoners have had little formal education and probably resisted whatever teaching they were exposed to. Material that

FIGURE VI–5. An Early Classroom at Elmira Reformatory (Courtesy American Correctional Association)

bored them as children or as truant teenagers is not likely to hold them enthralled as adults. What these mature felons do not need are "Dick and Jane" readers, or other textbooks designed for children. But because of the low priority and minimal funds assigned to education in most institutions, it is these useless texts that prisoners are offered, often by public schools that no longer use them. Small wonder that most prison programs are neither accredited nor enthusiastically supported by inmates. The surprising fact is that some educational services not only survive, but even contribute to inmate rehabilitation. In Ohio, the Department of Rehabilitation and Correction was finally able to establish a complete school district composed entirely of the educational programs within the state prison system.

Three major education-related programs that have been implemented, primarily with Safe Streets Act funds, are work release or furlough, educational release, and Project Newgate. The latter program brings the first years of college into the prison, along with instructors and a complete curriculum. In educational release, inmates are allowed to leave the institution to attend college, high school, or vocational-technical schools during the day, though they must return to the institution or an approved site when not at school, or at night. In the work release program, an inmate may be allowed to leave the limits of confinement to secure a job, thus developing a

FIGURE VI-6. Vocational Training in Construction Trades (Courtesy Federal Bureau of Prisons)

work history, learning a trade, supporting dependents, or making restitution to the victim of his or her crime. The use of educational release is becoming increasingly widespread in the United States.[5]

Education, medical care, and religious practice have served as the basic "treatment" programs in America's prisons since the days of the Walnut Street Jail. In recent years, this limited three-sided approach to treatment has expanded to include a wide variety of programs aimed at the rehabilitation of incarcerated offenders.

The Vocational-Rehabilitation Model

Vocational and technical training in prisons have been available to prisoners ever since the industrial prison was established in the early 1800s. This early training, however, was aimed not at prisoner rehabilitation but at institutional profit. Later, at the Elmira Reformatory, the concept of training for the purpose of providing a trade to ex-offenders was introduced, and it has slowly taken root over the years.

A major setback to adequate vocational training came with the passage of restrictive federal laws on the interstate transport of prison industry goods. These laws, passed in the mid-'30s, sounded the deathknell for many work programs in state prisons. Only in the past twenty years have institutions begun to re-emphasize vocational training programs.

The waste of prisoners' time in idleness is staggering. Neil Singer conducted an analysis of potential inmate economic benefits and found that 208,000 felons in prison could earn an average of $8,038 each year, or $1.67 billion in total.[6] Such economic realities cause legislators, managers, and citizens to wince when they appraise current forms of "treatment."

The critical relationship between prison industries and vocational training was addressed in the National Advisory Commission Report:

> Each correctional agency and each institution operating industrial and labor programs should take steps immediately to reorganize their programs to support the reintegrative purpose of correction institutions.
>
> 1. Prison industries should be diversified and job specifications defined to fit work assignments to offenders' needs as determined by release planning.
>
> 2. All work should form part of a designed training program with provisions for:
>
>   a. Involving the offender in the decision concerning his assignment.
>
>   b. Giving him the opportunity to achieve on a productive job to further his confidence in his ability to work.
>
>   c. Assisting him to learn and develop his skills in a number of job areas.
>
>   d. Instilling good working habits by providing incentives.
>
> 3. Joint bodies consisting of institution management, inmates, labor organizations, and industry should be responsible for planning and implementing a work program useful to the offender, efficient, and closely related to skills in demand outside the prison.
>
> 4. Training modules integrated into a total training plan for individual offenders should be provided. Such plans must be periodically monitored and flexible enough to provide for modification in line with individuals' needs.
>
> 5. Where job training needs cannot be met within the institution, placement in private industry on work-furlough programs should be implemented consistent with security needs.

6. Inmates should be compensated for all work
   performed that is of economic benefit to the
   correctional authority or another public or private
   entity. As a long-range objective to be implemented
   by 1978, such compensation should be at rates
   representing the prevailing wage for work of the
   same type in the vicinity of the correctional facility.[7]

The private sector should also contract with prisoners in their factories inside prisons (or miniature production communities), allowing prisoners to earn wages equal to those of nonprisoner employees, produce modern products for a competitive market, pay taxes, support their dependents (and relieve welfare rolls), amass a "nest egg" to supplement their release money, provide important continuity in their work histories, contribute toward retirement benefits, and so on. Such a plan is under consideration in a number of states, such as Georgia, and is frequently implemented in the Scandinavian countries.[8] Canada has also developed a model inmate employment and industrial program.[9]

These procedures, taken together, provide a realistic solution to one of the most serious problems impeding the successful return of offenders to an employment-oriented society.

Psychologists, Psychiatrists, and Sociologists

Psychology is concerned with the measurement and evaluation of an individual's intellectual capability and his or her ability to cope and adjust in society. The use of mass testing, popularized in World War I, clearly had possibilities for prisons. With the advent of the first classification program in New Jersey in 1918, the psychologist became a dominant force in the classification process. Today, IQ tests and other measurements developed by psychologists have become standard in classification and treatment decisions. The psychologists have continued to outnumber other professionals who seek to determine the cause of and cure for criminal behavior; with their measurements and questionnaires, psychologists are generally more acceptable to the correctional staff than psychiatrists.

Although psychiatrists became involved in prison activity early in the development of treatment programs, the correctional team has not accepted their presence as readily as that of psychologists. It is often difficult for the mission-orientzd custody staff to accept the abstract, seemingly indecisive approach that is the hallmark of psychiatric treatment. The correctional officer would prefer to have all offenders with psychiatric problems relegated to mental institutions. The suspicion of prison psychiatrists also stems from an awareness that competent psychiatrists in private practice can make several times the salaries offered by prisons.

Another stumbling block to really effective psychiatric service in prison is the institutional environment itself; many psychiatrists would argue that little can be done in the way of treatment inside the monolithic institutions. Their efforts in prisons, as a result, stress diagnosis rather than treatment. This combination of circumstances means that some state systems have very few full-time psychiatric staff members, and others have none. To gain maximum help from the psychiatrist, the whole function of most prisons would have to be changed. The new pattern envisioned by the psychiatrist would be along the lines of the hospital model, where treatment diagnoses can be seen through to completion. An alternative might be a small, urban-based, short-term treatment facility for handling moderately disturbed offenders.

Sociologists have been latecomers into correctional treatment programs. They are especially helpful in identifying and developing the roles and structures of the prison subcultures and the administrative personnel. Many of the current research projects in prisons and other areas of correctional treatment are being directed by sociologists. This group of professionals has also been helpful in the identification of the social factors that stimulate offenders to commit or repeat crimes. The findings and recommendations from many sociological studies are helping to push corrections back into the community. Sociologists have also worked their way into administrative positions in corrections, where they can exert more influence on the complex organization and its programs. Many of the higher education programs in corrections are housed in university sociology departments, where criminology is handled as an integral part of the discipline of sociology.

The Social Worker in Corrections

The social work profession became particularly important in the spectrum of corrections when the emphasis on rehabilitation increased. The caseworker is essential in the presentence investigation phase, and many probation officers and parole officers received their training in social work. It is reasonable that the social worker should become more involved in institutional programs as the latter's emphasis shifted toward treatment. Social workers had already taken their places in school programs, hospitals, and mental health institutions, among others. The basic concepts of social casework can be successfully applied in the authoritarian atmosphere of the prison. The social worker has the training to help the offender adapt to the prison situation inside the walls. Barnes and Teeters list four prerequisites for effective casework in prison:

First, it must be accepted by the administration that there are constructive elements in a prison experience; second, that these elements can be translated into a sound correctional program; third, that the staff dedicate itself to the task of helping the inmate find maturity as a mark of social responsibility; fourth, that the administration provide the structure or climate in which the case worker can operate effectively.[10]

Clearly the role of the social caseworker is especially suited to working out inmate problems.

Treatment and the Reintegration Model

The movement toward treatment and corrections in the community has highlighted the need to make programs inside the walls relate to circumstances in the outside world. Control of crime cannot be achieved by the reformation of prisoners alone. Continued reformation and reintegration efforts must take place in the community. Toward this end, many of the barriers shutting off the prison from the community have come down in the last decade. The treatment concept has been expanded to encompass the efforts of community-oriented professionals, and community volunteers have begun to provide offenders with the support and guidance needed to ensure successful reintegration. The main objective of the reintegration model is to return the offender to the community as a responsible and productive citizen, rather than a feared and shunned "ex-con" with little hope for success. Institutions dedicated to this objective have learned to overcome deficits in funding and personnel by using the ingenuity of prison staff and the resources available in the community. Teachers and graduate students are encouraged to provide courses on topics that will help reintegrate the inmate, such as social problems, mental health, and use of community resources. Other assistance and support by outsiders help to lessen the feeling of isolation and stigma that inevitably overtakes the incarcerated offender.

In many institutions, the barriers are coming down for traffic in both directions ("the door swings both ways"). Outside activity by inmates and prison personnel ranges from touring lecture programs to work and educational furloughs. These latter programs serve as a method of graduated release back to the community. The rationale for graduated release has been described as follows:

> There is convincing evidence that the periods immediately before and immediately after release from an institution stand as particularly critical times in an inmate's life. Occasional bravado notwithstanding, most inmates keenly appreciate the fact that they have failed in the past to remain within legal boundaries and that the same or similar conditions that led them to prison in the first place may catapult them back into custody. If nothing else, their incarceration brings into question their adequacy as criminals, that is, the quality of their skill

FIGURE VI–7. A Voluntary Class in Sign Language, for Staff and Inmates Who Wish to Communicate with Inmates Who Have Hearing and Speech Problems (Courtesy Federal Bureau of Prisons)

and intelligence, and their ability to evade capture in the future. For those inmates who desire to remain law abiding, the power of that commitment to withstand social and psychological erosion creates nagging doubts.[11]

This reintegration model allows the inmate to take on increasing responsibilities until he or she is ready for complete acceptance by the community. It is the wave of the future, and treatment programs built around such a comprehensive and integrated plan will have much higher potential for success than the old custody/control methods. The true reintegration model recognizes the need to provide the ex-offender with a reasonable means of support—hence the undeniable importance of good vocational training.

Treatment: An Eclectic Program

Many elements are involved in the correctional treatment process. From the more formalized approach of the social scientists, the medical professionals, and the educators to the efforts of community volunteers and release programs, the key to treatment is an organized program designed to prepare the inmate for successful reintegration with the free society. It is obvious how important the cooperation and understanding of the security and custody staff can be in the success of any of the efforts described as "treatment." As the single most influential agent of change, the correctional officer is the keystone to the success or failure of any kind of treatment program. A cooperative effort by custody and treatment staffs is the essence of an effective institutional program. Treatment cannot end at the prison gate. To be sure of maximum success, the treatment must be continued and reinforced in the community. These community programs are discussed in chapter 28.

REVIEW QUESTIONS

I. Find the answers to the following in the text:

1. What are the general categories of treatment services?

2. Is classification more properly a security or treatment function? Why?

3. Explain the various roles of psychologists, psychiatrists, and sociologists in correctional institutions.

4. Explain the rationale of the reintegration model and how it applies to graduated release.

5. Why does the custody staff seem to feel that most innovative treatment amounts to being "soft"?

II. Words to identify:

1. diagnostic workup

2. chaplain

3. counseling service

4. conventional treatment

5. social caseworker

6. vocational rehabilitation

7. eclectic programs

8. reintegration model

9. technical training

10. educational furlough

11. work release

NOTES

1. American Correctional Association, *Manual of Correctional Standards* (Washington, D.C.: ACA, 1966).

2. Wayne Morse, *The Attorney General's Survey of Release Procedures* (Washington, D.C.: U.S. Government Printing Office, 1940).

3. Ohio Citizens' Task Force on Corrections, *Final Report* (Columbus, Ohio: State of Ohio, 1972), pp. C-55–C-56.

4. National Advisory Commission on Criminal Justice Standards and Goals, *Corrections* (Washington, D.C.: U.S. Government Printing Office, 1973), p. 381.

5. David Shichor and Harry Allen, "Correctional Efforts in the Educated Society: The Case of Study Release," *Lambda Alpha Epsilon* 39 (June 1976): 18-24.

6. Neil Singer, *The Value of Inmate Manpower* (Washington, D.C.: American Bar Association Commission on Correctional Facilities and Manpower, 1973).

7. National Advisory Commission, *Corrections*, p. 387.

8. For an article on managing as a process, see John Conrad, "The Managing Model of Criminal Behavior," *British Journal of Criminology* 14 (April 1974).

9. Canadian Penitentiary Service, "Canada Launches New Approach to Inmate Employment," *American Journal of Corrections* 38 (November-December 1976): 10, 28.

10. Harry Elmer Barnes and Negley K. Teeters, *New Horizons in Criminology*, 3d ed. (Englewood Cliffs, N.J.: Prentice-Hall, 1959), pp. 472-473.

11. National Institute of Mental Health, *Graduated Release* (Washington, D.C.: U.S. Government Printing Office, 1972), p. 3.

RECOMMENDED READING LIST

Coffey, Alan; Eldefonso, Edward; and Hartinger, Walter. *An Introduction to the Criminal Justice System and Process*. Engelwood Cliffs, N.J.: Prentice-Hall, 1974.

Eldefonso, Edward, *Readings in Criminal Justice*. Beverly Hills, Calif.: Glencoe Press, 1973.

Felkenes, George T. *The Criminal Justice System: Its Function and Personnel*. Englewood Cliffs, N.J.: Prentice-Hall, 1973.

Frank, Benjamin. *Contemporary Corrections: A Concept in Search of Content*. Reston, Va.: Reston, 1973.

Killinger, George C., and Cromwell, Paul F. *Penology*. St. Paul, Minn.: West Publishing, 1973.

LeGrande, James L. *The Basic Processes of Criminal Justice*. Beverly Hills, Calif.: Glencoe Press, 1973.

Munro, Jim L. *Administrative Behavior and Police Organization*. Cincinnati, Ohio: W.H. Anderson Co., 1974.

National Advisory Commission on Criminal Justice Standards and Goals. *Corrections*. Washington, D.C.: U.S. Government Printing Office, 1973.

National Association of Attorneys General. *Religion in Correctional and Mental Institutions*. Raleigh, N.C.: Committee on the Office of Attorney General, 1976.

National Institute of Mental Health. *Community Based Correctional Programs: Models and Practices*. Washington, D.C.: U.S. Government Printing Office, 1971.

The President's Commission on Law Enforcement and Administration of Justice. *Task Force Report: Corrections*. Washington, D.C.: U.S. Government Printing Office, 1967.

Sansone, John M. *Sentencing, Corrections, and Special Treatment Services in Sweden, Denmark, and the Netherlands*. Hartford, Conn.: Hartford Institute of Criminal and Social Justice, 1976.

Schrag, Clarence. *Crime and Justice: American Style*. Washington, D.C.: U.S. Government Printing Office, 1971.

Whisenand, Paul M., and Ferguson, R. Fred. *The Managing of Police Organizations*. Englewood Cliffs, N.J.: Prentice-Hall, 1973.

PART VII

Correctional Systems

25 Jails and Detention Facilities

Jails are festering sores in the criminal justice system. The result is what you would expect, only worse. Jails are, without question, brutal, filthy cesspools of crime—institutions which serve to brutalize and embitter men, to prevent them from returning to a useful role in society.

RICHARD VELDE

Jails: A Grim History

The housing of offenders and suspected criminals in local detention facilities is a practice as old as the definition of crime. The local gaol, lockup, stockade, or jail has changed little over the centuries. Only recently has there been any attempt to develop treatment for jail inmates, and even these efforts must be continuously monitored or officials are likely to abandon them. Originally devised as a place to lock up and restrain all classes of misfits, the jail has a long and sordid history. As discussed in chapter 2, the great prison reformer, John Howard, was made keenly aware of the appalling conditions in jails in eighteenth-century England when he found himself the proprietor of one of the worst. His efforts to reform the practices and improve the conditions in the gaols and prisons of England and the rest of Europe parallel the periodic attempts by American reformers to clean up our jails.

Early jails in America were similar to those in Europe. Most were composed of small rooms in which as many as twenty to thirty prisoners were jammed together. The purpose of jails, as originally conceived by Henry II of England when he provided for construction of the first official English jail at the Assize of Clarendon in 1166, was to detain suspected or accused offenders until they could be brought before a court. Seldom were the jails adequately heated or ventilated, and food was either sold by the jailer or brought in by family or friends. Conditions within these early jails defy description, and problems of overcrowding and poor sanitation continue to plague many jails today. At best, most are warehouses for the misdemeanant, vagrant, petty offender, and common drunk. At worst, they are the festering sores described by Richard Velde, above. The jail, perhaps more than any other segment of the correctional subsystem, is resistant to change and tends to deteriorate more quickly than it can be improved.

Where Do We Put the Misdemeanant?

If overwork and overcrowding in felon institutions has increased the pressures for alternatives to incarceration, a veritable crush is seen at the misdemeanant level, where both convicted misdemeanants and pretrial felons jam the same facilities. Most misdemeanor arrests are handled by either a fine or a jail sentence. The local jail or workhouse is used as an alternative to a fine in those cases where the sentence is often stated as "30 days or $30." As long as the principal objective of the fine or jail term was punishment and/or deterrence, there was no particular problem. The sentence to the jail term usually resulted in a short period of "making little ones out of big ones,"[1] and the prisoner was *worked,* not treated. The shift to the goal of rehabilitation as the primary purpose for *all* corrections has complicated the simple punishment process of the misdemeanant system. Inadequate funds, low-quality staffing, ancient facilities, and insufficient time to work with the offender have hampered efforts to develop meaningful programs in jails and local corrections.

The jail has been the last institution in line for public and government support since John Howard inherited the abomination at Bedfordshire in 1773. The public's attention is focused on jails from time to time, usually when politicans or the media expose particularly appalling conditions in a certain jail, but they seem to revert to their original deplorable state rapidly. In a few progressive areas, facilities have been constructed to provide better conditions and programs for the misdemeanant prisoner, but these are all too few. Community programs and facilities are sometimes used to provide work and educational programs for these short-term prisoners—again, not very often. The recent availability of Law Enforcement Assistance Administration funds, however, has generated a number of pilot programs aimed at providing a workable model for the proper mix of custody and program for the future jail.

Of all the problems that plague the criminal justice system, none is more confused and irrational than the question of what should be done with the felon in the period preceding trial. Pretrial detention and procedures for pretrial liberty have been subjects of hot debate among personnel in the criminal justice subsystems for many decades. The presumption of innocence is difficult to maintain once the defendant has been arrested and detained in jail. The police find this presumption difficult to accept if they have acted on probable cause (high probability of guilt) in first making the arrest. Several projects studying the effects of pretrial decisions on sentencing are building a base of evidence that this period is critical to later correctional efforts. At least two studies have shown that pretrial detention,

TABLE 8. RELATIONSHIP BETWEEN DETENTION AND UNFAVORABLE DISPOSITION WHEN NUMBER OF FAVORABLE CHARACTERISTICS IS HELD CONSTANT

| | NUMBER OF FAVORABLE CHARACTERISTICS | | | | | | | |
| | None | | One | | Two | | Three | |
	Bail	Jail	Bail	Jail	Bail	Jail	Bail	Jail
Disposition	(%)	(%)	(%)	(%)	(%)	(%)	(%)	(%)
Sentenced to prison	[72]*	82	26	73	17	52	6	—
Convicted without prison	[6]	2	42	8	44	24	48	—
Not convicted	[22]	16	32	19	39	24	46	—
Number of defendants	(88)	(107)	(68)	(110)	(122)	(62)	(67)	(2)

*Brackets indicate the number of cases is small and the percentage should be read with caution.

TABLE 9. CASE DISPOSITIONS, BY JAIL STATUS AND CHARGE

| CHARGE | AT LIBERTY BEFORE TRIAL | | | DETAINED BEFORE TRIAL | | |
	Percent Con-victed	Percent Not Con-victed	Total Cases	Percent Con-victed	Percent Not Con-victed	Total Cases
Assault	23	77	126	59	41	128
Grand Larceny	43	57	96	72	28	156
Robbery	51	49	35	58	42	100
Dangerous Weapons	43	57	23	57	43	21
Narcotics	52	48	33	38	62	42
Sex Crimes	10	90	49	14	86	28
Others	30	70	47	78	22	23

when all other major factors are held constant, has an adverse effect on both sentencing and conviction rates. In Table 8, some of these effects are shown by data from a study in New York City.[2]

Possible extended confinement of innocent persons is recognized as a major problem, as with pretrial detention of the unadjudicated felon later found not guilty. Of those detained in jail in another New York project, the innocent detainees averaged 46 percent of the inmate population. Table 9 shows the breakdown of the figures.[3] The defendant who is innocent, and is exposed through pretrial confinement to the conditions that exist in most of the nation's jails, will probably build up considerable animosity toward the criminal justice system and corrections in particular. The convicted offender eventually sent to a correctional institution also will have negative feelings about the inequities of a system that appears to arbitrarily confine some defendants before trial, while others are released. Three goals for pretrial reform have been outlined by the National Advisory Commission:

1. Detention and other restrictions on liberty should be minimized to an extent consistent with the public interest. As noted throughout this report, incarceration as a criminal sanction is widely overused. While confinement is necessary for the small percentage of offenders who are dangerous, it has all too often been considered the standard response to crime. In the pretrial process the detention of persons awaiting trial is far too frequent and in practice is generally based not on any real or imagined public interest requirement but on the financial resources of the accused.

2. The treatment of persons awaiting trial should be consistent with the presumption of innocence. But persons awaiting trial in most jurisdictions are considered to be in the same class as persons already convicted and sentenced. They are housed together in the same degrading and inhumane facilities, they are deprived of the basic amenities of life, and they are treated as though their guilt had already been established. This is self-fulfilling prophecy, as the deprivations make preparation for trial more difficult and enhance the risk of conviction and harsher punishment.

3. The time prior to trial should be a constructive period in the life of the accused rather than one of idleness. Many persons awaiting trial require or could utilize assistance that only the state can provide. Many suffer from difficulties relating to alcohol, drugs, or physical or mental problems or defects. Frequently their confinement results from inability to cope with financial, employment, social, or family responsibilities. Yet few persons awaiting trial are accorded access to assistance. If detained, they are housed in local jails that typically have few resources, and there appears to be a feeling that programs for persons not yet convicted are neither authorized, desirable, nor deserving of high priority.[4]

The number of adult prisoners in state and federal institutions in January of 1977 was over 275,000, up sharply from the 1970 figure of 203,046. Although the percentage of prisoners in the total population has declined slightly since 1960, the *number* of prisoners has risen; we are placing prisoners into confinement at a slightly higher rate than the rate of population growth. In 1970, also, there were 153,063 adult prisoners in jails and detention centers of America, about half of them being held for trial.[5]

Again, numerous studies, like the following, have shown that at least a substantial portion of the pretrial detainees can be placed on bail or some other form of release without a significant increase in the number of those who fail to appear in court:

1. The Manhattan Summons Project—over 36,000 summonses were issued in two years, a saving of more than $2.5 million in police time plus the amount saved by not housing those who would otherwise have gone to jail.

2. The Manhattan Court Employment Project—as of June, 1970, charges against 366 men had been dropped due to their successful participation in the program.

3. The Manhattan Bail Project—of 3,505 persons released on recognizance by the end of the action phase of the project only 56 persons would have spent time in jail awaiting trial.[6]

The extensive use of probation is perhaps the most effective way to handle first offenders. Prisons tend to exacerbate offenders' weaknesses and decrease their ability to handle problems. Also, prisons often serve as schools for crime. Probation, by contrast, helps offenders adjust *to* society *in* society. The National Council on Crime and Delinquency reported some studies that point out the dramatic results *effective* probation can have:

In Michigan, fully trained officers carrying fifty-man caseloads brought about the following results:

- the number of offenders who required imprisonment was reduced 50 percent;

- 80 percent of felony offenders could be treated in the community with no significant threat to the public safety;

- the probation failure rate was reduced from 32.2 percent to 17.4 percent.

In California, a study was made of offenders in the state's Superior Court. Some were placed on probation; others were given probation plus a jail term; the remainder received straight jail sentences.
The results:

- 66 percent of felons given probation remained free of violations during the first year.

- 52 percent given *probation and jail* remained free of violations for the first year.

- 41 percent placed in *jail* remained free of violations for the first year.[7]

These and other studies reinforce the idea that imprisonment should be considered only as an alternative to community treatment, not the other way around.

Approximately 60 percent of the adult incarcarated felons across America are released on parole—100 percent of the felons in some states. It was estimated that as many as 142,000 offenders would be on conditional release from correctional institutions by 1975. The basic goal of parole authorities is to provide adequate supervision, control, assistance, and services to the parolee. The advantages and disadvantages of probation and parole were discussed in Part III. It is sufficient to state that community programs show better results than institutionalization.

Other Dispositions for the Misdemeanant

The confusion in the definition and enforcement of misdemeanor statutes is reflected in the absence of uniform techniques and systems for dealing with misdemeanants. While different states vary greatly in their approaches, and jurisdictions within states may also be inconsistent, some patterns are fairly constant. As mentioned earlier, the bulk of the misdemeanor cases are disposed of through confinement or probation. There are other alternatives for disposition as well, the most prevalent being the use of *fines*.

Fines are often called "price tag justice." In the case of the misdemeanor offenses, the fine is often offered as an *alternative* to a period of confinement, meaning that the offender who cannot pay is confined—in effect—for being *poor* rather than for the offense. The number of misdemeanor cases the lower courts must hear is a major obstacle to all but the most cursory justice. Some lower courts may hear as many as 100 or more misdemeanor cases in a single morning.[8] It is difficult, under such circumstances, to conduct any kind of in-depth diagnosis of the offender, the offense, or the offender's ability to pay a fine. The amount of fines for particular crimes is virtually standardized, and paying them is like paying forfeited bail. For the individual unable to pay, a term in the lockup is the only alternative. In some cases, however, fines can be paid on the installment plan. This procedure gives offenders a chance to keep their jobs or seek work to pay the fine. This system, combined with weekend confinement,[9] has been a major improvement in misdemeanor justice in recent years.

Other alternatives for the misdemeanant are *probation without adjudication* and *suspended sentence*. These are both variations on the same theme: holding formal disposition over the head of offenders for a period of time, often under specified conditions, and then nullifying the conviction. In probation without adjudication (also known as deferred prosecution), offenders can forego prosecution as long as they meet certain established conditions, usually for a specific period of time. The suspended sentence is used when offenders obviously do not require supervision to ensure their good behavior. This alternative is generally used in the case of first offenders considered to be so impressed with their arrest and conviction that further sanctions against them would be of little positive value.

The extent to which these alternatives are employed is not known with any degree of certainty, as little research has been performed in this area. It is apparent that the misdemeanants, like adult felons, often "fall out" of the correctional funnel before it narrows down. If they did not, the jails of the country simply could not hold them.

Misdemeanor Probation: Promise Unfulfilled

Another major alternative to confinement for the misdemeanant is *misdemeanor probation*. John Augustus was the first misdemeanant probation officer in America. Then, as today, the jails were populated mostly with drunks and vagrants. Probation, while finding its origins in the adult misdemeanor system, had its greatest growth in the juvenile and adult felon systems. While misdemeanor crime occurs in both urban and rural jurisdictions, the majority of adult misdemeanor probation services are available only in urban centers. In a large portion of the United States there is literally no probation service for the misdemeanant. In some jurisdictions probation services for felons and misdemeanants have been combined, but this has created even heavier caseloads for the already overworked probation officers.

A few states have at least nominal statewide systems for the supervision of adult misdemeanants on probation. In many of these systems, supervision is provided only if requested, making the service itself something of a farce—more of a check-in formality than a counseling process. Often the offender is seen only once a month for a few minutes, usually in the office of the probation officer. The hope and promise of the program started by Boston cobbler John Augustus have not been fulfilled in the modern version of misdemeanant probation. Some of the reasons are found in the general overload of the criminal justice system; others are found in the short-term nature of misdemeanor sentences.

Where to Make Changes

A serious problem with misdemeanant corrections lies in the hodgepodge of offenders and offenses thrown together in the short-term facilities built primarily for detention. In some misdemeanant facilities, the *felons* confined for various reasons—with no separation from misdemeanants—number as high as 50 percent. Thrown in with this group of *convicted* offenders, both misdemeanants and felons, is another large of *unconvicted* persons who are awaiting trial or other action. The unrestricted mingling of these categories of convicted and unconvicted felons and misdemeanants is the target for several pilot projects across the country. Their implementation is critical.

A number of high-impact treatment programs are specifically designed to be carried out in the brief periods covered by misdemeanant sentences. The development and expansion of these programs, with maximum involvement in the community, will greatly assist the local misdemeanor correctional workers in their efforts.

In Des Moines, Iowa, several innovative programs have been developed with significantly reduced jail population, costs, and collateral consequences of misdemeanant conviction, such as offender's loss of job, families having to go on welfare, repossession of possessions being purchased on time, and family dissolution. In implementing these programs, the state saved the average per diem cost of $4.00 per person for the literally thousands of misdemeanant cases diverted (some for over 110 days) from the jail on "Release On Personal Recognizance" (ROR): a promise by persons who could not raise bail bond to show up in court on the day of trial. Other persons not otherwise eligible for ROR (those who had committed serious crimes against the person), who were likewise unable to raise bail bond, were diverted to the Pretrial Supervision program (probation without adjudication). Still other misdemeanants (and a few felons) were diverted into the Ft. Des Moines Residential Facility for Men. In the latter, the offender contracts to perform certain tasks to resolve problems (such as getting a job, learning a trade, or participating in personal or marital counseling) which have led him to commit the crime. He is told not only that someone cares about him, but also that (1) only he can solve his own problems, (2) if he chooses not to do so he is choosing to be jailed, and (3) if he tries to solve his problems through the available opportunities he will be free.

All three of these programs have had remarkably low failure rates; only 1.8 percent of the ROR and Pretrial Supervision cases have failed to appear for trial, compared to 2.2 percent for the bail-bond procedure. The rearrest rate of the Residential Facility offenders was a mere 36 percent, compared with 50 to 70 percent for releases from penal institutions.[10]

These favorable results did not require heavy technical, vocational, professional, or academic expenditures; only those resources available in the community were used. Due to the effective use of such local resources and programs, as well as the remarkable outcomes, the National Institute of Law Enforcement and Criminal Justice has declared this to be an "exemplary project," suitable for replication in other jurisdictions. The correctional client who enters the criminal justice system as a misdemeanant may well be the future felon to be treated at the state prison. Effective correctional programs, designed to reform the misdemeanant at the earliest possible point, are crucial. The volume of misdemeanor offenders is so great that more resources *must* be provided for upgrading the facilities, programs, and the quality of personnel they encounter.

Characteristics of the Jail Today

Urban dwellers in America have responded to the need for local lockups and correctional facilities in a number of ways. The most common confinement facility is the lockup, but the size and quality of these facilities varies greatly. The difference between the one-cell lockup in a small southern town and the gigantic facilities in New York City is as great as the difference between a small-town resident and a native of New York. (The counterpart of the city lockup is the county jail, but jails, lockups, detention facilities, workhouses, and a number of other units are all commonly referred to as "jails." To simplify discussion in this chapter, we shall refer to all of these facilities as city or county jails, unless it is more meaningful to refer to them by another designation.) Policies and programs vary greatly between cities and counties, but some general descriptions and suggestions can be made in regard to city systems, dividing them into small, medium, and large categories.

It is difficult to determine just how many jails there are in America. The 1967 report by President Johnson's Commission found that in 1965 some 3,473 local jails were functioning.[11] In 1972, the National Jail Census revealed the existence of 3,921 locally administered jails which have the authority to retain adult offenders for forty-eight hours or longer.[12] These figures did not include federal and state prisons or other correctional institutions; institutions used exclusively for juveniles; or the state-operated jails of Connecticut, Delaware, and Rhode Island. The survey also did not include drunk tanks, lockups, and other facilities which retain persons for less than forty-eight hours. If one sticks to the criterion of forty-eight hours or more, the national survey figures are probably the most accurate that are available. These locally operated jails employed 44,298 persons and housed 141,588 inmates.

Since the 1970 national jail census,[13] federal funds, primarily from the Law Enforcement Assistance Administration (LEAA), have increased program and human services. For example, 86 percent of the institutions surveyed in 1970 had no exercise or recreational facilities, but in 1972 some form of recreational opportunity or entertainment was available in more than 60 percent of these facilities; almost 75 percent had exercise yards. While less than 10 percent of the jails offered adult basic education or vocational training programs, 35 percent offered alcohol treatment programs, 25 percent had drug addiction programs, and 40 percent had work release programs in which selected sentenced inmates spent part of their time working in the community. This represents a welcome increase in programming for jail residents, and is an example of programming which enlightened jail administrators can develop when funds are available. Whether these programs can continue in the absence of LEAA funds is the crucial question, and local reform groups may find their tasks even more difficult when it becomes necessary to persuade county and city commissioners to continue these programs with the support of local funds.

The latest national survey focusing on age of jail structures found 100,000 cells in 3,319 surveyed jails; more than 5,000 were at least 100 years old and another 25,000 had been in use for over 50 years. It is small wonder that the jails in America are looked upon as a disgrace by all professionals hoping for a change in the correctional system.

Physical Plants

An examination of the physical conditions in the nation's jails might best begin with a description in the 1960s of the District of Columbia Jail in the nation's capital:

> The District of Columbia Jail is a filthy example of man's inhumanity to man. It is a case study in cruel and unusual punishment, in the denial of due process, in the failure of justice.
>
> The Jail is a century old and crumbling. It is overcrowded. It offers inferior medical attention to its inmates, when it offers any at all. It chains sick men to beds. It allows—forces—men to live in crowded cells with rodents and roaches, vomit and excreta. It is the scene of arbitrary and capricious punishment and discipline. While there is little evidence of racial discrimination (the Jail "serves" the male population of the District of Columbia and is, therefore, virtually an all-black institution), there are some categories of prisoners who receive better treatment than others.
>
> The eating and living conditions would not be tolerated anywhere else. The staff seems, at best, indifferent to the horror over which it presides. This, they say, is the job society wants them to do. The facilities and amounts of time available for recreation and exercise are limited, sometimes by a guard's whim. Except for a few privileged prisoners on various details, there is no means by which an inmate may combat idleness—certainly nothing that could be called education, counselling or self-help.[14]

Unfortunately, the conditions described above are by no means unique; some jails are even worse. They range from overcrowded and overused facilities to underutilized ones, in the process of deterioration. In either case, the result is a physical plant in appalling condition. According to the 1970

National Jail Census, more than 25 percent of the jails then in use were built before 1920.

Most jails are fairly uniform in their basic structural arrangements. Usually they are designed to allow for a minimum staff while providing secure confinement for inmates. A large central cage-like structure called the "bullpen" is used for most of the nonviolent prisoners and the drunks (the latter use generated another nickname, the "tank"). Larger jails may contain several bullpens and a separate drunk tank. The central area is usually surrounded by rows of cells, facing inward toward the bullpens. Like keepers of caged animals, officials often limit contact with inmates by passing food into the bullpens and cells through slots in the doors. Thus, already minimal contact between inmates and staff is reduced still further. While lack of contact is usually justified in the name of security, it compounds the already highly impersonal atmosphere at most jails.

Sanitary facilities are another major problem, especially in the older jails. Even in those equipped with adequate plumbing and sanitary facilities, the violence and frustration of the inmates is often vented on these objects. The lack of privacy and the personal degradation associated with the open use of sanitary facilities heightens the resentment, leading inmates to vandalize the already limited equipment. Many jails visited by the 1970 National Jail Census did not have any functioning flush toilets; buckets and similarly medieval expedients still prevail in many American jails. Although toilets are a problem, the need for showers and washroom facilities is even more critical. The large percentage of drunks and others placed in the tank, some filthy with their own vomit and excrement, are often left in that condition due to a lack of adequate cleanup facilities. As stated in the National Advisory Commission: "If cleanliness is next to godliness, most jails are securely in the province of hell."[15]

Problems with Personnel

The physical plants used to house our jails reflect the multitude of problems faced by these facilities. Provision of adequate personnel is crucial to the improved operation of our jails. Most jails are operated by the law enforcement agency which has jurisdiction in the area served. Because of their mission, law enforcement officers are interested in keeping offenders *in* jail, and thus are less eager to provide correctional services than custody. Since most of the full-time operating jail personnel are also police officers, dedicated to putting offenders *into* jail, the primary emphasis is on "custodial convenience." This philosophy involves an almost fanatical concern with security, leaving responsibility for the internal operation of the jail to the inmates themselves. It is this situation that has produced the most reprehensible conditions in many of the large municipal jails. Where jail personnel are not sworn officers, but low-paid custodial individuals, the conditions become still worse. A critical need for pre-service and in-service training of jailers and other jail personnel has been clearly perceived by jail inspectors. The immediate requirement is not a vast influx of professional staff, but simple training aimed at breaking the habitual work patterns of uninterested, politically appointed, and unqualified jail personnel. Of course, the personnel situation would also be improved by higher-paid and better-qualified staffing for almost all jails. The national seven-day average ratio of jail workers to inmates is $1\frac{2}{3}:40$.[16] This ratio is only an average; the discrepancy becomes more acute during the night. The answer, however, is not so much people as *better* people in the jobs already available.

One problem with upgrading personnel and facilities has its roots in the long history of the jail "fee system," which stems from a practice in early England. The office of sheriff in those days was a position of pomp and prestige, but little work. The distasteful duty of caring for the jail and its inmates was usually sold as a concession to a "keeper" or "gaoler." Fees for the maintenance of inmates were extracted from their family, friends, or estate. Under this system, the greater the number of inmates and the longer they were kept, the more income accrued to the jailer. In order to increase his profit, the jailer cut his expenses to a minimum and operated the jail as cheaply as possible. This system remained unquestioned until 1773, when John Howard became the Sheriff of Bedfordshire.

The fee system was used in America for many years, until it was largely replaced by a variation. The inmates themselves are no longer required to pay for the privilege of remaining in jail; instead, the fees are paid to the sheriff or jailer from the county treasury. In some states, this per diem fee is paid by the state or by federal agencies with which the jail has a contract. Not surprisingly, a system that pays the sheriff to arrest and jail as many persons as possible is often exploited by the sheriffs who inherit it. Not until a salary or civil service program is devised to replace fee systems will the corruption they encourage be eliminated.

The standards for jailers and related personnel have been a matter of concern for many years. The United States Bureau of Prisons' manual *(The Jail: Its Operation and Management)* for the training of jail personnel is highlighted by the comments of Norman A. Carlson: "Changing the jail function from detention alone to one that includes correctional programming will make demands on jail personnel that they must be prepared to meet. This challenge can be met through training, leadership, and community support."[17] It is clear that the upgrading of personnel and their re-orientation to this new and challenging mission is as critical in the jail area as it is anywhere else in the criminal justice system.

The State's Role

Jails and lockups have been the traditional responsibility of city and county government. In recent years, however, the states have begun to move into this "preserve," generally by setting standards for operations and by inspections. The state's role in the reform of local adult corrections is hampered by the many political considerations involved. The states generally do not initiate programs that are action-oriented, but simply inspect and report the most glaring problems. Only a small number of states, with relatively small populations, have consolidated jail operations under state control.[18] A survey conducted in 1971 found that only seventeen states had established standards for both operational procedures and facility planning and construction.[19]

Because of the variety of needs within a state, the overall authority for jails may be most effectively organized by a comprehensive or regional community center approach, but this is difficult because of the expensive interjurisdictional planning and coordination that must take place. Nevertheless, this approach offers a valuable opportunity to achieve a balance between the overcrowded and underused facilities that are often located near each other, though in different jurisdictions. Regionalization is not a panacea, however, and the cost of transporting prisoners, along with the effect of removal from their home community, must be considered. In large urban centers a network of services may be more appropriate. The network concept envisions a group of facilities throughout an area, each designed to perform a particular function. Ideally, a network would allow for progression of inmates to programs or facilities geared to their individual needs. Whether a state chooses to develop regional or network jail service systems, the active participation of the state correctional agency is essential. Movement toward a statewide network of graduated correctional services can best be accomplished if the state has at least some control over jail operations.

Community Correctional Centers: A New Wave?

Whether regionally oriented or part of an urban network, in years to come the jail will eventually evolve into a "community correctional center." This center will be geared to provide residential care to the four major categories of inmates: persons awaiting trial, persons serving sentences, persons moving between major institutions, and short-term returnees. These inmates will be served in the center only after the court has exhausted all diversionary and alternative possibilities, such as release on own recognizance, release under supervision, use of summons and warrants by police, etc. In the case of pretrial inmates, it must be stressed that these individuals will not have been found guilty of a crime. Nothing in their treatment or detention programs should imply guilt. In the 1972 jail census it was found that 58 percent of the jail population had not been convicted, but was awaiting arraignment or trial. Yet because they were being held in jail, these suspects were subjected to conditions worse than those in many prisons for offenders convicted of major felonies. Unconvicted detainees should be kept separate from the convicted population and from those who are mentally or

FIGURE VII–1. The Cleveland Reintegration Center, a Former Home for Unwed Mothers (Courtesy Ohio Department of Rehabilitation and Correction)

physically ill. Community correctional centers can be planned to provide the categories of security and treatment needed. There are many pitfalls to avoid in this area of reform, however, and administrators must move with caution when trying to develop correctional care programs.

Another advantage of the community correctional center accrues to the sentenced offender. The jail has been used traditionally as the confinement ground for misdemeanants, while felons go to state prison. There is now considerable reason to believe that it might be effective to treat nondangerous felons the same as misdemeanants. This philosophy may be a bit advanced for most jurisdictions, and probably community correctional centers will continue to handle only the minor offender and misdemeanant, for some time. However, imaginative community treatments for the convicted offender, including work release, study release, and weekend sentences, have already been used by many jurisdictions. Some jurisdictions having small halfway houses may consider using these facilities for deserving jailed offenders.

In addition, early release opportunities, such as parole or release to a small halfway house, which are generally available for felons in state institutions, should be offered to community correctional center inmates. Such programs are less costly than incarceration, can serve as incentives for inmates, and avoid the dangers of protracted unnecessary confinement.

For too long the local jail has been used as a place of total confinement for all who were sent there. Much more imagination and variety need to be employed to assure that sentenced offenders are not worse off when leaving than upon arrival.[20]

Community correctional centers would allow offenders access to the kind of program found in halfway-*out* and halfway-*in* houses. Offenders preparing for release from state institutions could be transferred to community centers, from which they could be gradually reintegrated into the mainstream of life. They might also use the centers for help and guidance when they felt in danger of reverting to criminal behavior. This two-way model is used throughout the mental health field, where outpatient service and temporary voluntary recommitment have helped to avoid major problems and render more effective treatment.

The community correctional center is a reasonable alternative to the traditional jail and an important move toward the integration of all correctional services within a state or regional area. In order for these centers to be effective, emphasis must be placed on the proper programs, including:

- Accurate observation of the individual.

- Intensive staff-client interaction.

- Opportunities for reality confrontation and reality testing.

- Discussions.

- Choice.

- Positive leisure-time options.

- Optimal living and constructive learning situations.

- Community and group interaction.[21]

Jail Planning and Administration

Movement toward and acceptance of community correctional centers will probably come about slowly, and realistic jail administrators will have to plan carefully to change facilities and programs that already exist. Jail administrators are not expected to be planning experts. Many of the plans and programs that they initiate must be based on what the community will allow. But before new facilities are built or major changes implemented, jail administrators should assist in the planning in the following manner:

1. by defining the problem—presenting information that demonstrates the need to assess the jail;

2. by supplying information about present and future needs of the jail, including the physical plant and program;

3. by coordinating studies in the jail that will supply information to the study group;

4. by defining the role and objectives of the jail to the planning group and the community;

5. by influencing planning strategies—suggesting the kinds of persons who should be a part of the planning group; and

6. by insisting on a systematic approach to planning and involving other local and state criminal justice agencies in the planning process.[22]

An active role by the jail administrator will assure that change, no matter how well intended, does not develop in the wrong direction. The National Advisory Commission suggests ways to prevent this problem:

At least two kinds of investment should be *postponed* in any statewide jail reform program based on a phased-stage implementation of state standards; the building of new jails and the hiring of more personnel. Investment in new jails, or the major refurbishing of old ones, would merely cement in the old problems under somewhat more decent conditions. . . . Increasing the number of personnel in existing jails would only have the effect of giving more persons a vested interest in maintaining the status quo and contribute to greater resistance to future change. By and large, new buildings and more staff should come only after the potential effects of criminal law reform and diversion alternatives have been fully considered. Such collateral reforms, combined with an increasing tendency toward regionalization of jails, would require fewer jails and fewer, but better qualified and trained, jail personnel.[23]

The most important single need for jail reform is a strong and well-informed administration. Leadership such as that exhibited by Winston E. Moore, Executive Director of Cook County's Department of Corrections, can turn a system previously declared a disgrace into one that is a model for large urban jails. The Programmed Activity for Correctional Education

(PACE) program associated with the Cook County Jail is briefly described as follows:

> Pace Institute was founded in 1967 as a private philanthropic organization operating behind the walls of the Cook County Jail, as a demonstration that constructive educational and vocational training of youthful inmates will reduce considerably the number of men who return to prison. Pace Institute provides basic education in reading, writing and arithmetic; pre-vocational and vocational training in automotive repair, building trades, metal work, welding and soldering, electrical work, drafting, tailoring, pipe assembly. There are classes in science, constitutional government, in communication and social skills including listening and speaking. There is expert instruction in every case, to help insure the trainee's ability to enter a trade school, or high school, or college, or to secure employment at his level of competence.
>
> Through the methods it has developed and through the remarkable dedication of its staff, Pace Institute has become the means for motivating men and clothing them with the pride of some education, ability, achievement.
>
> With the facilities presently available, in its own building, Pace Institute has been able to serve 175 trainees each year. The backlog of applicants and the success of Pace's work have made it imperative that a new two-story building be built, so that a total of at least 400 trainees may be accommodated in Pace Institute's intensive educational and vocational programs.[24]

Jail administrators have an obligation to society to seek methods that can work in their own communities. Administrators are the practitioners who, with community involvement, must break the tradition of neglect and indifference that is the legacy of the jail. Unless vigorous and imaginative leadership is exhibited, even revitalized jails soon regress to their squalid past.

Jail Diversion Programs: A Better Way

While improvement in jail facilities and upgrading of jail personnel take a great deal of time and money, many other helpful procedures can be initiated more simply. Some were recommended back in 1937, by the National Jail Committee of the American Correctional Association. The fact that so many of these suggestions would still benefit jails today, almost forty years later, reflects the general esistance to change that characterizes most of our jail system.

I. *Measures to Keep People Out of Jail*

1. By law direct that the courts adopt a more extended use of bail, recognizance, and other approved measures of release from custody.

2. Secure a law providing for collection of fines by installment and for sufficient personnel to enforce it.

3. Develop an approved probation system, not only to prevent people from getting into jail, but to supervise and guide offenders released from custody.

II. *Fundamental Changes in Jail Set-up*

4. Abolish the locally controlled jail as a place for convicted prisoners.

5. Place the jail and all its present functions wholly within the state correction system and under centralized control.

6. Reorganize the system to provide for secure and suitable detention places, properly staffed and equipped for segregation, classification of prisoners charged with law breaking.

7. Establish regional farms and/or custodial centers for care, training, and needed treatment, with a regular work program under rigid discipline.

8. Eliminate the fee system in connection with arrest, trial, and custody of prisoners, and place all fee officers on fixed salary.

III. *Reform in Law and Court Action*

9. Simplify law and court procedures with regard to all arrested persons.

10. Adopt measures and reforms to shorten time spent in detention quarters by prisoners awaiting trial, witnesses, appeals, etc.

11. Secure an indeterminate sentence law with specified minimum sentence.

IV. *Standards and Records*

12. Fix minimum standards for custodians of prisoners and probation workers with merit system safeguards.

13. Establish a central state bureau of identification and records.

14. Create a uniform system of records and statistics for the whole correctional set-up, *jails included.*[25]

The most effective way to reform inmates is either to keep them out of jail or release them as soon as possible. Pretrial diversion,[26] increased use of bail and personal recognizance, more extensive use of fines (including time payments), and various forms of work and study release are all viable alternatives to the destructive and expensive enforced idleness in most jails. Jails have proven highly resistant to change in the past and can be expected to remain so in the future. Until jails as we know them become historical relics and are replaced by integrated community correctional centers, the best policy is to search for ways to keep people out of them and still protect the citizenry.

REVIEW QUESTIONS

I. Find the answers to the following in the text:

1. Why has the fee system been such a detriment to jail progress?

2. What effect does the changing role in corrections have on jail operations?

3. The community correctional center is a new concept. Does it differ much from the jails today? How?

4. What is the area of greatest weakness in the jails? Is more personnel the answer? Why or why not?

II. Words to identify:

1. lockup

2. stockade

3. bullpen

4. tank

5. fee system

6. *per diem* rates

7. community correctional center

   8. PACE

   9. jail diversion

  10. personal recognizance

NOTES

1. This refers to the practice at some early prisons of breaking large rocks into gravel and other road materials, by hand, with sledgehammers.

2. Charles E. Ares et al., "The Manhattan Bail Project: An Interim Report on the Use of Pretrial Parole," *New York University Law Review* 38 (1963): 67, 85.

3. Ann Rankin, "The Effect Pretrial Detention," *New York University Law Review* 39 (1964): 654.

4. National Advisory Commission on Criminal Justice Standards and Goals, *Corrections* (Washington, D.C.: U.S. Government Printing Office, 1973), p. 101.

5. Law Enforcement Assistance Administration, *National Jail Census, 1970: A Report on the Nation's Local Jails and Types of Inmates* (Washington, D.C.: U.S. Government Printing Office, 1973).

6. National Council on Crime and Delinquency, *Policies and Background Information* (Hackensack, N.J.: National Council on Crime and Delinquency, 1972), p. 19.

7. *Policies and Background Information,* p. 15.

8. National Advisory Commission on Criminal Justice Standards and Goals, *Courts* (Washington, D.C.: U.S. Government Printing Office, 1973), p. 161.

9. *Weekend confinement* is a system which allows convicted offenders to serve their sentence in a series of weekends. This allows them to continue to work in the community and to support their families.

10. Law Enforcement Assistance Administration, *A Handbook on Community Correction in Des Moines* (Washington, D.C.: U.S. Government Printing Office, 1972), p. 66.

11. The President's Commission on Law Enforcement and Administration of Justice, *Task Force Report: Corrections* (Washington, D.C.: U.S. Government Printing Office, 1967), p. 163.

12. U.S. Department of Justice, *The Nation's Jails* (Washington, D.C.: U.S. Government Printing Office, 1975), p. 1.

13. U.S. Department of Justice, *1970 National Jail Census* (Washington, D.C.: U.S. Government Printing Office, 1971), p. 1.

14. National Advisory Commission on Criminal Justice Standards and Goals, *Corrections* (Washington, D.C.: U.S. Government Printing Office, 1973), p. 275.

15. National Advisory Commission, *Corrections,* p. 276.

16. National Advisory Commission, *Corrections,* p. 276.

17. Nick Pappas, *The Jail: Its Operation and Management* (Lompoc, Calif.: Federal Prison Industries, 1971), p. v.

18. Alaska, Connecticut, Delaware, Rhode Island, and Vermont in 1972 (National Advisory Commission, *Corrections,* p. 292).

19. National Advisory Commission, *Corrections,* p. 278.

20. National Advisory Commission, *Corrections,* p. 287.

21. National Advisory Commission, *Corrections,* p. 287.

22. Pappas, *The Jail,* p. 175.

23. National Advisory Commission, *Corrections,* p. 279.

24. From promotional and information materials supplied by the PACE Institute, Chicago, 1973.

25. Harry Elmer Barnes and Negley K. Teeters, *New Horizons in Criminology,* 3d ed. (Englewood Cliffs, N.J.: Prentice-Hall, 1959), pp. 399-400.

26. Joan E. Jacoby, *Pre-Trial Screening in Perspective* (Washington, D.C.: U.S. Department of Justice, 1976).

26 State Prison Systems

In truth, then, it seems that our prisons are not correctional institutions at all but rather "crime hatcheries"
which produce men and women more deviant,
disturbed and finely skilled in criminal ways than when
they were first admitted.

CLAUDE PEPPER

Correctional Institutions: The Core of the System

This chapter discusses the systems which contain the correctional institutions in state-operated programs for offenders—approximately 200 major juvenile and 350 adult prisons.[1] Detention centers, jails, workhouses, and other facilities for misdemeanants and minor offenders are not included, since they are generally operated at the local level. The major correctional institutions contained in the state systems are maximum, medium, and minimum security prisons, modeled after the nineteenth-century concept. These institutions form the core of most state correctional programs, with the simultaneous functions of punishment and reform. Most are short on money and personnel, but they are still expected to prevent their graduates from returning to crime. Security and custody is the primary emphasis in these prisons, isolated in philosophy and location from the mainstream of urban life. A former director of the Federal Bureau of Prisons described the ironic situation in 1948:

> Even our modern prison system is proceeding on a rather uncertain
> course because its administration is necessarily a series of
> compromises. On the one hand, prisons are expected to punish; on the
> other, they are supposed to reform. They are expected to discipline
> rigorously at the same time that they teach self-reliance. They are built
> to be operated like vast impersonal machines, yet they are expected to
> fit men to live normal community lives. They operate in accordance
> with a fixed autocratic routine, yet they are expected to develop
> individual initiative. All too frequently restrictive laws force prisoners
> into idleness despite the fact that one of their primary objectives is to

teach men how to earn an honest living. They refuse a prisoner a voice in self-government, but they expect him to become a thinking citizen in a democratic society. To some, prisons are nothing but "country clubs" catering to the whims and fancies of the inmates. To others the prison atmosphere seems charged only with bitterness, rancor and an all-pervading sense of defeat. And so the whole paradoxical scheme continues, because our ideas and views regarding the function of correctional institutions in our society are confused, fuzzy and nebulous.[2]

Correctional institutions are both a blessing and a curse. Reflecting a positive and humane movement away from the cruel punishments of the eighteenth century, they provided an alternative to death and flogging. In terms of changing inmates so that they can lead a noncriminal life in the free world, prisons have obviously failed. Still, the public's perceived need for security and the prison's effectiveness in isolating offenders from society have unfortunately made it the primary answer to criminal misbehavior.

The almost 200,000 inmates confined in correctional institutions for adults in 1971 were distributed in maximum, medium, and minimum institutions as follows:[3]

TABLE 10. POPULATION OF STATE CORRECTIONAL FACILITIES FOR ADULTS, BY SECURITY CLASSIFICATION OF INMATES

CLASSIFICATION	INMATES	PERCENT OF TOTAL POPULATION
Maximum	109,920	56%
Medium	57,505	29
Minimum	28,485	15
Total	195,910	100%

The general trend today is toward medium rather than maximum security. Most medium security prisons were built in the twentieth century, in accordance with the development of behavioral science concepts. In fact, over fifty of the existing one hundred ten medium security correctional institutions were built in the last twenty-five years. While many of the ideals of early prison reformers could be realized in some medium security institutions, the primary emphasis remains security. The medium security correctional institution may well be the last resort in most state systems in the future, since it provides much the same security as the maximum security prison but without the latter's oppressive and destructive atmosphere. The minimum security prison all too frequently tends to sacrifice individual programs to the needs of the farm or work camp activities.

Organization of State Systems

Over 5,300 American correctional facilities were identified in 1971 in a national survey by the Law Enforcement Assistance Administration. Notably, only 16 percent of these facilities were under the control of state agencies. It is not surprising that the so-called correctional "system" in most states is not really systematized at all:

> All but four states have highly fragmented correctional systems, vesting various correctional responsibilities in either independent boards or noncorrectional agencies. In forty-one states, an assortment of health, welfare, and youth agencies exercise certain correctional responsibilities, though their primary function is not corrections.
>
> In over forty states, neither state nor local governments have full-scale responsibility for comprehensive correctional services. Some corrections services, particularly parole and adult and juvenile institutions, are administered by state agencies, while others, such as probation, local institutions and jails, and juvenile detention, are county or city responsibilities.
>
> More than half of the states provide no standard-setting or inspection services to local jails and local adult correctional institutions.[4]

Organizational rigidity has handicapped meaningful revision and modernization of corrections. Rehabilitation and reintegration require that organizational structures be concerned with more than just institutional programs. In at least five states, this organizational need has been met by exercising control over all correctional activities at the state level.

There are two general patterns for organization of corrections at the state level: the establishment of a separate department of corrections (with a director appointed by the governor), or a division within a larger state department. Most correctional administrators consider the *separate department* to be more effective. Having the director at the cabinet level adds great flexibility and prestige to the correctional operation. Without an intermediate level of organization, the director of a separate department has the ability to move more freely at the policy-making level. An autonomous department is more able to control the allocation of personnel and fiscal resources without competition from other divisions within the same department. Centralized control also has the advantage of providing more effective administration functions that are unique to correctional problems.

Corrections is a "human resource" organization. As such, it is not amenable to analysis by use of charts or the development of expenditure measures and empirical criteria. Human resources management presents special problems:

Managing a human resource organization is probably even more difficult than managing other public agencies because many traditional management tools are not directly applicable. Data describing effects of the correctional process relate to behavior or attitudes and are subject to subjective, frequently conflicting interpretations. The feedback loops necessary for judging the consequences of policies are difficult to create and suffer from incomplete and inaccurate information. There has not been in corrections an organized and consistent relation between evaluative research and management action.

The management of corrections as a human resource organization must be viewed broadly in terms of how offenders, employees, and various organization processes (communications, decisionmaking, and others) are combined into what is called "the corrections process."[5]

The corrections process must include a system of multi-level programs and facilities to provide the spectrum of services required to make a statewide program work. Most state correctional systems are concerned only with the major institutions and parole services, leaving the majority of correctional problems in the state to units of local government.

Classification and Assignment in a State System

Most state codes provide for the "separation or classification of prisoners, their division into different grades with promotion or degradation according to merit or demerit, their employment and instruction in industrial pursuits, and their education." Most also stipulate that reformation of prisoners is a primary goal, though there are some exceptions—California, for example, now advocates punishment.

One of the crucial areas in corrections is the initial classification and assignment of convicted offenders. The American Correctional Association *Manual of Correctional Standards* states that: "The primary objective of classification as a systematic process is the development and administration of an integrated and realistic program of treatment for the individual, with procedures for changing the program when indicated."[6] Five general approaches are recognized:

1. Analysis of individual problems through the use of every available diagnostic technique;

2. Evolution of a treatment and training program in staff conference, with participation of the inmate;

3. Implementation of the recommended program;

FIGURE VII-2. Classification Committee Hearing (Courtesy Federal
Bureau of Prisons)

4. Revision when indicated;

5. Relating of the institutional program to the planned parole program.

In line with these approaches, effective operation of a classification
system rests upon several elements—facilities and personnel to supply
diagnostic information, a philosophy of treatment directed at inmate needs
rather than institution convenience, diversification of treatment programs,
and genuine opportunity for the inmate to participate in planning his or her
own program.

Diagnostic information is assembled through several channels. One of the
most important documents is the presentence investigation provided by the
courts. Information can also be gathered from the inmates, their families,
community agencies, and official records. Other information is gathered by
administration of diagnostic examination, such as psychological aptitude and
educational tests. Observations by staff members who have contact with
inmates are also valuable. From these sources a picture of the needs and
aspirations of the individual inmates emerges.

In most systems, initial classification determines the institution to which
an inmate will be assigned. At the receiving institution, a determination is
made as to whether the individual shall remain in minimum security or be
transferred to a medium or maximum security penitentiary. (Each state has
at least one maximum security institution, designed to hold anyone assigned
to it.) In most states, transfer decisions rest to a considerable extent upon the
perceived ability of the individual to handle a lesser degree of security. Also

important is an evaluation of the individual's ability to adjust to a program geared primarily to work, to academic or vocational training, or to the needs of older offenders. A classification committee usually participates in making these decisions.

The classification process continues at the institutional level. While each transfer institution has different program emphases, each provides some version of education, counseling, and the other ingredients of a total program. Theoretically, individuals are assigned according to their needs; realistically, assignments are too often made to conform to institution needs. For example, an inmate may genuinely aspire to learn welding. If the welding class is filled—as it often may be—but there is a vacancy in the furniture shop, the inmate may be assigned to the furniture shop; no effort would be made to provide additional welding instruction. Also, inmates will often be assigned to a maintenance operation, such as food service or janitorial work, which is unlikely to conform to their own vocational ambitions.

An essential element of effective classification is provision for a periodic review of the inmate's progress through the recommended program. All institutions allow for this reevaluation, usually called reclassification. The purpose is to adjust the program in accordance with the inmate's progress and needs. Realistically, again, decisions are all too frequently made on the basis of available vacancies and institutional needs. Institution personnel may genuinely wish to provide the recommended program for an inmate; however, the need to keep the institution going inevitably shapes their decisions. They may rationalize maintenance assignments on the basis that many inmates need the experiences of accepting supervision, developing regular work habits, learning to relate to fellow-workers, and the like. This may be true, but treatment staff members are no less frustrated than inmates when prescribed programs are ignored. The classification and assignment process described above is only a composite example of what the more effective programs provide.

Development of State Systems

Each type of state correctional system has developed as a matter of historical accident as well as in response to the particular needs of the state. As might be expected, the large industrial prisons are more in evidence in the major industrial states, generally in the area between Illinois and New York. Most of these institutions were built early in the prison movement and designed to take advantage of the cheap labor force inmates represented. They were the hardest hit by the restrictions the government later placed on prison industries. At present, the industry allowed in these giant institutions does not provide full employment for the large inmate populations. In an effort to spread the few jobs among many inmates, personnel try to slow down

FIGURE VII-3. A Prison Farm of the 1960s (Courtesy Ohio
Department of Rehabilitation and Correction)

production and make the work last as long as possible. These procedures are
not likely to equip the inmate for job success on the outside. The general
picture of activity in the now-defunct industrial prisons is one of idleness
and boredom. Despite even the most dedicated attempts by the staff, there
are just not enough meaningful jobs or other programs to help the huge
populations housed in the Jacksons, Atticas, and San Quentins of the
country.

The prison farm pattern was developed in the southern states. These farms
became very profitable ventures for the states, and thus have been slow to
change. Prisoners serving on public works and state farms replaced slave
labor in many states, not only in the South. Here again, authorities might
rationalize that the training received from farm work helps to prepare
offenders for return to a basically agrarian Southern economy, but the intent
was to use free labor to produce farm products. Cheap prison labor was
often leased out to farm owners, at a great profit both to the farmer and to
the state that collected the fee. The practice of prison farms has become less
profitable, however, with the advent of highly mechanized farming methods
in the agricultural states.

Other regions in the country have designated certain institutions as
farm-oriented. The food produced in these institutions has been used to feed
the rest of the institutions in the state. Many states have now begun to
abandon this practice, since it has been realized that farming experience is of
little value to the primarily urban inmate found in most contemporary

prisons. Another problem has been the pressure from farm organizations, who argue that such competition from the state is unfair—much as union workers did with regard to prison industries.

Other states have chosen to set up work camps and other forms of prisoner activity appropriate to their particular needs. Lumber camps have been used, as have road prisons or camps to construct and maintain roads. Some more recent versions of the work camp concept have been geared to provide a combination of hard work in the outdoors and programmed treatment aimed at preparing the offender for release. In general, it is considered more beneficial for offenders to do time in the relatively healthful atmosphere of a small work camp than to languish in the idleness and boredom of the prison.

Inmates in State Prisons

In 1974, the Law Enforcement Assistance Administration commissioned a national survey of inmates[7] in correctional facilities in the United States and found an estimated 191,400 offenders under the jurisdiction of state correctional authorities. Since that study was conducted, the population of state prisons has skyrocketed to over 226,000. Almost all of these inmates (98 percent) had been sentenced, but 2 percent had been committed for study and observation prior to sentencing, were voluntarily committed drug addicts submitting to treatment in lieu of sentencing, were either awaiting trial or release on bond or were being held temporarily prior to transfer to other authorities, such as the military or another state's correctional system.

An overwhelming majority of the inmates (97 of every 100) were males. Whites outnumbered other racial groups by 51 to 49 percent, and blacks represented 47 percent of the total. All but a scant 1 percent were at least 18 years of age, and 75 percent of all inmates were between the ages of 18 and 34, a grouping which accounts for only 40 percent of the general population. The average age of inmates was between 20 and 24.

As a group, state prison inmates had less education than their counterparts in the civilian population. Sixty-one percent of the inmates had not received a high school diploma, in contrast to 36 percent of the general population 18 years of age or older.

Although a fairly young group, 48 percent had never been married, 25 percent were divorced or separated, 24 percent were married, and 3 percent were widowed. Since admission to prison, about 11 percent had changed their marital status, primarily through divorce. Inmates were underrepresented in terms of military service; only one in four had served in the armed forces. Of those who had served, 54 percent had received an honorable discharge.

Two out of three prisoners had been employed at least part-time prior to the crime which led to their incarceration (the instant offense). Almost 70 percent had worked primarily as nonfarm laborers, operatives, craftsmen, or service workers. Their use of alcohol and drugs was discouragingly high. Forty-three percent of the inmates had been drinking alcoholic beverages at the time of their instant offense, and another 26 percent had been under the influence of an illicit drug, primarily marijuana.

In terms of their criminal offenses, almost 60 percent had committed one of the "big three" crimes: robbery, burglary, or homicide. The average sentence length imposed was seven years, although 12 percent of the prisoners were incarcerated under life sentences. Seventy percent had incurred at least one other sentence, in addition to the instance offense, and roughly 1 in 3 had served time as a juvenile offender. There were many repeat offenders: 52 percent had been sentenced at least twice for the same type of offense. A total of 56 percent had previously been on probation as adult or youthful offenders, and almost 38 percent had previously received parole.

These data suggest the dimensions of the difficulties faced in the state systems, and indicate the inefficiency and general failure of current uncoordinated correctional systems.

A Citizens' Task Force Looks at a State System

Ohio is a fairly representative state, with its fair share of nineteenth-century institutions. But in contrast to many other states, Ohio is reaching for solutions to the prison dilemma, trying to improve and progress. In February 1971, the governor established a Citizens' Task Force in response to grievances of prison employees and inmates, and increasing difficulties facing correctional administrators. Because these problems were seen as symptomatic of broader, deeper, and more complicated issues, the Task Force decided to examine and evaluate the very nature of the correctional system itself, and to offer recommendations for solving immediate and long-range problems. In ten months this group studied in detail the areas of administration, institutional processes and services, correctional law and inmate affairs, and community-based services.[8]

The adult correctional system in Ohio was, at that time, one of the major divisions of the Department of Mental Hygiene and Correction. The division was responsible for seven major correctional institutions housing some 9,100 inmates, as well as an Adult Parole Authority which provided a variety of services to approximately 4,900 persons, the majority of whom were on parole.

The major institutions ranged in size from 2,000 (Ohio State Reformatory) to less than 300 (Ohio Reformatory for Women). In general, the prison population was found to be young, disproportionately black, from the lower classes, predominately male, and suffering from a variety of educational, vocational, social, medical, psychological, and psychiatric handicaps. These findings were reaffirmed by the 1974 national survey.

More than 70 percent had been previously incarcerated, at an average per-person operational cost to the state of $2,513 in 1970. Over 95 percent of those incarcerated were scheduled for eventual release into society, most on parole—at an annual cost per person of approximately $400. Of those paroled, it was predicted that approximately one in ten would return to crime while still on parole, and end up in prison as a result. In all, the estimated annual cost of crime in Ohio in 1971 exceeded one billion dollars.

The adult correctional system seemed to be predicated on an assumption that long sentences would further correctional rehabilitation of offenders. This assumption is patently false. In fact, most of Ohio's correctional administrators agreed that: (a) sentences are generally too long, and (b) many inmates derive the maximum benefit of incarceration during the first few years and often tend to go "downhill" in their behavior and attitudes after that, with resultant hostility and increased potential for further crime after release.

In attempting to make an evaluation, the Task Force asked: "What should Ohio expect of a correctional system?" Before any realistic and intelligent assessment of the state's prison system could be undertaken, that fundamental question had to be answered. The consensus of opinion suggested that it could be answered in one word: *PROTECTION*.

A correctional system should provide maximum feasible protection against violence, invasion of property rights, and all other lawlessness. The entire program of the system should be aimed toward that single objective. Mounting fear and anxiety engendered by an increase in lawlessness threatens the basic fabric of society. A free society simply will not endure in the atmosphere of pervasive terror which emerges when citizens feel increasingly vulnerable to criminal acts.

The increase of crime is a phenomenon which cannot be attributed entirely to an inadequate correctional program. But the system of prisons and corrections must share at least part of the blame. Prisons have been justifiably labeled "schools for crime." An intolerable rate of recidivism overwhelmingly attests to the bankruptcy of rehabilitative and educational programs in the penal institutions. And those who are sent there have already proven themselves threats to the peace and tranquility of our society.

If any correctional system hopes to achieve the sole purpose which can be legitimately assigned to it, that of protecting against the enormous cost and burden of criminal conduct—a cost which must be measured in loss of life as well as loss of property—the Task Force found that basic changes needed to be made:

1. Human beings cannot be placed in barbaric
   institutions, subjected to a total deprivation of any
   semblance of dignity and respect, with any
   reasonable expectation that upon their release they

will suddenly begin to conform their conduct to the requirements of the law and to act in a responsible fashion.

2. If prison society is itself lawless, if life within prison walls is regulated without regard to basic notions of justice and fair play, those who emerge from that society are apt to conduct themselves outside of prisons in the same manner in which they have learned to survive within prisons.

3. The rules which regulate those who are incarcerated should be designed to instill a respect for the rights of others and an awareness of the responsibilities of living in a free and open society.

4. Incarceration is employed altogether too frequently as a means of dealing with criminal offenders. Every conceivable alternative to imprisonment should be explored before any individual is committed to an institution.[9]

The Task Force, when it examined those problems, kept in mind the overwhelming public interest and stake in a safe and decent society. It asserted that *Ohio must cease sending so many people to prison as a "solution" to the crime problem, and that wherever possible, alternatives to incarceration must be found.*[10]

The public has been led to believe that the criminal justice system—particularly corrections—prevents crime. As presently structured, it does not. Corrections alone cannot deal effectively with the problems of crime. Consequently, alternatives to incarceration are publicly being examined and accepted by more citizens across the nation today than ever before. This is in part due to news media coverage of the criminal justice system, public forums, citizen task forces, and economic realities—all of which contribute to widespread questioning of the traditional correctional processes for handling and correcting law offenders. Correctional programs based in the community are not new: however, their potential has yet to be recognized and developed by corrections, and their effectiveness and economy have yet to be supported and accepted in many jurisdictions.

Included in the concept of community-based corrections are effective probation and parole services, selective use of work release, study release, and home furlough programs, and the development of halfway houses and prerelease guidance centers. These will be discussed in later chapters.

A Summary of State Systems

The state correctional systems in America are as diverse as the states themselves. It has been our intent to give an overview of some of the

FIGURE VII-4. One of the Newest State Prisons (Courtesy Ohio
Department of Rehabilitation and Correction)

problems that face most correctional administrators when they are trying to
model a unified and coordinated system of corrections within the framework
of fragmented and antiquated institutions and procedures. The prison remains the core of most state correctional systems, despite its patent failure as
a means of rehabilitation or reintegration of offenders, the current missions
of corrections. Classification of inmates and subsequent assignment and
reassignment is still based more on the needs of the institutions and security
than on individual programs. A few states have seen the advantage of a
correctional system that is controlled by the state at all levels, but most are
still moving toward an autonomous department of corrections for the 12 to
18 percent of offenders who now fall under state control. Movements to
absorb all correctional programs under the state's supervision and control
encounter almost insurmountable political and practical obstacles at every
step.

State correctional systems are composed of inheritances from a sometimes
well-intentioned but often inhumane past. The purposes that many of the
crumbling institutions were built for and the procedures for operating them
are no longer in tune with society or behavioral science. The cry to tear
down these monuments is a valid one, but practicalities dictate that public
safety must be assured before this can be done. While many new programs
outside the prisons are being attempted, they must be proven effective before
they will be widely accepted. Much progress is being made, sometimes at
the prodding of citizen groups such as the Ohio Citizens' Task Force on Corrections. The investigations of that group uncovered the general condition

of a typical state system of the 1970s. Programs and problems within particular types of institutions have been discussed in previous chapters. Next, we will examine a truly centralized and integrated correctional system, the federal system.

REVIEW QUESTIONS

I. Find the answers to the following in the text:

1. What is the paradox that faces the correctional institution when it attempts to rehabilitate and reintegrate offenders?

2. What problem derives from organizational rigidity in state correctional systems?

3. What is the general consensus of the primary mission expected of a state correctional system?

4. Why are alternatives to incarceration beginning to be so appealing to citizen groups and correctional administrators?

5. What characteristics were found to be prevalent among inmates of state prisons?

II. Words to identify:

1. organizational rigidity

2. corrections department

3. division of corrections

4. human resources management

5. classification and assignment

6. road camps

7. lumber camps

8. protection

9. citizens' task force

10. fragmentation of services

NOTES

1. U.S. Department of Justice, *Survey of Inmates in Adult Correctional Facilities: 1974* (Washington, D.C.: National Criminal Justice Information and Statistics Service, 1976). A national survey of inmates in 1974 identified 701 adult correctional facilities, including community correctional centers, work release centers, prison and road camps, reception and prerelease centers, etc. There are approximately 350 major prisons in America.

2. Quoted in Harry Elmer Barnes and Negley K. Teeters, *New Horizons in Criminology,* 3d ed. (Englewood Cliffs, N.J.: Prentice-Hall, 1959), pp. 461-462.

3. National Advisory Commission on Criminal Justice Standards and Goals, *Corrections,* (Washington, D.C.: U.S. Government Printing Office, 1973), p. 344.

4. National Advisory Commission, *Corrections,* p. 440.

5. National Advisory Commission, *Corrections,* p. 442.

6. American Correctional Association, *Manual of Correctional Standards* (Washington, D.C.: ACA, 1966).

7. *Survey of Inmates, 1974.* The 1977 prison population in state systems jumped to 226,000.

8. The bulk of this section is drawn form Section A of the *Final Report* by the Ohio Citizens' Task Force on Corrections (Columbus, O.: State of Ohio, 1971).

9. Ohio Citizens' Task Force, *Final Report,* p. A-4.

10. Ohio Citizens' Task Force, *Final Report,* p. A-5.

27 The Federal System

That there is hereby established in the Department of Justice a Bureau of Prisons . . . responsible for the safekeeping, care, protection, instruction and discipline of all persons charged with or convicted of offenses against the United States.

Acts Approved by President Hoover
May 14 and May 27, 1930

Creation of the Federal Bureau of Prisons

In 1930, there were only seven federal prisons, less than one-sixth of the number of institutions in the federal prison system today. The seven original prisons were all funded separately by Congress and operated under policies and regulations established individually by the wardens. The federal government had over 12,000 offenders in these institutions and an equal number in state and local facilities. All prisons of that era, federal as well as state, were little more than human warehouses. They were badly overcrowded, some containing double the population they were built for. Inmates often slept in basements, corridors, and makeshift dormitories.

In 1929, a congressional committee was established to study conditions in federal prisons. In the same year, a correctional study group chosen to develop the federal prison system outlined a penal philosophy providing practical steps to improve the national prisons. This philosophy recognized that the chief mission of prisons was to protect the public, but that protection could be best achieved by rehabilitation of inmates, almost all of whom would eventually be released from custody and returned to the community.

Based on the recommendations of the congressional committee and the correctional study group, legislation was proposed which resulted in an Act of Congress, signed by President Hoover on May 14, 1930. This legislation

The bulk of the material in this chapter has been adapted from *Federal Bureau of Prisons 1975* (Washington, D.C.: U.S. Department of Justice, 1975). The authors are grateful for the permission to use this material, modified only slightly to meet editorial, format, and space requirements.

established the Bureau of Prisons and directed it to develop an integrated system of institutions to provide custody and treatment based on the individual needs of offenders. Congress gave vigorous support to the new agency. Subsequent legislation approved open camps, the construction of new facilities, and a program of diversified industrial employment within the institutions. An independent three-man Board of Parole also was established, replacing the old system of institution boards. The young Bureau moved rapidly in planning and constructing the new institutions, improving existing facilities and living conditions, and upgrading and training personnel. As the Bureau grew, so did its goals of developing into a professional, effective service.

Through all these changes and improvements, the Bureau of Prisons, as an integral part of the federal criminal justice system, continued to perform its mission of protecting society, safeguarding federal offenders committed to the custody of the attorney general, and carrying out the judgments of the federal courts.

To achieve the Bureau's threefold concerns—care, custody, and corrections—its major objectives remained the same:

- To provide a level of supervision consistent with human dignity and offering maximum protection to the community, staff, and inmates.

- To increase the number of Federal offenders achieving a successful adjustment upon their return to the free community.

- To offer a wide variety of program alternatives for offenders, including those that do not require institutional confinement.

- To maintain institutional environments that minimize the corrosive effects of confinement.

- To increase the knowledge of correctional technology through systematic evaluation and research.

National Institute of Corrections

The National Institute of Corrections, established two years earlier, acquired a legislative mandate during fiscal 1975. The president, on September 7, 1974, signed into law the Juvenile Justice and Delinquency Prevention Act of 1974, Public Law No. 93-415. Title V, Part B of the Act established within the Bureau of Prisons the National Institute of Corrections. Previously the Institute had been operating under authority of the attorney general, using Bureau of Prisons personnel and Law Enforcement Assistance Administration funds.

The new act authorizes NIC to carry out a program of technical assistance and training for state and local correctional personnel, as well as for law enforcement officers, judges, judicial, probation and parole personnel, welfare workers, and other persons who work with offenders. NIC is also empowered to carry out correctional research and evaluation programs, to serve as a clearinghouse and information center, to help develop and implement improved corrections programs at state, local, and federal levels, and to help establish correctional policy, goals, and standards. The overall policy and operations of the Institute are under the direction and supervision of an advisory board appointed by the attorney general. This 16-member panel is composed of six federal officials serving ex-officio, five correctional practitioners, and five persons from the private sector.

A Time of Reexamination

The entire criminal justice systems of the United States are now the subject of a debate which has been prompted by the rapidly increasing rate of crime. According to Federal Bureau of Investigation figures, serious crime in the calendar year of 1974 rose 18 percent over the previous year, the largest increase in 14 years. And in the calendar year of 1975, the rate went up another 9.1 percent. The effectiveness of law enforcement agencies, the courts, probation, parole, and corrections have all come under question and reexamination.

In a special message on crime delivered on June 19, 1975, former President Ford asked Congress to enact mandatory prison sentences for federal offenses committed with dangerous weapons; for hijackers, kidnappers, and hard drug dealers; and for repeat federal offenders who commit crimes of violence. He also asked the states to establish similar mandatory sentencing systems. Ford also called for a crackdown on white-collar crime. At the same time, he asked for the construction of more modern and more humane institutions for the incarceration of criminal offenders. Ford noted that "grave questions have been raised by qualified experts about the ability of the corrections system to rehabilitate offenders. . . . While the problem of criminal rehabilitation is difficult, we must not give up on our efforts to achieve it, especially in dealing with youthful offenders."

The debate has sparked a reexamination by the Federal Bureau of Prisons of its own philosophy and a review of the medical model and its appropriateness for use in corrections. The use of medical terms where inappropriate was dropped, and the Bureau restated its position that a balanced system of corrections was needed—one that recognizes that rehabilitation, deterrence, and retribution are all legitimate goals of the criminal justice system.

Though the population of the federal prison system was 23,566 at the end of fiscal 1975—compared to 23,690 a year earlier—the figure was on the rise again by year's end. A temporary decline took place in the middle of fiscal 1975, largely because of such occurrences as the granting of paroles to drug offenders not previously eligible and the release of Selective Service violators under the presidential clemency program. Several indicators suggest that the prison population will continue to rise, and that the crowding of federal institutions will be worse in the months and years ahead.

The total population of federal prisons is above operational capacity, and this population would be double were it not for the fact that many offenders are being placed in contract nonfederal community-based facilities. But even these figures do not tell the whole story. The operational capacities of federal institutions (formerly called "planned capacities") are used as a guide for making daily designations and transfers to various institutions, and to show which institutions can best absorb additional population. Operational capacity figures often include the use of inadequate housing, such as basement areas and old shower facilities, and the placement of more inmates in a cell than it was originally designed to hold.

Humane standards advocated by the United Nations Standard Minimum Rules for Treatment of Offenders, the American Correctional Association, the National Clearinghouse on Correctional Planning and Architecture, and the National Advisory Commission on Criminal Justice Standards and Goals would provide each inmate with a private room or cell, or 75 to 80 square feet of space, or both. Newer federal institutions meet, or nearly meet, these standards. Unfortunately, most older institutions do not. Living space per inmate varies from 70 square feet at the Federal Reformatory at Petersburg, Virginia, down to 18 square feet at the U. S. Penitentiary at Leavenworth, Kansas.

The nature of the offenders in federal prisons is changing. More than 25 percent of all federal inmates have been convicted of a violent offense, compared to only 15 percent ten years ago. The best risks are being moved into community-based corrections, some through halfway houses but most through probation. The proportion of convicted federal offenders placed on probation has increased steadily the past several years and reached 54 percent in the second half of fiscal 1975. More than one-third of those released from federal prisons were sent to halfway houses, and the Bureau's goal is to increase this to 65 percent by fiscal 1979. The population pressures these programs can relieve, however, are necessarily limited. More modern and smaller facilities and updated correctional techniques will be needed to meet the needs of a growing and changing population.

Another critical factor was rising costs, particularly for food and energy. The cost of confinement per inmate per day rose from $13.85 in fiscal 1973 to $16.86 in 1974 and to $20.34 in 1975. More efficient use of energy, improved farm operations, and across-the-board cost-cutting (without sacrificing essential programs) have helped to offset price increases.

Organization

The work of the Federal Bureau of Prisons has been largely decentralized and is now carried out by five divisions and by five regional offices. The

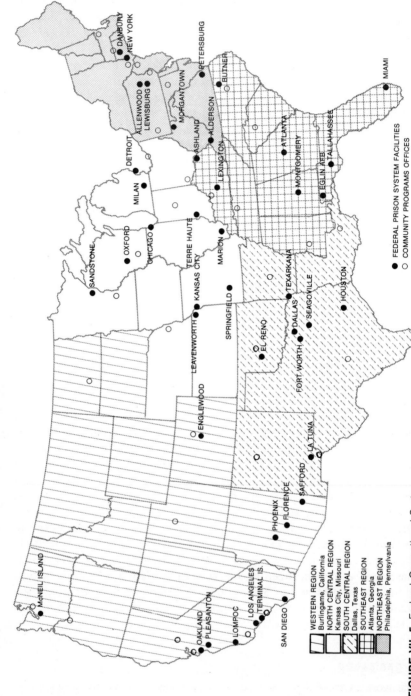

WESTERN REGION
Burlingame, California
NORTH CENTRAL REGION
Kansas City, Missouri
SOUTH CENTRAL REGION
Dallas, Texas
SOUTHEAST REGION
Atlanta, Georgia
NORTHEAST REGION
Philadelphia, Pennsylvania

● FEDERAL PRISON SYSTEM FACILITIES
○ COMMUNITY PROGRAMS OFFICES

FIGURE VII-5. Federal Correctional System

five divisions are Correctional Programs, Planning and Development, Medical and Services, Federal Prison Industries, Inc., and the National Institute of Corrections. The head of each reports to the director of the Bureau of Prisons. (Federal Prison Industries and the National Institute of Corrections each also have advisory boards.) The five regions are headquartered in Atlanta, Georgia, Burlingame (near San Francisco), California, Dallas, Texas, Kansas City, Missouri, and Philadelphia, Pennsylvania. Each is headed by a regional director. Heads of the Bureau's 50 correctional institutions, ranging from penitentiaries to halfway houses, report to the regional directors, who in turn report to the director of the Bureau of Prisons.

Regionalization, completed during fiscal 1975, means that functions truly national in scope have been assigned to appropriate divisions in the Washington central office. The rest have been delegated to the field. Thus, day-by-day administration of such functions as case management, health and drug abuse programs, education, vocational training, and correctional services has been transferred to the regions and to the individual institutions. National headquarters in Washington establishes policy, provides overall supervision, and does planning, development, data-gathering, evaluation, and research.

The U.S. Board of Parole has also been regionalized. The two agencies now have common regional boundaries and regional headquarters in adjacent offices in the same cities so that services can be shared. The two agencies are therefore able to work more closely together to carry out their joint responsibilities toward offenders under sentence by federal courts.

While decentralization was carried out for the federal prison system through regionalization, it was being accomplished within each institution in the system through establishment of functional units. Organizing an institution around these units means essentially, as in the case of regionalization, giving staff closest to the inmates the responsibility and authority to make operating decisions while reserving for the institution's central staff such management duties as monitoring and general supervision. Treatment for drug addiction and alcoholism, vocational training and education, and similar functions are decentralized. But many functions, such as those performed by the business office, health and food services, mechanical services, and safety and sanitation, remain centralized. Functional units make it possible for staff to work in a close relationship with inmates. Basically, the units are small, flexible, semi-autonomous subgroups, operating within the confines of the larger facility. They are made up of from 50 to 100 inmates, housed together, generally for a specific objective—for instance, vocational training or drug addiction treatment. Units are under supervision of a small, permanently assigned, multidisciplinary staff team, working directly in the unit. Typically, the staff team might consist of a unit manager, a caseworker, an education specialist, a vocational training representative, a psychologist, and a correctional counselor. The team has decision-making authority and is responsible for planning and managing correctional programs for all the inmates in the unit.

Reorganization of the structure of institutions along functional lines began in 1973. There are now 140 functional units in 22 completely unitized institutions. All of the Bureau's youth and young adult facilities have converted to functional units, and all of the adult institutions have at least one such unit in operation. The functional unit concept is not a panacea for all correctional problems. However, through better use of staff and program resources and improved inmate-staff relationships, preliminary assessments indicate it is a much more effective and humane approach to inmate management.

New Institutions

For years, the Federal Bureau of Prisons had been planning, designing, and building metropolitan correctional centers to house convicted federal offenders serving short sentences as well as persons awaiting federal trial. The centers were designed to demonstrate that such offenders could be housed under secure, humane conditions without the stark surroundings of the typical jail.

The first two centers were completed in fiscal 1975 in San Diego and New York, and a third was under construction in Chicago (and was dedicated in October 1975). These high-rise short-term detention facilities are located in the downdown areas of their respective cities, near the federal courts, the U.S. Marshals, and other components of the federal criminal justice system served by the Bureau of Prisons. The San Diego center, dedicated November 15, 1974, is 22 stories high and can accommodate 500 offenders. The 12-story New York center, also designed to house 500, was dedicated July 1, 1975.

These centers have several features that set them apart from the traditional jail or correctional institution:

- They are free of steel grilles, guard corridors, and other typical jail surroundings. Windows have no iron bars, but are designed to withstand escape attempts. Most inmates have private rooms which meet humane standards for privacy, dignity, and security.

- Housing areas are divided into semi-autonomous functional units, each with its own visiting area, indoor recreation facilities, and space for casework and food service.

- Since each unit is capable of operating independently, the centers have a functional flexibility which makes them readily adaptable to almost any type of correctional housing, from maximum security to

FIGURE VII–6. Metropolitan Correction Center, San Diego (Courtesy Federal Bureau of Prisons)

a community setting that permits some inmates to leave during the day to hold jobs or go to school.

The lower floors are devoted to services and administration. The top floors house inmates, both male and female. The centers can provide a variety of services, including education, work and study release, medical care, psychological diagnosis, religious counseling, and outdoor physical exercise.

The centers resemble office buildings on the outside and they are designed to blend with the surrounding architecture. They are also economical. The lack of steel and concrete—so visible in most jails—not only relieves the austerity typical of such institutions but permits savings in construction costs of many millions of dollars. The most important reason for the centers' modern design, however, is "to enhance the sense of safety and humaneness," said Bureau of Prisons Director Norman A. Carlson. "All of the inmates here will be staying for only a short time. The vast majority of them will be persons awaiting trial—individuals who have not yet been found guilty by the Courts of any offense. Certainly such people are entitled to a humane, safe environment."

Community-based Programs

The Bureau of Prisons operates a variety of community-based correctional programs to help ease the transition of inmates back into society. The Bureau has greatly liberalized its furlough policy, which permits inmates to leave the institutions, spend some time with their families, and otherwise begin the process of reintegrating themselves into their communities. As a result, a total of 19,810 overnight furloughs were granted in fiscal 1975, compared to 9,921 the previous year. Work and study release programs were also expanded. These programs permit inmates to leave the institution during the day to hold down a regular job or go to school in the outside community, returning to the institution at night.

The Bureau makes use of two kinds of halfway houses—its own, called community treatment centers, and contract facilities, operated by public and private agencies. A typical halfway house might be a wing of a small downtown hotel where inmates live under minimum supervision. During working hours, they are free to hold jobs or go to school. They are also free to spend weekends with their families. The remainder of their time is spent at the halfway house. The Bureau has 16 community treatment centers in operation in 12 metropolitan areas. These centers accommodate 600 offenders, who live there during the last 90 to 120 days of their sentences, and conduct programs to ease the transition to community life. The Bureau also furnishes residential and other prerelease services to federal offenders who are being released to areas not served by a community treatment center. The needs of these offenders are met through the use of over 475 contract facilities. The Bureau maintains a field staff of 48 community program officers in 43 metropolitan areas across the country. In addition to the contract residential and work release facilities, there are more than 5,000 federal offenders housed daily in over 800 contract jail facilities. Most of these individuals are serving short sentences or are being held pending trial or transfer to a federal institution for service of sentence.

A computerized information system provides up-to-date profiles on all the nonfederal community resources available by contract for federal offenders prior to or just after release from prison. These resources, located in the releasee's home community, include halfway houses, drug treatment outpatient units and work/study release units. The system also collects population and demographic data on federal offenders placed in these programs, and provides U.S. Marshals with data on nonfederal detention facilities available by contract for placement of pretrial detainees, service of sentence commitments, and transfers in route from one federal prison to another. Population and demographic data on federal offenders serving their sentences in these facilities is collected to assist in planning for federal offender population growth.

Federal Prison Industries

Federal Prison Industries (FPI) is a self-sustaining, wholly-owned government corporation which was established by Congress in 1934 with a mandate to employ and train Federal inmates. FPI has 51 industrial operations in 23 federal correctional institutions across the country, and employs approximately 5,000 inmates in providing manufactured goods and services to agencies of the U.S. government.

FPI operates a number of registered apprenticeship programs for inmate employees and has initiated a new concept called the production-training unit. These industrial units will combine formal training components and industrial work experience to maximize the skills and knowledge that inmates may acquire from employment.

Voluntary Surrender

The voluntary surrender program permits federal offenders considered good risks to report for incarceration without the expense of being transported by federal marshals. This program not only saves money, but also makes the whole process of incarceration more humane by sparing the inmate the experience of spending time in jail and then being escorted in handcuffs to prison.

In July, 1969, the Northern District of California began a pilot project that permitted certain sentenced prisoners to surrender themselves voluntarily to specific institutions designated for service of their sentences. The success of

FIGURE VII–7. Inmates Doing Computer Programming Work at Terminal Island, California (Courtesy Federal Bureau of Prisons)

that pilot project led to the implementation of voluntary surrender procedures for all U. S. District Courts in October, 1974. The program is administered by a new Population Control Section within the Bureau of Prisons. Each court wanting to use voluntary surrender commitment for a specific offender first asks the Bureau for designation of an institution and then orders the surrender at that institution at an agreed-upon date and time.

Education and Training

The Federal Bureau of Prisons has an education staff of 475 teachers and administrators at 31 major institutions located in 23 states across the country. On any given day of the year about 9,000 inmates are involved in some phase of educational programming. Hundreds of community volunteers and special education contractors associated with schools and other education agencies in the community are also involved in providing instruction in federal correctional programs. A staff of three professional educators in the central office and five regional administrators for education give the program policy guidance and technical assistance.

The total program is organized around the following key components and objectives:

Adult basic education (ABE).   Approximately one-third of all inmates are involved in adult basic education programs which essentially are remedial activities designed to bring each student with the need and ability to a minimum sixth grade level in reading, writing, and computation.

FIGURE VII–8. Inmates in a Blue Print Class at the Federal Correctional Institution at Terminal Island, California (Courtesy Federal Bureau of Prisons)

Adult secondary education.   These programs allow inmates to earn regular high school diplomas or equivalency certificates.

Post secondary education.   An estimated 3,000 inmates are involved in 9,000 college-level courses, earning associate of arts degrees, bachelor of arts degrees, and master of arts degrees.

Vocational training.   Approximately 12,000 trainees are enrolled in one or more of the different trade and occupation programs offered in the institutions. Preparing offenders for employment and assisting them in gaining an understanding of the world of work is a prime objective of Bureau vocational programs. To achieve this objective, institutional education programs provide exploratory and trade training, on-the-job training in maintenance and industrial shops, and registered apprenticeship programs. Currently 64 programs in 41 different trades in 17 institutions are registered by the U.S. Department of Labor's Bureau of Apprenticeship and Training and apprenticeship bureaus at the state level. In addition, joint apprenticeship training committees in local communities, trade advisory committees from local community colleges, and vocational-technical schools make their services available to Bureau employees by advising them on training and labor trends, and on the potential for new instructional activities either in the institutions or in community school programs on a study release basis.

Social education. This can be described as a process of creating a learning environment composed of experiences through which an individual gains the knowledge, skills, and attitudes necessary to shape, support, and maintain a worthwhile and positive self-image and to interact in responsible ways with other human beings. Upon evaluation of their need to further implement social education throughout their facilities, institutions requested assistance to develop realistic objectives and action plans for their individual situations. Social education coordinators have been designated at each institution.

Education programming in the federal prison system provides a variety of instructional styles with particular emphasis on self-paced study, the use of programmed materials in learning centers, and peer tutors. Multimedia instructional materials are available to reinforce learning experiences. In addition, the residential centers offer support and assistance for specialty programs (interpersonal communications training, training for trainers), meetings and workshops, and management training programs. Each faculty member works closely with assigned institution training coordinators to insure compatibility of training efforts and objectives. In past years, the Bureau's major training focus has been on the line employee; although a major portion of training resources continues to be directed at line staff programs, the Bureau is increasing its offerings in supervisory, management, and executive level training programs.

Personnel

Public Law 93-350 of July 12, 1974, established a mandatory retirement age of 55 after 20 years' service in a federal law enforcement position, effective January 1, 1975. All positions in federal correctional institutions were specifically included by Congress in the law. The law also permits heads of agencies to fix minimum and maximum age limits for initial appointment into covered positions with the concurrence of the U.S. Civil Service Commission. In June 1975, the CSC approved the attorney general's proposal to establish the maximum entry age as the date immediately preceding one's 35th birthday.

Except for entry-level positions, most vacancies in the federal prison service are filled through a strong internal merit promotional plan. Correctional treatment specialist and teacher positions, for example, are filled through merit promotion of employees who meet the basic educational requirements.

FIGURE VII–9. Female Corrections Officer at Federal Correctional
Institution, Terminal Island, California (Courtesy Federal Bureau
of Prisons)

Essential Services

A wide variety of services essential to the functioning of a modern prison system are made available to inmates of federal institutions. These include counseling, case management, religious worship, mental health, medical, dental, and food services.

The role of the correctional officer in federal prisons has changed substantially in recent years. He or she now functions as a counselor as well as an active participant in inmate management. In keeping with their new role, these officers now wear colorful blazers and slacks instead of the traditional gray guard's uniform of the past. These changes help relax the traditional tension between inmates and officers. Case management workers carry out classification and parole assignments and approve community programs for offenders. A total of 300 case management professionals work in federal institutions.

Religious freedom is considered a right, not a privilege, and maximum opportunity for pursuing individual religious beliefs is extended to federal inmates. All major facilities have full-time chaplains. They are aided by outside ministers, working under contract. A total of 57 chaplains serve federal prisoners' spiritual needs. Chaplains not only conduct worship services and provide pastoral care, but also coordinate community-related chapel activity that offers a wide variety of program options for inmates of all faiths. Community volunteers help in the development of religious programs.

The Bureau's mental health programs help inmates with drug abuse and alcoholism problems. More than 100 full-time professionals, including psychiatrists, psychologists, and psychiatric nurses, work in these programs. A large-scale psychiatric in-patient service is maintained at the Medical Center for Federal Prisoners, Springfield, Missouri. Two additional psychiatric referral centers were established during the year at the federal correctional institutions at Danbury, Connecticut, and Terminal Island, California. At these centers, care is given to sentenced psychiatric patients transferred for treatment from other Bureau facilities, and court evaluations are performed for competency hearings.

The Bureau operates 20 drug abuse programs at 16 institutions, under authority of the Narcotics Addicts Rehabilitation Act of 1966 and P.L. 93-292. Community care programs, carried out by contract treatment agencies, are available to all identified releasees and probationers as well. Alcohol abuse or alcoholism treatment units have been established at three Bureau institutions. Several other institutions have begun treatment units which combine alcohol and drug abuse programs.

The health care facilities in each federal prison vary in size from small dispensaries to 14 hospitals accredited by the Joint Commission on Hospital Accreditation. Some 483 medical professional, technical, and support staff are employed, supplemented by 500 local consultants in medical specialties.

FIGURE VII–10. A Living Room–Recreation–Dining Area at the
Metropolitan Corrections Center, San Diego (Courtesy Federal Bureau
of Prisons)

In food service, inmates receive nourishing meals. Much of the food is
produced on federal prison farms, particularly beef, pork, and dairy products. Six institutions have installed microwave ovens to provide appetizing
meals at significant savings in staff time and energy use. The commissary
program, which employs 75 civilians at 32 institutions, permits each inmate
to buy each month $45 worth of certain amenities, such as candy, cigarettes,
and hobbycraft items, which are not provided by the institution. Sales for the
year were $7.4 million. Profits are used to pay civilian and inmate salaries
and for other operating expenses.

Research

In addition to its research on functional unit management and furloughs, the
Bureau is also evaluating co-corrections and recidivism rates.

A recently completed study of recidivism, done in collaboration with the
U.S. Board of Parole, found that despite an increase in the percentage of
prisoners classified as high risks, the recidivism rate for federal prisoners has
gone down between 1970 and 1972. The main finding of the study was a
sharp rise in the proportion of "high risk" offenders (those most likely to
recidivate) in the Bureau of Prisons population. Fewer than 47 percent of all

releasees in 1970 were categorized as high risks, as compared to 54.7 percent in 1972. Despite this increase, the recidivism rate after two years for 1972 releasees was 31 percent, as compared to a 33 percent figure for 1970 releasees.

Research projects for the near future include an evaluation of the impact of metropolitan community centers and a field study of community treatment center releasees.

Assistance to Local and State Governments

The Bureau of Prisons provides technical assistance to state and local governments who request help in improving their correctional systems. Authorization for the Bureau to undertake these activities is provided by P.L. 90-371, which was enacted July 1, 1968, and by the legislation creating the new National Institute of Corrections. The conduct of this function is closely related to and coordinated with the activities of the Law Enforcement Assistance Administration.

State and local correctional officials are also permitted to attend training sessions held by the Bureau at its Atlanta and Dallas training centers. About 200 a year do so. Training packages are made available to local and state jurisdictions and to other agencies. The Bureau's regional offices are a primary source of aid to state and local correctional agencies. The National Institute of Corrections is expected in the years ahead to increase greatly the kinds and amounts of assistance the Federal Bureau of Prisons is able to provide to local and state correctional agencies.

Future Plans

While striving to create a better balance between rehabilitation, punishment, and deterrence in corrections, the Federal Bureau of Prisons will continue its efforts to make institutions more humane. This goal will be pursued by trying to replace present outdated facilities with more modern institutions; by introducing more voluntarism into inmate decisions on program participation; and by attempting to reduce tensions by liberalizing rules and enlarging inmate rights, to an extent that is consistent with security and safety.

Staff training will be enhanced through establishment of another training center in the western part of the United States. Inmate programs will be expanded and improved. Two-thirds of Federal inmates have not completed high school, and more than one in three function below the sixth grade level. Fewer than one in five have any substantial work experience. Many have drug and alcoholic addiction problems. Research will be stepped up through the National Institute of Corrections and through the new Federal Correctional Institution at Butner, North Carolina. The Bureau of Prisons plans to help create a more effective criminal justice system by continued and expanded cooperation with the U.S. Board of Parole, the U.S. Marshals, the federal courts, the probation officers, and other elements of the criminal justice system.

Summary

One objective of the Federal Bureau of Prisons is to be a *model* for state and local corrections. The Bureau has attacked some of the major issues head-on and has begun to make notable progress. But there are no simple solutions to the long-festering problems of corrections. Much hard work lies ahead—for the Bureau and all other correctional agencies in this country.

One of the bright spots on the horizon is the increasing use by the courts and corrections of community-based treatment as a humane, less costly alternative to incarceration for selected offenders. A substantial percentage of offenders, however, are not suitable for treatment in the relative freedom of community-based programs. In this category fall many multiple offenders who have long histories of serious, often violent crimes.

To achieve maximum correctional benefits for all offenders, the Bureau of Prisons has sought to develop a balanced approach, recognizing that no single, all-purpose treatment method can be expected to produce effective results. One of the main challenges of the future undoubtedly will be to sustain the present level of public and legislative interest, which demands a concerted effort by the correctional community and by concerned citizens.

While the Federal Bureau of Prisons is often described as a model that state systems might copy, it too has its problems and detractors. A study conducted by the Government Accounting Office (GAO) reported "limited success" in the federal system:

> The limited success of the Federal Bureau of Prisons in meeting rehabilitation objectives that would prepare inmates of federal prisons to re-enter society as useful citizens, has been analyzed in a detailed General Accounting Office (GAO) report.
>
> The GAO said the Bureau has made definite progress in developing educational, vocational, and related programs for rehabilitation of federal prisoners, but added that in relation to the total problem this progress has been limited. The GAO said it examined the case histories of 169 inmates released from five federal institutions during July 1971, which showed the inmates had a total of 342 basic needs when they entered prison in the areas of: sixth-grade reading proficiency; high school equivalency; character trait treatment; and marketable skills. The GAO said the federal prisons only met or treated 116, or 34 percent, of these prisoners' needs during their imprisonment. The GAO said that although this indicates the Federal Bureau of Prisons has achieved some success, more inmates still need more rehabilitation services.

The GAO report also stated that available rehabilitation programs already operating in the federal prison system are not being used to their greatest potential because inmates are simply not motivated to improve themselves. The report added that the system has a shortage of psychiatrists, psychologists and social case-workers which prevents treatment for some inmates needing help. The report said inmates have only limited opportunities to learn marketable skills because vocational programs are limited by the availability of Federal Prison Industries Inc. (FPI) funding and sufficient emphasis has not been placed on preparing inmates for jobs on the outside.[1]

In addition, the National Council on Crime and Delinquency has, based on its strong policy of nonimprisonment, suggested that the Federal Bureau of Prisons be disbanded.[2] This policy was further elaborated in March 1974:

> Imprisonment of non-dangerous offenders should be virtually abandoned, the National Council on Crime and Delinquency has declared in a new policy statement. The NCCD said that prison facilities have failed in their assigned tasks of rehabilitating offenders, deterring crime, and protecting society. Furthermore, according to the new policy statement adopted by the NCCD's Board of Directors, prisons "are probably incapable of being operated constitutionally, themselves productive of crime, and destructive of the keepers as well as the kept."
>
> NCCD called for greater use of alternatives to prisons, such as diversion from the criminal justice system before trial, probation and suspended sentences, deferred conviction on consent, fines, restitution, and boarding homes.[3]

Despite these controversies, the Federal Bureau of Prisons remains a model for many of the less progressive states to follow. If the model were adopted throughout the country, the problems in the reform of corrections would become much less staggering.

REVIEW QUESTIONS

I. Find the answers to the following in the text:

1. Explain the various categories of the institutions in the federal prison system.

2. What is the goal of the NIC?

3. Outline some of the community programs in which the Bureau is involved.

4. Why does the Bureau have such an advantage over state systems when it comes to evaluation of programs?

II. Words to identify:

    1. NIC

    2. regionalization

    3. functional units

    4. co-correctional

    5. social education

    6. MBO

    7. voluntary surrender

    8. ABE

    9. Community Treatment Center

    10. Metropolitan Correctional Center

NOTES

1. Washington Crime News Services, "GAO Reports 'Limited Success' of Federal Bureau of Prisons," *Criminal Justice Digest* 1 (November 1973): 3.

2. The National Council on Crime and Delinquency, "The Federal Bureau of Prisons," *Policies and Background Information* (Hackensack, N.J.: National Council on Crime and Delinquency, 1972), pp. 27-29. The basic statements in regard to the Federal Bureau of Prisons are:

   - Existing federal institutions should be phased out as state systems are upgraded and programmed to receive federal prisoners through transfer or direct commitment.

   - Offenders charged and convicted in federal courts can when necessary be detained and confined in state and local corrections and detention centers, a practice now being conducted in several parts of the country.

   - LEAA funds to state and local corrections systems merely serve to reinforce the existing national policy for prisons, minimizing noninstitutional corrections within the offenders' home communities.

   - A comprehensive federal correction agency must be established to provide the leadership in noninstitutional correctional services for states and localities as well as to assist in their funding.

   - Children should be diverted from the federal system and placed under the jurisdiction of the juvenile or family court in local communities.

   - The federal govenment should use probation far more frequently than it does at present; it should use imprisonment primarily for those too dangerous or assaultive to be allowed to live in the community.

3. Washington Crime News Services, "NCCD Policy on Non-Imprisonment," *Criminal Justice Digest* 2 (March 1974): 15.

28 Community Corrections

There is no effort within the criminal justice system that holds a fraction of the potential to reduce crime offered by a vigorous, thoughtful corrections program. Not even the efforts directed at the underlying causes of crime, such as health services, education, employment, or decent housing offer the same potential at near the cost.

RAMSEY CLARK

Prisons: At a Turning Point

For almost two centuries, prisons, reformatories, and training schools have embodied the primary societal response to criminal behavior in America. Increasingly, the public has become aware that these institutions are inefficient, ineffective, and expensive. Unrelieved confinement may be necessary for a small percentage of the inmate population, but to house all of the rest in these bleak and cheerless places is a waste not only of human potential but also of costly security measures. More recently, the correctional system has expanded to include three components: probation, parole, and institutional incarceration. The three have grown separately, often in competition for the same limited fiscal and personnel resources. In recent years authorities have recognized that an effective utilization of these scarce resources demands the coordination and consolidation of the three services. Still badly fragmented and divided in many ways, the correctional services in the United States are beginning to move toward the creation of an organized system. Foremost in this movement is the shift away from the total institution, toward alternatives to incarceration.

In today's correctional community the main thrust is toward the use of supportive treatment in the community to as great an extent as possible. The custodial institutions failed because most of them had virtually no access to treatment programs, professional services, or public support. Perhaps it would be better to raze them all and start over again, but this cannot be done until workable alternatives have been firmly established. The variety of alternatives is growing, however, and attempts to evaluate the effectiveness of these programs are under way.

Partial Incarceration: A Beginning

One of the earliest bases for releasing prisoners before their full sentences expired was the first work release legislation. The use of offenders for community work programs has its origins in the prisoners who helped construct the massive public works in ancient Rome. Those workers, however, had no hope for release; their work was just another form of slave labor. The work release philosophy, which permits inmates to work on their own in the free community, dates back to a 1913 Wisconsin statute which allowed misdemeanants to continue to work at their jobs while serving short sentences in jail. North Carolina applied the principles of the Wisconsin statute to felony offenders in 1957, under limited conditions; Michigan and Maryland soon followed suit with similar acts. In 1965, Congress passed the Federal Prisoner Rehabilitation Act, which provided for work release, furloughs, and community treatment centers for federal prisoners. This act, part of which follows, then served as a model for many additional states:

> The Attorney General may extend the limits of the place confinement of a prisoner as to whom there is reasonable cause to believe he will honor this trust, by authorizing him, under prescribed conditions, to . . .

1. visit a specifically designated place or places for a period not to exceed thirty days and return to the same or another institution or facility. An extension of limits may be granted only to permit a visit to a dying relative, attendance at the funeral of a relative, the obtaining of medical services not otherwise available, the contacting of prospective employers, or for any other compelling reason consistent with the public interest; or

2. work at paid employment or participate in a training program in the community on a voluntary basis while continuing as a prisoner of the institution or facility to which he is committed. . . .

    The willful failure of a prisoner to remain within the extended limits of his confinement, or to return within the time prescribed, to an institution or facility, designated by the Attorney General, shall be deemed an escape from the custody of the Attorney General.[1]

Work release is not intended to be a substitute for parole, but it can be a valuable tool for the correctional administrator and for the parole officer who must eventually supervise an individual who has participated in work release. The work release program is not really an alternative to incarceration in the either/or sense. It is a chance for offenders to test their work skills and personal control over their behavior in the community, and it allows them to spend the major part of the day away from the institution. Because offenders must still return to the institution, the work release program may be considered only a partial alternative.

Work release has other benefits besides allowing inmates to be outside the walls for a period of time each day. The income derived from the work can be used for a number of things. If the inmates have families, the earnings can be used to keep them off welfare rolls or to augment the assistance they might be receiving. Inmates can reimburse victims for their loss, if the judge has required it. They may be able to build a nest egg for the time when they will be released. One of the major fringe benefits is that their community becomes aware of their ability to maintain a job without creating problems for themselves or others. Also, the offenders' association with stable fellow-workers in the free world may give them support and guidance that they could not find inside the walls. In the American tradition, the ability to "do a good day's work" both heightens the offenders' self-esteem and commands respect from others.

Another form of partial incarceration is the furlough. Both work release and furlough extend the limits of confinement to unsupervised absences from the institution. Furloughs and home visits have been used for many years on an informal basis. The death of a family member or some other crisis situation were the most common reasons to use the furlough. As states have passed legislation making furloughs a legal correctional tool, they have been used for a number of purposes, including a home visit during holiday periods or just prior to release, so that the return to the free world is a graduated process. Education has been another reason for extensive use of the furlough, often allowing the inmate to be in residence at the school during the week, returning to the correctional institution on the weekend. A major benefit of home furloughs, obviously, is decreased sexual tension in institutions. More uses for the furlough practices will be explored as correctional administrators gain experience with them.

Graduated Release: Toward a Community-based Alternative

It has been generally recognized that an offender who has served a long sentence in a total institution will suffer culture shock when suddenly returned to the community from which he came. Just as astronauts must reenter the atmosphere in a series of shallow passes, so the offender needs to reenter society in a gradual series of steps. This program, referred to as graduated release, is intended to ease the pressures of culture shock experienced by institutionalized offenders. Some of the concepts planned to reduce the effect of reentry are presently being practiced, others must wait until there is a true correctional continuum available. Any preparation for release is better than none, but preparation that can include periods of nonincarcerated time is even more effective.

The periods immediately before and after release of an offender are especially crucial to the ex-offender's adjustment to society. Despite statements made with false bravado to the media, most ex-offenders know that they will have a serious problem trying to reestablish a life outside the institution. Their apprehension builds as they approach release. Many inmates become "jackrabbits" (escape) shortly before they are due for release.[2] Others commit some almost meaningless petty offense within a short period after their release. These actions can be seen as deliberate efforts to ensure their quick return to the "safety" of the institution, where all their needs are met and no demands (except obedience to the rules) are made on them. Awareness of this phenomenon has led many thoughtful correctional administrators to establish prerelease and postrelease programs aimed at assisting the ex-offender through those critical periods. Topics covered in such programs include getting a driver's license, how to spend money, how to find an apartment, sex, family adjustment, credit buying, and so on.

The whole experience of incarceration is a prelude to the eventual release of the inmate. Unfortunately, the institutional environment bears little relation to the free life. The inmate is not allowed to earn a wage, is deprived of heterosexual relations, and lives in an authoritarian world dominated by the needs of the institution. To expect an individual to switch overnight from that situation to a free world community is asking a great deal of even the strongest personality. The Sam Houston Institution of Contemporary Corrections has provided some pointers on the establishment of prerelease and graduated release programs:

1. Pre-release preparation should begin as early as possible in the sentence, and inmates should know in advance the purpose and intention of the program.

2. Reliance must be placed upon a sound program and not upon the use of special privileges as an enticement to participate.

3. The program should be organized with realistic goals in mind and should be part of the total treatment process.

4. The counseling program should be geared toward dealing with the immediate problems of adjustment rather than with underlying personality problems.

5. Participants should be carefully selected by the staff on an individual basis rather than according to predetermined arbitrary standards.

6. Employee-employer rather than custodian-inmate relationships should exist between the staff and the inmates.

7. Every effort should be made to enlist the support and participation of the community, and family contact should be encouraged.

8. Whenever possible, work release should be included. The center itself should be minimum security and should encourage personal responsibility. If pre-release programs are to be made a part of the treatment process, there should be some provision for determining their effectiveness.[3]

Again, graduated release and prerelease programs are not either/or alternatives to incarceration, but they can help to offset the destructive and dependency-producing effects of imprisonment. A clearcut movement toward an alternative to incarceration, outside the institution, is seen with the development of the halfway house: a place for offenders who can benefit from work or education in the free world, while residing in the community.

Halfway Houses as Alternatives to Incarceration

The interest in the halfway house as an alternative to imprisonment has grown in recent years. Although the original halfway houses served as residences for homeless men released from prison, they have since been used for a variety of purposes. Small residences to provide shelter have been managed by prison aid societies for over a century. In recent years, more attention has been given to halfway houses as the possible nuclei for community-based networks of residential treatment centers, or as prerelease guidance centers.

In 1961 the Federal Bureau of Prisons established prerelease guidance centers in major metropolitan areas. The offender is sent to these centers from a correctional institution several months before he or she is eligible for parole. Staff personnel are selected on the basis of their treatment orientation and aptitude for counseling. The offender is allowed to work and attend school in the community without supervision, and participates in a number of programs in the halfway house itself. This approach has been copied by many states and appears to be a viable program when properly staffed and supervised. The prerelease guidance centers of the Federal Bureau of Prisons are probably the best-known and most carefully researched of the halfway houses. As possible uses for the halfway house are explored and outcomes verified, they will serve not only for short-term residency prior to placement on parole but also as noninstitutional residence facilities for a number of different classes of offenders. At that point, they will constitute the first real alternative to institutional incarceration in the community.

A Changing Emphasis

In recent years, more and more people—in the correctional field and the general public—have come to favor community-based corrections. The concept is often advanced as a new and revolutionary idea, but in reality the concept of treating (or punishing) the offender in the community is one of the oldest forms of social control. By comparison, the concept of *imprisonment* is new, and many of the problems in the ex-offender's readjustment to the community stem from long isolation in the artificial prison environment. Even the harsh punishments common in our early history were performed in the community (e.g., stocks, pillories, and even executions). When correctional efforts eventually moved inside the prisons, the shift was really in *emphasis* rather than *procedures*. The treatment and rehabilitation movements for convicted felons and adjudicated delinquents have alerted communities to the fact that offenders they send away to prison almost always return. As a corollary, the public has begun to question the effectiveness of institutional corrections and to support the idea of community treatment.

Community involvement in correcting offenders is a reversal of the prison philosophy which held that isolation was the only answer. The combination of rising recidivism rates and skyrocketing costs for institutional programs has encouraged community programs, but many of them have not fulfilled the inflated claims made by supporters. "The most rigorous research designs generally have elicited the finding that offenders eligible for supervision in the community in lieu of institutionalization do *as well* in the community as they do in prison or training school. When intervening variables are controlled, recidivism rates appear to be about the same."[4] Even if the results are only equal, the *cost* of community corrections is so much lower than institutionalization that its emphasis can be justified on economics alone. And if the costs were the same, the community programs would be worth consideration on humanitarian grounds, as a more reasonable approach than the fortress prisons to social control.

Before we destroy the prisons, however, it is essential to recognize that the correctional Utopia promised by community-based correctional programs cannot be created overnight. Crime and violence will continue to generate public fear, concern, and overreaction. Overselling community-based programs as a panacea for *all* offenders misleads the public. Newspaper headlines seldom note that the ex-offender who returns to crime did *not* have the benefit of community-based treatment, and the public assumes community programs are worthless and that more offenders should be incarcerated.

A proper balance between small, humane, program-oriented maximum security institutions and community-based programs must be maintained for the foreseeable future. Until we develop effective programs for offenders who are so drug-dependent, violent, or disadvantaged that we cannot help them and they cannot help themselves, we must have some technique to keep society safe from them. The remaining offenders, however, should be given more and more opportunities for participation in community-based programs, which are generally divided into two subcategories: diversion programs, and programs designed to augment the existing correctional system.

One of the basic principles underlying community-based corrections is minimization of the offender's contact with institutional incarceration. The emphasis away from the dehumanizing and alienating effects of institutionalization mandates avoidance of jails, workhouses, and prisons, to an extent consistent with the protection of society. To be effective, community-based programs must take advantage of every aspect of the services available to the offender *in the outside world*. This goal requires a whole new set of roles for all involved in the correctional process. Citizens, correctional workers, and offenders themselves must adjust to new expectations and functions. The role of "social change agent" includes more responsibility than the correctional worker held in his or her earlier control function. Even the traditional community roles of the probation and parole officer must be changed in emphasis to provide the offender with the total services of the community-based system. This will require extensive recruiting and retraining within the present system to provide the quality personnel with the orientation needed to make the system work.

Diversion: Keeping the Offender Out of the System

Diversion from the criminal justice system has taken place in one form or another since social controls were first established. In most cases informal diversions merely involve an official's exercise of discretion at some point in the criminal process. More formal diversions involve suspension of the criminal process in favor of some noncriminal disposition. Only about 30 percent of the reported offenses in America result in an arrest, and only about one-third of these arrests result in a criminal conviction,[5] an indication that preconviction diversion is not uncommon. Diversion generally occurs at three points, as identified in the National Advisory Commission report:

> There are three main points at which diversion may occur: prior to
> police contact, prior to official police processing, and prior to official
> court processing. Analysis of each of these potential points of
> diversion yields three basic models in terms of responsibility for
> diversion: community-based diversion programs, police-based

diversion programs, and court-based diversion programs. While each of these models usually involves more than one agency or group, programs will be grouped according to who initiates and is primarily responsible for their operations.[6]

Most diversion programs now in effect constitute informal responses to the ambiguities of existing legislation. The value of such programs is difficult, if not impossible, to estimate. Their goals and procedures must be clearly articulated and integrated with the rest of the criminal justice system.

Diversion projects are most effective when integrated into a community-based correctional system with alternative levels of supervision and custody. Formalizing the currently informal options on an accountable basis must be done without rigidifying the process. If community-based programs are too restricted, they will become merely "institutions without walls." Diversion is seen as the first threshold of the community corrections system, designed to remove as many offenders as possible from the process *before* conviction and criminalization.

While these programs aimed at a total or partial alternative to incarceration are improvements, they do not eliminate the stigma of a conviction record. Diversion programs tied to treatment and services in the community, however, both avoid the problems of incarceration *and* remove the criminal label. These programs are not seen as a substitute for probation services, but as a method of filling the gap between offenders eligible for probation and cases where charges can be dropped. Diversion should be accompanied by a formalized agreement with offenders as to what they are to do in return for the elimination of their arrest records. A set of alternative treatment services and residential reinforcements may be needed to help diverted individuals handle their problems: The diverted individuals should have the advantages available to all other categories of offenders and ex-inmates being treated in the local network.

Police agencies have practiced diversion, in an informal manner, by using their great powers of discretion at the time of arrest. Several programs have been established to encourage more of these diversions on a formal basis. Police have been reluctant in the past to formalize their practice of discretion, because of public reaction to the practice as "weakness," or being "soft." Most formalized programs are aimed at the youthful offenders in an effort to keep them from beginning a career of crime. One example is found in Richmond, California:

[An] example of a police-based diversion program is occurring in Richmond, California. The Richmond Police Department's Juvenile Diversion Program, funded on a pilot basis by LEAA and subsequently aided by the California Youth Authority, is testing the feasibility of the police providing direct helping and counseling services to youth involved in pre-delinquent and certain delinquent activities. Program elements include crisis intervention, behavior management training for parents, counseling, tutorial services, and employment assistance. These services traditionally have been provided by other agencies such as probation staffs, the school department, or paroling authorities. The intent is to provide direct services and eliminate the wasted hours, days, and weeks of time that sometimes expire before offenders referred for service actually receive service.

The basic thrust of this project is that the police are on the cutting edge of the entire juvenile justice system and are in this sense the primary gatekeepers to that system. With adequate resources and properly trained staff, the police feel they are in the position to provide 24-hour services of a helping nature to youthful offenders who are at risk of coming into the formal juvenile justice system if care and service are not immediately provided.[7]

Another example of diversionary tactics at the police level is the Family Crisis Intervention approach. This approach, which has been used in several major cities, is exemplified by the New York experience:

There are indications that the police, by identifying conflict situations at an early stage of development, can prevent the escalation of violence. A conspicuous example is the Family Crisis Intervention Project in New York City. Officers from a high-risk precinct are trained to work in teams to intervene in family disturbance calls, attempting to resolve the conflict on the scene. If unsuccessful, they refer the antagonists to a community agency. The New York program has been successful in many other cities, including Oakland, Denver, and Chicago.

In the New York experience, not one homicide occurred in 926 families handled by intervention teams. Nor was a single officer injured, even though the teams were exposed to an unusually large number of dangerous incidents. Families having had experience with the teams referred other families to the project, and many troubled individuals sought out team members for advice. It is believed that police-community relations were improved as a result and that a number of incidents were averted that otherwise might have led to arrest.[8]

The courts are involved with diversion in several ways. One method is to use civil commitment for individuals who presumably will be more treatable in a hospital situation. However, the constitutionality of these civil commitment procedures has come under question, and their continued use is doubtful. A more common and reasonable use of diversion by the courts is found in pretrial intervention programs, which have been funded extensively by the United States Department of Labor. The general pattern and some sample results are as follows:

> At the end of the prescribed period of the continuance, the participant's counselor may recommend one of the following three actions to the court:
>
> • Dismissal of pending charges based on satisfactory project participation and demonstrated self-improvement.
>
> • Extension of the continuance to allow the program staff more time to work with the person (usually for an additional 30 to 90 days).
>
> • Return of the defendant to normal court processing, without prejudice, because of unsatisfactory performance in the program.
>
> Of 753 young first offenders enrolled in one of the first projects, charges were dropped for 468 who completed the program successfully, while 285 offenders were returned to face prosecution because of unsatisfactory performance. The recidivisim rate (using a 15-month period following arrest as the base) was 14 percent lower for project participants than for a control group of first offenders.[9]

Diversion is especially appropriate for the public drunk and the first-time drug abuser. The current alternative to incarceration for the public drunk is the *detoxification center*. New York and Washington, D.C., have had centers in operation for many years. Both centers draw the same conclusions:

> The response to the voluntary aspect of the Bowery and District of Columbia programs demonstrates the willingness of many problem drinkers to accept treatment, if only for free room and board. Opening the D.C. center to walk-ins has resulted in a patient population that is 50 percent self-referred.[10]

The severity of criminal sanctions and public reaction to most drug offenses makes the diversion of drug abuse cases a sensitive area. Some jurisdictions have braved public reprobation and set up progressive programs for nonviolent drug abuse cases. In Illinois a special act was passed in order to handle the drug problem cases in a diversionary manner:

The maximum referral period is two years for pre-adjudication cases. Under the statute, treatment can be successfully completed at any time during that period. If an offender leaves the program or if IDAP dismisses him, pending criminal charges are brought to court. If a person faithfully participates in the program for two years but cannot be certified cured by staff, the court exercises discretion in dropping the charges or resuming prosecution. The maximum term of treatment for persons assigned to the program as probationers is five years or the length of probation, whichever is less.

The program's minimum goal is to turn out law-abiding citizens. Its maximum goal is to enable its patients to lead productive, drug-free lives. Its multimodality approach serves the patients' diverse needs, and its flexibility allows for modifications.[11]

The spectrum of diversionary programs is geared toward the same goal: provision of a reasonable alternative to incarceration in large, punitive prisons. Again, as in the development of many other aspects of correctional services, such programs often begin as independent actions. These multifaceted efforts are all competing for the scarce dollars and personnel allotted to corrections as a whole; consequently, many of them are poorly staffed and underfunded. It is a real danger that the proliferation of these programs, without careful coordination at all levels of the criminal justice system, will produce *poor* results from *good* ideas—and the inevitable backlash to an emphasis on incarceration. Signs of such a backlash are already in evidence.

Probation and Parole: A Changing Role

Probation and parole have been traditional responses to release of offenders in the community. Probation gives nondangerous convicted offenders a chance to remain in their community and work toward eventual release from supervision. Parole has been developed for institutionalized offenders who are ready to return to the community under supervision before their sentence has expired. Both programs were discussed in detail in Part III. The essential element in successful community-based corrections is coordination of the activities and services available for *all* offenders, whether on diversion, probation, or parole. These programs presently function as separate entities, under the control of separate branches and local units of government. As a comprehensive, community-based correctional *system* is developed, traditional probation and parole officer roles will give way to that of "change agents," or agents with a similar label. Such agents will have an array of correctional treatment and service alternatives at their disposal, with the ability to move offenders as needed from one type of program to another (as opposed to the narrow options of returning offenders to court or prison, or ignoring their problems entirely).

Adjuncts to Institutionalization—An Intermediate Step

The sharp distinction between treatment methods in the institution and community-based treatment has become blurred as increasing numbers of offenders are released under supervision. The most effective response to their differential needs is to develop a differential spectrum of custody and supervision modalities. The problems of bridging the gap between the institution and the community have been recognized since the earliest prisons began to release offenders on "tickets of leave" in the mid-nineteenth century. The efforts of Ireland's Sir Walter Crofton provided the prisoner of that period a chance to work in the community for a period of time prior to his release. The concept of work release has since become an important adjunct to institutional programs. Under these programs, offenders are allowed to work at jobs in the community and still receive the benefit of certain programs available at an institution. Work release may often be the first phase in the establishment of some form of residential and custodial facility in the community for offenders who are able to function at their job but are still in need of treatment under supervision. Such community-based facilities are usually referred to as "halfway houses," because residents are considered to be halfway out of the institution.

Halfway houses are often operated by private organizations, under state supervision. As funds have been made available from various sources, halfway houses have developed with a number of different organizational and ideological orientations. Some states have begun to take a much closer look at their funding of halfway house programs and require a better accounting of results. Halfway houses are often located in depressed neighborhoods in older buildings originally designed for some other purpose.[12]

The increasing use of diversionary and probationary alternatives to imprisonment had resulted in the development of halfway-*in* houses for those offenders who need supportive residential treatment but are not so dangerous as to be sent to prison. It is probable that an integrated system of the future would place halfway-out and halfway-in offenders in the same residence, with the emphasis on the *kinds* of treatment provided rather than the *type* of offender. These two categories may well be joined by a third: the new reintegration centers will become an important part of the correctional system. The future emphasis on provision of residential care and custody will most likely center around referral to available community services and programs, rather than just personal contact with the offender.

The community correctional center mentioned in chapters 25 and 27 has been the most appealing development toward a community-based institution in recent years. These centers have been developed in a number of models, generally fairly open, located in the community, and utilizing community resources for its services. Centers serve a variety of purposes, including detention, treatment, holding, and pre-release, and are based in a variety of facilities ranging from existing jails to hotels and motels. With growing support, the centers will develop a specific and integrated set of services.

Is Cheaper Better?

Proponents of community-based corrections, as mentioned earlier, have often made exaggerated claims for their results. Upon examination, however, it appears that community programs are no more and no less effective than institutional corrections. But from a financial standpoint, community-based corrections are proving more practical. In the Des Moines project, it was found that residential corrections were approximately four times cheaper than the on-going state institutional programs.[13] In community-based programs that do not require a residential facility, the cost differential is even more pronounced. The cost of maintaining an inmate in a correctional institution is estimated to be approximately $4,500 a year, as opposed to $600 for probation and parole.

Economics is not the only measure of a correctional program, however; the major objective of such programs is to *protect the public*. Only when it is definitely established that shifts from institutional to community corrections can be accomplished with no increased danger to the public should they be made. It is clear that treatment in the community is more humane, and that it relieves the offender of the burden of institutionalization. It has been proven that subjecting offenders to custodial coercion in the fortress prisons places them in physical danger, destroys their community ties, and reduces their self-esteem. A system that avoids these problems, costs less, is more (or equally) effective, and still protects the community, is hard to fault. It is basically for these reasons that the movement toward community corrections has gained such great support in the past decade. Improvements and increased success for the programs now in an experimental status will make the community-based programs the keystone of corrections in the decades to come.

Incarceration: Is It All Bad?

The answer to all correctional problems may appear to lie in the closing and tearing down of America's prisons, but the total problem is not that simple. When we speak of alternatives to incarceration, we speak of a carefully selected group of convicted offenders and accused offenders. The primary mission of the correctional system is the *protection of the public*. All programs must be designed or proposed with that mission in mind, or they will be doomed to early failure and public rejection. All systems described above have a carefully executed evaluation of the prospective client built into their procedures. It is not proposed that *all* offenders be given the chance for diversion, or community treatment, or any of the programs described. What seems to be a critical need, however, is a system that provides as many alternatives to incarceration as possible for the individual *who appears to have some hope of benefitting from it,* and who will present little, if any, danger to the community. The residual population, as mentioned many times before, may be required to remain in maximum security institutions until new treatments are found for them. Institutions for these residual inmates can be made more humane, more oriented toward treatment, and more closely tied to the community as well. The community should be encouraged to come into the institution, providing models of behavior and friendship ties for the offenders who must remain incarcerated. The prison, in a modified form, still has a valuable place in the correctional system for the estimated 15 to 20 percent of the convicted offenders who require this level of control. For the vast majority of convicted and diverted offenders, however, the use of either partial or total alternatives is a more reasonable response than incarceration.

REVIEW QUESTIONS

I. Find the answers to the following in the text:

1. What are the traditional components of a correctional system? What are some recent additions?

2. Why is graduated release so beneficial to both the community and the offender?

3. Should all offenders be given the chance for diversion from the criminal justice system? Why or why not?

4. What is the primary mission of any correctional system?

II. Words to identify:

1. partial incarceration

2. work release

3. furlough

4. home visit

5. graduated release

6. pre-release programs

7. diversion

8. family crisis intervention

9. diversionary programs

10. halfway houses

NOTES

1. American Academy of Political and Social Science, "The Continuum of Corrections," in *The Future of Corrections (The Annals)* 381 (January 1969): 85.

2. *Jackrabbit* is a slang term for a prisoner with nervous jitters just prior to release. Many of these inmates will deliberately attempt to escape so that they will be kept in prison. For this reason, "short-timers" are often kept in tight security immediately preceding their release date.

3. Benjamin Frank, *Contemporary Corrections: A Concept in Search of Content* (Reston, Va.: Reston Publishing Co., 1973), pp. 228-229.

4. National Institute of Mental Health, *Community-Based Correctional Programs: Models and Practices* (Washington, D.C.: National Institutes of Health, 1971), p. 33.

5. National Advisory Commission on Criminal Justice Standards and Goals, *Corrections* (Washington, D.C.: U.S. Government Printing Office, 1973), p. 74.

6. National Advisory Commission, *Corrections*, p. 77.

7. National Advisory Commission, *Corrections*, p. 82.

8. National Advisory Commission, *Corrections*, p. 81.

9. National Advisory Commission, *Corrections*, pp. 84-85.

10. National Advisory Commission, *Corrections*, p. 87.

11. National Advisory Commission, *Corrections*, pp. 87-88.

12. *Halfway House Evaluation Project*, Program for the Study of Crime and Delinquency, The Ohio State University for the Department of Economics and Community Development, the Administration of Justice Division.

13. Department of Court Services, *A Handbook on Community Corrections in Des Moines* (Washington, D.C.: U.S. Department of Justice, 1973), p. 145.

RECOMMENDED READING LIST

American Correctional Association. *Manual of Correctional Standards*. Washington, D.C.: ACA, 1969.

Barnes, Harry Elmer, and Teeters, Negley K. *New Horizons in Criminology*. 3d ed. Englewood Cliffs, N.J.: Prentice-Hall, 1959.

Boorkman, David, et al. *Community-Based Corrections in Des Moines*. Washington, D.C.: U.S. Government Printing Office, 1976.

Carter, Robert; Glaser, Daniel; and Wilkens, Leslie T. *Correctional Institutions*. New York: J.B. Lippincott, 1972.

Coffey, Alan; Eldefonso, Edward; and Hartinger, Walter. *An Introduction to the Criminal Justice System and Process*. Englewood Cliffs, N.J.: Prentice-Hall, 1974.

Felkenes, George T. *The Criminal Justice System: Its Functions and Personnel.* Englewood Cliffs, N.J.: Prentice-Hall, 1973.

Frank, Benjamin. *Contemporary Corrections: A Concept in Search of Content.* Reston, Va.: Reston, 1973.

Glaser, Daniel. *The Effectiveness of a Prison and Parole System.* New York: Bobbs-Merrill, 1964.

Joint Commission on Correctional Manpower and Training. *Perspectives on Correctional Manpower and Training.* Washington, JCCMT, 1969.

LeGrande, James L. *The Basic Processes of Criminal Justice.* Beverly Hills, Calif.: Glencoe Press, 1973.

Lieberman, Joel B., et al. *The Bronx Sentencing Project of the Vera Institute of Justice.* Washington, D.C.: U.S. Government Printing Office, 1972.

Morris, Norval E., and Hawkins, Gordon. *The Honest Politician's Guide to Crime Control.* Chicago: University of Chicago Press, 1970.

Newman, Oscar. *Architectural Design for Crime Prevention.* Washington, D.C.: U.S. Government Printing Office, 1973.

Pappas, Nick. *The Jail: Its Operation and Management.* Lompoc, Calif.: U.S. Bureau of Prisons, 1970.

Radzinowicz, Leon, and Wolfgang, Marvin E. *The Criminal in Confinement.* New York: Basic Books, 1971.

Seiter, Richard P., et al. *Halfway Houses.* Washington, D.C.: U.S. Government Printing Office, 1977.

Sylvester, Sawyer F., Jr. *The Heritage of Modern Criminology.* Cambridge, Mass.: Schenkman Publishing, 1972.

U.S. Department of Justice. *The Change Process in Criminal Justice.* Washington, D.C.: U.S. Government Printing Office, 1973.

U.S. Department of Justice. *Prevention of Violence in Correctional Institutions.* Washington, D.C.: U.S. Government Printing Office, 1972.

U.S. Department of Justice. *The St. Louis Detoxification and Diagnostic Evaluation Center.* Washington, D.C.: U.S. Government Printing Office, 1973.

PART VIII

Summary and Overview

29 Corrections at the Crossroads

Incarceration costs more than control of the offender in the community, much more, sometimes as much as six or seven times the cost. Behavioral scientists and intuitive observers agree that although the harm that prisons do is hard to measure, whatever good they do is too elusive to discern.

JOHN CONRAD

Corrections in a Climate of Change

The last few decades have been a time of great social change. The industrialization of America eventually led to urbanization and the resulting problems connected with densely populated, low-income slums. Rising crime in the poorly designed urban centers contributed to an exodus to the suburbs by those who could afford the move. The inner city cores were left with the poor, the uneducated, and the minority groups. Cities became places of fear and so-called street crime developed into a political issue. Presidential hopeful Senator Barry Goldwater alerted the nation to "law and order" as a campaign issue in the 1964 general elections. Lyndon Johnson was elected, but he got the message that something had to be done about crime in the streets and appointed a commission to look into the problems of "Crime in a Free Society."

The task force reports of that commission, especially the report on corrections, detailed what was already common knowledge to practitioners in the field: failure at all levels of the system, high recidivism rates from institutions, prisons depicted as schools of crime, and a lack of alternatives to incarceration. All of these points were variations on the themes contained in the Wickersham Commission Report of 1931 and several other reports in between. As in the past, most correctional administrators expected the 1967 commission reports to end up on dusty shelves, causing little or no action. Fortunately, the federal government was to provide the means to do something about the recommendations of *this* commission.

The Law Enforcement Assistance Act of 1965 (Public Law 89-197) was enacted to provide funds for the development of programs to reduce the

FIGURE VIII-1. Road Gang in Prison Stripes—Not Too Long Ago
(Courtesy American Correctional Association)

burden of crime in the streets. The initial success of this legislation led to the development of the "Omnibus Crime Control and Safe Streets Act" of 1968 (P.L. 90-351). This legislation, implemented with generous funding by the Congress, has pumped billions of dollars into the nation's fight against crime. Important to the field of corrections was the *specific* requirement that at least 20 percent of the money provided to the Law Enforcement Assistance Administration be spent on action programs in corrections. These funds have encouraged innovation, education, and evaluation across the spectrum of correctional services. Continued federal funding has been matched by signficant permanent funds from the states as well, ensuring the continuation of the most promising of the pilot programs and procedures.

Prisons continue to be at least partial microcosms of the outside society. It is not surprising that issues that swept the cities in the 1960s spread to the prisons of America. The 1960s saw great advances in the development of civil rights, but radical groups to the left and right perceived change as either too slow or too fast. The result increased polarization between the races and caused especially serious problems in the institutional setting. Divisions along racial, political, and ideological lines are strongly accentuated by the total institution. Many of the riots and disturbances in the prisons have been aimed at achieving political ends rather than improving conditions in the institution. The pressure-cooker environment of a total institution means that the slightest friction can explode the surface calm almost immediately. Thus, the highly volatile issues of the 1960s and '70s have produced serious crises in the prisons. Left with the residual, often hard-core and radicalized problem offenders as their cadre, prisons have erupted into frequent violence. The serious overcrowding of the prisons, which contain almost 300,000 inmates, further exacerbates the problems of the administrator with a "living time-bomb" on his or her hands. As correctional administrators turn more and more to incarceration alternatives, this growing cadre of troublemakers will pose an even greater threat to the institutions.

Personnel Improvements: A Major Goal

Perhaps no issue in corrections is as critical as training, educating, and recruiting qualified staffs for the various systems. In the past, institutional guards have been stigmatized by the general public almost as much as the inmates they were expected to guard. In the nineteenth-century institution, the model of a strong, brutal guard was appropriate for the mission expected of him: *custody* and *control*. In today's correctional climate, however, that mission also includes *rehabilitation* and *reintegration*. The correctional officer, or "change agent," is expected to possess a number of skills and abilities that were never envisioned by the original architects of the penitentiary:

> In virtually every occupation and profession today, central themes of concern are the educational preparation, in-service training, and development of the manpower involved. In industry, the rapid advance of technology and automation has created a demand for higher levels of education and skills among workers. At the same time, the need for professionals and technicians in education, health, counseling, and the broad spectrum of other community services is growing faster than the education system can produce them. At the national level, a great deal of effort is going into a continuous and long-range study of the manpower resources of the country. Along with this is being developed a national policy dealing with the upgrading of educational levels and skills as well as with the distribution and most effective utilization of national manpower resources. In effect, the manpower problem is becoming defined more in terms of an educational and training crisis than in terms of manpower shortages.
>
> Corrections has not only been caught up in this complex of social and economic change but it is also feeling, more directly than in the past, the combined impact of new concepts and techniques in management, the technologies underlying the application of systems analysis to social problems, and the results of research on differential effectiveness of programs. Even the traditional boundaries which kept corrections confined within conventional limitations of institutions, probation, and parole are undergoing considerable re-examination.

Implied in all of this change are some very critical issues relating to utilization of professional and non-professional personnel, the validity of existing formulas for staffing correctional agencies, and the kinds of in-service training that will contribute most effectively to the programmatic changes which seem imminent.[1]

Several approaches to the critical shortage of qualified personnel are either in operation or proposed. In-service training is the first line of attack toward reshaping the ideological boundaries of corrections:

There are five kinds of in-service training: attitudinal, organizational, managerial, training for professional staff, and vocational training. I list attitudinal training first because persons come on our staffs through the indoctrination or orientation road. But it is my opinion that, in orientation or indoctrination training, in essence you are *not* orienting the employee to the company; you are *not* telling him about its benefits; you are *not* really answering his questions. What you are actually trying to do is to develop a productive attitude by means of what we call orientation. The truth of the matter is that trainees will remember only 10 percent of what they are told and will ask about these things again and again. The orientation-indoctrination for the new employee is really to set a productive attitude.[2]

In-service training is one of the easiest and least expensive ways for the correctional administrator to upgrade the quality and change the orientation of his or her current staff. Efforts to bring in new personnel with a different level of training and orientation may generate resentment in the present staff and strengthen their resistance to change. Including *all* staff members in the program of in-service training will ensure the establishment of uniform policies and approaches to treatment.

Other resources for raising the level of the correctional personnel are the local universities and other educational institutions. Many educational programs for staff members can be financed through the Law Enforcement Assistance Administration's Law Enforcement Educational Program (LEEP). The emphasis is on the social sciences and other courses designed to increase staff understanding of and sensitivity to the needs and problems faced by inmates. Many educational institutions have developed "package programs" for correctional administrators so that staff classes may be conducted inside the prisons. Using colleges and universities to upgrade personnel means that advanced-level courses will be available to some staff members whose previous education was extremely limited.

The latest source of personnel to be tapped for correctional employment has been the ex-offender. Radical though this approach may seem, it is not really all that new:

Two rose-tinted legends have long been current in that rather prosaic mosaic of myths known as "sound correctional policy." The first suggests that many correctional problems would be solved "if only our correctional personnel were better trained." The second, a logical consequence of the first, is that a major obstacle to correctional progress could be overcome "if only we could solve the problem of recruiting these better-trained personnel in adequate numbers." It has been suggested that many ex-offenders are peculiarly suited to fill this manpower gap and that their recruitment, by ameliorating the personnel shortage, would go far toward solving the correctional crisis. The fact that this conference is sponsored by the Joint Commission on Correctional Manpower and Training makes it seem all the more urgent that these implications be examined. Taking them in reverse order:

1. The massive use of offenders in correctional roles is not new but immemorially old, not uncommon but widespread, not radical but highly conventional. Moreover, it does not appear to be true that convicts have almost always occupied these roles without formal acknowledgement and reward. The recent episode in Arkansas reminds us that convicts have wielded both power and guns with official sanction and reward, and have often used them with a license as unchecked as that of a sheriff's posse. Sophisticated colonialists have long known that one of the best ways to keep a subject population in subjugation is to divide it from within by enlisting potential leaders of violent revolution as instruments of violent repression.

2. The notion that larger drafts of trained correctional manpower could solve correctional problems either begs or ignores the question of precisely what this manpower would be engaged in doing. During the witch craze that gripped New England, a time came in Salem when virtually anyone who was not a witch was a dedicated witch-hunter. Increasing the number of demonologists has rarely decreased the number of demons. For a modern example of the same lunatic logic, one need only quote the arguments of those who would rely on hard-nosed law enforcement as the only realistic solution of the riot problem. In order to solve a problem created in part by police harassment, one need only increase the number of persons engaging in the harassment.[3]

Ex-offenders have been used effectively in a number of programs throughout the nation. Most recently the Adult Parole Authority of the state of Ohio has been using ex-offenders as "Case Aides" to parole officers. This has been recognized as an "Exemplary Project" by the LEAA selection board, an accolade reserved for very few projects. The preliminary conclusions from that experiment are encouraging:

> Responses to interviews or questionnaires by parole supervisors,
> prison inmates, and parolees indicate general agreement that the Parole
> Officer Aide Program is worthwhile. Supervisors ranked parole officer
> aides higher than parole officers only on effort and ability to get jobs,
> yet saw them as a valuable source of information for parole officers
> and as able to teach parole officers how to relate to parolees. Inmates
> consistently indicated a preference for parole officer aides, with over
> two-thirds of them expressing a desire to be employed as an aide.
> Parolees supervised by aides consistently ranked aides higher on all
> questions or scales than did parolees supervised by parole officers. The
> researchers suggest this could be due to the smaller caseloads of parole
> officer aides which allows them to devote more time to each of their
> parolees.[4]

Achievement of the goal of correctional programs staffed with those who are highly motivated, well-educated, and oriented toward the mission of reintegration is still far down the road. The correctional system has traditionally been last in line for financial support, but the skyrocketing social cost of crime demands immediate personnel improvement. In-service training, educational opportunities, and imaginative recruiting are just a few methods for the correctional administrator to consider in moving toward crime reduction. It is ironic that, just as some movement is being made toward great improvement, the population crunch is causing the hiring of personnel to be done on a crisis basis—no doubt setting back progress in this critical area.

The Death of the Medical Model

Are we hearing the death knell of the medical model in corrections? Apparently so, if the research is to be believed.[5] Bailey, Logan and Martinson, among others, have looked at hundreds of treatment programs evaluated over a broad scale of rigorousness and, giving even biased evaluations the benefit of any doubt, conclude that none of these hundreds of rehabilitation programs are consistently effective.

The medical model in corrections was the outgrowth of the success of the biological and medical sciences, particularly in the last century. As the "ideology of evil" eroded in correctional practice, the medical model gradually became the dominant approach that governed correctional practices, especially in the last four decades. Wayson argues:

> The social sciences, guided by an empiricist philosophy, led corrections to the individual in the search for the causes of crime, because he was "sick," "anti-social" or "deprived." One only had to describe the etiology of the disease and prescribe appropriate "cures." Philosophically, the approach denies free will by positing that cultural, sociological, or psychological forces make the individual incapable of choosing. The objective of corrections, particularly incarceration, was to rehabilitate.[6]

Such significant correctional and criminal justice administrators and researchers as Raymond Procunier, Richard McGee, James Q. Wilson, David Fogel and William Nagel are opposed to the medical model and/or its requisite, the indeterminate sentence. Contemporary criticisms of the medical model do not follow political lines, and there are few distinctions between the right and left.

Increasingly, there are salient charges that institutions cannot rehabilitate, that prisoners are not sick, that incarceration does not cure, that treatment is a myth, and that nothing works. It might be better, conclude the disclaimers, if we faced reality and devoted our energies to more productive alternatives. Indeed, some states are seriously considering abandoning the existing model, including the Parole Board. Sources of disaffection are numerous, and include *inter alia* researchers, inmates, courts, and economists.

Criticisms: Researchers

The failure of the medical model can be readily documented. Martinson, for example, examined 231 treatment projects and found that very few were significantly or consistently successful. Indeed, he calls rehabilitation a myth. In his own words:

> There is no method for reversing the powerful tendency of offenders to persist in criminal activity. The tendency may be reduced somewhat by a given method, but percentage differences are small and the costs of achieving these small reductions may be high. In the face of such facts it seems absurd to insist that the official aim of the post adjudicatory process is to "rehabilitate" the offender. Worse, such a demand may tempt prison officials to achieve the impossible.[7]

Earlier, Bailey looked at 100 projects and was similarly disappointed:

Finally, how corrective is correctional treatment? Of the total sample of correctional outcome reports evaluated, 10% described effects of the treatment as resulting in either "harm" or "no change" in behavior. Thirty-eight percent reported a statistically significant difference in the direction of improvement for the group treated. Five percent of the reported results were classified as "not relevant" to the outcome problem posed by the study.

Thus, roughly one-half of the outcome reports evaluated concluded considerable improvement in the treatment group. Almost one-fourth of the reports concluded either harmful results or "no change." These results, based upon the reported findings themselves, raise some serious questions regarding the efficacy of correctional treatment.[8]

Thus, these and many other researchers suggest that treatment programs predicated on the notion of a sickness and a cure are doomed to failure from the start.

David J. Rothman calls prisons "the failure model."[9] He suggests that, rather than nourishing correctional myths, it would be better to admit failure and to plan for it, as is done in the business sector where insurance underwriting assuages the pain of unexpected fires and catastrophes. Rothman also feels that the American penchant for coping with failures by risk control would alleviate the failure of corrections.

Finally, the American Friends Service Committee, while remarking at length on the failure of the individual treatment model, gives a variety of reasons explaining why it is so firmly entrenched:

The underlying rationale of this treatment model is deceptively simple. It rejects inherited concepts of criminal punishment as the payment of a debt owed to society, a debt proportioned to the magnitude of the offender's wrong. Instead, it would save the offender through constructive measures of reformation, protect society by keeping the offender locked up until that reformation is accomplished, and reduce the crime rate not only by using cure-or-detention to eliminate recidivism, but hopefully also by the identification of potential criminals in advance so that they can be rendered harmless by preventive treatment. Thus the dispassionate behavioral expert displaces judge and theologian.[10]

Criticisms: Inmates

Another source of discontent with the existing rehabilitation model is the inmate population, some of whom are fond of misquoting R. D. Laing:

If you don't admit that you're sick—
  You're really sick,
If you admit that you're sick—
  You're obviously right.

In the United States today, our over 330 state prisons hold close to 270,000 people (excluding the approximately 28,000 federal prisoners). About 100,000 others are on parole throughout the country. In addition, there are 160,000 others in 4,037 municipal and county jails throughout the states. We also have close to 50,000 juveniles detained in 732 juvenile facilities. This is more than the population of fifteen of our states.

Prisoners, as correctional administrators are increasingly realizing, are acquiring a sizeable body politic. Through demonstrations, work stoppages, riots, and other manifestations of discontent, they have won sizeable concessions from grudging prison administrators. These concessions include inmate councils, grievance procedures, an elimination of censorship, and, in some jurisdictions, even union demands.

> As Martinson (1972) and others have noted, the nature of collective inmate action has undergone dramatic change since the early attempts at mass escape. Contemporary inmates are much more politically sophisticated and organizationally inclined. They no longer involve themselves in collective action for the exclusive purpose of communicating their displeasure to their immediate keepers. Instead, they are becoming aware that, in an age of instant communication through the mass media, their "audience" has widened considerably. Any perusal of inmate literature today will demonstrate to the reader that the modern prisoner is often acquainted, formally or informally, with the basic tenets of labeling theory and with the results of studies focusing on self-reported crime, police and judicial discretion and "white collar" crime. Increasingly he feels that he has been singled out to bear the burden of punishment by a society that is, from most indications, characterized by a tremendous discrepancy between idealized behavior (as reflected in its laws) and actual behavior (as reported by its citizens). The belief that they are "political prisoners" characterizes the conclusion drawn by an increasing number of our inmates. They are aware that the attributes which disproportionately distinguish them from the free citizens outside the walls are race, income level, and social status—not behavior or mens rea.[11]

Inmates are increasingly perceiving rehabilitation as a game to be played, and they are learning that, in exchange for minimal conformity to prison rules, the system can be corrupted. The demands for concessions are, in part, an outgrowth of that recognition.

Criticisms: Courts

The courts, in abandoning the "hands off" philosophy of Felix Frankfurter, have begun to express dismay over and disagreement with correctional practices. In one state (Alabama), the courts have threatened to close down the system. In others, courts have forced prison administrators to institute due process and humane practices. In some cases *(Sostre* v. *Rockefeller),* the courts have ruled against prison administrators and awarded punitive damages. Courts are paying increasing attention to an escalating number of inmate briefs. For example, the number of inmate briefs filed annually has increased from 2,000 in 1960 to 16,000 in 1970.[12] They constitute one out of every six civil findings.

In general the U.S. Supreme Court, in its unofficial role as a regulatory agency of the criminal justice system, has begun to limit discretion throughout the three basic components of the system, particularly in the police areas. In corrections, *Morrissey* v. *Brewer* is one case of note. *Furman* v. *Georgia* and *Gregg* v. *Georgia,* for example, address the death penalty, and there are lower court decisions which address the First Amendment and could have particularly adverse impacts on the medical model in corrections.

The basic rights granted to all citizens as defined by the various Constitutional Amendments have in large part been extended to prisoners, and in the next few years the right to treatment and the right to refuse treatment will be examined. These issues derive from the widespread use of the treatment model in corrections.

A future area of appeals which will eventually be heard and perhaps determined by the United States Supreme Court will relate to treatment programs that address the motivation of prisoners in contrast to the specific behavior that brought them to prison. One such program area is the behavior modification techniques, about which considerable controversy rages. In the 1973 case of *Mackey* v. *Procunier,* the Ninth Circuit Court raised the issue of "impermissible tinkering with the mental process." In that same year, a case involving a lobotomy operation *(Kaimowitz* v. *Michigan Department of Mental Health)* was decided; such impermissible tinkering with the mental process was held to be a violation of the First Amendment by the Michigan Circuit Court. Unless some highly effective "treatments" for criminal behavior are found which withstand the test of basic rights *and* are backed by solid evaluations, these programs and the medical model are in serious trouble.

Criticisms: Economists

Economists too are looking at our correctional model with some dismay. Only in recent years, when state money has been in increasingly short supply, has it become evident that criminal justice and corrections are very expensive. Total spending on federal, state, and local levels for police, prosecutors, courts, and prisons has shot up from $3.5 billion in 1969 to $17.2 billion in 1975.

Capital costs are astronomical. In Florida, for example, increased crime rates and court commitments have sorely taxed the correctional system. Florida's 11,500 inmates are housed in facilities designed for 9,000; Florida is now utilizing tent prisons, devoid of most correctional amenities. Some $58,000,000 worth of new institutions are either in the planning or construction state. By 1980, it is estimated that a quarter of a billion dollars will be required,[13] if present trends continue.

While capital costs are over $25,000 per cell,[14] the expense of keeping a felon incarcerated for one year can reach $12,000 per year. The waste of idleness is equally staggering. (Perhaps it is now time to repeal the Ashurst-Summers Act and the Hawes-Cooper Act.) An analysis of potential inmate economic benefits reveals that 290,000 felons in prison could earn an average of $8,038 per year or $2.33 billion. Such economic realities cause legislators, business managers, and the citizenry to wince while they reappraise "treatment."

Proposed Alternatives

Assuming the medical model will cease to be the major model in corrections and that the internal and external change agents will continue their current thrust and impact, a reintegrative model[15] is proposed as a possible alternative. Designed to allow for the weaknesses of the medical model and to incorporate recent innovations and predicted developments in corrections, the model is diagrammed in Figure VIII-2.

The reintegration model presented here assumes that:

1. Relatively few offenders perpetrate crime due to medical, psychiatric and/or psychological factors.

2. Offenders are apt to commit crime on their own volition and are not compelled by some irresistible impulse; criminals exercise "free will."

3. Most offenders can be handled through community-based corrections and relatively few (15-20 percent) require incapacitation and/or punishment.

4. Reintegration is a gradual process; there are few offenders who are able to escape an economically and socially marginal life-style in a brief period of time.

5. Sufficient community-based programs exist or can be coordinated to permit the gradual reintegration of offenders.

6. Offenders' problems arise in the community and must be handled in the community.

7. Given the option between punishment and community-based correctional programming, most offenders will not opt for punishment.

8. Some offenders are too dangerous to be handled even in a coordinated and comprehensive community-based program; for these offenders, prisons are necessary.

9. The courts must be an integral part of the overall reintegration of offenders.

10. The role of the defense attorney extends into the decision of the offender to participate in a punishment or reintegration package.

11. Both punishment and the reintegration model programming are the domain of any state's department of corrections.

The Contract

We need not detail the general procedures in processing offenders from the arrest-parole points of the criminal justice system, nor elaborate on the existence of varied alternatives to formal processing. These are briefly sketched in Figure VIII–2 and are assumed to exist to divert offenders for reintegration purposes. Our focus is on the offender pleading guilty or adjudicated guilty of a felony.

Once guilt is determined, and prior to disposition of the instant case, the judge will formally preside over and participate in the offender's choice of either punishment or reintegration. In this initial decision, the defense attorney would continue to provide legal advice and protect the offender's rights. Prosecution should remain a viable entity and would also participate in the final contract.

Upon conviction of those offenders not opting for punishment, the state's department of corrections would institute the development of a comprehensive reintegration plan predicated on maximizing the delivery of services, victim restitution, the least restrictive environment, and a detailed plan for the handling of the offender. Various options in the possible plans are in Figure VIII–2 and would include such programs as behavior modification, intrusive therapy, halfway houses, probation hostels for heavily dependent offenders, community treatment centers, community reintegration centers, education/vocation furlough programs, etc. The individualized plan would be presented to the court in the form of a proposed contract. Both defense and presecutorial attorneys could consent to or dissent from the plan; the court would retain authority in development of the final contract.

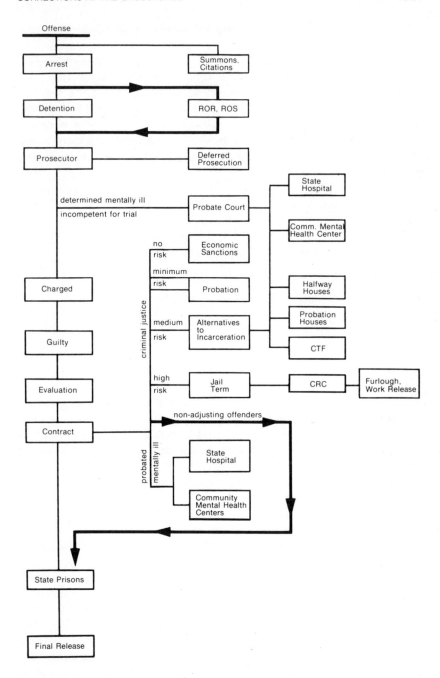

FIGURE VIII–2. A Reintegration Model (We are indebted to Dr. Richard P. Seiter for the original conception of this figure.)

Once the contracts were approved and signed by all parties, the court would formally dispose of the offender by his or her commitment as a probationer to the state's department of corrections, whose responsibility would include implementation of the contract, provision of services, and supervision, the levels of which could be varied in accordance with the offender's progress toward defined goals within the contractual time period. Serious deviation from the contract, absconding, and technical violations would be governed by at least the *Morrissey* conditions. The court would retain the right to formally revoke the reintegration contract and to impose prison as the alternative.

There would be six categories of offenders for whom this would not be necessary; mandatory prison terms would be required for those offenders who:

1. perpetrate murder in the first degree;

2. commit any crime in which a firearm was used;

3. are third-time felony conviction offenders;

4. are rapists;

5. are convicted as large-scale drug dealers;

6. are pedophiles (prefer children as sexual objects).

The philosophy of prison would be incapacitation; sentence lengths would be determinate, with minor reductions for "good time" behavior. Recidivists would receive multiples of the determinate sentence. Inasmuch as parole would not exist as a mandatory requirement and sentences would be determinate, a paroling agency would not be necessary. However, ex-prisoners desiring assistance would be eligible for all services, on a voluntary basis, available to probationers.

At present, this system is much more dream than reality. Yet the various elements that are its foundation exist in most jurisdictions today. The major difference between the social justice model and the standard criminal justice model is the establishment of graduated and integrated levels of correctional treatment, related less to the offense than to the offender's individual problems and needs. Most social agencies are taking this approach on a piecemeal basis now, but the added element of coordination and control would assure that all programs could maximally contribute toward the offender's rehabilitation. The social justice model seems to represent a logical conclusion for the present evolutionary trend in corrections. Like it or not, the correctional system today is under heavy fire; the emphasis is on accountability. Explanations must be given for the billions spent on corrections, rehabilitation, and processing of offenders. Excuses and glib platitudes are no longer the currency of the times. Results are.

The Role of Research in Corrections

One of the major handicaps to correctional reform is the lack of conclusive evidence as to which techniques work and which do not. Although many extensive research projects have attempted to explain, or justify, one or another of the hundreds of different approaches to correctional rehabilitation, most results are still inconclusive. In his massive examination of correctional research, Robert Martinson points out the crux of the evaluation problem in the field:

> In sum, even in the case of treatment programs administered outside penal institutions, we simply cannot say that this treatment in itself has an appreciable effect on offender behavior. On the other hand, there is one encouraging set of findings that emerges from these studies. For from many of them there flows the strong suggestion that even if we can't "treat" offenders so as to make them do better, a great many of the programs designed to rehabilitate them at least did not make them do *worse*. And if these programs did not show the advantages of actually rehabilitating, some of them did have the advantage of being less onerous to the offender himself without seeming to pose increased danger to the community. And some of these programs—especially those involving less restrictive custody, minimal supervision, and early release—simply cost fewer dollars to administer. The information on the dollar costs of these programs is just beginning to be developed but the implication is clear: *that if we can't do more for (and to) offenders, at least we can safely do less.*
>
> There is, however, one important caveat even to this note of optimism: In order to calculate the true costs of these programs, one must in each case include not only their administrative cost but also the cost of maintaining in the community an offender population increased in size. This population might well not be committing new offenses at any greater rate; but the offender population might, under some of these plans, be larger in absolute *numbers*. So the total number of offenses committed might rise, and our chances of victimization might therefore rise too. We need to be able to make a judgment about the size and probable duration of this effect; as of now, we simply do not know.
>
> [A] pattern has run through much of this discussion—of studies which "found" effects without making any truly rigorous attempt to exclude competing hypotheses, of extraneous factors permitted to intrude upon the measurements, of recidivism measures which are not all measuring the same thing, of "follow-up" periods which vary enormously and rarely extend beyond the period of legal supervision, of experiments never replicated, of "system effects" not taken into account, of categories drawn up without any theory to guide the

enterprise. It is just possible that some of our treatment programs *are* working to some extent, but that our research is so bad that it is incapable of telling.[16]

Massive attacks on the problems of corrections have been waged since the end of World War II—which produced new methods of helping people as well as killing them. These efforts have ensured that change is here to stay, and that the search for real solutions will continue. There is no doubt that correctional research has already altered many beliefs and practices with regard to the handling of inmates. Further research should be structured around specific objectives:

> Two complementary sources of research are required to meet correction's continuing needs. First, research must be incorporated as an integral instrument of correctional management. Modern administration depends on the collection and analysis of information as a basis for policy formulation and a guide for specific decisions. No information system can replace the decisionmaker, but availability of selected information, carefully interpreted, offers an invaluable aid to his reason and judgment. Every correctional manager should be afforded the tools of research methodology and the degree of objectivity an agency research program can provide.
>
> Second, there is need for research done outside the agency. Not all sources of innovation can be found within the confines of any one agency or system. Continued improvement of corrections can be expected only from the application of new ideas and models derived from basic research and prototype projects. The support of such research by national funding agencies insures contribution of ideas from the private sector, the academic community, and other sources. Also required is a continuing hospitality to the conduct of research in the operating correctional agencies.
>
> Research alone cannot create a new day in corrections. It offers the administrator opportunity to learn from the mistakes of others. The administrator's task in attempting to meet needs as they arise is to utilize all tools with which innovations are forged.[17]

As noted above, research alone cannot solve the problems of correctional administrators. In some cases it may dash cherished hopes and beliefs, but the knowledge gained can be used to progress in a sound, scientific manner.

The main purpose of most research in corrections is to evaluate the effectiveness of a particular system or program. It is easy to confuse these terms. A *system* refers to the entire correctional apparatus of a particular state, county, city, or region, or that of the federal government. A *program* refers to a certain approach to treatment (or punishment). The role of evaluative research has been outlined by the National Advisory Commission as follows:

Measurement and review should reflect these considerations:

1. For system reviews, measurement of recidivism should be the primary evaluative criterion. The following definition of recidivism should be adopted nationally by all correctional agencies to facilitate comparisons among jurisdictions and compilation of national figures:

    Recidivism is measured by (1) criminal acts that resulted in a conviction by a court, when committed by individuals who are under correctional supervision or who have been released from correctional supervision within the previous three years, and by (2) technical violations of probation or parole in which a sentencing or paroling authority took action that resulted in an adverse change in the offenders' legal status.

    Technical violations should be maintained separately from data on reconvictions. Also, recidivism should be reported in a manner to discern patterns of change. At a minimum, statistical tables should be prepared every six months during the three-year followup period, showing the number of recidivists. Discriminations by age, offense, length of sentence, and disposition should be provided.

2. Program review is a more specific type of evaluation that should entail these five criteria of measurement:

    a. Measurement of effort, in terms of cost, time, and types of personnel employed in the project in question.

    b. Measurement of performance, in terms of whether immediate goals of the program have been achieved.

    c. Determination of adequacy of performance, in terms of the program's value for offenders exposed to it as shown by individual followup.

    d. Determination of efficiency, assessing effort and performance for various programs to see which are most effective with comparable groups and at what cost.

    e. Study of process, to determine the relative contributions of process to goal achievement,

such as attributes of the program related to
success or failure, recipients of the program who
are more or less benefited, conditions affecting
program delivery, and effects produced by the
program. Program reviews should provide for
classification of offenders by relevant types (age,
offense category, base expectancy rating,
psychological state or type, etc.). Evaluative
measurement should be applied to discrete and
defined cohorts. Where recidivism data are to be
used, classifications should be related to
reconvictions and technical violations of
probation or parole as required in systems
reviews.

3. Assertions of system or program success should not
   be based on unprocessed percentages of offenders
   not reported in recidivism figures. That is, for
   individuals to be claimed as successes, their
   success must be clearly related in some
   demonstrable way to the program to which they were
   exposed.[18]

The following caveat is presented for researchers who are determined to
make their evaluation prove that the program in question is a good one:

Great caution should be used in making claims about correctional
successes. In point of fact, recidivism can tell us only about
correctional failures. Unless research and statistics can tell us about
how individuals were affected by different programs and how they
later developed as "successes," corrections cannot be expected to
move forward significantly. Avoidance of failure is not identical by
any stretch of logic with promotion of success. The attributes of
specific programs that had positive impact on specific offenders must
be identified. Furthermore, discrimination of program failures from
expected failures is essential to understanding recidivism.
Discrimination of program successes is equally essential, but these
successes must be individually verified, not inferred from statistical
class. That is, the fact that a cohort of released offenders had a
recidivism rate of 40 percent does not mean that the correctional
system can claim a 60 percent success rate for its programs.[19]

Research has a definite place in the development of corrections into an
effective social change agency. Combined with improved data-keeping and
processing procedures, scientific studies will assist the correctional administrator in selecting the most effective programs from the spectrum of those

available. Research is not a panacea, however; empirical results can only tell *what* happened, and any conclusions as to *why* it happened must be theoretical at best. It will be up to the correctional administrator to use the research to improve, and sometimes eliminate, programs and policies shown to be unsatisfactory.

Current and Future Trends

The most obvious trend in corrections today is toward the use of alternatives to incarceration whenever possible. In large part, the decreasing prison population reflects a favorable view of community-based alternatives to the destructive and ineffective institutional programs. The correctional ideology has shifted from punishment to treatment and reintegration. The public has finally become aware that after imprisonment, offenders return to the community in worse shape than ever. Too many of these uncorrected individuals see crime as the answer to their problems. Thus, every effort is expended to correct the offender in the community before an institutional alternative must be employed; community reintegration centers provide many of the programs and much of the security of the fortress prisons.

The general movement away from punishment includes attempts to reduce or eliminate the stigma of a criminal conviction, particularly in the case of victimless crimes such as public drunkenness. Detoxification centers, located in many jurisdictions, have been extremely effective in helping public drunks cope with their problem while avoiding the stigma of a criminal conviction. This procedure also releases critical police resources to combat serious crime. Other alternatives to the criminal justice system presently being evaluated are: deferred prosecution, prosecution without adjudication, and the use of a summons or citation in lieu of arrest.

Viable incarceration alternatives, among other benefits, enable offenders to earn a living, complete an education, or work to repay the victim of their crime. Development and extension of victim compensation and restitution statutes is a likely move over the next few years. If work release and similar programs are not provided to help offenders earn money to repay their victims, the state will have to make restitution out of *public* funds. Thus, failure to establish such programs may prove very expensive for the state, as television and other media continue to encourage public awareness of the victim's needs.

The Fear of Crime: Where It Begins

Emphasis on violence in the media, instant visual coverage of criminal acts, and deterioration in the cities have intensified public fear of crime. It seems that these fears are justified by the rising crime rates, especially with regard to crimes of violence. The public has been told again and again that the majority of these crimes are committed by individuals who have been arrested and processed through the correctional system before. The inevitable result has been a loss of faith in the rehabilitative capability of our correctional systems, and a cry for more punitive confinement. As noted in a brochure distributed by the United States Chamber of Commerce, "The conditions within many prisons achieve nothing but an increase in the number of recidivists (those released from institutions who commit additional crimes). Eighty percent of all felonies are committed by repeaters."[20] This kind of statement, while based on facts, is damaging to the entire correctional system. It reflects, unfortunately, only the actions of those few offenders who passed through the entire correctional funnel and ended up in *institutions*.

We have already shown that those offenders who are selectively funneled into our prisons are the very ones most likely to return to criminal behavior. The increasing use of alternatives to incarceration is rapidly placing the largest portion of the correctional population *outside* the institution. Some diversionary and probation programs claim success rates as high as 60 to 90 percent. Since offenders involved in these programs are not usually included in the calculations used to arrive at repeater rates, the public receives a distorted picture of the total system. Based on the figures above, an equally valid conclusion would be that offenders who participated in a noninstitutional program, or were dealt with entirely outside the criminal justice system, are committing *only 20 percent* of the felonies. The point is that statistics can be interpreted in several ways, and public fear of the repeat offender is not often based on an accurate picture. Greater effort must be expended in the future to present the complete story to the public, so they can understand the successes as well as the failures.

The reduction of public fear, when *all* the facts are presented, will help establish the value of alternatives to incarceration for most offenders. These facts will suggest that offenders who are not amenable to reintegration should be treated on the basis of their social dysfunctions, not simply as long as a specific sentence happens to last. Crime is a real danger, and some fear is certainly justified. But fear based on incomplete information can do more harm than good to the cause of safer streets.

Victims as Inmates: Needed Change

When a child is abused by a parent, the traditional response has been to take action to remove the child from the family for placement in a juvenile care facility. In rare cases these are highly specialized centers in which the juvenile *victim* is given a chance to feel cared about. In most cases, far too many, the juvenile victim is processed in the same manner and by the same system as juvenile *offenders*. It is small wonder that so many juvenile institutions are known as "schools for crime." Juvenile victims are hard pressed to understand that they are in an institution because of *parens patriae*—not to be punished, like others in the same environment. Embittered at being the only ones removed from the family and institutionalized, juveniles turn away from the authorities and toward the inmate subculture for support. Prior to the recognition of the need for "status offender" legislation, this has been the familiar picture.

Society has begun to realize what has been done to juveniles who were victims of crime (abused children, incest victims, and children exploited for pornography, prostitution, and child labor), and has begun to recommend that family units be maintained intact for treatment. If one member needs to be punished for the crime, it clearly should not be the victim.

The handling of so-called "victimless" crimes has also come under close scrutiny and criticism. The users (victims) of drug and alcohol are finding that possession and use of such substances is beginning to be decriminalized. Marijuana is the current target for decriminalization, as was alcohol in the early 1930s. Whether the use of "pot" is good or bad is yet to be decided, but those who use it are victims of the dealers of such substances, just as alcohol users were victims of the bootleggers in the "roaring twenties." We do not advocate legalization or decriminalization of marijuana; we only posit this as another case in which the victim of illegal activity becomes the one most often punished. Prostitution is another "victimless" crime that does indeed have victims. The prostitute is victimized by the pimps who profit financially from her way of life. The customer may also be seen as a victim—of uncontrollable urges and a convincing sales pitch. Both of these "victims" of victimless crime can be, and are, punished as offenders. Gambling is yet another crime that punishes the victim in many cases. A more realistic approach to these crimes is being taken, but the tide of public opinion is hard to turn. From the standpoint of pragmatic correctional administration, removing these victims from the already overcrowded systems, both juvenile and adult, would help to relieve some of the deadly pressures that now plague corrections.

Where Now?

It is extremely difficult to decide when to stop writing about this fascinating, complex, and dynamic field we call "corrections." But, reluctantly, we shall now close with a few observations. This text has been designed to give the student a broad view of the history, processes, systems, clientele, and problems shaping the functions and facilities that constitute corrections in America. In the beginning we asked the question, "What is corrections?" It should be apparent by now that corrections is a goal in search of a process, a process that works. The history of corrections is long, but in America we are actually dealing with less than two centuries of experience. The main response to crime in the corrections systems of America has been the penitentiary—a persistent idea, but in terms of reintegration of offenders into the free community, an unsuccessful one. The industrial prisons built with such great expectations in the nineteenth century were not designed for reintegration, and efforts to make them serve that purpose have inevitably failed. In recent years, the advent of community-based treatment has created a correctional revolution in America, even during a period of skyrocketing populations in our fortress prisons.

The new correctional goals of rehabilitation and reintegration are difficult if not impossible to attain in the maximum security institution. The validity of these goals was reinforced with the infusion of many middle- and upper-class persons into the jails and prisons of America in the turbulent 1960s. The problems of criminalization and prisonization are also addressed by the new correctional concepts. Maximum use of diversion from the criminal justice system allows many nondangerous offenders to receive treatment and support without incurring the stigma of a criminal record. The negative effects of a criminal record have been examined in detail, and the next great move in this area will be some form of mandatory expungement, after the ex-offender has lived in the community for a specified period without criminal involvement.

The correctional systems in America are slowly moving toward a philosophy that emphasizes treatment aimed at the nonviolent offender's individual problems, rather than punishment aimed at the offense. At the same time, paradoxically, there is great pressure to *punish* the violent offender, with overcrowded prisons nearing the boiling point as a result. We look forward to writing about the outcome of this situation a few years hence. It is hard to break down the boundaries that exist between felonies and misdemeanors, federal and state crimes, and federal, state, and local correctional systems. All these divisions encourage the development of separate programs, separate systems, and separate drains on fiscal and personnel resources. It will probably be some time before individual offenders are treated in a network of separate programs and facilities geared toward *classes of offenders,* not *offenses* or *jurisdictions.* This movement is slowly getting under way, however, and it clearly heralds the direction of corrections in the next decades. It will be up to the professionals in the field to ensure that the new approaches do not jeopardize public safety, and to provide alternatives for those who refuse to be reintegrated. It is a big job, but it represents the only source of an effective solution to America's rising crime problem.

NOTES

1. Joint Commission on Correctional Manpower and Training, *Targets for In-Service Training* (Washington, D.C.: Joint Commission on Correctional Manpower and Training, 1968), p. 1.

2. Joint Commission on Correctional Manpower and Training, *Targets for In-Service Training,* p. 3.

3. Joint Commission on Correctional Manpower and Training, *Offenders as a Manpower Resource* (Washington, D.C.: Joint Commission on Correctional Manpower and Training, 1969), p. 73.

4. Joseph E. Scott and Pamela A. Bennett, *Ex-Offenders as Parole Officers: An Evaluation of the Parole Officer Case Aid Program in Ohio* (Columbus, Ohio: Ohio State University Research Foundation, 1973), p. 95.

5. Constance Holden, "Prisons: Faith in 'Rehabilitation' Is Suffering a Collapse," *Science* 188 (May 1975): 815-817.

6. William Wayson, "Correctional Myths and Economic Realities," *Proceedings, The Second National Workshop on Correctional and Parole Administration* (College Park, Md.: American Correctonal Association, 1974), pp. 26-27.

7. Robert Martinson, "What Works?—Questions and Answers about Prison Reform," *Public Interest* (Spring 1974): 22-55. Martinson's review does not include reports made since 1967. The National Institute of Law Enforcement and Criminal Justice, U.S. Department of Justice, is contracting privately to determine the effectiveness of programs in more recent years.

8. Walter C. Bailey, "Correctional Outcome: An Evaluation of 100 Reports," *Journal of Criminal Law, Criminology and Police Science* 57 (June 1966): 153-160.

9. David Rothman, "Prisons: The Failure Model," *The Nation* 219 (December 21, 1974): 656-659. See his *The Discovery of the Asylum* (Boston: Little, Brown and Company, 1971).

10. Friends Service Committee, *Struggle for Justice* (New York: Hill and Wang, 1971).

11. Ronald Huff, "Unionization Behind Walls," *Criminology* 12:2 (August 1974): 175-194. Quotation from pp. 176-177.

12. National Advisory Commission on Criminal Justice Standards and Goals, *A National Strategy to Reduce Crime* (Washington, D.C.: U.S. Government Printing Office, 1973), p. 115.

13. *Criminal Justice Newsletter* 6:3 (February 3, 1975).

14. The U.S. Bureau of Prisons completed a new 500-bed facility in San Diego in November of 1975 at a cost of $14,859,000 or $29,718 per cell.

15. See the excellent articel by Vincent O'Leary and David Duffee, "Correctional Policy: A Classification of Goals Designed for Change," *Crime and Delinquency* 17:4 (October 1971): 373-386. We are indebted to these authors, but differ significantly from their position, particularly in the area of parole.

16. Martinson, "What Works?," pp. 47-79.

17. National Advisory Commission on Criminal Justice Standards and Goals, *Corrections* (Washington, D.C.: U.S. Government Printing Office, 1973), p. 496.

18. National Advisory Commission, *Corrections,* pp. 528-529.

19. National Advisory Commission, *Corrections,* p. 530.

20. Chamber of Commerce of the United States, *Marshaling Citizen Power to Modernize Corrections* (Washington, D.C.: Chamber of Commerce of the United States, 1972), p. 5.

Glossary

The authors are grateful to the Law Enforcement Assistance Administration for the publication of the *Dictionary of Criminal Justice Data Terminology*, from which the following terms and definitions have been extracted. It is in the spirit of that effort to standardize Criminal Justice terminology that we have decided to include this section. We hope that students, especially those new to the field, will take the time to read and absorb the meanings of these "tools of the trade." To obtain more detailed information about the terms in this glossary, the student should write to: U.S. Department of Justice, National Criminal Justice Information and Statistics Service, LEAA, Washington, D.C. 20531.

Abscond (corrections): To depart from a geographical area or jurisdiction prescribed by the conditions of one's probation or parole, without authorization.

Abscond (court): To intentionally absent or conceal oneself unlawfully in order to avoid a legal process.

Acquittal: A judgment of a court, based either on the verdict of a jury or a judicial officer, that the defendant is not guilty of the offense(s) for which he or she has been tried.

Adjudicated: Having been the subject of completed criminal or juvenile proceedings, and convicted, or adjudicated a delinquent, status offender, or dependent.

Adjudication (criminal): The judicial decision terminating a criminal proceeding by a judgment of conviction or acquittal, or a dismissal of the case.

Adjudication (juvenile): The juvenile court decision, terminating an adjudicatory hearing, that the juvenile is either a delinquent, status offender, or dependent, or that the allegations in the petition are not sustained.

Adjudicatory hearing: In juvenile proceedings, the fact-finding process wherein the juvenile court determines whether or not there is sufficient evidence to sustain the allegations in a petition.

Adult: A person who is within the original jurisdiction of a criminal, rather than a juvenile, court because his or her age at the time of an alleged criminal act was above a statutorily specified limit.

Alias: Any name used for an official purpose that is different from a person's legal name.

Appeal: A request by either the defense or the prosecution that a case be removed from a lower court to a higher court in order for a completed trial to be reviewed by the higher court.

Appearance: The act of coming into a court and submitting to the authority of that court.

Appearance, first (initial appearance): The first appearance of a juvenile or adult in the court which has jurisdiction over his or her case.

Appellant: A person who initiates an appeal.

Arraignment: The appearance of a person before a court in order that the court may inform him of the accusation(s) against him and enter his plea.

Arrest: Taking a person into custody by authority of law, for the purpose of charging him or her with a criminal offense or for the purpose of initiating juvenile proceedings, terminating with the recording of a specific offense.

Arson: The intentional destruction or attempted destruction, by fire or explosive, of the property of another, or of one's own property with the intent to defraud.

Assault: Unlawful intentional inflicting, or attempted or threatened inflicting, of injury upon another.

Assault, aggravated: Unlawful intentional causing of serious bodily injury with or without a deadly weapon or unlawful intentional attempting or threatening of serious bodily injury or death with a deadly weapon.

Assault on a law enforcement officer: A simple or aggravated assault, where the victim is a law enforcement officer engaged in the performance of his or her duties.

Assault, simple: Unlawful intentional threatening, attempted inflicting, or inflicting of less than serious bodily injury, in the absence of a deadly weapon.

Assault with a deadly weapon: Unlawful intentional inflicting, or attempted or threatened inflicting, of injury or death with the use of a deadly weapon.

Assigned counsel: An attorney, not regularly employed by a government agency, assigned by the court to represent a particular person(s) in a particular criminal proceeding.

Attorney/lawyer/counsel: A person trained in the law, admitted to practice before the bar of a given jurisdiction, and authorized to advise, represent, and act for other persons in legal proceedings.

Backlog: The number of pending cases which exceed the capacity of the court, in that they cannot be acted upon because the court is occupied in acting upon other cases.

Bombing incident: The detonation or attempted detonation of an explosive or incendiary device with willful disregard of risk to the person or property of another, or for a criminal purpose.

Booking: A police administrative action officially recording an arrest and identifying the person, the place, the time, the arresting authority, and the reason for the arrest.

Burglary: Unlawful entry of a structure, with or without force, with intent to commit a felony, or larceny.

Camp/ranch/farm: Any of several types of similar confinement facilities, usually in a rural location, which contain adults or juveniles committed after adjudication.

Case: At the level of police or prosecutorial investigation, a set of circumstances under investigation involving one or more persons; at subsequent steps in criminal proceedings, a charging document alleging the commission of one or more crimes; a single defendant; in juvenile or correctional proceedings, a person who is the object of agency action.

Case (court): A single charging document under the jurisdiction of a court; or a single defendant.

Caseload (corrections): The total number of clients registered with a correctional agency or agent during a specified time period, often divided into active and inactive, or supervised and unsupervised, thus distinguishing between clients with whom the agency or agent maintains contact and those with whom it does not.

Caseload (court): The total number of cases filed in a given court or before a given judicial officer during a given period of time.

Caseload, pending: The number of cases at any given time which have been filed in a given court, or are before a given judicial officer, but have not reached disposition.

CCH: An abbreviation for "computerized criminal history."

Charge: A formal allegation that a specific person(s) has committed a specific offense(s).

Charging document: A formal written accusation, filed in a court, alleging that a specified person(s) has committed a specific offense(s).

Check fraud: The issuance or passing of a check, draft, or money order that is legal as a formal document, signed by the legal account holder but with the foreknowledge that the bank or depository will refuse to honor it because of insufficient funds or closed account.

Chief of police: A local law enforcement officer who is the appointed or elected head of a police department.

Child abuse: A willful action or actions by a person causing physical harm to a child.

Child neglect: Willful failure by the person(s) responsible for a child's well-being to provide for adequate food, clothing, shelter, education, and supervision.

Citation (appear): A written order issued by a law enforcement officer directing an alleged offender to appear in a specific court at a specified time in order to answer a criminal charge.

Commitment: The action of a judicial officer ordering that an adjudicated and sentenced adult, or adjudicated delinquent or status offender who has been the subject of a juvenile court disposition hearing, be admitted into a correctional facility.

Community facility (nonconfinement facility, adult or juvenile): A correctional facility from which residents are regularly permitted to depart, unaccompanied by any official, for the purpose of daily use of community resources such as schools or treatment programs, and seeking or holding employment.

Complaint: A formal written accusation made by any person, often a prosecutor, and filed in a court, alleging that a specified person(s) has committed a specific offense(s).

Complaint denied: The decision by a prosecutor to decline a request that he or she seek an indictment or file an information or complaint against a specified person(s) for a specific offense(s).

Complaint granted: The decision by a prosecutor to grant a request that he or she seek an indictment or file an information or complaint against a specified person(s) for a specific offense(s).

Complaint requested (police): A request by a law enforcement agency that the prosecutor seek an indictment or file a complaint or information against a specified person(s) for a specific offense(s).

Confinement facility: A correctional facility from which the inmates are not regularly permitted to depart each day unaccompanied.

Convict: An adult who has been found guilty of a felony and who is confined in a federal or state confinement facility.

Conviction: A judgment of a court, based either on the verdict of a jury or a judicial officer or on the guilty plea of the defendant, that the defendant is guilty of the offense(s) for which he or she has been tried.

Correctional agency: A federal, state, or local criminal justice agency, under a single administrative authority, of which the principal functions are the investigation, intake screening, supervision, custody, confinement, or treatment of alleged or adjudicated adult offenders, delinquents, or status offenders.

Correctional day program: A publicly financed and operated nonresidential educational or treatment program for persons required, by a judicial officer, to participate.

Correctional facility: A building or part thereof, set of buildings, or area enclosing a set of buildings or structures operated by a government agency for the custody and/or treatment of adjudicated and committed persons, or persons subject to criminal or juvenile justice proceedings.

Correctional institution: A generic name proposed in this terminology for those long-term adult confinement facilities often called "prisons," "federal or state correctional facilities," or "penitentiaries," and juvenile confinement facilities called "training schools," "reformatories," "boy's ranches," and the like.

Correctional institution, adult: A confinement facility having custodial authority over adults sentenced to confinement for more than a year.

Correctional institution, juvenile: A confinement facility having custodial authority over delinquents and status offenders committed to confinement after a juvenile disposition hearing.

Corrections: A generic term which includes all government agencies, facilities, programs, procedures, personnel, and techniques concerned with the investigation, intake, custody, confinement, supervision, or treatment of alleged or adjudicated adult offenders, delinquents, or status offenders.

Count: Each separate offense, attributed to one or more persons, as listed in a complaint, information, or indictment.

Counterfeiting: The manufacture or attempted manufacture of a copy or imitation of a negotiable instrument with value set by law or convention, or the possession of such a copy without authorization, with the intent to defraud by claiming the genuineness of the copy.

Court: An agency of the judicial branch of government, authorized or established by statute or constitution, and consisting of one or more judicial officers, which has the authority to decide upon controversies in law and disputed matters of fact brought before it.

Court of appellate jurisdiction: A court which does not try criminal cases, but which hears appeals.

Court of general jurisdiction: Of criminal courts, a court which has jurisdiction to try all criminal offenses, including all felonies, and which may or may not hear appeals.

Court of limited jurisdiction: Of criminal courts, a court of which the trial jurisdiction either includes no felonies or is limited to less than all felonies, and which may or may not hear appeals.

Credit card fraud: The use or attempted use of a credit card in order to obtain goods or services with the intent to avoid payment.

Crime (criminal offense): An act committed or omitted in violation of a law forbidding or commanding it for which an adult can be punished, upon conviction, by incarceration and other penalties or a corporation penalized, or for which a juvenile can be brought under the jurisdiction of a juvenile court and adjudicated a delinquent or transferred to adult court.

Crime Index offenses, (index crimes): A UCR classification that includes all Part I offenses with the exception of involuntary (negligent) manslaughter.

Crimes against business (business crimes), (commerical crimes): A summary term used by the National Crime Panel reports, including: burglary (against businesses) and robbery (against businesses).

Crimes against households (household crimes): A summary term used by the National Crime Panel reports, including: burglary (against households), household larceny, and motor vehicle theft.

Crimes against persons: A summary term used by UCR and the National Crime Panel reports, but with different meanings:

UCR	**National Crime Panel**
murder	forcible rape
non-negligent (voluntary) manslaughter	robbery (against persons) aggravated assault
negligent (involuntary) manslaughter	simple assault personal larceny
forcible rape	
aggravated assault	

Crimes against property (property crime): A summary term used by UCR, both as a subclass of the Part I offenses and as a subclass of Crime Index offenses, but with different meanings:

As a subset of UCR Part I offenses	**As a subset of UCR Crime Index offenses**
robbery	burglary
burglary	larceny–theft
larceny–theft	motor vehicle theft
motor vehicle theft	

Crimes of violence (violent crime): A summary term used by UCR and the National Crime Panel, but with different meanings:

As a subset of UCR Index Crimes	**As a subset of National Crime Panel crimes against persons**
murder	forcible rape
non-negligent (voluntary) manslaughter	robbery (against persons)

        forcible rape   aggravated assault
        robbery   simple assault
        aggravated assault

Criminal history record information: Information collected by criminal justice agencies on individuals, consisting of identifiable descriptions and notations of arrests, detentions, indictments, informations, or other formal criminal charges, and any disposition(s) arising therefrom, sentencing, correctional supervision, and release.

Criminal justice agency: Any court with criminal jurisdiction and any other government agency or subunit which defends indigents, or of which the principal functions or activities consist of the prevention, detection, and investigation of crime; the apprehension, detention, and prosecution of alleged offenders; the confinement or official correctional supervision of accused or convicted persons, or the administrative or technical support of the above functions.

Criminal proceedings: Proceedings in a court of law undertaken to determine the guilt or innocence of an adult accused of a crime.

Culpability: A state of mind on the part of one who has committed an act which makes him or her liable to prosecution for that act.

Defendant: A person against whom a criminal proceeding is pending.

Defense attorney: An attorney who represents the defendant in a legal proceeding.

Delinquency: Juvenile actions or conduct in violation of criminal law, and, in some contexts, status offenses.

Delinquent: A juvenile who has been adjudicated by a judicial officer of a juvenile court as having committed a delinquent act, which is an act for which an adult could be prosecuted in a criminal court.

Delinquent act: An act committed by a juvenile for which an adult could be prosecuted in a criminal court, but for which a juvenile can be adjudicated in a juvenile court, or prosecuted in a criminal court if the juvenile court transfers jurisdiction.

De novo: Anew, afresh, as if there had been no earlier decision.

Dependency: The legal status of a juvenile over whom a juvenile court has assumed jurisdiction because the court has found his or her care by parent, guardian, or custodian to fall short of a legal standard of proper care.

Dependent: A juvenile over whom a juvenile court has assumed jurisdiction because the court has found his or her care by parent, guardian, or custodian to fall short of a legal standard of proper care.

Detention: The legally authorized holding in confinement of a person subject to criminal or juvenile court proceedings, until the point of commitment to a correctional facility or release.

Detention center: A government facility which provides temporary care in a physically restricting environment for juveniles in custody pending court disposition.

Detention facility: A generic name proposed in this terminology as a cover term for those facilities which hold adults or juveniles in confinement pending adjudication, adults sentenced for a year or less of confinement, and in some instances postadjudicated juveniles, including facilities called "jails," "county farms," "honor farms," "work camps," "road camps," "detention centers," "shelters," "juvenile halls," and the like.

Detention facility, adult: A confinement facility of which the custodial authority is 48 hours or more and in which adults can be confined before adjudication or for sentences of a year or less.

Detention facility, juvenile: A confinement facility having custodial authority over juveniles confined pending and after adjudication.

Detention hearing: In juvenile proceedings, a hearing by a judicial officer of a juvenile court to determine whether a juvenile is to be detained, to continue to be detained, or to be released, while juvenile proceedings are pending in his or her case.

Diagnosis or classification center: A functional unit within a correctional institution, or a separate facility, which holds persons held in custody for the purpose of determining to which correctional facility or program they should be committed.

Dismissal: A decision by a judicial officer to terminate a case without a determination of guilt or innocence.

Disposition: The action by a criminal or juvenile justice agency which signifies that a portion of the justice process is complete and jurisdiction is relinquished or transferred to another agency, or which signifies that a decision has been reached on one aspect of a case and a different aspect comes under consideration, requiring a different kind of decision.

Disposition, court: The final judicial decision which terminates a criminal proceeding by a judgment of acquittal or dismissal, or which states the specific sentence in the case of a conviction.

Disposition hearing: A hearing in juvenile court, conducted after an adjudicatory hearing and subsequent receipt of the report of any predisposition investigation, to determine the most appropriate disposition of a juvenile who has been adjudicated a delinquent, a status offender, or a dependent.

Disposition, juvenile court: The decision of a juvenile court, concluding a disposition hearing, that a juvenile be committed to a correctional facility, or placed in a care or treatment program, or required to meet certain standards of conduct, or released.

Diversion: The official halting or suspension, at any legally prescribed processing point after a recorded justice system entry, of formal criminal or juvenile justice proceedings against an alleged offender, and referral of that person to a treatment or care program administered by a nonjustice agency, or a private agency, or no referral.

Driving under the influence—alcohol (drunk driving): The operation of any vehicle after having consumed a quantity of alcohol sufficient to potentially interfere with the ability to maintain safe operation.

Driving under the influence—drugs: The operation of any vehicle while attention or ability is impaired through the intake of a narcotic or an incapacitating quantity of another drug.

Drug law violation: The unlawful sale, transport, manufacture, cultivation, possession, or use of a controlled or prohibited drug.

Embezzlement: The misappropriation, misapplication, or illegal disposal of legally entrusted property with intent to defraud the legal owner or intended beneficiary.

Escape: The unlawful departure of a lawfully confined person from a confinement facility, or from custody while being transported.

Expunge: The sealing or purging of arrest, criminal, or juvenile record information.

Extortion: Unlawful obtaining or attempting to eventually obtain the property of another by the threat of eventual injury or harm to that person, or the person's property, or another person.

Felony: A criminal offense punishable by death, or by incarceration in a state or federal confinement facility for a period of which the lower limit is prescribed by statute in a given jurisdiction, typically one year or more.

Filing: The commencement of criminal proceedings by entering a charging document into the official record of a court.

Finding: The official determination of a judicial officer or administrative body regarding a disputed matter of fact or law.

Fine: The penalty imposed upon a convicted person by a court requiring that he or she pay a specified sum of money.

Forgery: The creation or alternation of a written or printed document which, if validly executed, would constitute a record of a legally binding transaction, with the intent to defraud by affirming it to be the act of an unknowing second person.

defining features
- making or altering a written or printed document or record
- act is falsely attributed to an unknowing second person
- intent to illegally deprive a person of property or legal rights

Fraud: An element of certain offenses consisting of deceit or intentional misrepresentation with the aim of illegally depriving a person of property or legal rights.

Fugitive: A person who has concealed himself or fled a given jurisdiction in order to avoid prosecution or confinement.

Group home: A nonconfining residential facility for adjudicated adults or juveniles, or those subject to criminal or juvenile proceedings, intended to reproduce as closely as possible the circumstances of family life, and at minimum providing access to community activities and resources.

recommended conditions of use Classify government facilities fitting this definition as *community facilities*.

annotation "Group home" is variously defined in different jurisdictions. Most of the facilities known by this name are privately operated, though they may be financed mainly from government funds. Classification problems unique to private facilities have not been dealt with in this terminology, although most recommended standard descriptors for publicly operated facilities are also applicable to the private sector. See *correctional facility* for a list of recommended standard descriptors. The data collection questionnaire for the LEAA series "Children in Custody" defines "group home" as, "Allows juveniles extensive contact with the community, such as through jobs and schools, but none or less than half are placed there on probation or aftercare/ parole." It is distinguished from *halfway house* in this series by the percent of residents on probation or parole.

Halfway house: A nonconfining residential facility for adjudicated adults or juveniles, or those subject to criminal or juvenile proceedings, intended to provide an alternative to confinement for persons not suitable for probation, or needing a period of readjustment to the community after confinement.

recommended conditions of use Classify government facilities fitting this definition as *community facilities*.

annotation "Halfway house" is variously defined in different jurisdictions. Most of the facilities known by this name are privately operated, though they may be financed mainly from government funds. Classification problems unique to private facilities have not been dealt with in this terminolgy, although most recommended standard descriptors for publicly operated facilities are also applicable to the private sector. See *correctional facility* for a list of recommended standard descriptors. The data collection questionnaire for the LEAA series "Children in Custody" defines "halfway house" as, "Has 50 percent or more juveniles on probabtion or aftercare/parole, allowing them extensive contact with the community, such as through jobs and schools." It is distinguished from *group home* in this series by the percent of residents on probation or parole.

Hearing: A proceeding in which arguments, evidence, or witnesses are heard by a judicial officer or administrative body.

Hearing, probable cause: A proceeding before a judicial officer in which arguments, evidence, or witnesses are presented and in which it is determined whether there is sufficient cause to hold the accused for trial or whether the case should be dismissed.

Homicide: Any killing of one person by another.

Homicide, criminal: The causing of the death of another person without justification or excuse.

equivalent terms

UCR term—for police reporting level	dictionary entry term
criminal homicide	criminal homicide
murder (often used as cover term for murder and non-negligent manslaughter)	murder
non-negligent manslaughter	voluntary manslaughter
negligent manslaughter	involuntary manslaughter
(included in negligent manslaughter)	vehicular manslaughter

Homicide, excusable: The intentional but justifiable causing of the death of another or the unintentional causing of the death of another by accident or misadventure, without gross negligence. Not a crime.

Homicide, justifiable: The intentional causing of the death of another in the legal performance of an official duty or in circumstances defined by law as constituting legal justification. Not a crime.

Homicide, willful: The intentional causing of the death of another person, with or without legal justification.

Indictment: A formal written accusation made by a grand jury and filed in a court, alleging that a specified person(s) has committed a specific offense(s).

Infraction: An offense punishable by fine or other penalty, but not by incarceration.

Inmate: A person in custody in a confinement facility.

Institutional capacity: The officially stated number of inmates or residents which a correctional facility is designed to house, exclusive of extraordinary arrangements to accommodate overcrowded conditions.

Intake: The process during which a juvenile referral is received and a decision is made by an intake unit either to file a petition in juvenile court, to release the juvenile, to place him under supervision, or to refer him elsewhere.

Intake unit: A government agency or agency subunit which receives juvenile referrals from police, other government agencies, private agencies, or persons, and screens them, resulting in closing of the case, referral to care or supervision, or filing of a petition in juvenile court.

Jail: A confinement facility, usually administered by a local law enforcement agency, intended for adults but sometimes also containing juveniles, which holds persons detained pending adjudication and/or persons committed after adjudication for sentences of a year or less.

Jail (sentence): The penalty of commitment to the jurisdiction of a confinement facility system for adults, of which the custodial authority is limited to persons sentenced to a year or less of confinement.

Judge: A judicial officer who has been elected or appointed to preside over a court of law, whose position has been created by statute or by constitution, and whose decisions in criminal and juvenile cases may only be reviewed by a judge of a higher court and may not be reviewed de novo.

Judgment: The statement of the decision of a court that the defendant is convicted or acquitted of the offense(s) charged.

Judicial officer: Any person excercising judicial powers in a court of law.

Jurisdiction: The territory, subject matter, or person over which lawful authority may be exercised.

Jurisdiction, original: The lawful authority of a court or an administrative agency to hear or act upon a case from its beginning and to pass judgment on it.

Jury, grand: A body of persons who have been selected and sworn to investigate criminal activity and the conduct of public officials and to hear the evidence against an accused person(s) to determine whether there is sufficient evidence to bring that person(s) to trial.

Jury, trial (jury, petit), (jury): A statutorily defined number of persons selected according to law and sworn to determine certain matters of fact in a criminal action and to render a verdict of guilty or not guilty.

Juvenile: A person subject to juvenile court proceedings because a statutorily defined event was alleged to have occurred while his or her age was below the statutorily specified limit of original jurisdiction of a juvenile court.

  annotation Jurisdiction is determined by age at the time of the event, not at the time of judicial proceedings, and continues until the case is terminated. Thus a person may be described in a given data system as a juvenile because he or she is still subject to *juvenile court* proceedings even though his or her actual age may be several years over the limit. Conversely, criminal process data systems may include juveniles if the juvenile court has waived jurisdiction. ● Although the age limit varies in different states, it is most often the 18th birthday. The variation is small enough to permit nationally aggregated data to be meaningful, although individual states should note their age limit in communications with other states. • UCR defines juvenile as anyone under eighteen years of age. • See *youthful offender*.

Juvenile court: A cover term for courts which have original jurisdiction over persons statutorily defined as juveniles and alleged to be delinquents, status offenders, or dependents.

Juvenile justice agency: A government agency, or subunit thereof, of which the functions are the investigation, supervision, adjudication, care, or confinement of juveniles whose conduct or condition has brought or could bring them within the jurisdiction of a juvenile court.

Juvenile record: An official record containing, at a minimum, summary information pertaining to an identified juvenile concerning juvenile court proceedings, and, if applicable, detention and correctional processes.

Kidnapping: Unlawful transportation of a person without his or her consent, or without the consent of his or her guardian, if a minor.

Larceny (larceny–theft): Unlawful taking or attempted taking of property, other than a motor vehicle, from the possession of another.

Law enforcement agency: A federal, state, or local criminal justice agency of which the principal functions are the prevention, detection, and investigation of crime, and the apprehension of alleged offenders.

Law enforcement agency, federal: A law enforcement agency which is an organizational unit, or subunit, of the federal government.

Law enforcement agency, local: A law enforcement agency which is an organizational unit, or subunit, of local government.

Law enforcement agency, state: A law enforcement agency which is an organizational unit, or subunit, of state government.

Law enforcement officer (peace officer), (policeman): An employee of a law enforcement agency who is an officer sworn to carry out law enforcement duties, or a sworn employee of a prosecutorial agency who primarily performs investigative duties.

Law enforcement officer, federal: An employee of a federal law enforcement agency who is an officer sworn to carry out law enforcement duties, or a sworn employee of a federal prosecutorial agency who primarily performs investigative duties.

Law enforcement officer, local: An employee of a local law enforcement agency who is an officer sworn to carry out law enforcement duties, or a sworn employee of a local prosecutorial agency who primarily performs investigative duties.

Law enforcement officer, state: An employee of a state law enforcement agency who is an officer sworn to carry out law enforcement duties, or a sworn employee of a state prosecutorial agency who primarily performs investigative duties.

Level of government: The federal, state, regional, or local county or city location of administrative and major funding responsibility of a given agency.

Manslaughter, involuntary (negligent manslaughter): Causing the death of another by recklessness or gross negligence.

Manslaughter, vehicular: Causing the death of another by grossly negligent operation of a motor vehicle.

Manslaughter, voluntary (non-negligent manslaughter): Intentionally causing the death of another with reasonable provocation.

Misdemeanor: An offense usually punishable by incarceration in a local confinement facility for a period of which the upper limit is prescribed by statute in a given jurisdiction, typically limited to a year or less.

Model Penal Code: A generalized modern codification of that which is considered basic to criminal law, published by the American Law Institute in 1962.

Motion: An oral or written request made by a party to an action, before, during or after a trial, that a court issue a rule or order.

Motor vehicle theft: Unlawful taking, or attempted taking, of a motor vehicle owned by another with the intent to deprive the owner of it permanently or temporarily.

Murder: Intentionally causing the death of another without reasonable provocation or legal justification, or causing the death of another while committing or attempting to commit another crime.

Nolo contendere: A defendant's formal answer in court to the charges in a complaint, information, or indictment in which the defendant states that he or she does not contest the charges, and which, while not an admission of guilt, subjects the defendant to the same legal consequences as a plea of guilty.

Offender (criminal): An adult who has been convicted of a criminal offense.

Offender, alleged: A person who has been charged with a specific criminal offense(s) by a law enforcement agency or court, but has not been convicted.

Offense: An act committed or omitted in violation of a law forbidding or commanding it.

Offenses, Part I: A class of offenses selected for use in UCR, consisting of those crimes which are most likely to be reported, which occur with sufficient frequency to provide an adequate basis for comparison, and which are serious crimes by nature and/or volume.

annotation The Part I offenses are:

1. Criminal homicide
   a. Murder and non-negligent [voluntary] manslaughter
   b. Manslaughter by negligence [involuntary manslaughter]

2. Forcible rape
   a. Rape by force
   b. Attempted forcible rape

3. Robbery
   a. Firearm
   b. Knife or cutting instrument
   c. Other dangerous weapon
   d. Strongarm

4. Aggravated Assault
   a. Firearm
   b. Knife or cutting instrument
   c. Other dangerous weapon
   d. Hands, fist, feet, etc.—aggravated injury

5. Burglary
   a. Forcible entry
   b. Unlawful entry—no force
   c. Attempted forcible entry

6. Larceny–theft [larceny]

7. Motor vehicle theft
   a. Autos
   b. Trucks and buses
   c. Other vehicles

The various subclassifications of Part I offenses are described in the entry for UCR, in the subsection *UCR offense classifications*.

Offenses, Part II: A class of offenses selected for use in UCR, consisting of specific offenses and types of offenses which do not meet the criteria of frequency and/or seriousness necessary for Part I offenses.

annotation The Part II offenses are:

other assaults (simple,* nonaggravated)
arson*
forgery* and counterfeiting*
fraud*
embezzlement*
stolen property; buying, receiving, possessing
vandalism
weapons; carrying, possessing, etc.
prostitution and commercialized vice
sex offenses (except forcible rape, prostitution, and commercialized vice)
narcotic drug laws
gambling

offenses against the family and children
driving under the influence*
liquor laws
drunkenness
disorderly conduct
vagrancy
all other offenses (excepting traffic law violations)
suspicion*
curfew and loitering laws (juvenile violations)
runaway* (juveniles)

Terms marked with an asterisk (*) are defined in this glossary, though not necessarily in accord with UCR usuage. • UCR does not collect reports of Part II offenses. Arrest data concerning such offenses, however, are collected and published.

Parole: The status of an offender conditionally released from a confinement facility prior to the expiration of his or her sentence, and placed under the supervision of a parole agency.

Parole agency: A correctional agency, which may or may not include a parole authority, and of which the principal functions are the supervision of adults or juveniles placed on parole.

Parole authority: A person or a correctional agency which has the authority to release on parole adults or juveniles committed to confinement facilities, to revoke parole, and to discharge from parole.

Parolee: A person who has been conditionally released from a correctional institution prior to the expiration of his or her sentence, and who has been placed under the supervision of a parole agency.

Parole violation: An act or a failure to act by a parolee which does not conform to the conditions of his or her parole.

Penalty: The punishment annexed by law or judicial decision to the commission of a particular offense, which may be death, imprisonment, fine, or loss of civil privileges.

Person: A human being, or a group of human beings considered a legal unit, which has the lawful capacity to defend rights, incur obligations, prosecute claims, or can be prosecuted or adjudicated.

Petition (juvenile): A document filed in juvenile court alleging that a juvenile is a delinquent, a status offender, or a dependent, and asking that the court assume jurisdiction over the juvenile, or asking that the juvenile be transferred to a criminal court for prosecution as an adult.

Petition not sustained: The finding by a juvenile court in an adjudicatory hearing that there is not sufficient evidence to sustain an allegation that a juvenile is a delinquent, status offender, or dependent.

Plea: A defendant's formal answer in court to the charges brought against him or her in a complaint, information, or indictment.

Plea bargaining: The exchange of prosecutorial and/or judicial concessions, commonly a lesser charge, the dismissal of other pending charges, a recommendation by the prosecutor for a reduced sentence, or a combination thereof, in return for a plea of guilty.

Plea, final: The last plea, to a given charge, entered in a court record by or for a defendant.

Plea, guilty: A defendant's formal answer in court to the charges in a complaint, information, or indictment, in which the defendant states that the charges are true and that he or she has committed the offense as charged, or that he or she does not contest the charges.

Plea, initial: The first plea to a given charge, entered in a court record by or for a defendant.

Plea, not guilty: A defendant's formal answer in court to the charges in a complaint, information, or indictment, in which the defendant states that he or she is not guilty.

Police department: A local law enforcement agency directed by a chief of police or a commissioner.

Police officer: A local law enforcement officer employed by a police department.

Population movement: Entries and exits of adjudicated persons, or persons subject to judicial proceedings, into or from correctional facilities or programs.

Predisposition report: The document resulting from an investigation undertaken by a probation agency or other designated authority, which has been requested by a juvenile court, into the past behavior, family background, and personality of a juvenile who has been adjudicated a delinquent, a status offender, or a dependent, in order to assist the court in determining the most appropriate disposition.

Presentence report: The document resulting from an investigation undertaken by a probation agency or other designated authority, at the request of a criminal court, into the past behavior, family circumstances, and personality of an adult who has been convicted of a crime, in order to assist the court in determining the most appropriate sentence.

Prior record: Criminal history record information concerning any law enforcement, court, or correctional proceedings that have occurred before the current investigation of, or proceedings against, a person; or statistical descriptions of the criminal histories of a set of persons.

Prison: A confinement facility having custodial authority over adults sentenced to confinement for more than a year.

Prisoner: A person in custody in a confinement facility, or in the personal custody of a criminal justice official while being transported to or between confinement facilities.

Prison (sentence): The penalty of commitment to the jurisdiction of a confinement facility system for adults, of which the custodial authority extends to persons sentenced to more than a year of confinement.

Probable cause: A set of facts and circumstances which would induce a reasonably intelligent and prudent person to believe that an accused person had committed a specific crime.

Probation: The conditional freedom granted by a judicial officer to an alleged offender, or adjudicated adult or juvenile, as long as the person meets certain conditions of behavior.

Probation agency (probation department): A correctional agency of which the principal functions are juvenile intake, the supervision of adults and juveniles placed on probation status, and the investigation of adults or juveniles for the purpose of preparing presentence or predisposition reports to assist the court in determining the proper sentence or juvenile court disposition.

Probationer: A person required by a court or probation agency to meet certain conditions of behavior, who may or may not be placed under the supervision of a probation agency.

Probation officer: An employee of a probation agency whose primary duties include one or more of the probation agency functions.

Probation (sentence): A court requirement that a person fulfill certain conditions of behavior and accept the supervision of a probation agency, usually in lieu of a sentence to confinement but sometimes including a jail sentence.

Probation violation: An act or a failure to act by a probationer which does not conform to the conditions of his or her probation.

Pro se (in propria persona): Acting as one's own defense attorney in criminal proceedings; representing oneself.

Prosecutor: An attorney employed by a government agency or subunit whose official duty is to initiate and maintain criminal proceedings on behalf of the government against persons accused of committing criminal offenses.

Prosecutorial agency: A federal, state, or local criminal justice agency of which the principal function is the prosecution of alleged offenders.

Public defender: An attorney employed by a government agency or subdivision, whose official duty is to represent defendants unable to hire private counsel.

Public defender's office: A federal, state, or local criminal justice agency or subunit of which the principal function is to represent defendants unable to hire private counsel.

Purge (record): The complete removal of arrest, criminal, or juvenile record information from a given records system.

Rape: Unlawful sexual intercourse with a female, by force or without legal or factual consent.

Rape, forcible: Sexual intercourse or attempted sexual intercourse with a female against her will, by force or threat of force.

Rape, statutory: Sexual intercourse with a female who has consented in fact but is deemed, because of age, to be legally incapable of consent.

Rape without force or consent: Sexual intercourse with a female legally of the age of consent, but who is unconscious, or whose ability to judge or control her conduct is inherently impaired by mental defect, or impaired by intoxicating substances.

Recidivism: The repetition of criminal behavior; habitual criminality.

annotation In statistical practice, a recidivism rate may be any of a number of possible counts of instances of arrest, conviction, correctional commitment, and correctional status changes, related to counts of repetitions of these events within a given period of time. • Efforts to arrive at a single standard statistical description of recidivism have been hampered by the fact that the correct referent of the term is the actual repeated criminal or delinquent behavior of a given person or group, yet the only available statistical indicators of that behavior are records of such system events as rearrests, reconvictions, and probation or parole violations or revocations. It is recognized that these data reflect agency decisions about events and may or may not closely correspond with actual criminal behavior. Different conclusions about degrees of correspondence between system decisions and actual behavior consequently produce different definitions of recidivism, that is, different judgments of which system event repetition rates best measure actual recidivism rates. This is an empirical question, and not one of definition to be resolved solely by analysis of language usage and system logic. • Resolution has also been delayed by the limited capacities of most criminal justice statistical systems, which do not routinely make available the standardized offender-based transaction data (OBTD) which may be needed for the best measurement of recidivism. • Pending the adoption of a standard statistical description of recidivism, and the ability to implement it, it is recommended that recidivism analyses include the widest possible range of system events that can correspond with actual recidivism, and that sufficient detail on offenses charged be included to enable discrimination between degrees of gravity of offenses. The units of count should be clearly identified and the length of community exposure time of the subject population stated. • The National Advisory Commission on Criminal Justice Standards and Goals recommends a standard definition of recidivism in its volume *Corrections* (1973): "Recidivism is measured by (1) criminal acts that resulted in conviction by a court, when committed by individuals who are under correctional supervision or who have been released from correctional supersision within the previous three years, and by (2) technical violations of probation or parole in which a sentencing or paroling authority took action that resulted in an adverse change in the offender's legal status." Neither of these formulations is endorsed as adequate for all purposes. Both limit the measure and concept of recidivism to populations which are or have been under correctional supervision. Yet the ultimate significance of data concerning the repetition of criminal behavior often depends upon the comparison of the behavior of unconfined or unsupervised offenders with the behavior of those with correctional experience.

Referral to intake: In juvenile proceedings, a request by the police, parents, or other agency or person that a juvenile intake unit take appropriate action concerning a juvenile alleged to have committed a delinquent act or status offense, or to be dependent.

Release from detention: The authorized exit from detention of a person subject to criminal or juvenile justice proceedings.

Release from prison: A cover term for all lawful exits from federal or state confinement facilities primarily intended for adults serving sentences of more than a year, including all conditional and unconditional releases, deaths, and transfers to other jurisdictions, excluding escapes.

release on parole conditional release	release while still under jurisdiction of correctional agency, before expiration of sentence
discretionary	release date determined by parole authority
mandatory	release date determined by statute
discharge from prison unconditional release	release ending all agency jurisdiction
discretionary	pardon, commutation of sentence
mandatory	expiration of sentence
temporary release	authorized, unaccompanied temporary departure for educational, employment, or other authorized purposes
transfer of jurisdiction	transfer to jurisdiction of another correctional agency or a court
death	death from homicide, suicide, or natural causes
execution	execution of sentence of death

In some systems "release on parole" represents only discretionary conditional release. It is recommended that mandatory conditional releases be included, as both types describe conditional releases with subsequent parole status.

Release on bail: The release by a judicial officer of an accused person who has been taken into custody, upon the accused's promise to pay a certain sum of money or property if he or she fails to appear in court as required, which promise may or may not be secured by the deposit of an actual sum of money or property.

Release on own recognizance: The release, by a judicial officer, of an accused person who has been taken into custody, upon the accused's promise to appear in court as required for criminal proceedings.

Release, pretrial: A procedure whereby an accused person who has been taken into custody is allowed to be free before and during his or her trial.

Release to third party: The release by a judicial officer of an accused person who has been taken into custody, to a third party who promises to return the accused to court for criminal proceedings.

Residential treatment center: A government facility which serves juveniles whose behavior does not necessitate the strict confinement of a training school, often allowing them greater contact with the community.

Retained counsel: An attorney, not employed or compensated by a government agency or subunit, nor assigned by the court, who is privately hired to represent a person(s) in a criminal proceeding.

Revocation: An administrative act performed by a parole authority removing a person from parole, or a judicial order by a court removing a person from parole or probation, in response to a violation on the part of the parolee or probationer.

Revocation hearing: An administrative and/or judicial hearing on the question of whether or not a person's probation or parole status should be revoked.

Rights of defendant: Those powers and privileges which are constitutionally guaranteed to every defendant.

Robbery: The unlawful taking or attempted taking of property that is in the immediate possession of another, by force or the threat of force.

Robbery, armed: The unlawful taking or attempted taking of property that is in the immediate possession of another, by the use or threatened use of a deadly or dangerous weapon.

Robbery, strongarm: The unlawful taking or attempted taking of property that is in the immediate possession of another by the use or threatened use of force, without the use of a weapon.

Runaway: A juvenile who has been adjudicated by a judicial officer of a juvenile court as having committed the status offense of leaving the custody and home of his or her parents, guardians, or custodians without permission and failing to return within a reasonable length of time.

Seal (record): The removal, for the benefit of the subject, of arrest, criminal, or juvenile record information from routinely available status to a status requiring special procedures for access.

Security: The degree of restriction of inmate movement within a correctional facility, usually divided into maximum, medium, and minimum levels.

Security and privacy standards: A set of principles and procedures developed to insure the security and confidentiality of criminal or juvenile record information in order to protect the privacy of the persons identified in such records.

Sentence: The penalty imposed by a court upon a convicted person, or the court decision to suspend imposition or execution of the penalty.

Sentence, indeterminate: A statutory provision for a type of sentence to imprisonment where, after the court has determined that the convicted person shall be imprisoned, the exact length of imprisonment and parole supervision is afterwards fixed within statutory limits by a parole authority.

Sentence, mandatory: A statutory requirement that a certain penalty shall be imposed and executed upon certain convited offenders.

Sentence, suspended: The court decision postponing the pronouncing of sentence upon a convicted person, or postponing the execution of a sentence that has been pronounced by the court.

Sentence—suspended execution: The court decision setting a penalty but postponing its execution.

Sentence—suspended imposition: The court decision postponing the setting of a penalty.

Shelter: A confinement or community facility for the care of juveniles, usually those held pending adjudication.

Sheriff: The elected or appointed chief officer of a county law enforcement agency, usually responsible for law enforcement in unincorporated areas, and for the operation of the county jail.

Sheriff, deputy: A law enforcement officer employed by a county sheriff's department.

Sheriff's department: A law enforcement agency organized at the county level, directed by a sheriff, which exercises its law enforcement functions at the county level, usually within unincorporated areas, and operates the county jail in most jurisdictions.

Speedy trial: The right of the defendant to have a prompt trial.

State highway patrol: A state law enforcement agency of which the principal functions consist of prevention, detection, and investigation of motor vehicle offenses, and the apprehension of traffic offenders.

State highway patrol officer: An employee of a state highway patrol who is an officer sworn to carry out law enforcement duties, primarily traffic code enforcement.

State police: A state law enforcement agency whose principal functions may include maintaining statewide police communications, aiding local police in criminal investigation, police training, guarding state property, and highway patrol.

State police officer: An employee of a state police agency who is an officer sworn to carry out law enforcement duties, sometimes including traffic enforcement duties.

Status offender: A juvenile who has been adjudicated by a judicial officer of a juvenile court as having committed a status offense, which is an act or conduct which is an offense only when committed or engaged in by a juvenile.

Status offense: An act or conduct which is declared by statute to be an offense, but only when committed or engaged in by a juvenile, and which can be adjudicated only by a juvenile court.

Subjudicial officer: A judicial officer who is invested with certain judicial powers and functions, but whose decisions in criminal and juvenile cases are subject to de novo review by a judge.

Subpoena: A written order issued by a judicial officer requiring a specified person to appear in a designated court at a specified time in order to serve as a witness in a case under the jurisdiction of that court, or to bring material to that court.

Summons: A written order issued by a judicial officer requiring a person accused of a criminal offense to appear in a designated court at a specified time to answer the charge(s).

Suspect: A person, adult or juvenile, considered by a criminal justice agency to be one who may have committed a specific criminal offense, but who has not been arrested or charged.

Suspicion: Belief that a person has committed a criminal offense, based on facts and circumstances that are not sufficient to constitute probable cause.

Theft: Larceny, or in some legal classifications, the group of offenses including larceny, and robbery, burglary, extortion, fraudulent offenses, hijacking, and other offenses sharing the element of larceny.

Time served: The total time spent in confinement by a convicted adult before and after sentencing, or only the time spent in confinement after a sentence of commitment to a confinement facility.

Training school: A correctional institution for juveniles adjudicated to be delinquents or status offenders and committed to confinement by a judicial officer.

Transfer hearing: A preadjudicatory hearing in juvenile court for the purpose of determining whether juvenile court jurisdiction should be retained or waived over a juvenile alleged to have committed a delinquent act(s), and whether he or she should be transferred to criminal court for prosecution as an adult.

Transfer to adult court: The decision by a juvenile court, resulting from a transfer hearing, that jurisdiction over an alleged delinquent will be waived and that he or she should be prosecuted as an adult in a criminal court.

Trial: The examination of issues of fact and law in a case or controversy, beginning when the jury has been selected in a jury trial, or when the first witness is sworn, or the first evidence is introduced in a court trial, and concluding when a verdict is reached or the case is dismissed.

Trial, court (trial, judge): A trial in which there is no jury, and in which a judicial officer determines the issues of fact and law in a case.

Trial, jury: A trial in which a jury determines the issues of fact in a case.

UCR: An abbreviation for the Federal Bureau of Investigation's uniform crime reporting program.

Venue: The geographical area from which the jury is drawn and in which trial is held in a criminal action.

Verdict: In criminal proceedings, the decision made by a jury in a jury trial, or by a judicial officer in a court trial, that a defendant is either guilty or not guilty of the offense(s) for which he or she has been tried.

Verdict, guilty: In criminal proceedings, the decision made by a jury in a jury trial, or by a judicial officer in a court trial, that the defendant is guilty of the offense(s) for which he or she has been tried.

Verdict, not guilty: In criminal proceedings, the decision made by a jury in a jury trial, or by a judicial officer in a court trial, that the defendant is not guilty of the offense(s) for which he or she has been tried.

Victim: A person who has suffered death, physical or mental suffering, or loss of property as the result of an actual or attempted criminal offense committed by another person.

Warrant, arrest: A document issued by a judicial officer which directs a law enforcement officer to arrest a person who has been accused of an offense.

Warrant, bench: A document issued by a judicial officer directing that a person who has failed to obey an order or notice to appear be brought before the court.

Warrant, search: A document issued by a judicial officer which directs a law enforcement officer to conduct a search for specified property or persons at a specific location, to seize the property or persons, if found, and to account for the results of the search to the issuing judicial officer.

Witness: A person who directly perceives an event or thing, or who has expert knowledge relevant to a case.

Youthful offender: A person, adjudicated in criminal court, who may be above the statutory age limit for juveniles but is below a specified upper age limit, for whom special correctional commitments and special record sealing procedures are made available by statute.

Index